A Short History of

Latin America

A Short History of

Latin America

SECOND EDITION

BENJAMIN KEEN

MARK WASSERMAN
Rutgers University

HOUGHTON MIFFLIN COMPANY   BOSTON
DALLAS   GENEVA, ILLINOIS   HOPEWELL, NEW JERSEY
PALO ALTO

Printed in the U.S.A.

Library of Congress Catalog Card
Number: 83-80894

ISBN: 0-395-34362-3

Maps by Dick Sanderson.

Cover: *Andean Family*, by Hector Poleo of Venezuela, Oil, 1943. Museum of Modern Art of
Latin America, Washington, D.C. Photo courtesy
of OAS Audio-Visual Program.

BCDEFGHIJ-H-8987654

Contents

v

List of Maps

Preface

The second edition of *A Short History of Latin America* has two major objectives. First, it seeks to make available to teachers and students of Latin American history a text based on the best recent historical scholarship and enriched with data and concepts drawn from the sister social sciences of economics, anthropology, and sociology. Since it is a history of Latin American *civilization*, we devote considerable space to the way of life and culture at different periods of the area's history. To enable students to deepen their knowledge of Latin American history on their own, we have added an annotated bibliography, "Suggestions for Further Reading," limited for the most part to titles in English.

Our second objective has been to set Latin American history within a broad interpretive framework. This framework is the "dependency theory," the most influential contemporary theoretical model for social scientists concerned with understanding Latin America. Not all followers of the theory understand it in precisely the same way, but most probably agree with the definition of *dependency* offered by the Brazilian scholar Theotonio dos Santos: "A situation in which the economy of certain countries is conditioned by the development and expansion of another economy to which the former is subject." We give the name *neocolonialism* to the dependency or external economic domination to which Latin America has been subject since the last quarter of the nineteenth century. We believe that neocolonialism, despite its façade of modernity, has sharpened the economic, social, and political problems that the region inherited from its colonial past, and we view with frank sympathy the efforts of the Latin American nations in recent decades to eliminate the consequences of the old colonialism and the new.

Since 1980, when the first edition of this book appeared, the neocolonial model of Latin American development, based on foreign loans and investments, has entered a crisis for which no solution appears in sight. The near default of Brazil and Mexico on their foreign debts in 1982—a default averted by financial rescue packages organized by Western governments and banks on the basis of agreements that by mid-1983 were unraveling—signaled the start of this deep crisis. A mountain of debt hangs over Latin America and also threatens the Western banks that reaped enormous profits by flooding the area with dollars (in 1982 Latin America paid $35 billion in interest on a debt of $300 billion). There is no prospect that this immense debt can be repaid without large write-offs and long delays. Thus, it is reasonable to assume that the flow of loans to Latin America will never resume on its former vast scale.

This suggests that sooner or later the Latin American model of "dependent development" will need to be replaced by more autonomous, inward-directed strategies of development, based on more rational exploitation of the area's natural and human resources and aimed at raising the pitifully low living standards of the masses rather than the enrichment of small rul-

ing classes. It would be naive to suppose that these strategies can be implemented without profound changes in Latin America's economic and social structures, or without overcoming the bitter opposition of traditional elites and their foreign allies.

A word about the organization of our text. We have decided against the approach that tries to cover the post-independence history of the twenty Latin American nations in detail, including mention of every general who ever passed through a presidential palace. We believe that this approach turns students off by miring them in a bog of tedious facts. We have preferred to limit our coverage of the national period in the nineteenth century to four countries—Mexico, Argentina, Chile, and Brazil—whose history seemed to illustrate best the major issues and trends of the period. In addition to the countries named above, our survey of the twentieth century broadens to include the central Andean area, with a special concentration on Peru; Cuba, the scene of a socialist revolution with continental repercussions; and Central America, where a revolutionary storm, having toppled the U.S.-supported Somoza tyranny in Nicaragua, threatens to bring down the rickety structures of oligarchical and military rule in El Salvador and Guatemala. This selective approach toward national history has permitted a reasonably full treatment of Latin American society and culture in the nineteenth and twentieth centuries.

The chapter on Central America is entirely new for the second edition. Other chapters have been substantially updated, however, to cover recent events and incorporate current scholarship. Several new maps enhance this edition as well. The authors have profited from one another's advice and criticism, but each assumes primary responsibility for his own chapters. Benjamin Keen wrote Chapters 1–12, 15, 16, 18, and 19; Mark Wasserman wrote Chapters 13, 14, 17, and 20.

We gratefully acknowledge our debt to the

following colleagues for their careful scrutiny of the second edition of our text and their many valuable suggestions for revision:

George D. Beelen
Youngstown State University

John Coatsworth
University of Chicago

Ismael de la Rocha
Ventura Community College

Gerald Michael Greenfield
University of Wisconsin, Parkside

Craig Hendricks
Long Beach City College

Thomas Holloway
Cornell University

Roderick McDonald
Rider College

Barbara A. Tenenbaum
University of South Carolina-Columbia

Ralph H. Vigil
University of Nebraska-Lincoln

Thomas W. Walker
Ohio University

Joseph Richard Werne
Southeast Missouri State University

Ralph Lee Woodward
Tulane University

We have adopted many but not all of these colleagues' suggestions; they bear no responsibility for any remaining errors of fact or interpretation. We also wish to recall the many students, graduate and undergraduate, who helped us to define our views on Latin American history through the give-and-take of classroom discussion and the reading and discussion of their own papers and theses. In particular, Benjamin Keen wishes to thank Stephen Niblo and Keith Haynes for sharing with him the findings of their important researches into the political economy of the *Porfiriato* and the ideology of the Mexican Revolution, respectively.

B. K.
M. W.

A Short History of

Latin America

PART ONE

THE COLONIAL
HERITAGE
OF LATIN AMERICA

For most North Americans, perhaps, the colonial past is a remote, picturesque time that has little relevance to the way we live now.* The situation is very different in Latin America. "Even the casual visitor to Latin America," says the historian Woodrow Borah, "is struck by the survival of institutions and features that are patently colonial." The inventory of colonial survivals includes many articles and practices of everyday life, systems of land use and labor, and a wealth of social relations and attitudes.

Characteristic of the Latin American scene is the coexistence and mingling of colonial and modern elements: The digging stick, the foot plow, and the handloom coexist with the tractor, the conveyer belt, and the computer. In Latin America the colonial past is not a nostalgic memory but a harsh reality. It signifies economic backwardness; political arbitrariness, corruption, and nepotism; a hierarchical social order and attitudes of condescension and contempt on the part of elites toward the masses.

We begin our survey of the colonial period of Latin American history with some account of Ancient America, the name we give to that long span of time during which the Indians— the first Americans—developed their cultures in virtual isolation from the Old World. The Indian past profoundly influenced the character of the colonial era. By no accident, the chief capitals of the Spanish Empire in America arose in the old Indian heartlands—the Mexican and Peruvian areas—the homes of millions of industrious natives accustomed to performing tribute labor for their ruling classes. The Indians, the Spaniards well knew, were the true wealth of the Indies. Territories that held few Indians failed to attract them or remained marginal in the Spanish colonial scheme of things.

Equally decisive for the character of the colo-

* The material in the section on colonial Latin America is based in part on Benjamin Keen's article, "Latin America and the Caribbean, Colonial," in *Encyclopaedia Britannica* (the 15th edition), © Encyclopaedia Britannica, Inc., 1980.

nial period was the Hispanic background. The conquistadors came from a Spain where five centuries of struggle against the Moslems had made warfare almost a way of life and had created a large *hidalgo* (noble) class that regarded manual labor with contempt. To some the conquest of America appeared to be an extension of the reconquest of Spain from the Moors. "The conquest of Indians," wrote the Spanish chronicler Francisco López de Gómara, "began when the conquest of the Moors had ended, in order that Spaniards may always war against the infidels." Spain's economic backwardness and immense inequalities of wealth, which sharply limited opportunities for advancement or even a decent livelihood for most Spaniards, help to explain the desperate valor of the conquistadors. It also explains their harshness in dealing with the Indians, and sometimes with each other, and the dog-eat-dog atmosphere of the Conquest. It seems significant that many great captains of the Conquest—Cortés, Pizarro, Valdivia, Balboa—came from the bleak land of Estremadura, Spain's poorest province.

On the ruins of the old Indian societies Spain laid the foundations of a new colonial order. Two important aspects of that order need to be stressed. One is the mixture of capitalist and feudal elements in its economic structure, its social organization, and its ideology. This blend of feudal and capitalist elements formed part of Spain's (and Portugal's) legacy to independent Latin America and serves to explain the tenacious hold of some anachronistic institutions on the area today.

Another important aspect of that order is the continual struggle, sometimes open, sometimes muffled, between the Spanish crown and the conquistadors and their descendants for control of Indian labor and tribute. In that struggle the colonists gradually gained the upper hand. The emergence in the sixteenth and seventeenth centuries of a hereditary colonial aristocracy rich in land and peons represented a defeat for the Crown and for the Indian community whose interests, however feebly and vacillatingly, the Crown defended. When in the late eighteenth century Spain's kings sought to tighten their control over the colonies, exclude Creoles (American-born Spaniards) from high official posts, and institute reforms that sometimes clashed with Creole vested interests, it was too late. These policies only alienated a powerful colonial elite whose members already felt a dawning sense of nationality and dreamed of the advantages of a free trade with the outside world.

A parallel development occurred during the same period in the relations between Portugal and Brazil. Between 1810 and 1822, American elites, taking advantage of Spain's and Portugal's distresses, seized power in most of Spanish America and Brazil. These aristocratic rebels wanted no radical social changes or economic diversification; their interests as producers of staples for export to western Europe required the continuance of the system of large estates worked by peons or slaves. As a result, independent Latin America inherited almost intact the colonial legacy of a rigidly stratified society and an externally oriented economy dependent on a foreign country for capital and finished goods.

CHAPTER ONE

Ancient America

A great number of Indian groups, speaking many different languages and having different ways of life, occupied America at the time of its discovery by Columbus. For at least ten thousand years before its discovery, the New World had existed in virtual isolation from the Old. Sporadic and transient contacts between America and Asia no doubt occurred, and some transfer of culture traits, mainly stylistic embellishments, probably took place through trans-Pacific diffusion. But there is no convincing evidence that people or ideas from China, India, or elsewhere significantly influenced the cultural development of Indian America.

ENVIRONMENT AND CULTURE IN ANCIENT AMERICA

During its thousands of years of isolation, America was a unique social laboratory in which the Indians worked out their own destinies, adapting in various ways to their special environments. By 1492 this process had produced results that suggest that the patterns of early human cultural evolution are basically similar the world over. The first Europeans found native groups in much the same stages of cultural development through which parts of the Old World had once passed: Old Stone Age hunters and food gatherers, New Stone Age farmers, and finally, empires as complex as those of Bronze Age Egypt and Mesopotamia.

Racially, the inhabitants of Ancient America were blends of several Asiatic physical types and shared with the modern Indian the typical physical features of dark eyes, straight or wavy black hair, and yellowish or copper skin. Their remote ancestors had probably come from Asia across the Bering Strait in waves of migration that began between forty thousand and a hundred thousand years ago and continued until about 10,000 B.C. These firstcomers brought with them little more than fire, the domesticated dog, a few stone tools and weapons, and some kind of clothing.

Two waves of migrations appear to have taken place. The first brought extremely primitive groups who lived by gathering wild fruit, fishing, and hunting small game. A recent archaeological discovery suggests that these primitive hunters and gatherers passed through Peru about twenty-two thousand years ago. The second series of invasions brought big-game hunters who, like their predecessors, spread out through the continent. By 9000 B.C., these Asiatic invaders or their descendants had reached Patagonia, the southern tip of the continent.

This first colonization of America took place in the last part of the great geological epoch known as the Pleistocene, a period of great climatic changes. Glacial ages, during which blankets of ice covered extensive areas of the Old and New Worlds, alternated with periods of thaw, when temperatures rose to approximately present-day levels. Even in ice-free areas, precipitation often increased markedly during the glacial ages, creating lush growth of pastures and woodlands that supported many varieties of game. Consequently, large sections of America in this period were a hunter's paradise. Over its plains and through its forests roamed many large, prehistoric beasts. The projectile points of prehistoric hunters have been found near the remains of such animals from one end of America to the other.

Around 9000 B.C., the retreat of the last great glaciation (the Wisconsin), accompanied by drastic climate changes, caused a crisis for the Indian hunting economy. A warmer, drier climate settled over vast areas. Grasslands decreased, and the large animals that had pastured on them gradually died out. The improved techniques of late Pleistocene hunting also may have contributed to the disappearance of these animals. The hunting folk now had to adapt to their changing environment or vanish with the animals that had sustained them.

Southwestern United States, northern Mexico, and other areas offer archaeological evidence of a successful adjustment to the new conditions. The Indians increasingly turned for food to smaller animals, such as deer and jack rabbits, and to edible wild plants, especially seeds, which were ground into a palatable meal. This new way of life eventually led to the development of agriculture. At first, agriculture merely supplemented the older pursuits of hunting and food collecting; its use hardly constituted an "agricultural revolution." The shift from food gathering to food producing was more likely a gradual accumulation of more and more domesticated plants that gradually replaced the wild edible plants. Over an immensely long period, time and energy formerly devoted to hunting and plant collecting were diverted to such agricultural activities as clearing, planting, weeding, gardening, picking, harvesting, and food preparation. But in the long run, agriculture, in the New World as in the Old, had revolutionary effects: People began to lead a more disciplined and sedentary life, the food supply increased, population grew, and division of labor became possible.

In caves in the Mexican highlands, archaeologists have found the wild plants that the Indians gradually domesticated; among the more important are pumpkins, beans, and maize. Domestication of these plants probably occurred between 7000 and 2300 B.C. Among these achievements, none was more significant than the domestication of maize, the mainstay of the great cultures of Ancient America. Manioc (a starchy root cultivated in the tropics as a staple food) and the potato (in Peru) were added to the list of important Indian domesticated plants between 5000 and 1000 B.C.

From its place or places of origin, agriculture swiftly spread over the American continents. By 1492 maize was under cultivation from the northern boundary of present-day United States to Chile. But not all Indian peoples adopted agriculture as a way of life. Some, like the Indians who inhabited the bleak wastes of Tierra del Fuego at the far tip of South America, were forced by severe climatic conditions either to hunt and collect food or starve. Others, like the prosperous, sedentary Indians of the Pacific northwest coast, who lived by waters teeming with fish and forests filled with game, had no reason to abandon their good life in favor of agriculture.

Where agriculture became the principal economic activity, its yield depended on such natural factors as soil fertility and climate and on the farming techniques employed. Forest tribes usually employed the slash-and-burn method of cultivation. Trees and brush were cut down and burned, and maize or other staples were planted in the cleared area with a digging stick. Because this method soon exhausted the soil, the clearing had to be left fallow and a new one made. After this process had gone on long enough, the whole village had to move to a new site or adopt a dispersed pattern of settlement that would allow each family group sufficient land for its needs. Slash-and-burn ag-

riculture thus had a structural weakness that usually sharply limited the cultural development of the Indian peoples who employed it. That a strong controlling authority could at least temporarily overcome the defects of this method is suggested by the success of the Maya: Their brilliant civilization arose in a tropical forest environment on a base of slash-and-burn farming directed by a powerful priesthood, but there is now abundant evidence that from very early times this was supplemented by more intensive methods of agriculture.

A more productive agriculture developed in the rugged highlands of Middle America and the Andean altiplano and on the desert coast of Peru. In such arid or semiarid country, favored with a temperate climate and a naturally rich soil, the land could be tilled more easily and its fertility preserved longer with digging-stick methods. Most important, food production could be increased with the aid of irrigation, which led to larger populations and a greater division of labor. The need for cooperation and regulation on irrigation projects favored the rise of strong central governments and the extension of their authority over larger areas. The Aztec and Inca empires arose in natural settings of this kind.

NUCLEAR AMERICA

Mexico and Peru were the centers of an extensive Indian high culture area that included central and southern Mexico, Central America, and the Andean zone of South America. This is the heartland of Ancient America, the home of its first agricultural civilizations. Evidence of early village life and the basic techniques of civilization—agriculture, pottery, weaving—has been found in almost every part of this territory. Specialists often refer to this important region as Nuclear America.

In recent decades, this region has been the scene of major archaeological discoveries. In the Valley of Mexico, in southern Mexico and on its gulf coast, on the high plateau of Bolivia, and in the desert sands of coastal Peru, excavations have uncovered the remains of splendid temples, mighty fortresses, large cities and towns, and pottery and textiles of exquisite artistry. Combining the testimony of the spade with that provided by Indian and Spanish historical accounts, specialists have attempted to reconstruct the history of Nuclear America. The framework for this effort is a sequence of stages based on the technology, social and political organization, religion, and art of a given period. To this sequence of stages specialists commonly assign the names Archaic, Formative or Preclassic, Classic, and Postclassic. This scheme is tentative in detail, with much chronological overlap between stages and considerable variation in the duration of some periods from area to area.

The *Archaic* stage began about nine thousand years ago when a gradual shift from food gathering and hunting to agriculture began in many parts of Nuclear America. This incipient agriculture, however, did not cause revolutionary changes in Indian society. For thousands of years, people continued to live in much the same primitive fashion as before. Social groups were small and probably seminomadic. Weaving was unknown, but a simple pottery appeared in some areas toward the end of the period.

Between 2500 and 1500 B.C., a major cultural advance in various regions of Nuclear America opened the *Formative*, or *Preclassic*, period. Centuries of haphazard experimentation with plants led to the selection of improved, high-yield varieties. These advances ultimately produced an economy solidly based on agriculture and sedentary village life. Maize and other important domesticated plants were brought under careful cultivation; irrigation came into use in some areas; a few animals were domesticated. By the end of the period, pottery and weaving were highly developed. Increased food production enabled villagers to support a class of priests who acted as intermediaries between people and gods. More abundant food also re-

leased labor for the construction of ceremonial sites—mounds of earth topped by temples of wood or thatch.

The social unit of the Formative period was a village community composed of one or more kinship groups, but by the end of the period small states uniting several villages had appeared. Since land and food were relatively plentiful and populations small, warfare must have been infrequent. Religion centered on the worship of water and fertility gods; human sacrifice was probably absent or rare.

The advances of the Formative period culminated in the *Classic* period, which began around the opening of the Christian era and lasted until approximately A.D. 1000. The term Classic refers to the flowering of material, intellectual, and artistic culture that marked this stage. There was no basic change in technology, but the extension of irrigation works in some areas caused increases in food production and freed manpower for construction and technical tasks. Population also increased, and in some regions genuine cities arose. Architecture, pottery, and weaving reached an impressive level of style. Metallurgy flourished in Peru, as did astronomy, mathematics, and writing in Mesoamerica (central and south Mexico and adjacent upper Central America). The earlier earth mounds gave way to huge stone-faced pyramids, elaborately ornamented and topped by great temples. The construction of palaces and other official buildings nearby made each ceremonial center the administrative capital of a state ruled by a priest-king. Social stratification was already well developed, with the priesthood the main ruling class. However, the growing incidence of warfare in the late Classic period (perhaps caused by population pressure, with greater competition for land and water) brought more recognition and rewards to successful warriors. Religion became an elaborate polytheism served by a large class of priests.

Typical cultures of the Classic period were the Teotihuacán civilization of central Mexico, the Monte Albán culture in southwestern Mexico, and the lowland Maya culture of southern Yucatán and northern Guatemala. The Olmec civilization of the Mexican gulf lowlands displays some Classic features, but falls within the time span usually allotted to the Formative. In Peru the period is best represented by the brilliant Mochica and Nazca civilizations of the coast. The available evidence suggests that the Classic stage was limited to Mesoamerica, the central Andean area (the highlands and coasts of Peru and Bolivia), and the Ecuadorian coast.

The Classic era ended abruptly in both the northern and southern ends of Nuclear America. Shortly before or after A.D. 1000 most of the great Classic centers in Mesoamerica and Peru were abandoned or destroyed by civil war or foreign invasion. Almost certainly, the fall of these civilizations came as the climax of a longer period of decline. Population pressure, soil erosion, and peasant revolts caused by excessive tribute demands are among the explanations that have been advanced for the collapse of the great Classic city-states and kingdoms.

A Time of Troubles, of obscure struggles and migrations of peoples, followed these disasters. Then new civilizations arose on the ruins of the old. The *Postclassic* stage, from about A.D. 1000 to 1500, seems to have repeated on a larger, more complex scale, the rise-and-fall pattern of the previous era. Chronic warfare, reflected in the number of fortifications and fortified communities, and an increased emphasis on urban living were distinguishing features of this stage. Another was the formation of empires through the subjugation of a number of states by one powerful state. The dominant state appropriated a portion of the production of the conquered people, primarily for the benefit of its ruling classes. The Aztec and Inca empires typify this era.

No important advances in technology occurred in the Postclassic period, but in some regions the net of irrigation works was extended. The continuous growth of warfare and the rise of commerce sharpened economic distinctions between nobles and commoners, between rich and poor. The warrior class replaced the priesthood as the main ruling class. Imperialism also influenced the character of religion, enhancing the importance of war gods and human sacrifice. The arts and crafts showed some decline from Classic achievements; there was a tendency toward standardization and mass production of textiles and pottery in some areas.

After reaching a peak of power, the empires displayed the same tendency toward disintegration as their Classic forerunners. The Tiahuanaco civilization and the Inca Empire in Peru may have represented two cycles of empire growth, while the first true Mexican imperial cycle, that of the Aztec conquests, had not ended when the Spaniards conquered America.

Three high civilizations, the Aztecs of Mexico, the Maya of Central America, and the Incas of Peru, have held the center of attention to the virtual exclusion of the others. This partiality is understandable. We know more about these peoples and their ways of life. The Aztec and Inca civilizations still flourished at the coming of the Spaniards, and some conquistadors wrote vivid accounts of what they saw. The colorful story of the Conquest of Mexico and Peru and the unhappy fate of their emperors Moctezuma (Montezuma) and Atahualpa have also served to focus historical and literary attention on the Aztecs and the Incas. Unfortunately, the fame and glamour surrounding these peoples have obscured the achievements of their predecessors, who laid the cultural foundations on which the Maya, Aztecs, and Incas built.

THE AZTECS OF MEXICO

At the opening of the sixteenth century, most of central Mexico, from the fringes of the arid northern plateau southward to the lowlands of Tehuantepec, paid tribute to the Aztecs of the Valley of Mexico. These Aztecs were latecomers in a region that had been the home of highly

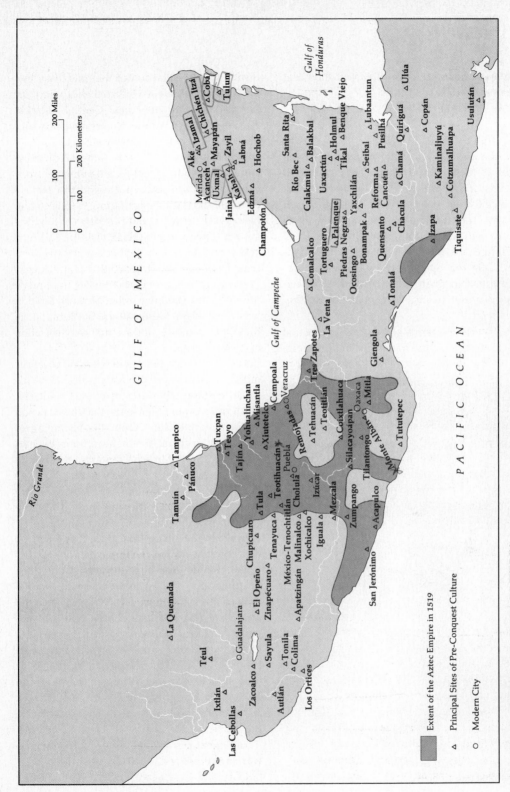

GULF OF MEXICO

Gulf of Campeche

Gulf of Honduras

PACIFIC OCEAN

Río Grande

△ La Quemada

○ Guadalajara

△ Téul
Téul

△ Zacoalco
△ Sayula
○ Ixtlán
Las Cebollas ○
Los Ortices
△ Colima
△ Tonila
△ Autlán

△ El Opeño
△ Chupícuaro
△ Zinapécuaro
△ Tenayuca
△ Apatzingán
México-Tenochtitlán
△ Malinalco
Xochicalco △
Iguala △
△ Mezcala
△ Acapulco
San Jerónimo

△ Tamuín
△ Tampico
△ Pánuco
△ Tuxpan
△ Teayo
△ Tula
△ Tajín ○ Yohualinchan
△ Misantla
△ Xiutetelco
Cempoala △
Veracruz △
Remojadas △△
△ Teotihuacán ○ Puebla
Cholula ○
Izúcar ○
△ Tehuacán
△ Teotitlán
△ Coixtlahuaca
△ Silacayoapan
Zumpango △
Tilantongo △○ Oaxaca
Monte Albán △△ Mitla
△ Tututepec
△ Zapotes
Tres Zapotes △
△ La Venta
△ Comalcalco
△ Tortuguero
△ Palenque
△ Piedras Negras
Ocosingo △
△ Yaxchilán
Bonampak △
Quensanto △
Giengola △
Tonalá △
Izapa △
Tiquisate △

Mérida ○ Aké ○
Acanceh △ △ Izamal
△ Uxmal △ Chichén Itzá
Jaina △ Mayapán △ Cobá
Kabah △ △ Zayil Tulum △
Edzná △ Labná △
Champotón △ △ Hochob
Santa Rita △
Río Bec △
Calakmul △ △ Balakbal
Uaxactún △ △ Holmul
Tikal △ Benque Viejo △
△ Seibal Lubaantun △
Reforma △ Pusilhá △
Cancuén △
Chacula △ △ Chamá Quiriguá △
△ Kaminaljuyú
△ Cotzumalhuapa
△ Copán
Ulúa △
Usulután △

200 Miles
200 Kilometers
100
100
0
0

* lo-classic

PRINCIPAL SITES OF PRE-CONQUEST CULTURE IN
MESOAMERICA

▨ Extent of the Aztec Empire in 1519

△ Principal Sites of Pre-Conquest Culture

○ Modern City

developed civilizations for almost a thousand years before their arrival.

Pre-Aztec Civilizations

As early as 1000 B.C., the inhabitants of the Valley of Mexico lived in small villages set in the midst of their maize, bean, and squash fields. They cultivated the land with slash-and-burn methods, produced a simple but well-made pottery, and turned out large numbers of small clay figures that suggest a belief in fertility goddesses. By the opening of the Christian era, there appeared small, flat-topped mounds, evidence of a more formal religion and a directing priesthood.

Much earlier (perhaps spanning the period 1500 to 400 B.C.), arose the precocious and enig-

matic Olmec civilization of the gulf coast lowlands, whose influence radiated widely into the central Mexican plateau and Central America. The origins, development, and disappearance of the Olmec culture remain a mystery.

Important elements of the Olmec civilization were its ceremonial centers, monumental stone carving and sculpture (including the famous colossal heads whose significance is conjectural), hieroglyphic writing, and probably a calendrical system. The principal Olmec sites are La Venta and Tres Zapotes, in the modern state of Veracruz. Discovery of Olmec culture and evidence of the wide diffusion of its art style have made untenable the older view that Maya civilization was the first in Mesoamerica. It seems likely that Olmec culture was the mother civilization of Mesoamerica.

The technical, artistic, and scientific advances of the Formative period made possible the climactic cultural achievements of the Classic era. In Mexico's central highlands, the Classic period opened in splendor. About the beginning of the Christian era, at Teotihuacán, some twenty-eight miles from Mexico City, arose the mighty pyramids later given the names of the Sun and the Moon, which towered over clusters of imposing temples and other buildings. The stone sculpture used in the decoration of the temples, as well as the marvelous grace and finish of the cement work and the fresco painting, testify to the high development of the arts among the Teotihuacans. The ancient water god, known to the Aztecs as Tlaloc, seems to have been the chief deity. But the feathered serpent with jaguar fangs, later known as Quetzalcoatl, is also identified with water and fertility and appears prominently in the greatest temple. There is little evidence of war or human sacrifice until a relatively late phase. Priests in benign poses and wearing the symbols of their gods dominate the mural paintings.

This great ceremonial center at Teotihuacán was sacred ground. Probably only the priestly nobility and their servants lived here. Farther

Colossal stone head by Olmec sculptors. (Inge Morath/Magnum Photos)

out were the residential quarters inhabited by officials, artisans, and merchants. Teotihuacán is estimated to have had a population of between 125,000 and 200,000. On the outskirts of the city, which covered an area of seven square miles, lived a large rural population that supplied the metropolis with its food. It is likely that an intensive agriculture using canal irrigation and terracing on hillslopes formed the economic foundation of the Teotihuacán civilization. Despite the predominantly peaceful aspect of its religion and art, Teotihuacán seems to have been not only a major trading center but a military state that directly controlled regions as remote as highland Guatemala.

Contemporary with Teotihuacán, but overshadowed by that great city, were other centers of Classic culture in Mesoamerica. To the southwest, at Monte Albán in the rugged mountains of Oaxaca, the Zapotecs erected a great ceremonial center that was also a true city. One of their achievements, probably of Olmec origin, was a complicated system of hieroglyphic writing. In the same period, the Maya Classic civilization flowered in the Petén region of northern Guatemala.

By A.D. 800, the Mesoamerica world had been shaken to its foundations by a crisis that seemed to spread from one Classic center to another. Teotihuacán, Rome of that world, itself perished at the hands of invaders, who burned down the city sometime between A.D. 650 and 800. Toward the latter date, the great ceremonial center at Monte Albán was abandoned. And by A.D. 800, the process of disintegration had reached the Classic Maya heartland of southern Yucatán and northern Guatemala, whose deserted or destroyed centers returned one by one to the bush.

From this Time of Troubles in Mesoamerica (approximately A.D. 700 to 1000) a new Postclassic order emerged, sometimes appropriately called Militarist. Whereas priests and benign nature gods may have sometimes presided over Mesoamerican societies of the Classic era, warriors and terrible war gods clearly dominated the states that arose on the ruins of the Classic world. In central Mexico the sway of Teotihuacán, probably based above all on cultural and economic supremacy, gave way to strife among new states that warred with one another for land, water, and tribute.

The most important of these, successor to the power of Teotihuacán, was the Toltec "empire," with its capital at Tula, about fifty miles from Mexico City. Lying on the periphery of the Valley of Mexico, Tula may have once been an outpost of Teotihuacán, guarding its frontiers against the hunting tribes of the northern deserts. Following the collapse of Teotihuacán, one such tribe, the Toltecs, swept down from the north, entered the Valley of Mexico, and overwhelmed the pitiful survivors among the Teotihuacán people.

Toltec power and prosperity reached its peak under a ruler named Topiltzin, who moved his capital to Tula in about 980. Apparently renamed Quetzalcoatl in his capacity of high priest of the ancient god worshiped by the Teotihuacáns, Topiltzin-Quetzalcoatl reigned for nineteen years with such splendor that he and his city became legendary. The Song of Quetzalcoatl tells of the wonders of Tula, a true paradise on earth where cotton grew colored and the soil yielded fruit of such size that small ears of corn were used, not as food, but as fuel to heat steam baths. The legends of ancient Mexico celebrate the Toltecs' superhuman powers and talents; they were described as master artisans, as creators of culture. Over this Golden Age presided the great priest-king Quetzalcoatl, who thus revived the glories of Teotihuacán.

Toward the end of Quetzalcoatl's reign, Tula seems to have become the scene of an obscure struggle between two religious traditions. One was associated with the worship of Tezcatlipoca, a Toltec tribal god pictured as an all-powerful and capricious deity who demanded human sacrifice. The other was identified with the cult of the ancient god Quetzalcoatl, who had

The Departure of Quetzalcoatl, by José Clemente Orozco. (Dartmouth College, Hanover, N.H.)

brought men and women maize, all learning, and the arts. In a version of the Quetzalcoatl legend that may reflect post-Conquest Christian influence, the god demanded of them only the peaceful sacrifice of jade, snakes, and butterflies. This struggle found fanciful expression in the native legend that tells how the black magic of the enchanter Tezcatlipoca caused the saintly priest-king Quetzalcoatl to fall from grace and drove him into exile from Tula.

Whatever its actual basis, the Quetzalcoatl legend, with its promise that an Indian Redeemer would someday return to reclaim his kingdom, profoundly impressed the mind of ancient Mexico and played its part in the destruction of the Aztec Empire. By a singular coincidence, the year in the Aztec cycle of years in which Quetzalcoatl promised to return was the very year in which Cortés landed at Veracruz. Aztec belief in the legend helps to explain the vacillation and contradictory moves of the doomed Moctezuma.

Topiltzin-Quetzalcoatl was succeeded by lesser kings, who vainly struggled to solve the growing problems of the Toltec state. The causes of this crisis are obscure: Tremendous droughts may have caused crop failure and famines, perhaps aggravated by Toltec neglect of agriculture in favor of collection of tribute from conquered peoples. A series of revolutions reflected the Toltec economic and social difficulties. The last Toltec king, Huemac, apparently committed suicide about 1174, and the Toltec state disappeared with him. In the following year, a general dispersion or exodus of the Toltecs took place. Tula itself fell into the hands of barbarians in about 1224.

The fall of Tula, situated on the margins of the Valley of Mexico, opened the way for a general invasion of the valley by Nahuatl-speaking northern peoples. These newcomers, called Chichimecs, may be compared to the Germanic invaders who broke into the dying Roman Empire. Like them, the Chichimec leaders respected and tried to absorb the superior culture of the vanquished people. They were eager to intermarry with the surviving Toltec royalty and nobility.

These invaders founded a number of succession-states in the lake country at the bottom of the Valley of Mexico. Legitimately or not, their rulers all claimed the honor of Toltec descent. In artistic and industrial development, the Texcocan kingdom, organized in 1260, easily excelled its neighbors. Texcocan civilization reached its climactic moment two centuries later in the reign of King Nezahualcoyotl (1418–1472), distinguished poet, philosopher, and lawgiver, perhaps the most remarkable figure to emerge from the mists of ancient America.

The Arrival of the Aztecs

Among the last of the Chichimec tribes to arrive in the valley were the Aztecs, or Mexica. The date of their departure from the north was probably about A.D. 1111. Led by four chiefs and a woman who carried a medicine bundle housing the spirit of their tribal god, Huitzilopochtli, they arrived in the Valley of Mexico in about 1218 after obscure wanderings. They were basically a hunting and gathering people, but had some acquaintance with agriculture. Finding the most desirable sites occupied by other tribes, they had to take refuge on marshy lands around Lake Texcoco. Here in 1344 or 1345, they began to build the town of Tenochtitlán. At this time, the Aztec tribe was composed of a small number of kinship groups called *calpulli*.

The patches of solid ground that formed the Aztec territory were gradually built over with huts of cane and reeds. They were followed later by more ambitious structures of turf, adobe, and light stone. As the population increased, a larger cultivable area became necessary. For this purpose the Aztecs borrowed from their neighbors the technique of making *chinampas*— artificial garden beds formed of masses of earth

and rich sediment dredged from the lake bed and held in place by wickerwork. Eventually the roots, striking downward, took firm hold in the lake bottom and created solid ground. On these chinampas the Aztecs grew maize, beans, and other products.

For a long time, the Aztecs were subservient to their powerful neighbors in Atzcapotzalco, the dominant power in the lake country in the late fourteenth and early fifteenth centuries. A turning point in Aztec history came in 1428. Led by their new war chief Itzcoatl, the Aztecs joined the rebellious city-state of Texcoco and the smaller town of Tlacopan to destroy the tyranny of Atzcapotzalco. Their joint victory (1430) led to the rise of a Triple Alliance for the conquest first of the valley, then of much of the Middle American world. Gradually, the balance of power shifted to the aggressive Aztec state. Texcoco became a junior partner, and Tlacopan was reduced to a satellite. The strong position of their island fortification and a shrewd policy of forming alliances and sharing the spoils of conquest with strategic mainland towns, which they later came to dominate, help to explain Aztec success in gaining control of the Valley of Mexico. In turn, conquest of the valley offered a key to the conquest of Middle America. The valley possessed the advantages of short internal lines of communication surrounded by easily defensible mountain barriers. Openings to the north, east, west, and south gave Aztec warriors easy access to adjacent valleys.

Conquest of Atzcapotzalco gave the Aztecs their first beachhead on the lakeshore. Most of the conquered land and the peasantry living on it were assigned to warrior-nobles who had distinguished themselves in battle. Originally assigned for life, these lands tended to become fiefs held in permanent inheritance. Thus, warfare created new economic and social cleavages within Aztec society.

These developments were accompanied by ideological changes. They included the elevation of the tribal god Huitzilopochtli to a position of equality with, or supremacy over, the great gods traditionally worshiped in the Valley of Mexico. Other ideological changes included the burning of the ancient picture writings because these books slighted the Aztecs and the creation of a new history that recognized the Aztec grandeur. A new emphasis was placed on getting prisoners of war to sacrifice on the altars of the Aztec gods to assure the continuance of the universe.

The successors of Itzcoatl, sometimes individually, sometimes in alliance with Texcoco, extended Aztec rule over and beyond the Valley of Mexico. By the time Moctezuma became ruler in 1503, the Triple Alliance was levying tribute on scores of towns, large and small, from the fringes of the arid northern plateau to the lowlands of Tehuantepec, and from the Atlantic to the Pacific. Within this extensive area only a few states or kingdoms, like the fierce Tarascans' state or the city-state of Tlaxcala, retained complete independence. Others, like Cholula, were left at peace in return for their benevolent neutrality or cooperation with the Aztecs.

The Aztecs waged war with or without cause. Refusal by a group to pay tribute to the Aztec ruler was sufficient pretext for invasion by the Aztecs. Injuries to the far-ranging Aztec merchants by people of the region they visited sometimes served as motive for invasion. Aztec merchants also prepared the way for conquest by reporting on the resources and defenses of the areas in which they traded; sometimes they acted as spies in hostile territory. If they returned home safely, these valiant merchants were honored by the ruler with amber lip plugs and other gifts. If their enemies discovered them, however, the consequences were horrid. "They were slain in ambush and served up with chili sauce," says a native account.

Victory in war always had the same results: Long lines of captives made the long journey to Tenochtitlán to be offered up on the altars of the gods. In addition, periodic tribute payments of maize, cotton mantles, cacao beans,

or other products—depending on the geography and resources of the region—were imposed on the vanquished. Certain lands were also set aside to be cultivated by them for the support of the Aztec crown, priesthood, and state officials or as fiefs given to warriors who had distinguished themselves in battle. A steward or tribute collector, sometimes assisted by a resident garrison, was stationed in the town. For the rest, the conquered people continued to enjoy autonomy in government, culture, and customs.

Aztec Culture and Society

The Aztec capital of Tenochtitlán had a population estimated to be between 150,000 and 200,000. An Indian Venice, the city was an oval island connected with the mainland by three causeways that converged at the center of the city and served as its main arteries of traffic. There were few streets; their place was taken by numerous canals, thronged with canoes and bordered by footpaths giving access to the thousands of houses that lined their sides. An aqueduct in solid masonry brought fresh water from the mountain springs of Chapultepec.

On the outlying chinampas, the Aztec farmers, who paddled their produce to town in tiny dugouts, lived in huts with thatched roofs resting on walls of wattle smeared with mud. Inside each hut were a three-legged *metate* (grinding stone), a few mats that served as beds and seats, some pottery, and little more. The majority of the population—artisans, priests, civil servants, soldiers, and entertainers—lived in more imposing homes. These were sometimes built of adobe, sometimes of a reddish *tezontli* lava, but they were always lime-washed and painted. Far more pretentious than most were the homes of clan leaders, merchants, and nobles.

As in housing, Aztec clothing differed according to the individual's economic and social status. For men the essential garments were a loincloth with broad flaps at front and back, usually decorated with fringes and tassels as well as embroidery work, and a blanket about two yards by one in size. This blanket hung under the left arm and was knotted on the right shoulder. Commoners wore plain blankets of maguey fiber or coarse cotton; rich merchants and nobles displayed very elaborate cotton mantles adorned with symbolic designs. Women wore shifts, wraparound skirts of white cotton tied with a narrow belt, and loose, short-sleeved tunics. Both shifts and tunics were decorated with vivid embroidery. Men wore sandals of leather or woven maguey fiber; women went barefoot.

As with dress, so with food: Wealth and social position determined its abundance and variety. The fare of the ordinary Aztec consisted of ground maize meal, beans, and vegetables cooked with chili. Meat was rarely seen on the commoner's table, but on festive occasions a dog might be served. It was otherwise with the nobility. A native account of the foods eaten by the lords includes many varieties of tortillas and tamales, roast turkey hen, roast quail, turkey with a sauce of small chilies, tomatoes, and ground squash seeds, venison sprinkled with seeds, many kinds of fish and fruits—and such delicacies as maguey grubs with a sauce of small chilies, winged ants with savory herbs, and rats with sauce. They finished their repast with chocolate, a divine beverage forbidden to commoners.

Education among the Aztecs was highly formal and served the dual purpose of preparing the child for his or her duties in the world and of indoctrinating him or her with the ideals of the tribe. Boys were sent to school at the age of ten or twelve. Sons of commoners, merchants, and artisans attended the *Telpochcalli* (House of Youth), where they received instruction in religion, good usage, and the art of war. The *Calmecac* (Priests' House), a school of higher learning, was reserved in principle for the sons of the nobility, but there is evidence that at least some children of merchants and commoners were admitted. Here, in addition to

ordinary training, students received instruction that prepared them to be priests, public officials, and military leaders. The curriculum included what we would today call rhetoric, or a noble manner of speaking, study of religious and philosophical doctrines as revealed in the divine songs of the sacred books, the arts of chronology and astrology, and training in history through study of the *Xiuhamatl* (Books of the Years). The *tlamatinime* (sages) who taught in the Aztec schools were also concerned with the formation of "a true face and heart," the striking Nahuatl metaphor for personality. Self-restraint, moderation, devotion to duty, a stoic awareness that "life is short and filled with hardships, and all comes to an end," an impeccable civility, modesty: These were among the qualities and concepts that the Aztec sages instilled in their charges.

Girls had special schools, where they were taught such temple duties as sweeping, offering incense three times during the night, and preparing food for the idols; weaving and other womanly tasks; and general preparation for marriage. Education for the men usually terminated at the age of twenty or twenty-two; for girls, at sixteen or seventeen. These were also the ages at which marriage was contracted.

In a society with such a complex economic and social life, disputes and aggressions inevitably arose and necessitated the development of an elaborate legal code. A hierarchy of courts was topped by two high tribunals that met in the royal palace in Tenochtitlán. The punishments of the Aztecs were severe. Death was the penalty for murder, rebellion, wearing the clothes of the other sex, and adultery; theft was punished by slavery for the first offense, by hanging for the second.

By the time of the Conquest, division of labor among the Aztecs had progressed to the point where a large class of artisans no longer engaged in agriculture. The artisan class included carpenters, potters, stonemasons, silversmiths, and featherworkers. In the same category belonged such specialists as fishermen, hunters, dancers, and musicians. All these specialists were organized in guilds, each with its guild hall and patron god; their professions were probably hereditary. The artist and the craftsman enjoyed a position of high honor and responsibility in Aztec society. Assigning the origin of all their arts and crafts to the Toltec period, the Aztecs applied the name Toltec to the true or master painter, singer, potter, or sculptor.

Advances in regional division of labor and the growth of the market for luxury goods also led to the emergence of a merchant class, which was organized in a very powerful guild. The wealth of this class and its important military and diplomatic services to the Aztec state made the merchants a third force in Aztec society, ranking only after the warrior nobility and the priesthood. The wealth of the merchants sometimes aroused the distrust and hostility of the Aztec rulers and nobility. Popular animosity toward the merchants is reflected in the words of a native account: "The merchants were those who had plenty, who prospered; the greedy, the well-fed man, the covetous, the niggardly, the miser, who controlled wealth and family . . . the mean, the stingy, the selfish."

The priesthood was the main integrating force in Aztec society. Through its possession of a sacred calendar that regulated the performance of agricultural tasks, it played a key role in the life of the people. The priesthood was also the repository of the accumulated lore and history of the Aztec tribe. By virtue of his special powers of intercession with the gods, his knowledge and wisdom, the priest was called on to intevene in every private or collective crisis of the Aztec. Celibate, austere, continually engaged in the penance of bloodletting, priests wielded an enormous influence over the Aztec people.

The priesthood shared authority and prestige with the nobility, a class that had gained power through war and political centralization. In addition to many warriors, this class consisted of a large bureaucracy made up of tribute collectors,

judges, ambassadors, and the like. Such officeholders were rewarded for their services by the revenue from public lands assigned to support them. Their offices were not hereditary. They were, however, normally conferred on sons of fathers who had held the same positions.

The wealth of the warrior nobility consisted chiefly of landed estates. Originally granted for life, these lands eventually became private estates that were handed down from father to son and could be sold or exchanged. The former free peasants on these lands were probably transformed into *mayeques* (serfs) tied to the land. With the expansion of the Aztec Empire, the number of private estates steadily grew.

On the margins of Aztec society was a large class of slaves. Slavery was the punishment for a variety of offenses, including failure to pay debts. Slavery was sometimes assumed by poor people in return for food. Slave owners frequently brought their chattels to the great market at Atzcapotzalco for sale to rich merchants or nobles for personal service or as sacrificial offerings to the gods.

The Aztec political system on the eve of the Conquest was a mixture of royal despotism and theocracy. Political power was concentrated in a ruling class of priests and nobles, over which presided an absolute ruler resembling an Oriental despot. Originally, the ruler had been chosen by the whole Aztec tribe, assembled for that purpose. Later he was chosen by a tribal council or electoral college dominated by the most important priests, officials, and warriors, including close relatives of the king. The council, in consultation with the kings of Texcoco and Tlacopan, selected the monarch from among the sons, brothers, or nephews of the previous ruler. The new ruler was assisted by a council of four great nobles. At the time of the Conquest the emperor was the luckless Moctezuma II, who succeeded his uncle Ahuitzotl.

Barbaric splendor and intricate ceremonies prevailed in Moctezuma's court. The great nobles of the realm took off their rich ornaments of feather, jade, and gold before entering his presence; barefoot, eyes on the ground, they approached the basketry throne of their king. Moctezuma dined in solitary magnificence, separated by a wooden screen from his servitors and the four great lords with whom he conversed.

This wealth, luxury, and ceremony revealed the great social and economic changes that had taken place in the small, despised Aztec tribe that came to live in the marshes of Lake Texcoco less than two centuries before. The Aztec Empire had reached a peak of pride and power. Yet the Aztec leaders lived in fear; the Aztec chronicles register a deep sense of insecurity. The mounting demands of the Aztec tribute collectors caused revolts on the part of tributary towns. Though repressed, they broke out afresh. The haunted Aztec imagination saw portents of evil on earth and in the troubled air. A child was born with two heads; the volcano Popocatepetl became unusually active; a comet streamed across the sky. The year 1519 approached, the year in which according to Aztec lore the god-king Quetzalcoatl might return to reclaim the realm from which he had been driven centuries before by the forces of evil.

THE MAYA OF
CENTRAL AMERICA

If the Aztecs excelled in war and conquest, the Maya were preeminent in cultural achievement. Certainly, no other Indian group ever demonstrated such extraordinary abilities in architecture, sculpture, painting, mathematics, and astronomy.

The ancient Maya lived in a region comprising portions of southeastern Mexico, almost all of Guatemala, the western part of Honduras, all of Belize, and the western half of El Salvador. But the Maya civilization attained its highest development in the tropical forest lowland area whose core is the Petén region of Guatemala, at the base of the Yucatán Peninsula. This was

the primary center of Maya Classic civilization from about AD. 250 to 900. The region was rich in wild game and building materials (limestone and fine hardwoods). In almost every other respect it offered immense obstacles to the establishment of a high culture. Clearing the dense forests for planting and controlling weeds were extremely difficult tasks with the primitive implements available. There was no metal, the water supply was uncertain, and communication facilities were poor. Yet it was here that the Maya built some of their largest ceremonial centers.

The contrast between the forbidding environment and the Maya achievement led some specialists to speculate that Maya culture was a transplant from some other, more favorable area. This view has been made obsolete by the discovery of long Preclassic sequences at lowland sites. There is, however, linguistic and archaeological evidence that the lowland Maya were descendants of groups who lived in or near the Olmec area before 1000 B.C. and who brought with them the essential elements of Mesoamerican civilization. In time they developed these elements into their own unique achievements in the sciences, art, and architecture.

Just as puzzling as the rise of the Maya lowland culture in such an inhospitable setting is the dramatic decline that led to a gradual cessation of building activity and eventual abandonment of the ceremonial centers after A.D. 800. Specialists have advanced various explanations for this decline. They include soil exhaustion as a result of slash-and-burn farming, invasion of cornfields by grasslands from the same cause, failure of the water supply, peasant revolts against the ruling priesthood, and the disruptive effects of the fall of Teotihuacán, which had close commercial and political ties with the Maya area. None of these explanations by itself, however, appears completely satisfactory.

Recently a more complex explanation of the Classic Maya collapse has emerged. According to this theory, the cessation of political and commercial contacts with Teotihuacán after about A.D. 550 led to a breakdown of centralized authority—perhaps previously exerted by Tikal, the largest and most important ceremonial center of the southern lowlands—and increased autonomy of local Maya elites. These elites expressed their pride and power by constructing ever more elaborate ceremonial centers, which added to the burdens of commoners. Growing population size and density strained food resources and forced the adoption of more intensive agricultural methods. These, in turn, increased competition for land, which was reflected in the growth of warfare and militarism. Improved agricultural production relieved population pressures for a time and made possible the late Classic flowering (A.D. 600–800), marked by a revival of ceremonial center construction, architecture, and the arts. But renewed population pressures, food shortages, and warfare between regional centers, perhaps aggravated by external attacks, led to a severe cultural and social decline in the last century of the Classic period. The build-up of pressure—so runs the theory—"resulted in a swift and catastrophic collapse accompanied by widespread depopulation through warfare, malnutrition, and disaster, until those who survived were again able to achieve a stable agricultural society at a much lower level of population density and social organization."[1]

No such decline occurred in northern Yucatán, a low, limestone plain covered in most places with dense thickets of thorny, scrub forest. This area had been occupied by the Maya fully as long as the south, although with less impressive cultural achievements. But here, too, there arose great ceremonial centers complete with steep pyramids, multistoried palaces, and large

quadrangles. Into this area, in about 900, poured invaders from the central Mexican highlands, probably Toltec emigrants from strife-torn Tula. Toltec armies overran northern Yucatán and established their rule over the Maya, governing from the temple city of Chichén Itzá. The invaders introduced Toltec styles in art and architecture, including colonnaded halls, warrior columns, and the reclining stone figures called Chac Mools. Toltec influence was also reflected in an increased obsession with human sacrifice. After 1200, Maya cultural and political influence revived. Chichén Itzá was abandoned, and power passed to the city-state of Mayapan, a large, walled town from which Maya rulers dominated much of the peninsula, holding tribal chiefs and their families as hostages to exact tribute from surrounding provinces. But in the fifteenth century, virtually all centralized rule disappeared. A successful revolt overthrew the tyranny of Mayapan and destroyed the city itself in 1441. By this time, Maya civilization was in full decline. By the arrival of the Spaniards, all political unity or imperial organization in the area had disappeared.

Maya Economy and Society

Archaeological discoveries of the past two decades have radically revised our notions about the subsistence base of the ancient Maya. Until recently, the prevailing view assumed the primary role of maize in the diet and the almost exclusive reliance on the slash-and-burn (swidden) system of agriculture (explained on page 6). Since this system excluded the possibility of such dense populations as were found at Teotihuacán and other Mesoamerican Classic or Postclassic centers, the traditional interpretation assumed a dispersed peasant population whose houses—typically one-room pole-and-thatch structures—were widely scattered or grouped in small hamlets across the countryside between the ceremonial and administrative

[1] Norman Hammond, *Ancient Maya Civilization* (New Brunswick, N.J.: Rutgers University Press, 1982), p. 140.

Mayan ceremonial site at Tikal. (National Tourist Board, Guatemala)

centers. These centers, containing temples, pyramids, ritual ball courts, and other structures, were denied the character of true "cities"; it was believed that only the Maya elites—a few priests, nobles, and officials and their attendants—lived in them. The rural population, on the other hand, living out among their *milpas* (farm plots), only visited these centers for religious festivals and other special occasions.

This traditional view began to be seriously questioned in the late 1950s, when detailed mapping of the area around the Tikal ceremonial precinct revealed that dense suburbs spread out behind the center for several miles. Similar dense concentrations of house clusters were later found at other major and even minor centers of the Classic period. In the words of Norman Hammond, "the wide-open spaces between the Maya centers, with their scattered bucolic farmers, suddenly became filled with closely packed and hungry suburbanites."

These revelations of the size and density of Classic Maya settlements forced a reassessment of the economic system that supported them.

It has now been clearly established that, in addition to slash-and-burn farming, the Maya practiced an intensive and permanent agriculture that included highly productive kitchen gardens with root crops as staples, arboriculture, terracing, and raised fields—artificial platforms of soil built up from low-lying areas.

The evidence of dense suburban populations around ceremonial centers like Tikal has also provoked a debate about the degree of urbanism present in the Maya lowlands. The traditional view that the Classic Maya centers were virtually deserted for most of the year has become untenable. There is, however, no agreement as to whether they were "cities" in the sense that Teotihuacán was clearly a city. Tikal, in the heart of the Petén, was certainly a metropolitan center with a population of perhaps 50,000 and a countryside heavily populated over an area of some fifty square miles. There is also evidence of some genuine urbanization in northern Yucatán during the Postclassic period, possibly a result of Toltec influence and the tendency to develop the city or town as a fortified position. Chichén Itzá, an old Classic ceremonial center, was greatly enlarged under Toltec influence, while Mayapan, which succeeded Chichén Itzá as a political and military center, constituted a large urban zone encircled by a great wall.

Awareness of the large size and density of Classic Maya populations, the intensive character of much of their agriculture, and the strict social controls that such complex conditions require has also led to a reassessment of Maya social organization. The older view that the ruling class was a small theocratic elite that ruled over a dispersed peasant population from basically empty ceremonial centers has been abandoned. Increased ability to decipher glyphs on the stelae (carved monuments) periodically erected at Classic Maya centers has contributed to a better understanding of the Maya social order. It was once believed that the content of these inscriptions was exclusively religious and astronomical.

In recent decades, however, evidence has accumulated that many of the glyphs carved on stelae, lintels, and other monuments record accessions, wars, and other milestones in the lives of secular rulers. The new interpretation assumes a very complex social order with large distance between the classes. At the apex of the social pyramid stood a hereditary ruler who combined the political, military, and religious leadership of the state. He was surrounded by an aristocracy or nobility, from which were drawn the administrative and executive bureaucracy. Intellectual specialists such as architects, priests, and scribes may have formed another social level. Below them were the numerous artisans required for ceremonial and civil construction—potters, sculptors, stoneworkers, painters, and the like. At the bottom of the social pyramid were the common laborers and peasant farmers who supplied the labor and food that supported this massive superstructure. The weight of their burdens must in time have become crushing, and their discontent may have ignited revolts that brought the ultimate collapse of the lowland Maya civilization.

Archaeological investigations have thrown new light on Classic Maya family and settlement patterns. The fact that the residential platforms on which most Maya houses rested occur in groups of three or more suggests that the Maya family was extended rather than nuclear. It probably consisted of two or more nuclear families spanning two or more generations with a common ancestor. Male predominance is suggested by the richer furnishings of male graves and the preeminence of men in monumental art, leading to the conclusion that descent was patrilineal, from father to son. Maya dress and diet, like its housing, reflected class distinctions. Maya clothing was much the same as the Aztec: cotton loincloths, leather sandals, and sometimes a mantle knotted about the shoulder for men; and wraparound skirts of cotton and blouses with holes for the head and arms for the women.

The same articles of clothing, much more ornately decorated, were worn by the upper classes.

Maya Religion and Learning

The great object of Maya religion, as the Spanish bishop Diego de Landa concisely put it, was "that they [the gods] should give them health, life, and sustenance." The principal Maya divinities, like those of the Aztecs, represented those natural forces and objects that most directly affected the material welfare of the people. The supreme god in the Maya pantheon was Itzam Na, a creator god who incorporated in himself the aspects of many other gods; not only creation, but fire, rain, crops, and earth were among his functions or provinces. Other important divinities were the sun god, the moon goddess, the rain gods, the maize god, and the much-feared god of death. Like the Aztecs, the Maya believed that a number of worlds had successively appeared and been destroyed; this present world, too, would end in catastrophe.

The Maya view of the afterlife also closely resembled that of the Aztecs. They believed in an Upper World constituted of thirteen layers and an Under World of nine. Over each layer presided a certain god; over the lowest layer of the Under World presided the God of Death, Ah Puch. In common with the Aztecs and other peoples of Middle America, the Maya worshiped and placated the gods with a variety of ritual practices that included fasting, penance by bloodletting, the burning of incense, and human sacrifice. But the scale of human sacrifice markedly increased in the Postclassic period under Toltec influence.

The Maya priests were obsessed with time, to which they assigned an occult or magical content. They developed a calendar that was more accurate than ours in making adjustments in the exact length of the solar year. Maya theologians thought of time as burdens carried on the backs of the gods. At the end of a certain period one god laid down his burden for another god to pick up and continue on the journey of time. A given day or year was lucky or unlucky depending on whether the god-bearer was benevolent or malevolent. Thus, the Maya calendars were primarily divinatory in character; that is, they were used to predict conditions in a particular time period.

Like the Aztecs, the Maya had two almanacs. One was a sacred round of 260 days, corresponding to the pattern of ceremonial life. This calendar was composed of two intermeshing and recurrent cycles of different length: one of thirteen days, recorded as numbers; and the second of twenty days, recorded as names. The name of the fourteenth day-name began with one again. A second cycle was the solar year of 365 days, divided into eighteen "months" of twenty days each, plus a final period of five unlucky days during which all unnecessary activity was banned. Completion of these two cycles coincided every fifty-two years. The Aztecs awaited the end of the fifty-two-year period with great anxiety, because they believed that the world might come to an end at this time. A similar belief may have existed among the Maya. Carved monuments (stelae) bearing hieroglyphic texts indicating the date and other calendrical data, such as the state of the moon, the position of the planet Venus, and so on, were frequently erected at the end of the fifty-two-year cycle and at other intervals.

The Maya developed the science of mathematics further than any of their Middle American neighbors. Their units were ones, fives, and twenties, with ones designated by dots, fives by bars, and positions for twenty and multiples of twenty. Place-value numeration, based on a sign for zero, was perhaps the greatest intellectual development of Ancient America. In this system, the position of a number determined its value, making it possible for a limited quantity of symbols to express numbers of any size. Its simplicity made it far superior to the contemporary western European arithmetical system, which employed the cumbersome Roman numeration consisting of distinct symbols for each higher unit. It remained for the Arabs to bring their numeration concept to Europe from India, the only other place where it had been invented. However, Maya mathematics appears to have been applied chiefly to calendrical and astronomical calculation; there is no record of Maya enumeration of people or objects.

Until recently it was believed that Maya hieroglyphic writing, like the mathematics, chiefly served religious and divinatory rather than utilitarian ends. We now have abundant evidence that many of the glyphs carved on the monuments are historical, recording milestones in the lives of Maya rulers. In addition to the inscriptions that appear on stone monuments, lintels, stairways, and other monumental remains, the Maya had great numbers of sacred books or codices, of which only three survive today. These books were painted on folding screens of native paper made of bark. Concerned above all with astronomy, divination, and related topics, they reveal that Maya astronomers made observations and calculations of truly astounding complexity.

The Maya had no alphabet, properly speaking; that is, the majority of their characters represent ideas or objects rather than sounds. But Maya writing, like the Aztec, had reached the stage of syllabic phonetics through the use of rebus writing, in which the sound of a word is represented by combining pictures or signs of things whose spoken names resemble sounds in the word to be formed. Thus, the Maya word for drought, *kintunyaabil*, was written with four characters, the signs of sun or day (*kin*), stone or 360-day unit of time (*tun*), solar year (*haab*), and the affix *il*. Certain Russian scholars have advanced a theory that Maya writing was truly syllabic and hence can be deciphered by matching the most frequent sound elements in modern Maya to the most frequent signs in the ancient writing, using computers to speed the process of decipherment. The existence of purely phonetic glyphs in the Maya script is now generally accepted by scholars, but they seem to be relatively rare in the deciphered material.

Maya writing was not primarily used to record literature or history, but the Maya, like the Aztecs, had a large body of myth, legends, poetry, and traditional history that was transmitted orally from generation to generation. Examples of such material are found in the *Popol Vuh*, the so-called Sacred Book of the Quiche Maya of Guatemala. This book deals, among other matters, with the adventures of the heroic twins Hunahpu and Xbalanque, who after many exploits ascended into heaven to become the sun and the moon. It was written in post-Conquest times in the Spanish alphabet by a native who drew on the oral traditions of his people.

In certain types of artistic activity the Maya surpassed all other Middle American peoples. The temples and pyramids at Teotihuacán and Tenochtitlán were often larger than their Maya counterparts but lacked their grace and subtlety. A distinctive feature of Maya architecture was the corbeled vault, or false arch. Other Middle American peoples used horizontal wooden beams to bridge entrances, producing a heavy and squarish impression. The Maya solved the same problem by having the stones on either side of the opening project farther and farther inward, bridging the two sides at the apex by a capstone. Other characteristics of the Maya architectural style were the great façades richly decorated with carved stone and high ornamental roof combs in temples and palaces. Inner walls were frequently covered with paintings, a few of which have survived. The most celebrated of these paintings are the frescoes discovered in 1946 at Bonampak, an isolated site in the tropical forests of the northeastern corner of the Mexican state of Chiapas. They date from about A.D. 800. These frescoes completely cover the inner walls of a small building of three rooms. They tell a story that begins with a ritual dance, goes on to portray an expedition to obtain sacrificial victims, which is followed by a battle scene, and ends with a human sacrifice, ceremonies, and dance. Despite the highly conventionalized and static style, the absence of perspective and shading, and obvious errors in the human figure, there is an effect of realism that is often missing from Aztec or Toltec art.

Students of the Maya have frequently testified to the admirable personal qualities of the people who, with a very limited technology and in a most forbidding environment, created one of the greatest cultural traditions of all time. Bishop Diego de Landa, who burned twenty-seven Maya codices as "works of the devil," nevertheless observed that the Maya were very generous and hospitable. No one could enter their houses, he wrote, without being offered food and drink. The observations of modern anthropologists confirm Landa's judgment; mildness, generosity, and honesty, they report, are all prominent traits of the contemporary Maya Indians.

THE INCAS OF PERU

In the highlands of Peru in the mid-fourteenth century, a small tribe rose from obscurity to create by 1500 the mightiest empire of Ancient America. From the time of the discovery and conquest of Peru by Pizarro to the present, the Inca achievements in political and social organization have attracted intense interest. Soon after the Conquest a debate began on the nature of Inca society that continues to the present day. For some it is a "socialist empire"; others view it as a forerunner of the "welfare state" of our own time; for still others the Inca realm anticipated the totalitarian tyrannies of the twentieth century.

The physical environment of the central Andean area offers a key to the remarkable cultural development of this region. In Peru high mountains rise steeply from the sea, leaving a narrow coastal plain that is a true desert. The Humboldt Current runs north along the coast from the Antarctic, making the ocean much colder than the land; hence the rains fall at sea. But lack of rainfall is compensated for by short rivers that make their precipitous way down from the high snowfields. These rivers create oases at intervals along the coast and provide water for systems of canal irrigation. The aridity of the climate preserves the great natural wealth of the soil, which in areas of heavy rainfall is leached away. The coastal waters of Peru are rich in fish, and its offshore islands, laden in Inca times with millions of tons of guano, made available an inexhaustible source of fertilizer for agriculture.

To be sure, the rugged highlands of Peru and Bolivia offer relatively little arable land. But the valleys are fertile and well watered and support a large variety of crops. Maize is grown at lower levels (up to about eleven thousand feet), potatoes and quinoa (a hardy grain resembling buckwheat) at higher altitudes. Above the agricultural zone the *puna* (plateau) provides fodder for herds of llamas and alpacas, domesticated members of the camel family, which were important in Inca times as a source of meat and wool. Potentially, this environment offered a basis for large food production and a dense population.

Origins of Inca Culture

Like the Aztecs of Mexico, the Incas of Peru were heirs to a cultural tradition of great antiquity. This tradition had its origin not in the highlands but on the coast. By 2500 B.C., a village life, based chiefly on fishing and food gathering and supplemented by the cultivation of squash, lima beans, and a few other plants, had arisen about the mouths of rivers in the coastal area. Maize, introduced into Peruvian

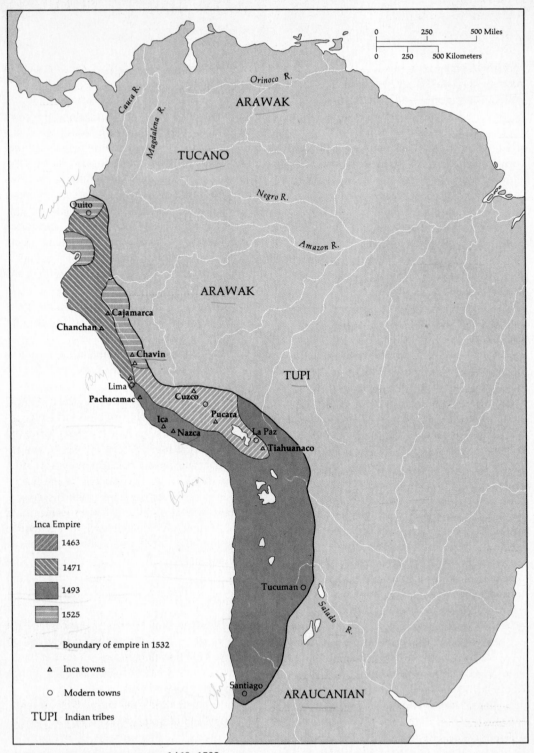

Inca Empire

```
▨  1463
▧  1471
▓  1493
▤  1525
```

——— Boundary of empire in 1532

△ Inca towns

○ Modern towns

TUPI Indian tribes

GROWTH OF THE INCA EMPIRE, 1460–1532

agriculture about 1500 B.C., did not become important until many centuries later.

The transition from the Archaic to the Preclassic period seems to have come later and more suddenly in Peru than in Mesoamerica. After long centuries of the simple village life just described, a strong advance of culture began on the coast about 900 B.C. This advance seems to have been associated with progress in agriculture, especially greater use of maize, and with a movement up the river valleys from the littoral (coastal area), possibly as a result of population pressure. Between 900 and 500 B.C., a distinctive style in building, art, ceramics, and weaving, known as Chavín (from the name of the site of a great ceremonial center discovered in 1946), spread along the coast and even into the highlands. The most distinctive feature of Chavín is its art style, which features a feline being, presumably a deity whose cult spread over the area of Chavín influence.

The Classic period that emerged in Peru at or shortly before the beginning of the Christian era reflected further progress in agriculture, notably in the use of irrigation and fertilization. The brilliant culture called Nazca displaced the Chavín along the coast and highlands of southern Peru at this time. Nazca pottery is distinguished by its use of color. Sometimes there are as many as eleven soft pastel shades on one pot. The lovely Nazca textiles display an enormous range of colors.

Even more remarkable was the Mochica culture of the northern Peruvian coast. The Mochica built pyramids and temples, roads and large irrigation canals, and evolved a complex, highly stratified society with a directing priesthood and a powerful priest-king. Metallurgy was well developed, as evidenced by the wide use of copper weapons and tools and the manufacture of alloys of gold, copper, and silver. But as craftsmen and artists the Mochica are best known for their red and black pottery, never surpassed in the perfection of its realistic modeling. The

so-called portrait vases, apparently representing actual individuals, mark the acme of Mochica realism. The pottery was also frequently decorated with realistic paintings of the most varied kind, including erotic scenes, which today are collectors' items. The pottery frequently depicts war scenes, suggesting chronic struggles for limited arable land and sources of water. The aggressive Mochica were themselves finally conquered by invaders who ravaged their lands, and a time of turbulence and cultural decline came to northern Peru.

About A.D. 600, the focus of Andean civilization shifted from the coast to the highlands. At the site called Tiahuanaco, just south of Lake Titicaca on the high plateau of Bolivia, there arose a great ceremonial center famed for its megalithic architecture, which was constructed with great stone blocks perfectly fitted together,

Mochica portrait vase with stirrup spout. (Jack Howard/Editorial Photocolor Archives, Inc.)

and for its monumental human statuary. Tiahuanaco seems to have been the capital of a military state that eventually controlled all of southern Peru from Arequipa south to highland Bolivia and Chile. Another people, the Huari, embarked on a career of conquest from their homeland near modern Ayacucho; their territory ultimately included both the coast and highlands as far north as Cajamarca and south to the Tiahuanaco frontier. After a few centuries of domination, the Huari Empire broke up about A.D. 1000. At about the same time the Tiahuanaco sway also came to an end. The disintegration of these empires was followed by a return to political and artistic regionalism in the southern Andean area.

By A.D. 1000, a number of Postclassic states, differing from their predecessors in their greater size, had established their control over large portions of the northern Peruvian coast. Their rise was accompanied by the growth of cities. Each river valley had its own urban center, and an expanded net of irrigation works made support of larger populations possible. The largest of these new states was the Chimu kingdom. Its capital, Chanchan, was an immense city spread over eight square miles, with houses made of great molded adobe bricks grouped into large units or compounds. The Chimu kingdom survived until its conquest by the Inca in the mid-fifteenth century.

Inca Economy and Society

In the highlands, meanwhile, where less settled conditions prevailed, a new power was emerging. The Incas (so called after their own name for the ruling lineage) made a modest appearance in history as one of a number of small tribes that inhabited the Cuzco region in the Andean highlands and struggled with each other for possession of land and water. A strong strategic situation in the Valley of Cuzco and some cultural superiority over their neighbors favored

the Incas as they began their career of conquest. Previous empires—Huari, Tiahuanaco, and Chimu—no doubt provided the Incas with instructive precedents for conquest and the consolidation of conquest through a variety of political and socioeconomic techniques. Like other imperialist nations of antiquity, the Incas had a body of myth and legend that ascribed a divine origin to their rulers and gave their warriors a comforting assurance of supernatural favor and protection.

True imperial expansion seems to have begun in the second quarter of the fifteenth century, in the reign of Pachacuti Inca, who was crowned in 1438. Together with his son Topa Inca, also a great conqueror, Pachacuti obtained the submission of many provinces by the skillful use of claims of divine aid, fair promises, threats, and naked force. Reputed to be a great organizer as well as a mighty warrior, Pachacuti is credited with many reforms and innovations, including the establishment of the territorial divisions and elaborate administrative bureaucracy that made the wheels of the Inca Empire go round. By 1527, the boundary markers of the Children of the Sun rested on the modern frontier between Ecuador and Colombia to the north and on the Maule River in Chile to the south. A population of perhaps 16 million people owed allegiance to the emperor. When the Spaniards arrived, the ruler was Atahualpa, who had just won the imperial mantle by defeating his half-brother Huascar.

The Incas maintained their authority with an arsenal of devices that included the spread of their Quechua language (still spoken by five-sixths of the Indians of the central Andean area) as the official language of the empire, the imposition of a unifying state religion, and a shrewd policy of incorporating chieftains of conquered regions into the central bureaucracy. An important factor in the Inca plan of unification was the policy of resettlement, or colonization. This consisted of deporting dissident populations and replacing them with loyal *mitimaes* (colonists) from older provinces of the empire. An excellent network of roads, or rather footpaths, linked administrative centers and made it possible to send armies and messengers quickly from one part of the empire to another. Some roads were paved, others were cut into solid rock. Where the land was marshy, the roads passed over causeways; suspension bridges spanned gorges, and pontoon bridges of buoyant reeds were used to cross rivers. The Incas had no system of writing, but they possessed a most efficient means of keeping records in a memory aid called the *quipu*, a stick or cord with a number of knotted strings tied to it. Strings of different colors represented different articles, people, or districts; knots tied in the strings ascended in units representing ones, tens, hundreds, thousands, and so on.

The economic basis of the Inca Empire was its intensive irrigation agriculture capable of supporting without serious strain not only the producers but the large Inca armies, a large administrative bureaucracy, and many other persons engaged in nonproductive activities. The Incas did not develop this agriculture. By the time of their rise, the original coastal irrigation systems had probably been extended over all suitable areas in coastal and highland Peru. But along with their political and religious institutions, the Incas introduced the advanced practices of irrigation, terracing, and fertilization among conquered peoples of more primitive culture. Terracing was widely used to extend the arable area and to prevent injury to fields and settlements in the narrow Andean valleys from run-off from the steep slopes during the rainy season. Irrigation ditches, sometimes mere trenches, sometimes elaborate stone channels, conducted water to the fields and pastures where it was needed.

Agricultural implements were few and simple. They consisted chiefly of a foot plow, used to break up the ground and dig holes for planting, and a hoe with a bronze blade for general cultivation. As previously noted, the potato and quinoa were staple crops in the higher valleys; maize was the principal crop at lower altitudes; and a wide variety of plants, including cotton, coca, and beans, was cultivated in the lower and hotter valleys. A major function of the Inca state was to regulate the exchange of the products of these multiple environments, primarily through the collection of tribute and its redistribution to various groups in Inca society. The Inca state also promoted self-sufficiency by allowing members of a given community to exploit the resources of different levels of the Andean "vertical" economy.

The basic unit of Inca social organization was the *ayllu*, a kinship group whose members claimed descent from a common ancestor and married within the group. A village community typically consisted of several ayllu. Each ayllu owned certain lands, which were assigned in lots to heads of families. Each family head had the right to use and pass on the land to male descendants but not to sell or otherwise dispose of it. Villagers frequently practiced mutual aid in agricultural tasks, in the construction of dwellings, and in other projects of a private or public nature. The Inca rulers took over this communal principle and utilized it for their own ends in the form of corvée, or unpaid forced labor.

Before the Inca conquest, the ayllu were governed by *curacas* (hereditary chiefs) assisted by a council of elders. Under Inca rule, the kinship basis of ayllu organization was weakened through the planned removal of some of its members and the settlement of strangers in its midst (the system of mitimaes). A varying amount of land was taken from the villages and vested in the Inca state and the state church. In addition to working their own lands and those of their curaca, ayllu members were required to till the Inca state and church lands. The Inca government also used the forced labor of villagers to create new arable land by leveling and terracing slopes. This new land was often turned over as private estates to curacas and Inca military leaders and nobles who had rendered conspicuous service to the Inca state. The Inca himself possessed private estates, and others were owned by the lineages of dead emperors and used to maintain the cult of these former rulers. These private estates were not worked by ayllu members but by a new servile class, the *yanacona*,[2] defined by Spanish sources as "permanent servants"; each ayllu had to contribute a number of such servants or retainers, who also worked in the Inca temples and palaces and performed personal service.

In addition to agricultural labor, ayllu members had to work on roads, irrigation channels, and fortresses, in the mines, and so on, in a system called the *mita*, later adopted by the Spaniards for their own purposes. Another requirement was that villages produce specified quantities of cloth for the state to use in clothing soldiers and retainers. All able-bodied commoners between certain ages were subject to military service. There is no trace of socialism or a welfare state in these arrangements, which favored not the commoners but the Inca dynasty, nobility, priesthood, warriors, and officials. Many of the activities cited as reflecting the benevolence and foresight of the Inca state were actually traditional village and ayllu functions. One such activity was the maintenance of storehouses of grain and cloth by the community for times of crop failure. The Inca state merely took over this principle, as it had taken over the principle of cooperative labor for communal ends, and established storehouses containing the goods produced by the peasants' forced labor on state and church lands. The cloth and grain stored in these warehouses were used primarily to clothe and feed the army, the Crown artisans,

the conscript labor for public works, and the officials who lived in Cuzco and other towns.

The relations between the Inca and the peasantry were based on the principle of reciprocity, expressed in an elaborate system of gifts and countergifts. The peasantry cultivated the lands of the Inca, worked up his wool and cotton into cloth, and performed various other kinds of labor for him. The Inca, the divine, universal lord, in turn permitted them to cultivate their communal lands, supported the aged and sick who could not support themselves, and in time of famine released to the villages the surplus grain in his storehouses. Since the imperial gifts were the products of the peasants' own labor, this "reciprocity" amounted to intensive exploitation of the commoners by the Inca rulers and nobility. We must not underestimate, however, the hold of this ideology, buttressed by a religious world view that regarded the Inca as responsible for defending the order and very existence of the universe, on the Inca peasant mentality.

At the time of the Conquest, a vast gulf separated the regimented and laborious life of the commoners from the luxurious life of the Inca nobility. At the apex of the social pyramid were the Inca and his kinsmen, composed of twelve lineages. Members of these lineages had the privilege of piercing their ears and distending the lobes with large ornaments; hence the name *orejones* (big ears) assigned to the Inca kinsmen by the Spaniards. The orejones were exempt from tribute labor and military service; the same was true of the curacas, who had once been chieftains in their own right, and of a numerous class of specialists—servants, retainers, quipu keepers and other officials, and entertainers. Side by side with the Inca state, which drained off the peasants' surplus production, regulated the exchange of goods between the various regions, and directed vast public works, there arose the incipient feudalism of the Inca nobility and curacas. Their loyalty and services to the

---

[2] A plural term in Quechua but treated by the Spaniards as singular.

Inca were rewarded with rich gifts of land, llamas, and yanacona. Their growing resources enabled them to form their own local clienteles, achieve a certain relative independence of the Crown, and play an important role in the disputes over the succession that sometimes followed the emperor's death.

Inca rule over the peasant masses was largely indirect, exercised through local chieftains. It probably did not seriously affect the round of daily life in the villages. The typical peasant home in the highlands was a small hut with walls of fieldstone or adobe and a gable roof thatched with grass. The scanty furniture consisted of a raised sleeping platform, a clay stove, and some clay pots and dishes. Men wore a breechcloth, a sleeveless tunic, and a large cloak over the shoulders with two corners tied in front; the fineness of the cloth used and the ornamentation varied according to social rank. Women wore a wraparound cloth extending from beneath the arms to the ankles, with the top edges drawn over the shoulders and fastened with straight pins. An ornamented sash around the waist and a shoulder mantle completed the woman's apparel. Men adorned themselves with earplugs and bracelets; women wore necklaces and shawl pins.

Inca Religion and Learning

The Inca state religion existed side by side with the much older ancestor cults and the worship of innumerable *huacas* (local objects and places). Chief of the Inca gods was a nameless creator called Viracocha and Pachayachachic (lord and instructor of the world). His cult seems to have been a philosophical religion largely confined to the priesthood and nobility. First in importance after Viracocha was the Sun God, claimed by the Inca royal family as its divine ancestor. Other notable divinities were the Thunder God, who sent the life-giving rain, and the Moon, wife of the Sun, who played a vital role in the

regulation of the Inca festival calendar. The Inca idols were housed in numerous temples attended by priests who directed and performed ceremonies that included prayer, sacrifice, confession, and the rite of divination. Another priestly function was the magical cure of disease. The priests were assisted in their religious duties by a class of *mamacuna* (holy women) who had taken vows of permanent chastity. Human sacrifice was performed on very momentous occasions, such as an important victory or some great natural calamity.

Inca art was marked by a high level of technical excellence. The architecture was solid and functional, characterized by massiveness rather than beauty. The stone sculpture, more frequent in the highlands than on the coast, has been described as ponderous and severe. But the tapestries of Inca weavers are among the world's textile masterpieces, so fine and intricate is the weaving. Inca metallurgy was also on a high technical and artistic plane. Cuzco, the Inca capital, abounded in gold objects: The imperial palace had gold friezes and panels of gold and silver, and the Temple of the Sun contained a garden with lifelike replicas of plants and animals, all made of hammered gold.

Although the Incas had no system of writing and hence no written literature, narrative poems, prayers, and tales were handed down orally from generation to generation. The Inca hymns and prayers that have been preserved are notable for their lofty thought and beauty of expression. Of the long narrative poems that dealt with Inca mythology, legends, and history, there remain only summaries in Spanish prose.

A melancholy and nostalgic spirit pervades many of the traditional Inca love songs, and the same plaintiveness characterizes the few examples of their music that have come down to us. Based on the five-toned, or pentatonic, scale, this music was performed with an assortment of instruments: flutes, trumpets, and whistles; gongs, bells, and rattles; and several kinds of skin drums and tambourines. The dances that accompanied the music sometimes represented an elementary form of drama.

Spanish conquistadors destroyed Inca political organization and dealt shattering blows to all aspects of Inca civilization, but elements of that culture survive everywhere in the central Andean area. These survivals, tangible and intangible, include the Quechua speech of great numbers of Indians; the numerous Indian communities, or ayllu, still partly based on cooperative principles; the widespread pagan beliefs and rites of the people; and of course the monumental ruins of Sacsahuaman, Ollantaytambo, Machu Picchu, Pisac and Cuzco itself. Inca civilization also lives in the writings of Peruvian historians, novelists, and statesmen who evoke the vanished Inca greatness and praise the ancient virtues of their people. In the 1960s, one Peruvian president, Fernando Belaúnde Terry, urged his nation to imitate the industry, energy, and foresight of its Indian forebears in order to make Peru once again the flourishing garden that it was under the Incas. His successor, the military reformer Juan Velasco Alvarado, gave the name Inca to his program for the economic, social, and political reconstruction of Peru.

NEW LIGHT ON
ANCIENT AMERICA

As a result of the patient researches of anthropologists and historians, the volume of information on Ancient America is growing at a rapid rate. Students are more and more impressed with the complexity of the civilizations of Nuclear America and commonly compare them with such advanced Old World cultures as ancient Egypt and Mesopotamia. Recent studies of the population history of Ancient America have contributed to the rising respect for the Indian cultural achievement. If we assume, as many social scientists do, that population density is correlated with a certain tech-

nological and cultural level, then a high estimate of the Indian population of America in 1492 is in some measure a judgment on the old Indian societies and on the colonial societies that arose on their ruins.

Beginning in the 1940s, three professors at the University of California, Woodrow Borah, Sherburne Cook, and Lesley B. Simpson, opened a new line of inquiry into the demographic history of Ancient America with a remarkable series of studies focusing on central Mexico. Using a variety of Indian and Spanish records and sophisticated statistical methods, the Berkeley school projected backward from a base established from Spanish counts of the Indians for tax purposes and arrived at a figure of 25.3 million for central Mexico on the eve of the Conquest.

Later, Cook and Borah extended their inquiries into other areas. Particularly striking are their conclusions concerning the population of Hispaniola in 1492. Previous estimates of the island's population had ranged from a low of 60,000 to the 3 to 4 million proposed by the sixteenth-century Spanish friar Bartolomé de Las Casas, but those high figures had long been regarded as the patent exaggerations of a pro-Indian enthusiast. After careful study of a series of statements and estimates on the aboriginal population of Hispaniola made between 1492 and 1520, Cook and Borah not only confirmed the reliability of Las Casas's figures but offered even higher probable figures of from 7 to 8 million.

Aside from Borah's suggestion in 1964 that the population of America in 1492 may have been "upwards of 100 million," the Berkeley school did not attempt to estimate the pre-Columbian population of the continent as a whole. A systematic effort of this kind was made by the American anthropologist Henry Dobyns. Assuming that the Indian population was reduced by roughly 95 percent after contact with the Europeans, he estimated a pre-Conquest population of between 90 and 112 million;

of this number he assigned 30 million each to central Mexico and Peru.

The methods and findings of the Berkeley school and Dobyns have provoked some bitter dissent, and the debate continues. In general, however, the evidence of the last quarter-century of research in this field quite consistently points to larger populations than were accepted previously. The most recent effort to generalize from this evidence, taking account both of the findings of the Berkeley school and its critics, is that of Professor William M. Denevan (1976), who postulates a total population of 57.3 million—a far cry from the 1939 estimate of 8.5 million by the American anthropologist A. L. Kroeber.

CHAPTER TWO

The Hispanic

Background

Conquest was a major theme of Spanish history from very remote times. The prehistoric inhabitants of the peninsula, whose unknown artists produced the marvelous cave paintings of Altamira, were overrun by tribes vaguely called Iberians and by the Celts, who are believed to have come from North Africa and central Europe, respectively, probably before 1000 B.C. New waves of invasion brought the Phoenicians, Greeks, and Carthaginians, commercial nations that established trading posts and cities on the coast but made no effort to dominate the interior. Still later, Spain became a stake of empire in the great struggle for commercial supremacy between Rome and Carthage that ended with the decisive defeat of the latter in 201 B.C. For six centuries thereafter, Rome was the dominant power in the peninsula.

Unlike earlier invaders, the Romans attempted to establish their authority throughout Spain (the name comes from the word *Hispania,* applied by the Romans to the whole peninsula) and to impose their language and institutions on the native peoples. From Latin, made the official language, sprang the various dialects and languages still spoken by the Hispanic peoples. Roman law replaced the customary law of the Celts, Iberians, and other native groups. Native tribal organization was destroyed through forced changes of residence, concentration in towns, and the planting of Roman colonies that served as agencies of pacification and assimilation. Agriculture, mining, and industry developed, and Roman Spain carried on an extensive trade in wheat, wine, and olive oil with Italy. Roman engineers constructed great public roads and aqueducts, some of which are still in use. Roman education and literary culture were brought to Spain, and a number of Spaniards by birth or residence (the satirical poet Martial, the epic poet Lucan, and the philosopher Seneca) made notable contributions to Latin literature.

Early in the fifth century A.D., as a result of the decline of Roman military power, a number of barbarian peoples of Germanic origin invaded Spain. By the last half of the century, one group of invaders, the Visigoths, had gained mastery over most of the peninsula. As a result of long contact with the empire, the Visigoths had already lost part of their barbarism. Their assimilation of Roman culture continued in Spain through contact with the Hispano-Romans. The Visigothic kingdom was Christian; its speech became Latin with a small admixture of Germanic terms; in administration it followed the Roman model. But the succession to the kingship followed Germanic tradition in being elective, a frequent source of great internal strife.

SPAIN'S MEDIEVAL HERITAGE

The divisions among the Goths caused by struggles over kingship played into the hands of the new Moslem power in North Africa. In 711 the Moslems crossed the straits and decisively defeated Roderic, the last Gothic king.

Within a few years, all of Spain, aside from the remote region north of the Cantabrian Mountains, had fallen into Moslem hands. But the Moslems' hold on the bleak uplands of Castile was never strong; they preferred the fertile plains and delightful climate of southern Spain, which they called Al-Andalus, the land of Andalusia.

The Moslems, heirs to the accumulated cultural wealth of the ancient Mediterranean and Eastern worlds, enriched this heritage with their own magnificent contributions to science, arts, and letters. In the tenth and eleventh centuries, Moslem Spain, with its capital at Córdoba, was an economic and intellectual showplace from which new knowledge and ideas flowed into Christian lands. Spanish agriculture gained by the introduction of new irrigation and water-lifting devices and new crops: sugar, saffron, cotton, silk, and citrus fruits. Industry was broadened through the introduction of such new products as paper and glass, hitherto unknown to the West. Moslem metalwork, pottery, silk, and leatherwork were esteemed throughout Europe. Many Moslem rulers were patrons of literature and learning; the scholar-king Al-Haquem II built up a library said to have numbered four hundred thousand volumes.

As a rule, the Moslem conquerors did not insist on the conversion of the vanquished Christians, preferring to give them the option of accepting the Islamic faith or paying a special poll tax. The relatively tolerant Moslem rule was favorable to economic and cultural advance. The Jews, who had suffered severe persecution under the Visigoths, enjoyed official protection and made major contributions to medicine, philosophy, and Talmudic studies. The condition of the peasantry probably improved, for the conquerors distributed the vast estates of the Visigothic lords among the serfs, who paid a certain portion of the produce to the new Moslem lords and kept the rest for themselves. But in later centuries, these trends were reversed; great landed estates again arose, taxation increased, and severe persecution of Jews and

Mozárabes (Christians who had adopted Arab speech and customs) drove many to flee to Christian territory.

Despite its noble achievements, Moslem civilization rested on insecure foundations. The Arab conquerors never fully threw off the tribal form of social organization under which they began their prodigious advance, and the Moslem world was torn by fierce political and religious feuds over control of the empire. In Spain these internal differences were complicated by conflicts between the Arabs and the North African Berbers, recent converts to Islam who were more fanatically devout than their teachers. By the mid-eleventh century, the caliphate of Córdoba had broken up into a large number of *taifas* (states) that constantly warred with each other. These discords enabled the petty Christian kingdoms that had arisen in the north to survive, grow strong, and eventually launch a general advance against the Moslems. In the west, Portugal, having achieved independence from Castile by the mid-twelfth century, attained its historic boundaries two centuries later. In the center, the joint realm of León and Castile pressed its advance; to the east, the kingdom of Aragon steadily expanded at the expense of the disunited Moslem states.

The Reconquest began as a struggle of Christian kings and nobles to regain their lost lands and serfs; only later did it assume the character of a crusade. Early in the ninth century, the tomb of St. James, supposedly found in northwest Spain, became the center of the famous pilgrimage of Santiago de Compostela and gave Spain a warrior patron saint who figured prominently in the Reconquest and the conquest of the New World. But the career of the famous Cid, whose Arabic title of "lord" was given by his Moslem soldiers to Ruy Díaz de Vivar, illustrates the absence of religious fanaticism in the first stage of the struggle. True to the ideals of his time, the Cid placed feudal above religious loyalties, and as a vassal of the Moslem kings of Saragossa and Valencia fought Moorish and Christian foes alike. When he captured Valencia

for himself in 1094, he allowed the Moslems to worship freely and retain their property, requiring only the payment of tributes authorized by the Koran.

The Moslems vainly sought to check the Christian advance by calling on newly converted, fanatically religious Berber tribes in North Africa to come to their aid. The Christian victory at Las Navas de Tolosa (1212) in Andalusia over a large Berber army marked a turning point in the Reconquest. Ferdinand III of Castile captured Córdoba, the jewel of Moslem Spain, in 1236; the surrender of Seville in 1248 gave him control of the mouth of the Guadalquivir River and communication with the sea. By the time of Ferdinand's death in 1252, the Moslem territory in Spain had been reduced to the small kingdom of Granada. The strength of its position, protected by steep mountains and impassable gorges, and the divisions that arose within the Christian camp gave Granada two and a half more centuries of independent life.

Castile

Castile, the largest and most powerful of the Spanish kingdoms, played the leading role in the Reconquest. The great movement left an enduring stamp on the Castilian character. Centuries of struggle against the Moor made war almost a Castilian way of life and created a large class of warrior-nobles who regarded manual labor with contempt. In the Castilian scale of values, the military virtues of courage, endurance, and honor took the first place. Not only the nobles but the commoners accepted these values. The lure of plunder, land, and other rewards drew many peasants and artisans into the armies of the Reconquest and diffused militarist and aristocratic ideals throughout Castilian society. To these ideals the crusading spirit of the Reconquest, especially in its later phase, added a strong sense of religious superiority and mission.

The Reconquest also helped to shape the character of the Castilian economy. As the

Fifteenth century Spanish castle in Caceres, Extremadura. (United Press International Photo)

Moslems fell back, vast tracts of land came into the possession of the Crown, and the kings assigned the lion's share of this land to the nobility, the church, and the three military orders of Calatrava, Alcántara, and Santiago. As a result, Castile, especially the area from Toledo south (New Castile), became a region of enormous estates and a very wealthy, powerful aristocracy.

The Reconquest also insured the supremacy of sheep raising over agriculture in Castile. In a time of constant warfare, of raids and counter-raids, the mobile sheep was a more secure and valuable form of property than land. With the advance of the Christian frontier, much new territory—frequently too arid for easy agricultural use—was opened to the sheep industry. The introduction of the merino sheep into Spain from North Africa around 1300, coinciding with a sharply increased demand in northern Europe for Spanish wool, gave a marked stimulus to sheep raising. By the late thirteenth century, there had arisen a powerful organization of sheep raisers, the Mesta. In return for large subsidies to the Crown, this organization received extensive privileges, including the right to move great flocks of sheep across Spain from summer pastures in the north to winter pastures in the south, with frequent injury to the farmlands and woods in their path. The great nobles dominated the sheep industry as well as agriculture. Their large rents and the profits from the sale of their wool gave them an economic, social, and military power that threatened the supremacy of the king.

The Castilian towns represented the only counterpoise to this power. The advance of the Reconquest and the need to consolidate its gains promoted municipal growth. To attract settlers to the newly conquered territory, the king gave generous fueros (charters of liberties) to the towns that sprang up one after another. These charters endowed the towns with administrative autonomy and vast areas of land that extended their jurisdiction into the surrounding countryside. The towns were governed by elected judicial officials known as alcaldes and by members of the town council, called regidores. The economic expansion of the thirteenth and fourteenth centuries and the growth of the wool trade, above all, made the Castilian towns bustling centers of industry and commerce. The wealth of the towns gave them a peculiar importance in the meetings of the consultative body, or parliament, known as the Cortes. Since the nobles and the clergy were exempt from taxes, the deputies of the towns had to vote the money needed by the king. Their price for voting it became the redress of grievances presented in the form of petitions that royal approval transformed into laws.

The Castilian towns had their time of splendor, but in the last analysis the middle class remained small and weak; it was overshadowed by the enormous power of the great nobles. Aware of their weakness, the towns joined their forces in *hermandades*, military associations that resisted the aggressions of the nobles and sometimes of the king. But the posture of the towns was essentially defensive. Without the aid of the king, they could not hope to impose their will on the aristocracy.

As the Moslem power waned, the great nobles turned from fighting the infidel to battling the king, the towns, and each other. In the course of the fourteenth and fifteenth centuries, the nobles gained the upper hand in their struggle with the king, usurping royal lands and revenues and often transforming the monarch into their pawn. The degradation of the Crown reached its lowest point in the reign of Henry IV (1454–1474), when there was an almost total breakdown of central government and public order. Beneath this anarchy, however, the continued expansion of economic life inspired a growing demand for a strong monarchy capable of establishing peace and order.

Aragon

The medieval history of the smaller, less populous kingdom of Aragon differed in important ways from that of Castile. The king of Aragon ruled over three states: Aragon, Valencia, and Catalonia, each regarded as a separate *reino* (kingdom), each having its own Cortes. The upland state of Aragon was the poorest, most backward of the three. Valencia was the home of a large Moorish peasant population subject to a Christian landowning nobility. The dominant role in the union was played by Catalonia and its great city of Barcelona, which had given Aragon its dynasty and most of its revenues. A thriving industry and powerful fleets had made Barcelona the center of a commercial empire based on the export of textiles. Catalan arms had also won Sardinia and Sicily for the crown of Aragon. In Aragon, therefore, the ruling class was not the landed nobility, which was relatively poor, but the commercial and industrial oligarchy of Barcelona. The constitutional system of Aragon reflected the supremacy of this class by giving legislative power to the Cortes of Catalonia and by providing special watchdog committees of the Cortes, which guarded against any infringement of the rights and liberties of the subjects.

In the fourteenth and fifteenth centuries, the prosperity of Barcelona was undermined by the ravages of the Black Death, agrarian unrest in the Catalan countryside, struggles between the merchant oligarchy and popular elements in Barcelona, and above all by the loss of traditional Catalan markets to Genoese competitors. This economic decline sharpened Catalan internal struggles, in which the Crown joined on the side of the popular elements. The result was the civil war of 1462–1472, which ended in a qualified victory for the king, John II, but which completed the ruin of Catalonia. The weakness of Aragon on the eve of its union with Castile insured Castilian leadership of the coming new Spain.

The chain of events leading to Spanish unity began with the secret marriage in 1469 of Isabella, sister of Henry IV of Castile, and Ferdinand, son of John II of Aragon. This match was the fruit of complex intrigues in which the personal ambitions of the young couple, the hostility of many Castilian nobles to their king, and the desire of John II to add Castile to his son Ferdinand's heritage all played their part. On the death of Henry IV in 1474, Isabella proclaimed herself queen of Castile with the support of a powerful faction of Castilian nobles and towns that declared that Henry's daughter Juana was illegitimate. This claim led to a dynastic war in which Portugal supported Juana. By 1479 the struggle had ended in Isabella's favor. In the same year, John II died and Ferdinand succeeded to his dominions. Ferdinand and Isabella now became joint rulers of Aragon and Castile, but the terms of their marriage contract carefully subordinated Ferdinand to Isabella in the government of Castile and excluded Isabella from the administration of Aragon. The process of Spanish unification, however, had begun. Under the leadership of Castile, Spain embarked on a remarkable career of domestic progress and imperial expansion.

THE SPAIN OF FERDINAND AND ISABELLA

Restoration of Order

The young monarchs faced an urgent problem of restoring peace and order in their respective kingdoms. Catalonia was still troubled by struggles between feudal lords and serfs determined to end their legal servitude. Ferdinand intervened to bring about a solution relatively favorable to the peasantry. His ruling of Guadalupe (1486) ended serfdom in Catalonia and enabled fifty thousand peasants to become small landowners. But he made no effort to reform Aragon's archaic constitutional system, which set strict limits on the royal power. As a result, Castile and Aragon, despite their newfound unity, continued to move along divergent political courses.

The task of restoring order was greater in Castile. The age of anarchy under Henry IV had transformed cities into battlefields and parts of the countryside into a desert. To eradicate the evils of banditry and feudal violence, Isabella counted above all on the support of the towns and the middle classes. The Cortes of Madrigal (1476) forged a solid alliance between the Crown and the towns for the suppression of disorder. Their instrument was the *Santa Hermandad*, a police force paid for and manned principally by the towns but under the direct control of the Crown. The efficiency of this force and the severe and prompt punishments meted out by its tribunals gradually restored peace in Castile.

But Isabella's program went beyond this immediate goal. She proposed to bend to the royal will all the great institutions of medieval Castile: the nobility, the church, and the towns themselves. The Cortes of Toledo of 1480 reduced the power of the grandees (nobles of the first rank) in various ways. An Act of Resumption compelled them to return to the Crown about half the revenues they had usurped since 1464. Another reform reorganized the Council of Castile, the central governing agency of the kingdom. This reform reduced the grandees who had dominated the old royal council to holders of empty dignities. It vested effective responsibility and power in *letrados* (officals usually possessed of legal training), who were drawn from the lower nobility, the middle class, and *conversos* (converted Jews). The same end of curbing aristocratic power was served by the establishment of a hierarchy of courts and magistrates that ascended from the *corregidor* (the royal officer who watched over the affairs of a municipality) through the *cancillerías* (the high law courts of Castile) up to the Council of Castile, the highest court as well as the supreme administrative body of the country. At all levels, the Crown asserted its judicial primacy, including the right of intervention in the feudal jurisdiction of the nobility.

The vast wealth of the military orders made them veritable states within the Castilian state. The Crown determined to weaken their power by securing for itself control of these orders. When the grand mastership of Santiago fell vacant in 1476, Isabella personally appeared before the dignitaries of the order to insist that they confer the headship on her husband; they meekly assented. When the grand masterships of Calatrava and Alcántara fell vacant, they too were duly conferred on Ferdinand. By these moves, the Crown gained important new sources of revenue and patronage.

The towns had served the Crown well in the struggle against anarchy, but in the past two centuries their democratic traditions had declined, and many had fallen under the control of selfish oligarchies. Some, like Seville, had become battlefields of aristocractic factions. These disorders provided Isabella with pretexts for resuming the policy, initiated by some of her predecessors, of intervening in municipal affairs by introducing corregidores into the towns. These officials combined administrative and judicial functions and steadily usurped the roles of the alcaldes and regidores. Ferdinand and Isabella also carried forward another practice begun by their predecessors. The offices of alcalde and regidor in towns with royal charters were made appointive by the Crown instead of elective by the householders. *Villas de señorío* (towns under noble or ecclesiastical jurisdiction) were permitted to function under the traditional system, but with the right of royal intervention in the event of miscarriage of justice.

The taming of the towns was accompanied by a decline in the importance of the Cortes. An important factor in this decline was the large increase in revenues from royal taxes, such as the *alcabala* (sales tax), which freed the Crown from excessive dependence on the grants of the Cortes. The increased supervision of the Crown over the municipalities also decreased the likelihood of resistance by their deputies in the Cortes to royal demands. The sovereigns summoned the Castilian Cortes only when they needed money. When the treasury was full or when peace prevailed they ignored them.

Religious and Economic Reforms

In their march toward absolute power, the monarchs did not hesitate to challenge the church. Under their pressure, the weak popes of this period yielded to them the right of *patronato* (the right of appointment to all major ecclesiastical benefices in the Spanish realms). Although, unlike Henry VIII of England, Ferdinand and Isabella never despoiled the church of its vast landed possessions, they did drain off for themselves a part of the ecclesiastical wealth by taking one-third of all the tithes paid to the Castilian church and the proceeds from the sale of indulgences.

To insure the loyalty of the church, to make it an effective instrument of royal policy, the sovereigns had to purge it of many abuses: plural benefices, absenteeism, concubinage, and the like. The pious Isabella found a strong ally in the work of reform in a dissident faction of the regular clergy (those belonging to a monastic order or religious community). This group, who called themselves Observants, protested against the worldliness of their colleagues and demanded a return to the strict simplicity of the primitive church. The struggle for reform began within the Franciscan order under the leadership of the ascetic Francisco Jiménez de Cisneros, whom Isabella appointed archbishop of Toledo in 1495, and spread to the other orders. It grew so heated that four hundred Andalusian friars preferred moving to North Africa and becoming Moslems, rather than accept the new rule. The dispute ended in the complete victory of the Observants over their more easygoing brethren.

Isabella was less successful in efforts to reform the secular (or nonmonastic) clergy, but here too an improvement took place. The great ecclesiastical offices ceased to be a monopoly of the aristocracy. Isabella preferred to select prelates from the lower nobility and the middle class, taking account of the morals and learning of the candidates. The Isabelline religious reform had a special meaning for the New World: It insured that the Faith would be carried to the Indies by an elite force of clergy often distinguished for their zeal, humanity, and learning.

The sovereigns also gave attention to the need for economic reform. They attempted to promote Castilian industry and commerce by protectionist measures. They forbade the export of gold and silver, sporadically barred the import of cloth that competed with native products, and encouraged Italian and Flemish artisans to settle in Spain. They promulgated navigation acts that gave preference to domestic shipping and subsidies to domestic shipbuilding. They suppressed all the internal tolls that had been established in Castile since 1464 and made an effort to standardize weights and measures. Under Isabella's predecessors, a serious depreciation of the currency had taken place. To restore the credit of the coinage, Isabella suppressed all private mints and struck an excellent money that equaled foreign coins in value. All these measures contributed to an economic expansion and consequently to a rapid increase of Crown revenues, from 885,000 *reales* in 1474 to 26,283,334 *reales* in 1504.

Despite their basically pragmatic outlook, the sovereigns had broad intellectual and artistic interests. To their court they summoned Italian humanists like Alessandro Geraldini, Lucio Marineo Siculo, and Peter Martyr de Anghera to tutor their children and the sons of the greatest houses of Spain. Enlightened prelates like Archbishop Jiménez de Cisneros founded new schools and universities to rival the famed University of Salamanca. Spain herself produced some distinguished practitioners of the new learning, such as Antonio de Nebrija, grammarian, historian, and lexicographer, who in 1492 published and presented to Isabella a Castilian grammar—the first grammar of any modern European language. The vitality of the Castilian language and life found expression in a realistic masterpiece, the novel *La Celestina* (1499) by Fernando de Rojas. Meanwhile, Spanish architecture and sculpture developed its own distinctive style, known as plateresque, an ornamental blend of Moorish arabesques, flowers, foliage, and Renaissance motifs.

Foreign Policy

The restoration of domestic peace enabled the sovereigns to turn their attention to questions of foreign policy. For the Castilian Isabella, the conquest of Granada came first. Hardly had their authority been firmly restored when the sovereigns demanded of the Granadan ruler the tribute paid by his predecessors to Castile. Abdul Hassan replied that his mints now coined steel, not gold. The wealth of the Granadan kingdom and its mountainous terrain enabled the Moors to hold out for ten years. But the superior Spanish military power, especially the formidable new arm of artillery, finally broke the Moslem resistance. In January 1492, Granada surrendered to Ferdinand and Isabella, on whom Pope Alexander VI bestowed the title "The

Catholic Sovereigns" in honor of their crusading piety.

Whereas Isabella's heart was set on the conquest of Granada, Ferdinand, heir to Aragon's Mediterranean empire and the traditional rivalry between France and Aragon, looked eastward to Aragon's borders with France and to Italy. He achieved most of his goals after Isabella's death in 1504. Employing an adroit blend of war and diplomacy, he obtained the return of two Aragonese provinces lost to France by previous rulers, the incorporation of the kingdom of Naples into the Aragonese empire, and the checkmating of French designs in Italy. In the course of Ferdinand's Italian wars, his commanders, especially the "Great Captain," Gonzalo de Córdoba, created a new-style Spanish army armed with great firepower and strong offensive and defensive weapons. The new system, first tested in Italy, established Spain's military supremacy in Europe. Before his death, Ferdinand rounded out his conquests with the acquisition of Navarre (1512), which gave Spain a strongly defensible frontier with France.

The Catholic Sovereigns rendered major services to the Spanish people. They tamed the arrogant nobility, expelled the Moors, and united the Spanish kingdoms in the pursuit of common goals. They encouraged the growth of trade and industry and showed themselves to be intelligent patrons of learning and the arts. Their prudent diplomacy gave Spain a place among the first powers of Europe. In the same period, America was discovered under Castilian auspices, the Caribbean became a Spanish lake, and Spanish explorers and adventurers, by the end of the reign, were at the approaches to the great Indian empires of Mexico and Peru. Small wonder that monarchs who presided over such victories became for succeeding generations of Spaniards the objects of a national cult and legend.

Reappraisal of Ferdinand and Isabella's Policies

For modern historians, the fame of the Catholic Sovereigns has lost some of its luster. These

Ferdinand and Isabella at the Surrender of
Granada in 1492, which ended the Reconquest.
(Historical Pictures Service, Inc.)

historians charge Ferdinand and Isabella with mistaken policies that nullified much of the sound part of their work. One of these errors was a definite bias in favor of the economic and social interests of the aristocracy. If the nobility lost most of its political power under Ferdinand and Isabella, nothing of the kind happened in the economic sphere. Concentration of land in noble hands actually increased during their reign. The Cortes of 1480, which forced the nobility to surrender about half the lands and revenues usurped from the Crown since 1464, explicitly authorized the nobles to retain the vast holdings acquired prior to that date. A policy of assigning a lion's share of the territory reconquered from the Moslems to the grandees also favored the growth of land monopoly. As a result of these policies, about 2 or 3 percent of the population owned 95 percent of the land by 1500.

This land monopoly reduced the great majority of the Castilian peasants to the condition of tenants heavily burdened by rents, seigneurial dues, tithes, and taxes. True, serfdom in the strict sense had apparently disappeared from most parts of Castile by 1480; the Castilian peasant was legally free to sell his land and move elsewhere at will. But since the nobility owned virtually all the land, the peasant's liberty was, as the Spanish historian Jaime Vicens Vives puts it, the liberty "to die of hunger."

The royal policy of favoring sheep raising over agriculture was equally harmful to long-range Spanish economic interests. Like their predecessors, the sovereigns were influenced by the taxes and export duties paid by the sheep

SPAIN IN THE TIME OF CHRISTOPHER COLUMBUS

farmers and by the inflow of gold in payment for Spanish wool. As a result, they granted extensive privileges to the sheep raisers' guild, the Mesta. The climax of these favors was a 1501 law that reserved in perpetuity for pasture all land on which the migrant flocks had ever pastured. This measure barred vast tracts of land in Andalusia and Estremadura from being used for agriculture. The privilege granted the shepherds to cut branches from trees for fuel or to make fences and to trim or even fell trees whenever pasturage was scarce, together with the practice of burning the trees in autumn to produce better spring pasturage, contributed heavily to deforestation and soil erosion. Moreover, the overflow of sheep from their legal passage caused much damage to crops and soil. In a time of growing population, these policies and conditions inevitably produced serious food deficits. Chronic shortages climaxed in a devastating food crisis in the early sixteenth century.

Modern historians also question the traditional

view that Spanish industry made spectacular advances under the Catholic Sovereigns. These historians claim that the only true industries of the period were the iron industry of the Basque provinces and the cloth industry of the Castilian central zone, which received a strong stimulus from the discovery of America and the opening of American markets. The resulting industrial prosperity lasted until shortly after the middle of the sixteenth century. But the level of industrial production never reached that of England, the Low Countries, and Italy. The abject poverty of the peasantry, which composed 80 percent of the population, sharply limited the effective market for manufactured goods. Shortages of capital and skilled labor also acted as a brake on industrial expansion. Other obstacles to industrial growth were the excessive costs of transport by mule train and oxcarts across the rugged peninsula and the customs barriers that continued to separate the Spanish kingdoms. Nor were the paternalistic measures of the sovereigns invariably helpful to industry. Through Ferdinand's influence, a guild system modeled on the rigid Catalan model was introduced into the Castilian towns. In this the sovereigns did Castilian industry no service, for they fastened the straitjacket of guild organization on it precisely at the time when the discovery and colonization of America, the influx of American gold and silver, and the resulting economic upsurge challenged Spanish industry to transform its techniques, lower costs, increase output and quality, and thereby establish Spanish economic as well as political supremacy in Europe.

No policy of the sovereigns has come under harsher attack than their anti-Semitic measures. During the early Middle Ages, the Jews formed an influential and prosperous group in Spanish society. Down to the close of the the thirteenth century, a relatively tolerant spirit prevailed in Christian Spain. Relations among Jews, Christians, and Moslems were so close and neighborly as to provoke protests by the church. In the fourteenth century, these relations began to de-

teriorate. Efforts by the clergy to arouse hatred of the Jews and popular resentment of such specialized Jewish economic activities as usury and tax farming,[1] which caused severe hardship for peasants and other groups, contributed to this process. The rise of anti-Semitism led to the adoption of repressive legislation by the Crown and to a wave of attacks on Jewish communities. To save their lives, many Jews accepted baptism; they came to form a very numerous class of conversos, or Jewish converts to the Catholic faith.

The converts soon achieved a marked prosperity and influence as tax farmers, court physicians, counselors, and lawyers. Wealthy, unhampered by feudal traditions, intellectually curious, intensely ambitious, the conversos incurred the hostility not only of peasants but of the church and of many nobles and burghers. Whether heretics or not, they posed a threat to the feudal order based on landed wealth, hereditary status, and religious orthodoxy. The envy and hostility they aroused help to explain why the sovereigns, who had surrounded themselves with Jewish and converso advisers, and one of whom (Ferdinand) had Jewish blood in his veins, established the Inquisition and expelled the Jews from Spain. When the Crown had tamed the nobility and the towns, when it had acquired large new sources of revenue, its dependence on the Jews and conversos was reduced; these groups became dispensable. The sacrifice of the Jews and conversos sealed the alliance between the absolute monarchy and the church and nobility.

The conversos first felt the blows of religious persecution with the establishment of the Spanish Inquisition in Castile in 1478. The task of this tribunal was to detect, try, and punish heresy, and its special target was the mass of conversos, many of whom were suspected of secretly adhering to Judaism. As a result of the

---

[1] Tax farming was the collection of taxes by individuals who paid the Crown a fixed sum and retained the moneys collected.

Inquisition's activities, some two thousand conversos were burned at the stake; a hundred and twenty thousand fled abroad. As certain Spanish towns pointed out in memorials protesting the establishment of the Inquisition, the purge had a disastrous effect on the Spanish economy by causing this great flight of the conversos and their capital.

The Jews had a breathing space of twelve years during the costly War of Granada, for they were among the largest contributors to the royal finances. The surrender of Granada, however, brought near a decision on the fate of the Jews. The conquest of a rich territory and an industrious Moorish population, ending the drain of the war, meant that the Jews were no longer financially indispensable. After some hesitation, the sovereigns yielded to anti-Semitic pressure and, on March 30, 1492, signed the edict giving the Jews the choice of conversion or expulsion.

The destruction or flight of many conversos and the expulsion of the Jews certainly contributed to the dreary picture presented by the Spanish economy at the close of the sixteenth century. The purge of the conversos eliminated from Spanish life its most vital capitalist elements, the groups that in England and Holland were preparing the ground for the Industrial Revolution. The flight of converso artisans dealt Spanish industry a heavy blow and was directly responsible for royal edicts (1484) inviting foreign artisans to settle in Castile with exemption from taxes for ten years.

The anti-Semitic policies of the sovereigns also harmed Spanish science and thought in general. The Inquisition helped to blight the spirit of free inquiry and discussion in Spain at a time when the Renaissance was giving an extraordinary impulse to the play of European intellect in all fields. The sovereigns, who laid the foundations of Spain's greatness in so short a time, bear much of the responsibility for its premature decline. But the contradictions in their policies, the incorrect decisions that nullified much of the sound part of their work, resulted from more than personal errors of judgment; they reflected the structural weakness and backwardness of Spanish society as it emerged from seven centuries of struggle against the Moor.

THE HAPSBURG ERA: TRIUMPH AND TRAGEDY

Isabella's death in 1504 placed all of the Iberian Peninsula except Portugal under the rule of Ferdinand. Isabella's will had named her daughter Juana as successor, with the provision that Ferdinand should govern in case Juana proved unable. Since Juana's growing mental instability made her unfit to govern, Ferdinand assumed the regency. Juana's husband, Philip the Fair of Burgundy, supported by a considerable number of Castilian nobles, challenged Ferdinand's right to rule Castile, but Philip's sudden death in 1506 left Ferdinand undisputed master of Spain. Ferdinand himself died in 1516. To the Spanish throne ascended his grandson Charles, eldest son of Juana and Philip the Fair. Through his maternal grandparents, Charles inherited Spain, Naples and Sicily, and the Spanish possessions in Africa and America. Through his paternal grandparents, Marie of Burgundy and the Holy Roman emperor Maximilian, he inherited the territories of the house of Burgundy, which included the rich Netherlands, and the German possessions of the house of Hapsburg.

The Reign of Charles V

A solemn youth with the characteristic jutting underjaw of the Hapsburgs, Charles (first of that name in Spain and fifth in the Holy Roman Empire) had been born and reared in Flanders and knew no Spanish. Ferdinand had hoped that his younger grandson of the same name, who had been educated in Spain, would succeed him on the throne, but on his deathbed the old king had reluctantly consented to rescind his previous will and name Charles his heir. As the result of the accession of Charles to the throne of Spain, the course of Spanish history underwent a decisive change.

The Catholic Sovereigns, whatever their errors, had attempted to foster Spain's economic development and its partial unity; their prudent diplomacy set for itself limited goals. They had advanced toward absolute monarchy discreetly, respecting both the sensitivities of their peoples and those traditions that did not stand in the way of their designs. Charles, reared at the court of Burgundy in a spirit of royal absolutism, had a different notion of kingship. On his arrival in Spain he immediately alienated his subjects by his haughty manner and by the greed of his Flemish courtiers, whom he placed in all key positions. He aroused even greater resentment by attempting to make the Castilians pay the bill for his election as Holy Roman emperor to succeed his grandfather Maximilian. Having achieved his ambition by expending immense sums of money, which placed him deeply in debt to the German banking house of Fugger, Charles hurried off to Germany.

For Castilians the election appeared to mean an absentee king and heavier tax burdens. Popular wrath burst forth in the revolt of the Castilian towns, or communes, in 1520–1521. The revolt of the *Comuneros* has been called the first bourgeois revolution in Europe, but it began as an essentially conservative movement: The rebels demanded that Charles return to Spain and make his residence there, that the drain of money abroad end, that no more foreigners be appointed to offices in Spain. Many nobles supported the rebellion at this stage, although the grandees remained neutral or hostile. But the leadership of the revolution soon fell into more radical hands. Simultaneously, there arose in Valencia a revolt of the artisans and middle classes against the great landowners. As a result of these developments, the Comunero movement lost almost all aristocratic support. In April 1521 the Comunero army suffered a total defeat, and the revolt began to fall apart. In July 1522, Charles was able to return to Spain, with four

thousand German troops at his side. The last effort of the Spanish people to turn the political clock back, to prevent the final success of the centralizing and absolutist policies initiated by the Catholic Sovereigns, had failed.

For a time, at least, the dazzling successes of Charles V in the New and the Old Worlds reconciled the Spanish people to the new course. Spaniards rejoiced over the conquests of Cortés and Pizarro and the victories of the invincible Spanish infantry in Europe. They set to dreaming of El Dorados, universal empires, and a universal church. The poet Hernando de Acuña gave voice to Spain's exalted mood:

One Fold, one Shepherd only on the earth . . . One Monarch, one Empire, and one Sword.

War dominated Charles's reign: war against France, against the Protestant princes of Germany, against the Turks, even against the pope, whose holdings in central Italy were threatened by Spanish expansionism. Actually, only one of these wars vitally concerned Spain's national interests; this was the struggle with the Turkish Empire, whose growing naval power endangered Aragon's possessions in Italy and Sicily and even threatened Spain's coasts with attack. Yet Charles, absorbed in the Protestant problem and his rivalry with France, pursued this struggle against the infidel less consistently than the others; in the end, it declined to a mere holding operation.

The impressive victories of Spanish arms on land and sea had few tangible results, for Charles, embroiled in too many quarters, could not take full advantage of his successes. In 1556, Charles renounced the Spanish throne in favor of his son Philip. Charles had failed in all his major objectives. The Protestant heresy still flourished in the north; the Turks remained solidly entrenched in North Africa, and their piratical fleets prowled the Mediterranean. Charles's project of placing his son Philip on the imperial throne had broken on the opposition of German princes, Protestant and Catholic, and of Charles's own brother Ferdinand, who wished to make the title of Holy Roman emperor hereditary in his own line. Charles's other dream of bringing England into the empire by marrying Philip to Mary Tudor collapsed when Mary died in 1558.

Meanwhile, Spaniards groaned under a crushing burden of debts and taxes, with Castile bearing the main part of the load. German and Italian merchant-princes and bankers, to whom an ever-increasing part of the royal revenue was pledged for loans, took over important segments of the Spanish economy. The Fuggers assumed the administration of the estates of the military orders and the exploitation of the mercury mines of Almadén. Their rivals, the Welsers, took over the Galician mines and received the American province of Venezuela as a fief whose Indians they barbarously exploited. To find money for his fantastically expensive foreign enterprises, Charles resorted to extraordinary measures: He extracted ever larger grants from the Cortes of Castile and Aragon; he multiplied royal taxes; he appropriated remittances of American treasure to private individuals, compensating the victims with *juros* (bonds). When his son Philip came to the throne in 1556, Spain was bankrupt.

The Reign of Philip II and the Remaining Hapsburgs

The reign of Philip (1556–1598) continued in all essential respects the policies of his father, with the same general results. Spain won brilliant military victories, which Philip failed to follow up from lack of funds or because some new crisis diverted his attention to another quarter. His hopes of dominating France by playing on the divisions between Huguenots and Catholics were frustrated when the Protestant Henry of Navarre entered the Catholic church, a move that united France behind Henry and forced Philip to sign a peace with him. The war against the Turks produced the great sea victory of Lepanto (1571), which broke the Turkish naval

power, but when Philip's reign ended, the Turks remained in control of most of North Africa. In the prosperous Netherlands, the richest jewel in his imperial crown, Philip's policies of religious repression and absolutism provoked a great revolt that continued throughout his reign and imposed a terrible drain on the Spanish treasury. War with England flowed from the accession of the Protestant Elizabeth to the throne, from her unofficial support to the Dutch rebels, and from the encroachments of English corsairs and smugglers in American waters. The crushing defeat of the Invincible Armada in 1588 dealt a heavy blow to Spain's self-confidence and virtually sealed the doom of Philip's crusade against the heretical north. Philip succeeded in another enterprise, the annexation of Portugal (1580), which gave Spain considerably more naval strength and a long Atlantic seaboard to use in a struggle against the Protestant north. But Philip failed to exploit these strategic opportunities, and Portugal, whose colonies and ships now became fair game for Dutch and English seafarers, grew increasingly discontent with a union whose disadvantages exceeded its gains.

At his death in 1598, Philip II left a Spain in which the forces of disintegration were at work but which was still powerful enough militarily and territorially to be feared and respected. Under his successors, Spain entered a rapid decline. This decline first became visible in the area of diplomacy and war. The truce of 1609 with the Dutch, which tacitly recognized Dutch independence, was an early sign of waning Spanish power. The defeat of the famous Spanish infantry at the battle of Rocroi (1643) revealed the obsolescence of Spanish military organization and tactics and marked the end of Spanish military preponderance on the Continent. By the third quarter of the century, Spain, reduced to the defensive, had been compelled to sign a series of humiliating treaties by which she lost the Dutch Netherlands, part of Flanders, Luxembourg, and a string of lesser possessions.

The crisis existed at home as well as abroad.

Efforts to make other Spanish kingdoms bear part of the burdens of the wars in which Castile had been so long engaged caused resentment and resistance. The able but imprudent favorite of Philip IV, Count Olivares, aroused a storm by his efforts to billet troops in Catalonia and otherwise make Catalonia contribute to the Castilian war effort at the expense of the ancient fueros, or privileges, of the principality. In 1640 a formidable revolt broke out; it continued for twelve years and shattered the economy of Catalonia. In the same year, Portugal, weary of a union that brought more losses than gains, successfully revolted against Spanish rule. Lesser insurrections took place in Biscay, Andalusia, Sicily, and Naples.

A decline in the quality of Spain's rulers no doubt contributed to this political decline. Philip II, "a glorious failure," had worked diligently to achieve his goals of Spanish predominance in Europe and the liquidation of Protestantism. His successors, Philip III (1598–1621) and Philip IV (1621–1665), were weak and incompetent kings who preferred to leave the work of government in the hands of favorites. The last Hapsburg king of Spain, Charles II (1665–1700), was a pathetic imbecile, totally incapable of ruling.

The Waning Economy and Society

The quality of Spain's rulers had less to do with its decay than the crumbling of the economic foundations on which the empire rested. By the 1590s, the Castilian economy had begun to crack under the strain of costly Hapsburg adventures in foreign policy. Philip II several times resorted to bankruptcy to evade payments of debts to foreign bankers. His successors, lacking Philip's resources, were driven to currency inflation, which caused a flight of gold and silver abroad, until the national currency consisted largely of copper. But the development that contributed most to the Spanish economic crisis was a drastic decline in the inflow of American treasure in the middle decades of the seven-

teenth century—from about 135 million pesos in the decade from 1591 to 1600 to 19 million pesos in the decade from 1651 to 1660 (the complex causes of this decline will be discussed in Chapter 4).

By the end of the first quarter of the seventeenth century, signs of economic decline were on every hand. In the reign of Charles V, Seville had sixteen thousand looms producing silk and wool; at the death of Philip III in 1621, only four hundred remained. Toledo had fifty woolen manufacturing establishments in the sixteenth century; it had thirteen in 1665. The plight of agriculture was shown by a chronic shortage of foodstuffs, sometimes approaching famine conditions, and by the exodus of peasants from the countryside. Castile became a land of deserted villages. In the period from 1600 to 1700, Spain also suffered an absolute loss of population, from about 8 million to 6 million. The ravages of epidemics, aggravated by near-famine conditions; the expulsion of the Moriscos, or converted Moors, between 1609 and 1614; and emigration to the Indies contributed to this heavy loss.

The economic decline caused a contraction of Spain's artisan and merchant class, strengthened the domination of aristocratic values, and fostered the growth of parasitism. In the seventeenth century, ambitious young Spaniards looked above all to the church and the court for an assured living. In 1626, Spain had nine thousand monasteries; at the end of the century, there were about 200,000 monks and priests in a population of 6 million. The nobility formed another very large unproductive class. At the end of the century, according to one calculation, Spain had four times as many nobles as France with its much larger population. The highest rung of the ladder of nobility was occupied by a small number of grandees—counts, dukes, marquis—who possessed enormous wealth and immense prerogatives; the lowest was occupied by a great number of hidalgos, petty nobles whose sole capital often was their honor and the precious letters patent that attested to their rank and their superiority over base *pecheros* (taxpayers), peasants, artisans, and burghers. The noble contempt for labor infected all classes. The number of vagabonds steadily grew; meanwhile, agriculture lacked enough laborers to till the land.

Literary and Artistic Developments

Spreading into all areas of Spanish life, the *decadencia* (decadence) inspired moods of pessimism, fatalism, and cynicism. Spanish society presented extreme contrasts: great wealth and abject poverty, displays of fanatical piety and scandalous manners, desperate efforts to revive the imperial glories of a past age by kings who sometimes lacked the cash to pay their servants and supply the royal table. The paradoxes of Spanish life, the contrast between the ideal and the real, stimulated the Spanish literary imagination. In this time, so sterile in other respects, Spain enjoyed a Golden Age of letters. As early as 1554, the unknown author of *Lazarillo de Tormes*, first of the picaresque novels, captured the seamy reality of a Spanish world teeming with rogues and vagabonds. Its hero relates his adventures under a succession of masters—a blind beggar, a stingy priest, a hungry hidalgo; he finally attains his highest hope, a sinecure as a town crier, secured for him by a priest whose mistress he had married.

The picaresque genre reached its climax in the *Guzmán de Alfarache* of Mateo de Alemán (1599), with its note of somber pessimism: "All steal, all lie. . . . You will not find a soul who is man unto man." The cleavage in the Spanish soul, the conflict between the ideal and the real, acquired a universal meaning and symbolism in the *Don Quijote* (1605) of Miguel Cervantes de Saavedra. The corrosive satires of Francisco Quevedo (1580–1645) gave voice to the despair of many seventeenth-century intellectuals. "There are many things here," wrote Quevedo, "that seem to exist and have their being, and

yet they are nothing more than a name and an appearance."

By contrast, Spanish drama of the Golden Age only faintly reflected the national crisis. The plays of Lope de Vega (1562–1645) are rich in invention, sparkling dialogue, and melodious verse; his gallant hidalgos, courageous and clever heroines, and dignified peasants evoke the best traditions of Spain's past with a curious disregard for the dismal present. The dramas of Calderón de la Barca (1600–1681), however, suggest the defeatist temper of late seventeenth-century Spain by their tragic view of life and their stress on the illusory nature of reality: "*La vida es sueño, y los sueños sueño son*" ("Life is a dream, and our dreams are part of a dream").

Spanish painting of the Golden Age, like the literature, mirrors the transition from the confident and exalted mood of the early sixteenth century to the disillusioned spirit of the late seventeenth century. The great age of painting began with El Greco (1541–1616), whose work blends naturalism, deliberate distortion, and intense emotion to convey the somber religious passion of the Spain of Philip II. Yet some of El Greco's portraits are done with a magnificent realism. The mysticism of El Greco is completely absent from the canvases of Diego Velázquez (1599–1660). With a sovereign mastery of light, coloring, and movement, Velázquez captured for all time the palace life of two Spanish kings, presenting with the same detachment the princes and princesses and the dwarfs and buffoons of the court.

The death of the wretched Charles II in 1700 brought the Hapsburg era to its end. Even before that symbolic death there had been some signs of a Spanish demographic and economic revival, notably in Catalonia, which by the 1670s had made a strong recovery from the depths of the great depression. Under a new foreign dynasty, the Bourbons, who were supported by all the progressive elements in Spanish society, Spain was about to begin a remarkable, many-sided effort at national reconstruction.

CHAPTER THREE

The Conquest of *America*

The discovery of America resulted from European efforts to find a sea road to the East that would break the monopoly of Egypt and Venice over the lucrative trade in spices and other Oriental products. The drain of their scanty stock of gold and silver into the pockets of Italian and Levantine middlemen had grown increasingly intolerable to the merchants and monarchs of western Europe. Portugal took a decisive lead in the race to find a waterway to the land of spices. She had important advantages over her rivals: a long Atlantic seaboard with excellent harbors, a large class of fishermen and sailors, and an aristocracy that early learned to supplement its meager revenue from the land with income from trade and shipbuilding. Earlier than any other European country, Portugal became a unified nation-state under an able dynasty, the house of Avis, which formed a firm alliance with the merchant class and took a personal interest in the expansion of commerce.

This fact helps explain Portugal's head start in the work of discovery. The Portuguese victory of Aljubarrota (1385), gained with English support, ended for a time Castile's efforts to absorb its smaller neighbor and released Portuguese energies for an amibitious program of overseas expansion.

THE GREAT VOYAGES

Exploration Under Prince Henry

The famous Prince Henry (1394–1460) initiated the Portuguese era of exploration and discovery. Henry, somewhat misleadingly known as "the Navigator" since he never sailed beyond sight of land, united a medieval crusading spirit with the more modern desire to penetrate the secrets of unknown lands and seas and reap the profits of expanded trade. In 1415, Henry participated in the capture of the Moroccan seaport of Ceuta, a great Moslem trading center from which caravans crossed the desert to Timbuktu, returning with ivory and gold obtained by barter from the Negroes of the Niger basin. Possession of the African beachhead of Ceuta opened up large prospects for the Portuguese. By penetrating to the sources of Ceuta gold, they could relieve a serious Portuguese shortage of the precious metal; Henry also hoped to reach the land of the fabled Christian ruler Prester John. Prester John was already identified with the emperor of Abyssinia, but no one knew how far his empire extended. An alliance with this ruler, it was hoped, would encircle the Moslems in North Africa with a powerful league of Christian states.

Efforts to expand the Moroccan beachhead, however, made little progress. If the Portuguese could not penetrate the Moslem barrier that separated them from the southern sources of gold and the kingdom of Prester John, could they not reach these goals by sea? In 1419, Henry set up a headquarters at Sagres on Cape St. Vincent, the rocky tip of southeast Portugal.

Here he assembled a group of expert seamen and scientists. At the nearby port of Lagos, he began the construction of stronger and larger ships, equipped with the compass and the improved astrolabe. Beginning in 1420, he sent ship after ship to explore the western coast of Africa. Each captain was required to enter in his log data concerning currents, winds, and calms and to sketch the coastline. An eminent converso map maker, Jehuda Crespes, used these data to produce ever more detailed and accurate charts.

The first decade of exploration resulted in the discovery of the Madeiras and the Azores. But progress southward was slow; the imaginary barriers of a flaming torrid zone and a green sea of darkness made sailors excessively cautious. Passage in 1434 around Cape Bojador, the first major landmark on the West African coast, proved these fears groundless. Before Henry's death in 1460, the Portuguese had pushed as far as the Gulf of Guinea and had begun a lucrative trade in gold dust and slaves captured in raids or bought from coastal chiefs. Henry's death brought a slackening in the pace of exploration. But the advance down the African coast continued, under private auspices and as an adjunct to the slave trade—the first bitter fruit of European overseas expansion. In 1469 a wealthy merchant, Fernão Gomes, secured a monopoly of the trade to Guinea (the name then given to the whole African coast), on condition that he explore farther south at the rate of a hundred miles a year. Complying with his pledge, Gomes sent his ships eastward along the Gold, Ivory, and Slave coasts and then southward almost to the mouth of the Congo.

The Sea Route to the East

Under the energetic John II, who came to the throne in 1481, the Crown resumed control and direction of the African enterprise. At Mina, on the Gold Coast, John established a fort that became a center of trade in slaves, ivory, gold dust, and a coarse black pepper, as well as a base for further exploration. If Henry had dreamed of finding gold and Prester John, the project of reaching India by rounding Africa was now uppermost in John's mind. In 1483 an expedition commanded by Diogo Cão discovered the mouth of the Congo River and sailed partway up the mighty stream. On a second voyage in 1484, Cão pushed as far south as Cape Cross in southwest Africa. The Portuguese monarch sensed that victory was near. In 1487 a fleet headed by Bartholomeu Dias left Lisbon with orders to pass the farthest point reached by Cão and if possible sail round the tip of Africa. After he had cruised farther south than any captain before him, a providential gale blew Dias's ships in a wide sweep around the Cape of Good Hope and to a landfall on the coast of East Africa. He had solved the problem of a sea road to the Indies and returned to Lisbon to report his success to King John.

The route to the East lay open. But domestic and foreign problems distracted John's attention from the Indian enterprise. He died in 1495 without having sent the expedition for which he had made elaborate preparations. His successor, Manuel I, known as the Fortunate, carried out John's plan. In 1497 a fleet of four ships, commanded by the tough, surly nobleman Vasco da Gama, sailed from Lisbon on a voyage that inaugurated the age of European imperialism in Asia. After rounding the Cape, de Gama sailed into the Indian Ocean and up the coast of East Africa. At Malinda, in modern Kenya, he took on an Arab pilot who guided the fleet to Calicut, the great spice trade center on the west coast of India. Received with hostility by the dominant Arab traders and with indifference by the local Indian potentate, who scorned his petty gifts, the persistent da Gama managed to load his holds with a cargo of pepper and cinnamon and returned to Lisbon in 1499 with two of the four ships with which he had begun his voyage. A new fleet, commanded by Pedro Álvares Cabral, was quickly outfitted and sent to India. Swinging far west in the south Atlantic, Cabral made a landfall on the coast of Brazil in early 1500 and sent one ship back to Lisbon to report his discovery before continuing to India. He returned to Portugal with a cargo of spices and a story of severe fighting with Arab merchants determined to resist the Portuguese intruders.

The great soldier and administrator Afonso de Albuquerque, who set out in 1509, completed the work begun by da Gama. He understood that in order to squeeze out the Egyptian and Venetian competition and gain a total monopoly of the spice trade he must conquer key points on the trade routes of the Indian Ocean. Capture of Malacca on the Malay Peninsula gave the Portuguese control of the strait through which East Indian spices entered the Indian Ocean. Capture of Muscat and Ormuz barred entrance to the Persian Gulf and closed that route to Europe to other nations' ships. The Portuguese strategy was not completely successful, but it diverted to Lisbon the greater part of the spice supply.

For a time, Portugal basked in the sun of an unprecedented prosperity. But the strain of maintaining its vast Eastern defense establishment was too great for Portugal's limited manpower and financial resources, and expenses began to outrun revenues. To make matters worse, under Spanish pressure King Manuel decreed the expulsion of all unbaptized Jews in 1496. As a result, Portugal lost the only native group financially capable of exploiting the investment opportunities offered by the Portuguese triumph in the East. Florentine and German bankers quickly moved in and diverted most of the profits of the Eastern spice trade abroad. Lisbon soon became a mere depot. Cargoes arriving there from the East were shipped almost at once to Antwerp or Amsterdam, better situated as centers of distribution to European customers. In time, Dutch and English rivals snatched most of the Asiatic colonies from Portugal's failing hands.

The Voyages of Columbus

The search for a sea road to the Indies inspired more than one solution. If some believed that the route around Africa offered the answer to the Eastern riddle, others favored sailing due west across the Atlantic. This view had the support of an eminent authority, the Florentine scientist Paolo Toscanelli, who in 1474 advised the Portuguese to try the western route as "shorter than the one which you are pursuing by way of Guinea." His letter came to the attention of an obscure Italian seafarer, Christopher Columbus, who had been reflecting on the problem, and helped to confirm his belief that such a passage from Europe to Cipangu (Japan) and Cathay (China) would be easy. This conception rested on a gross underestimate of the earth's circumference and an equal overestimate of the size and eastward extension of Asia. Since all educated Europeans believed that the world was round, that question never entered into the dispute between Columbus and his opponents. The main issue was the extent of the ocean between Europe and Asia, and on this point the opposition was right.

For Columbus the idea of reaching the East by sailing west acquired all the force of an obsession. A figure of transition from the dying Middle Ages to the world of capitalism and science, a curious combination of mystic and practical man, Columbus became convinced that God himself had revealed to him "that it was feasible to sail from here to the Indies, and placed in me a burning desire to carry out this plan."

About 1484, Columbus, who then resided in Lisbon, offered to make a western voyage of discovery for John II, but a committee of experts who listened to his proposal advised the king to turn it down. Undismayed by his rebuff, Columbus next turned to Castile. After eight years of discouraging delays and negotiation, Isabella—in a last-minute change of mind—agreed to support the "Enterprise of the Indies."

The *capitulación* (contract) made by the queen with Columbus named him admiral, viceroy, and governor of the lands he should discover and promised him a generous share in the profits of the venture.

On August 3, 1492, Columbus sailed from Palos with three small ships, the *Pinta*, the *Santa María*, and the *Niña*, manned not by the jailbirds of legend but by experienced crews under competent officers. The voyage was remarkably prosperous, with fair winds the whole way out. But the great distance beyond sight of land began to worry some of the men, and by the end of September there was grumbling aboard the *Santa María*, Columbus's flagship. According to Columbus's son Ferdinand, some sailors proposed to heave the admiral overboard and return to Spain with the report that he had fallen in while watching the stars. Columbus managed to calm his men, and soon floating gulfweed and bosun birds gave signs of land. On October 12, they made landfall at an island in the Bahamas that Columbus named San Salvador, probably modern Watling Island.

Cruising southward through the Bahamas, Columbus came to the northeast coast of Cuba, which he took for part of Cathay. An embassy sent to find the Great Khan failed in its mission but returned with reports of a hospitable reception by natives who introduced the Spaniards to the use of "certain herbs the smoke of which they inhale"—an early reference to tobacco. Next Columbus sailed eastward to explore the northern coast of an island (that today is occupied by the Dominican Republic and Haiti) he named Española (Hispaniola). Here the Spaniards were cheered by the discovery of some alluvial gold and gold ornaments, which the natives bartered for Spanish trinkets.

From Hispaniola, on whose coast Columbus lost his flagship, he returned to Spain to report his supposed discovery of the Indies. The sovereigns received him with signal honors and ordered him to prepare immediately a second expedition to follow up his discovery. In

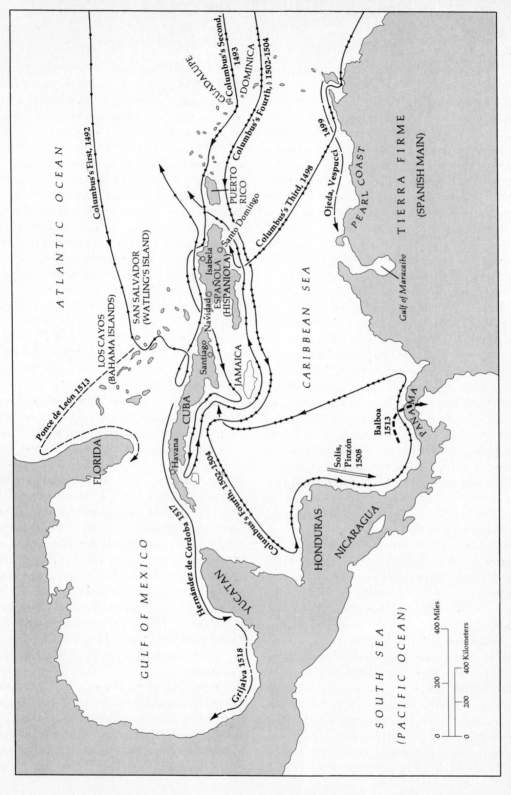

EARLY SPANISH VOYAGES IN THE CARIBBEAN

response to Portuguese charges of encroachment on an area in the Atlantic reserved to Portugal by a previous treaty with Castile, Ferdinand and Isabella appealed for help to Pope Alexander VI, himself a Spaniard. The pontiff complied by issuing a series of bulls in 1493 that assigned to Castile all lands discovered or to be discovered by Columbus and drew a line from north to south a hundred leagues west of the Azores and Cape Verdes; west of this line was to be a Spanish sphere of exploration. To John II this demarcation line seemed to threaten Portuguese interests in the south Atlantic and the promising route around Africa to the East. Yielding to Portuguese pressure, Ferdinand and Isabella signed in 1494 the Treaty of Tordesillas, which established a boundary 270 leagues farther west. Portugal obtained exclusive rights of discovery and conquest east of this line; Castile gained the same rights to the west.

Columbus returned to Hispaniola at the end of 1493 with a fleet of seventeen ships carrying twelve hundred people, most of them artisans and peasants, with a sprinkling of "caballeros, hidalgos, and other men of worth, drawn by the fame of gold and the other wonders of that land." The American reality frustrated the hopes of Columbus and the sovereigns for an orderly settlement of the land. The settlers soon gave themselves up to gold hunting and preying on the Indians. A foreigner of obscure origins, Columbus lacked the powers and personal qualities needed to control this turbulent mass of fortune hunters.

After founding the town of Isabella on the north coast of Hispaniola, Columbus sailed again in quest of Cathay. He coasted down the southern shore of Cuba almost to its western end. The great length of the island convinced him that he had reached the Asiatic mainland. To extinguish all doubts he made his officers and crews take solemn oath, "on pain of a hundred lashes and having the tongue slit if they ever gainsaid the same," that Cuba was the mainland of Asia. In 1496 he returned to Spain to report

his discoveries and answer charges sent by disgruntled settlers to the court. He left behind his brother Bartholomew, who removed the settlement from Isabella to a healthier site on the south shore, naming the new town Santo Domingo.

The first two voyages had not paid their way, but the sovereigns still had faith in Columbus and outfitted a third fleet in 1498. On this voyage he discovered Trinidad and the mouths of the Orinoco. The mighty current of sweet water discharged by the great river made Columbus conclude that he was on the shores of a continent, but his crotchety mysticism also suggested that the Orinoco was one of the four rivers of Paradise and had its source in the Garden of Eden.

Columbus arrived in Hispaniola to find chaos. The intolerable demands of the greedy Castilian adventurers had provoked the peaceable Taino Indians to the point of war. The Spaniards, disappointed in their hopes of quick wealth, blamed the Columbus brothers for their misfortunes and rose in revolt under a leader named Roldán. To appease the rebels Columbus had to issue pardons and grant land and Indian slaves. Meanwhile, acting on a stream of complaints against Columbus, the sovereigns had sent out an agent, Francisco de Bobadilla, to supersede Columbus and investigate the charges against the discoverer. On arrival in the island, the irascible Bobadilla seized Columbus and his brother and sent them to Spain in chains. Although Isabella immediately disavowed Bobadilla's arbitrary actions, Columbus never again exercised the functions of viceroy and governor in the New World.

Still gripped by his great illusion, Columbus continued to dream of finding a western way to the land of spices. He was allowed to make one more voyage, the most difficult and disastrous of all. He was now convinced that between the mainland he had recently discovered and the Malay Peninsula shown on ancient maps there must be a strait that would lead into the

Indian Ocean. In 1502 he sailed in search of this strait and a route to southern Asia. From Hispaniola, where he was not permitted to land, he crossed the Caribbean to the coast of Central America and followed it south to the Isthmus of Panama. Here he believed he was ten days' journey from the Ganges River. In Panama he found some gold, but the hoped-for strait continued to elude him. He finally departed for Hispaniola with his two remaining ships but was forced to beach the worm-riddled craft on Jamaica, where he and his men were marooned for a year awaiting the arrival of a relief ship. In November 1504, Columbus returned to Europe. Broken in health, convinced of the ingratitude of princes, he died in 1506 a rich but embittered man.

Balboa and Magellan

Other explorers followed in the wake of Columbus's ships and gradually made known the immense extent of the mainland coast of South America. In 1499, Alonso de Ojeda, accompanied by the pilot Juan de la Cosa and the Florentine Amerigo Vespucci, sailed to the mouths of the Orinoco and explored the coast of Venezuela. Vespucci took part in another voyage in 1501–1502 under the flag of Portugal. This expedition, sent to follow up the discovery of Brazil by Pedro Alvares Cabral in 1500, explored the Brazilian coast from Salvador da Bahia to Rio de Janeiro before turning back. Vespucci's letters to his patrons, Giovanni and Lorenzo de' Medici, reveal an urbane, cultivated Renaissance figure with a flair for lively and realistic description of the fauna, flora, and inhabitants of the New World. His letters were published and circulated widely in the early 1500s. One (whose authenticity is disputed) told of a nonexistent voyage in 1497 and gave him the fame of being the first European to set foot on the South American continent. A German geographer, Martin Waldseemuller, decided to honor Vespucci by assigning the name America to the area of Brazil

in a map of the newly discovered lands. The name caught on and presently was applied to the whole of the New World.

A growing shortage of Indian labor and the general lack of economic opportunities for new settlers on Hispaniola incited Spanish slave hunters and adventurers to explore and conquer the remaining Greater Antilles. Puerto Rico, Jamaica, and Cuba were occupied between 1509 and 1511. In the same period, efforts to found colonies on the coast of northern Colombia and Panama failed disastrously, and the remnants of two expeditions were united under the energetic leadership of the conquistador Vasco Núñez de Balboa to form the new settlement of Darien on the Isthmus of Panama. Moved by Indian tales of a great sea, south of which lay a land overflowing with gold, Balboa led an expedition across the forests and mountains of Panama to the shores of the Pacific. He might have gone on to discover the Inca Empire of Peru if he had not aroused the jealousy of his terrible father-in-law, the "two-legged tiger," Pedrarias Dávila, sent out by Charles V in 1514 as governor of the isthmus. Charged with treason and desertion, the discoverer of the Pacific was tried, condemned, and beheaded in 1519.

The discovery of the "South Sea" confirmed Columbus's reports on his fourth voyage of a narrow isthmus beyond which lay a sea that led to India. Although further exploration was required to dispel the lingering belief that the whole American landmass was a peninsula projecting from southeast Asia, the work of discovery after 1513 centered on the search for a waterway to the East through or around the American continent. Ferdinand Magellan, a Portuguese who had fought in India and the East Indies, was convinced that a short passage to the East existed south of Brazil. Failing to interest the Portuguese king in his project, Magellan turned to Spain, with greater success. The resulting voyage of circumnavigation of the globe, 1519–1522, the first in history, represented an immense navigational feat and greatly increased Europe's stock of geographical knowledge. But, aside from the acquisition of the Philippines for Spain, Magellan's exploit had little practical value, for his new route to the East was too long to have commercial significance. The net result was to enhance the value of America in Spanish eyes. Disillusioned with the dream of easy access to the riches of the East, Spain turned with concentrated energy to the task of extending her American conquests and to the exploitation of the human and natural resources of the New World.

THE CONQUEST OF MEXICO

Early Contact with Moctezuma

A disturbing report reached the Aztec capital of Tenochtitlán in 1518. Up from the coast of the Gulf of Mexico hurried the tribute collector Pinotl to inform King Moctezuma of the approach from the sea of winged towers bearing men with white faces and heavy beards. Pinotl had communicated with these men by signs and had exchanged gifts with their leader. Before departing, the mysterious visitors had promised (so Pinotl interpreted their gestures) to return soon and visit Moctezuma in his city in the mountains.

Indian accounts agree that the news filled Moctezuma with dismay. Could the leader of these strangers be the redeemer-god Quetzalcoatl, returning to reclaim his lost kingdom? According to one Aztec source, Moctezuma exclaimed: "He has appeared! He has come back! He will come here, to the place of his throne and canopy, for that is what he promised when he departed!"

The "winged towers" were the ships of the Spanish captain Juan de Grijalva, sent by Governor Diego Velázquez of Cuba to explore the coasts whose existence the slave-hunting expedition of Francisco Hernández de Córdoba (1517) had already made known. Córdoba had discovered the peninsula of Yucatán, inhabited by Maya Indians whose cotton cloaks and brilliant plumes, stone pyramids, temples, and gold ornaments revealed a native culture far more advanced than any the Spaniards had hitherto encountered. Córdoba met with disastrous defeat at the hands of the Maya and returned to Cuba to die of his wounds. He brought back enough gold and other signs of Indian wealth, however, to encourage Velázquez to outfit a new venture, which he entrusted to his kinsman Juan de Grijalva.

Grijalva sailed from Santiago in April 1518, touched at the island of Cozumel on the northeastern corner of Yucatán, then coasted down the peninsula, following Córdoba's route. In June they reached the limits of Moctezuma's empire. At a river that Grijalva named Banderas they were greeted by natives waving white flags and inviting them by signs to draw near. Here Grijalva's flagship was boarded by the Aztec official Pinotl, whose report was to cause so much consternation in Tenochtitlán. A lively trade developed, with Indians bartering gold for Spanish green beads. Grijalva was now convinced that he had come to a wealthy kingdom filled with many large towns. Near the present port of Veracruz, Grijalva sent Pedro de Alvarado back to Cuba with the gold that had been gained by barter. Alvarado was to report to Velázquez what had been accomplished, request authority to found a colony, and seek reinforcements. Grijalva himself sailed on with three other ships, perhaps as far as the river Pánuco, which marked the northern limits of the Aztec Empire. Then he turned back and retraced his course, arriving in Cuba in November 1518.

Cortés-Quetzalcoatl

Velázquez was already planning a third expedition to conquer the Mexican mainland. He passed over his kinsman Grijalva and chose as leader of the expedition the thirty-four-year-old Hernando Cortés, a native of Medellín in the

— Church
— Military

Spanish province of Estremadura. Cortés was born in 1485 into an hidalgo family of modest means. At the age of fourteen he went to Salamanca, seat of a great Spanish university, to prepare for the study of law, but left some years later, determined on a military career. He had to choose between Italy, the great battlefield of Europe, where Spanish arms were winning fame under the great captain Gonzalo de Córdoba, and the Indies, land of gold, Amazons, and El Dorados. In 1504, aged nineteen, he embarked for Hispaniola.

struct'd relatshp bt. Spanish + Indians

Soon after arriving on the island he participated in his first military exploit, the suppression of a revolt of Indians made desperate by Spanish mistreatment. His reward was an *encomienda* (a grant of Indian tribute and labor). In 1511 he served under Velázquez in the easy conquest of Cuba. The following year he was appointed alcalde of the newly founded town of Santiago in Cuba. In 1518 he persuaded Velázquez to give him command of the new expedition to the Mexican mainland. At the last moment the distrustful governor decided to recall him, but Cortés simply disregarded Velázquez's messages. In February 1519, he sailed from Cuba with a force of some six hundred men. Because Velázquez had not completed negotiations with the emperor Charles for an agreement authorizing the conquest and settlement of the mainland, Cortés's instructions permitted him only to trade and explore.

Cortés's fleet first touched land at the island of Cozumel, where they rescued a Spanish castaway, Jerónimo de Aguilar, who had lived among the Maya for eight years. In March 1519, Cortés landed on the coast of Tabasco, defeated local Indians in a sharp skirmish, and secured from them along with pledges of friendship the Mexican girl Malinche, who was to serve him as interpreter, adviser, and mistress. In April he dropped anchor near the site of modern Veracruz. He had contrived a way to free himself from Velázquez's irksome authority. In apparent deference to the wishes of a majority of his

followers, who claimed that conquest and settlement would serve the royal interest better than mere trade, Cortés founded the town of Villa Rica de la Vera Cruz and appointed its first officials, into whose hands he surrendered the authority he had received from Velázquez. These officials then conferred on Cortés the title of captain general with authority to conquer and colonize the newly discovered lands. Cortés thus drew on Spanish medieval traditions of municipal autonomy to vest his disobedience in a cloak of legality.

Some days later, Moctezuma's ambassadors appeared in the Spanish camp. The envoys brought precious gifts, the finery of the great gods Tlaloc, Tezcatlipoca, and Quetzalcoatl. Reverently, they arrayed Cortés in the finery of Quetzalcoatl. On his face they placed a serpent mask inlaid with turquoise, with a crossband of quetzal feathers and a golden earring hanging down on either side. On his breast they fastened a vest decorated with quetzal feathers; about his neck they hung a collar of precious stones with a gold disc in the center. They fastened a mirror encrusted with turquoises to his hips, placed a cloak with red borders about his shoulders, and adorned his feet with greaves set with precious stones and hung with little bells. In his hand they placed a shield with ornaments of gold and mother-of-pearl and a fringe and pendant of quetzal feathers. They also set before him sandals of fine, soft rubber, black as obsidian.

The Aztec account relates that the god was not satisfied. "Is this all?" Cortés is said to have asked. "Is this your gift of welcome? Is this how you greet people?" The stricken envoys departed and returned with gifts more to the god's liking, including a gold disc in the shape of the sun, as big as a cartwheel, an even larger disc of silver in the shape of the moon, and a helmet full of small grains of gold.

The envoys reported to Moctezuma what they had heard and seen, supplementing their accounts with painted pictures of the gods and their possessions. They described the firing of a cannon, done on Cortés's order to impress the Aztec emissaries:

A thing like a ball of stone comes out of its entrails; it comes out shooting sparks and raining fire. The smoke that comes out with it has a pestilent odor, like that of rotten mud. . . . If the cannon is aimed against a mountain, the mountain splits and cracks open. If it is aimed against a tree, it shatters the tree into splinters.

Vividly, they described other weapons, the armor, and the mounts of the Spaniards.

Of the terrible war dogs of the Spaniards the envoys said:

Their dogs are enormous, with flat ears and long dangling tongues. The color of their eyes is burning yellow; their eyes flash fire and shoot off sparks. Their bellies are hollow, their flanks long and narrow. They are tireless and very powerful. They bound here and there, panting, with their tongues hanging out. And they are spotted like an ocelot.[1]

Moctezuma's envoys assured Cortés that they would serve him in every way during his stay on the coast but pleaded with him not to seek a meeting with their king. This pleading was part of Moctezuma's pathetic strategy of plying Cortés-Quetzalcoatl with gifts in the hope that he would be dissuaded from advancing into the interior and reclaiming his lost throne. Suavely, Cortés informed the ambassadors that he had crossed many seas and journeyed from very distant lands to see and speak with Moctezuma and could not return without doing so.

The March to Tenochtitlán

Becoming aware of the bitter discontent of tributary towns with Aztec rule, Cortés began to

play a double game. He encouraged the Totonac Indians of the coast to seize and imprison Moctezuma's tax collectors but promptly obtained their release and sent them to the king with expressions of his regard and friendship. He took two other steps before beginning the march on Tenochtitlán. To Spain he sent a ship with dispatches for the emperor Charles in which he sought to obtain approval for his actions by describing the great extent and value of his discoveries. To help in gaining the emperor's goodwill, Cortés persuaded his men to send Charles not only his *quinto* (royal fifth) but all the treasure received from Moctezuma. In order to stiffen the resolution of his followers by cutting off all avenues of escape, he scuttled and sank all his remaining ships on the pretext that they were not seaworthy. Then Cortés and his small army began the march on Mexico-Tenochtitlán.

Advancing into the sierra, Cortés entered the territory of the tough Tlaxcalan Indians, traditional enemies of the Aztecs. The Spaniards had to prove in battle the superiority of their weapons and their fighting capacity before they obtained an alliance with this powerful tribe. Then Cortés marched on Cholula, an ancient center of Classic cultural traditions and the cult of Quetzalcoatl. Here, claiming that the Cholulans were conspiring to attack him, Cortés staged a mass slaughter of the Cholulan nobility and warriors after they had assembled in a great courtyard. When news of this event reached Tenochtitlán, terror spread throughout the city.

The Spaniards continued their inexorable advance:

They came in battle array, as conquerors, and the dust rose in whirlwinds on the roads. Their spears glinted in the sun, and their pennons fluttered like bats. They made a loud clamor as they marched, for their coats of mail and their weapons clashed and rattled. Some of them were dressed in glistening iron from head to foot; they terrified everyone who saw them.[2]

[1] Miguel Leon-Portilla, ed., *The Broken Spears: The Aztec Account of the Conquest of Mexico* (Boston: Beacon Press, 1962), pp. 30–31.

[2] Ibid., p. 41.

These photographs from the Codex Mendoza extol the virtues and rewards of being a warrior in Aztec society. (Bodleian Library, Oxford. MS. Arch. Seld. A.1, folio 65R upper.)

Moctezuma's fears and doubts had by now reduced him to a hopelessly indecisive state of mind. He wavered between submission and resistance, between the conviction that the Spaniards were gods and half-formed suspicions that they were less than divine. He sent new envoys, who brought rich gifts to Cortés but urged him to abandon his plan of visiting the Aztec capital. Moctezuma's naive efforts to bribe or cajole the terrible strangers who "longed and lusted for gold," who "hungered like pigs for gold," in the bitter words of an Indian account, proved vain. As Moctezuma's doom approached, his own gods turned against him. A group of sorcerers and soothsayers sent by the king to cast spells over the Spaniards were stopped by the young god Tezcatlipoca, who conjured up before their terrified eyes a vision of Mexico-Tenochtitlán burning to the ground. His forces spent, Moctezuma ended by welcoming Cortés at the entrance to the capital as a rightful ruler returning to his throne. The

Aztec king completed his degradation by allowing himself to be kidnapped from his palace by Cortés and a few comrades and taken to live as a hostage in the Spanish quarters.

The Aztec nation had not said its last word. In Cortés's absence from the city—he had set off for the coast to face an expedition sent by Governor Velázquez to arrest him—his lieutenant Pedro de Alvarado ordered an unprovoked massacre of the leading Aztec chiefs and warriors as they celebrated with song and dance a religious festival in honor of Huitzilopochtli. The result was a popular uprising that forced the Spaniards to retreat to their own quarters. This was the situation that Cortés, having won over most of the newcomers and defeated the rest, found when he returned to Tenochtitlán to rejoin his comrades. His efforts to pacify the Aztecs failed. The tribal council deposed the captive Moctezuma and elected a new chief, who launched heavy attacks on the invaders. As the fighting raged, Moctezuma died, killed by stones cast by his own people as he appealed for peace, according to Spanish accounts; strangled by the Spaniards themselves, according to Indian sources. Fearing a long siege and famine, Cortés evacuated Tenochtitlán at a heavy cost in lives. The surviving Spaniards and their Indian allies at last reached friendly Tlaxcala.

Strengthened by the arrival of Spanish reinforcements from Cuba and by thousands of Indians who joined the fight against their old masters, Cortés again marched on Tenochtitlán in December 1520. A ferocious struggle began in late April 1521. On August 23, after a siege in which the Aztecs fought for four months with extraordinary bravery, their last king, Cuauhtemoc, surrendered amid the laments of his starving people. Cortés took possession of the ruins that had been the city of Tenochtitlń.

The Aftermath of Conquest

From the Valley of Mexico the process of conquest was extended in all directions. Guatemala was reduced by Pedro de Alvarado, Honduras by Cortés himself. In 1527, Francisco de Montejo began the conquest of Yucatán, but as late as 1542 the Maya rose in a desperate revolt that was crushed with great slaughter. Meanwhile, expeditions from Darien subjugated the Indians of Nicaragua. Thus did the two streams of Spanish conquest, both originally starting from Hispaniola, come together again.

For a brief time, Cortés was undisputed master of the old Aztec Empire, renamed the Kingdom of New Spain. He made grants of encomienda to his soldiers, reserving for himself the tributes of the richest towns and provinces. The Crown rewarded his services by granting him the title of marquis of the Valley of Oaxaca and the tributes of twenty-three thousand Indian vassals; he lived in almost kingly style, dining "with minstrels and trumpets." But royal distrust of the great conquerors soon asserted itself. He was removed from his office of governor, his authority was vested in an *audiencia* (high court), pending the appointment of a viceroy, and all his actions came under close legal scrutiny. In 1539 he returned to Spain and served with distinction in the expedition against Algiers in the following year, but he was ignored and snubbed by the king. Filled with bitterness, he retired to live in seclusion in Seville. He died in 1547, leaving his title and estates to his eldest legitimate son, Martin Cortés.

THE CONQUEST OF PERU

The conquest of Mexico challenged other Spaniards to match the exploits of Cortés and his companions. The work of discovering a golden kingdom rumored to lie beyond the "South Sea" was begun by Balboa but cut short by his death at the hands of Pedrarias Dávila. In 1519, Dávila founded the town of Panama on the western side of the isthmus, and this town became a base for explorations along the Pacific coast. Three years later, Pascual de Andagoya crossed the Gulf of San Miguel and returned with more information concerning a land of gold called "Biru."

Pizarro and Atahualpa

Dávila entrusted direction of a voyage of discovery southward to Francisco Pizarro, an illiterate soldier of fortune little of whose early history is known. Pizarro recruited two partners for the Peruvian venture: Diego de Almagro, an adventurer of equally obscure origins, and Hernando de Luque, a priest who acted as financial agent for the trio. Two preliminary expeditions, fitted out from Panama in 1524 and 1526, yielded enough finds of gold and silver to confirm the existence of the elusive kingdom. Pizarro now left for Spain to obtain royal sanction for the enterprise of Peru. He returned to Panama with the titles of captain general and *adelantado* (commander), accompanied by his four brothers and other followers. Almagro, dissatisfied with the allotment of titles and other rewards in the royal contract, accused Pizarro of slighting his services to the king. The quarrel was patched up, but it contained the seeds of a deadly feud.

In December 1531, Pizarro again sailed from Panama for the south with a force of some two hundred men and landed several months later on the Peruvian coast. On arrival the Spaniards learned that civil war was raging in the Inca Empire. Atahualpa, son of the late emperor Huayna Capac by a secondary wife, had risen against another claimant of the throne, his half brother, Huascar, defeated him in a war marked by great slaughter, and made him prisoner. Atahualpa was advancing toward the imperial capital of Cuzco when messengers brought him news of the arrival of white strangers. After an exchange of messages and gifts between the leaders, the two armies advanced to a meeting at the town of Cajamarca, high in the mountains.

Perhaps in direct imitation of Cortés, Pizarro proposed to win a quick and relatively bloodless

victory by seizing the Inca Atahualpa, through whom he may have hoped to rule the country, much as Cortés had done with Moctezuma. In one important respect, however, the Peruvian story differs from that of Mexico. If Moctezuma's undoing was his passive acceptance of the divinity of the invaders, Atahualpa's mistake was to underestimate the massed striking power of the small Spanish force. He had been led to believe that the swords were no more dangerous than women's weaving battens, that the firearms were capable of firing only two shots, and that the horses were powerless at night. This last delusion apparently led to his delayed entry into Cajamarca at dusk, instead of noon, as Pizarro had been told to expect.

When Atahualpa and his escort appeared for the rendezvous in the square of Cajamarca, he found it deserted, for Pizarro had concealed his men in some large buildings opening on the square. Then the priest Vicente de Valverde came forward, accompanied by an interpreter, to harangue the bewildered Inca concerning his obligations to the Christian God and the Spanish king until the angry emperor threw down a Bible, which Valverde had handed him. At a signal from Pizarro, his soldiers, supported by cavalry and artillery, rushed forward to kill hundreds of the terrified Indians and take the Inca prisoner. "It was a very wonderful thing," wrote a Spanish observer, "to see so great a lord, who came in such power, taken prisoner in so short a time."

Atahualpa vainly sought to gain his freedom by offering to fill his spacious cell higher than a man could reach with gold objects as the price of his ransom. Pizarro accepted the offer, and hundreds of llama-loads of gold arrived from all parts of the empire until the room had been filled to the stipulated height. But Pizarro had no intention of letting the emperor go; he remained in "protective custody," a puppet ruler who was to insure popular acceptance of the new order. Soon, however, the Spaniards began to suspect that Atahualpa was becoming the

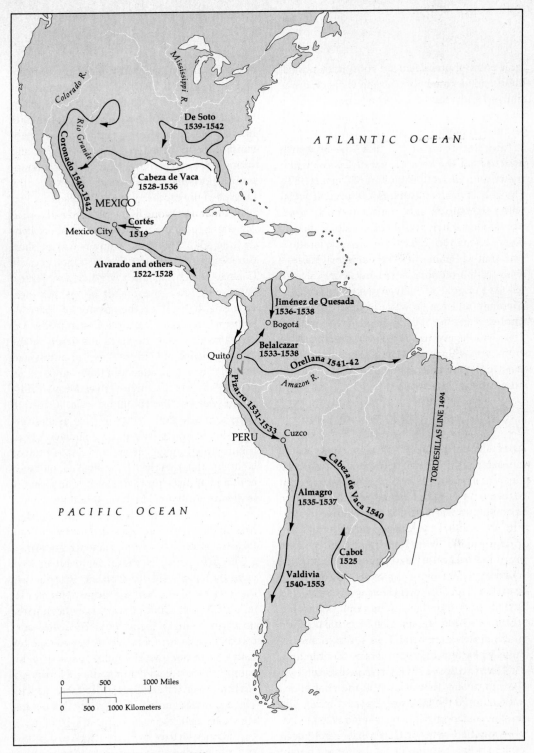

EARLY SPANISH OVERLAND EXPEDITIONS

focal point of a widespread conspiracy against them and decided that he must die. He was charged with treason and condemned to death by burning, a sentence commuted to strangling on his acceptance of baptism.

After the death of the Inca, the Spaniards marched on the Inca capital of Cuzco, which they captured and pillaged in November 1533. The gold and silver looted from Cuzco, together with Atahualpa's enormous ransom of gold, was melted down and divided among the soldiers. Hernando Pizarro, Francisco's brother, was sent to Spain with the emperor Charles's share of the plunder. Hernando's arrival with his load of gold and silver caused feverish excitement, and a new wave of Spanish fortune hunters sailed for the New World. Meanwhile, Francisco Pizarro had begun construction of an entirely new Spanish capital, Lima, the City of the Kings, conveniently near the coast for communication with Panama.

Post-Conquest Troubles

After Atahualpa's death, Pizarro, posing as the defender of the legitimate Inca line, proclaimed Huascar's brother Manco as the new Inca. But Manco was not content to play the role of a Spanish puppet. A formidable insurrection, organized and led by Manco himself, broke out in many parts of the empire. A large Indian army laid siege to Cuzco for ten months but failed by a narrow margin to take the city. Defeated by superior Spanish weapons and tactics and by food shortages in his army, Manco retreated to a remote stronghold in the Andean mountains, where he and his successors maintained a kind of Inca government-in-exile until 1572, when a Spanish military expedition entered the mountains, broke up the imperial court, and captured the last Inca, Tupac Amaru, who was beheaded in a solemn ceremony at Cuzco.

The Indian siege of Cuzco had barely been broken when fighting began between a group of the conquerors headed by the Pizarro brothers and a group led by Diego de Almagro over possession of the city of Cuzco. Defeated in battle, Almagro suffered death by strangling but left behind him a son and a large group of supporters to brood over their poverty and supposed wrongs. Twelve of them, contemptuously dubbed by Pizarro's secretary "the knights of the cape" because they allegedly had only one cloak among them, planned and carried out the assassination of the conqueror of Peru in June 1541. But their triumph was of short duration. From Spain came a judge, Vaca de Castro, sent by Charles V to advise Pizarro concerning the government of his province. Assuring himself of the loyalty of Pizarro's principal captains, Vaca de Castro made war on Almagro's son, defeated his army on the "bloody plains of Chupas," and promptly had him tried and beheaded as a traitor to the king.

Presently, fresh troubles arose. Early in 1544, a new viceroy, Blasco Núñez Vela, arrived in Lima to proclaim the edicts known as the New Laws of the Indies. These laws regulated Indian tribute, freed Indian slaves, and forbade forced labor by the Indians. They evoked outraged cries and appeals for their suspension from the Spanish landowners in Peru. When these pleas were not heeded, the desperate conquistadors rose in revolt and found a leader in Gonzalo Pizarro, brother of the murdered Francisco.

The first phase of the great revolt in Peru ended auspiciously for Gonzalo Pizarro with the defeat and death of the viceroy Núñez Vela in a battle near Quito. Pizarro now became the uncrowned king of the country. The rebel leader owed much of his initial military success to the resourcefulness and demoniac energy of his eighty-year-old field commander and principal adviser, Francisco de Carbajal. To these qualities Carbajal united an inhuman cruelty that became legendary in Peru.

After his victory over the viceroy, Carbajal and other advisers urged Pizarro to proclaim himself king of Peru. But Pizarro, a weaker man than his iron-willed lieutenant, hesitated to avow the revolutionary meaning of his actions. The arrival of a smooth-tongued envoy of the Crown, Pedro de la Gasca, who announced suspension of the New Laws and offered pardons and rewards to all repentant rebels, caused a trickle of desertions from Pizarro's ranks that soon became a flood. As his army melted away, Carbajal is said to have hummed the words of an old Spanish song: "These my hairs, mother, two by two the breeze carries them away."

Finally, the rebellion collapsed almost without a struggle, and its leaders were executed. Before the civil wars in Peru had run their course, four of the Pizarro "brothers of doom" and the Almagros, father and son, had met violent deaths; a viceroy had been slain; and numberless others had lost their lives. Peace and order were not solidly established in the country until the administration of Viceroy Francisco de Toledo, who came out in 1569, a quarter-century after the beginning of the great civil wars.

THE QUEST FOR EL DORADO

Exploration in North America

From its original base in the West Indies and from the two new centers of Mexico and Peru, the great movement of Spanish exploration radiated in all directions. While Spanish ships were launched on the waters of the Pacific to search for the Spice Islands, land expeditions roamed the interior of North and South America in quest of new golden kingdoms.

The North American mainland early attracted the attention of Spanish gold hunters and slave hunters based in the West Indies. In 1513, Ponce de León, governor of Puerto Rico, sailed west and discovered a subtropical land to which he gave the name La Florida. His subsequent efforts to colonize the region ended with his death at

the hands of Indians. In the 1520s another expedition, ineptly led by Pánfilo de Narváez, met with disaster in the vast, indefinite expanse of La Florida. Only four survivors of the venture, among them its future chronicler, the honest and humane Alvar Núñez Cabeza de Vaca, reached Mexico safely after a great, circuitous trek over the plains of Texas. In the last stages of his journey, Cabeza de Vaca was followed by thousands of adoring Indians, "clouds of witnesses" to his reputation as a medicine man of great powers.

Cabeza de Vaca's tales of adventure, with their hints of populous cities just beyond the horizon, inspired the conquistador Hernando de Soto, a veteran of the conquest of Peru, to try his fortune in La Florida. In 1542, after three years of unprofitable wanderings and struggles with Indians in the great area between South Carolina and Arkansas, the discoverer of the Mississippi died in the wilderness of a fever.

The strange tales told by Cabeza de Vaca and his three companions on their arrival in Mexico in 1536, and the even stranger story told by a certain Fray Marcos, who claimed to have seen in the far north one of the Seven Cities of the mythical golden realm of Cibola (from a great distance, it was true), persuaded Viceroy Antonio de Mendoza in 1540 to send an expedition northward commanded by Francisco Vásquez de Coronado. For two years, Spanish knights in armor pursued the elusive realm of gold through the future states of Arizona, New Mexico, Colorado, Oklahoma, Kansas, and possibly Nebraska. Disillusioned by the humble reality of the Zuñi pueblos of Arizona, the apparent source of the Cibola myth, Coronado went on to discover the Grand Canyon of the Colorado and then pushed east in search of still another El Dorado, this time called Quivira. Intruders who left no trace of their passage, the Spaniards were repelled by the immensity of the great plains and returned home bitterly disappointed with their failure to find treasure.

Further Exploration in South America

The golden will-o'-the-wisp that lured Spanish knights into the deserts of the Southwest also beckoned to them from South America's jungles and mountains. From the town of Santa Marta, founded in 1525 on the coast of modern Colombia, an expedition led by Gonzalo Jiménez de Quesada set out in 1536 on a difficult journey up the Magdalena River in search of gold and a passage to the Pacific. They suffered incredible hardships before they finally emerged onto the high plateau east of the Magdalena inhabited by the Chibcha. These Indians were primarily farmers, were skillful in casting gold and copper ornaments, lived in palisaded towns, and were ruled by a chieftain called the Zipa. After defeating them in battle, Jiménez de Quesada founded in 1538 the town of Sante Fé de Bogatá, future capital of the province of New Granada. The immense treasure in gold and emeralds looted from the Chibcha fired Spanish imaginations and inspired fantasies about yet other golden kingdoms. The most famous of these legends was that of El Dorado (the Golden Man), which in one version told of an Indian ruler who every morning was anointed with gold dust, which he washed off at night.

The dream of spices also played its part in inspiring the saga of Spanish exploration and conquest. Attracted by accounts of an eastern land where cinnamon trees grew in profusion, Gonzalo Pizarro led an expedition in 1539 from Quito in modern Ecuador across the Andes and down the forested eastern slopes of the mountains. Cinnamon was found, but in disappointingly small quantities. Lured on by the customary Indian tall tales of rich kingdoms somewhere beyond the horizon, designed to trick the intruders into moving on, the treasure hunters plunged deep into the wilderness. Gonzalo's lieutenant, Francisco de Orellana, sent with a party down a certain stream in search of food, found the current too strong to return and went on to enter a great river whose course

he followed in two makeshift boats for a distance of eighteen hundred leagues, eventually emerging from its mouth to reach Spanish settlements in Venezuela. Meanwhile, the disgruntled Pizarro and his men made their way back home as best they could. On the banks of the great river, Orellana fought Indians whose women joined the battle. For this reason, he gave the river its Spanish name of Amazonas—an illustration of the myth-making process among the Spaniards of the Conquest.

Among others who pursued phantom kingdoms in the wilderness of the Amazon and Orinoco river systems was Sir Walter Raleigh, wise in other things but naive and credulous in the matter of El Dorado. Raleigh staked and lost his head on his promise to find a gold mine for King James of England. His description of the "Rich and Beautiful Empire of Guiana" incorporated just about all the elements of the legend of El Dorado, including the themes of lost Inca treasure, the Golden Man who was anointed with gold dust, which he washed off in a sacred lake, and a warlike tribe of women.

In the southern reaches of the continent, which possessed little gold or silver, new agricultural and pastoral settlements arose. In 1537, Pizarro's comrade and rival, Diego de Almagro, made a fruitless march across the rugged Andean altiplano and the sun-baked Chilean desert in search of gold. He returned, bitterly disappointed, to a final confrontation with Pizarro. Two years later, Pizarro authorized Pedro de Valdivia to undertake the conquest of the lands to the south of Peru. After crossing the desert of northern Chile, Valdivia reached the fertile Central Valley and founded there the town of Santiago. In constant struggle with the Araucanian Indians, Valdivia laid the foundations of an agricultural colony based on the servile labor of other, more pacific Indians. He was captured and killed by the Araucanians during an expedition southward in 1553.

In the same period (1535), the town of Buenos Aires was founded on the estuary of the Rio de la Plata by the adelantado Pedro de Mendoza, who brought twenty-five hundred colonists in fourteen ships. But Buenos Aires was soon abandoned by its famished inhabitants, who moved almost a thousand miles upstream to the newly founded town of Asunción in Paraguay, where a genial climate, an abundance of food, and a multitude of docile Guarani Indians created more favorable conditions for Spanish settlement. Asunción became the capital of Paraguay and all the Spanish territory in southeastern South America. Not until 1580 was Buenos Aires permanently resettled by colonists coming from Asunción.

The Conquistadors

What sort of men were the conquistadors? The conquest of America attracted a wide variety of types. There was a sprinkling of professional soldiers, some with backgrounds of service in the Italian wars and some with pasts that they preferred to forget. The old conquistador Gonzalo Fernández de Oviedo had such men in mind when he warned the organizers of expeditions against "fine-feathered birds and great talkers" who "will either slay you or sell you or forsake you when they find that you promised them more in Spain than you can produce." In one of his *Exemplary Tales*, Cervantes describes the Indies as "the refuge and shelter of the desperate men of Spain, sanctuary of rebels, safeconduct of homicides." No doubt men of this type contibuted more than their share of the atrocities that stained the Spanish Conquest. But the background of the conquistadors was extemely varied, running the whole gamut of the Spanish social spectrum. The majority were commoners, but there were many marginal hidalgos, poor gentlemen who wished to improve their fortunes; some were *segundones* (second sons), disinherited by the Spanish laws of primogeniture and entail. Of the 168 men who captured Atahualpa at Cajamarca in 1532, 38 were hidalgos and 91 plebeians, with the back-

ground of the rest unknown or uncertain. According to James Lockhart, who has studied the men of Cajamarca, 51 members of the group were definitely literate and about 76 "almost certainly functioning literates." The group included 19 artisans, 12 notaries or clerks, and 13 "men of affairs."

Of the Spanish kingdoms, Castile provided the largest contingent, with natives of Andalusia predominating in the first, or Caribbean, phase of the Conquest; men from Estremadura, the poorest region of Spain, made up the largest single group in the second, or mainland, phase. Cortés, Pizarro, Almagro, Valdivia, Balboa, Orellana, and other famous conquistadors all came from Estremadura. Foreigners were not absent from the Conquest. Oviedo, in an attempt to clear Spaniards of sole responsibility for the crimes committed in the Indies, assures us that men had come there from every part of Christendom: There were Italians, Germans, Scots, Englishmen, Frenchmen, Hungarians, Poles, Greeks, Portuguese, and men "from all the other nations of Asia, Africa, and Europe."

By the 1520s, an institution inherited from the Spanish *Reconquista*, the *compaña* (warrior band), whose members shared in the profits of conquest according to certain rules, had become the principal instrument of Spanish expansion in the New World. At its head stood a military leader who usually possessed a royal capitulación, which vested him with the title of adelantado and with the governorship of the territory to be conquered. Sometimes these men were wealthy in their own right and contributed large sums or incurred enormous debts to finance the expedition. Italian, German, and Spanish merchant capitalists and royal officials grown wealthy through the Indian slave trade or other means provided much of the capital needed to fit out ships, acquire horses and slaves, and supply arms and food.

The warrior band was in principle a military democracy, with the distribution of spoils carried out by a committee elected from among the entire company. After subtracting the quinto and the common debts, the remaining booty was divided into equal shares. In the distribution of Atahualpa's treasure, there were 217 such shares, each worth 5,345 gold pesos—a tidy sum for that time. Distribution was made in accordance with the individual's rank and contribution to the enterprise. The norm was one share for a *peón* or foot soldier, two for a *caballero* or horseman (one for the rider, another for the horse), and more for a captain.

Despite its democratic aspect, the captains, large investors, and royal officials dominated the enterprise of conquest and took the lion's share for themselves. Some of the men were servants or slaves of the captains and investors, and their shares went entirely or in part to their employers or masters; in other cases, conquistadors had borrowed or bought on credit to outfit themselves, and the greater part of their earnings went to their creditors. Contemporary accounts complain of the predatory ways of some captains, who sold supplies to their men in time of need at profiteering prices. At a later stage of each conquest came the distribution of encomiendas. Craftsmen and other plebeians received encomiendas after the conquest of Mexico and Peru; later, however, only the leaders and hidalgo members of expeditions were rewarded with such grants.

Bravery, tenacity, and an incredible capacity for enduring hardships were among the conspicuous virtues of the conquistador. The legendary Castilian austerity prepared the conquistador for the difficulties he encountered in the New World. The Spanish common solider of the War of Granada ate only once a day, fortifying himself occasionally with swigs of the thin, sharply bitter wine he carried in a leather bottle. His single meal was a salad of onions, garlic, cucumbers, and peppers chopped very finely and mixed with bread crumbs, olive oil, vinegar, and water. Soldiers with such traditions were capable of marching a day's journey on a handful of toasted corn.

A fierce nationalism and a religious fanaticism—more often manifested in a brutal contempt for the Indian than in a desire for his or her conversion—were essential elements in the psychological make-up of the conquistador. Add to these traits the quality of romanticism. The Reconquest, filled with a thousand combats, raids, and ambushes, had heated the Spanish imagination to an incandescent pitch. Spanish romanticism found expression in a rich literature of romances, popular ballads that celebrated the exploits of the frontier wars against the Moors and that were frequently on the lips of the conquistadors. The literate soldiers of the Conquest were also influenced by their reading of classic literature, especially of the romances of chivalry with their prodigious line of perfect knights and their mythical islands, Amazons, and giants, which the fantasy of the conquistadors placed in one or another part of the Indies. The conquistador was romantically conscious of his historical role. Some of Cortés's soldiers boasted to him that neither the Romans nor Alexander had ever performed deeds equal to theirs, to which Cortés replied that "far more will be said in future history books about our exploits than has ever been said about those of the past."

Of the trinity of motives (God, Gold, and Glory) commonly assigned to the Spanish conquistador, the second was certainly upper-most in the minds of most. "Do not say that you are going to the Indies to serve the king and to employ your time as a brave man and an hidalgo should," observed Oviedo in an open letter to would-be conquerors, "for you know the truth is just the opposite; you are going solely because you want to have a larger fortune than your father and your neighbors." Pizarro put it even more plainly in his reply to a priest who urged the need for spreading the Faith among the Indians. "I have not come for any such reasons. I have come to take away from them their gold." The conquistador and chronicler of the conquest of Mexico, Bernal Díaz del Castillo, ingenuously declared that the conquerors died "in the service of God and of His Majesty, and to give light to those who sat in darkness—and also to acquire that gold which most men covet." But the worthy Bernal wrote with the self-serving end of gaining additional rewards for his "great and notable service" to the king, and his book was meant for the eyes of their grave worships, the members of the Royal Council of the Indies.

Most conquistadors dreamed of eventually returning to Spain with enough money to found a family and live in a style that would earn them the respect and admiration of their neighbors. Only a minority, chiefly large merchants and *encomenderos,* acquired the capital needed to fulfill this ambition, and not all of them returned to Spain. The majority, lacking encomiendas or other sources of wealth, remained and often formed ties of dependency with more powerful Spaniards, usually encomenderos whose service they entered as artisans, military retainers, or overseers of their encomiendas or other enterprises. After 1535, as more and more would-be conquistadors came to the Indies while the opportunities for joining profitable conquests diminished, the problem of a large number of unemployed and turbulent Spaniards, many of whom wandered about, robbing and abusing the Indians, caused serious concern to royal officials and to the Crown itself.

Most conquistadors and other early Spanish settlers in the Indies were single young males, with a sprinkling of married men who had left their wives at home while they sought their fortunes. Aside from an occasional mistress or camp follower, few Spanish women accompanied the expeditions. Once the fighting had stopped, however, a small stream of Spanish women began to cross the Atlantic. Some were wives coming to rejoin their husbands (there were laws, generally unenforced, requiring that a married man must have his wife come to live with him or be deported to Spain); others were mothers, sisters, or nieces of the settlers. Marriages with Indian women were not uncommon; even hidalgos were happy at the opportunity to marry a wealthy Indian noblewoman like Moctezuma's daughter, Tecuixpo (Isabel Moctezuma), who was wed to three Spanish husbands in turn. After mid-century, however, most Spaniards of all social levels tended to marry Spanish women, either immigrants or those born in the Indies. By the last quarter of the century, the Spanish family and household, based on strong clan and regional loyalties, had been reconstituted in the Indies.

Of the thousands of bold captains and their followers who rode or marched under the banner of Castile to the conquest of America, few lived to enjoy in peace and prosperity the fruits of their valor, their sufferings, and their cruelties. "I do not like the title of adelantado," wrote Oviedo, "for actually that honor and title is an evil omen in the Indies, and many who bore it have come to an evil end." Of those who survived the battles and the marches, a few received the lion's share of spoils, land, and Indians; the majority remained in modest or worse circumstances, and frequently in debt. The conflict between the haves and the have-nots among the conquerors contributed significantly to the explosive, tension-ridden state of affairs in the Indies in the decades following the Conquest.

CHAPTER FOUR

The Economic
Foundations
of Colonial Life

From the first days of the Conquest, the Spanish government faced a problem of harmonizing the demand of the conquistadors for cheap Indian labor, which they frequently employed in a wasteful and destructive manner, with the Crown's interest in the preservation of a large, tribute-paying Indian population. The first decades of colonial experience demonstrated that the Indians, left to the tender mercies of the colonists, might either become an extinct race, as actually happened on the once densely populated island of Hispaniola, or rise in revolts threatening the very existence of the Spanish Empire in America. The Crown naturally regarded these alternatives with distaste.

The Indian question had other facets. There was a political issue, for excessive concentration of land and Indians in the hands of colonists might lead to the rise of a class of feudal lords independent of royal authority, a development the Spanish kings were determined to prevent. The church also had a major interest in the Indian problem. If the Indians died out as a result of Spanish mistreatment, the great task of saving pagan souls would remain incomplete and the good name of the church would suffer. Besides, who then would construct churches and monasteries and support the servants of God in the Indies?

The dispute over Indian policy immediately assumed the dramatic outward form of a struggle of ideas. For reasons deeply rooted in Spain's medieval past, Spanish thought of the sixteenth century had a strongly legalistic and scholastic character. At a time when scholasticism[1] was dying in other Western lands, it retained great vitality in Spain as a philosophic method and as an instrument for the solution of private and public problems. The need "to discharge the royal conscience," to make the royal actions conform to the natural and divine law, helps to explain Spanish preoccupation with the doctrinal foundations of Indian policy. What was the nature of the Indians? What was their cultural level? Were they the slaves by nature described by Aristotle, a race of subhumans who might properly be conquered and made to serve the Spaniards? What rights and obligations did the papal donation of America to the Spanish monarchs confer on them? Summoned by the monarchs to answer these and similar questions, jurists and theologians waged a battle of books in which they bombarded each other with citations from Aristotle, the church fathers, and medieval philosophers. Less frequently, they supported their positions with materials based on direct observation or written accounts of Indian life.

TRIBUTE AND LABOR IN THE SPANISH COLONIES

Behind the subtle disputations over Spain's obligations to the Indians, however, went on a

[1] A system of theological and philosophical doctrine and inquiry that predominated in the Middle Ages. It was based chiefly on the authority of the church fathers and of Aristotle and his commentators.

complex struggle over the question of who should control Indian labor and tribute, the foundations of the Spanish Empire in America. The main parties to this struggle were the Crown, the church, and the colonists.

The Encomienda and Slavery

Hispaniola was the first testing ground of Spain's Indian policy. The situation created on the island by the arrival of Columbus's second expedition has been aptly summed up by Samuel Eliot Morison in the phrase "Hell on Hispaniola." Eager to prove to the Crown the value of his discoveries, Columbus compelled the natives to bring in a daily tribute of gold dust. When the hard-pressed Indians revolted, they were hunted down, and hundreds were sent to Spain as slaves. Later, yielding to the demands of rebellious settlers, Columbus distributed the Indians among them, with the grantees enjoying the right to use the forced labor of the natives.

This temporary arrangement, formalized in the administration of Governor Nicolás de Ovando and sanctioned by the Crown, became the encomienda. This system, which had its origin in the Spanish medieval practice of granting jurisdiction over lands and people captured from the Moors to leading warriors, consisted in the assignment to a colonist of a group of Indians who were to serve him with tribute and labor. He in turn assumed the obligation of protecting his Indians, paying for the support of a parish priest, and helping to defend the colony. In practice, the encomienda in the West Indies proved a hideous slavery. Basically as a result of this mistreatment and the disorganization of Indian society, the Indian population of Hispaniola dwindled from several million to 29,000 within two decades. This decline was not the result of epidemic disease, for there is no record of any epidemic among the Indians of the Antilles before 1518.

The first voices raised against this state of affairs were those of a company of Dominican friars who arrived in Hispaniola in 1510. Their spokesman was Father Antonio Montesinos, who on Advent Sunday, 1511, ascended the church pulpit to threaten the Spaniards of the island with damnation for their offenses against the natives. The angry colonists and the Dominicans soon carried their dispute to the court. King Ferdinand responded by approving a code of Spanish-Indian relations, the Laws of Burgos (1512–1513). For all its fine-sounding phrases, however, the code did little more than sanction and regularize the existing situation.

The agitation begun by the Dominicans raised the larger question of the legality of Spain's claim to the Indies. To satisfy the royal conscience, a distinguished jurist, Dr. Juan López de Palacios Rubios, drew up a document, the *Requerimiento*, which the conquistadors were supposed to read to the Indians before making war on them. This curious manifesto called on the natives to acknowledge the supremacy of the church and the pope and the sovereignty of the Spanish monarchs over their lands by virtue of the papal donation of 1493, on pain of suffering war and enslavement. Not until they had rejected those demands, which were to be made known to them by interpreters, could war be legally waged against them. Some conquistadors took the Requirement lightly, mumbling it into their beards before an attack or reading it to captured Indians after a raid; the chronicler Oviedo relates that Palacios Rubios himself laughed heartily when told of the strange use made of the document by these captains.

Bartolomé de Las Casas (1484–1566), a former encomendero who had repented of his ways and later turned friar, now joined the struggle against Indian slavery and the doctrines of Palacios Rubios. Of the Requirement, Las Casas said that on reading it he could not decide whether to laugh or weep. Las Casas argued that the papal grant of America to the crown of Castile had been made solely for the purpose of conversion; it gave the Spanish crown no temporal power or possession in the Indies.

The Indians had rightful possession of their lands by natural law and the law of nations. All Spanish wars and conquests in the New World were illegal. Spain must bring Christianity to the Indians by the only method "that is proper and natural to men . . . namely, love and gentleness and kindness."

Las Casas hoped for a peaceful colonization of the New World by Spanish farmers who would live side by side with the Indians, teach them to farm and live in a civilized way, and gradually bring into being an ideal Christian community. A series of disillusioning experiences, including the destruction of an experiment along those lines on the coast of Venezuela (1521) by Indians who had suffered from the raids of Spanish slave hunters, turned Las Casas's mind toward more radical solutions. His final program called for the suppression of all encomiendas, liberation of the Indians from all forms of servitude except a small voluntary tribute to the Crown in recompense for its gift of Christianity, and the restoration of the ancient Indian states and rulers, the rightful owners of those lands. Over these states the Spanish king would preside as "Emperor over many kings" in order to fulfill his sacred mission of bringing the Indians to the Catholic faith and the Christian way of life. The instruments of that mission should be friars, who would enjoy special jurisdiction over the Indians and protect them from the corrupting influence of lay Spaniards. Although Las Casas's proposals appeared radical, they in fact served the royal aim of curbing the power of the conquistadors and preventing the rise of a powerful colonial feudalism in the New World. Not humanitarianism but selfinterest, above all, explains the partial official support that Las Casas's reform efforts received in the reign of Charles V (1516–1556).

The question of Indian policy became crucial with the discovery and conquest of the rich, populous empires of Mexico and Peru. The most elementary interests of the Crown demanded that the West Indian catastrophe should not be repeated in the newly conquered lands. In 1523, Las Casas appeared to have won a major victory. King Charles sent Cortés an order forbidding the establishment of encomiendas in New Spain, because "God created the Indians free and not subject." Cortés, who had already assigned encomiendas to himself and his comrades, did not enforce the order. Backed by the strength and needs of his hard-bitten soldiers, he argued so persuasively for the encomienda system as necessary for the welfare and security of the colony that the royal order was revoked. Encomienda tribute and labor continued to be the main source of income for the colonists until the middle of the sixteenth century. The labor of encomienda Indians was supplemented by that of Indian slaves captured in wars or obtained from Indian slave owners.

The New Laws of the Indies and the Encomienda

Despite its retreat in the face of Cortés's disobedience, the Crown renewed its efforts to bring Indian tribute and labor under royal control. Cautiously, it moved to curb the power of the conquistadors. The second audiencia (high court) of New Spain, established in 1531–1532, took the first steps in the direction of regulating Indian tribute and labor. It moderated the tribute paid by many Indian towns, provided for registration with the audiencia of tribute assessments, and forbade, in principle, the use of Indians as carriers without their consent. The climax of royal intervention came with proclamation of the New Laws of the Indies (1542). These laws appeared to doom the encomienda. They prohibited the enslavement of Indians, ordered the release of slaves to whom legal title could not be proved, barred compulsory personal service by the Indians, regulated tribute, and declared that existing encomiendas were to lapse on the death of the holder.

In Peru the New Laws provoked a great revolt; in New Spain they caused a storm of protest

by the encomenderos and a large part of the clergy. Under this pressure the Crown again retreated. The laws forbidding Indian slavery and forced labor were reaffirmed, but the right of inheritance by the heir of an encomendero was recognized and even extended by stages to a third, fourth, and sometimes even a fifth life. Thereafter, or earlier in the absence of an heir, the encomienda reverted to the Crown. In the natural course of events, the number of encomiendas steadily diminished and that of Crown towns increased.

By about 1560, the encomienda had been partially "tamed." Royal intervention had curbed the power of the encomenderos and partially stabilized the tribute and labor situation, at least in areas near the colonial capitals. Tribute was now assessed in most places by the audiencias, which made a continuing effort to adjust it to the fluctuations of population and harvests on appeal from the Indians. The institution of *visita* and *cuenta* was employed to make such adjustments. The visita (inspection of an Indian town) yielded information concerning its resources or capacity to pay, which was needed to determine its per capita quota. The cuenta (count), made at the same time, gave the number of tribute payers. About 1560, the annual tribute paid to the king or to an encomendero by each married tributary Indian in New Spain was usually one silver peso and four-fifths of a bushel of maize or its equivalent in other produce.

This mechanism of assessment and copious protective legislation did not bring significant or enduring relief to the Indians. Padding of population counts and other abuses by encomenderos and other interested parties were common. More important, recounts and reassessments consistently lagged behind the rapidly shrinking number of tribute payers, with the result that the survivors had to bear the tribute burdens of those who had died or fled. Moreover, from the accession to the throne of Philip II (1556), the dominant motive of Spain's Indian policy became the increase of royal revenues in order to relieve the Crown's desperate financial crisis. Indian groups hitherto exempt from tribute lost their favored status, and the tribute quota was progessively raised. As a result of these measures and the gradual reversion of encomiendas to the Crown, the amount of royal tribute collected annually in New Spain rose from about 100,000 pesos to well over 1 million pesos between 1550 and the close of the eighteenth century.

For the colonists, however, the encomienda steadily declined in economic value. They lost the right to demand labor from their tributaries (1549); they also lost their fight to make the encomienda perpetual. The heaviest blow of all to the encomendero class was the catastrophic decline of the Indian population in the second half of the sixteenth century. In central Mexico, the Indian population dropped from perhaps 25 million in 1519 to slightly over 1 million in 1605. On the central coast of Peru, the tributary population seems to have fallen by 1575 to 4 percent of what it had been before the Conquest. For reasons that remain unclear, the rates of population decline in both Mexico and Peru appear to have been considerably higher on the coast than in the highlands. Disease, especially diseases of European origin against which the Indians had no acquired immunity, was the major direct cause of this demographic disaster. But overwork, malnutrition, severe social disorganization, and the resulting loss of will to live underlay the terrible mortality associated with the great epidemics and even with epidemic-free years. In Peru the great civil wars and disorders of the period from 1535 to 1550 undoubtedly contributed materially to Indian depopulation.

As the number of their tributaries fell, the encomenderos' income from tribute dropped proportionately, while their expenses, which included the maintenance of a steward to collect tribute, support of a parish priest, and heavy taxes, remained steady or even increased. As a result, many encomenderos, as well as other

Spaniards without encomiendas, began to engage in the more lucrative pursuits of agriculture, stock raising, and mining. The decline of the Indian population, sharply reducing the flow of foodstuffs and metals, stimulated a rapid growth of *haciendas* (Spanish estates) producing grain and meat.

Thus, in central Mexico by the 1570s, and in the northern and central Andean highlands by the end of the sixteenth century, the encomienda had lost its original character of an institution based on the use of Indian labor without payment. Its importance as a source of revenue to Spanish colonists had greatly diminished, and it had been placed in the way of extinction through the progressive reversion of individual encomiendas to the Crown. These changes, however, did not take place everywhere. In areas that lacked precious metals or where Indian agricultural productivity was low, and where consequently there was little danger of the colonists acquiring excessive power, the Crown permitted encomenderos to continue exploiting the forced labor of their Indians. This was the case in Chile, where the encomienda based on personal service continued until 1791; in Venezuela, where it survived until the 1680s; and in Paraguay, where it still existed in the early 1800s. The crown also allowed the encomienda as a labor system to continue in such areas of New Spain as Oaxaca and Yucatán.

The Repartimiento, Yanaconaje, and Free Labor

In the key areas of central Mexico and the Andean highlands, however, a new system, the *repartimiento*, replaced forced labor under the encomienda after 1550. Under this system, all adult male Indians had to give a certain amount of their time in rotation throughout the year to work in Spanish mines and workshops, on farms and ranches, and on public works. By this means, the Crown sought to regulate the use of an ever-diminishing pool of Indian labor and give access to such labor to both encomenderos and the growing number of Spaniards without encomiendas. The Indians received a token wage for their work, but the repartimiento, like the encomienda, was essentially disguised slavery. Indians who avoided service and community leaders who failed to provide the required quotas were subject to imprisonment, fines, and physical punishment.

In Peru, where the condition of the Indians seems to have been generally worse than in New Spain, the repartimiento (here known as the *mita*) produced especially disastrous effects. The silver mines of Potosí and the Huancavelica mercury mine were notorious deathtraps for Indian laborers under the mita. In Peru and Bolivia, the mita remained a major source of labor in mining to the end of the colonial period.

In the Andean area, the repartimiento was supplemented by another institution taken over from Inca society—the system of yanaconas, Indians who were separated from their communities and served Spaniards as personal servants or were attached to their estates. Like European serfs, the yanaconas were transferred from one landowner to another together with the estate. It is estimated that by the end of the sixteenth century the number of yanaconas on Spanish haciendas was almost equal to the number of Indians who lived in their own communities.

Although the repartimiento offered a temporary solution for the critical labor problem, many Spanish employers found it unsatisfactory, for it did not provide a dependable and continuing supply of labor. From an early date, mine owners and *hacendados* in New Spain turned increasingly to the use of free or contractual Indian wage labor. The heavy weight of tribute and repartimiento obligations on a diminishing native population and Spanish usurpation of Indian communal lands induced many Indians to accept an hacendado's invitation to become farm laborers working for wages, mostly paid in kind. Some traveled back and forth to work from their communities; others became resident peons on the haciendas. Other Indians were drawn to the northern silver mines by the lure of relatively high wages.

By 1630, when the Crown abolished the agricultural repartimiento in central Mexico, the move provoked little or no protest, for most landowners relied on free labor. The mining repartimiento continued longer in New Spain. It was still employed intermittently in the eighteenth century but had little importance, for the mines of New Spain operated mainly with contractual labor. In Peru and Bolivia, where the mita, supplemented by *yanaconaje*, was the dominant labor system, providing a mass of cheap workers for the high-cost silver mines, free labor was less important. However, there were as many as forty thousand free Indian miners (known as *mingas*) employed at the Potosí mines in the seventeenth century.

From the first, this so-called free labor was often associated with debt servitude. The second half of the seventeenth century saw the growth of the system of *repartimiento* or *repartimiento de mercancías*,[2] the compulsory purchase by Indians of goods from district governors (corregidores, alcaldes mayores). In combination with their other burdens, repartimiento was a powerful inducement for them to accept advances of cash and goods from Spanish hacendados; the tribute payment was usually included in the reckoning. An Indian so indebted had to work for his employer until the debt was paid. Despite its later evil reputation, peonage, whether or not enforced by debts, had definite advantages for many Indians. It usually freed them from the recurrent tribute and repartimiento burdens of the Indian community and often gave some security in the form of a plot of land the Indian could work for himself and his family. But if the hacienda offered some Indians escape from their intolerable conditions,

[2] The term *repartimiento*, it will be recalled, was also applied to the periodic conscription of Indians for labor useful to the Spanish community.

it aggravated the difficulties of those who remained on their ancestral lands. The hacienda expanded by legal or illegal means at the expense of the Indian pueblo, absorbing whole towns and leaving others without enough land for their people when the long population decline finally ended in the first half of the seventeenth century and a slow recovery began. The hacienda also lured laborers from the pueblo, making it difficult for the Indian town to meet its tribute and repartimiento obligations. Between the two *repúblicas* (commonwealths), the *república de indios* and the *república de españoles*, as Spanish documents frequently called them, stretched a gulf of hostility and distrust.

The importance of debt servitude as a means of securing and holding labor seems to have varied according to the availability of free labor. It was used extensively in northern Mexico, where such labor was scarce, but appears to have been less important in central Mexico, where it was more abundant. Some recent studies stress that debt peonage was "more of an inducement than a bond," with the size of advances reflecting the bargaining power of labor in dealing with employers and that hacendados sometimes made no special effort to recover their peons who had fled without repayment of loans. But the evidence for such relative lack of concern about fugitive peons comes chiefly from late eighteenth-century Mexico, when labor was increasingly abundant. For earlier, labor-scarce periods, there is much evidence of strenuous efforts to compel Indians to remain on estates until their debts had been paid off. Indeed, hacendados and officials sometimes likened Mexican peons to European serfs who were bound to their estates, with the right to their services passing with the transfer of the land from one owner to another.

Widely used in agriculture and mining, debt servitude assumed its harshest form in the numerous *obrajes* (workshops) producing cloth and other goods that sprang up in many areas in the sixteenth and seventeenth centuries. Convict labor, assigned to employers by Spanish judges,

was early supplemented by the "free" labor of Indians who were ensnared by a variety of devices. Indians were often tempted into these workshops by an offer of liquor or a small sum of money and, once inside the gates, were never let out again. "In this way," wrote a seventeenth-century observer, "they have gathered in and duped many married Indians with families, who have passed into oblivion here for twenty years, or longer, or their whole lives, without their wives or children knowing anything about them; for even if they want to get out, they cannot, thanks to the great watchfulness with which the doormen guard the exits."[3]

Black Slavery

Side by side with the disguised slavery of repartimiento and debt servitude existed black slavery. For a variety of reasons, including the fact that Spaniards and Portuguese were accustomed to the holding of black slaves, the tradition that blacks were descendants of the biblical Ham and bore his curse, and the belief that they were better able to support the hardships of plantation labor, Spanish defenders of the Indian did not display the same zeal on behalf of the enslaved Africans.

In fact, the rapid development of sugar cane agriculture in the West Indies in the early 1500s brought an insistent demand for black slave labor to replace the vanishing Indians. There arose a lucrative slave trade, chiefly carried on by foreigners under a system of *asiento* (contract between an individual or company and the Spanish crown). The high cost of slaves tended to limit their use to the more profitable plantation cultures or to domestic service in the homes of the wealthy. Large numbers lived on the coasts of Venezuela and Colombia, where they were employed in the production of such crops as

---

[3] Antonio Vasquez de Espinosa, *Compendium and Description of the West Indies*, tr. by C. U. Clark (Washington, D.C.: The Smithsonian Institution, 1942), p. 134.

cacao, sugar, and tobacco, and in the coastal valleys of Peru, where they labored on sugar and cotton plantations, but smaller concentrations were found in every part of the Indies. In Chapter 5, we shall consider the much disputed question whether African slavery in Hispanic America was "milder" than in other European colonies.

In summary, all colonial labor systems rested in varying degrees on servitude and coercion. Although contractual labor gradually emerged as the theoretical norm, all the labor systems just described coexisted throughout the colonial period. Indian slavery, for example, was abolished in 1542, but Indian wars and enslavement continued in frontier areas on various pretexts into the eighteenth century. Which labor system dominated at a given time and place depended on such factors as the area's natural resources, the number of Europeans in the area and the character of their economic activities, the size and cultural level of its Indian population, and the Crown's economic and political interests. Finally, it should be noted that in the course of the sixteenth and seventeenth centuries the labor pool was gradually expanded by the addition of mestizos (mixtures of Indians and whites), free blacks and mulattos, and poor whites. Since most of these people were exempt from encomienda and repartimiento obligations, they usually worked for wages and enjoyed freedom of movement, but like the Indians were subject to control through debts. In Chapter 7, we will discuss eighteenth-century changes in the labor system.

THE COLONIAL ECONOMY

The Conquest disrupted the traditional subsistence-and-tribute economy of the Indians. War and disease took a heavy toll of lives, to the detriment of production; in some areas the complex irrigation networks established and maintained by Indian centralized authorities were destroyed or fell into ruin. The Conquest also transformed the character and tempo of Indian economic activity. When the frenzied scramble for treasure had ended with the exhaustion of the available gold and silver objects, the encomienda became the principal instrument for the extraction of wealth from the vanquished. The peoples of the Aztec and Inca empires were accustomed to paying tribute in labor and commodities to their rulers and nobility. But the tribute demands of the old ruling classes, although apparently increasing on the eve of the Conquest, had been limited by custom and by the capacity of Indian ruling groups to utilize tribute goods. The greater part of such tribute was destined for consumption or display, not for trade. The demands of the new Spanish masters, on the other hand, were unlimited. Gold and silver were the great objects; if these could not be obtained directly, the encomenderos proposed to obtain them by sale in local or distant markets of the tribute goods produced by their Indians. Driven by visions of infinite wealth, the Spaniards took no account of what the Indians had formerly given in tribute and exploited them mercilessly. A compassionate missionary, writing in 1554, complained that before the Conquest the Indians in his part of Mexico

never used to give such large loads of mantas [pieces of cotton cloth], nor had they ever heard of beds, fine cotton fabrics, wax, or a thousand other fripperies like bed sheets, tablecloths, shirts, and skirts. All they used to do was cultivate the fields of their lords, build their houses, repair the temples, and give of the produce of their fields when their lords asked for it.[4]

Cortés as a Businessman

The business career of Hernando Cortés illustrates the large variety and scale of the economic

---

[4] *Life and Labor in Ancient Mexico: The Brief and Summary Relation of the Lords of New Spain* by Alonso de Zorita, tr. and ed. by Benjamin Keen (New Brunswick, N.J.: Rutgers University Press, 1963), pp. 279–280.

activities of some encomenderos. By 1528, Cortés was already worth 500,000 gold pesos, at least $2.5 million in our money. Part of this wealth represented Cortés's share of the loot taken in Tenochtitlán and other places during and immediately after the Conquest. But his chief source of income was his encomienda holdings. To himself he assigned the richest tribute areas in the former Aztec Empire. At the time of his death in 1547, although many of his encomiendas had been drastically reduced and tribute assessments lowered, he was still receiving 30,000 gold pesos annually from this source. He received large quantities of gold dust, textiles, maize, poultry, and other products from encomienda towns. The pueblo of Cuernavaca (near Mexico City) alone gave as part of its annual tribute cloth worth 5,000 gold pesos. Cortés's agents sold the tribute cloth and other products to traders who retailed them in Mexico City and other Spanish towns. Cortés had his own extensive real estate holdings in Mexico City. On or near the central square he erected shops, some of which he used for his own trading interests, others of which he rented out.

Cortés was an empire builder in the economic as well as political sense of the word. He invested the capital he acquired from encomienda tribute and labor in many enterprises. Mining attracted his special attention. In the Oaxaca and Michoacán districts, he had gangs of Indian slaves, more than a thousand in each, panning gold; many of these slaves died from hard labor and inadequate food. In 1529 these mining areas brought him 12,000 pesos in gold annually. In addition to his own mining properties, Cortés held others, such as silver mines in the Taxco area of Mexico, in partnerships. In such cases, his investment usually consisted of goods, livestock, or the labor of his encomienda Indians or his Indian and Negro slaves.

After encomienda tribute, agriculture and stock raising were Cortés's largest sources of income. He had large landholdings in various parts of Mexico, some acquired by royal grant, others usurped from Indians. He employed en-

comienda labor to grow maize on his land. His fields in the vicinity of Oaxaca alone produced ten to fifteen thousand bushels a year. Part of this grain he sold in the Spanish towns and at the mines, part went to feed his gangs of slaves at the gold washings and his Indian carriers. Cortés also raised great numbers of cattle and hogs, which were butchered in his own slaughterhouses. Near Tehuantepec he had herds of more than ten thousand wild cattle, which supplied hides and tallow for export to Panama and Peru.

The restless Cortés also pioneered in the development of the Mexican sugar industry. By 1547 his plantations were producing more than three hundred thousand pounds of sugar annually, most of which was sold to agents of European merchants for export. If he was not the first to experiment with silk raising in New Spain, as he claimed, he certainly went into the business on a large scale, laying out thousands of mulberry trees with the labor of Indians paid in cash or cacao beans. In this venture, however, he suffered heavy losses. Nonetheless, the variety and extent of Cortés's business interests suggest how misleading is the familiar portrait of the conquistador as a purely feudal type devoted only to war and plunder, disdainful of all trade and industry.

The Growth of the Haciendas

Among the first generation of colonists, large-scale enterprises such as those of Cortés were rare. The typical encomendero was content to occupy a relatively small land grant and draw tribute from his Indians, who continued to live and work in large numbers on their ancestral lands. The major shift from reliance on encomienda tribute to the development of Spanish commercial agriculture and stock raising came after 1550 in response to the massive Indian population decline and the Crown's restrictive legislation, which combined to deprive the encomienda of much of its economic value. Acute food shortages in the Spanish towns created new economic opportunities for Spanish farmers and ranchers. Simultaneously, the reduction of Indian populations left vacant large expanses of Indian land, which Spanish colonists hastened to occupy for wheat raising or, more commonly, as sheep or cattle ranges.

By the end of the sixteenth century, the Spanish-owned hacienda was responsible for the bulk of agricultural commercial production and pressed ever more aggressively on the shrinking Indian sector of the colonial economy. Spanish colonists used various methods to "free" land from Indian occupation: purchase, usurpation, and *congregación* (forced concentration of Indians in new communities, ostensibly to facilitate control and Christianization). Although Spain's declared policy was to protect Indian community land, the numerous laws forbidding encroachment on such land failed to halt the advance of the hacienda. The power of the hacendados, whose ranks included high royal officials, churchmen, and wealthy merchants, usually carried all before it.

In the seventeenth century, the Crown actually encouraged usurpation of Indian lands by adopting the device of *composición* (settlement), which legalized the defective title of the usurper through payment of a fee to the king. Not only Indian communities but communities of Spanish or mestizo small farmers saw their lands devoured by the advancing hacienda. A striking feature of this process was that land was sometimes primarily acquired not for use but to obtain Indian day laborers and peons by depriving them of their fields or to eliminate competition by Indian or other small producers. The establishment of a *mayorazgo* (entail) assured the perpetuation of the consolidated property in the hands of the owner's descendants.

The tempo of land concentration, however, varied from region to region according to its resources and proximity to markets. In the Valley of Mexico, for example, the bulk of the land was held by great haciendas by the end of the colonial period. Indian commoners and chiefs, on the other hand, retained much of the land

in the province of Oaxaca, which had limited markets for its crops.

Spanish Agriculture in the New World

Spanish agriculture differed from Indian land use in significant ways. First, it was extensive, cultivating large tracts with plows and draft animals, by contrast with the intensive Indian digging-stick agriculture. Second, Spanish agriculture was predominantly commercial, producing commodities for sale in local or distant markets, by contrast with the subsistence character of traditional Indian agriculture. Through the need to pay tribute and other obligations in cash, the Indian farmer came under increasing pressure to produce for the market. But, as a rule, the hacendado's superior resources made it difficult for the Indian farmer to compete except in times of abundant harvests, and he tended to fall back to the level of subsistence agriculture, whose meager yield he sometimes supplemented by labor for the local hacendado.

Spanish colonial agriculture early produced wheat on a large scale for sale in urban centers like Mexico City, Lima, Veracruz, and Cartagena; maize was also grown on haciendas for the sizable Indian consumers' market in Mexico City and Lima. Sugar, like wheat, was one of Europe's agricultural gifts to America. Spaniards brought it from the Canary Islands to Hispaniola, where it soon became the foundation of the island's prosperity. By 1550 more than twenty sugar mills processed cane into sugar, which was shipped in great quantities to Spain. "The sugar industry is the principal industry of those islands," wrote José de Acosta at the end of the sixteenth century, "such a taste have men developed for sweets." From the West Indies sugar quickly spread to Mexico and Peru. Sugar refining, with its large capital outlays for equipment and Negro slaves, was the largest-scale enterprise in the Indies.

In the irrigated coastal valleys of Peru, wine and olives, as well as sugar, were produced in quantity. The silk industry had a brief period of prosperity in Mexico, but soon declined in the face of labor shortages and competition from Chinese silk brought in the Manila galleons from the Philippines to the port of Acapulco. Spain's sporadic efforts to discourage the production of wine, olives, and silk, regarded as interfering with Spanish exports of the same products, seem to have had little effect. Other products cultivated by the Spaniards on a capitalist plantation basis included tobacco, cacao, and indigo. A unique Mexican and Central American export, highly valued by the European cloth industry, was cochineal, a blood-red dye made from the dried bodies of insects parasitic on the nopal cactus.

Spain made a major contribution to American economic life with the introduction of various domestic animals—chickens, mules, horses, cattle, pigs, and sheep. The mules and horses revolutionized transport, gradually eliminating the familiar spectacle of long lines of Indian carriers loaded down with burdens. Horses and mules became vital to the mining industry for hauling and for turning machinery. Cattle and smaller domesticated animals greatly enlarged the food resources of the continent. Meat was indispensable to the mining industry, for only a meat diet could sustain the hard work of the miners. "If the mines have been worked at all," wrote a Spanish judge in 1606, "it is thanks to the plentiful and cheap supply of livestock." In addition to meat, cattle provided hides for export to Spain and other European centers of leather manufacture, as well as hides and tallow (used for lighting) for the domestic market, especially in the mining areas. Sheep raisers found a large market for their wool in the textile workshops that arose in many parts of the colonies.

In a densely settled region like central Mexico, the explosive increase of Spanish cattle and sheep had catastrophic consequences. A horde of animals swarmed over the land, often invading not only the land vacated by the dwindling Indian population but the reserves of land needed by the Indian system of field rotation.

Cattle trampled the Indian crops, causing untold damage; torrential rains caused massive erosion on valley slopes close cropped by sheep. By the end of the sixteenth century, however, the Mexican cattle industry had become stabilized. Exhaustion of virgin pasturelands, mass slaughter of cattle for their hides and tallow, and official efforts to halt grazing on Indian harvest lands had produced a marked reduction in the herds. Gradually, the cattle ranches and sheep herds moved to new, permanent grazing grounds in the sparsely settled, semiarid north.

An equally rapid increase of horses, mules, and cattle took place in the empty pampas (grasslands) of the Río de la Plata (modern Argentina). Their increase in this area of almost infinite pasturage soon outstripped potential demand and utilization, and herds of wild cattle became a common phenomenon in La Plata as in other parts of Spanish America. Barred by Spanish law from seaborne trade with the outside world, the inhabitants of this remote province, lacking precious metals or abundant Indian labor, relieved their poverty by illegal commerce with Dutch and other foreign traders, who carried their hides and tallow to Europe. In addition, they also sent mules and horses, hides and tallow to the mining regions of Upper Peru (Bolivia).

Another center of the cattle industry was the West Indies. José de Acosta wrote in about 1590 that

the cattle have multiplied so greatly in Santo Domingo, and in other islands of that region that they wander by the thousands through the forests and fields, all masterless. They hunt these beasts only for their hides; whites and Negroes go out on horseback, equipped with a kind of hooked knife, to chase the cattle, and any animal that falls to their knives is theirs. They kill it and carry the hide home, leaving the flesh to rot; no one wants it, since meat is so plentiful.[5]

[5] José de Acosta, *Historia natural y moral de las Indias* (Mexico, 1940), p. 318.

Colonial Mining and Industry

Mining, as the principal source of royal revenue in the form of the quinto, or royal fifth of all gold, silver, or other precious metals obtained in the Indies, received the special attention and protection of the Crown. Silver, rather than gold, was the principal product of the American mines. Spain's proudest possession in the New World was the great silver mine of Potosí in upper Peru, whose flow of treasure attained gigantic proportions between 1579 and 1635. Potosí was discovered in 1545; the rich Mexican silver mines of Zacatecas and Guanajuato were opened up in 1548 and 1558, respectively. In the same period, important gold placers (sand or gravel deposits containing eroded particles of the ore) were found in central Chile and in the interior of New Granada (Colombia). The introduction of the patio process for separating the silver from the ore with mercury (1556) gave a great stimulus to silver mining. The chief source of mercury for Potosí silver was the Hunancavelica mine in Peru, where labor was "a thing of horror"; Mexican silver was chiefly processed with mercury from the Almadén mine in Spain. As in other times and places, the mining industry brought prosperity to a few, failure or small success to the great majority.

Lack of capital to finance technical improvements required by the increasing depth of mines, flooding, and similar problems, combined with shortages and the high cost of mercury (a Crown monopoly), caused a precipitous decline of silver production in the viceroyalty of Peru after 1650. In Mexico production levels fluctuated, with output declining in some old centers and rising in new ones, but here the long-range trend for the seventeenth century seems to have been upward. (An older view claimed that an acute labor shortage caused by the catastrophic fall of the Indian population was the root cause of a supposed decline in silver production in New Spain, but it now appears that mine owners in general had little difficulty in filling their labor needs.) As silver production fell, colonial agriculture and stock raising, which had expanded to satisfy the demands of the mining centers for grain, meat, hides, tallow, and work animals, also entered a period of contraction. There was a shift from large-scale commercial enterprise to an emphasis on self-sufficiency. A simultaneous crisis of the European economy reduced the demand for such colonial staples as hides, sugar, and indigo.

The colonial depression was not total, however, for the economic picture is a mixed one. It has been argued, for example, that the spectacular decline in silver remittances to Castile, cited in support of the thesis of a colonial seventeenth-century economic crisis, was caused in part by a growing colonial self-sufficiency that reduced dependence on European goods. In New Spain, proceeds from the alcabala (the sales tax), a significant indicator of the state of the economy, increased until 1638 and declined only slightly thereafter. Although trade with Seville declined, the same was not generally true of interprovincial trade; in the 1620s a vigorous trade in cacao, Venezuela's principal export, developed between that colony and Mexico. Trade also flourished between Chile and Peru. On balance, however, the description of the colonial seventeenth century as a century of depression is probably correct. It also seems likely that the reduced tempo of economic activity in mining and agriculture lessened the worst exploitation of Indian labor and helped to initiate the slow Indian population recovery that was under way by the last quarter of the seventeenth century.

The Spaniards found a flourishing handicrafts industry in the advanced culture areas of Mexico, Central America, and Peru. Throughout the colonial period, the majority of the natives continued to supply their own needs for pottery, clothing, and household goods. In the Spanish towns, craft guilds modeled on those of Spain arose in response to the high prices for all Spanish imported goods. To avoid competition

Gold mining in Spanish America in the sixteenth
century: Indian workers overseen by their Spanish
conquerors. (Historical Pictures Service, Inc.)

from Indian and mestizo artisans, who quickly
learned the Spanish crafts, they were soon incorporated into the Spanish-controlled guilds
but were barred from becoming masters. These
guilds attempted to maintain careful control over
the quantity and quality of production in industries serving the needs of the colonial upper
class.

The period up to about 1630 saw a steady
growth of factory-type establishments, the previously mentioned obrajes, many of which produced cheap cotton and woolen goods for popular consumption. Most of these enterprises
were privately owned, but some were operated
by Indian communities to meet their tribute
payments. A number of towns in New Spain
(Mexico City, Puebla, Tlaxcala, among others)
were centers of this textile industry. Other primitive factories produced such articles as soap,
chinaware, and leather. The seventeenth-century
depression seems to have blighted the once-
flourishing textile industry of New Spain but
does not appear to have had the same harmful
effects elsewhere. To some extent, the depression, by reducing the capacity to purchase foreign imports, may have promoted the growth

of colonial industry. The population increase of the late seventeenth century may have also stimulated the growth of manufacturing. There is little evidence that sporadic Spanish legislative efforts to restrict the growth of colonial manufactures achieved their purpose.

The Framework of the Economy

Was the colonial economy capitalist, feudal, or a mixture of both? Scholars have hotly debated this question in recent decades. Some deny the relevance of the concepts of feudalism and capitalism, taken from a European context, to a unique colonial reality, but most students will admit the presence of capitalist, feudal, and even more archaic elements—such as the pre-Columbian Indian communities based on communal land tenure—in the colonial economy. The feudal or quasi-feudal elements included labor systems based in varying degrees on servitude and coercion; the nonmonetary character of many economic transactions; and the technical backwardness of industry and agriculture, which reflected the very low level of investment for production by contrast with high levels of expenditure for conspicuous consumption, the church, and charities. Regulations (such as those that forbade Indians to wear European clothes or own land privately) that seriously hampered the development of a market economy also demonstrated feudal characteristics.

The colonial economy also contained capitalist elements. From the first it was geared to external markets (as shown by the entrepreneurial activities of Cortés and other conquistadors) and reflected the vicissitudes of European capitalism. But the development of colonial capitalism remained embryonic, stunted by the overwhelming weight of feudal relations and attitudes and the continuous siphoning off of wealth to Spain, itself an economic satellite of the more developed capitalist powers of northwest Europe. The double character of the hacienda—often self-sufficient and nonmonetary in its internal re-

lations but oriented externally toward European markets—reflected the dualism of the colonial economy. For lack of a better term, that economy may perhaps be best described as "semifeudal" or "semicapitalist."

COMMERCE, SMUGGLING, AND PIRACY

The Colonial Commercial System

Spain's colonial commercial system was restrictive, exclusive, and regimented in character, in conformity with the mercantilist standards of that day. Control over all colonial trade, under the Royal Council of the Indies, was vested in the Casa de Contratación (House of Trade), established in 1503 in Seville. This agency licensed and supervised all ships, passengers, crews, and goods passing to and from the Indies. It also collected import and export duties and the royal share of all precious metals and stones brought from the Indies, licensed all pilots, and maintained a *padrón real* (standard chart) to which all charts issued to ships in the Indies trade had to conform. It even operated a school of navigation that trained the pilots and officers needed to sail the ships in the transatlantic trade.

Commerce with the colonies was restricted until the eighteenth century to the wealthier merchants of Seville and Cádiz, who were organized in a guild that exercised great influence in all matters relating to colonial trade. With the aim of preventing contraband trade and safeguarding the Seville monopoly, trade was concentrated in three American ports, Veracruz in New Spain, Cartagena in new Granada, and Nombre de Dios (later Portobelo) on the Isthmus of Panama. The Seville merchant oligarchy and corresponding merchant groups in the Indies, particularly the merchant guilds in Mexico City and Lima, deliberately kept the colonial markets understocked. In general they played into each other's hands at the expense of the colonists, who were forced to pay exorbitant prices for all European goods acquired through legal channels. Inevitably, the system generated colonial discontent and stimulated the growth of contraband trade.

With the object of enforcing the close-port policy and protecting merchant vessels against foreign attack, a fleet system was developed and made obligatory in the sixteenth century. As perfected about the middle of the century, it called for the annual sailing under armed convoy of two fleets, each numbering fifty or more ships, one sailing in the spring for Veracruz and taking with it ships bound for Honduras and the West Indies, the other sailing in August for Panama and convoying ships for Cartagena and other ports on the northern coast of South America. Veracruz supplied Mexico and most of Central America; from Portobelo goods were carried across the isthmus and shipped to Lima, the distribution point for Spanish goods to places as distant as Chile and Buenos Aires. Having loaded their returns of silver and colonial produce, the fleets were to rendezvous at Havana and sail for Spain in the spring, before the onset of the hurricane season. In the seventeenth century, as a result of Spain's economic decadence and the growing volume of contraband trade, fleet sailings became increasingly irregular.

Danger and difficulty attended the long voyage to the Indies from the time a ship left Seville to thread its careful way down the shoal-ridden Guadalquivir to the Mediterranean. Hunger and thirst, seasickness and scurvy at sea, and yellow fever and malaria in tropical harbors like Veracruz and Portobelo were familiar afflictions. Storms at sea took a heavy toll of ships; foreign pirates and privateers posed a chronic threat. Gluts of goods in the colonial markets as a result of competition from foreign smugglers, and frequent confiscation of silver by the Crown, with tardy or inadequate compensation, often reduced merchants' profits to the vanishing point. But the heaviest damage to Spanish commercial interests stemmed from the activities of foreign smugglers and pirates, who seized the opportunity presented by Spain's growing economic and military weakness.

Spanish industry, handicapped by its guild organization and technical backwardness, could not supply the colonies with cheap and abundant manufactures in return for colonial foodstuffs and raw materials, as required by the implied terms of the mercantilist bargain. Indeed, it was not in the interest of the merchant monopolists of Seville and Cádiz, who throve on a regime of scarcity and high prices, to permit an abundant flow of manufactures to the colonies. Prices to the colonial consumer were also raised by a multitude of taxes: the *avería* (convoy tax), the *almojarifazgo* (import duty), and the alcabala (sales tax). Inevitably, the manufacturers and merchants of the advanced industrial nations of northern Europe sought to enter by force or guile into the large and unsatisfied Spanish-American markets. The ambitious monarchs of those lands scoffed at Spain's claim of dominion over all the Western Hemisphere except that portion that belonged to Portugal; they defied Spanish edicts forbidding foreigners to navigate American waters or trade on American coasts on pain of destruction of ships and crews. The ironic query said to have been addressed by Francis I of France to the kings of Spain and Portugal summed up the foreign viewpoint: "Show me, I pray you, the will of our father Adam, that I may see if he has really made you his only universal heirs."

The English Threat and Sir Francis Drake

England soon emerged as the principal threat to Spain's empire in America. The accumulation of capital and development of manufacturing under the fostering care of the Tudor kings produced an explosion of English commercial energies in the reign of Queen Elizabeth. The Old World did not provide sufficient outlets for these erupting energies, and England's merchant adventurers eagerly turned to America. The historic slave-trading voyage of John Hawkins to the West Indies in 1562 opened

England's drive to break into the closed Spanish-American markets. Half honest trader, half corsair, Hawkins came to the Indies heavily armed and ready to compel the colonists to trade with him at cannon point, but he showed himself scrupulously honest in his business dealings with the Spaniards, even to the point of paying the royal license and customs dues. Hawkins owed the success of his first two American voyages to the needs of the Spanish settlers, who were ready to trade with a Lutheran heretic or the devil himself to satisfy their desperate need for slave labor and European wares. To cover up these violations of Spanish law, the venal local officials made a thin pretense of resistance. But by 1567 the pretense had worn too thin, the Spanish government had taken alarm, and angry orders went out to drive the English smugglers away. Stiffening Spanish resistance culminated in the near-destruction of Hawkins's trading fleet by a Spanish naval force at Veracruz in 1568.

Only two of the English ships managed to get away; one was commanded by Hawkins, the other by his cousin, Francis Drake. Four years later, Drake left England with four small ships, bound for the Isthmus of Panama. In actions marked by audacity and careful planning, he stormed and plundered the town of Nombre de Dios, escaping at dawn. Later, he made the most lucrative haul in the history of piracy by capturing the pack train carrying Peruvian silver from the Pacific side of the isthmus to Nombre de Dios. In 1577, Drake set sail again on an expedition that had the secret sponsorship and support of Queen Elizabeth. Its objects were to "singe the King of Spain's beard" by seizing his treasure ships and ravaging his colonial towns; to explore the whole Pacific coast of America, taking possession of the regions beyond the limits of Spanish occupation; and to display English maritime prowess by means of a second circumnavigation of the globe. In the 1580s, Drake made other voyages of reprisal against Cartagena, St. Augustine, and Santo Domingo. Small wonder that the name of Drake became a word of fear to the inhabitants of colonial coastal towns.

Inroads by Other Europeans

In the seventeenth century, piracy and smuggling were supplemented by efforts to found colonies, not only on the mainland of North America but in the forbidden waters of the Spanish Main. The Dutch, intermittently at war with Spain since 1576, launched a formidable military and commercial offensive against the Spanish West Indies. Their principal instrument was the Dutch West India Company, organized in 1621. A brilliant admiral, Piet Heyn, captured the whole homebound Veracruz treasure fleet off the coast of Cuba in 1628. That victory brought a dividend of 50 percent to the company's shareholders and financed a new company offensive against Brazil that resulted in Dutch occupation of the rich sugar-producing Brazilian northeast for a quarter-century (1630–1654).

Dutch capture of Curaçao, hard off the coast of Venezuela (1634), gave them an invaluable smuggling base and emboldened the French and English to seize both unoccupied and occupied Spanish islands—Barbados and St. Kitts, Martinique and Guadeloupe. In 1655, an English Puritan fleet, defeated in an effort to capture Santo Domingo, turned on Jamaica and easily captured the thinly settled island. In the same period, French corsairs based in the pirate lair of Tortuga began to settle the adjacent northwest corner of Hispaniola, virtually abandoned by Spaniards since 1605. By 1665 this region had become the French colony of St. Domingue, with a governor appointed by the trading Compagnie des Indes.

The Effects of Privateers and Smugglers on Spanish Prosperity

In this period, piracy in the West Indies became a highly organized, large-scale activity often enjoying the open or covert protection of the

English pirates periodically plundered Spanish ships that were loaded with gold and silver from the New World. (The Bettmann Archive, Inc.)

was quite free of patriotic or religious zeal and plied his trade in the calculating spirit of a businessman engaged in a likely speculation.

Piracy entered on a decline following the signing of the Treaty of Madrid in 1670 between England and Spain, by which the British government agreed to aid in the suppression of the corsairs in return for Spanish recognition of its sovereignty over the British and West Indian islands. French buccaneers, however, continued active until the signing of the Treaty of Ryswick in 1697, by which Spain formally recognized French possession of St. Domingue.

The injury inflicted on Spanish prosperity and prestige by pirates and privateers, great as it was, was dwarfed by the losses caused by the less spectacular operations of foreign smugglers. Contraband trade steadily increased in the course of sixteenth and seventeenth centuries. The European establishments in Jamaica, St. Domingue, and the Lesser Antilles became so many bases for contraband trade with the Spanish colonies. Buenos Aires was another funnel through which Dutch and other foreign traders poured immense quantities of goods that reached markets as distant as Peru. By the end of the seventeenth century, French companies operating behind the façades of Spanish merchant houses in Seville and Cádiz dominated even the legal trade with the Indies.

A shrewd English observer put his finger on the major source of Spain's misfortunes: her economic weakness. The Spaniards, he remarked, were said to be stewards for the rest of Europe:

Their galleons bring the silver into Spain, but neither wisdom nor power can keep it there; it runs out as fast as it comes in, nay, and faster; insomuch that the little [Swiss] Canton of Bern is really richer, and has more credit, than is the king of Spain, notwithstanding his Indies. At first sight this seems to be strange and incredible; but when we come to examine it, the mystery is by no means impenetrable. The silver and rich commodities which come from the Indies come not for nothing (the king's duties

English governors of Jamaica and the French governors of St. Domingue. Two leading figures in this unsavory business were the ferocious French pirate L'Olonnois and the equally unscrupulous English buccaneer Henry Morgan. Romantic literature has cast a false glamour about these gangsters of the sea. Unlike the nationalistic and fervently Protestant Drake, the typical pirate captain of the seventeenth century *excepted) and very little of the goods or manufactures for which they come, belong to the subjects of the crown of Spain. It is evident, therefore, that the Spanish merchants are but factors, and that the greatest part of the returns from the West Indies belong to those foreigners for whom they negotiate.*[6]

[6] John Campbell, *The Spanish Empire in America* (London, 1747), p. 299.

Spanish economists of the seventeenth century understood the causes of Spain's plight. Their writings offered sound criticisms of the existing state of affairs and constructive proposals for reform. But their arguments were powerless to change the course of Spanish policy, dictated by small mercantile and aristocratic cliques whose special interests and privileges were wholly incompatible with the cause of reform.

CHAPTER FIVE

State, Church, and Society

The political organization of the Spanish Empire in America reflected the centralized, absolutist regime by which Spain itself was governed. By the time of the discovery and conquest of America, Castilian parliamentary institutions and municipal liberties had lost most of their former vitality. The process of centralization begun by the Catholic Sovereigns reached its climax under the first two Hapsburgs. In Castile there arose a ponderous administrative bureaucracy capped by a series of royal councils appointed by and directly responsible to the king. Aragon, which stubbornly resisted royal encroachments on its fueros (charters of liberties), retained a large measure of autonomy until the eighteenth century. Even in Castile, however, Hapsburg absolutism left largely intact the formal and informal power of the great lords over their peasantry. In Aragon, in whose soil feudal relations were more deeply rooted, the arrogant nobility claimed a broad seigneurial jurisdiction, including the right of life and death over its serfs, as late as the last decades of the seventeenth century. This contrast between the formal concentration of authority in the hands of royal officials and the actual exercise of supreme power on the local level by great landowners was to characterize the political structure of Spanish America as well.

POLITICAL INSTITUTIONS OF THE SPANISH EMPIRE

Formation of Colonial Administration

The pattern of Spain's administration of its colonies was formed in the critical period between 1492 and 1550. The final result reflected the steady growth of centralized rule in Spain itself and the application of a trial-and-error method to the problems of colonial government. To Columbus, Cortés, Pizarro, and other great expeditionary leaders, the Spanish kings granted sweeping political powers that made these men practically sovereign in the territories that they had won or proposed to subdue. But once the importance of these conquests had been revealed, royal jealousy of the great conquistadors was quick to show itself. Their authority was soon revoked or strictly limited, and the institutions that had been employed in Spain to achieve centralized political control were transferred to America for the same end. By the middle of the sixteenth century, the political organization of the Indies had assumed the definitive form that it was to retain, with slight variations, until late in the eighteenth century.

The Council of the Indies, originally a standing committee of the all-powerful Council of Castile but chartered in 1524 as a separate agency, stood at the head of the Spanish imperial administration almost to the end of the colonial period. Although great nobles and court favorites were appointed to the council, especially in the seventeenth century, its membership consisted predominantly of lawyers. Under the king, whose active participation in its work varied from monarch to monarch, it was the supreme legislative, judicial, and executive institution of government. One of its most important functions was the nomination to the king of all high colonial officials. It also framed a vast body of legislation for the Indies—the famous Laws of the Indies, first codified in 1681—which combined decrees of the most important kind with others of a very trivial character. Although the council was frequently staffed by conscientious and highly capable officials in the early Hapsburg period, the quality of its personnel tended to decline under the inept princes of the seventeenth century. Nonetheless, historians owe the council a particular debt for its initiative in seeking to obtain detailed information on the history, geography, resources, and population of all the colonies. The *relaciones* (reports) that incorporated this information represent a rich mine of materials for students of colonial Spanish America.

The Royal Agents

The principal royal agents in the colonies were the viceroys, the captains general, and the audiencias. The viceroys and captains general had essentially the same functions, differing only in the greater importance and extent of the territory assigned to the jurisdiction of the former. Each was the supreme civil and military officer in his realm, having in his charge such vital matters as the maintenance and increase of the royal revenues, defense, Indian welfare, and a multitude of other responsibilities. At the end of the Hapsburg era, in 1700, there were two great American viceroyalties. The viceroyalty of New Spain, with its capital at Mexico City, included all Spanish possessions north of the Isthmus of Panama; that of Peru, with its capital at Lima, embraced all of Spanish South America except for the coast of Venezuela. Captains general, theoretically subordinate to the viceroys but in practice virtually independent of them, governed large subdivisions of these vast

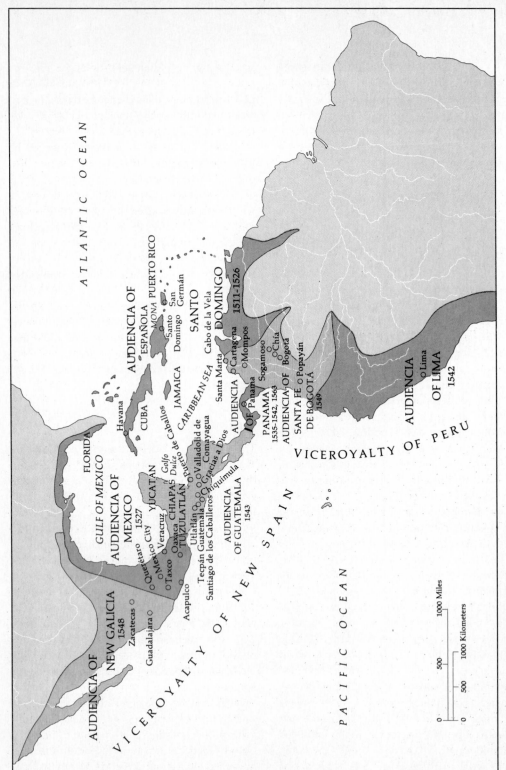

ATLANTIC OCEAN

AUDIENCIA OF
ESPAÑOLA

MONA PUERTO RICO

Santo   San
Domingo Germán

SANTO
DOMINGO
1511-1526

Havana

CUBA

JAMAICA

CARIBBEAN SEA

Cabo de la Vela

Santa Marta

Cartagena   Mompos

Sogamoso
Chia
Bogotá

AUDIENCIA OF
PANAMA   Popayán
1535-1542, 1563

SANTA FE   AUDIENCIA
DE BOGOTA
1549

AUDIENCIA
OF LIMA
1542

Lima

VICEROYALTY OF PERU

FLORIDA

GULF OF MEXICO

AUDIENCIA OF
MEXICO
1527

Querétaro
Mexico City
Taxco
Veracruz
Oaxaca CHIAPAS
TUZULATLÁN
YUCATAN

Golfo
Dulce de Caballos
Puerto de
Valladolid de
Comayagua
Utlatlán   Gracias a Dios
Tecpán Guatemala
Santiago de los Caballeros Chiquimula

AUDIENCIA
OF GUATEMALA
1543

AUDIENCIA
OF
PANAMA
Panama

Acapulco

AUDIENCIA OF
NEW GALICIA
1548

Zacatecas
Guadalajara

VICEROYALTY OF NEW SPAIN

PACIFIC OCEAN

1000 Miles

1000 Kilometers

500

500

0

VICEROYALTIES AND AUDIENCIAS IN THE
SIXTEENTH CENTURY

territories. Other subdivisions, called *presidencias*, were governed by audiencias. Their judge-presidents acted as governors, but military authority was usually reserved to the viceroy. Overlapping and shifting of jurisdiction was common throughout the colonial period and formed the subject of frequent disputes among royal officials.

A colonial viceroy, regarded as the very image of his royal master, enjoyed an immense delegated authority, which was augmented by the distance that separated him from Spain and by the frequently spineless or venal nature of lesser officials. He might be a lawyer or even a priest by background but was most commonly a representative of one of the great noble and wealthy houses of Spain. A court modeled on that of Castile, a numerous retinue, and the constant display of pomp and circumstance bore witness to his exalted status. In theory, his freedom of action was limited by the laws and instructions issued by the Council of the Indies, but a sensible recognition of the need to adapt the laws to existing circumstances gave him a vast discretionary power. The viceroy employed the formula *obedezco pero no cumplo*—"I obey but do not carry out"—to set aside unrealistic or unenforceable legislation.

The sixteenth century saw some able and even distinguished viceroys in the New World. The Viceroy Francisco de Toledo (1569–1581), the "supreme organizer of Peru," was certainly an energetic, hard-working administrator who consolidated Spanish rule and imposed royal authority in Peru. His Indian resettlement program and his institution of *mita*, the system of forced Indian labor in the mines, however, profoundly disrupted Indian social organization and took a heavy toll of Indian lives. In New Spain, such capable officials as Antonio de Mendoza (1530–1550) and his successor, Luis de Velasco (1550–1564) wrestled with the problems left by the Conquest. They strove to curb the power of the conquistadors and to promote economic advance; sometimes they also tried, to a limited degree, to protect the interests of the Indians. But the predatory spirit of the colonists, royal distrust of excessive initiative on the part of high colonial officials, and opposition from other sectors of the official bureaucracy largely thwarted their efforts. In the seventeenth century, in an atmosphere of growing financial crisis, corruption, and cynicism at the Spanish court, the quality of the viceroys inevitably declined. In 1695, by way of illustration, the viceroyships of Peru and Mexico were, in effect, sold to the highest bidders.

Each viceroy or captain general was assisted in the performance of his duties by an audiencia, which was the highest court of appeal in its district and also served as the viceroy's council of state. The joint decisions of viceroy and audiencia, taken in administrative sessions, had the force of law, giving the audiencia a legislative character roughly comparable to that of the Council of the Indies in relation to the king. Although the viceroy had supreme executive and administrative power and was not legally obliged to heed the advice of the audiencia, its immense prestige and its right to correspond directly with the Council of the Indies made it a potential and actual check on the viceregal authority. The Crown, ever distrustful of its colonial officers, thus developed a system of checks and balances that assured ample deliberation and consultation on all important questions but that also encouraged indecision and delay.

In addition to hearing appellate cases and holding consultative meetings with their viceroy or captain general, *oidores* (judges) were required to make regular tours of inspection of their respective provinces with the object of making a searching inquiry into economic and social conditions, treatment of the Indians, and other matters of interest to the Crown. Although viceroys and oidores were well paid by colonial standards, the style of life their positions demanded was expensive, and the viceroy or oidor who did not take advantage of his office to enrich himself could expect to return to Spain poor.

Provincial Administration

Provincial administration in the Indies was entrusted to royal officials who governed districts of varying size and importance from their chief towns and who usually held the title of corregidor or alcalde mayor. Some were appointed by the viceroy (from whom they often bought their jobs), others by the Crown. They possessed supreme judicial and political authority in their districts and represented the royal interest in the *cabildos* (town councils). Certain civil and criminal cases could be appealed from the municipal magistrates to the corregidor, and from him to the audiencia. If not trained as a lawyer, the corregidor was assisted by an *asesor* (legal counsel) in the trial of judicial cases.

Corregidores were of two kinds. Some presided over Spanish towns; others, *corregidores de indios*, administered Indian pueblos, or towns, which paid tribute to the Crown. One of the principal duties of the corregidor de indios, who was usually appointed for three years, was to protect the natives from fraudulent or extortionate practices on the part of the whites, but there is ample testimony that the corregidor was himself the worst offender in this respect. Indian *caciques* (chiefs) often were his accomplices in these extortions. Perhaps the worst abuses of his authority arose in connection with the practice of *repartimiento* or *repartimiento de mercancías*, the mandatory purchase of goods from the corregidor by the Indians of his district. Ostensibly designed to protect the Indians from the frauds or wiles of private Spanish traders, the corregidor's exclusive right to trade with the Indians became an instrument for his own speedy enrichment at the expense of the natives.

The Crown employed an arsenal of regulations to insure good and honest performance on the part of public officials. Viceroys and oidores were forbidden to engage in trade or hold land within their jurisdictions or to accept gifts or fees; even their social life was hedged about with many restrictions. All royal officials, from the viceroy down, faced a *residencia* (judicial review) of their conduct at the end of their term of office. This took the form of a public hearing at which all who chose could appear before the judge of residence to present charges or testify for or against the official in question. At the end of the process, the judge found the official guilty or innocent of part or all of the charges and handed down a sentence that could be appealed to the Council of the Indies. Another device, the *visita*, was an investigation of official conduct, usually made unannounced by a *visitador* specially appointed for this purpose by the Crown or, in the case of lesser officials, by the viceroy in consultation with the audiencia. As a rule, the visita was no more effective than the residencia in preventing or punishing official misdeeds.

The only political institution in the Indies that satisfied to some degree local aspirations for self-rule was the town council, known as the cabildo or *ayuntamiento*. Any suggestion, however, that the cabildo had some kind of democratic character has no basis in fact. At an early date, the Crown assumed the right to appoint the regidores and alcaldes. Under Philip II and his successors, it became the established practice for the king to sell these posts to the highest bidder, with a right of resale or bequest, on condition that a certain portion of the value be paid to the Crown as a tax at each transfer. In some towns, however, cabildo members elected their successors.

Throughout the colonial period, the municipal governments were closed, self-perpetuating oligarchies of rich landowners, mine owners, and merchants. These men frequently received no salaries for their duties and used their positions to distribute municipal lands to themselves, to assign themselves Indian labor, and in general to serve the narrow interests of their class. Their official tasks included supervision of local markets, distribution of town lands, and local taxation. They also elected the alcaldes, who administered justice as courts of first instance. Vigilantly supervised by the provincial governor, or corregidor, who frequently intervened in its affairs, the cabildo soon lost such autonomy as it may have possessed in the early days. Yet, despite its undemocratic character, inefficiency, and waning prestige and autonomy, the cabildo was not without potential significance. As the only political institution in which the Creoles (American-born Spaniards) were largely represented, it was destined to play an important part in the coming of the nineteenth-century wars of independence.

The officials and agencies just described represented only a small part of the apparatus of colonial government. A large number of secretaries (*escribanos*) attended to the paperwork of the various departments. As a rule, they collected no salaries but were reimbursed by fees for their services. There was a multitude of police officers, collectors of the royal fifth, alcaldes with special jurisdiction, and the like. Under Charles V, control of such offices often lay in the hands of high Spanish officials, who sold them to persons who proposed to go to the Indies to exploit their fee-earning possibilities. Beginning with Philip II, many of these offices were withdrawn from private patronage and sold directly by the Crown, usually to the highest bidder. In the second half of the seventeenth century, the sale of offices by the Crown or the viceroy spread from fee-earning positions to higher, salaried posts. As a rule, the beneficiaries of such transactions sought to return to Spain rich, having made the highest possible profit on their investment. Consequently, corruption in this period became structural in the government of the Indies. Colonial officials, high and low, abused their trusts in innumerable and ingenious ways.

If the royal authority, represented by viceroys, oidores, corregidores, and other officials, was more or less supreme in the capitals and the surrounding countryside, the same was not true of more distant and isolated regions. In such areas, the royal authority was very remote, and the power of the great landowners was virtually absolute. On their large, self-sufficient estates, they dispensed justice in the manner of feudal lords, holding court and imprisoning peons in their own jails; they raised and maintained their own private armies; and they generally acted as monarchs of all they surveyed. Sometimes these powerful individuals combined their de facto military and judicial power with an official title, which made them representatives of the Crown in their vicinities. Spain's growing economic and political weakness in the late seventeenth century, which loosened the ties between the mother country and her colonies, favored this decentralization of power. The contrast between the nominal concentration of power in the central government and the effective supremacy of great landowners on the local level was one of the legacies of the colonial period to independent Latin America; to this day it remains a characteristic of the political life of many Latin American republics.

Ineffectiveness of Much Spanish Colonial Law

The frequent nonobservance of Spanish colonial law was a fact of colonial political life. In considerable part, this situation reflected the dilemma of royal officials faced with the task of enforcing laws bitterly opposed by powerful colonial elites with whom they generally had close social and economic ties. This dilemma found its most acute expression in the clash between the Crown's protective Indian legislation, which reflected its awareness that the conservation of the Indians—the real wealth of the Indies—was clearly in the royal interest, and the drive of colonial elites for maximum profits. The result was that the protective Indian laws were systematically flouted. The Crown often closed its eyes to the violations, not only because it wished to avoid confrontation with powerful colonial elites but because those laws sometimes collided with the Crown's own narrow, short-range interests (its need for revenue to finance wars and diplomacy and to support a parasitic nobility).

Hence the contradiction between that admirable legislation, so often cited by defenders of Spain's work in America, and the reality of Indian life and labor in the colonies. In a report to Philip II, Alonso de Zorita, a judge who retired to an honorable poverty in 1566 after nineteen years of administrative activity in the Indies, wrote:

The wishes of Your Majesty and his Royal Council are well known and are made very plain in the laws that are issued every day in favor of the poor Indians and for their increase and preservation. But these laws are obeyed and not enforced, wherefore there is no end to the destruction of the Indians, nor does anyone care what Your Majesty decrees.[1]

Not all colonial legislation, however, was so laxly enforced. There was a considerable body of exploitative or discriminatory Indian laws that was in general vigorously enforced, including laws requiring the Indians to pay tribute and perform forced labor for token wages, permitting the forced sale of goods to them at fixed prices, and limiting Indian landownership to a low maximum figure while allowing the indefinite growth of Spanish estates.

THE CHURCH IN THE INDIES

The Spanish church emerged from the long centuries of struggle against the Moslems with immense wealth and an authority second only to that of the Crown. The Catholic Sovereigns,

Ferdinand and Isabella, particularly favored the clergy and the spread of its influence as a means of achieving their ends of national unity and royal absolutism. The Spanish Inquisition, which they founded, had political as well as religious uses, and under their great-grandson, Philip II, it became the strongest support of an omnipotent crown. While the Spanish towns sank first into political and then into economic decadence, and the great nobles were reduced to the position of a courtier class aspiring for favors from the Crown, the church steadily gained in wealth and influence. Under the last Hapsburgs, it threatened the supremacy of its royal master. It remained for the enlightened Bourbon kings of the eighteenth century to curb in some measure the excessive power of the church.

Royal control over ecclesiastical affairs, both in Spain and the Indies, was solidly founded on the institution of the *patronato real* (royal patronage). As applied to the colonies, this consisted of the absolute right of the Spanish kings to nominate all church officials, collect tithes, and found churches and monasteries in America. Under diplomatic pressure from King Ferdinand, Pope Julius II had accorded this extraordinary privilege to Spain's rulers in 1508, ostensibly to assist them in their pious work of converting New World heathen. The Spanish monarchs regarded the patronato as their most cherished privilege and reacted sharply to all encroachments on it.

The Spiritual Conquest of America

Beginning with Columbus's second voyage, one or more clergymen accompanied every expedition that sailed for the Indies, and they came in swelling numbers to the conquered territories. The friars formed the spearhead of the second religious invasion that followed on the heels of the Conquest. The friars who came to America in the first decades after the Conquest were, on the whole, an elite group. They were products of one of the periodic revivals of asceticism and

[1] *Life and Labor in Ancient Mexico: The Brief and Summary Relation of the Lords of New Spain by Alonso de Zorita,* tr. and ed. by Benjamin Keen (New Brunswick, N.J.: Rutgers University Press, 1963), p. 216.

Introducing Indians to Christianity. (The British Museum, London)

discipline in the medieval church, especially of the reform of the orders instituted in Spain by the Catholic Sovereigns and carried out with implacable energy by Cardinal Cisneros. This vanguard group of clergy frequently combined with missionary zeal a sensitive social conscience and a love of learning. The missionaries were frequently impressed by the admirable qualities of the Indians, by their simplicity and freedom from the greed and ambitions of Europe, by the plasticity of the Indian character. Wrote Vasco de Quiroga, royal judge and later bishop of the province of Michoacán in Mexico:

Anything may be done with these people, they are most docile, and, proceeding with due diligence, may easily be taught Christian doctrine. They possess innately the instincts of humility and obedience, and the Christian impulses of poverty, nakedness, and contempt for the things of this world, going barefoot and bareheaded with the hair long like apostles; in fine, with very tractable minds void of error and ready for impression.[2]

The friars converted prodigious numbers of natives, who as a rule willingly accepted the new and more powerful divinities of the invaders. In Mexico, the Franciscans claimed to have converted more than a million Indians by 1531; one of the most famous and vigorous of the Franciscan apostles, usually known by his Indian name of Motolinia, asserted that he had converted more than fifteen hundred in one day! Where persuasion failed, pressures of various kinds, including force, were used to obtain conversions. In order to facilitate the missionary effort, the friars studied the native languages and wrote grammars and vocabularies that are still of value to scholars.

[2] Quoted in Sir Arthur Helps, *The Spanish Conquest in America*, 4 vols. (London, 1902), 3:146.

The religious, especially the Franciscans, also assigned a special importance to the establishment of schools in which Indian upper-class youth might receive instruction in the humanities, including Latin, logic, and philosophy, as well as Christian doctrine. The most notable of these centers was the Franciscan Colegio de Santa Cruz in Mexico. Before it entered on a decline in the 1560s as a result of lay hostility or disinterest and the waning fervor of the friars themselves, the school had produced a harvest of graduates who often combined enthusiasm for European culture with admiration for their own pagan past. These men were invaluable to the missionaries in their effort to reconstruct the history, religion, and social institutions of the ancient Indian civilizations.

Although some of the early friars undertook to destroy all relics of the pagan past—idols, temples, picture writings—the second generation of missionaries became convinced that paganism could not be successfully combated without a thorough study and understanding of the old pre-Conquest Indian way of life. In Mexico there arose a genuine school of ethnography devoted to making an inventory of the rich content of Indian culture. If the primary and avowed motive of this effort was to arm the missionary with the knowledge he needed to discover the concealed presence of pagan rites and practices, intellectual curiosity and delight in the discovery of the material, artistic, and social achievements of the vanished Indian empires also played a part.

The work of conversion, by the subsequent admission of the missionaries themselves, was less than wholly successful. The result of the missionary effort was generally a fusion in Indian minds of old and new religious ideas, in which the cult of the Virgin Mary sometimes merged with the worship of pagan divinities. Writing half a century after the conquest of Mexico, the Dominican Diego Durán saw a persistence of paganism in every aspect of Indian life, "in their dances, in their markets, in their baths, in the songs which mourn the loss of their ancient gods." In the same period, the great scholar-missionary Sahagún complained that the Indians continued to celebrate their ancient festivals, in which they sang songs and danced dances with concealed pagan meanings. To this day, Indians in such lands as Guatemala and Peru continue to perform rites and ceremonies dating from the time of the Maya and the Incas.

The friars had to battle not only the Indian tendency toward backsliding but divisions within their own camp. Violent disputes arose among the orders over the degree of prebaptismal instruction required by Indian converts, with the Dominicans and Augustinians demanding stiffer standards than the Franciscans. Other disputes arose as to which order should have jurisdiction over a particular area or pueblo. A more serious conflict arose between the secular and the regular clergy. The pastoral and sacramental duties performed by the regular clergy in America were normally entrusted only to parish priests. Special papal legislation (1522) had been required to grant these functions to the regulars, a concession made necessary by the small number of seculars who came to the Indies in the early years. But after mid-century their number increased, and the bishops increasingly sought to create new parishes manned by seculars. These seculars were intended to replace the regulars in the spiritual direction of Indian converts. The friars resisted by every means at their disposal, but they fought a losing battle. The secular clergy had various advantages in their favor. One was a ruling of the Council of Trent that only clergy under episcopal authority could have parochial jurisdiction. Another was the preference accorded to the episcopal hierarchy by Philip II, who disliked the excessive independence of spirit shown by members of the orders in disputes over Indian policy and other matters.

In 1574 the seculars gained a decisive victory through the issuance of a royal edict giving each bishop virtual control over the number of friars in his diocese and their assignment to parishes. A subsequent decree (1583) stated the principle that secular clergy were to be preferred over friars in all appointments to parishes. But these rulings did not settle this and related questions; from first to last the colonies were a scene of unedifying strife among the clergy over their fields of jurisdiction.

The Moral Decline of the Clergy and the Missionary Impulse

To the factors contributing to the decline of the intellectual and spiritual influence of the orders one must add the gradual loss of a sense of mission and of morale among the regular clergy. Apostolic fervor inevitably declined as the work of conversion in the central areas of the empire approached completion; many of the later arrivals among the clergy preferred a life of ease and profit to one of austerity and service. By the last decades of the sixteenth century, there were frequent complaints against the excessive number of monasteries and their wealth. The principal sources of this wealth were legacies and other gifts from rich donors—for a rich man not to provide for the church in his will was a matter of scandal. The resources thus acquired became inalienable in the form of mortmain, or perpetual ownership. Invested in land and mortgages, this wealth brought in more wealth. The enormous economic power of the church gave it a marked advantage over competitors and enabled it to take advantage of weaker lay property owners, especially in time of recession. The last important order to arrive in Spanish America, the Society of Jesus (1572), was also the most fortunate in the number of rich benefactors and the most efficient in running its numerous enterprises, which, it should be said in its favor, were largely used to support its excellent system of *colegios* (secondary schools) and its missions.

Inevitably, this concern with the accumulation of material wealth weakened the ties between the clergy and the humble Indian and mixed-blood masses whose spiritual life they were supposed to direct. As early as the 1570s, there were many complaints of excessive ecclesiastical fees and clerical exploitation of Indian labor. A viceroy of New Spain, the marqués de Monteclaros, assured King Philip III in 1607 that the Indians suffered the heaviest oppression at the hands of the friars and that one Indian paid more tribute to his parish priest than twenty paid to His Majesty. Hand in hand with a growing materialism went an increasing laxity of morals. Concubinage became so common among the clergy of the later colonial period that it seems to have attracted little official notice or rebuke. By the last decades of the colonial period, the morals of the clergy had declined to a condition that the Mexican historian Lucas Alamán, himself a leader of the clerical party in the period of independence, could only describe as scandalous. From this charge one must in general exclude the Jesuits, noted for their high moral standards and strict discipline; and of course men of excellent character and social conscience were to be found among both the secular and regular clergy.

The missionary impulse of the first friars survived longest on the frontier, "the rim of Christendom." Franciscans first penetrated the great northern interior of New Spain, peopled by hostile Chichimeca, "wild Indians." Franciscans accompanied the Oñate expedition of 1598 into New Mexico and dominated the mission field there until the end of the colonial period; they were also found in such distant outposts of Spanish power as Florida and Georgia. After the expulsion of the Jesuits from the Indies in 1767, the Franciscans took their place directing missionary work among the Indians of California. In addition to their pioneering efforts in California, the early Jesuits were active in the conversion and pacification of the Chichimeca of the north central plateau of Mexico and had exclusive charge of the conversion of the Indian tribes of the northwest coast of Mexico.

The mission was one of three closely linked institutions—the other two being the *presidio* (garrison) and the civil settlement—designed to serve the ends of Spanish imperial expansion and defense on the northern frontier. The mission, it was hoped, would gather the Indian converts into self-contained religious communities, train them to till the land, herd cattle, and practice various crafts, until they became fully Christianized and Hispanicized. The presidios would provide military protection for the neighboring missions and insure a cooperative attitude on the part of the Indian novices. Finally, attracted by the lure of free land, Spaniards of modest means would throng into the area, forming civil settlements that would become bustling centers of life and trade. By all these means, the frontier would be pushed back, pacified, and maintained against foreign encroachment.

This three-pronged attack on the wilderness was not very successful. Romantic literature has created a myth of an idyllic mission society in the American Southwest that does not correspond to reality. Certain tribes on the northern frontier, such as the powerful Apaches of Arizona, New Mexico, and Texas and the Comanches of Texas, never were reduced to mission life. The missionaries had greater success among such sedentary tribes as the Pueblo Indians of New Mexico, the Pima and Opata of Sonora in northwest Mexico, and the Hasinai of east Texas. Even among these peaceful tribes, however, Indian revolts and desertions were frequent. In 1680 the supposedly Christianized Pueblo Indians of New Mexico revolted, slaughtered the friars, and maintained a long, tenacious resistance against Spanish efforts at reconquest. The rise of native leaders who proclaimed that the old gods and way of life were best often sparked wholesale desertions. Mistreatment by soldiers in nearby presidios and the terror inspired by Apache and Comanche raiding parties also provoked frequent flight by mission Indians.

The authoritarian paternalism of the fathers enforced by the use of stocks, prisons, and whipping posts, produced cultural change in the desired directions, but at the cost of reduced vitality on the part of the Indians affected. One indication of the maiming effect of mission life was the reduced birthrate among the neophytes. Spanish census records show that the mission Indian birthrate in 1783 in Texas was far below that among the Spanish inhabitants of the province. This and desertions made necessary constant recruitment of converts, but the presence of hovering Apache and Comanche bands, mounted on swift horses introduced by the Spaniards, made this hazardous. An indication of the failure of the mission enterprise was the unwillingness of the Spanish government in the late eighteenth century to finance the search for converts.

The civil settlements proved no more successful. By the end of the colonial period, there were only a few scattered towns on the northern frontier, and the continuous raids made life and property so insecure that in New Mexico settlers who petitioned for permission to leave outnumbered recruits coming to the area. Ultimately, the whole task of defending and civilizing the future American Southwest fell on a chain of presidios stretching approximately along the present border between the United States and Mexico. Successive reverses in the open field compelled the Spanish troops to take refuge behind the security of the high presidio walls. In the end, Spain was forced to adopt a policy of neutralizing the Apaches and Comanches by periodic distribution of gifts to these warlike tribes. When the outbreak of the wars of independence stopped the flow of gifts, the hostile Indians again took to the warpath, driving by the useless line of presidios into the interior of Mexico.

The most notable instance of successful missionary effort, at least from an economic point of view, was that of the Jesuit establishments in Paraguay. In this region, favored by a genial climate and fertile soil, the Jesuits established more than thirty missions; these formed the principal field of Jesuit activity in America until the expulsion of the Jesuits in 1767. Their strict discipline, centralized organization, and absolute control over the labor of thousands of docile Indians producing large surpluses enabled the Jesuits to turn their missions into a highly profitable business enterprise. Great quantities of such goods as cotton, tobacco, and hides were shipped down the Paraná River to Buenos Aires for export to Europe. Rather than "Christian socialism," the Jesuit mission system could more correctly be described as "theocratic capitalism."

To protect the missions against slave raiders from the Portuguese colony of São Paulo, the fathers created a native militia armed with European weapons. Every effort was made to limit contact with the outside world. The life of the Indians was rigidly regimented in dress, housing, and the routines of work, play, and rest. The self-imposed isolation of the Jesuit mission empire aroused the curiosity of eighteenth-century European philosophers and literati; Voltaire gave an ironic and fanciful description of it in his witty satire on the follies and vices of the age, *Candide.*

Jesuit rule in Paraguay and Jesuit mission activity everywhere in the colonies ended when a royal decree expelled the order from the colonies in 1767. Among the motives for this action were the conflict between the nationalistic church policy of the Bourbons and Jesuit emphasis on papal supremacy, suspicions of Jesuit meddling in state affairs generally, and the belief that the Jesuit mission system constituted a state within a state. The expulsion of the Jesuits from Paraguay resulted in intensified exploitation of the Indians by Spanish officials and landowners and in a shedding by the Indians of much of the thin veneer of European culture imposed on them by the missionaries. Within a generation the previously thriving Jesuit villages were in ruins.

The Inquisition in the New World

The Inquisition formally entered the Indies with the establishment by Philip II of tribunals of the Holy Office in Mexico and Lima in 1569. Prior to that time, its functions were performed by clergy who were vested with or assumed inquisitorial powers. Its great privileges, its independence of other courts, and the dread with which the charge of heresy was generally regarded by Spaniards made the Inquisition an effective check on "dangerous thoughts," whether religious, political, or philosophical. The great mass of cases tried by its tribunals, however, had to do with offenses against morality or minor deviations from orthodox religious conduct, such as blasphemy.

As in Spain, the Inquisition in the Indies relied largely on denunciations by informers and employed torture to secure confessions. As in Spain, the damage done by the Inquisition was not limited to the snuffing out of lives and the confiscation of property but included the creation of an atmosphere of fear, distrust, and rigid intellectual conformity. Indians, originally subject to the jurisdiction of inquisitors, were later removed from their control as recent converts of limited mental capacity and hence not fully responsible for their deviations from the Faith.

THE STRUCTURE OF CLASS AND CASTE

The social order that arose in the Indies on the ruins of the old Indian societies was based, like that of Spain, on feudal principles. Race, occupation, and religion were the formal criteria that determined an individual's social status. All mechanical labor was regarded as degrading, but large-scale trade (as opposed to retail trade) was compatible with nobility, at least in the Indies. Great emphasis was placed on *limpieza de sangre* (purity of blood), meaning above all descent from "Old Christians," without mixture of converso or Morisco (Moslem) blood. Proofs of such descent were jealously guarded, and sometimes manufactured.

The various races and racial mixtures were

carefully distinguished and graded in a kind of hierarchy of rank. A trace of Negro blood legally sufficed to deprive an individual of the right to hold public office or enter the professions, as well as depriving him of the other rights and privileges of white men. The same taint attached to the great mass of mestizos (mixtures of Indians and Spaniards). True, the Laws of the Indies assigned perfect legal equality with whites to mestizos of legitimate birth, but to the very end of the colonial period the charters of certain colonial guilds and schools excluded all mestizos, without distinction.

The White Ruling Class

In practice, racial lines were not very strictly drawn. In the Indies, a white skin was a symbol of social superiority, roughly the equivalent of *hidalguía,* a title of nobility in Spain, but it had no cash value. Not all whites belonged to the privileged economic group. Colonial records testify to the existence of a large class of "poor whites"—vagabonds, beggars, or worse—who disdained work and frequently preyed on the Indians. A Spaniard of this group, compelled by poverty to choose his mate from the colored races, generally doomed his descendants to an inferior economic and social status. The mestizo or even mulatto son of a wealthy Spanish landowner or merchant, on the other hand, if acknowledged and made his legal heir, could pass into the colonial aristocracy. If traces of Indian or Negro descent were too strong, the father might reach an understanding with the parish priest, who had charge of baptismal certificates; it was also possible for a wealthy mestizo or mulatto to purchase from the Crown a document establishing his legal whiteness. Wealth, not gentle birth or racial purity, was the distinguishing characteristic of the colonial aristocracy. Granted this fact, it remains true that the apex of the colonial pyramid was composed overwhelmingly of whites.

This white ruling class was itself divided by group jealousies and hostilities. The Spaniards brought to the New World their regional rivalries and feuds—between Old Castilians and Andalusians, between Castilians and Basques—and in the anarchic, heated atmosphere of the Indies these rivalries often exploded into brawls or even pitched battles. But the most abiding cleavage within the upper class was the division between the Spaniards born in the colonies, called Creoles, and the European-born Spaniards, called Peninsulars or referred to by such disparaging nicknames as *gachupín* or *chapetón* (tenderfoot). Legally, Creoles and Peninsulars were equal; indeed Spanish law called for preference to be given in the filling of offices to the descendants of conquistadors and early settlers. In practice, the Creoles suffered from a system of discrimination that during most of the colonial period virtually denied them employment in high church and government posts and large-scale commerce. The preference shown for Peninsulars over natives sprang from various causes, among them the greater access of Spaniards to the court, the fountainhead of all favors, and royal distrust of the Creoles. By the second half of the sixteenth century, the sons or grandsons of conquistadors were complaining of the partiality of the Crown and its officials for unworthy newcomers from Spain. The Creoles viewed with envenomed spite these Johnny-come-latelies, who often won out in the scramble for *corregimientos* and other government jobs. A Mexican poet, Francisco de Terrazas, expressed the Creole complaint in rhyme:

Spain: to us a harsh stepmother you have been,
A mild and loving mother to the stranger,
On him you lavish all your treasures dear,
With us you only share your cares and danger.[3]

[3] Francisco de Terrazas, *Poesías,* ed. Antonio Castro Leal (Mexico, 1941), p. 87. From *The Aztec Image in Western Thought* by Benjamin Keen, p. 90. Copyright © 1971 by Rutgers University, the State University of New Jersey. Reprinted by permission of Rutgers University Press.

The resulting cleavage in the colonial upper class grew wider with the passage of time. Both groups developed an arsenal of arguments to defend their positions. Peninsulars often justified their privileged status by reference to the alleged indolence, incapacity, and frivolity of the Creoles, which they sometimes solemnly attributed to the American climate or other environmental conditions. The Creoles responded in kind by describing the Europeans as mean and grasping parvenus (new rich). The growing wealth of the Creoles from mines, plantations, and cattle ranches only sharpened their resentment at the discrimination from which they suffered. The split within the colonial upper class must be regarded as a major cause of the Creole wars of independence.

The Mestizo: An Ambiguous Status

The mestizo arose from a process of racial mixture that began in the first days of the Conquest. In the post-Conquest period, when white women were scarce, the Crown and the church viewed Indian-white marriages with some favor; mixed marriages were not uncommon in those years. But this attitude soon changed as the Crown, for its own reasons, adopted a policy of systematic segregation of the Indians from the white community. By the first quarter of the seventeenth century, the authoritative writer on Spain's colonial legislation, Juan Solórzano Pereira, could write: "Few Spaniards of honorable position will marry Indian or Negro women." Consequently, the great mass of mestizos had their origin in irregular unions between Spaniards and Indian women. The stigma of illegitimacy, unredeemed by wealth, doomed the majority to the social depths. Some became peons, resembling the Indian in their way of life; others swelled the numerous class of vagabonds; still others enrolled in the colonial militia. Mestizos also formed part of the lower middle class of artisans, overseers, and shopkeepers. Without roots in either Indian or

Spanish society, scorned and distrusted by both, small wonder that the lower-class mestizo acquired a reputation for violence and instability.

The Indians: A Separate Nation

By contrast with the mestizo, no ambiguity marked the position of the Indian in Spanish law and practice. The Indians constituted a separate nation, the república de indios, which also constituted a hereditary tribute-paying caste. The descendants of the Indian rulers and hereditary nobility, however, received special consideration, partly from Spanish respect for the concept of señor natural (the natural or legitimate lord), partly because they played a useful role as intermediaries between the Spanish rulers and Indian tribute payers. The Indian nobles were allowed to retain all or part of their patrimonial estates and enjoyed such special privileges as the right to ride horses, wear European dress, and carry arms.

There is ample evidence that members of the Indian aristocracy were among the worst exploiters of their own race. Their role as collectors of Indian tribute for the Spaniards offered large opportunities for enrichment at the expense of the commoners. They also usurped communal lands, imposed excessive rents on their Indian tenants, and forced the commoners to labor for them. In part, as Charles Gibson points out, these inordinate demands represented a "response to strain, an effort to maintain position and security" in the face of Spanish encroachments on the lands and prerequisites of the native nobility.

By the end of the sixteenth century, the Indian aristocracy was in full decline. One cause of this decline was Spanish invasion of their lands, to which the Indian nobles often responded with costly but futile litigation. Another cause of their downfall was their responsibility for the collection of tribute from the commoners. When the number of tribute payers in a town declined because of an epidemic or other circumstances, the Indian governor had to make up the arrears on the town's fixed quota or go to jail. In order to make good the deficit, he might have to sell or mortgage his lands. However, at the end of the colonial period, especially in the Andean area, there remained a minority of Indian nobles who had grown wealthy through trade, stock raising, or agriculture, and who enjoyed high social position. Perhaps typical of this small class of wealthy Indian or mestizo nobles was the famous late eighteenth-century Peruvian cacique José Gabriel Condorcanqui (Tupac Amaru). Lillian Fisher writes that he lived like a Spanish nobleman, wearing "a long coat and knee-breeches of black velvet, a waistcoat of gold tissue worth seventy or eighty *duros* (dollars), embroidered linen, silk stockings, gold buckles at his knees and on his shoes, and a Spanish beaver hat valued at twenty-five duros. He kept his hair curled in ringlets that extended nearly down to his waist."[4] His source of wealth included the ownership of 350 mules, which he used to transport mercury and other goods to Potosí and other places, and a large cacao estate.

By contrast with the privileged treatment accorded to the Indian hereditary nobility, Indian commoners suffered under crushing burdens of tribute, labor, and ecclesiastical fees. Viewed as a constitutionally inferior race and hence as perpetual wards of the Spanish state, they repaid the Spanish tutelage with the obligation to pay tribute and give forced labor. *Gente sin razón* ("people of weak minds") was a phrase commonly applied to the Indians in colonial documents. Their juridical inferiority and status as wards found expression in laws (universally disregarded) forbidding them to make binding contracts or to contract debts in excess of five pesos and in efforts to minimize contact between Indians and other racial groups. These and many other restrictions on Indian activity had an os-

tensible protective character. But an enlightened Mexican prelate, Bishop Manuel Abad y Queipo, pointed out that these so-called privileges

do them little good and in most respects injure them greatly. Shut up in a narrow space of six hundred rods, assigned by law to the Indian towns, they possess no individual property and are obliged to work the communal lands. . . . Forbidden by law to commingle with the other castes, they are deprived of the instruction and assistance that they should receive from contact with these and other people. They are isolated by their language, and by a useless, tyrannical form of government.

He concluded that the ostensible privileges of the Indians were "an offensive weapon employed by the white class against the Indians, and never serve to defend the latter."[5]

Most of the Indians lived in their own towns, some of pre-Hispanic origin, others created by a process of resettlement of dispersed Indian populations in new towns called "reductions" or "congregations." To serve the ends of Spanish control and tribute collection, the Indian towns were reorganized on the peninsular model, with municipal governments patterned on those of Spanish towns. The Indian cabildo had its regidores, its alcaldes who tried minor cases, and its *gobernador*, who was responsible for the collection and delivery of tribute to the corregidor or the encomendero. These offices as a rule became hereditary in certain aristocratic families.

The Indian town typically was composed of one or more kinship groups (calpulli in Mexico, ayllu in the Andean region), each with its hereditary elders who represented the group in interclan disputes, acted as intermediaries in arranging marriages, supervised the allotment of land to clan members, and otherwise served their communities. A certain degree of Hispanicization of Indian commoners took place,

---

[4] Lillian E. Fisher, *The Last Inca Revolt, 1780–1783* (Norman: University of Oklahoma Press, 1966), p. 23.

[5] Cited in José María Luis Mora, *Obras sueltas*, 2 vols. (Paris, 1837), 1:55–57.

reflected above all in religion but also in the adoption of various tools and articles of dress and food. But the barriers erected by Spain between the two communities and the fixed hostility with which they regarded each other prevented any thoroughgoing acculturation. In response to the aggressions and injustices inflicted on it by the white world, the Indian community drew into itself and fought stubbornly not only to preserve its land but its cultural identity, speech, social organization, and traditional dances and songs. After the clan, the most important Indian instrumentality for the maintenance of collective identity and security was the *cofradía* (religious brotherhood), whose members were responsible for the maintenance of certain cult activities.

The Conquest and its aftermath inflicted not only heavy material damage on Indian society but serious psychological injury as well. Spanish accounts frequently cite the lament of Indian elders over the loss of the severe discipline, strong family ties, and high moral standards of the pre-Conquest regimes. The Spanish judge Zorita quoted approvingly the remark of an Indian elder that with the coming of the Spaniards to Mexico "all was turned upside down . . . liars, perjurers, and adulterers are no longer punished as they once were because the principales (nobles) have lost the power to chastise delinquents. This, say the Indians, is the reason why there are so many lies, disorders, and sinful women."[6] A symptom as well as cause of Indian social disorganization was widespread alcoholism.

Blacks, Mulattos, Zambos: The Lowest Class

Blacks, mulattos, and *zambos* (mixtures of Indians and blacks) occupied the bottom rungs of the colonial social ladder. By the end of the sixteenth century some 75,000 African slaves had been introduced into the Spanish colonies under the

[6] *Life and Labor in Ancient Mexico*, p. 126.

system of *asiento*, which was discussed in Chapter 4. The infamous Middle Passage (the journey of slaves across the Atlantic) was a thing of horror; the Jesuit Alonso de Sandoval, who had charge of conversion of slaves, left this harrowing description of the arrival of a cargo of slaves in the port of Cartagena in New Granada:

They arrive looking like skeletons; they are led ashore, completely naked, and are shut up in a large court or enclosure . . . and it is a great pity to see so many sick and needy people, denied all care or assistance, for as a rule they are left to lie on the ground, naked and without shelter. . . . I recall that I once saw two of them, already dead, lying on the ground on their backs like animals, their mouths open and full of flies, their arms crossed as if making the sign of the cross . . . and I was astounded to see them dead as a result of such great inhumanity.

By the end of the eighteenth century some 9.5 million slaves had been brought to the Americas. Especially dense concentrations were found in Brazil and in the Caribbean area, which were dominated by plantation economies. Historians have hotly disputed the character of Latin American black slavery. What may be called the traditional view, expressed in books like Gilberto Freyre's *The Masters and the Slaves* (1946), Frank Tannenbaum's *Slave and Citizen: The Negro in the Americas* (1947), and Herbert Klein's *Slavery in the Americas: A Comparative Study of Virginia and Cuba* (1967), claimed that cultural factors tended to make slavery in Latin America milder than in the United States. Particularly influential was Tannenbaum's little book, which explained this greater leniency by such factors as medieval Iberian legislation, which recognized the unnaturalness of slavery; the church's insistence on the slave's right to marry and its protection of the slave family; and the elaborate body of Spanish law defining slave rights, including the slave's right to purchase his freedom and that of other members of his family. Marvin Harris subjected the

Tannenbaum thesis to sharp criticism in his *Patterns of Race in the Americas* (1964), which argued that the supposed mildness of Latin American black slavery was a myth, that the protective legislation was often ignored, and that economic rather than cultural factors determined the specific differences between slave societies.

Recent studies generally support the view that the tempo of economic activity was decisive in determining the intensity of slave exploitation and the harshness of plantation discipline. Certainly manumission of slaves was more frequent in the Hispanic than in the English, Dutch, or French colonies, but it is likely that the unprofitability of slavery under certain conditions contributed more than cultural traditions to this result. Whatever the reasons, by the close of the colonial period slaves formed a minority of the total black and mulatto population. Whatever their treatment, slaves retained the aspiration for freedom. Fear of slave revolts haunted the white ruling class, and slaves frequently fled from their masters. Some of them formed independent communities in remote jungles or mountains that successfully resisted Spanish punitive expeditions.

This stubborn attachment of the black slaves to freedom, reflected in frequent revolts, flights, and other forms of resistance, suggests that the debate over the relative mildness or severity of black slavery in Latin America evades the main issue—the dehumanizing character of even the "mildest" slavery. Brought from Africa by force and violence, cut off from their kindred and peoples, the uprooted slaves were subjected in their new environment to severe deculturation. For reasons of security, slaveowners preferred to purchase slaves of diverse tribal origins, language, and religious beliefs and deliberately promoted tribal disunity among them. The economic interest of the planters dictated that the great majority of the imported slaves should be young (between the ages of 15 and 20), and this contributed to the process of deculturation,

for very few aged blacks, the repositories of tribal lore and traditions in African societies, came in the slaveships. The scarcity of women (the proportion of females in the slave population on Cuban plantations between 1746 and 1822 ranged between 9 and 15 percent) distorted the sexual life of the slaves, creating a climate of intense sexual repression and instability. The church might insist on the right of the slave to proper Christian marriage and the sanctity of his marriage, but not until the nineteenth century was the separate sale of husbands, wives, and children forbidden in the Spanish colonies. The right of the master to sell or remove members of the slave's family and his free sexual access to slave women made difficult if not impossible a normal family life. The world of the slave plantation, resembling a prison rather than a society, left to independent Latin America a bitter heritage of racism, discrimination, and backwardness, problems that in most Latin American countries still await full solution.

Because of harsh treatment, poor living conditions, and the small number of women in the slave population, its rate of reproduction was very low. Miscegenation between white masters and slave women, on the other hand, produced a steady growth of the mulatto population. As noted above, by the end of the colonial period, for a variety of reasons, slaves formed a minority of the total black and mulatto population. Free blacks and mulattos made important contributions to the colonial economy, both in agriculture and as artisans of all kinds. Free blacks and mulattos, like Indians, were required to pay tribute.

Life in the City and on the Hacienda

Social life in the Spanish colonies had two centers: the colonial city and the hacienda, or large landed estate. Unlike its European counterpart, the colonial city as a rule did not arise spontaneously as a center of trade or industry but developed in planned fashion to serve the ends of Spanish settlement and administration of the

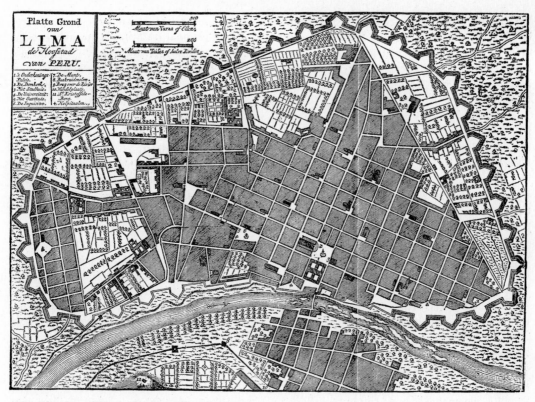

An early plan of Lima. (Historical Pictures Service, Inc.)

surrounding area. Sometimes it was founded on the ruins of an Indian capital, as in the case of Mexico City. More often it was founded on a site chosen for its strategic or other advantages, as in the case of Lima. By contrast with the usually anarchical layout of Spanish cities, the colonial town typically followed the gridiron plan, with a large central plaza flanked by the cathedral, the governor's *palacio*, and other public buildings. From this central square originated long, wide, and straight streets that intersected to produce uniform, rectangular blocks. This passion for regularity reflected both the influence of Renaissance neoclassical works on architecture and the regulatory zeal of the Crown. In sharp contrast to the carefully planned nucleus of the colonial city was the disorderly layout of the surrounding native *barrios*, slum districts inhabited by a large Indian and mestizo population that provided the Spanish city with cheap labor and combustible material for the riots that shook the cities in times of famine or other troubles.

Into the capitals flowed most of the wealth produced by the mines, plantations, and cattle ranches of the surrounding area. In these cities, in houses whose size and proximity to the center reflected the relative wealth and social position of their owners, lived the rich mine owners and landowners of the colonies. They displayed their wealth by the magnificence of their homes, furnishings, dress, and carriages, and by the multitude of their servants and slaves. By the end of the sixteenth century, Mexico City had already acquired fame for the beauty of its women, horses, and streets, the riches of its shops, and the reckless spending, gaming, and generosity of its aristocracy. The poet Bernardo de Balbuena, in a long poem devoted to "La Grandeza Mexicana" ("The Grandeur of Mexico City"), wrote of

That lavish giving of every ilk,
Without a care how great the cost
Of pearls, of gold, of silver, and of silk.[7]

By the close of the seventeenth century, Mexico City had a population estimated to number 200,000.

Lima, founded in 1534, proud capital of the viceroyalty of Peru, and Potosí, the great Peruvian mining center whose wealth became legendary, were two other major colonial cities. By 1650, when its wealth had already begun to decline, Potosí, with a population of 160,000 inhabitants, was the largest city in South America.

Before the eighteenth century, when changes in government and manners brought a greater stability, violence was prevalent in the colonial city. Duels, assassinations, even pitched battles between different Spanish factions were events frequently mentioned in official records and private diaries. From time to time, the misery of the masses in the native and mixed-blood wards exploded in terrifying upheavals. In 1624 the mobs of Mexico City, goaded by famine and a decree of excommunication issued by the archbishop against an unpopular viceroy, rose with cries of "Death to the evil government" and "Long live the church." They vented their wrath in widespread destruction and looting. In 1692 similar circumstances caused an even greater explosion, which ended in many deaths, the sacking of shops, and the virtual destruction of the viceroy's palace and other public buildings.

[7] Bernardo de Balbuena, *Grandeza Mexicana* (Mexico, 1954), p. 40.

The hacienda constituted the second great center of colonial social life. On the haciendas lived those Creole aristocrats who could not support the expense of a city establishment or whose estates were in remote provinces or frontier areas. By the end of the seventeenth century, the hacienda in many areas had become a largely self-sufficient economic unit, combining arable land, grazing land for herds of sheep and cattle, timberland for fuel and construction, and even workshops for the manufacture and repair of the implements used on the hacienda. The hacienda was often also a self-contained social unit, with a church or chapel usually served by a resident priest, a store from which workers could obtain goods charged against their wages, and even a jail to house disobedient peons. In the hacendado's large, luxuriously appointed house often lived not only his immediate family but numerous relatives who laid claim to his protection and support.

The hacienda often contained one or more villages of Indians who had once been owners of the land on which they now lived and worked as virtual serfs. These Indians lived in one-room adobe or thatch huts whose only furniture often was some sleeping mats and a stone used for grinding maize (called metate in New Spain). Like the slaves in other New World areas, the peons had learned to make the appropriate responses of resigned servility to the master. The hacienda, with its characteristic economic and social organization, represented the most authentic expression of the feudal side of colonial society. Its long shadow still falls over Latin America today.

Marital and familial relationships in white elite society were characterized by male domination, expressed in the right of fathers to arrange marriages for their daughters and in a double standard of sexual morality that enjoined strict chastity or fidelity for wives and daughters without corresponding restrictions on the sexual activity of husbands and sons. Male domination, however, was to some extent limited by the

Hispanic property law, which gave women the right to control their dowries and inheritances during and beyond marriage. There is evidence that some colonial women operated as entrepreneurs independently of their husbands; women were often appointed executors of their husbands' wills and frequently managed a husband's business after his death. At least some women of the white elite group were able to attain positions of political, economic, or intellectual leadership. (In the last category, the best known case is that of the Mexican poet Sor Juana Inés de la Cruz, who is discussed in Chapter 6.) But there was no common female colonial experience, since that experience varied with the different social backgrounds of individual women. Unfortunately, little as yet is known of the affairs of non-Hispanic women of the lower classes. What little in known suggests, paradoxically, that early post-Conquest society provided more opportunities for Indian females than for Indian males. The scarcity of white women forced Spaniards to take available Indian women as their mates, "allowing them to fill roles and positions that would ordinarily have been reserved for white women." Their positions in household work, sewing, and small-scale trade placed them in closer contact with Spanish society and helped strengthen their economic and social situation. With the arrival of growing numbers of white women by the late sixteenth century, however, the opportunities and mobility of Indian women became more limited.

CHAPTER SIX

The Bourbon Reforms and Spanish America

The death of the sickly Charles II in November 1700 marked the end of an era in Spanish history and the beginning of a new and better day, although the signs under which the new day began were far from hopeful. On his deathbed the wretched Charles, more kingly in his dying than he had ever been before, fought desperately to prevent the triumph of an intrigue for the partition of the Spanish dominions among three claimants of that inheritance, the prince of Bavaria, the archduke Charles of Austria, and Louis XIV's grandson, Philip of Anjou. In one of his last acts, Charles signed a will naming the French Philip, who became Philip V, successor to all his dominions.

English fears at the prospect of a union of France and Spain under a single ruler precipitated the War of the Spanish Succession (1702–1713). The war ended with the Treaty of Utrecht (1713), which granted to Great Britain Gibraltar and Minorca, major trade concessions in the Spanish Indies, and a guarantee against a union of the French and Spanish thrones under Philip. Another peace treaty, concluded the following year, gave the Spanish Netherlands and Spain's Italian possessions to Austria.

REFORM AND RECOVERY

Spain's humiliating losses deepened the prevailing sense of pessimism and defeatism, but there were compensations: The shock of defeat in the succession war drove home the need for sweeping reform of Spanish institutions; the loss of the Netherlands and the Italian possessions left Spain with a more manageable, more truly Spanish empire, consisting of the kingdoms of Castile and Aragon and the Indies.

The War of the Spanish Succession also brought a forcible solution of the Aragonese problem, which had long plagued the Hapsburg monarchy. Fearing the authoritarian tendencies of the new Bourbon dynasty and recalling the injuries suffered at French hands during the seventeenth century, the Catalans rose in support of the Austrian claimant in 1705; Aragon and Valencia also invited and received the support of English and Austrian troops. But Aragon and Valencia fell to Philip V's armies in 1707 and suffered immediate loss of their fueros as punishment for supporting the wrong side. The Catalans, abandoned by Great Britain when it signed the peace of Utrecht in 1713, held out until September 1714, when Barcelona surrendered to the Bourbon forces. The fall of the city was followed by the destruction of Catalan liberties and autonomy, with the province being placed under a captain general who governed with the aid of a royal audienca. The new regime made a systematic but unsuccessful effort to extinguish the Catalan language and nationality.

The Bourbon Reforms

The return of peace permitted the new dynasty to turn its attention to implementing a program of reform inspired by the French model. The reform and ensuing revival of Spain is associated with three princes of the House of Bourbon: Philip V (1700–1746) and his two sons, Ferdinand VI (1746–1759) and Charles III (1759–1788). Under the aegis of "enlightened despotism," the Bourbon kings attempted nothing less than a total overhaul of existing political and economic structures, a total renovation of the national life. Only such sweeping reform could close the gap that separated Spain from the foremost European powers and arm the country with the weapons—a powerful industry, a prosperous agriculture, a strong middle class—it needed to prevent its defeat by England and her allies in the struggle for empire that dominated the eighteenth century.

The movement for reform, although carried out within the framework of royal absolutism and Catholic orthodoxy, inevitably provoked the hostility of reactionary elements within the church and the nobility. As a result, the Bourbons, although supported by such liberal grandees as the count of Floridablanca and the count of Aranda, recruited many of their principal ministers and officials from the ranks of the lesser nobility and the small middle class. These men were strongly influenced by the rationalist spirit of the French Encyclopedists,[1] although they rejected French anticlericalism and deism. They were characteristic of the Spanish Enlightenment in their rigid orthodoxy in religion and politics combined with enthusiastic pursuit of useful knowledge, severe criticism of defects in the church and clergy, and belief in the power of informed reason to improve society by reorganizing it along more rational lines.

The work of national reconstruction began under Philip V but reached its climax under Charles III. This great reformer-king attempted to revive Spanish industry by removing the stigma attached to manual labor, establishing

---

[1] Writers of the famous *Encyclopédie* (1751–1780), who were identified with the Enlightenment and advocated deism and a rationalist world outlook.

state-owned textile factories, inviting foreign technical experts into Spain, and encouraging technical education. He aided agriculture by curbing the privileges of the Mesta, or stockbreeders' corporation, and by settling colonies of Spanish and foreign peasants in abandoned regions of the peninsula. He continued and expanded the efforts of his predecessors to encourage shipbuilding and foster trade and communication by the building of roads and canals. Clerical influence declined as a result of the expulsion of the Jesuits in 1767 and of decrees restricting the authority of the Inquisition. Under the cleansing influence of able and honest ministers, a new spirit of austerity and service began to appear among public officials.

But the extent of the changes that took place in Spanish economic and social life under the Bourbons must not be exaggerated. The Crown, linked by a thousand bonds to the feudal nobility and church, never touched the foundation of the old order, the land monopoly of the nobility, with its corollaries of mass poverty and archaic agricultural methods. As a result of these weaknesses, added to the lack of capital for industrial development and the debility of the Spanish middle class, Spain, despite marked advances in population and production, remained at the close of the era a second- or third-class power by comparison with Great Britain, France, or Holland.

The outbreak of the French Revolution, which followed by a few months the death of Charles III in December 1788, brought the reform era effectively to a halt. Frightened by the overthrow of the French monarchy and the execution of his royal kinsman, Charles IV and his ministers turned sharply to the right. The leading reformers were banished or imprisoned, and the importation of French rationalist and revolutionary literature was forbidden. Yet the clock could not be and was not entirely turned back, either in Spain or in the colonies. It was under the corrupt government of Charles IV, for example, that the expedition of Francisco Xavier

Balmis sailed from Spain (1803) to carry the procedure of vaccination to the Spanish dominions in America and Asia—an act that probably saved innumerable lives.

In the field of colonial reform, the Bourbons moved slowly and cautiously, as was natural in view of the powerful vested interests identified with the old order of things. There was never any thought of giving a greater measure of self-government to the colonists or of permitting them to trade more freely with the non-Spanish world. On the contrary, the Bourbons centralized colonial administration still further, with a view to making it more efficient. In addition, their commercial reforms were designed to diminish smuggling and strengthen the exclusive commercial ties between Spain and her colonies, to "reconquer" the colonies economically for Spain.

Revival of Colonial Commerce and Breakdown of Trading Monopoly

The first Bourbon, Philip V, concentrated his efforts on an attempt to reduce smuggling and to revive the fleet system, which had fallen into decay in the late seventeenth century. With the Treaty of Utrecht, the English merchant class had scored an impressive victory in the shape of the asiento; the South Sea Company was granted the exclusive right to supply slaves to Spanish America, with the additional right of sending a shipload of merchandise to Portobelo every year. It was well known that the slave ships carried contraband merchandise, as did the provision ships that accompanied the annual ship and reloaded her with goods. Buenos Aires, where the South Sea Company maintained a trading post, was another funnel through which English traders poured large quantities of contraband goods that penetrated as far as Peru.

The Spanish government sought to check smuggling in the Caribbean by commissioning private warships (guardacostas), which prowled the main lanes of trade in search of ships loaded

A typical urban market. (From Carl Nebel, *Voyage Pittoresque . . . [au] Mexique*, Paris, 1836.)

with contraband. The depredations of the guardacostas led to English demands for compensation and finally to war between England and Spain in 1739. During this war, the British again disrupted the fleet sailings Philip V had attempted to revive. In 1740 they were suspended. Their place was taken by swifter and more economical register ships, which sailed singly, under license from the Crown. Ships bound for Peru used the route around Cape Horn; others sailed directly to Buenos Aires. The end of the South American fleet, known as the *galeones*, brought the death of the Portobelo Fair. The New Spain fleet was alternately revived and suspended, but in 1789 it was abandoned. The convoy system, says John H. Parry, "had long outlived its usefulness; in war it had become inadequate, in peace unnecessary."

The introduction of register ships did not, however, end the monopoly of the Cádiz *consulado* (merchant guild), whose members alone could load these vessels. The first breach in the wall of this monopoly came in the 1720s, with the organization of the Caracas Company, which was founded with the aid of capitalists in the Biscay region. In return for the privilege of trade with Venezuela, this company undertook to police the coast against smugglers and develop the resources of the region. The Caracas Company was on the whole a remarkable success. Dutch interlopers were driven away. Shipments of cacao to Spain doubled, and the price in Spain fell nearly to half. Exports of tobacco, cotton, dyewoods, and indigo also increased.

Biscayan and Catalan capital organized similar companies for trade with Havana, Hispaniola, and other places the old system of colonial trade had left undeveloped. These enterprises, however, were financial failures, in part because of inadequate capital, in part because of poor management. These breaches of the Cádiz monopoly brought no benefits to Creole merchants, who continued to be almost completely excluded from the legal trade between Spain and her colonies.

The first Bourbons made few changes in the administrative structure of colonial government, contenting themselves with efforts to improve the quality of administration by more careful selection of officeholders. One major reorganization was the separation of the northern Andean region (present-day Ecuador, Colombia, and Venezuela) from the viceroyalty of Peru. In 1739 it became a viceroyalty, named New Granada, with its capital at Santa Fe (modern Bogotá). This change had strategic significance, reflecting a desire to provide better protection for the Caribbean coast, especially the fortress of Cartagena. It also reflected the rapid growth of population in the central highlands of Colombia. Within the new viceroyalty, Venezuela was named a captaincy general, with its capital at Caracas, and became virtually independent of Santa Fe.

The movement for colonial reform, like the program of domestic reform, reached a climax in the reign of Charles III. Part of this reform had been foreshadowed in the writings of a remarkable Spanish economist and minister of finance and war under Ferdinard VI, José Campillo. Shortly before his death in 1743, Campillo wrote a memorial on colonial affairs that advocated the abolition of the Cádiz monopoly, a reduction of duties on goods bound for America, the organization of a frequent mail service to America, the encouragement of trade between the colonies, and the development of colonial agriculture and other economic activities that did not compete with Spanish manufacturers. Most of these recommendations were incorporated in a report made to Charles III by a royal commission in 1765. The shock of Spain's defeat in the Seven Years' War, which cost her the loss of Florida and almost the loss of Cuba, provided impetus for a program of imperial reorganization and reform.

In this period, the trading monopoly of Cádiz was gradually eliminated. In 1765, commerce with the West Indies was thrown open to seven other ports besides Cádiz and Seville; this reform, coming at a time when Cuban sugar production was beginning to expand, gave a sharp stimulus to the island's economy. This privilege was gradually extended to other regions until, by the famous decree of free trade of 1778, commerce was permitted between all qualified Spanish ports and all the American provinces except Mexico and Venezuela. In 1789, New Spain and Venezuela were thrown open to trade on the same terms.[2] The burdensome duties levied on this trade were also replaced by simple ad valorem duties of 6 or 7 percent. Restrictions on intercolonial trade were also progressively lifted, but this trade was largely limited to non-European products. A major beneficiary of this change was the Río de la Plata area, which in 1776 was opened for trade with the rest of the Indies. Meanwhile, the Casa de Contratación, symbol of the old order, steadily declined in importance until it closed its doors in 1789. A similar fate overtook the venerable Council of the Indies. As a consultative body it lingered on into the nineteenth century, but most of its duties were entrusted to a powerful colonial minister appointed by the king.

The success of the "free trade" policy was reflected in a spectacular increase in the value of Spain's commerce with Spanish America, an increase said to have amounted to about 700 percent between 1778 and 1788. The entrance of new trading centers and merchant groups into the Indies trade and the reduction of duties and the removal of irksome restrictions had the effect of increasing the volume of business, reducing prices, and perhaps diminishing con-

---

[2] It must be stressed, however, that these reforms did not seriously weaken the dominant role of the Cádiz monopolists and their American agents in colonial trade. As late as 1790, more than 85 percent of the trade moved through Cádiz, thanks to its superior facilities for shipping, insurance, warehousing, and communication.

traband (although one cannot speak with certainty here, for the easing of restrictions inevitably facilitated the activity of smugglers).

But the achievements of the Bourbon commercial reform must not be overestimated. The reform ultimately failed in its aim of reconquering colonial markets for Spain for two basic reasons: first, Spain's industrial weakness, which the best efforts of the Bourbons were unable to overcome; and, second, Spain's closely related inability to keep her sea-lanes to America open in time of war with England, when foreign traders again swarmed into Spanish-American ports. Indeed, the Spanish government openly confessed its inability to supply the colonies with needed goods in time of war by lifting the ban against foreign vessels of neutral origin (which meant United States ships, above all) during the years from 1797 to 1799 and again in the years from 1805 to 1809. This permission to trade with neutrals gave rise to a spirited United States commerce with the Caribbean area and with the Río de la Plata.

Increased Economic Activity

Perhaps the most significant result of the Bourbon commercial reform was the stimulus it gave to economic activity in Spanish America. To what extent this increased economic activity should be ascribed to the beneficial effects of the Bourbon reform and to what degree it resulted from the general economic upsurge in western Europe in the eighteenth century cannot be stated with certainty. What is certain is that the latter part of the century saw a rising level of agricultural, pastoral, and mining production in Spanish America. Stimulated by the Bourbon reform and by the growing European demand for sugar, tobacco, hides, and other staples, production of these products rose sharply in this period. There developed a marked trend toward regional specialization and monoculture in the production of cash crops. After 1770, coffee, grown in Venezuela and Cuba, joined

cacao and sugar as a major export crop of the Caribbean area. The gradual increase in population also stimulated the production of food crops for local markets, notably wheat, preferred over maize by the European population. Tithe collections offer an index of agricultural growth: In the decade from 1779 to 1789, tithe collections in the principal agricultural areas were 40 percent greater than in the previous decade.

It appears, however, that agricultural prosperity was largely limited to areas producing export crops or with easy access to domestic markets. David Brading paints a gloomy picture of the financial condition of the Mexican haciendas in the eighteenth century. Except in the Valley of Mexico, the Bajío,[3] and the Guadalajara region, markets were too small to yield satisfactory returns. Great distances, poor roads, and high freight costs prevented haciendas from developing their productive capacity beyond the requirements of the local market. Private estates were worse off than church haciendas, because they had to pay tithes and sales taxes and bore the double burden of absentee landowners and resident administrators. Great landed families who possessed numerous estates in different regions, producing varied products for multiple markets, were more fortunate; their profits averaged from 6 to 9 percent of capital value in the late eighteenth century. However, thanks to cheap labor, even a low rate of return yielded large revenues, which enabled hacendados to maintain a lavish, seigneurial style of life. Many haciendas were heavily indebted to ecclesiastical institutions, the principal bankers of the time.

The increase in agricultural production, it should be noted, resulted from more extensive use of land and labor rather than from the use of improved implements or techniques. The inefficient great estate (*latifundio*), which used

---

[3] A relatively urbanized area with a diversified economy (agriculture, mining, manufacturing) lying within the modern Mexican states of Guanajuato and Querétaro.

poorly paid peon labor, and the slave plantation accounted for the bulk of commercial agricultural production. The Prussian traveler Alexander von Humboldt, commenting on the semifeudal land tenure system of Mexico, observed that "the property of New Spain, like that of Old Spain, is in a great measure in the hands of a few powerful families, who have gradually absorbed the smaller estates. In America, as well as in Europe, large commons are condemned to the pasturage of cattle and to perpetual sterility."

The increasing concentration of landownership in Mexico and the central Andes in the second half of the eighteenth century reflected the desire of hacendados to eliminate the competition of small producers in restricted markets and to maintain prices at a high level. Given the low productivity of colonial agriculture, however, such natural disasters as drought, premature frosts, or excessive rains easily upset the precarious balance between food supplies and population, producing frightful famines like that of 1785–1787 in central Mexico. Thousands died of hunger or diseases induced by that famine.

What sugar, cacao, and coffee were for the Caribbean area, hides were for the Río de la Plata. The rising European demand for leather for shoewear and industrial purposes and the permission given in 1735 for direct trade with Spain in register ships sparked an economic upsurge in the Plata area. The unregulated hunting of wild cattle on the open pampa soon gave way to the herding of cattle on established *estancias* (cattle ranches). By the end of the century, these were often of huge size—15 to 20 square leagues—with as many as eighty or a hundred thousand head of cattle. By 1790, Buenos Aires was exporting nearly a million and a half hides annually. The meat of the animal, hitherto almost worthless except for the small quantity that could be consumed immediately, now gained in value as a result of the demand for salt beef, processed in large-scale *saladeros* (salting plants). Markets for salt beef were found

above all in the Caribbean area, especially Cuba, where it was chiefly used for feeding the slave population. The growth of cattle raising in La Plata, however, was attended by the concentration of land in ever fewer hands and took place at the expense of agriculture, which remained in a very depressed state.

The eighteenth century also saw a marked revival of silver mining in the Spanish colonies. Peru and Mexico shared in this advance, but the Mexican mines forged far ahead of their Peruvian rivals in the Bourbon era. The mine owners included Creoles and Peninsulars, but the Spanish merchants who financed the mining operations received most of the profits. As in the case of agriculture, the increase in silver production was not due primarily to improved technique, it resulted from the opening of many new as well as old mines and the growth of the labor force. The Crown, however, especially under Charles III, contributed materially to the revival by offering new incentives to entrepreneurs and by its efforts to overcome the backwardness of the mining industry. The incentives included reductions in taxes and in the cost of mercury, a government monopoly.

In New Spain the Crown promoted the establishment of a mining guild (1777) whose activities included the operation of a bank to finance development. Under this guild's auspices was founded the first school of mines in America (1792). Staffed by able professors and provided with modern equipment, it offered excellent theoretical and practical instruction and represented an important source of Enlightenment thought in Mexico. Foreign and Spanish experts, accompanied by teams of technicians, came to Mexico and Peru to show the mine owners the advantages of new machinery and techniques. These praiseworthy efforts were largely frustrated by the traditionalism of the mine owners, by lack of capital to finance changes, and by mismanagement. Yet the production of silver steadily increased. Supplemented by the gold of Brazil, it helped to spark the Industrial Revolution in northern Europe and to stimulate commercial activity on a worldwide scale. In addition, American silver helped the Bourbons meet the enormous expenses of their chronic wars.

Colonial manufacturing, after a long and fairly consistent growth, began to decline in the last past of the eighteenth century, principally because of the influx of cheap foreign wares with which the domestic products could not compete. The textile and wine industries of western Argentina fell into decay as they lost their markets in Buenos Aires and Montevideo to lower-priced foreign wines and cloth. The textile producers of the province of Quito in Ecuador complained of injury from the same cause. In the Mexican manufacturing center of Puebla, production of chinaware, of which the city had long been a leading center, slumped catastrophically between 1793 and 1802.

Although Spain adopted mercantilist legislation designed to restrict colonial manufacturing—especially of fine textiles—this legislation seems to have been only a small deterrent to the growth of large-scale manufacturing. More important deterrents were lack of investment capital, the characteristic preference of Spaniards for land and mining as fields of investment, and a semiservile system of labor that was equally harmful to the workers and to productivity. Humboldt, who visited the woolen workshops of Querétaro in 1803, was disagreeably impressed

not only with the great imperfection of the technical process in the preparation for dyeing, but in a particular manner also with the unhealthiness of the situation, and the bad treatment to which the workers are exposed. Free men, Indians, and people of color are confounded with the criminals distributed by justice among the manufactories, in order to be compelled to work. All appear half naked, covered with rags, meagre, and deformed. Every workshop resembles a dark prison. The doors, which are double, remain constantly shut, and the workmen are not permitted

to quit the house. Those who are married are only allowed to see their families on Sunday. All are unmercifully flogged, if they commit the smallest trespass on the order established in the manufactory.[4]

One of the few large-scale lines of industry was the manufacture of cigars. In the same town of Querétaro, Humboldt visited a cigar factory that employed three thousand workers, including nineteen hundred women.

Labor Systems in the Eighteenth Century

Humboldt's comments testify to the persistence of servitude and coercion as essential elements of the labor system from the beginning to the end of the colonial period. Despite the Bourbons' theoretical dislike of forced labor, they sought to tighten legal enforcement of debt peonage in the Indies. Concerned with more efficient collection of Indian tribute, José de Gálvez, the reforming minister of Charles III, tried to attach the natives more firmly to their pueblos and haciendas. In 1769, he introduced in New Spain the system of clearance certificates, documents that certified that peons had no outstanding debts and could seek employment with other landowners. The mobility of peons who lacked these papers could be restricted. Debt peonage was authorized by the Mining Ordinances of New Spain and was also practiced in the gold and silver mines of Chile, where a system of clearance certificates like that used in Mexico was employed.

In practice, as previously noted, the importance of debt peonage and the severity of its enforcement depended on the availability of labor. In New Spain, by the late eighteenth century, the growth of the labor force through population increase and the elimination of small producers had sharply reduced the importance of debt as a means of securing and holding

[4] Alexander von Humboldt, *Political Essay on the Kingdom of New Spain*, 4 vols. (London, 1822–1823), 3:463–464.

laborers. Eric Van Young, for example, has documented a reduction of the per capita indebtedness of resident peons in the Guadalajara area, suggesting their decreased bargaining power in dealing with employers. The new situation enabled hacendados to retain or discharge workers in line with changing levels of production. Thus in late eighteenth-century Mexico, landowners simply dismissed workers when crop failures occurred in order to save on their rations. These changes were accompanied by a tendency for real wages and rural living standards to decline.

In the Andean area, the forced labor system of the mita continued to provide the bulk of the labor force working in mining almost to the end of the colonial period. Agricultural labor was theoretically free, but heavy tribute demands and the operations of the repartimiento de mercancías (the forced purchase of goods by the Indians from corregidores) created a need for cash that compelled many natives to seek employment on Spanish haciendas. They included a large number of so-called *forasteros* ("outsiders") who had fled their native pueblos to escape the dreaded mita service and tribute burdens. In addition to working the hacendado's land, these laborers or sharecroppers and their families had to render personal service in the master's household. Theoretically free, their dependent status must have sharply limited their mobility.

Political Reforms

Under Charles III, the work of territorial reorganization of the sprawling empire continued. The viceroyalty of Peru, already diminished by the creation of New Granada, was further curtailed by the creation in 1776 of the viceroyalty of the Río de la Plata, with its capital at Buenos Aires. This act reflected official Spanish concern over the large volume of contraband in the estuary. It also reflected fear of a possible foreign attack on the area by the British, who had recently entrenched themselves in the nearby Falkland Islands, or the Portuguese who, advancing southward from Brazil, had established the settlement of Sacramento on the banks of the estuary, a base from which they threatened shipping and the town of Montevideo. To put an end to this danger the Spanish government mounted a major military expedition designed to establish full control of both banks of the river. The commander Pedro de Cevallos came out with the temporary title of viceroy of Buenos Aires. In 1778 the viceroyalty was made permanent with the appointment of the viceroy Juan José de Vértiz y Salcedo, whose rule of over a decade saw a remarkable growth in the prosperity of the area. This prosperity owed much to the decree of "free trade" of 1778, which authorized direct trade between Buenos Aires and Spain and permitted intercolonial trade. In 1783 the establishment of a royal audiencia at Buenos Aires completed the liberation of the Río de la Plata provinces from the distant rule of Lima. The inclusion of Upper Peru in the new viceroyalty, with the resulting redirection of the flow of Potosí silver from Lima to Buenos Aires, signified a stunning victory for the landowners and merchants of Buenos Aires over their mercantile rivals in Lima.

The trend toward decentralization in the administration of Spanish America reflected not only the struggle against foreign military and commercial penetration but an enlightened awareness of the problems of communication and government posed by the great distances between the various provinces, an awareness spurred by advances in cartography and knowledge of the geography of the continent in general. Two indications of this tendency were the greater autonomy enjoyed by the captaincies general in the eighteenth century and the increase in their number. Thus, in 1777 Venezuela was raised to a captaincy general, as previously mentioned. Similarly, in 1778 Chile was raised from the status of a presidency to that of a captaincy general. The increased autonomy enjoyed by the captains general enabled an enlightened ruler like Ambrosio O'Higgins in Chile to attempt major economic reforms, stimulate mining and manufacturing, introduce new crops, and in general try to promote not only the interests of the Spanish crown but the welfare of the Chilean people.

The creation of new viceroyalties and captaincies general went hand in hand with another major political reform, the transfer to the colonies between 1782 and 1790 of the intendant system, already introduced to Spain by France. This reform was made in the interests of greater administrative efficiency and in the hope of increasing royal revenues from the colonies. The intendants, provincial governors who ruled from the capitals of their provinces, were expected to relieve the overburdened viceroys of many of their duties, especially in financial matters. Among their other duties, the intendants were expected to further the economic development of their districts by promoting the cultivation of new crops, the improvement of mining, the building of roads and bridges, and the establishment of consulados and economic societies. Under their prodding, the lethargic cabildos or town councils were in some cases stirred to greater activity. The Ordinance of Intendants also abolished the offices of corregidor and alcalde mayor, notorious vehicles for the oppression of the natives. These officials were replaced as governors of Indian towns by men called *subdelegados,* who were nominated by the intendants and confirmed by the viceroys.

Many of the intendants at the height of the reform era were capable and cultivated men who not only achieved the objectives of increased economic activity and revenue collection but promoted education and cultural progress generally. But the same could not be said of the majority of their subordinates, the subdelegados, who, like their predecessors, soon became no-

torious for their oppressive practices. A common complaint was that they continued to compel the Indians to trade with them, although the repartimiento had been forbidden by the Ordinance of Intendants. The great popular revolts of the 1780s were fueled in large part by the failure of the Indian and mixed-blood masses to share in the fruits of the eighteenth-century economic advance, whose principal beneficiaries were Spanish and Creole landowners, mine owners, and merchants.

Strengthening the Defenses

Increased revenue, as previously indicated, was a major objective of the Bourbon commercial and political reforms. A major purpose to which that revenue was applied was the strengthening of the sea and land defenses of the empire. Before the eighteenth century, primary dependence for defense had been placed on naval power: convoy escorts and cruiser squadrons. Before the middle of the eighteenth century, standing armed forces in the colonies were negligible, and authorities relied on local forces raised for particular emergencies. The disasters of the Seven Years' War and the loss of Havana and Manila (1762) to the English, in particular, resulted in a decision to correct the shortcomings in the defense system of the colonies. Fortifications of important American ports were strengthened, and colonial armies created. These included regular units stationed permanently in the colonies or rotated between peninsular and overseas service and colonial militia whose ranks were filled by volunteers or drafted recruits.

To make military service attractive to the Creole upper class, which provided the officer corps of the new force, the Crown granted extensive privileges and exemptions to Creole youths who accepted commissions. To the lure of prestige and honors, the grant of the *fuero militar* added protection from civil legal jurisdiction and liability, except for certain specified offenses. The special legal and social position thus accorded to the colonial officer class helped to form a tradition, which has survived to the present in Latin America, of the armed forces as a special caste with its own set of interests, not subject to the civil power, that acted as the arbiter of political life, usually in the interests of conservative ruling classes. Under the Bourbons, however, the power of the colonial military was held in check by such competing groups as the church and the civil bureaucracy.

Although the expansion of the colonial military establishment under the Bourbons offered some opportunities and advantages to upper-class Creole youth, it did nothing to allay the long-standing resentment of Creoles against their virtual exclusion from the higher offices of state and church and from large-scale commerce. Bourbon policy in regard to the problem went through two phases. In the first half of the eighteenth century, wealthy Creoles could sometimes purchase high official posts, and for a time they dominated the prestigious audiencias of Mexico City and Lima. But in the second half of the century, an anti-Creole reaction took place. José de Gálvez, Charles III's colonial minister, was the very embodiment of the spirit of enlightened despotism that characterized his reign. Gálvez distrusted Creole capacity and integrity and removed high-ranking Creoles from positions in the imperial administration. The new upper bureaucracy, such as the intendants who took over much of the authority of viceroys and governors, was in the great majority Spanish-born.

Other Bourbon policies injured Creole vested interests or wounded their sensibilities and traditions. An example was the sudden expulsion of the Jesuits (1767), who enjoyed much favor among the Creole aristocracy. Thus, despite and partly because of the reformist spirit of the Bourbon kings, the Creoles became progressively alienated from the Spanish crown. Their alienation intensified an incipient Creole nationalism

that, denied direct political outlets, found its chief expression in the areas of culture and religion.

COLONIAL CULTURE AND THE ENLIGHTENMENT

Colonial culture in all its aspects was a projection of Spanish culture of the time. If we leave aside the very important work done in the study of Indian antiquity and religions, colonial culture only faintly reflected its American milieu in respect to subject matter and treatment. At least until the eighteenth century, a neomedieval climate of opinion, enforced by the authority of church and state, sharply restricted the play of the colonial intellect and imagination. Colonial culture thus suffered from all the infirmities of its parent but inevitably lacked the breadth and vitality of Spanish literature and art, the product of a much older and more mature civilization. Despite these and other difficulties, such as the limited market for books, colonial culture left a remarkably large and valuable heritage.

The Church and Education

The church enjoyed a virtual monopoly of colonial education at all levels. The primary and secondary schools maintained by the clergy, with few exceptions, were open only to children of the white upper class and the Indian nobility. Poverty condemned the overwhelming majority of the natives and mixed castes to illiteracy. Admission to the universities, which numbered about twenty-five at the end of the colonial era, was even more restricted to youths of ample means and pure white blood.

The universities of Lima and Mexico City, both chartered by the Crown in 1551, were the first permanent institutions of higher learning. Patterned on similar institutions in Spain, the colonial university faithfully reproduced their medieval organization, curricula, and methods of instruction. Indifference to practical or scientific studies, slavish respect for the authority of the Bible, Aristotle, the church fathers, and certain medieval schoolmen, and a passion for hairsplitting debate of fine points of theological or metaphysical doctrine were among the features of colonial academic life. Theology and law were the chief disciplines; until the eighteenth century, science was a branch of philosophy, taught from the *Physics* of Aristotle.

A strict censorship of books (no book could be published in either Spain or the colonies without the approval of the Royal Council) limited the spread of new doctrines in colonial society. In recent decades it has been shown that the laws prohibiting the entry of works of fiction into the Spanish colonies were completely ineffective, but this tolerance did not extend to heretical or subversive writings. The records of the colonial Inquisition reveal many tragic cases of imprisonment, torture, and even death for individuals who were charged with the possession and reading of such writings. At least until the eighteenth century, when the intellectual iron curtain surrounding Spanish America began to lift, the people of the colonies were effectively shielded from literature of an unorthodox religious or political tendency.

Yet, within the limits imposed by official censorship and their own backgrounds, colonial scholars were able to make impressive contributions, especially in the fields of Indian history, anthropology, linguistics, and natural history. The sixteenth century was the Golden Age of Indian studies in Spanish America. In Mexico a large group of missionaries, especially members of the Franciscan order, carried out long, patient investigations of the native languages, religion, and history. With the aid of native informants, Friar Bernardino de Sahagún compiled a monumental *General History of the Things of New Spain*, a veritable encyclopedia of information on all aspects of Aztec culture; scholars have only begun to mine the extraordinary wealth of ethnographic materials in Sahagún's work. Another Franciscan, usually known by his Indian name of Motolinia (Friar Toribio de Benavente), wrote a *History of the Indians of New Spain* that is an invaluable guide to Indian life before and after the Conquest. Basing his work on Aztec picture writings and a chronicle, now lost, written by an Indian noble in his own language, Father Diego Durán wrote a history of ancient Mexico that preserves both the content and spirit of Aztec tribal epics and legends. The Jesuit José de Acosta sought to satisfy Spanish curiosity about the natural productions of the New World and the history of the Aztecs and Incas in his *Natural and Moral History of the Indies*. His book, simply and pleasantly written, displays a critical spirit rare for its time; it achieved an immediate popularity in Spain and was quickly translated into all the major languages of western Europe.

Not a few historical works were written by Indian or mestizo nobles actuated by a variety of motives: interest and pride in their native heritage joined to a desire to prove the important services rendered by their forebears to the Conquest and the validity of their claims to noble titles and land. Products of convent schools or colegios, they usually combined Christian piety with nostalgic regard for the departed glories of their ancestors. A descendant of the kings of Texcoco, Fernando de Alva Ixtlilxochitl, wrote a number of historical works that show a mastery of European historical method. These works combine a great amount of valuable information with a highly idealized picture of Texcocan civilization. Another writer of the early seventeenth century, the mestizo Garcilaso de la Vega, son of a Spanish conquistador and an Inca princess, gives in his *Royal Commentaries of the Incas*, together with much valuable information on Inca material culture and history, an idyllic picture of Peruvian life under the benevolent rule of the Inca kings. His book, written in a graceful, fluent Spanish, is more than a history; it is a first-class work of art. No other Spanish history was as popular in Europe as Garcilaso's *Royal Commentaries;* its favorable image of Inca civilization continues to influence our view of ancient Peru down to the present.

Science, Literature, and the Arts

The second half of the seventeenth century saw a decline in the quantity and quality of colonial scholarly production. This was the age of the baroque style in literature, a style that stressed word play, cleverness, and pedantry, that subordinated content to form, meaning to ornate expression. Yet two remarkable men of this period, Carlos Sigüenza y Góngora in Mexico and Pedro de Peralta Barnuevo in Peru, foreshadowed the eighteenth-century Enlightenment by the universality of their interests and their concern with the practical uses of science. Sigüenza, mathematician, archaeologist, and historian, attacked the ancient but still dominant superstition of astrology in his polemic with the Jesuit father Kino over the nature of comets; he also defied prejudice by providing in his will for the dissection of his body in the interests of science. He made careful observations of comets and eclipses of the sun and exchanged his observations with scientists in Europe. Yet the prevailing baroque spirit of fantasy appeared in his speculation that the Greek god Poseidon was the great-grandson of Noah and the forebear of the American Indians.

Peralta Barnuevo, cosmographer and mathematician, made astronomical observations that were published in Paris in the *Proceedings* of the French Royal Academy of Sciences, of which he was elected corresponding member; he also superintended the construction of fortifications in Lima. Yet this able and insatiably curious man of science also sought refuge in a baroque mysticism, and in one of his last works concluded that true wisdom, the knowledge of God, was not "subject to human comprehension."

Colonial literature, with some notable exceptions, was a pallid reflection of prevailing literary trends in the mother country. The isolation from foreign influences, the strict censorship of all

reading matter, and the limited audience for writing of every kind made literary creation difficult. "A narrow and dwarfed world," the discouraged Mexican poet Bernardo de Balbuena called the province of New Spain. To make matters worse, colonial literature in the seventeenth century succumbed to the Spanish literary fad of *Gongorismo* (so called after the poet Luis de Góngora)—the cult of an obscure, involved, and artificial style.

Amid a flock of "jangling magpies," as one literary historian describes the Gongorist versifiers of the seventeenth century, appeared an incomparable songbird, known to her admiring contemporaries as "the tenth muse"—Sor Juana Inés de la Cruz (1651–1695). This remarkable nun, who also assembled in her convent one of the finest mathematical libraries of the time, wrote poetry of matchless beauty and grace. But Sor Juana could not not escape the pressures of her environment. Rebuked by the bishop of Puebla for her worldly interests, she ultimately gave up her books and scientific interests and devoted the remainder of her brief life to religious devotion and charitable works.

Colonial art drew its principal inspiration from Spanish sources, but, especially in the sixteenth century, Indian influence was sometimes visible in design and ornamentation. Quito in Ecuador and Mexico City were among the chief centers of artistic activity. The first school of fine arts in the New World was established in Mexico City in 1779 under royal auspices. As might be expected, religious motifs dominated painting and sculpture. In architecture the colonies followed Spanish examples, with the severe classical style of the sixteenth century giving way in the seventeenth to the highly ornamented baroque and in the eighteenth to a style that was even more ornate.

The intellectual atmosphere of the Spanish colonies was not conducive to scientific inquiry or achievement. As late as 1773, the Colombian botanist Mutis was charged with heresy for giving lectures in Bogotá on the Copernican system.

The prosecutor of the Inquisition asserted that Mutis was "perhaps the only man in Latin America to uphold Copernicus." In the last decades of the eighteenth century, however, the growing volume of economic and intellectual contacts with Europe, and the patronage and protection of enlightened governors, created more favorable conditions for scientific activity. Science made its greatest strides in the wealthy province of New Spain, where the expansion of the mining industry stimulated interest in geology, chemistry, mathematics, and metallurgy. In Mexico City there arose a school of mines, a botanical garden, and an academy of fine arts. The Mexican scientific renaissance produced a galaxy of brilliant figures that included Antonio de León y Gama, an astronomer of whose writings Humboldt commented that they displayed "a great precision of ideas and accuracy of observation"; Antonio de Alzate, whose *Gaceta de Literatura* brought to Creole youth the knowledge of Europe's scientific advances and who championed the intelligence and capacity of the Indian; and Joaquín Velázquez Cárdenas y León, astonomer, geographer, and mathematician, whose services to his country included the founding of the school of mines. These men combined Enlightenment enthusiasm for rationalism, empiricism, and progress with a strict Catholic orthodoxy; Alzate, for example, vehemently denounced in his *Gaceta* the "infidelity" and skepticism of Europe's philosophes.

Spain, now under the rule of the enlightened Bourbon kings, itself contributed to the intellectual renovation of the colonies. A major liberalizing influence, in both Spain and its colonies, was exerted by the early eighteenth-century friar Benito Feijóo, whose numerous essays waged war on folly and superstition of every kind. Feijóo helped to naturalize the Enlightenment in the Spanish-speaking world by his lucid exposition of the ideas of Bacon, Newton, and Descartes. Spanish and foreign scientific expeditions to Spanish America, authorized and

sometimes financed by the Crown, also stimulated the growth of scientific thought and introduced the colonists to such distinguished representatives of European science as the Frenchman La Condamine and the German Alexander von Humboldt.

Among the clergy, the Jesuits were most skillful and resourceful in the effort to reconcile church dogma with the ideas of the Enlightenment, in bridging the old and the new. In Mexico, Jesuit writers like Andrés de Guevara, Pedro José Marquez, and Francisco Javier Clavigero praised and taught the doctrines of Bacon, Descartes, and Newton. These Jesuits exalted physics above metaphysics and the experimental method over abstract reasoning and speculation; but all of them combined these beliefs with undeviating loyalty to the teachings of the church. Thus, the expulsion of the Jesuits from Spanish America (1767) removed from the scene the ablest, most subtle defenders of the traditional Catholic world view. In their Italian exile—for it was in Italy that most of the Jesuit exiles settled—some of them occupied their leisure time writing books designed to make known to the world the history and geography of their American homelands. The most important of these works by Jesuit exiles was the *History of Ancient Mexico* (1780–1781) of Francisco Clavigero, the best work of its kind written to date and an excellent illustration of the characteristic Jesuit blend of Catholic orthodoxy with the critical, rationalist approach of the Enlightenment.

Despite their frequent and sincere professions of loyalty to the Crown, the writings of colonial intellectuals revealed a sensitivity to social and political abuses, a discontent with economic backwardness, and a dawning sense of nationality that contained potential dangers for the Spanish regime. Colonial newspapers and journals played a significant part in the development of a critical and reformist spirit among the educated Creoles of Spanish America. Subjected to an oppressive censorship by church and state and beset by chronic financial difficulties, they generally had short and precarious lives. More important than the routine news items they carried were the articles on scientific, economic, and social problems they housed and the ideas of social utility, progress, and the conquest of nature they vigorously announced.

The circulation and influence of forbidden books among educated colonials steadily increased in the closing decades of the eighteenth century and the first years of the nineteenth. It would nevertheless be incorrect to conclude, as some writers have done, that the Inquisition became a toothless tiger in the eighteenth century and that radical ideas could be advocated with almost total impunity. It is true that the influence of the Inquisition weakened under the Bourbons, especially Charles III, because of the growth of French influence. But the censorship was never totally relaxed, the Inquisition continued vigilant, and with every turn of the diplomatic wheel that drew Spain and France apart the inquisitorial screws were tightened. Thus, the outbreak of the French Revolution brought a wave of repression against advocates of radical ideas in Mexico, culminating in a major auto-da-fé (public sentencing) in Mexico City at which long prison sentences and other severe penalties were handed out. How powerless these repressions were to check the movement of new thought is illustrated by the writings of the fathers of Spanish-American independence. Their works reveal a thorough knowledge of the ideas of Locke, Montesquieu, Raynal, and other important figures of the Enlightenment.

CREOLE NATIONALISM

The incipient Creole nationalism, however, built on other foundations than the ideas of the European Enlightenment, which were alien and suspect to the masses. Increasingly conscious of themselves as a class and of their respective provinces as their *patrias* (fatherlands), Creole intellectuals of the eighteenth century assembled an imposing body of data designed to refute the attacks of such eminent European writers as the comte de Buffon and Cornelius de Pauw, who proclaimed the inherent inferiority of the New World and its inhabitants.

In the largest sense, the Creole patria was all America. As early as 1696, the Mexican Franciscan Agustín de Vetancurt claimed that the New World was superior to the Old in natural beauty and resources. New Spain and Peru, he wrote in florid prose, were two breasts from which the whole world drew sustenance, drinking blood changed into the milk of gold and silver. In a change of imagery, he compared America to a beautiful woman adorned with pearls, emeralds, sapphires, chrysolites, and topazes, drawn from the jewel boxes of her rich mines.

In the prologue to his *History of Ancient Mexico*, Clavigero stated that his aim was "to restore the truth to its splendor, truth obscured by an incredible multitude of writers on America." The epic, heroic character that Clavigero gave the history of ancient Mexico reflected the Creole search for origins, for a classical antiquity other than the European, to which the Peninsulars could lay better claim. The annals of the Toltecs and the Aztecs, he insisted, offered as many examples of valor, patriotism, wisdom, and virtue as the histories of Greece and Rome. Mexican antiquity displayed such models of just and benevolent rule as the wise Chichimec king Xolotl and philosopher-kings such as Nezahualcoyotl and Nezahualpilli. In this way, Clavigero provided the nascent Mexican nationality with a suitably dignified and heroic past. The Chilean Jesuit Juan Ignacio Molina developed similar themes in his *History of Chile* (1782).

The Creole effort to develop a collective self-consciousness also found expression in religious thought and symbolism. In his *Quetzalcoatl and Guadalupe: The Formation of Mexican National Consciousness* (1976), Jacques Lafaye has shown how Creole intellectuals exploited two powerful myths in the attempt to achieve Mexican spiritual autonomy and even superiority vis-á-vis Spain. One was the myth that the Virgin Mary appeared in 1531 on the hill of Tepeyac, near Mexico City, to an Indian called Juan Diego and through him commanded the bishop of Mexico to build a church there. The proof demanded by the bishop came in the form of winter roses from Tepeyac, enfolded in Juan Diego's cloak, which was miraculously painted with the image of the Virgin. From the seventeenth century, the *indita*, the brown-faced Indian Virgin (as opposed to the Virgin of Los Remedios, who had allegedly aided Cortés) was venerated throughout Mexico as the Virgin of Guadalupe. Under her banner, in fact, Miguel Hidalgo in 1810 was to lead the Indian and mestizo masses in a great revolt against Spanish rule.

The other great myth was that of Quetzalcoatl, the Toltec redeemer-king and god. Successive colonial writers had suggested that Quetzalcoatl was none other than the Christian apostle St. Thomas. On December 12, 1794, the Creole Dominican Servando Teresa de Mier arose in his pulpit in the town of Guadalupe to proclaim that Quetzalcoatl was in fact St. Thomas, who long centuries before had come with four disciples to preach the Gospel in the New World. In this the Apostle had succeeded, and at the time of the Conquest, Christianity—somewhat altered, to be sure—reigned in Mexico. If Mier was right, America owed nothing to Spain, not even her Christianity. Spanish officials, quickly recognizing the revolutionary implications of Mier's sermon, arrested him and exiled him to Spain.

The preceding episode illustrates the devious channels through which Creole nationalism moved to achieve its ends. One of those ends was Creole hegemony over the Indian and mixed-blood masses, to be based on their awareness of their common patria, on their collective adherence to such national cults as that of the Virgin of Guadalupe in Mexico. In the 1780s, however, the accumulated wrath of those masses broke out in a series of explosions that

Antonio García's *Virgen de Guadalupe*, 1946–1947. Fresco. (Sacred Heart Church, Corpus Christi, Texas)

threatened the very existence of the colonial social and political order. In this crisis the Creole upper class showed that their aristocratic patria did not really include the Indians, mestizos, and blacks among its sons, that their rhetorical sympathy for the dead Indians of Moctezuma's and Atahualpa's time did not extend to the living Indians of their own time.

THE REVOLT OF THE MASSES

Innumerable Indian and Negro slave revolts punctuated the colonial period of Spanish-American history. Before Spanish rule had been firmly established, the Indians rose against their new masters in many regions. In Mexico the Mixton war raged from 1540 to 1542. The Maya of Yucatán staged a great uprising in 1546. A descendant of the Inca kings, Manco II, led a nationwide revolt against the Spanish conquerors of Peru. In Chile the indomitable Araucanians began a struggle for independence that continued into the late nineteenth century. In the jungles and mountains of the West Indies, Central America, and northern South America, groups of runaway Negro slaves established communities that successfully resisted Spanish efforts to destroy them. The revolutionary wave subsided in the seventeenth century but rose again to great heights in the eighteenth, as a result of new burdens imposed on the common people.

The Bourbon reforms helped to enrich colonial landowners, merchants, and mine owners, beautified their cities, and broadened the intellectual horizons of upper-class youths, but the multitude did not share in these benefits. On the contrary, Bourbon efforts to increase the royal revenues by the creation of governmental monopolies and privileged companies and the imposition of new taxes actually made more acute the misery of the lower classes. This circumstance helps to explain the popular character of the revolts of 1780–1781, as distinct from the Creole wars of independence of the next generation. With rare exceptions, the privileged Creole group either supported the Spaniards against the native uprisings or joined the revolutionary movements under pressure, only to desert them at a later time.

Revolt in Peru

In Peru the corrupt government of the corregidores, the abuse of the repartimiento, the death-dealing mita of Potosí and Huancavelica, and increases in sales taxes (alcabalas) caused intense discontent that reached a climax as a result of the measures taken by the visitador José de Areche, who was sent out by Charles III in 1777 to reform conditions in the colony. Areche tightened up the collection of tribute and sales taxes and broadened the tributary category to include all mestizos. As a result,

the contribution of the Indians was increased by 1 million pesos annually. These measures not only caused great hardships to the commoners but created greater difficulties for the native caciques, or chiefs, who were responsible for the collection of tribute quotas. Areche himself foretold the storm to come when he wrote: "The lack of righteous judges, the mita of the Indians, and provincial commerce have made a corpse of this America. Corregidores are interested only in themselves. . . . How near everything is to ruin if these terrible abuses are not corrected, for they have been going on a long time."

The great revolt of 1780–1781 in Peru had its forerunner. From 1742 to 1755, a native leader called Juan Santos, "the invincible," waged partisan warfare against the Spaniards from his base in the eastern slopes of the Andes. The memory of his exploits was still alive when the revolt of José Gabriel Condorcanqui began. A well-educated, wealthy mestizo descendant of the Inca kings, he had made repeated, fruitless efforts to obtain relief for his people through legal channels. In November 1780, he raised the standard of revolt by ambushing the hated corregidor Antonio de Arriaga near the town of Tinta and putting him to death after a summary trial. At this time he also took the name of the last head of the neo-Inca state and became Tupac Amaru II. His actions were preceded by an uprising led by the Catari brothers in the territory of present-day Bolivia. By the first months of 1780, the southern highlands of the viceroyalty of Peru were aflame with revolt. Although the various revolutionary movements lacked a unified direction, the rebel leaders generally recognized Tupac Amaru as their chief and continued to invoke his name even after his death.

The objectives of Tupac Amaru himself are not entirely clear. In public, the Indian chieftain proclaimed his loyalty to the Spanish king and church, limiting his demands to the abolition of the mita, the repartimiento, the alcabala, and other taxes; the suppression of the corregidores; and the appointment of Indian governors for the provinces. But it is difficult to believe that the well-educated Tupac Amaru, who had had years of experience in dealing with Spanish officialdom, seriously believed that he could obtain sweeping reforms from the Crown by negotiation, even from a position of strength, especially after his execution of the corregidor Arriaga. His protestations of loyalty were contradicted by certain documents in which he styled himself king of Peru, by the war of fire and blood that he urged against peninsular Spaniards, excepting only the clergy, and by the effective government, headed by a junta of five members, that he established for the territory under his control.

More plausible is the view that his professions of loyalty to Spain represented a mask by means of which he could utilize the still strong faith of the Indians in the mythical benevolence of the Spanish king and perhaps soften his punishment in case of defeat.

Tactical errors, such as Tupac Amaru's failure to attack Cuzco before the arrival of Spanish reinforcements, poor communications between the rebel forces, the superior arms and organization of the royalist armies, divisions among the native nobility, and the failure of the great majority of Creoles to support the revolt, doomed it to defeat. Many of the Indian caciques, jealous of Tupac Amaru or fearful of losing their privileged status, led their subjects into the Spanish camp. Despite some initial successes, the rebel leader soon suffered a complete rout. Tupac Amaru, members of his family, and his leading captains were captured and put to death, some with ferocious cruelty. In the territory of present-day Bolivia the insurrection continued two years longer, reaching its high point in two prolonged sieges of La Paz (March–October 1781).

The last Inca revolt was not entirely in vain, however. Among the reforms hastily instituted by the Crown were abolition of the repartimiento, a lightening of mita burdens, the replacement of the hated corregidores by the system of intendants, and the establishment of an audiencia, or high court, in Cuzco—another of Tupac Amaru's goals. As a result of these and other reforms under the able viceroy Teodoro de Croix, there was at least a temporary improvement in the condition of the Peruvian Indians.

Insurrection in New Granada (1781)

The revolt of the Comuneros in New Granada, like that in Peru, had its origin in intolerable economic conditions. Unlike the Peruvian upheaval, however, it was more clearly limited in its aims to the redress of grievances. Increases in the alcabala and a whole series of new taxes, including one on tobacco and a poll tax, all designed principally to pay the costs of defense of New Granada against English attack, provoked an uprising in Socorro, an important agricultural and manufacturing center in the north. The disturbances soon spread to other communities. The reformist spirit of the revolt was reflected in the insurgent slogan: *viva el rey y muera el mal gobierno!* (Long live the king, down with the evil government!)

In view of its organization and its effort to form a common front of all colonial groups with grievances against Spanish authority (excepting the Negro slaves), the revolt of the Comuneros marked an advance over the rather chaotic course of events to the south. A *común* (central committee), elected in the town of Socorro by thousands of peasants and artisans from adjacent towns, directed the insurrection. Each of the towns in revolt also had its común and a captain chosen by popular election.

Under the command of hesitant or unwilling Creole leaders, a multitude of Indian and mestizo peasants and artisans marched on the capital of Bogotá, capturing or putting to flight the small forces sent from the capital. Playing for time until reinforcements could arrive from the

VICEROYALTIES IN LATIN AMERICA IN 1780

coast, the royal audiencia dispatched a commission headed by the archbishop to negotiate with the Comuneros. The popular character of the movement and the unity of oppressed groups that it represented were reflected in the terms that the rebel delegates presented to the Spanish commissioners and that the latter signed and later repudiated: These terms included reduction of Indian and mestizo tribute and sales taxes, return to the Indians of land usurped from them, abolition of the new tax on tobacco, and preference for Creoles over Europeans in the filling of official posts.

An agreement, reached on June 4, 1781, satisfied virtually all the demands of the rebels and was sanctified by the archbishop by a special religious service. Secretly, however, the Spanish commissioners signed another document declaring the agreement void because it was obtained by force. The jubilant insurgents scattered and returned to their homes. Only José Antonio Galán, a young mestizo peasant leader, maintained his small force intact and sought to keep the revolt alive.

Having achieved their objective of disbanding the rebel army, the Spanish officials prepared to crush the insurrection completely. The viceroy Manuel Antonio Flores openly repudiated the agreement with the Comuneros. Following a pastoral visit to the disaffected region by the archbishop, who combined seductive promises of reform with threats of eternal damnation for confirmed rebels, Spanish troops brought up from the coast moved into the region and took large numbers of prisoners. The Creole leaders of the revolt hastened to atone for their political sins by collaborating with the royalists. Galán, who had vainly urged a new march on Bogotá, was seized by a renegade leader and handed over to the Spaniards, who put him to death by hanging on January 30, 1782. The revolt of the Comuneros had ended.

CHAPTER SEVEN

Colonial Brazil

Brazil's existence was unknown when the Treaty of Tordesillas (1494) between Spain and Portugal, fixing the dividing line between the overseas possessions of the two powers 370 leagues west of the Cape Verde Islands, assigned a large stretch of the coastline of South America to the Portuguese zone of exploration and settlement. In 1500, Pedro Álvares Cabral sailed with a large fleet to follow up Vasco da Gama's great voyage to India. He was, according to one explanation, driven by a storm farther west than he had intended and therefore made landfall on the Brazilian coast on April 22. Some historians speculate that he purposely changed course to investigate reports of land to the west or to verify a previous discovery. Whatever the reason for his westward course, Cabral promptly claimed the land for his country and sent a ship to report his discovery to the king.

THE BEGINNING OF COLONIAL BRAZIL

Portugal's limited resources, already committed to the exploitation of the wealth of Africa and the Far East, made it impossible to undertake a full-scale colonization of Brazil. But Portugal did not entirely neglect its new possession. Royal expeditions established the presence of a valuable dyewood, called brazilwood, that grew abundantly on the coast between the present states of Pernambuco and São Paulo. Merchant capitalists soon obtained concessions to engage in the brazilwood trade and established a scattering of trading posts where European trinkets and other goods were exchanged with the Indians for brazil logs and other exotic commodities. A small trickle of settlers, some castaways, others *degredados* (criminals exiled from Portugal to distant parts of the empire) began; these exiles were often well received by the local Indians and lived to sire a large number of mixed-bloods who gave valuable assistance to Portuguese colonization. Meanwhile, French merchant ships, also drawn by the lure of brazilwood, began to appear on the Brazilian coast. Alarmed by the presence of these interlopers, King João III sent in 1530 an expedition under Martim Affonso de Sousa to drive away the intruders and found permanent settlements in Brazil. In 1532 the first Portuguese town in Brazil, named São Vicente, was founded near the present port of Santos.

The Captaincy System

The limited resources of the Portuguese crown, combined with its heavy commitments in the spice-rich East, forced the king to assign to private individuals the major responsibility for the colonization of Brazil. This responsibility took the form of the captaincy system, already used by Portugal in Madeira, the Azores, and the Cape Verde Islands. The Brazilian coastline was divided into fifteen parallel strips extending inland to the uncertain line of Tordesillas. These strips were granted as hereditary captaincies to a dozen individuals, each of whom agreed to colonize, develop, and defend his captaincy or captaincies at his own expense. The captaincy system represented a curious fusion of feudal and capitalist elements. The grantee or donatory was not only a vassal owing allegiance to his lord the king, but a businessman who hoped to derive large profits from his own estates and from taxes obtained from the colonists to whom he had given land. This fusion of feudal and capitalist elements characterized the entire Portuguese colonial enterprise in Brazil from the first.

Few of the captaincies proved successful from either the economic or political point of view, since few donatories possessed the combination of investment capital and administrative ability required to attract settlers and defend their captaincies against Indian attacks and foreign intruders. One of the most successful was Duarte Coelho, a veteran of the India enterprise who was granted the captaincy of Pernambuco. His heavy investment in the colony paid off so well that by 1575 his son was the richest man in Brazil, collecting large amounts in quitrents (rents paid in lieu of feudal services) from the fifty sugar mills of the province and himself exporting more than fifty shiploads of sugar a year.

By the mid-sixteenth century, sugar had replaced brazilwood as the foundation of the Brazilian economy. Favored by its soil and climate, the northeast (the provinces of Pernambuco and Bahia) became the seat of a sugar cane civilization characterized by three features: the *fazenda* (large estate), monoculture, and slave labor. There soon arose a class of large landholders whose extensive plantations and wealth marked them off from their less affluent neighbors. Only the largest planters could afford to erect the *engenhos* (mills) needed to process the sugar before export. Small farmers had to bring their sugar to the millowner for grinding, paying one-fourth to

ATLANTIC OCEAN

GRÃO PARÁ

Negro R.

Solimões R.

Amazonas R.

Ilha
Marajó

Belem

São Luis
Maranhão

MARANHÃO

Xingu R.

Araguaia R.

PIAUÍ

Fortaleza

CEARÁ

RIO
GRANDE DO
NORTE

Natal

PARAÍBA

PERNAMBUCO

Olinda

Recife

ALAGOAS

SERGIPE

São Francisco R.

BAHIA

Salvador

MATO GROSSO

Cuiabá R.

GOIÁS

Santa Cruz

Pôrto Seguro

MINAS GERAIS

Vila Rica do
Ouro Preto

ESPÍRITO SANTO

Paraguay R.

Paraná R.

Tietê R.

SÃO PAULO

RIO DE JANEIRO

São Paulo

São Vicente

Santos

Rio de Janeiro

PARANÁ

Paraná R.

Uruguay R.

SANTA CATARINA

Ilha Santa Catarina

Treaty boundary 1777

RIO GRANDE DO SUL

Colônia do Sacramento

0   600 miles

0   600 kilometers

COLONIAL BRAZIL

one-third of the harvest for the privilege. Since Europe's apparently insatiable demand for sugar yielded quick and large profits, planters had no incentive to diversify crops, and food agriculture was essentially limited to small farms. Technical backwardness characterized all agricultural processes. The slash-and-burn system of clearing the land for cultivation, copied from the Indians, depleted the soil, forcing planters to leave the land idle for longer and longer periods, until finally exhaustion was complete. The same backwardness was apparent in the operation of the sugar mills, which continued in Brazil to be driven chiefly by oxen long after West Indian planters had adopted waterpower, which almost doubled the output.

Portugal's Indian Policy

The problem of labor was first met by raids on Indian villages, the raiders returning with trains of captives who were sold to planters and other employers of labor. These aggressions were the primary cause of the chronic warfare between the Indians and the Portuguese. But Indian labor was unsatisfactory from an economic point of view, since the natives, lacking any tradition of organized work of the kind required by plantation agriculture, worked poorly and offered many forms of resistance, ranging from attempts at escape to suicide.

As a result, after 1550 planters turned increasingly to the use of Negro slave labor imported from Africa. But the supply of Negro slaves was often cut off or sharply reduced by the activity of Dutch pirates and other foreign foes, and Brazilian slave hunters continued to find a market for their wares throughout the colonial period. The most celebrated slave hunters were the *bandeirantes* (from the word *bandeira* meaning "banner" or "military company") from the upland settlement of São Paulo. Unable to compete in sugar production with the more favorably situated plantation areas of the northeast, these men, who were themselves part Indian in most cases, made slave raiding in the interior their principal occupation. The eternal hope of finding gold or silver in the mysterious interior gave added incentive to their expeditions. As the Indians near the coast dwindled in numbers or fled before the invaders, the bandeirantes pushed ever deeper south and west, expanding the frontiers of Brazil in the process.

The Brazilian Indian did not accept the loss of land and liberty without a struggle, but his resistance was handicapped by the fatal tendency of tribes to war against each other, a situation that the Portuguese utilized for their own advantage. Forced to retreat into the interior by the superior arms and organization of the whites, the natives often returned to make destructive forays on isolated Portuguese communities. As late as the first part of the nineteenth century, stretches of the Brazilian shore were made uninhabitable by the raids of Indians who lurked in the forests and mountains back of the coast.

But the unequal struggle at last ended here, as in the Spanish colonies, in the total defeat of the natives. Overwork, loss of the will to live, and the ravages of European diseases to which the Indians had no acquired immunity caused very heavy loss of life among the enslaved Indians. Punitive expeditions against tribes that resisted enslavement or gave some other pretext for sanctions also caused depopulation. The Jesuit father Antônio Vieira, whose denunciations of Portuguese cruelty recall the accusations of Las Casas, claimed that Portuguese mistreatment of Indians had caused the loss of more than 2 million lives in Amazonia in forty years. A distinguished English historian, Charles R. Boxer, considers this claim exaggerated but concedes that the Portuguese "often exterminated whole tribes in a singularly barbarous way."[1]

[1] Charles R. Boxer, *The Golden Age of Brazil, 1695–1750* (Berkeley: University of California Press, 1962), p. 278.

This scene of cannibalism among Brazilian Indians
is from *Les Singularitez de la France Antarctique* by
André Thevet, Paris, 1558. (The British Library,
London)

Almost the only voices raised in protest against
the enslavement and mistreatment of Indians
were those of the Jesuit missionaries. The first
fathers, led by Manoel da Nóbrega, came in
1549 with the captain general Tomé de Sousa.
Four years later, another celebrated missionary,
José de Anchieta, arrived in Brazil. Far to the
south, on the plains of Piratininga, Nóbrega
and Anchieta established a colegio or school
for Portuguese, mixed-blood, and Indian children that became a model institution of its kind.
Around this settlement gradually arose the town
of São Paulo, an important point of departure

into the interior for "adventurers in search of
gold and missionaries in search of souls."

The Jesuits followed a program for the settlement of their Indian converts in *aldeias* (villages) where they lived under the care of the
priests, completely segregated from the harmful
influence of the white colonists. This program
provoked many clashes with the slave hunters
and the planters, who had very different ends
in view. In an angry protest to the *Mesa da
Consciência*, a royal council entrusted with responsibility for the religious affairs of the colony,
the planters sought to turn the tables on the

Jesuits by claiming that the Indians in the Jesuit villages were "true slaves, who labored as such not only in the colegios but on the so-called Indian lands, which in the end became the estates and sugar mills of the Jesuit fathers."

The clash of interests between the planters and slave hunters, on the one hand, and the Jesuit missionaries, on the other, reached a climax about the middle of the seventeenth century, an era of great activity on the part of the bandeirantes of São Paulo. In various parts of Brazil, the landowners rose in revolt, expelled the Jesuits, and defied royal edicts proclaiming the freedom of the Indians. In 1653 the Jesuit Antônio Vieira, a priest of extraordinary oratorical and literary powers, arrived in Brazil with full authority from the king to settle the Indian question as he saw fit. During Lent Vieira preached a famous sermon to the people of Maranhão, in which he denounced Indian slavery in terms comparable to those used by Father Montesinos on Santo Domingo in 1511. The force of Vieira's tremendous blast was somewhat weakened by his suggestion that Indian slavery should be continued under certain conditions and by the well-known fact that the society itself had both Indian and Negro slaves. Yet there can be no doubt that the condition of the Indians in the Jesuit mission villages was superior to that of the Indian slaves in the Portuguese towns and plantations. A stronger argument against Jesuit practices is the fact that the system of segregation, however benevolent in intent, represented an arbitrary and mechanical imposition of alien cultural patterns on the Indian population and that it hindered rather than facilitated true social integration of the Indian.

The Crown, generally sympathetic to the Jesuit position but under strong pressure from the planter class, pursued for two centuries a policy of compromise that satisfied neither Jesuits nor planters. A decisive turn came during the reform ministry of the marquis de Pombal (1750–1777),

who expelled the Jesuits from Portugal and Brazil and secularized their missions. His legislation, forbidding Indian raids and enslavement, accepted the Jesuit thesis of Indian freedom; he also accepted the need for preparing the natives for civilized life and even the principle of concentrating the Indians in communities under the care of administrators responsible for their education and welfare. But his policy did not segregate the Indians from the Portuguese community; it made them available for use as paid workers by the colonists and actually encouraged contact and mingling between the two races, including interracial marriage. In the meantime, the growth of the African slave trade, also encouraged by Pombal, diminished the demand for Indian labor and thus brought a greater measure of peace to the Indians. Whether Pombal's reform legislation significantly improved the material condition of the Indian population is doubtful, but it contributed to the absorption of the Indians into the colonial population and ultimately into the Brazilian nation. The decisive factor here was race mixture, which increased as a result of the passing of the Jesuit temporal power.

The French and Dutch Challenges

The dyewood, the sugar, and the tobacco of Brazil early attracted the attention of foreign powers. The French were the first to challenge Portuguese control of the colony. With the aid of Indian allies, they made sporadic efforts to entrench themselves on the coast, and in 1555 founded Rio de Janeiro as the capital of what they called Antarctic France. One cultural by-product of French contact with the Indians was the creation of a French image of the Brazilian Indian as a "noble savage," immortalized by the sixteenth-century French philosopher Montaigne in his essay "On Cannibals." But the French offensive in Brazil was weakened by Catholic-Huguenot strife at home, and in 1567 the Portuguese commander Mem de Sá ousted the French and occupied the settlement of Rio de Janeiro.

A more serious threat to Portuguese sovereignty over Brazil was posed by the Dutch, whose West India Company seized and occupied for a quarter of a century (1630–1654) the richest sugar-growing portions of the Brazilian coast. Under the administration of Prince Maurice of Nassau (1637–1644), Dutch Brazil, with its capital at Recife, became the site of brilliant scientific and artistic activity. The Portuguese struggle against the Dutch became an incipient struggle for independence, uniting elements of all races from various parts of Brazil. These motley forces won victories over the Dutch at the first and second battles of Guararapes (1648–1649). Weakened by tenacious Brazilian resistance and a simultaneous war with England, the Dutch withdrew from Pernambuco in 1654. But they took with them the lessons they had learned in the production of sugar and tobacco, and their capital, and transferred both to the West Indies. Soon the more efficient plantations and refineries of Barbados and other Caribbean islands gave serious competition to Brazilian sugar in the world market, with a resulting fall of prices. By the last decade of the seventeenth century, the Brazilian sugar industry had entered a long period of stagnation.

The Mineral Cycle, the Cattle Industry, and the Commercial System

In this time of gloom, news of the discovery of gold in the southwestern region later known as Minas Gerais reached the coast in 1695. This discovery opened a new economic cycle, led to the first effective settlement of the interior, and initiated a major shift in Brazil's center of economic and political gravity from north to south. Large numbers of colonists from Bahia, Pernambuco, and Rio de Janeiro, accompanied by their slaves and servants, swarmed into the mining area. Their exodus from the older regions caused an acute shortage of field hands that continued until the gold boom had run its course by the middle of the eighteenth century. The Crown tried to stem the exodus by legislation and by policing the trails that led to the mining area, but its efforts were in vain. For two decades (1700–1720), it had no success in asserting royal authority and collecting the royal fifth in the gold fields. Violence between rival groups, especially pioneers from São Paulo and European-born newcomers, reached the scale of civil war in 1708. The mutual weakening of the two sides as a result of these struggles finally enabled the Crown to restore order.

In 1710 a new captaincy of "São Paulo and the Mines of Gold" was established; in 1720 it was divided into "São Paulo" and "Minas Gerais." In 1729, wild excitement was caused by the discovery that certain stones found in the area, hitherto thought to be crystals, were in reality diamonds; many adventurers with their slaves turned from gold to diamond washing. The great increase in the supply of diamonds to Europe upset the market, causing a serious fall in price. As a result, the Portuguese government instituted a regime of drastic control over the *Diamantina* (Diamond District) to limit mining and prevent smuggling and thus maintain prices; this regime effectively isolated the district from the outside world.

Like its predecessor, the mineral cycle was marked by rapid and superficial exploitation of the new sources of wealth, followed by an equally swift decline. By 1750 the river gold washings of Minas Gerais were nearly exhausted. The Diamond District also suffered a progressive exhaustion of deposits. By 1809 the English traveler John Mawe could describe the gold-mining center of Villa Rica as a town that "scarcely retains a shadow of its former splendor."

Yet the mineral cycle left a permanent mark on the Brazilian landscape in the form of new centers of settlement in the southwest, not only in Minas Gerais but in the future provinces of Goias and Matto Grosso, Brazil's Far West, which was penetrated by pioneers in search of gold. If the mining camps became deserted, the new towns survived, although with diminished vitality. The decline of the mining industry also spurred efforts to promote the agricultural and pastoral wealth of the region. The shift of the center of economic and political gravity southward from Pernambuco and Bahia to Minas Gerais and Rio de Janeiro was formally recognized in 1763, when Rio de Janeiro became the seat of the viceregal capital.

As the provinces of Minas Gerais and Goias sank into decay, the northeast experienced a partial revival based on increasing European demand for sugar, cotton, and other semitropical products. Between 1750 and 1800, Brazilian cotton production made significant progress but then declined as rapidly as a result of competition from the more efficient cotton growers of the United States. The beginnings of the coffee industry, future giant of the Brazilian economy, also date from the late colonial period.

Cattle raising also made its contribution to the advance of the Brazilian frontier and the growing importance of the south. The intensive agriculture of the coast and the concentration of population in coastal cities like Bahia and Pernambuco created a demand for fresh meat that gave an initial impulse to cattle raising. Since the expanison of plantation agriculture in the coastal zone did not leave enough land for grazing, the cattle industry inevitably had to move inland.

By the second half of the seventeenth century, the penetration of the distant São Francisco Valley from Bahia and Pernambuco was well under way. Powerful cattlemen, with their herds of cattle, their cowboys (*vaqueiros*), and their slaves, entered the *sertão* (backcountry), drove out the Indians, and established fortified ranches and villages for their retainers. Such occupation

was legitimized before or after the fact by the official grant of a huge tract of land, a virtual feudal domain, to the cattle baron in question, whose word became law on his estate. The landowner's cattle provided meat for the coastal cities and mining camps, draft animals for the plantations, and hides for export to Europe.

The cattle industry later expanded into the extreme southern region of Rio Grande do Sul, which was colonized by the government in the interests of defense against Spanish expansionist designs. Here too vast land grants were made. The counterpart of the vaqueiro in the south was the *gaúcho*. Like the vaqueiro, the gaúcho was an expert horseman, but he reflected the blend of cultures in the Río de la Plata in his speech, a mixture of Portuguese, Spanish, and Indian dialects; in his dress, the loose, baggy trousers of the Argentine cowboy; and in his chief implement, the *bolas*, balls of stone attached to a rawhide rope, a loan from the pampas Indians, which was used for entangling and bringing down animals.

Portugal, like Spain (with which she was united during the so-called Babylonian Captivity, 1580–1640), pursued a mercantilist commercial policy, though not as consistently or rigorously. During the period of Spanish domination, the commerce of Brazil was firmly restricted to Portuguese nationals and ships. The Dutch, who had been the principal carriers of Brazilian sugar and tobacco to European markets, responded with extensive smuggling and a direct attack on the richest sugar-growing area of Brazil.

Following the successful Portuguese revolt against Spain, a most favorable trade treaty was made with England, Portugal's protector and ally. By this treaty, British merchants were permitted to trade between Portuguese and Brazilian ports. But English ships frequently neglected the formality of touching at Lisbon and plied a direct contraband trade with the colony. Since Portuguese industry was incapable of supplying the colonists with the required quantity and

quality of manufactured goods, a large proportion of the outward-bound cargoes consisted
of foreign textiles and other products, of which
England provided the lion's share. Thus, Portugal, mistress of Brazil, itself became a colony
of Dutch and English merchants with offices
in Lisbon.

In the eighteenth century, during the reign
of Dom José I (1750–1777), his able prime minister, the marquis de Pombal, launched an administrative and economic reform of the Portuguese Empire that bears comparison with the
Bourbon reforms in Spain and Spanish America
that were taking place at the same time. Pombal's
design was to nationalize Portuguese-Brazilian
trade by creating a Portuguese merchant class
with enough capital to compete with British
merchants and a national industry whose production could dislodge English goods from the
Brazilian market. The program required an active
state intervention in the imperial economy
through the creation of a Board of Trade, which
subsidized merchant-financiers with lucrative
concessions in Portugal and Brazil; the formation
of companies that were granted monopolies over
trade with particular regions of Brazil and were
expected to develop the economies of those
regions; and the institution of a policy of import
substitution through state assistance to old and
new industries. Despite mistakes, failures, and
a partial retreat from Pombal's program after
he was forced out of office in 1777, the Pombaline
reform achieved at least partial success in its
effort to reconquer Brazilian markets for Portugal. Between 1796 and 1802, 30 percent of all
the goods shipped to Brazil consisted of Portuguese manufactures, especially cotton cloth.
But the flight of the Portuguese royal family
from Lisbon to Brazil in 1808 as a result of
Napoleon's invasion of Portugal, followed two
years later by the signing of a treaty with England
that gave the British all the trade privileges they
requested, effectively "dismantled the protective
edifice so painfully put together since 1750."

Britain once again enjoyed a virtual monopoly
of trade with Brazil.

GOVERNMENT AND CHURCH

The donatory system of government first established in Brazil by the Portuguese crown
soon proved unsatisfactory. There was a glaring
contradiction between the vast powers granted
to the donatories and the authority of the monarch; moreover, few donatories were able to
cope with the tasks of defense and colonization
for which they had been made responsible. The
result was a governmental reform. In 1549, Tomé
de Sousa was sent out as governor general to
head a central colonial administration for Brazil.
Bahia, situated about midway between the
flourishing settlements of Pernambuco and São
Vicente, became his capital. Gradually, the hereditary rights and privileges of the donatories
were revoked, as they were replaced by governors appointed by the king. As the colony
expanded, new captaincies were created. In 1763,
as previously noted, the governor of Rio de
Janeiro replaced his colleague at Bahia as head
of the colonial administration, with the title of
viceroy. In practice, however, his authority over
the other governors was negligible.

The Administrators and Their Deficiencies

The government of Portuguese Brazil broadly
resembled that of the Spanish colonies in its
spirit, structure, and vices. One notable difference, however, was the much smaller scale
of the Portuguese administration. The differing
economies of the two empires help to explain
this divergence. The Spanish Indies had a relatively diversified economy that served local
and regional, as well as overseas, markets and
a large Indian population that was an important
source of labor and royal tribute. Combined
with a Spanish population that numbered
300,000 in 1600 (when only 30,000 Portuguese

lived in Brazil), these conditions created an economic base for the rise of hundreds of towns and the need for a numerous officialdom charged with the regulation of Indian labor, the collection of Indian tribute, and many other fiscal and administrative duties. In Portuguese America, on the other hand, the establishment of an elaborate bureaucracy was rendered unnecessary by several factors: the overwhelming importance of exports, especially of sugar, which could be taxed when it was unloaded in Lisbon; the economic and social dominance of the plantation, which made for a weak development of urban life; and the minor role of the Indian population as a source of labor and royal revenue.

During the "Babylonian Captivity," the colonial policies of Spain and Portugal were aligned by the creation in 1604 of the *Conselho de India*, whose functions resembled those of the Spanish Council of the Indies. In 1736, the functions of the conselho were assumed by a newly created ministry of *Marinha e Ultramar* (Marine and Overseas). Under the king, this body framed laws for Brazil, appointed governors, and supervised their conduct. The governor, captain general, or viceroy combined in himself military, administrative, and even some judicial duties. His power tended to be absolute but was tempered by certain factors: the constant intervention of the home government, which bound him with precise, strict, and detailed instructions; the counter-weights of other authorities, especially the *relações* (high courts), which were both administrative and judicial bodies; and the existence of special administrative organs, such as the intendancies created in the gold and diamond districts, which were completely independent of the governor. Thus in Brazil, as in the Spanish colonies, there functioned a system of checks and balances that reflected above all the distrust felt by the home government for its agents. Other factors that tended to diminish the authority of the governor were the vastness of the country, the scattered population,

the lack of social stability, and the existence of enormous landholdings in which the feudal power of the great planters and cattle barons was virtually unchallenged.

The most important institution of local government was the *Senado de Câmara* (municipal council). The influence of this body varied with the size of the city. Whether elected by a restricted property-owning electorate or chosen by the Crown, its membership represented the ruling class of merchants, planters, and professional men. Elections were often marked by struggles for control by rival factions, planters and Creoles on one side, merchants and peninsulars on the other. The authority of the câmara extended over its entire *comarca* (district), which often was very large. But its power was limited by the frequent intervention of the *ouvidor* (royal judge), who usually combined his judicial functions with the administrative duties of *corregedor*. Generally speaking, the greater the size and wealth of the city, and the farther it was from the viceregal capital, the greater its powers.

Both the Crown and the municipal councils levied numerous taxes, whose collection was usually farmed out to private collectors. In return for making a fixed payment to the treasury, these men collected the taxes for the Crown and could keep the surplus once the set quota had been met. The system, of course, encouraged fraud and extortion of every kind. Another crippling burden on the population was tithes, which came to 10 percent of the total product, originally payable in kind but later only in cash. Tithes, writes the Brazilian historian Caio Prado Júnior, "ran neck and neck with conscription as one of the great scourges inflicted on the population by the colonial administration."[2]

The besetting vices of Spanish colonial administration—inefficiency, bureaucratic atti-

---

[2] Caio Prado Júnior, *The Colonial Background of Modern Brazil* (Berkeley: University of California Press, 1967), p. 377.

tudes, slowness, and corruption—were equally prominent in the Portuguese colonial system. Justice was not only costly but incredibly slow and complicated. Cases brought before lower courts ascended the ladder of the higher tribunals: ouvidor, relação, and on up to the Crown Board of Appeals, taking as long as ten to fifteen years for resolution.

Over vast areas of the colony, however, administration and courts were virtually non-existent. Away from the few large towns, local government often meant the rule of great landowners, who joined to their personal influence the authority of office, for it was from their ranks that the royal governors invariably appointed the capitães móres (district militia officers). Armed with unlimited power to enlist, command, arrest, and punish, the capitão mor became a popular symbol of despotism and oppression. Sometimes these men used the local militia as feudal levies for war against a rival family; boundary questions and questions of honor were often settled by duels or pitched battles between retainers of rival clans. The feudalism that still dominates much of the Brazilian backcountry may be traced back to these colonial origins.

Corruption pervaded the administrative apparatus from top to bottom. The miserably paid officials prostituted their trusts in innumerable ways: Embezzlement, graft, and bribery were well-nigh universal. The Jesuit Antônio Vieira referred to this universal corruption when he conjugated the verb rapio (I steal) in all its inflections in his sermon on the "Good Thief."

Some improvement, at least on the higher levels of administration, took place under the auspices of the extremely able and energetic marquis de Pombal. The same tendency toward centralization that characterized Bourbon colonial policy appeared in Portuguese policy in this period. Pombal abolished the remaining hereditary captaincies, restricted the special privileges of the municipalities, and increased the

power of the viceroy. In a mercantilist spirit, he sought to promote the economic advance of Brazil with a view to promoting the reconstruction of Portugal, whose condition was truly forlorn.

Typical of the enlightened viceroys of the Pombaline period was the marquis de Lavradio (1769–1779), whose achievements included the transfer of coffee from Pará into São Paulo, in whose fertile red soil it was to flourish mightily. How little changed, however, the administration of Brazil was by the Pombaline reform is suggested by Lavradio's letter of instructions to his successor, in which he gloomily observed that

> as the salaries of these magistrates [the judges] are small . . . they seek to multiply their emoluments by litigation and discord, which they foment, and not only keep the people unquiet, but put them to heavy expenses, and divert them from their occupations, with the end of promoting their own vile interest and that of their subalterns, who are the principal concocters of these disorders.

During the twelve years that he had governed in Brazil, wrote the viceroy, he had never found one useful establishment instituted by any of these magistrates.[3]

The Church and the State

In Brazil, as in the Spanish colonies, church and state were intimately united. By comparison with the Spanish monarchs, however, the Portuguese kings seemed almost niggardly in their dealings with the church. But their control over its affairs, exercised through the padroado—the ecclesiastical patronage granted by the pope to the Portuguese king in his realm and overseas

[3] E. Bradford Burns, ed., A Documentary History of Brazil (New York: Alfred A. Knopf, 1966), p. 144.

possessions—was as absolute. The king exercised his power through a special board, the *Mesa da Consciência e Ordens* (Board of Conscience and Orders). Rome, however, long maintained a strong indirect influence through the agency of the Jesuits, who were very influential in the Portuguese court until they were expelled from Portugal and Brazil in 1759.

With some honorable exceptions, notably that of the entire Jesuit order, the tone of clerical morality and conduct in Brazil was deplorably low. The clergy were often criticized for their extortionate fees and for the negligence they displayed in the performance of their spiritual duties. Occasionally, priests combined those duties with more mundane activities. Many were planters; others carried on a variety of businesses. One high-ranking Crown official summed up his impressions of the clergy in the statement "All they want is money, and they care not a jot for their good name."

Yet the church and the clergy made their own contributions to the life of colonial Brazil. The clergy provided such educational and humanitarian establishments as existed in the colony. From its ranks—which were open to talent and even admitted individuals of mixed blood despite the formal requirement of a special dispensation—came most of the few distinguished names in Brazilian colonial science, learning, and literature. Among them, Jesuit writers again occupy a prominent place. We must mention Manoel da Nóbrega and José de Anchieta for their lucid, informative letters and their studies of the Tupi Indian language; Antônio Vieira for his powerful sermons; Fernão Cardim for his *Treatise on the Land and People of Brazil*, first published in 1925; and the important *Culture and Opulence of Brazil* (1711) by the author who signed himself André João Antonil (João Antônio Andreoni). The chronicler and planter Gabriel Soares de Sousa contributed a detailed account of Brazilian geography, Indians, and natural resources in his *A Description of Brazil* (1587);

and in the late colonial period José da Rocha Pitta published the first history of Brazil, *History of Portuguese America* (1730). But the cultural poverty of colonial Brazil is suggested by the fact that throughout the colonial period there was not a single university or even a printing press.

MASTERS AND SLAVES

Race mixture played a decisive role in the formation of the Brazilian people. The scarcity of white women in the colony, the freedom of the Portuguese from puritanical attitudes, and the despotic power of the great planters over their Indian and Negro slave women all gave impetus to miscegenation. Of the three possible race combinations—white-Negro, white-Indian, Negro-Indian—the first was the most common. The immense majority of these unions were outside wedlock. In 1755 the marquis de Pombal, pursuing the goals of population growth and strengthening of Brazil's borders, issued an order encouraging marriages between Portuguese and Indians and proclaiming the descendants of such union eligible to positions of honor and dignity, but this favor was not extended to Negro-white unions.

Color, Class, and Slavery

In principle, color lines were strictly drawn. A "pure" white wife or husband, for example, was indispensable to a member of the upper class. But the enormous number of mixed unions outside wedlock and the resulting large progeny, some of whom, at least, were regarded with affection by white fathers and provided with some education and property, inevitably led to some blurring of color lines and a fairly frequent phenomenon of "passing." There was a tendency to classify individuals racially, if their color was not too dark, on the basis of social and

Working conditions in Brazil were so harsh that the average slave endured for only seven years after arriving from Africa. (The Bettmann Archive, Inc.)

economic position rather than on their physical appearance. The English traveler Henry Koster alludes to this "polite fiction" in his anecdote concerning a certain great personage, a capitão mor, whom Koster suspected of being a mulatto. In response to his question, his servant replied, "He was, but is not now." Asked to explain, the servant continued, "Can a capitão mor be a mulatto man?"

Slavery played as important a role in the social organization of Brazil as race mixture did in its ethnic make-up. The social consequences of the system were entirely negative. Slavery corrupted both master and slave, fostered harmful attitudes with respect to the dignity of labor, and distorted the economic development of Brazil. The tendency to identify labor with slavery sharply limited the number of socially acceptable occupations in which whites or free mixed-bloods

could engage. This gave rise to a populous class of vagrants, beggars, "poor whites," and other degraded or disorderly elements who would not or could not compete with slaves in agriculture and industry. Inevitably, given the almost total absence of incentive to work on the part of the slave, the level of efficiency and productivity of his or her labor was very low.

Much historical writing has fostered the idea that Brazilian slavery was mild by comparison with slavery in other colonies. In part, this tradition owes its popularity to the writings of the Brazilian sociologist Gilberto Freyre, who emphasized the patriarchal relations existing between masters and slaves in the sugar plantation society of the northeast. But the slaves described by Freyre were usually house slaves who occupied a privileged position. Their situation was very different from that of the great majority of slaves, who worked on the sugar and tobacco plantations of Bahia and Pernambuco. During harvest time and when the mills were grinding the cane, says Charles Boxer, the slaves sometimes worked round the clock and often at least from dawn to dusk. In the off season, the hours were not so long. But "discipline was maintained with a severity that often degenerated into sadistic cruelty where the infliction of corporal punishment was concerned." A royal dispatch of 1700 denounced the barbarity with which owners of both sexes treated their slaves and singled out for special condemnation the practice of lady owners who forced their women slaves to engage in prostitution.[4]

Obviously, the treatment of slaves varied considerably with the temperament of the individual slave owner. Although the Crown provided slaves with legal means of redress, there is little evidence that these were effective in relieving their plight. The church, represented on the plantation by a chaplain paid and housed

[4] Boxer, *The Golden Age of Brazil*, pp. 8, 173.

by the landowner, probably exerted little influence on the problem. A very low rate of reproduction among slaves and frequent suicides speak volumes concerning their condition. Many slaves ran away and formed *quilombos* (settlements of fugitive slaves in the bush). The most famous of these was the so-called republic of Palmares, founded in 1603 in the interior of the northeastern captaincy of Alagoas. A self-sufficient African kingdom with several thousand inhabitants who lived in ten villages spread over a 90-mile territory, Palmares was exceptional among quilombos in its size, complex organization, and ability to survive repeated expeditions sent against it by colonial authorities. Not until 1694 did a Paulista army destory it after a two-year siege. But the quilombos continued to alarm planters and authorities; as late as 1760 they complained of the threat posed by quilombos around Bahia.

Slavery played a decisive role in the economic life of colonial Brazil and placed its stamp on all social relations. In addition to masters and slaves, however, there existed a large free peasant population of varied racial make-up who lived on estates and in villages and hamlets scattered throughout the Brazilian countryside. Some were small landowners, often possessing a few slaves of their own, who brought their sugar cane for processing or sale to the *senhor de engenho* (sugar-mill owner). Their economic inferiority made their independence precarious, and their land and slaves tended to pass into the hands of the great planters in a process of concentration of landownership and growing social stratification. The majority, however, were tenant farmers or sharecroppers (*lavradores, moradores, foreiros*), who owed labor and allegiance to a great landowner in return for the privilege of farming a parcel of land. Other free peasants were squatters who in the seventeenth and eighteenth centuries pushed out of the coastal zone to settle in the backcountry and were regarded as intruders by the cattle barons

and other great landowners who laid claim to to those lands.

Other free commoners were the artisans, including many black or mulatto freedmen, who served the needs of the urban population. An important group of salaried workers—overseers, mechanics, coopers, and the like—supplied the special skills required by the sugar industry.

Large Estates and Colonial Towns

The nucleus of Brazilian social as well as economic organization was the large estate, or fazenda, which usually rested on a base of Negro slavery. The large estate centered about the *Casa Grande* (Big House) and constituted a patriarchal community that included the owner and his family, his chaplain and overseers, his slaves, his sharecroppers (known as *obrigados*), and his *agregados* (retainers)—freemen of low social status who received the landowner's protection and assistance in return for a variety of services.

In this self-contained world, an intricate web of relations arose between the master and his slaves and white or mixed-blood subordinates. No doubt, long contact sometimes tended to mellow and humanize these relationships and added to mere commercial relationship of a variety of emotional ties. The protective role of the master found expression in the relationship of *compadrio* (godfathership), in which the master became sponsor or godfather of a baptized child or a bridal pair whose marriage he witnessed. The system implied relations of mutual aid and a paternalistic interest in the welfare of the landowner's people. But it by no means excluded intense exploitation of those people or the display of the most ferocious cruelty if they should cross him or dispute his absolute power.

In the sugar-growing northeast the great planters became a distinct aristocratic class, possessed of family traditions and pride in their name and blood. In the cattle-raising regions of the sertão and the south, the small number of slaves, the self-reliant character of the vaqueiro or gaúcho, and the greater freedom of movement of workers gave society a somewhat more democratic tone. Everywhere, however, says the Brazilian historian Caio Prado Júnior, "the existence of pronounced social distinctions and the absolute and patriarchal domination of the owner and master were elements invariably associated with all the colony's large landed estates."[5]

By contrast with the decisive importance of the fazenda, most colonial towns were mere appendages of the countryside, dominated politically and socially by the rural magnates. Even in the few large cities like Bahia and Rio de Janeiro, the dominant social group was composed of *fazendeiros* and sugar-mill owners. These men often left the supervision of their estates to majordomos and overseers, preferring the pleasures and bustle of the cities to the dreary routines of the countryside. But in the city lived other social groups that disputed or shared power with the great landowners: high officials of the colonial administration; dignitaries of the church; wealthy professional men, especially lawyers; and the large merchants, almost exclusively Peninsulars, who monopolized the export-import trade and financed the industry of the planters.

The social position of the merchant was not very high, because of the medieval prejudice against commerce brought over from Portugal (a prejudice that did not prevent the highest officials from engaging in trade, albeit discreetly), but nothing barred the merchants from membership on the municipal councils. The conflict

between native-born landowners and European-born merchants, aggravated by nationalistic resentment against upstart immigrants, sometimes broke out into armed struggle. An illustration is the petty War of the Mascates (1710–1711) between Olinda, provincial capital of Pernambuco, which was dominated by the sugar planters, and its neighboring seaport of Recife, which was controlled by the merchants.

This struggle between *mazombos* (Brazilian-born whites) and *reinóis* (Peninsulars) foreshadowed the later rise of a broader Brazilian nationalism and the first projects of Brazilian independence. In the late eighteenth century, Minas Gerais, the most urbanized Brazilian region, had the most diversified economy. It became a seat of much unrest as a result of official efforts to reinforce the area's dependency on Portuguese exporters, collect large amounts of delinquent taxes, and impose a new head tax. A conspiracy to revolt and establish a republic on the American model was hatched in 1788–1789 by a group of dissidents, most of whom were highly placed members of the colonial elite. The only leading conspirator who was not a member of the aristocracy was José da Silva Xavier, a military officer of low rank who practiced the part-time profession of "Toothpuller," whence the name of *Tiradentes* by which he is known in Brazilian history. An enthusiast for the American Revolution, Silva Xavier apparently possessed copies of the Declaration of Independence and American state constitutions. When the conspiracy was discovered, all the principal conspirators were condemned to death, but the sentences were commuted to exile for all but the plebeian Silva Xavier. His barbarous execution, which he faced with great courage, made him a martyr as well as a precursor of Brazilian independence.

[5] Prado, *The Colonial Background of Modern Brazil*, p. 339.

CHAPTER EIGHT

The Independence of Latin America

The Bourbon reforms, combined with the up-surge of the European economy in the eighteenth century, brought material prosperity and less tangible benefits to many upper-class Creoles of Spanish America. Enlightened viceroys and intendants introduced improvements and re-finements that made life in the colonial city more healthful and attractive. Educational re-forms, the influx of new books and ideas, and increased opportunities to travel and study in Europe widened the intellectual horizons of Creole youth.

These gains, however, did not strengthen Creole feelings of loyalty to the mother country. Instead, they enlarged their aspirations and sharpened their sense of grievance. The growing wealth of some sections of the Creole elite made more galling its virtual exclusion from important posts in administration and the church. Mean-while, the swelling production of Creole ha-ciendas, plantations, and ranches pressed against the trade barriers maintained by Spanish

t of Caracas, José
Majesty does not
freedom of trade
cannot count on
e, Bourbon policy
ers the protection
competition from

in ill-paid Indian curacies and minor government jobs, bitterly resented the institutionalized discrimination that barred their way to advancement.

As a result, although some wealthy and powerful Creoles maintained excellent relations with the Peninsular establishment, Creoles and Peninsulars tended to become mutually hostile castes. The Peninsulars sometimes justified their privileged position by charging the Creoles with innate indolence and incapacity, qualities that some Spanish writers, following the Comte Georges de Buffon and Cornelius de Pauw, attributed to the noxious effects of the American climate and soil; the Creoles retorted by describing the Europeans as mean and grasping parvenus. So intense was the hatred between many members of these groups that a Spanish bishop in New Spain, Joseph Joaquín Granados, protested against the feeling of some young Creoles that "if they could empty their veins of the Spanish part of their blood, they would gladly do so." This cleavage inevitably fostered the growth of Creole nationalism; Humboldt, who traveled in Spanish America in the twilight years of the colony, reports a common saying: "I am not a Spaniard, I am an American."

The entrance of Enlightenment ideas into Latin America certainly contributed to the growth of Creole discontent, but the relative weight of various influences is uncertain. Bourbon Spain itself contributed to the Creole awakening by the many-sided effort of reforming officials to improve the quality of colonial life. Typical of this group was the intendant Juan Antonio Riaño, who introduced to the Mexican city of Guanajuato, the capital of his province, a taste for the French language and literature; he was also responsible "for the development of interest in drawing and music, and for the cultivation of mathematics, physics, and chemistry in the school that had been formerly maintained by the Jesuits."[1]

NCE

lar Spaniards

n Spain and its
xpressed in the
d the peninsular
stantly renewed
rds. In the late
migrant was a
ifty Basque or
entice to a Pen-
e. In the course
nition, the im-
r of the house
ed to the own-
he merchant's

ow... Creole sons would be given a landed estate—often a bottomless well in which mercantile and mining profits disappeared; other sons would enter the church or the law, both overcrowded professions.

Peninsular Spaniards thus continued to dominate the lucrative export-import trade and provincial trade. Spanish-born merchants, organized in powerful consulados, or merchant guilds, also played a key role in financing mining and the repartimiento business carried on among the Indians by Spanish officials. Not unnaturally, some upper-class Creoles, excluded from mercantile activity and responsible posts in the government and church, developed the aristocratic manners and idle, spendthrift ways with which the Peninsulars reproached them. Many other Creoles of the middling sort, vegetating

[1] Lucas Alamán, *Historia de Mejico*, 5 vols. (Mexico, 1849–1852), 1:76.

Many educated Creoles read the forbidden writings of Raynal, Montesquieu, Voltaire, Rousseau, and other radical philosophes, but another, innocuous-seeming agency for the spread of Enlightenment ideas in Latin America consisted of scientific texts, based on the theories of Descartes, Leibnitz, and Newton, which circulated freely in the colonies. By 1800, through all these channels, the Creole elite had become familiar with the most advanced thought of contemporary Europe.

The American Revolution contributed to the growth of "dangerous ideas" in the colonies. Spain was well aware of the ideological as well as political threat the United States posed to its empire. Spain had reluctantly joined its ally France in war against England during the American Revolution, but it kept the rebels at arm's length, refused to recognize American independence, and in the peace negotiations attempted unsuccessfully to coop the United States up within the Alleghenies. After 1783, a growing number of American ships touched legally or illegally at Spanish-American ports. Together with "Yankee notions," these vessels sometimes introduced such subversive documents as the writings of Thomas Paine and Jefferson.

The French Revolution probably exerted a greater influence on the Creole mind. Recalled the Argentine revolutionary Manuel Belgrano,

Since I was in Spain in 1789, and the French Revolution was then causing a change in ideas, especially among the men of letters with whom I associated, the ideals of liberty, equality, security, and property took a firm hold on me, and I saw only tyrants in those who would restrain a man, wherever he might be, from enjoying the rights with which God and Nature had endowed him."[2]

Another cultivated Creole, the Colombian Antonio Nariño, incurred Spanish wrath in 1794

by translating and printing on his own press the French Declaration of the Rights of Man of 1789. Sentenced to prison in Africa for ten years, Nariño lived to become leader and patriarch of the independence movement in Colombia and to witness its triumph.

But the French Revolution soon took a radical turn, and the Creole aristocracy became disenchanted with it as a model. Scattered conspiracies in some Spanish colonies and Brazil owed their inspiration to the French example, but they were invariably the work of a few radicals, drawing their support almost exclusively from lower-class elements. The most important result directly attributable to the French Revolution was the slave revolt in the French part of Haiti under talented Negro and mulatto leaders: Toussaint L'Ouverture, Jean Jacques Dessalines, Henri Christophe, and Alexandre Pétion. By January 1, 1804, Toussaint's lieutenant, General Dessalines, could proclaim the independence of the new state of Haiti. Black revolutionaries had established the first liberated territory in Latin America. But their achievement dampened rather than aroused support for independence among the Creole elite of other colonies. Thus, fear that secession from Spain might touch off a slave revolt helped to keep the planter class of neighboring Cuba loyal to Spain during and after the Latin American wars of independence.

Despite the existence of small conspiratorial groups, organized in secret societies, with correspondents in Europe as well as America, the movement for independence might have long remained puny and ineffectual. As late as 1806, when the precursor of revolution, Francisco de Miranda, landed on the coast of his native Venezuela with a force of some two hundred foreign volunteers, his call for revolution evoked no response, and he had to make a hasty retreat. Creole timidity and political inexperience and the apathy of the masses might have long postponed the coming of independence if external developments had not hastened its arrival. The revolution that Miranda and other forerunners

---

[2] Richardo Levene, ed., *Los sucesos de mayo contados por sus actores* (Buenos Aires, 1928), p. 60.

could not set in motion came as a result of decisions by European powers with very different ends in view.

The Causes of Revolution

Among the causes of the revolutionary crisis that matured from 1808 to 1810, the decline of Spain under the inept Charles IV was certainly a major one. The European wars unleashed by the French Revolution glaringly revealed the failure of the Bourbon reforms to correct the structural defects in Spanish economic and social life. In 1793, Spain joined a coalition of England and other states in war against the French republic. The struggle went badly for Spain, and in 1795 the royal favorite and chief minister, Manuel de Godoy, signed the Peace of Basel. The next year, Spain became France's ally. English sea power promptly drove Spanish shipping from the Atlantic, virtually cutting off communication between Spain and her colonies. Hard necessity compelled Spain to permit neutral ships, sailing from Spanish for foreign ports, to trade with her overseas subjects. United States merchants and shipowners were the principal beneficiaries of this departure from the old, restrictive system.

Godoy's disastrous policy of war with England had other results. An English naval officer, Sir Home Popham, undertook on his own initiative to make an attack on Buenos Aires. His fleet sailed from the Cape of Good Hope for La Plata in April 1806 with a regiment of soldiers on board. In its wake followed a great number of English merchant ships eager to pour a mass of goods through a breach in the Spanish colonial system. A swift victory followed the landing of the British troops. The viceroy, the Marquis of Sobremonte, fled from the capital at the approach of the enemy. The English soldiers entered Buenos Aires, meeting only token resistance. Hoping to obtain the support of the population, the English commander issued a proclamation guaranteeing the right of private property, free trade, and freedom of religion. But the English had mistaken the temper of the *porteños,* as the inhabitants of Buenos Aires were called. Creoles and Peninsulars joined to expel their unwanted liberators. A volunteer army, secretly organized, attacked and routed the occupation troops, capturing the English general and twelve hundred of his men. To an English officer who tempted him with ideas of independence under a British protectorate, the Creole Manuel Belgrano replied: "Either our old master or none at all."

The British government, meanwhile, had sent strong reinforcements to La Plata. This second invasion force was met with a murderous hail of fire as it tried to advance through the narrow streets of Buenos Aires and was beaten back with heavy losses. Impressed by the tenacity of the defense, the British commander gave up the struggle and agreed to evacuate both Buenos Aires and the previously captured town of Montevideo. This defeat of a veteran British army by a people's militia spearheaded by the legion of *patricios* (Creoles) was a large step down the road toward Argentine independence. The Creoles of Buenos Aires, having tasted power, would not willingly relinquish it again.

In Europe, Spain's distresses now reached a climax. Napoleon, at the helm of France, gradually reduced Spain to a helpless satellite. In 1807, angered by Portugal's refusal to cooperate with his Continental System by closing her ports to English shipping, Napoleon obtained from Charles IV permission to invade Portugal through Spain. French troops swept across the peninsula; as they approached Lisbon, the Portuguese royal family and court escaped to Brazil in a fleet under British convoy. A hundred thousand French troops continued to occupy Spanish towns. Popular resentment at their presence, and at the pro-French policies of the royal favorite Godoy, broke out in stormy riots that compelled Charles IV to abdicate in favor of his son Ferdinand. Napoleon now intervened and offered his services as a mediator in the dispute between father and son. Foolishly, the trusting pair accepted Napoleon's invitation to confer with him in the French city of Bayonne. There Napoleon forced both to abdicate in favor of his brother Joseph, his candidate for the Spanish throne. Napoleon then summoned a congress of Spanish grandees, which meekly approved his dictate.

The Spanish people had yet to say their word. On May 2, 1808, an insurrection against French occupation troops began in Madrid and spread like wildfire throughout the country. The insurgents established local governing juntas in the regions under their control. Later, a central junta assumed direction of the resistance movement in the name of the captive Ferdinand VII. This junta promptly made peace with England. When the Spanish armies fought the superbly trained French troops in conventional battles in the field, they usually suffered defeat, but guerrilla warfare pinned down large French forces and made Napoleon's control of conquered territory extremely precarious.

By early 1810, however, French victory seemed inevitable, for French armies had overrun Andalusia and were threatening Cádiz, the last city in Spanish hands. The central junta now dissolved itself and appointed a regency to rule Spain; this body in turn yielded its power to a national Cortes, or parliament, which met in Cádiz from 1810 to 1814 under the protection of English naval guns. Since most of the delegates actually came from Cádiz, whose liberal, cosmopolitan atmosphere was hardly typical of Spain, their views were much more liberal than those of the Spanish people as a whole. The constitution the Cortes approved in 1812 provided for a limited monarchy, promised freedom of speech and assembly, and abolished the Inquisition. But the Cortes made few concessions to the American colonies. It invited American delegates to join its deliberations but made clear that the system of peninsular domination and commercial monopoly would remain essentially intact.

In Spanish America, Creole leaders, anticipating the imminent collapse of Spain, considered how they might turn this dramatic rush of events to their own advantage. Those events had transformed the idea of independence, until lately a remote prospect, into a realistic goal. Confident that the armies of the invincible Napoleon would crush all opposition, some Creole leaders prepared to take power into their hands with the pretext of loyalty to the "beloved Ferdinand." They could justify their action by the example of the Spanish regional juntas formed to govern in the name of the captive king. The confusion caused among Spanish officials by the coming of rival emissaries who proclaimed both Ferdinand and Joseph Bonaparte the legitimate king of Spain also played into Creole hands.

In the spring of 1810, with the fall of Cádiz apparently imminent, the Creole leaders moved into action. Charging viceroys and other royal officials with doubtful loyalty to Ferdinand, they organized popular demonstrations in Caracas, Buenos Aires, Santiago, and Bogotá that compelled those authorities to surrender control to local juntas dominated by Creoles. But Creole hopes of a peaceful transition to independence were doomed to failure. Their claims of loyalty did not deceive the groups truly loyal to Spain, and fighting soon broke out between patriots and royalists.

THE LIBERATION OF SOUTH AMERICA

The Latin American struggle for independence suggests comparison with the American Revolution. Some obvious parallels exist between the two upheavals. Both sought to throw off the rule of a mother country whose mercantilist system hindered the further development of a rapidly growing colonial economy. Both were led by well-educated elites who drew their slogans and ideas from the ideological arsenal of the Enlightenment. Both were civil wars in which large elements of the population sided with the mother country. Both owed their final success in part to foreign assistance (although the North American rebels received far more help from their French ally than came to Latin America from outside sources).

The differences between the two revolutions are no less impressive, however. Unlike the American Revolution, the Latin American struggle for independence did not have a unified direction or strategy. This lack was due not only to vast distances and other geographical obstacles to unity but to the economic and cultural isolation of the various Latin American regions from each other. Moreover, the Latin American movement for independence lacked the strong popular base provided by the more democratic and fluid society of the English colonies. The Creole elite, itself part of an exploitative white minority, feared the oppressed Indians, Negroes, and castes, and as a rule sought to keep their intervention in the struggle to a minimum. This lack of unity of regions and classes helps to explain why Latin America had to struggle so long against a power like Spain, weak and beset by many internal and external problems.

The struggle for independence had four main centers. In Spanish South America there were two principal theaters of military operations, one in the north, another in the south. One stream of liberation flowed southward from Venezuela; another ran northward from Argentina. In Peru, last Spanish bastion on the continent, these two currents joined. Brazil achieved its own swift and relatively peaceful separation from Portugal. Finally, Mexico had to travel a very difficult, devious road before gaining its independence.

Simón Bolívar, the Liberator

Simón Bolívar is the symbol and hero of the liberation struggle in northern South America. Born in Caracas, Venezuela, in 1783, he came from an aristocratic Creole family rich in land, slaves, and mines. His intellectual formation was greatly influenced by his reading of the rationalist, materialist classics of the Enlightenment. Travel in various European countries between 1803 and 1807 further widened his intellectual horizons. He returned to Caracas in the latter year and soon became involved in conspiratorial activity directed at the overthrow of the Spanish regime.

In April 1810, the Creole party in Caracas organized a demonstration that forced the abdication of the captain general. A Creole-dominated junta that pledged to defend the rights of the captive Ferdinand took power, but its assurances of loyalty deceived neither local Spaniards nor the Regency Council in Cádiz. A considerable number of wealthy Creoles of the planter class also opposed independence, and when it triumphed many emigrated to Cuba or Puerto Rico. The patriots were also divided over what policy to follow; some, like Bolívar, favored an immediate declaration of independence, while others preferred to postpone the issue.

Perhaps to get Bolívar out of the way, the junta sent him to England to solicit British aid. He had no success in this mission but convinced the veteran revolutionary Francisco de Miranda to return to Venezuela and take command of the patriot army. In 1811 a Venezuelan congress proclaimed the country's independence and framed a republican constitution that abolished Indian tribute and special privileges (fueros) but retained Negro slavery, made Catholicism the state religion, and limited the rights of full citizenship to property owners. This last provision excluded the large free *pardo* (black and mulatto) population.

Fighting had already broken out between patriots and royalists. In addition to Peninsulars, the troops sent from Puerto Rico by the Regency Council, and a section of the Creole aristocracy, the royalist cause had the support of some free blacks and mulattos, angered by the republic's

A portrait of Símon Bolívar. (Courtesy of the Organization of American States)

earthquake of March 26, 1812, which caused great loss of life and property in Caracas and other patriot territories but spared the regions under Spanish control. The royalist clergy proclaimed this disaster a divine retribution against the rebels. A series of military defeats completed the discomfiture of the revolutionary cause.

With his forces disintegrating, Miranda attempted to negotiate a treaty with the royalist commander and then tried to flee the country, taking with him part of the republic's treasury. He may have intended to continue working for independence, but the circumstances made it appear as if he wished to save his own skin. Bolívar and some of his comrades, regarding Miranda's act as a form of treachery, seized him before he could embark and turned him over to the Spaniards. He died in a Spanish prison four years later. Bolívar, saved from the Spanish reaction by the influence of a friend of his family, received a safe conduct to leave the country.

Bolívar departed for New Granada (present-day Colombia), which was still partially under patriot control. Here, as in Venezuela, Creole leaders squabbled over forms of government. Two months after his arrival, Bolívar issued a Manifesto to the Citizens of New Granada in which he called for unity, condemned the federalist system as impractical under war conditions, and urged the liberation of Venezuela as necessary for Colombian security. Given command of a small detachment of troops to clear the Magdalena River of enemy troops, he employed a strategy that featured swift movement, aggressive tactics, and the advancement of soldiers for merit without regard to social background or color.

A victory at Cúcuta gained Bolívar the rank of general in the Colombian army and approval of his plan for the liberation of Venezuela. In a forced march of three months, he led five hundred men through Venezuela's Andean region toward Caracas. In Venezuela the Spaniards had unleashed a campaign of terror against all

denial of full citizenship to them. In many areas, the black slaves took advantage of the chaotic situation to rise in revolt, impartially killing Creole and Spanish hacendados. But the majority of the population remained neutral, fleeing from their villages at the approach of royal or republican conscription officers; if conscripted, they often deserted when they could or changed to the other side if its prospects seemed better.

On the patriot side, differences arose between the commander-in-chief, Miranda, and his young officers, especially Bolívar, who were angered by Miranda's military conservatism and indecisiveness. Amid these disputes came the patriots. At Trujillo, midway in his advance on Caracas, Bolívar proclaimed a counterterror, a war to the death against all Spaniards. As Bolívar approached the capital, the Spanish forces withdrew. He entered Caracas in triumph and received from the city council the title of liberator; soon afterward the grateful congress of the restored republic voted to grant him dictatorial powers.

Bolívar's success was short-lived, for developments abroad and at home worked against him. The fall of Napoleon in 1814 brought Ferdinand VII to the Spanish throne, released Spanish troops for use in America, and gave an important lift to the royal cause. Meanwhile, the republic's policies alienated large sectors of the lower classes. The Creole aristocrats stubbornly refused to grant freedom to their slaves. As a result, the slaves continued their struggle, independent of Spaniards and Creoles, and republican forces had to be diverted for punitive expeditions into areas of slave revolt.

The *llaneros* (cowboys) of the Venezuelan *llanos* (plains) also turned against the republic as a result of agrarian edicts that attempted to end the hunting or rounding up of cattle in the llanos without written permission from the owner of the land in question. These edicts also sought to transform the llaneros into semiservile peons by forcing them to carry an identity card and belong to a ranch. These attacks on their customary rights and freedom angered the llaneros. Under the leadership of the formidable José Tomás Boves, a mass of cowboys, armed with the dreaded lance, invaded the highlands and swept down on Caracas, crushing all resistance. In July 1814, Bolívar hastily abandoned the city and retreated toward Colombia with the remains of his army. Although Boves died in battle in late 1814, he had destroyed the Venezuelan "second republic."

Bolívar reached Cartagena in September to find that Colombia was on the verge of chaos. Despite the imminent threat of a Spanish invasion, the provinces quarreled with each other and defied the authority of the weak central government. Having determined that the situation was hopeless, Bolívar left in May 1815 for the British island of Jamaica. Meanwhile, a strong Spanish army under General Pablo Morillo had landed in Venezuela, completed the reconquest of the colony, and then sailed to lay siege to Cartagena. Cut off by land and sea, the city surrendered in December, and the rest of Colombia was pacified within a few months. Of all the provinces of Spanish America, only Argentina remained in revolt. Had Ferdinand made the concession (as one of his generals urged him to do) of granting legal equality with whites to the mixed-bloods who supported his cause, the Spanish Empire in America might have survived much longer. But the reactionary Ferdinand would make no concessions of any kind.

Bolívar still had an unshakeable faith in the inevitable triumph of independence. From Jamaica he sent a famous letter in which he affirmed that faith and offered a remarkable analysis of the situation and prospects of Spanish America. He scoffed at the ability of Spain, that "aged serpent," to maintain Spanish America forever in subjection.

Can that nation carry on the exclusive commerce of one-half the world when it lacks manufactures, agricultural products, crafts and sciences, and even a policy? Assume that this mad venture were successful, and further assume that pacification ensued, would not the sons of the Americans today, together with the sons of the conquistadores *twenty years hence, conceive the same patriotic designs that are now being fought for?*

Bolívar also looked into the political future of the continent. Monarchy, he argued, was foreign to the genius of Latin America; only a republican regime would be accepted by its peoples. A single government for the region was impracticable, divided as it was by "climatic differences, geographic diversity, conflicting interests, and dissimilar characteristics." Bolívar boldly forecast the destiny of the different regions, taking account of their economic and social structures. Chile, for example, seemed to him to have a democratic future; Peru, on the other hand, was fated to suffer dictatorship because it contained "two factors that clash with every just and liberal principle: gold and slaves."[3]

From Jamaica, Bolívar went to Haiti, where he received a sympathetic hearing and the offer of some material support from the mulatto president Alexandre Pétion, who asked in return for the freedom of the slaves in the territory that Bolívar should liberate. In March 1816, Bolívar and a small band of followers landed on the island of Margarita off the Venezuelan coast. Two attempts to gain a foothold on the mainland were easily beaten back, and soon Bolívar was back in the West Indies. Reflecting on his failures, he concluded that the effort to invade the well-fortified western coast of Venezuela was a mistake and decided to establish a base in the Orinoco River valley, distant from the centers of Spanish power. Roving patriot bands still operated in this region, and Bolívar hoped to win the allegiance of the llaneros, who were becoming disillusioned with their Spanish allies. In September 1816, Bolívar sailed from Haiti for the Orinoco River delta, which he ascended until he reached the small town of Angostura (modern Ciudad Bolívar), which he made his headquarters.

The tide of war now began to flow in Bolívar's favor. The patriot guerrilla bands accepted his leadership; even more important, he gained the support of the principal llanero chieftain, José Antonio Páez. European developments also favored Bolívar. The end of the Napoleonic wars idled a large number of British soldiers; many of these veterans came to Venezuela, forming a British Legion that distinguished itself in battle by its valor. English merchants made loans that enabled Bolívar to secure men and arms for the coming campaign. Helpful too was the mulish attitude of Ferdinand VII, whose refusal to consider making any concessions to the colonists caused the English government to lose patience and regard with more friendly eyes the prospect of Spanish-American independence.

On the eve of the decisive campaign of 1819, Bolívar summoned to Angostura a makeshift congress that vested him with dictatorial powers. To this congress he presented a project for a constitution for Venezuela in which he urged the abolition of slavery and the distribution of land to revolutionary soldiers. But the proposed constitution also had some nondemocratic features. They included a president with virtually royal powers, a hereditary senate, and restriction of the suffrage and officeholding to the propertied and educated elite. The congress disregarded Bolívar's reform proposals but elected him president of the republic and adopted a constitution embodying many of his ideas.

The war, however, still had to be won. Bolívar's bold strategy for the liberation of Venezuela and Colombia envisaged striking a heavy blow at Spanish forces from a completely unexpected direction. While llanero cavalry under Páez distracted and pinned down the main body of Spanish troops in northern Venezuela with swift raids, Bolívar advanced with an army of some twenty-five hundred men along the winding Orinoco and Arauco rivers, across the plains, and then up the towering Colombian Andes until he reached the plateau where lay Bogotá, capital of New Granada. On the field of Boyacá the patriot army surprised and defeated the royalists in a short, sharp battle that netted sixteen hundred prisoners and considerable supplies. Bogotá lay defenseless, and Bolívar entered the capital to the cheers of its people, who had suffered greatly under Spanish rule.

---

[3] *Selected Writings of Bolívar*, compiled by Vicente Lecuna and edited by Harold A. Bierck, Jr., 2 vols. (New York: Colonial Press, 1951), 1:103–122.

Leaving his aide, Francisco Santander, to organize a government, Bolívar hurried off to Angostura to prepare the liberation of Venezuela. Then thrilling news arrived from Spain; on January 1, 1820, a regiment awaiting embarkation for South America had mutinied, starting a revolt that forced Ferdinand to restore the liberal constitution of 1812 and give up his plans for the reconquest of the colonies. This news caused joy among the patriots, gloom and desertions among the Venezuelan royalists. In July 1821, the troops of Bolívar and Páez crushed the last important Spanish force in Venezuela at Carabobo. Save for some coastal towns and forts still held by beleaguered royalists, Venezuela was free.

Bolívar had already turned his attention southward. The independence of Spanish America remained precarious as long as the Spaniards held the immense mountain bastion of the central Andes. While Bolívar prepared a major offensive from Bogotá against Quito, he sent his able young lieutenant, Antonio José Sucre, by sea from Colombia's Pacific coast to seize the port of Guayaquil. Before Sucre even arrived, the Creole party in Guayaquil revolted, proclaimed independence, and placed the port under Bolívar's protection. With his forces swelled by reinforcements sent by the Argentine general José de San Martín, Sucre advanced into the Ecuadorian highlands and defeated a Spanish army on the slopes of Mount Pichincha, near Quito. Bolívar, meanwhile, advancing southward from Bogotá along the Cauca River valley, encountered stiff royalist resistance, but this crumbled on news of Sucre's victory at Pichincha. The provinces composing the former viceroyalty of New Granada—the future republics of Venezuela, Colombia, Ecuador, and Panama—were now free from Spanish control. They were temporarily united into a large state named Colombia or Gran Colombia, established at the initiative of Bolívar by the union of New Granada and Venezuela in 1821.

The Southern Liberation Movement and San Martín

The time had come for the movement of liberation led by Bolívar to merge with that flowing northward from Argentina. Ever since the defeat of the British invasions of 1806–1807, the Creole party, although nominally loyal to Spain, had effectively controlled Buenos Aires. The hero of the invasions and the temporary viceroy, Santiago Liniers, cooperated fully with the Creole leaders. A new viceroy, sent by the Seville junta to replace Liniers, joined with the viceroy at Lima to crush abortive Creole revolts in Upper Peru (Bolivia). But in Buenos Aires he walked softly, for he recognized the superior power of the Creoles. Under their pressure he issued a decree permitting free trade with allied and neutral nations, a measure bitterly opposed by representatives of the Cádiz monopoly. But this concession could not save the Spanish regime. Revolution was in the air, and the Creole leaders waited only, in the words of one of their number, for the figs to be ripe.

In May 1810, when word came that French troops had entered Seville and threatened Cádiz, the secret patriot society organized a demonstration that forced the viceroy to summon an open town meeting to decide the future government of the colony. This first Argentine congress voted to depose the viceroy and establish a junta to govern in the name of Ferdinand. The junta promptly attempted to consolidate its control of the vast viceroyalty. The interior provinces were subdued after sharp fighting. Montevideo, across the Río de la Plata on the Eastern Shore (modern Uruguay), remained in Spanish hands until 1814, when it fell to an Argentine siege. The junta met even more tenacious resistance from the gauchos of the Uruguayan pampa, led by José Gervasio Artigas, who demanded Uruguayan autonomy in a loose federal connection with Buenos Aires. The porteños would have nothing to do with Artigas's gaucho democracy, and a new struggle began. It ended when Artigas, caught between the fire of Buenos Aires and that of Portuguese forces claiming Uruguay for Brazil, had to flee to Paraguay. Uruguay did not achieve independence until 1828.

The Creole aristocracy in another portion of the old viceroyalty of La Plata, Paraguay, also suspected the designs of the Buenos Aires junta and defeated a porteño force sent to liberate Asunción. This done, the Creole party in Asunción rose up, deposed Spanish officials, and proclaimed the independence of Paraguay. A key figure in this uprising was the remarkable Dr. José Rodríguez de Francia, soon to become his country's first president and dictator.

Efforts by the Buenos Aires junta to liberate the mountainous northern province of Upper Peru also failed. Two thrusts by a patriot army into this area were defeated and the invaders rolled back. The steep terrain, long lines of communication, and the apathy of the Bolivian Indians contributed to these defeats.

The Buenos Aires government also had serious internal problems. A dispute broke out between liberal supporters of the fiery Mariano Moreno, secretary of the junta and champion of social reform, and a conservative faction led by the great landowner Cornelio Saavedra. This dispute foreshadowed the liberal-conservative cleavage that dominated the first decades of Argentine history after independence. In 1813 a national assembly gave the country the name of the United Provinces of La Plata and enacted such reforms as the abolition of mita, encomienda, titles of nobility, and the Inquisition. A declaration of independence, however, was delayed until 1816.

Also 1816 was the year in which the military genius of José de San Martín broke the long-standing military stalemate. San Martín, born in what is now northeastern Argentina in 1778, was a colonel in the Spanish army with twenty years of service behind him when revolution broke out in Buenos Aires. He promptly sailed for La Plata to offer his sword to the patriot junta. He was soon raised to the command of the army of Upper Peru, which was recuperating in Tucumán after a sound defeat at royalist hands. Perceiving that a frontal attack on the Spanish position in Upper Peru was doomed to failure, San Martín offered a plan for total victory that gained the support of the director of the United Provinces, Juan Martín de Pueyrredón. San Martín proposed a march over the Andes to liberate Chile, where a Spanish reaction had toppled the revolutionary regime established by Bernardo O'Higgins and other patriot leaders in 1810. This done, the united forces of La Plata and Chile would descend on Peru from the sea.

To mask his plans from Spanish eyes and gain time for a large organizational effort, San Martín obtained an appointment as governor of the province of Cuyo, whose capital, Mendoza, lay at the eastern end of a strategic pass leading across the Andes to Chile. He spent two years recruiting, training, and equipping his Army of the Andes. Like Bolívar, he used the promise of freedom to secure Negro and mulatto volunteers, and later declared they were his best soldiers. Chilean refugees fleeing the Spanish reaction in their country also joined his forces.

San Martín, methodical and thorough, demanded of the Buenos Aires government arms, munitions, food, and equipment of every kind. The director Pueyrredón ended one letter to San Martín on a note of humorous desperation:

I am sending the world, the flesh, and the devil! I don't know how I shall get out of the scrape I'm in to pay for all this, unless I declare bankruptcy, cancel my accounts with everyone, and clear out to join you, so that you can give me some of the dried beef I'm sending you. Damn it, don't ask me for anything else unless you want to hear that they found me in the morning dangling from a beam in the Fort!

In January 1817, the army began the crossing of the Andes. Its march over the frozen Andean passes equaled in difficulty Bolívar's scaling of the Colombian sierra. Twenty-one days later, the army issued on Chilean soil. A decisive defeat of the Spanish army at Chacabuco in February opened the gates of Santiago to San Martín. He won another victory at Maipú (1818), in a battle that ended the threat to Chile's independence. Rejecting Chilean invitations to become supreme ruler of the republic, a post assumed by O'Higgins, San Martín began to prepare the attack by sea on Lima, fifteen hundred miles away.

The execution of his plan required the creation of a navy. He secured a number of ships in England and the United States and engaged a competent though eccentric naval officer, Thomas, Lord Cochrane, to organize the patriot navy. In August 1820, the expedition sailed for Peru in a fleet made up of seven ships of war and eighteen transports. San Martín landed his army about a hundred miles south of Lima but delayed moving on the Peruvian capital. He hoped to obtain its surrender by economic blockage, propaganda, and direct negotiation with the Spanish officials. The desire of the Lima aristocracy, Creole and Peninsular, to avoid an armed struggle that might unleash an Indian and slave revolt worked in favor of San Martín's strategy. In June 1821, the Spanish army evacuated Lima and retreated toward the Andes. San Martín entered the capital and in a festive atmosphere proclaimed the independence of Peru.

But his victory was far from complete. He had to deal with counterrevolutionary plots and the resistance of Lima's corrupt elite to his program of social reform, which included the end of Indian tribute and the grant of freedom to the children of slaves. San Martín's assumption of supreme military and civil power in August 1821 added to the factional opposition. Meanwhile, a large Spanish army maneuvered in front of Lima, challenging San Martín to a battle he dared not join with his much smaller force. Disheartened by the atmosphere of intrigue and

hostility that surrounded him, San Martín became convinced that only monarchy could bring stability to Spanish America and sent a secret mission to Europe to search for a prince for the throne of Peru.

Such was the background of San Martín's depature for Guayaquil, where he met in conference with Bolívar on July 26 and 27, 1822. The agenda of the meeting included several points. One concerned the future of Guayaquil. San Martín claimed the port city for Peru; Bolívar, however, had already annexed it to Gran Colombia, confronting San Martín with a fait accompli. Another topic was the political future of all Spanish America. San Martín favored monarchy as the solution for the emergent chaos of the new states; Bolívar believed in a governmental system that would be republican in form, oligarchical in content. But the critical question before the two men was how to complete the liberation of the continent by defeating the Spanish forces in Peru.

San Martín's abrupt retirement from public life after the conference, the reluctance of the two liberators to discuss what was said there, and the meager authentic documentary record of the proceedings have surrounded the meeting with an atmosphere of mystery and produced two opposed and partisan interpretations. A view favored by Argentine historians holds that San Martín came to Guayaquil in search of military aid but was rebuffed by Bolívar, who was unwilling to share with a rival the glory of bringing the struggle for independence to an end; San Martín then magnanimously decided to leave Peru and allow Bolívar to complete the work he had begun. Venezuelan historians, on the other hand, argue that San Martín came to Guayaquil primarily in order to recover Guayaquil for Peru. They deny that he asked Bolívar for more troops and insist that he left Peru for personal reasons having nothing to do with the conference.

Both interpretations tend to diminish the stature and sense of realism of the two liberators.

San Martín was no martyr, nor was Bolívar an ambitious schemer who sacrificed San Martín to his passion for power and glory. San Martín must have understood that Bolívar alone combined the military, political, and psychological assets needed to liquidate the factional hornet's nest in Peru and gain final victory over the powerful Spanish army in the sierra. Given the situation in Lima, San Martín's presence there could only hinder the performance of those tasks. In this light, the decision of Bolívar to assume sole direction of the war and of San Martín to withdraw reflected a realistic appraisal of the Peruvian problem and the solution it required.

San Martín returned to Lima to find that in his absence his enemies had rallied and struck at him by driving his reforming chief minister, Bernardo Monteagudo, out of the country. San Martín made no effort to reassert his power. In September 1822, before the first Peruvian congress, he announced his resignation as protector and his impending departure. He returned to Buenos Aires by way of Chile, where the government of his friend O'Higgins was on the verge of collapse. In Buenos Aires the people seemed to have forgotten his existence. Accompanied by his daughter, he sailed for Europe at the end of 1823. He died in France in 1850 in virtual obscurity. His transfiguration into an Argentine national hero began a quarter-century later.

San Martín's departure left Lima and the territory under its control in serious danger of reconquest by the strong Spanish army in the sierra. Bolívar made no move to rescue the squabbling factions in Lima from their predicament; he allowed the situation to deteriorate until May 1823, when the Peruvian congress called on him for help. Then he sent Sucre with only a few thousand men, for he wanted to bring the Lima politicians to their knees. The scare produced by a brief reoccupation of the capital by the Spanish army prepared the Creole leaders to accept Bolívar's absolute rule.

Bolívar arrived in Peru in September 1823.

He required almost a year to achieve political stability and to weld the army he brought with him and the different national units under his command into a united force. After a month of difficult ascent of the sierra, in an altitude so high that Bolívar and most of his men suffered from mountain sickness, cavalry elements of the patriot and royalist armies clashed near the lake of Junín, and the Spaniards suffered defeat (August 6, 1824). The royalist commander, José de Canterac, retreated toward Cuzco. Leaving Sucre in command, Bolívar returned to Lima to gather reinforcements. To Sucre fell the glory of defeating the Spanish army in the last major engagement of the war, at Ayacucho (December 9, 1824). Only scattered resistance at some points in the highlands and on the coast remained to be mopped up. The work of continental liberation was achieved.

The Achievement of Brazilian Independence

In contrast to the political anarchy, economic dislocation, and military destruction in Spanish America, the drive toward independence of Brazil proceeded as a relatively bloodless transition between 1808 and 1822. The idea of Brazilian independence first arose in the late eighteenth century as a Brazilian reaction to the Portuguese policy of tightening political and economic control over the colony in the interests of the mother country. The first significant conspiracy against Portuguese rule, we recall, was organized in 1788–1789 in Minas Gerais, where rigid governmental control over the production and prices of gold and diamonds, as well as heavy taxes, caused much discontent, and where there existed a group of intellectuals educated in Europe and familiar with the ideas of the Enlightenment. But this conspiracy never went beyond the stage of discussion and was easily discovered and crushed. Other conspiracies in Río de Janeiro (1794), Bahia (1798), and Pernambuco (1801), and a brief revolt in Pernambuco (1817), reflected the influence of republican ideas over sections of the elite and even the lower strata of urban society. All proved abortive or were soon crushed. The stagnation of Brazilian life and the fear of slave owners that resistance to Portugal might spark slave insurrections effectively inhibited the spirit of revolt. Were it not for an accident of European history, the independence of Brazil might have long been delayed.

The French invasion of Portugal (1807), followed by the flight of the Portuguese court to Rio de Janeiro, brought large benefits to Brazil. Indeed, the transfer of the court in effect signified achievement of Brazilian independence. The Portuguese prince regent João opened Brazil's ports to the trade of friendly nations, permitted the rise of local industries, and founded a Bank of Brazil. In 1815 he elevated Brazil to the legal status of a kingdom co-equal with Portugal. In one sense, however, Brazil's new status signified the substitution of one dependence for another. Freed from Portuguese control, Brazil came under the economic domination of England, which obtained major tariff concessions and other privileges by the Strangford Treaty of 1810. One result was an influx of cheap machine-made goods that swamped the handicrafts industry of the country.

Brazilian elites took satisfaction in Brazil's new role and the growth of educational, cultural, and economic opportunities for their class. But this feeling was mixed with resentment at the thousands of Portuguese courtiers and hangers-on who came with the court and who competed with Brazilians for jobs and favors. Portuguese merchants in Brazil, for their part, were bitter over the passing of the Lisbon monopoly. Thus, the change in the status of Brazil sharpened the conflict between mazombos and reinóis.

The event that precipitated the break with the mother country was the revolution of 1820 in Portugal. The Portuguese revolutionists framed a liberal constitution for the kingdom, but they were conservative or reactionary in relation to Brazil. They demanded the immediate return of Dom João to Lisbon, an end to the system of dual monarchy that he had devised, and the restoration of the Portuguese commercial monopoly. Timid and vacillating, Dom João knew not which way to turn. Under the pressure of his courtiers, who hungered to return to Portugal and their lost estates, he finally approved the new constitution and sailed for Portugal. He left behind him, however, his son and heir, Dom Pedro, as regent of Brazil, and in a private letter advised him, in the event the Brazilians should demand independence, to assume leadership of the movement and set the crown of Brazil on his head. Pedro received the same advice from José Bonifacio de Andrada, a Brazilian scientist whose stay in Portugal had completely disillusioned him about the Portuguese capacity for colonial reform.

Soon it became clear that the Portuguese Côrtes intended to set the clock back by abrogating all the liberties and concessions won by Brazil since 1808. One of its decrees insisted on the immediate return of Dom Pedro from Brazil in order that he might complete his political education. The pace of events moved more rapidly in 1822. On January 9 Dom Pedro, urged on by José Bonifácio de Andrada and other Brazilian advisers who perceived a golden opportunity to make an orderly transition to independence without the intervention of the masses, refused an order from the Côrtes to return to Brazil and issued his famous *fico* ("I remain"). On September 7, regarded by all Brazilians as Independence Day, he issued the even more celebrated Cry of Ipiranga, "Independence or Death!", and in December 1822, having overcome slight resistance by Portuguese troops, was formally proclaimed constitutional emperor of Brazil.

MEXICO'S ROAD TO INDEPENDENCE

In New Spain, as in other colonies, the crisis of the Bourbon monarchy in 1808–1810 encouraged Creole leaders to strike a blow for independence under "the mask of Ferdinand." But in Mexico the movement for independence took an unexpected turn. Here the masses, instead of remaining aloof, joined the struggle and for a time managed to convert it from a private quarrel between two elites into a social revolution.

The special economic and social conditions of Mexico help to explain this development. The growth of industry, mining, and commercial agriculture in central Mexico had led to the rise of a large Indian proletariat. This group had become partially Europeanized. Many of its members no longer lived in isolated Indian communities ruled by hereditary caciques but in Spanish mining camps and towns. These people, together with many mestizos, mulattos, and free Negroes, bitterly resented not only their heavy tribute burdens but the many regulations that excluded them from full entry into the white, European world. This class formed the spearhead of the Hidalgo revolt, and its demands gave a distinctive stamp to the first stage of the Mexican struggle for independence.

In 1810 a Creole plot for independence was taking shape in the important industrial center of Querétaro. Although the leaders included some wealthy and aristocratic figures, from the first the conspirators seem to have planned to mobilize the Indian and mixed-blood proletariat, probably because they lacked confidence in their ability to win over the majority of their own class. If the motive of most of the plotters was the hope of raising troops, a genuine sympathy with the natives inspired Miguel Hidalgo y Costilla, a priest in the town of Dolores and one-time rector of the colegio of San Nicolas at Valladolid. The scholarly Hidalgo had already called the attention of Spanish authorities to himself by his freethinking ideas; he was also known for his scientific interests and his efforts to develop new industries in his parish.

Informed that their plot had been denounced to Spanish officials, the conspirators held an urgent council and decided to launch their revolt although arrangements were not complete. On September 16, 1810, Hidalgo called on the Indians of his parish to rise against their Spanish rulers. He appealed to the religious devotion of the natives by proclaiming the Virgin of Guadalupe the patron of his movement. As Hidalgo began his march on the capital, his forces grew; a horde of Indians and mixed-bloods, armed with machetes, slings, and pikes, swarmed after him. Many urban workers, including an entire regiment of miners from Guanajuato, joined his forces. After his first victories, Hidalgo issued decrees abolishing slavery and Indian tribute. Three months later, from his headquarters at Guadalajara, in his first and only reference to the land problem, he ordered that Indian communal lands in the vicinity of the city that had been rented to Spaniards be returned to the Indians. It was his wish that "only the natives in their respective pueblos should enjoy the use of those lands." Moderate though they were, these reforms gave the Mexican revolution a popular character absent from the movement for independence in South America. However, they alienated many Creoles who also desired independence—but without social revolution.

Hidalgo proved unable to weld his Indian horde into a disciplined army or to capitalize on his early victories. Less than one year after the revolt had begun, he was captured as he fled toward the United States border, condemned as a heretic and subversive by an inquisitorial court, and executed by a firing squad. A mestizo priest, José María Morelos, assumed leadership of the revolutionary struggle. He was a brilliant guerrilla leader who substituted strict discipline, training, and centralized direction for the loose methods of Hidalgo. Morelos liberated most of southern Mexico, then summoned a congress that proclaimed independence and framed a republican constitution for the country.

Morelos extended Hidalgo's program of social reform by prohibiting all forced labor and for-

Father Hidalgo proclaims the Grito de Dolores in
1810. Detail from the "Retablo de la
Independencia," by Juan O'Gorman. (Courtesy of
the Museo Nacional de Historia, Mexico)

bidding the use of racial terms. He went beyond
Hidalgo in his advocacy of land reform; in a
"plan" found among his papers he proposed
a "scorched earth" policy against all haciendas
more than two leagues in extent, denounced a
situation in which "a single individual owns
vast extents of uncultivated land and enslaves
thousands of people who must work that land
as peons (gañanes) or slaves," and proclaimed
the social benefits of the small landholding. But
Morelos, like Hidalgo, was surrounded and restrained by Creole lieutenants who wanted no
revolutionary social change, whose sole desire
was to oust the Peninsulars from power. Like

Hidalgo, Morelos had differences with his Creole associates that seriously hampered his military efforts. In 1815 he was captured by the royalist officer Agustín de Iturbide and after a summary trial suffered the fate of Hidalgo.

After the death of Morelos, the revolution declined into a guerrilla war waged by many rival chiefs, some of whom were mere brigands. Royalist armies gradually extinguished the remaining centers of resistance. By 1820 only two patriot leaders—Vicente Guerrero and Guadalupe Victoria—were carrying on the struggle for independence.

The Spanish revolution of 1820 abruptly altered this state of affairs. News that the rebels had compelled Ferdinand VII to swear allegiance to the liberal constitution of 1812 threw conservative clergy, army officers, and merchants, whether Creole or Peninsular, into a panic. Fearing the loss of their privileges, they schemed to separate Mexico from the mother country and establish independence under conservative auspices. Their instrument was the Creole officer Agustín de Iturbide, who had waged implacable war against the patriots. Iturbide offered peace and reconciliation to the principal rebel leader, Vicente Guerrero. His plan combined independence, monarchy, the supremacy of the Roman Catholic church, and the civil equality of Creoles and Spaniards. Guerrero was a sincere liberal and republican, Iturbide an unprincipled opportunist who dreamed of placing a crown on his own head. For the moment, however, Iturbide's program offered advantages to both sides. The united forces of Iturbide and Guerrero swiftly overcame scattered loyalist resistance. On September 28, 1821, Iturbide proclaimed Mexican independence, and eight months later a congress selected by Iturbide confirmed him as emperor of Mexico.

Despite its tinsel splendor, Iturbide's empire had no popular base. Within a few months, Agustín I had to abdicate and depart for Europe, with a warning never to return. Hoping for a comeback, Iturbide returned from England in 1824 and landed on the coast with a small party. He was promptly captured by troops of the new republican regime and shot.

LATIN AMERICAN INDEPENDENCE: A RECKONING

After more than a decade of war, accompanied by immense loss of life and property, most of Latin America had won its political independence. The revolutions were accompanied or quickly followed by a number of social changes. Independence brought the death of the Inquisition, the end of legal discrimination on the basis of race, and the abolition of titles of nobility in most lands. It also gave an impetus to the abolition of slavery, to the founding of public schools, and to similar reforms. All these changes, however, were marginal; independence left intact the existing economic and social structures. This was natural, for the Creole elite that headed the movement had no intention of transforming the existing order. They sought to replace the Peninsulars in the seats of power and to open their ports to the commerce of the world but desired no change of labor and land systems. Indeed, their interests as producers of raw materials and foodstuffs for sale in the markets of Europe and North America required the maintenance of the system of great estates worked by a semiservile native proletariat. No agrarian reform accompanied independence. The haciendas abandoned by or confiscated from loyalists usually fell into the hands of the Creole aristocracy. Some land also passed into the possession of mestizo or mulatto officers, who were assimilated into the Creole elite and as a rule promptly forgot the groups from which they had come.

Instead of broadening the base of landownership in Latin America, the revolutions actually helped to narrow it. The liberal, individualist ideology of the revolutionary governments undermined Indian communal land tenure in some cases by requiring the division of community lands among its members. This process facilitated the usurpation of Indian land by Creole landlords and hastened the transformation of the Indian peasantry into a class of peons or serfs on white haciendas, as will be discussed in Chapters 9 and 10. Since no structural economic change took place, despite an elaborate façade of republican constitutions and law codes, aristocratic values continued to dominate in Latin American society.

PART TWO

LATIN AMERICA IN THE NINETEENTH CENTURY

After winning their independence, the new Latin American states began a long, uphill struggle to achieve economic and political stability. They faced immense obstacles, for independence, as previously noted, was not accompanied by economic and social changes that could spur rapid progress—for example, no redistribution of land and income in favor of the lower classes took place. The large estate, generally operated with primitive methods and slave or peon labor, continued to dominate economic life. Far from diminishing, the influence of the landed aristocracy actually increased as a result of the leading military role it played in the wars of independence and of the passing of Spanish authority.

Economic life stagnated, for the anticipated large-scale influx of foreign capital did not materialize, and the European demand for Latin American staples remained far below expectations. Free trade brought increased commercial activity to the coasts, but this increase was offset by the near destruction of some local craft industries by cheap, factory-made European goods. The sluggish pace of economic activity and the relative absence of interregional trade and true national markets encouraged local self-sufficiency, isolation, political instability, and even chaos.

As a result of these adverse factors, the period from about 1820 to about 1870 was for many Latin American countries an age of violence, of alternate dictatorship and revolution. Its symbol was the *caudillo* (strong man), whose power was always based on force, no matter what kind of constitution the country had. Usually, the caudillo ruled with the aid of a coalition of lesser caudillos, each supreme in his region. Whatever their methods, the caudillos generally displayed some regard for republican ideology and institutions. Political parties, bearing such labels as "conservative" and "liberal," "unitarian" and "federalist," were active in most of the new states. Conservatism drew most of its support from the great landowners and their urban allies. Liberalism typically attracted provincial landowners, professional men, and other groups that had enjoyed little power in the past and were dissatisfied with the existing order. As a rule, conservatives sought to retain many of the social arrangements of the colonial era and favored a highly centralized government. Liberals, often inspired by the example of the United States, usually advocated a federal form of government, guarantees of individual rights, lay control of education, and an end to special privileges for the clergy and military. Neither party displayed much interest in the problems of the Indian peasantry and other lower-class groups.

Beginning in about 1870, the accelerating tempo of the Industrial Revolution in Europe stimulated a more rapid change in the Latin American economy and politics. European capital flowed into the area, creating the facilities needed to expand and modernize production and trade. The pace and degree of economic progress of the various countries were very uneven depending largely on their geographic position and natural resources.

Extreme one-sidedness was a feature of the new economic order. One or two products became the basis of each country's prosperity, making it highly vulnerable to fluctuations in the world demand and the price of these commodities. Meanwhile, other sectors of the economy remained stagnant or even declined through diversion of labor and land to other industries.

The late nineteenth-century expansion had two other characteristics: In the main, it took place within the framework of the hacienda system of land tenure and labor, and it was accompanied by a steady growth of foreign control over the natural and man-made resources of the region. Thus, by 1900 a new structure of dependency, or colonialism, had arisen, called neocolonialism, with Great Britain and later the United States replacing Spain and Portugal as the dominant power in the area.

The new economic order demanded peace and continuity in government, and after 1870 political conditions in Latin America did, in fact, grow more stable. Old party lines dissolved as conservatives adopted the positivist dogma of science and progress, while liberals abandoned their concern with constitutional methods and civil liberties in favor of an interest in material prosperity. A new type of "progressive" caudillo—Porfirio Díaz in Mexico, Rafael Núñez in Colombia, Antonio Guzmán Blanco in Venezuela—symbolized the politics of acquisition. The cycle of dictatorship and revolution continued in many lands, but the revolutions became less frequent and devastating.

These are some major trends in the political and economic history of Latin America in the period extending from about 1820 to 1900. Naturally, these trends were accompanied by other changes in the Latin American way of life and culture, notably the development of a powerful literature that often sought not only to mirror Latin American society but to change it. In the chapters that follow we shall present short histories of four leading Latin American countries—Mexico, Argentina, Chile, and Brazil—in the nineteenth century. All four contain themes and problems common to the area in that period, but each displays variations that reflect the specific backgrounds of the different states.

CHAPTER NINE

Dictators and

Revolutions

Independence did not bring Latin America the ordered freedom and prosperity that the liberators had hoped for. In most of the new states, decades of civil strife followed the passing of Spanish and Portuguese rule. Bolívar reflected the disillusionment of many patriot leaders when he wrote in 1829: "There is no good faith in America, nor among the nations of America. Treaties are scraps of paper; constitutions, printed matter; elections, battles; freedom, anarchy; and life, a torment." The contrast between Latin American stagnation and disorder and the meteoric advance of the former English colonies—the United States—intensified the pessimism and self-doubt of some Latin American leaders and intellectuals.

THE FRUITS OF INDEPENDENCE

Frustration of the great hopes with which the struggle for liberation began was inevitable, for independence was not accompanied by economic and social changes that could shatter the colonial mold. Aside from the passing of the

Spanish and Portuguese trade monopolies, the colonial economic and social structures remained intact. The hacienda, fazenda, or estancia, employing archaic techniques and a labor force of peons or slaves, continued to dominate agriculture; no significant class of small farmers arose to challenge the economic and political might of the great landowners. Indeed, the revolutions strengthened the power of the landed aristocracy by removing the agencies of Spanish rule—viceroys, audiencias, intendants—and by weakening the ingrained habits of obedience to a central authority. In contrast, all other colonial elites—the merchant class, weakened by the expulsion or emigration of many loyalist merchants; the mine owners, ruined by wartime destruction or confiscation of their properties; and the church hierarchy, often in disgrace for having sided with Spain—emerged from the conflict with diminished weight.

To their other sources of influence the landed aristocracy added the prestige of a military elite crowned with the laurels of victory, for many revolutionary officers had arisen from its ranks. The militarization of the new states as a result of years of destructive warfare and postwar instability assured a large political role for this officer group. Standing armies that often consumed more than half of the national budgets arose. Not content with the role of guardians of order and national security, the military became arbiters of political disputes, as a rule intervening in favor of the conservative land-owning interests and the urban elites with whom the great landowners were closely linked.

Economic Stagnation

Revolutionary leaders had expected that a vast expansion of foreign trade, which would aid economic recovery, would follow the passing of Spanish commercial monopoly. In fact, some countries, favored by their natural resources or geographic position, soon recovered from the revolutionary crisis and scored modest to large economic advances; they included Brazil (coffee and sugar), Argentine (hides), and Chile (metals and hides). But others, such as Mexico, Bolivia, and Peru, whose mining economies had suffered shattering blows, failed to recover colonial levels of production.

Several factors accounted for the economic stagnation that plagued many of the new states in the first half of the nineteenth century. Independence was not accompanied by a redistribution of land and income that might have stimulated a growth of internal markets and productive forces. The anticipated large-scale influx of foreign capital did not materialize, partly because political disorder discouraged foreign investment, partly because Europe and the United States, then financing their own industrial revolutions, had as yet little capital to export. Exports of Latin American staples also remained below expectations, for Europe still viewed Latin America primarily as an outlet for manufactured goods, especially English textiles. The resulting flood of cheap, factory-made European products damaged local craft industries and drained the new states of their stocks of gold and silver, creating a chronic balance-of-trade problem. The British conquest of the Latin American markets further weakened the local merchant class, which was unable to compete with its English rivals. By mid-century the wealthiest and most prestigious merchant houses, from Mexico City to Buenos Aires and Valparaíso, bore English names. Iberian merchants, however, continued to dominate the urban and provincial retail trade.

In their totality, these developments retarded the development of native capitalism and capitalist relations and reinforced the dominant role of the hacienda in the economic and political life of the new states. The deepening stagnation of the interior of these nations, which was aggravated by lack of roads and by natural obstacles to communication (such as jungles and mountains), intensified tendencies toward regionalism and the domination of regions by caudillos (strong men) great and small, who were usually local large landowners. The sluggish tempo of economic activity encouraged these caudillos to employ their private followings of peons and retainers as pawns in the game of politics and revolution on a national scale. Indeed, politics and revolution became in some countries a form of economic activity that compensated for the lack of other opportunities, since the victors, having gained control of the all-important customhouse (which collected duties on imports and exports) and other official sources of revenue, could reward themselves and their followers with government jobs, contracts, grants of public land, and other favors.

Politics: The Conservative and Liberal Programs

The political systems of the new states made large formal concessions to the liberal bourgeois ideology of the nineteenth century. With the exception of Brazil, all the new states adopted the republican form of government (Mexico had two brief intervals of imperial rule) and paid their respects to the formulas of parliamentary and representative government. Their constitutions provided for presidents, congresses, and courts; often they contained elaborate safeguards of individual rights.

These façades of modernity, however, poorly concealed the dictatorial or oligarchical reality beneath. Typically, the chief executive was a caudillo whose power rested on force, no matter what the constitutional form; usually, he ruled with the support of a coalition of lesser caudillos, each more or less supreme in his own domain. The supposed independence of the judicial and legislative branches was a fiction. As a rule, elections were exercises in futility. Since the party in power generally counted the votes, the opposition had no alternative but revolt.

Literacy and property qualifications disfranchised most Indians and mixed-bloods; where they had the right to vote, the *patrón* (master) often herded them to the polls to vote for him

or his candidates. Whether liberal or conservative, all sections of the ruling class agreed on keeping the peasantry, gauchos, and other "lower orders" on the margins of political life, on preventing their emergence as groups with collective philosophies and goals. The very privileges that the new Creole constitutions and law codes granted the Indians—equality before the law, the "right" to divide and dispose of their communal lands—weakened the solidarity of the native masses and their ability to resist the competitive individualism of the Creole world. However, especially gifted, ambitious, and fortunate members of these marginal groups were sometimes co-opted into the Creole elite and provided some of its most distinguished leaders; two examples are the Zapotec Indian Benito Juárez in Mexico and the mestizo president Andrés Santa Cruz in Bolivia.

At first glance, the political history of Latin America in the first half-century after independence, with its dreary alternation of dictatorship and revolt, seems pointless and trivial. But the political struggles of this period were more than disputes over spoils between sections of a small upper class. Genuine social and ideological cleavages helped to produce those struggles and the bitterness with which they were fought. Such labels as "conservative" and "liberal," "unitarian" and "federalist," assigned by the various parties to themselves or each other, were more than masks in a pageant, although opportunism contributed to the ease with which some leaders assumed and discarded these labels.

Generally speaking, conservatism reflected the interests of the traditional holders of power and privilege, men who had a stake in maintaining the existing order. Hence, the great landowners, the upper clergy, the higher ranks of the military and the civil bureaucracy, and monopolistic merchant groups tended to be conservatives. Liberalism, in contrast, appealed to those groups that in colonial times had little or no access to the main structures of economic and political power and were naturally eager to alter the existing order. Thus, liberalism drew much support from provincial landowners, lawyers and other professional men (the groups most receptive to new ideas), shopkeepers, and artisans; it also appealed to ambitious, aspiring Indians and mixed-bloods. But regional conflicts and clan or family loyalties often cut across the lines of social and occupational cleavage, complicating the political picture.

Liberals wanted to break up the hierarchical social structure inherited from the colonial period. They had a vision of their countries remade into dynamic middle-class states on the model of the United States or England. Inspired by the success of the United States, they usually favored a federal form of government, guarantees of individual rights, lay control of education, and an end to a special legal status for the clergy and military. In their modernizing zeal, liberals sometimes called for abolition of entails (which restricted the right to inherit property to a particular descendant or descendants of the owner), dissolution of convents, confiscation of church wealth, and abolition of slavery. The federalism of the liberals had a special appeal for secondary regions of the new states, eager to develop their resources and free themselves from domination by capitals and wealthy primary regions.

Conservatives typically upheld a strong centralized government, the religious and educational monopoly of the Roman Catholic church, and the special privileges (fueros) of the clergy and military. They distrusted such radical novelties as freedom of speech and the press and religious toleration. Conservatives, in short, sought to salvage as much of the colonial social order as was compatible with the new republican system. Indeed, some conservative leaders ultimately despaired of that system and dreamed of implanting monarchy in their countries.

Neither conservatives nor liberals displayed much interest in the problems of the Indian, black, and mixed-blood masses that formed the majority of people in most Latin American countries. Liberals, impatient with the supposed backwardness of the Indians, regarded their communalism as an impediment to the development of a capitalist spirit of enterprise and initiated legislation providing for the division of communal lands—a policy that favored land grabbing at the expense of Indian villages. Despite their theoretical preference for small landholdings and a rural middle class, liberals recoiled from any program of radical land reform. Conservatives, for their part, correctly regarded the great estate as the very foundation of their power. As traditionalists, however, the conservatives sometimes claimed to continue the Spanish paternalist policy toward the Indians and enjoyed some support among the natives, who tended to be suspicious of all innovations.

This summary of the conservative and liberal programs for Latin America in the first half-century after independence inevitably overlooks variations from the theoretical liberal and conservative norms—variations that reflected the specific conditions and problems of the different states. An examination of the history of four leading Latin American countries in this period, Mexico, Argentina, Chile, and Brazil, reveals not only certain common themes but a rich diversity of political experience.

MEXICO

The struggle for Mexican independence, begun by the radical priests Hidalgo and Morelos, was completed by the Creole officer Agustín de Iturbide, who headed a coalition of Creole and Peninsular conservatives terrified at the prospect of being governed by the liberal Spanish constitution of 1812, which was reestablished in 1820. Independence, achieved under such conservative auspices, meant that Mexico's economic and social patterns underwent little change. The great hacienda continued to dominate the countryside in many areas. Although Indian villages managed to retain substantial community lands until after mid-century and even improved their economic and political position somewhat with the passing of Spanish centralized authority, the trend toward usurpation of Indian lands grew stronger as a result of the lapse of Spanish protective legislation. Peons and tenants on the haciendas often suffered from debt servitude, miserable wages, oppressive rents, and excessive religious fees. At the constitutional convention of 1856–1857, the liberal Ponciano Arriaga declared:

With some honorable exceptions, the rich landowners of Mexico . . . resemble the feudal lords of the Middle Ages. On his seigneurial lands, with more or less formalities, the landowner makes and executes laws, administers justice and exercises civil power, imposes taxes and fines, has his own jails and irons, metes out punishments and tortures, monopolizes commerce, and forbids the conduct without his permission of any business but that of the estate.[1]

The church continued to wield an immense economic and spiritual power. An anonymous contemporary writer reflected the disillusionment of the masses with the fruits of independence: "Independence is only a name. Previously they ruled us from Spain, now from here. It is always the same priest on a different mule. But as for work, food, and clothing, there is no difference."

The Mexican Economy

The ravages of war had left mine shafts flooded, haciendas deserted, the economy stagnant. The end of the Spanish commercial monopoly, however, brought a large increase in the volume of foreign trade; the number of ships entering Mexican ports jumped from 148 in 1823 to 639 in 1826. But exports did not keep pace with imports, leaving a trade deficit that had to be covered by exporting precious metals. The drain of gold and silver aggravated the problems of the new government, which inherited a bankrupt treasury and had to support a swollen bureaucracy and an officer class ready to revolt against any government that suggested a cut in their numbers or pay. The exodus of Spanish merchants and their capital added to the economic problems of the new state.

Foreign loans appeared to be the only way out of the crisis. In 1824–1825, English bankers made loans to Mexico amounting to 32 million pesos, guaranteed by Mexican customs revenues. Of this amount the Mexicans received only a little more than 11 million pesos, as the bankers, Barclay and Company, went bankrupt before all the money due to Mexico from the loan proceeds was paid. By 1843 unpaid interest and principal had raised the nation's foreign debt to more than 54 million pesos. This mounting foreign debt not only created crushing interest burdens but threatened Mexico's independence and territorial integrity, for behind foreign capitalists stood governments that might threaten intervention in case of default.

Foreign investments, mainly from Britain, however, made possible a partial recovery of the decisive mining sector. Old mines, abandoned and flooded during the wars, were reopened, but the available capital proved inadequate, the technical problems of reconstruction were greater than anticipated, and production remained on a relatively low level.

An ambitious effort to revive and modernize Mexican industry also got under way, spurred by the founding in 1830 of the *Banco de Avío*, which provided governmental assistance to industry. Manufacturing, paced by textiles, made some limited progress in the three decades after independence. Leading industrial centers included Mexico City, Puebla, Guadalajara, Durango, and Veracruz. But shortages of capital,

[1] Francisco Zarco, *Historia del congreso estraordinario constituyente de 1856 y 1857,* 2 vols. (Mexico, 1857), 1:555.

ATLANTIC OCEAN

M E X I C O
1821

San Antonio

Rio Grande

GULF OF MEXICO

BAHAMA IS.
(Br.)

Mexico City   Veracruz

CUBA
(Sp.)

PUERTO RICO
(Sp.)

BR. HONDURAS

HAITI
1804

Guatemala

CARIBBEAN SEA

TRINIDAD
(Br.)

UNITED PROVINCES OF
CENTRAL AMERICA
1823-1839

Panama

Caracas

BR. GUIANA

DUTCH GUIANA

FR. GUIANA

Bogotá

GRAN COLOMBIA
1819-1830

GALAPAGOS IS.

Quito

Indefinite Boundary

EMPIRE OF BRAZIL
1822

PERU
1821

Lima

BOLIVIA
1825

Bahia

Sucre

PACIFIC OCEAN

PARAGUAY
1813

Asunción

Rio de Janeiro

CHILE
1817

UNITED
PROVINCES
OF
LA PLATA
1816

Santiago

Montevideo

URUGUAY
1828

Buenos Aires

0   500   1000 Miles

0   500   1000 Kilometers

LATIN AMERICA IN 1830

lack of a consistent policy of protection for domestic industry, and a socioeconomic structure
that sharply limited the internal market hampered the growth of Mexican factory capitalism.
By 1843 the Banco de Avío had to close its doors
for lack of funds. The Mexican economy, therefore, continued to be based on mining and agriculture. Mexico's principal exports were precious metals, especially silver, and such
agricultural products as tobacco, coffee, vanilla,
cochineal, and henequen (a plant fiber used in
rope and twine). Imports consisted primarily
of manufactured goods that Mexican industry
could not supply.

Politics: Liberals Versus Conservatives

A liberal-conservative cleavage dominated
Mexican political life in the half-century after
independence. That conflict was latent from the
moment that the "liberator" Iturbide, the former
scourge of insurgents, rode into Mexico City
on September 27, 1821, flanked on either side
by two insurgent generals, Vicente Guerrero
and Guadalupe Victoria, firm republicans and
liberals. The fall of Iturbide in 1823 cleared the
way for the establishment of a republic. But it
soon became apparent that the republicans were
divided into liberals and conservatives, federalists and centralists.

The constitution of 1824 represented a compromise between liberal and conservative interests. It appeased regional economic interests,
which were fearful of a too-powerful central
government, by creating nineteen states that
possessed taxing power; their legislatures, each
casting one vote, chose the president and vice
president for four-year terms. The national legislature was made bicameral, with an upper
house (Senate) and a lower house (Chamber of
Deputies). By assuring the creation of local civil
bureaucracies, the federalist structure also satisfied the demand of provincial middle classes
for greater access to political activity and office.

But the constitution had a conservative tinge
as well: Although the church lost its monopoly
of education, Catholicism was proclaimed the
official religion, and the fueros of the church
and the army were specifically confirmed.

A hero of the war of independence, the liberal
general Guadalupe Victoria, was elected first
president under the new constitution. Anxious
to preserve unity, Victoria brought the conservative Lucas Alamán into his cabinet. But
this era of good feeling was very short-lived;
by 1825, Alamán was forced out of the government. The liberal-conservative cleavage now
assumed the form of a rivalry between two
Masonic lodges, the York Rite lodge, founded
by the American minister Joel Roberts Poinsett,
and the Scottish Rite lodge, sponsored by the
British chargé d'affaires Henry Ward. Their rivalry reflected the Anglo-American competition
for economic and political influence in Mexico.
The old mining and landowning aristocracy,
which looked to Great Britain for leadership
and assistance in the economic and political
reconstruction of Mexico on a sound conservative
basis, formed a pro-British faction; the liberals
and federalists, who regarded the United States
as a model for their own reform program, formed
a pro-American *Yorkino* faction.

The fate of the thousands of Spaniards, including many wealthy merchants, who remained
in Mexico after the fall of the colonial regime
soon became a major political issue. Spain's
continued occupation of the fortress of Veracruz
until 1825, its refusal (until 1836) to recognize
Mexican independence, and the discovery of
plots against independence in which Spaniards
were implicated created much anti-Spanish
feeling. But conservative leaders like Alamán
strongly opposed ouster of the Spaniards as
being harmful to the economy and to the Mexican upper class, threatened by the ambitions
of upstart middle-class politicians. Nonetheless,
in 1827 the liberal Yorkinos pushed through
congress a decree of expulsion against the

Spaniards. Although not fully enforced, the decree hastened the transformation of the conservative and liberal factions into political parties.

The Conservative party represented the old landed and mining aristocracy, the clerical and military hierarchy, monopolistic merchants, and some manufacturers. Its intellectual spokesman and organizer was Lucas Alamán, statesman, champion of industry, and author of a brilliant history of Mexico from the conservative point of view. The Liberal party represented a Creole and mestizo middle class—provincial landowners, professional men, artisans, the lower ranks of the clergy and military—determined to end special privileges and the concentration of political and economic power in the upper class. A priest-economist, José María Luis Mora, presented the liberal position with great force and lucidity. But the Liberal party was divided; its right wing, the *moderados,* wanted to proceed slowly and sometimes joined the conservatives; its left wing, the *puros,* advocated sweeping antifeudal, anticlerical reforms.

The election of 1828 produced the first political crusis of the republic. The conservatives united behind Manuel Gómez Pedraza, a leader of the moderados; the puro candidate was Vicente Guerrero, a hero of the war for independence whose popularity should have assured his election. But Gómez Pedraza was secretary of war, and army pressure on the state legislatures produced a vote of ten to nine for him and the conservative vice-presidential candidate, Anastasio Bustamante. Liberal indignation was great, and General Antonio López de Santa Anna, who had overthrown Iturbide and saw another opportunity to make political capital by assuming the role of liberator, rose in revolt against Gómez Pedraza. By January 1829, the liberals had triumphed, and Congress declared Guerrero president of the republic. Hoping to promote unity, Guerrero asked Bustamante to remain as vice president—a serious error, as events proved.

An honest but uneducated man who doubted his own ability to govern, a mestizo scorned by the aristocratic Creole society of the capital, Guerrero lasted barely one year in office. He coped successfully with a Spanish effort to reconquer Mexico (1829), but was overthrown the next year by an army revolt organized by Bustamante with the aid of the unprincipled Santa Anna. For two years, a conservative dictatorship dominated by Lucas Alamán used the army to remove liberal governors and legislatures in the states, suppress newspapers, and jail, shoot, or exile puro leaders. The climax of this reign of terror was the execution of the veteran revolutionary Guerrero by a firing squad in 1831.

Growing unrest informed Santa Anna that the political pendulum was swinging toward the liberals, and in 1832 this careerist, a true conservative at heart, led a revolt against Bustamante. Province after province joined the revolt, and by the end of the year Bustamante had been forced into exile. Following congressional elections in March 1833, a new liberal government, dominated by the puros, was formed. Santa Anna, still posing as a liberal, was elected president, and Valentín Gómez Farías, a physician who remained a pillar of the liberal cause for a quarter-century, was chosen vice president. But Santa Anna would not assume responsibility for carrying out the liberal program; pleading ill health, he retired to his hacienda on the Veracruz coast and turned over to Gómez Farías the reins of office.

The year 1833 was a high-water mark of liberal achievement. Aided by José María Luis Mora, his minister of education, Gómez Farías pushed through Congress a series of radical reforms: abolition of the special privileges and immunities of the army and church (meaning that officers and priests would now be subject to the jurisdiction of civil courts), abolition of tithes, secularization of the clerical University of Mexico, creation of a department of public instruction, reduction of the army, and creation of a civilian militia. These measures were accompanied by a program of internal improvements designed to increase the prosperity of the interior by linking it to the capital and the coasts. In their use of the central government to promote education and national economic development, the liberals showed that they were not doctrinaire adherents of laissez faire.

The liberal program inevitably provoked clerical and conservative resistance. Army officers began to organize revolts; priests proclaimed from their pulpits that the great cholera epidemic of 1833 was a sign of divine displeasure with the works of the impious liberals. Santa Anna waited until the time was ripe. Then, in April 1834, he placed himself at the head of the conservative rebellion, occupied the capital, and sent Gómez Farías and Mora into exile. Resuming the presidency, he summoned a hand-picked reactionary congress that repealed the reform laws of 1833 and suspended the constitution of 1824. Under the new conservative constitution of 1836, the states were reduced to departments completely dominated by the central government, upper-class control of politics was assured through high property and income qualifications for holding office, and the fueros of the church and army were restored.

Santa Anna and the conservatives ruled Mexico for the greater part of two decades, 1834 to 1854. Politically and economically, the conservative rule subordinated the interests of the regions and the country as a whole to a wealthy, densely populated central core linking Mexico City, Puebla, and Veracruz. Its centralist trend was reflected in the tariff act of 1837, which restored the alcabala, or sales tax system, inland customhouses, and the government tobacco monopoly, insuring the continuous flow of revenues to Mexico City.

War and Territorial Losses

Conservative neglect and abuse of outlying or border areas like northern Mexico and Yucatán contributed to the loss of Texas and almost led to the loss of Yucatán. Santa Anna's destruction of provincial autonomy enabled American colonists in Texas, led by Sam Houston, to pose as patriotic federalists in revolt against Santa Anna's tyranny. Santa Anna's incompetent generalship contributed to the defeat of his miserable Indian and mestizo conscripts at the battle of San Jacinto (1837), which secured the de facto independence of Texas. In Yucatán, the Caste or Social War of 1839 combined elements of a regional war against conservative centralism and an Indian war against feudal landlords. For almost a decade, Yucatán remained outside Mexico.

After the definitive loss of Texas through annexation by the United States in 1845 came the greater disaster of the Mexican War (1846–1848). Its immediate cause was a dispute between Mexico and the United States over the boundary of Texas, but the decisive factor was the determination of the Polk administration to acquire not only Texas but California and New Mexico. The war ended in a catastrophic Mexican defeat, basically due to American superiority in resources, military training, and leadership, but the irresponsible, selfish attitudes of the Mexican aristocracy and church contributed to the debacle.

In 1846, after conservative generals had suffered a series of reverses, a liberal revolt returned the puros to power and re-established the constitution of 1824. Led by Gómez Farías, the puros had a plan for winning the war that produced a curious replay of the events of 1834. The plan called for recalling Santa Anna—still regarded as the best of Mexico's generals—from the exile to which his own conservatives had consigned him. Having been allowed by the Americans to slip through their blockade and re-enter Mexico, Santa Anna was named president and commander in chief of the Mexican armies.

Gómez Farías, meanwhile, undertook to finance the war by seizure of church property.

This proposal horrified the clergy and their aristocratic supporters. Some aristocratic militia regiments in the capital, mobilized to fight the Americans, decided it was more urgent to save the church from the puros and rose in revolt against Gómez Farías. At the critical moment, Santa Anna repeated his betrayal of 1834. Returning to the capital, he ousted Gómez Farías, installed the moderado General Pedro María de Anaya as president, then turned to meet the advance of General Winfield Scott from Veracruz. Despite the tenacious resistance of a volunteer army at the approaches to the capital, the American invaders entered Mexico City in September 1847.

Mexican armies had been beaten in the field, but guerrilla warfare, joined with the ravages of disease, was taking a heavy toll of American lives; continued resistance and refusal to admit defeat might have secured a better peace for Mexico. But the aristocratic Creoles—some of whom favored a total take-over of Mexico by the United States—and their clerical allies feared the consequences of partisan warfare to their wealth and privileges and hastened to make peace. While Santa Anna fled to a new exile in Jamaica, a moderado government, formed at Querétaro, opened negotiations with the Americans. By the treaty of Guadalupe Hidalgo (1848), Mexico ceded Texas, California, and New Mexico to the United States; in return, Mexico received $15 million and the cancellation of certain claims against it.

La Reforma, *Civil War, and the French Intervention*

A succession of moderado administrations, mildly conservative but reasonably honest and efficient, struggled with the myriad problems of postwar Mexico. Meanwhile, the disasters suffered by Mexico under conservative rule had created a widespread revulsion against conservative policies and stimulated a revival of puro Liberalism. In 1846, during the war, liberal administrations had come to power in the states of Oaxaca and Michoacán. In Michoacán the new governor was Melchor Ocampo, a scholar and scientist profoundly influenced by Rousseau and French utopian socialist thought, who was described by Justo Sierra as a "man of thought and action, agriculturalist, naturalist, economist, a public man from love of the public good, with no other ambition than that of doing something for his country." In Oaxaca a Zapotec Indian, Benito Juárez, became governor. Aided by a philanthropic Creole, Juárez had worked his way through law school and established a law office in the city of Oaxaca. As governor, he gained a reputation for honesty, efficiency, and the democratic simplicity of his manners.

Ocampo and Juárez were two leaders of a renovated liberalism that ushered in the movement called *La Reforma.* Like the older liberalism of the 1830s, the Reforma sought to destroy feudal vestiges and implant capitalism in Mexico. Its ideology, however, was more spirited than the aristocratic, intellectual liberalism of Mora; and its puro left wing included a small number of figures, such as Ponciano Arriaga and Ignacio Ramírez, who rose above the general level of liberal ideology by their attacks on the latifundio, defense of labor and women's rights, and other advanced ideas.

The revived liberal ferment, with its demand for the abolition of fueros and secularization of church property, inspired alarm among the reactionary forces. They feared that the moderado regime of Mariano Arista, who became president in 1850, did not offer adequate insurance against radical change. In January 1853, a coalition of high clergy, generals, and great Creole landowners, headed by the aged Alamán, organized a successful revolt against Arista and named Santa Anna, then living in Venezuela, dictator for one year. On his arrival in Mexico City on April 20, Santa Anna was formally proclaimed president.

For Alamán, the old dictator was merely a stopgap for an imported foreign prince. Alamán died on June 2, 1853, and with him died what intelligence and integrity remained in the conservative camp. Free from Alamán's restraining influence, Santa Anna returned to his familiar ways of graft and plunder, looting the public treasury for his own benefit and that of his sycophants. In December he had himself proclaimed perpetual dictator, with the title of His Most Supreme Highness.

Santa Anna's return to power, accompanied by a terrorist campaign against all dissenters, spurred a gathering of opposition forces, including many disgruntled moderados and conservatives. In early 1854, the old liberal caudillo from the state of Guerrero, Juan Álvarez, and the moderado general Ignacio Comonfort issued a call for revolt, the Plan of Ayutla, demanding the end of the dictatorship and the election of a convention to draft a new constitution. Within a year, Santa Anna's regime began to disintegrate, and in August 1855, seeing the handwriting on the wall, he went into exile for the last time. Some days later, a puro-dominated provisional government took office in Mexico City. The seventy-five-year-old Juan Álvarez was named provisional president; to his cabinet he named Benito Juárez as minister of justice and Miguel Lerdo de Tejada as minister of the treasury.

One of Juárez's first official acts was to issue a decree abolishing clerical and military fueros (the *Ley Juárez*). The decree raised a storm of conservative wrath, and Comonfort, now minister of war, himself disapproved of the measure. By December, moderado and conservative pressure, wielded through Comonfort, had brought a shift to the right in the cabinet. Melchor Ocampo, the most radical of the puros, was forced out, and a few days later Álvarez himself resigned, turning over the presidency to Comonfort, who proposed to steer a cautious middle course that he hoped would satisfy both liberals and conservatives.

The *Ley Lerdo* (Lerdo Law) of June 1856, drafted by Comonfort's minister of the treasury, Miguel

Lerdo de Tejada, was poorly designed to achieve such a reconciliation, for it struck a heavy blow at the material base of the church's power, its landed wealth. The law barred the church from holding land not used for religious purposes and compelled the sale of all such property to tenants, with the rent considered to be 6 percent of the sale value of the property. Real estate not being rented was to be auctioned to the highest bidder, with payment of a large sales tax to the government.

The intent of the law was to create a rural middle class, but since it made no provision for division of the church estates, the bulk of the land passed into the hands of great landowners, merchants, and capitalists, both native and foreign. What was worse, the law barred Indian villages from owning land and ordered that such land be sold in the same manner as church property, excepting only land and buildings used exclusively for the "public use" of the inhabitants and for communal pastures (*ejidos*). As a result, land-grabbers descended on the Indian villages, "denounced" their land to the local courts, and proceeded to buy it at auction for paltry sums. The law provided that the Indian owners should have the first opportunity to buy, but few natives could pay the minimum purchase price. When the Indians responded with protests and revolts, Lerdo explained in a circular that the intent of his law was that Indian community lands should be divided among the natives, not sold to others. But he insisted that "the continued existence of the Indian communities ought not to be tolerated . . . , and this is exactly one of the goals of the law." He was also adamant on the right of those who rented Indian lands to buy them if they chose to do so. As a result, during the summer and fall of 1856 many Indian pueblos lost crop and pasture lands from which they had derived revenues vitally needed to defray the cost of their religious ceremonies and other communal expenses. Indian resistance and the liberals' need to attract popular support during their struggle with the conservative counter-revolution and French interventionists in the decade 1857–1867 seem to have slowed enforcement of the Lerdo Law as it applied to Indian villages, but the long-range tendency of liberal agrarian policy was to compel division of communal lands, facilitating their acquisition by hacendados and even small and middle-sized farmers. The result was a simultaneous strengthening of the latifundio and some increase in the size of the rural middle class.[2]

While the provisional government was causing consternation among conservatives with the Ley Juárez and the Ley Lerdo, a constitutional convention dominated by moderate liberals had been completing its work. The constitution of 1857 proclaimed freedom of speech, press, and assembly; abolished fueros; forbade ecclesiastical and civil corporations to own land; and proclaimed the sanctity of private property. It restored the federalist structure of 1824, with the same division of Mexico into states, but replaced the bicameral national legislature with a single house and eliminated the office of vice-president (the chief justice of the Supreme Court should succeed if the office of president became vacant). An effort by the puro minority to incorporate freedom of religion in the constitution failed; the resulting compromise neither mentioned toleration nor explicitly adopted Catholicism as the official faith.

A few voices were raised against the land monopoly, peonage, and the immense inequalities of wealth. "We proclaim ideas and forget realities," complained the radical delegate Ponciano Arriaga. "How can a hungry, naked, miserable people practice popular government? How can we condemn slavery in words, while the lot of most of our fellow citizens is more grievous than that of the black slaves of Cuba or the United States?" Despite his caustic attack on the land monopoly, Arriaga offered a relatively moderate solution: The state should seize and auction off large uncultivated estates. The conservative opposition promptly branded Arriaga's project "communist"; the moderate majority in the convention passed over it in silence.

Having completed its work, the convention disbanded, and elections followed for the first Congress and president and the members of the Supreme Court. Comonfort, who had already expressed unhappiness with the constitution, was elected president, and Juárez chief justice of the Supreme Court.

Since the new constitution incorporated the Lerdo Law and the Juárez Law abolishing fueros, the church now openly entered the political struggle by excommunicating all public officials who took the required oath of loyalty. Counterrevolution had been gathering its forces for months and found an instrument in the vacillating president Comonfort. In December 1857, General Félix Zuloaga "pronounced" in favor of a Comonfort dictatorship, occupied the capital, and arrested Juárez. Pressed by the reactionaries to repeal the Juárez and Lerdo laws, Comonfort refused and finally found the strength to break with his reactionary supporters. He released Juárez, declared the constitution re-established, and himself went into exile, unmolested by the victorious rebels. Meanwhile, the liberals in the provinces had raised an army; proclaiming that Comonfort had violated the constitution and ceased to be president, they declared Juárez president of Mexico. For their part, the conservatives, in control of Mexico City, Puebla, and other major cities, declared the constitution void and the Juárez and Lerdo laws repealed.

The tremendous Three Years' War (1857–1860) had begun. In regional terms, the war pitted

---

[2] In 1863, in order to finance the struggle against the French intervention, the liberal Juárez issued a decree that authorized the sale of *tierras baldías* (vacant lands) to which there was no valid title. Since the Indians often lacked titles that were regarded as valid, their lands were exposed to "denunciation" and purchase from the state by land-grabbing landlords and speculators. In four years, Juárez issued titles to nearly 4.5 million acres of land, further stimulating the spoliation of Indian lands and the growth of peonage.

the rich central area, dominated by the conservatives, against the liberal south, north, and
Veracruz. Controlling extensive regions and
enjoying the support of a clear majority of the
population, the liberals nevertheless suffered
serious defeats in the first stage of the war. The
main reason was that most of the permanent
army had gone over to the conservatives, while
the liberals had to create their own armed forces.
The liberal armies, composed of elements of
the national guard and guerrilla bands, were
at the outset inevitably inferior in discipline and
equipment to the conservative troops, which
won almost all the pitched battles. In March
1858, conservative troops occupied the important
mining center of Guanajuato and approached
Querétaro, the seat of Juárez's government. He
was forced to move his headquarters, first to
Guadalajara and later to Veracruz, which remained the liberal capital until the end of the
war.

As the struggle progressed, both sides found
themselves in serious financial difficulties. The
conservatives, however, had the advantage of
generous support from the church. In July 1859,
Juárez struck back at the clergy with reform
laws that nationalized without compensation
all ecclesiastical property except church buildings; the laws also suppressed all monasteries,
established freedom of religion, and separated
church and state. The reform laws were designed
to encourage peasant proprietorship by dividing
church estates into small farms, but this goal
proved illusory; thanks to the Ley Lerdo, wealthy
purchasers had already acquired much of the
church land.

By the middle of 1860, the tide of war had
turned in favor of the liberals. In August 1860,
the best conservative general, Miguel Miramón,
was routed at Silao. In October, Guadalajara
fell to the liberals. And by the beginning of
January 1861, Juárez had re-entered the capital,
and the conservative leaders had fled the country. The war was effectively over, although

Benito Juárez. (Courtesy of the Organization of
American States)

conservative bands in the provinces continued
to make devastating raids.

Beaten in the field, the reactionaries looked
for help abroad. The conservative governments
of England, France, and Spain had no love for
the Mexican liberals and their leader Juárez.
Moreover, there were ample pretexts for intervention, for both sides had seized or destroyed foreign property without compensation,
and foreign bondholders were clamoring for
payments from an empty Mexican treasury. The
three European powers demanded compensation for damages to their nationals and payment of just debts. Juárez vainly pleaded poverty
and noted the dubious nature of some of the
claims.

In October 1861, the three powers agreed on a joint intervention in Mexico, and in January 1862, they sent occupation forces to Veracruz. England and Spain, having received assurances of future satisfaction of their claims, soon withdrew, but the French government rejected all Mexican offers, and its troops remained. Napoleon III wanted more than payment of debts. A group of Mexican conservative exiles had convinced the ambitious emperor that the Mexican people would welcome a French army of liberation and the establishment of a monarchy. Napoleon had visions of a French-protected Mexican Empire that would yield him great political and economic advantages. It remained only to find a suitable unemployed prince, and one was found in the person of Archduke Ferdinand Maximilian of Hapsburg, brother of the Austrian emperor Franz Josef.

To prepare the ground for the arrival of the new ruler of Mexico, the French army advanced from Veracruz into the interior toward Puebla. At Puebla, instead of being received as liberators, the interventionists met determined resistance on the part of a poorly armed Mexican garrison and were thrown back with heavy losses. The date—May 5, 1862—is still celebrated as a Mexican national holiday. Reinforced by the arrival of thirty thousand fresh troops, General Elie-Frédéric Forey again besieged Puebla in March 1863, and by May 17 the starving garrison had been forced to surrender. The fall of Puebla and the loss of its garrison of some thirty thousand men left Juárez without an adequate force to defend the capital, and at the end of May his government and the remnants of his army abandoned it and retreated northward. On June 10, the French entered the city to the rejoicing of the clergy; by the end of the year the interventionists had occupied Querétaro, Monterrey, San Luis Potosí, and Saltillo. But the invaders had secure control only of the cities; republican guerrilla detachments controlled most of the national territory.

Meanwhile, in October 1863, a delegation of conservative exiles called on Maximilian to offer him a Mexican crown. As a condition of acceptance, the prince insisted that the Mexican people be consulted, and the French authorities obligingly staged a plebiscite that supposedly gave an overwhelming vote in favor of Maximilian. In April 1864, he accepted the Mexican throne and presently departed with his wife Carlota for their new home.

The conservative conspirators had counted on Maximilian to help them recover their lost wealth and privileges, but the emperor, mindful of realities, would not consent to their demands; the purchase of church lands by native and foreign landlords and capitalists had created new interests that Maximilian refused to antagonize. Confident of conservative support, Maximilian even wooed moderate liberals and won the support of such intellectual lights as the historians José Fernando Ramírez and Manuel Orozco y Berra, who were impressed by Maximilian's good will and cherished the illusion of a stable and prosperous Mexico ruled by an enlightened monarch.

But the hopes of both conservatives and misguided liberals were built on quicksand. The victories of Maximilian's generals could not destroy the fluid and elusive liberal resistance, firmly grounded in popular hatred for the invaders and aided by Mexico's geography (a rugged terrain with vast, thinly populated territories and few roads). A turning point in the war came in the spring of 1865 in the United States, with the Union triumph over the Confederacy. American demands that the French evacuate Mexico, a region regarded by Secretary of State William Seward as an American zone of economic and political influence, grew more insistent, and American troops were massed along the Rio Grande. Facing serious domestic and diplomatic problems at home, Napoleon decided to cut his losses and liquidate the Mexican adventure.

Marshal Achille François Bazaine, preparing to embark with the remaining French troops, urged Maximilian to abdicate and leave Mexico, but his conservative advisers, who still believed that defeat could be avoided, prevailed on him to stay. With liberal armies converging on Querétaro, the same die-hard conservatives persuaded Maximilian to go there and assume supreme command. Together with the imperialist generals Miguel Miramón and Tomás Mejía, he was captured on May 14, 1867. After a trial by court-martial, all three were found guilty of treason, sentenced to death, and executed by a *Juarista* firing squad.

Postwar Attempts at Reconstruction and the Death of La Reforma

Juárez, symbol of the successful Mexican resistance to a foreign usurper, resumed his office of president in August 1867. His government inherited a devastated country. Agriculture and industry were in ruins; as late as 1873, the value of Mexican exports was below the level of 1810. To reduce the state's financial burdens and end the danger of military control, Juárez dismissed two-thirds of the army, an act that produced discontent and uprisings, which his generals managed to suppress.

Juárez devoted a considerable part of the state's limited resources to the development of a public school system, especially on the elementary level; by 1874 there were about eight thousand schools with some three hundred and fifty thousand pupils. One of the few material achievements of his administration was the construction of an important railroad line running from Veracruz through Puebla to Mexico City, completed after his death in 1872.

In his agrarian policy, Juárez continued the liberal program of seeking to implant capitalism in the countryside, at the expense not of the hacienda but of the Indian communities. Indeed, the period of the "Restored Republic" (1868–1876) saw an intensified effort by the federal government to implement the Lerdo Law by compelling dissolution and partition of Indian communal lands, opening the way for a new wave of frauds and seizures by neighboring hacendados and other land-grabbers. The result was a series of nationwide peasant revolts, the most serious occurring in the state of Hidalgo (1869–1870). Proclaiming the rebels to be "communists," the hacendados, aided by state and federal authorities, restored order by the traditional violent methods. A few liberals raised their voices in protest, but were ignored; one was Ignacio Ramírez, who condemned the frauds and usurpations practiced by the hacendados with the complicity of corrupt judges and officials and called for suspension of the law. On the other hand, the period saw the first legislative efforts to improve labor conditions and the formation in the cities of numerous trade unions whose leaders combined liberal and trade unionist principles.

Re-elected president in 1871, Juárez was able to put down a revolt by a hero of the wars of the Reforma, General Porfirio Díaz, who charged Juárez with attempting to become a dictator. But Juárez died the next year of a heart attack and was succeeded as acting president by the chief justice of the Supreme Court, Sebastián Lerdo de Tejada. Lerdo scheduled new elections for October 1872, ran against, and easily defeated Díaz, but in turn faced a growing movement of opposition that accused him of violations of republican legality. When Lerdo announced in 1876 that he intended to seek re-election, Díaz again rose in revolt, defeated troops loyal to Lerdo, and sent him into flight.

Díaz had seized power in the name of the ideals of the Reforma. In fact, the year 1876 marked the death of the Reforma and the idealistic principles of natural law that formed its theoretical base. The age of Díaz continued the efforts of the Reforma to construct a bourgeois society, but with new men, new methods, and a new ideology. The libertarian creed to which Juárez subscribed, no matter how often he deviated from it, was replaced by the ideology of positivism as propounded by its French founder, Auguste Comte—ideology that ranked order and progress above freedom.

The Reforma had paved the way for this change by transforming the Mexican bourgeoisie from a revolutionary class into a ruling class that was more predatory and acquisitive than the old Creole aristocracy. The remnants of that aristocracy speedily adapted to the ways of the new ruling class and merged with it. The interests of the old and the new rich required political stability, a docile labor force, internal improvements, and a political and economic climate favorable to foreign investments. The mission of the "honorable tyranny" of Porfirio Díaz was to achieve those ends.

ARGENTINA

In 1816 delegates to the congress of Tucumán proclaimed the independence of the United Provinces of the Río de la Plata. "Disunited," however, would have better described the political condition of the area of La Plata, for the Creole seizure of power in Buenos Aires in 1810 brought in its train a dissolution of the vast viceroyalty of the Río de la Plata.

The Liberation of Paraguay, Uruguay, and Upper Peru

Paraguay, having repelled efforts by the junta of Buenos Aires to "liberate" it, declared its own independence and fell under the dictatorial rule of the Creole lawyer José Gaspar Rodríguez de Francia, who effectively sealed it off from its neighbors. Francia had his reasons for the system of isolation: The rulers of Buenos Aires controlled Paraguay's river outlets to the sea, and isolation and self-sufficiency were the alternatives to submission and payment of tribute to Buenos Aires. Francia did permit a limited licensed trade with the outside world by way of Brazil, chiefly to satisfy military needs.

Francia's state-controlled economy brought certain benefits: The planned diversification of agriculture, which reduced production of such export crops as yerba maté, tobacco, and sugar, insured a plentiful supply of foodstuffs and the well-being of the Indian and mestizo masses. An interesting feature of Francia's system was the establishment of state farms or ranches— called *estancias de la patria*—that successfully specialized in the raising of livestock and ended Paraguay's dependence on livestock imports from the Argentine province of Entre Ríos. The principal sufferers under Francia's dictatorship were Spaniards, many of whom he expelled or penalized in various ways, and Creole aristocrats, who were kept under perpetual surveillance and subjected to severe repression.

Uruguay, then known as the Banda Oriental, was led toward independance by the gaucho chieftain José Gervasio Artigas, who resisted the efforts of the junta of Buenos Aires to dominate the area. In 1815 the junta abandoned these efforts, evacuated Montevideo, and turned it over to Artigas. No ordinary caudillo, Artigas not only defended Uruguayan nationality but sought to achieve social reform. In 1815 he issued a plan for distributing royalist lands to the landless, with preference shown to blacks, Indians, zambos, and poor whites. But he was not given the opportunity to implement this radical program. In 1817 a powerful Brazilian army invaded Uruguay and soon had a secure grip on the Banda Oriental. Artigas had to flee across the Paraná River into Paraguay. He received asylum from Francia but was never allowed to leave again; he died in Paraguay thirty years later.

Soon Uruguay again became a battlefield when a small group of Uruguayan exiles, supported by Buenos Aires, crossed over the estuary in 1825 and launched a general revolt against Brazilian domination. Brazil retaliated by declaring war against the United Provinces. The three-sided military conflict ended in a stalemate. Uruguay finally achieved independence in 1828 through the mediation of Great Britain, which was unwilling to see Uruguay fall under the control of either of its more powerful neighbors.

Upper Peru, the mountainous northern corner of the old viceroyalty of La Plata, also escaped the grasp of Buenos Aires after 1810. Three expeditions were sent into the high country, won initial victories, then were rolled back by Spanish counteroffensives. Logistical problems, the apathy of the Indian population, and the hostility of the Creole aristocracy, which remained loyal to Spain until it became clear that the royalist cause was doomed, contributed to the patriot defeats. Not until 1825 was Upper Peru liberated by General Antonio José de Sucre, Bolívar's lieutenant. Renamed Bolivia in honor of the liberator, it began its independent life the next year under a complicated, totally impractical constitution drafted by Bolívar himself.

The Struggle for Progress and National Unity

Even among the provinces that had joined at Tucumán to form the United Provinces of La Plata, discord grew and threatened the dissolution of the new state. The efforts of the wealthy port and province of Buenos Aires to impose its hegemony over the interior met with tenacious resistance. The end of the Spanish trade monopoly brought large gains to Buenos Aires and lesser gains to the littoral (coastal) provinces of Santa Fe, Entre Ríos, and Corrientes; their exports of meat and hides increased, and the value of their lands rose. But the wine and textile industries of the interior, which had been protected by the colonial monopoly, suffered from the competition of cheaper and superior European wares imported through the port of Buenos Aires.

The interests of the interior provinces required a measure of autonomy or even independence in order to protect their primitive industries, but Buenos Aires preferred a single free-trade zone under a government dominated by the port city. This was one cause of the conflict between Argentine *federales* (federalists) and *unitarios* (unitarians). By 1820 the federalist solution had triumphed; the United Provinces had in effect dissolved into a number of independent republics, with the interior provinces ruled by caudillos, each representing the interests of the local ruling class and having a gaucho army at his back.

A new start toward unity came with the appointment in 1821 of Bernardino Rivadavia as chief minister under Martín Rodríguez, governor of the province of Buenos Aires. An ardent liberal, strongly influenced by the English philosopher Jeremy Bentham, Rivadavia launched an ambitious program of educational, social, and economic reform. He promoted primary education, founded the University of Buenos Aires, abolished the ecclesiastical fuero and the tithe, and suppressed some monasteries. Rivadavia envisioned a balanced development of industry and agriculture, with a large role assigned to British investment and colonization. But the obstacles in the way of industrialization proved too great, and little came of efforts in this direction. The greatest progress was made in cattle raising, which expanded rapidly southward into former Indian territory.

In 1822, hoping to raise revenue and increase production, Rivadavia introduced the system of emphyteusis, a program of distribution of public lands through long-term leases at fixed rentals. Some writers have seen in this system an effort at agrarian reform, but there were no limits on the size of grants, and the measure actually contributed to the growth of latifundia. The lure of large profits in livestock raising induced many native and foreign merchants, politicians, and members of the military to join the rush for land. The net result was the creation not of a small farmer class but of a new and more powerful *estanciero* class that was the enemy of Rivadavia's progressive ideals.

Rivadavia's planning went beyond the province of Buenos Aires; he had a vision of a unified

Argentina under a strong central government that would promote the rounded economic development of the whole national territory. In 1825 a constituent congress met in Buenos Aires at Rivadavia's call to draft a constitution for the United Provinces of the Río de la Plata. Rivadavia, who was elected president of the new state, made a dramatic proposal to federalize the city and port of Buenos Aires. The former capital of the province would henceforth belong to the whole nation, with the revenues of its customhouse to be used to advance the general welfare.

Rivadavia's proposal reflected his nationalism and the need to mobilize national resources for a war with Brazil (1825–1828) over Uruguay. Congress approved Rivadavia's project, but the federalist caudillos of the interior, fearing that the rise of a strong national government would mean the end of their power, refused to ratify the constitution and even withdrew their delegates from the congress. In Buenos Aires a similar stand was taken by the powerful estancieros, who had no intention of surrendering the privileges of their province and regarded Rivadavia's program of social and economic reform as a costly folly.

Defeated on the issue of the constitution, Rivadavia suffered a further loss of prestige when his agent signed a peace treaty with Brazil recognizing Uruguay as a province of the Brazilian Empire. Rivadavia rejected the treaty, but popular anger at the agreement combined with opposition to his domestic program had sealed his political doom. In July 1827, he resigned the presidency and went into exile. The liberal program for achieving national unity had failed.

After an interval of factional struggles, the federalism espoused by the landed oligarchy of Buenos Aires triumphed in the person of Juan Manuel Rosas, who became governor of the province in 1829. Under his influence there was forged (1831) a federal pact under which Buenos Aires assumed representation for the other provinces in foreign affairs but left them

Juan Manuel Rosas. (Courtesy of the Organization of American States)

free to run their own affairs in all other respects. Federalism, as defined by Rosas, meant that Buenos Aires retained the revenues of its customhouse for its exclusive use and controlled trade on the Río de la Plata system for the benefit of its merchants. A network of personal alliances between Rosas and provincial caudillos, backed by use of force against recalcitrant leaders, insured for him a large measure of control over the interior.

Rosas' long reign saw a total reversal of Rivadavia's progressive policies. For Rosas and the ruling class of estancieros, virtually the only economic concern was the export of hides and salted meat and the import of foreign goods. The dictator also showed some favor to wheat farming, which he protected by tariff laws, but he neglected artisans and machine industry. Rosas himself was a great estanciero and owner of a saladero that enjoyed a monopoly on the curing of meat and hides. He vigorously pressed the conquest of Indian territory, bringing much new land under the control of the province of Buenos Aires; this land was sold for low prices to estancieros, and Rivadavia's policy of retaining ownership of land by the state was abandoned. Rosas also discarded Rivadavia's policy of promoting immigration and education. Rosas handed over what schools remained to the Jesuits, who were recalled from exile in 1836 (ultimately, Rosas found the order too independent and expelled it).

By degrees, the press and all other potential dissidents were cowed or destroyed. To enforce the dictator's will there arose a secret organization known as the *Mazorca* (ear of corn—a reference to the close unity of its members). In collaboration with the police, this terrorist organization beat up or even murdered Rosas' opponents. The masthead of the official journal and all official papers carried the slogan "Death to the savage, filthy unitarians!" Even horses had to display the red ribbon that was the federalist symbol. Those opponents who did not knuckle under and escaped death fled by the thousands to Montevideo, Chile, Brazil, or other places of refuge.

Under Rosas, the merchants of the city and the estancieros of the province of Buenos Aires enjoyed a measure of prosperity, although an Anglo-French blockade of the estuary of La Plata from 1845 to 1848, caused by Rosas' mistreatment of English and French nationals and his efforts to subvert Uruguayan independence, resulted in severe losses to both groups. But this prosperity bore no proportion to the possibilities of economic growth; technical backwardness marked all aspects of livestock raising and agriculture, and port facilities were totally inadequate.

Meanwhile, the littoral provinces, which had experienced some advance of livestock raising and agriculture, became increasingly aware that Rosas' brand of federalism was harmful to their interests and that free navigation of the river system of La Plata was necessary to assure their prosperity. In 1852 the anti-Rosas forces formed a coalition that united the liberal émigrés with the caudillo Justo José de Urquiza of Entre Ríos, who was joined by the great majority of the provincial caudillos, and Brazil and Uruguay. At Monte Caseros, their combined forces defeated Rosas' army and sent him fleeing to an English exile.

Victory over Rosas did not end the dispute between Buenos Aires and the other provinces, between federalism and unitarianism. Only the slower process of economic change would forge the desired unity. A rift soon arose between the liberal exiles who assumed leadership in Buenos Aires and the caudillo Urquiza of Entre Ríos, who was backed by his victorious army. Urquiza, who still sported the red ribbon of federalism, proposed a loose union of the provinces, with all of them sharing the revenues of the Buenos Aires customhouse. But the leaders of Buenos Aires feared the loss of their economic and political predominance to Urquiza, whom they wrongly considered a caudillo of the Rosas type; in fact, Urquiza was a sincere convert to the gospel of modernity and civilization.

Within the province of Buenos Aires, opinions were divided. Some favored entry into a new confederation but with very precise guarantees of the interests of their province; others argued for total separation from the other thirteen provinces. After Urquiza had unsuccessfully attempted to make Buenos Aires accept unification by armed force, the two sides agreed to a peaceful separation. As a result, delegates from Buenos Aires were absent from the constitutional convention that met at Santa Fe in Entre Ríos in 1852.

The constitution of 1853 reflected the influence of the ideas of the journalist Juan Bautista Alberdi on the delegates. His forcefully written pamphlet, *Bases and Points of Departure for the Political Organization of the Argentine Republic,* offered the United States as a model for Argentina. The new constitution strongly resembled that of the United States in certain respects. The former United Provinces became a federal republic, presided over by a president with significant power who served a six-year term without the possibility of immediate reelection. Legislative functions were vested in a bicameral legislature, a senate and a house of representatives. The Catholic religion was proclaimed the official religion of the nation, but freedom of worship for non-Catholics was assured. The states were empowered to elect governors and legislatures and frame their own constitutions, but the federal government had the right of intervention— including armed intervention—to insure respect for the provisions of the constitution. General Urquiza was elected the first president of the Argentine Republic.

The liberal leaders of Buenos Aires, joined by the conservative estancieros who had been Rosas' firmest supporters, refused to accept the constitution of 1853, for they feared the creation of a state they did not control. As a result, two Argentinas arose: The Argentine Confederation, headed by Urquiza, and the province of Buenos Aires. For five years, the two states maintained their separate existence. In Paraná, capital of the confederation, Urquiza struggled to repress gaucho revolts, stimulate economic development, and foster education and immigration. Modest advances were made, but the tempo of growth lagged far behind that of the wealthy city and province of Buenos Aires, which prospered on the base of a steadily increasing trade with Europe in hides, tallow, salted beef, and wool.

Hoping to increase the confederation's scanty revenues, Urquiza began a tariff war with Buenos Aires, levying surcharges on goods landed at the Paraná River port of Rosario if duties had been paid on them at Buenos Aires. Buenos Aires responded with sanctions against ships sailing to Rosario and threatened to close commerce on the Paraná altogether. In 1859 war between the two Argentine states broke out. Defeated at the battle of Cepeda, Bartolomé Mitre, the commander of the Buenos Aires forces, accepted a compromise whereby Buenos Aires would join the confederation after a constitutional reform that protected its special interests. But the peace was short-lived; war broke out again in the presidency of Santiago Derqui, Urquiza's successor and personal rival. In the decisive battle of Pavón (1861), in which Mitre, now governor of the province of Buenos Aires, commanded the Buenos Aires army, the forces of the confederation, led by Urquiza, suffered defeat.

The military and economic superiority of Buenos Aires, the need of the other provinces to use its port, and an awareness on all sides of the urgent need to achieve national unity dictated a compromise. At a congress representing all the provinces, held at Buenos Aires in 1862, it was agreed over the opposition of a die-hard group of Buenos Aires federalists that the city should be the provisional capital of both the Argentine Republic and the province and that the Buenos Aires customhouse should be nationalized, with the proviso that for a period of five years the revenues of the province would not fall below the 1859 level. In conformity with decisions of the congress, elections to choose the first president of a united Argentina were held the same year, and Bartolomé Mitre—distinguished historian, poet, soldier, and statesman—was elected president for a six-year term.

Mitre's term of office saw continued economic progress and consolidation of national unity. The customhouse was nationalized, as had been promised, and plans were made for the federalization of the capital. The construction of railways and telegraph lines that would forge closer links between Buenos Aires and the interior was begun, and European immigrants arrived in growing numbers. Some advances were made in the establishment of a public school system. But great problems remained. The shadow of the provincial caudillo continued to fall on the Argentine Republic; in the north, a revolt by one of Rosas' old allies had to be put down by armed force. The most difficult problem Mitre had to deal with, however, was the long, exhausting Paraguayan War (1865–1870).

The Paraguayan War

On the death of the dictator Francia in 1840, power in Paraguay was assumed by a triumvirate in which Carlos Antonio López soon emerged as the dominant figure. In essence, López continued Francia's dictatorial system but gave it a thin disguise of constitutional, representative government. Since he had inherited a stable, prosperous state, López could afford to rule in a less repressive fashion than his predecessor. More flexible than Francia, too, with a better understanding of the outside world, López made a successful effort to end Paraguay's diplomatic and commercial isolation. After the fall of Rosas, a stubborn enemy of Paraguayan independence, López obtained Argentine recognition of his country's independence, and the Paraná was at last opened to Paraguayan trade. López also established diplomatic relations with a series of countries, including England, France, and the United States. A special diplomatic mission to Europe, headed by his son, Francisco Solano López, also made important economic and cultural contacts, purchasing machines, placing orders for ship construction, and inviting engineers and other specialists to work in Paraguay.

The end of the policy of isolation was accompanied by a major expansion of the Paraguayan economy. Although agriculture (especially the production of such export crops as tobacco and yerba maté) continued to be the principal economic activity, López assigned great importance to the development of industry. One of his proudest achievements in this field was the construction of an iron foundry, the most modern enterprise of its type in Latin America. Transportation was improved with the building of roads and canals, the creation of a fleet of merchant ships, and the construction of a short railroad line.

Continuing Francia's policy, López enlarged the role of the state sector in the national economy. In 1848 he transferred to state ownership forest lands producing yerba maté and other commercial wood products and much arable land. The lucrative export trade in yerba maté and some other products became a government monopoly, and the number of state-owned ranches rose to sixty-four. López promoted education as well as economic growth; by the time of his death, Paraguay had 435 elementary schools with some 25,000 pupils, and a larger proportion of literate inhabitants than any other Latin American country.

At the same time, López took advantage of his position to concentrate ownership of land and various commercial enterprises in his own hands and those of his children, relatives, and associates; thus, there arose a bourgeoisie that profited by its close connection with the state apparatus, which enabled it to promote its own interests. The number of large private estates, however, was small; the private agricultural sector was dominated by small or medium-sized farms cultivated by owners or tenants, sometimes aided by a few hired laborers. By contrast with the situation in other Latin American countries, peonage and debt servitude were rare (slavery had been put in the way of extinction by a gradual manumission law in 1842). The relative absence of peonage and feudal survivals contributed to a rapid growth of Paraguayan capitalism and the well-being of its predominantly Indian and mestizo population. When López died in 1862, Paraguay was one of the most progressive and prosperous states in South America.

His son, Francisco Solano, whom López designated his heir apparent when his death approached, succeeded his father as dictator. The younger López inherited a tradition of border disputes with Brazil that erupted into open war when Brazil sent an army into Uruguay in 1864 to insure the victory of a pro-Brazilian faction in that country's civil strife. López could not be indifferent to this action, which threatened the delicate balance of power in the basin of

La Plata. López also feared that Brazilian control over Uruguay would end unrestricted Paraguayan access to the port of Montevideo, which would make Paraguayan trade dependent entirely on the good will of Buenos Aires.

When the Brazilian government disregarded his protests, López sent an army to invade the Brazilian province of Mato Grosso, but this foray into virtually empty territory had no military significance, and he soon withdrew his troops. Hoping to strike a more effective blow at Brazil, López requested President Mitre's permission in January 1865 to cross Argentine territory (the state of Corrientes) en route to Uruguay. López regarded Mitre's refusal as an unfriendly act. In March 1865, the Paraguayan congress declared war on Argentina, and Paraguayan troops occupied the town of Corrientes. On May 1, 1865, Brazil, Argentina, and the Brazilian-sponsored Flores regime in Uruguay concluded a Triple Alliance against Paraguay; a separate secret treaty between Brazil and Argentina provided for the partition of more than half of Paraguay's territory between them. Mitre was named commander in chief of the allied forces. Paraguay thus faced a coalition that included the two largest states in South America, with an immense superiority in manpower and other resources.

Yet the war dragged on for five years, for at its outset Paraguay possessed an army of some seventy thousand well-armed and disciplined soldiers that outnumbered the combined forces of its foes. Expelled from the territory they had overrun in Argentina and Brazil, the Paraguayan troops stubbornly defended themselves against the allied forces that crossed the Paraná into Paraguay in mid-April 1866. In August 1868, Fort Humaitá was stormed by Brazilian troops under Marshal Luis Alves de Lima Caxias, at the cost of two thousand men. In January 1869, the allies occupied Asunción. Retreating northward, López attempted to organize a new defense against overwhelming numerical odds. The end came on March 1, 1870. With a few followers, López made his last stand at a point near the Brazilian border. Although seriously wounded,

he refused to surrender, allegedly exclaiming: "I die with my fatherland." López was slain by a Brazilian soldier on the field of battle. With his death, effective Paraguayan resistance ended.

For Paraguay the war's consequences were tragic. Approximately three-fourths of the prewar population of some 500,000 perished as a result of military action, famine, disease, and a devastating Brazilian occupation. The adult male population fell to some 30,000. The peace treaty assigned much Paraguayan territory to the victors and burdened Paraguay with extremely heavy reparations. Brazil, the occupying power, installed a puppet regime composed of former López generals, who began a radical reconstruction of the Paraguayan economy and state. The essence of the new policy was to liquidate the progressive changes made under the Francia and López regimes. Most of the state-owned lands were sold to land speculators and foreign businessmen at bargain prices, with no restriction on the size of holdings. Tenants who could not present the necessary documents were ejected even though they and their forebears had cultivated the land for decades. By the early 1890s, the state-owned lands were almost gone. Foreign penetration of the economy through loans, concessions, and land purchases soon deprived Paraguay of its economic as well as its political independence.

The Paraguayan War caused increased taxes and other hardships; for these reasons, it was unpopular in Argentina. The burdens of the war revived the dying spirit of provincial separatism and compelled Mitre to leave the front to direct the suppression of revolts in different provinces. By 1867 these domestic difficulties had virtually taken Argentina out of the war; when it ended, however, Argentina obtained its share of Paraguayan reparations and territorial concessions (Formosa, Chaco, and Misiones).

Progress and Development Under Sarmiento

At the close of his presidential term, Mitre returned to civilian life. He was succeeded by

Domingo Faustino Sarmiento (1868–1874), a gifted essayist, sociologist, and statesman, former Argentine minister to the United States, and an enthusiast for its institutions. Like Mitre, Sarmiento worked for Argentine unity and economic and social progress.

After the Paraguayan War, a flood of technological change began to sweep over Argentina. Railways penetrated the interior, extending the stock-raising and farming area. The gradual introduction of barbed-wire fencing and alfalfa ranges made possible a dramatic improvement in the quality of livestock. In 1876 the arrival of an experimental shipload of chilled carcasses from France prepared the way for the triumph of frozen over salted meat, which led to a vast expansion of European demand for Argentine beef. Labor was needed to exploit the rapidly expanding pasturelands and farmlands; during Sarmiento's administration alone, some three hundred thousand immigrants poured into the country. But Sarmiento taught that it was not enough to build railroads and expand acreage; it was necessary to change people's minds. Believing in the need for an educated citizenry in a democratic republic, he labored to expand and improve the public school system; to this end he introduced to Argentina teacher-training institutions of the kind his friend Horace Mann had founded in the United States.

When Sarmiento left office, Argentina presented the appearance of a rapidly developing, prosperous state. But there were clouds in the generally bright Argentine sky. The growth of exports and the rise in land values did not benefit the forlorn gauchos, aliens in a land over which they had once freely roamed, or the majority of European immigrants. Little was done to provide these newcomers with homesteads. Immigrants who wished to farm usually found the price of land out of reach; as a result, many preferred to remain in Buenos Aires or other cities of the littoral, where they began to form an urban middle class largely devoted to trade. Meanwhile, foreign economic influence grew as a result of increasing dependence on foreign—chiefly British—capital to finance the construction of railways, telegraph lines, gasworks, and other needed facilities. The growing concentration of landownership reinforced the colonial land tenure pattern; the tightening British control of markets and the country's economic infrastructure reinforced the colonial pattern of dependence on a foreign metropolis, with London replacing Seville as commercial center. But Mitre, Sarmiento, and other builders of the new Argentina, dazzled by their success in nation-building and by a climate of prosperity they believed permanent, did not suspect the extent of the problems that were in the making and that future generations of Argentines would have to attempt to solve.

CHILE

The victories of José de San Martín's Army of the Andes over royalist forces at Chacabuco and Maipú in 1817 and 1818 gave Chile its definitive independence. From 1818 until 1823, Bernardo O'Higgins, a hero of the struggle for Chilean liberation and a true son of the Enlightenment, ruled the country with the title of supreme director. O'Higgins energetically pushed a program of reform designed to weaken the landed aristocracy and the church and promote a rapid development of the Chilean economy along capitalist lines. His abolition of titles of nobility and entails angered the great landowners of the fertile Central Valley between the Andes and the Pacific; his expulsion of the royalist bishop of Santiago and his restrictions on the number of religious processions and the veneration of images infuriated the church. The opposition to O'Higgins was joined by dissident liberals who resented his sometimes heavy-handed rule. In 1823, faced with a spreading revolt, O'Higgins resigned and went into exile in Lima. There followed seven turbulent years, with presidents and constitutions rising and falling.

Portales and Economic Growth

In Chile, as in other Latin American countries, the political and armed struggle gradually assumed the form of a conflict between conservatives, who usually were also centralists, and liberals, who were generally federalists. The conservative-centralists were the party of the great landowners of the Central Valley and the wealthy merchants of Santiago; the liberal-federalists spoke for the landowners, merchants, and artisans of the northern and southern provinces, who were resentful of political and economic domination by the wealthy central area. The victory of the conservative General Joaquín Prieto over the liberal General Ramón Freire in the decisive battle of Lircay (1830) brought to power a government headed by Prieto as president but dominated by one of his cabinet ministers, Diego Portales.

From 1830 until his death in 1837, Portales, who never held on elective office, placed the enduring stamp of his ideas on Chilean politics and society. A businessman of aristocratic origins, owner of a successful import house, he faithfully served the interests of an oligarchy of great landlords and merchants that dominated the Chilean scene for decades. Although Portales expressed atheist views in private, he supported the authority of the church as an instrument for keeping the masses in order. He understood the importance of trade, industry, and mining and promoted their interests. Assisted by his able finance minister, Manuel Rengifo, Portales continued the work of O'Higgins in removing remaining obstacles to internal trade. He introduced income and property taxes to increase the state's revenues and trimmed government spending by dismissing unnecessary employees. Agriculture was protected by high tariffs on agricultural imports. Port facilities were improved, measures were taken to strengthen the Chilean merchant marine, and in 1835 a steamship line began to connect the Chilean ports. Under the fostering care of the conservative regime and in response to a growing European demand for Chilean silver, copper, and hides, the national economy made steady progress in the 1830s. As a result of this economic growth, government revenues almost doubled between 1830 and 1835.

Measures designed to stimulate economic growth were accompanied by others that fortified the social and political power of the oligarchy. In order to tighten the bond between the conservative government and the church, Portales restored the privileges the church had lost under liberal rule and normalized relations between Chile and the papacy.

In 1833 a conservative-dominated assembly adopted a constitution that further consolidated the power of the oligarchy. Elections were made indirect, with the suffrage limited to men of the age of twenty-five who could satisfy literacy and property qualifications. Still higher property qualifications were required of members of the lower and upper houses. The constitution restored entails, insuring perpetuation of the latifundio. Catholicism was declared the state religion, and the church was given control over marriage. The president enjoyed an absolute veto over congressional legislation, appointed all high officials, and could proclaim a state of siege. The process of amending the constitution was made so difficult (it required the consent of two-thirds of Congress and the president) as to be virtually impossible. Since the president controlled the electoral machinery, the outcome of elections was a foregone conclusion. In 1836, Prieto was re-elected president for a second five-year term.

Realizing the futility of legal opposition to the conservative dictatorship, many liberals boycotted the election and later took to arms. This revolt, led by General Freire, was quickly crushed, and Freire was exiled to Australia. The Freire revolt had been organized in Peru, and this fact added to the tensions created by a tariff war between Peru and Chile. Relations between the two countries deteriorated further in 1836 as a result of the formation of a Peruvian-Bolivian confederation under the auspices of the ambitious Bolivian president, Andrés Santa Cruz. Portales saw in this union a threat to Chile's northern borders and obtained a congressional declaration of war on Peru in November 1836. The war lasted three years; it ended with a Chilean victory and dissolution of the confederation. Meanwhile, however, Portales had caused much resentment at home by his high-handed use of the extraordinary powers vested in him in wartime to arrest and jail all critics of the war. In June 1837, mutinous troops seized Portales and killed him before loyal troops could gain his release. The brilliant Portales had died, but his conservative system of politics and economics survived.

Recovery Under Bulnes

In 1841, Prieto was succeeded in the presidency by General Manuel Bulnes, who was re-elected to a second five-year term in 1846. Victorious at home and abroad, the conservative leadership decided it could relax the strict discipline of the Portales period. Chile's economic life quickly recovered from the strains caused by the war of 1836–1839 and began a renewed advance. Commerce, mining, and agriculture prospered as never before. The Crimean War and the gold rushes to California and Australia of the 1850s, created large new markets for Chilean wheat, stimulating a considerable expansion of the cultivated area. In 1840 an American, William Wheelright, established a steamship line to operate on the Chilean coasts, using coal from newly developed hard coal mines. Wheelright also founded a company that in 1852 completed Chile's first railroad line, providing an outlet to the sea for the production of the mining district of Copiapó. The major Santiago-Valparaíso line, begun in 1852, was not completed until 1863. Foreign—especially British—capital began to penetrate the Chilean economy; it dominated foreign trade and had a large interest in mining and railroads, but national capitalists

constituted an important, vigorous group and displayed much initiative in the formation of joint stock companies and banks.

The great landowners were the principal beneficiaries of this economic upsurge; their lands appreciated in value without any effort on their part. Some great landowners invested their money in railroads, mining, and trade. But the essential conservatism of the landed aristocracy and the urge to preserve a semifeudal control over its peons discouraged the transformation of the great landowners into capitalist farmers. A pattern of small landholdings arose in southern Chile, to which German as well as Chilean colonists came in increasing numbers in the 1840s and 1850s, but the rich Central Valley continued to be dominated by the latifundio, characterized by inefficient techniques and reliance on the labor of *inquilinos*—sharecroppers who also had to work the master's fields. Thus, alongside an emerging capitalist sector based on mining, trade, banking, intensive agriculture, and some industry, there existed a semifeudal sector based on the latifundio, peonage, and aristocratic life values that was a serious drag on the development of Chilean capitalism.

Yet Chile at this period presented a more progressive aspect than most other Latin American states. President Bulnes continued the law-and-order system initiated by Portales but tempered its authoritarian rigor. His minister of justice and instruction, Manuel Montt, established a system of public instruction that included special schools of fine arts, music, teacher training, and technical subjects. In 1842 the University of Chile was founded. Its first rector was the distinguished Venezuelan poet, scholar, and educator Andrés Bello. Although conservative in politics and letters, Bello helped to train a whole generation of Chilean intellectuals, some of whom broke with their master to embrace liberalism in politics and romanticism in literature.

One of Bello's disciples was José Victorino Lastarria, historian, sociologist, and a deputy of the Liberal party, which he helped to revive.

Dissatisfied with the modest concessions to modernity of the new conservatives, liberals like Lastarria, representing the left wing of the bourgeoisie, wanted to accelerate the rate of change. They demanded radical revision of the constitution of 1833 and an end to oligarchical rule.

To the left of Lastarria stood the firebrand Francisco Bilbao, author of a scorching attack on the church and the Hispanic heritage, "The Nature of Chilean Society" (1844). Later, he spent several years in France, where he was profoundly influenced by utopian socialist and radical republican thought. He returned to Chile in 1850 to found, with Santiago Arcos, the Society of Equality, which advocated these advanced ideas. The society carried on an intensive antigovernmental campaign. Within a few months it had reached a membership of four thousand, including representatives of the nascent Chilean working class.

Montt's Moderate Reforms

The Society of Equality was founded on the eve of the election of 1850, for which President Bulnes had designated Manuel Montt his heir. Despite Montt's progressive educational policies and patronship of the arts and letters, liberals identified him with the repressive system of Portales and the constitution of 1833. Liberals like Lastarria and radical democrats like Bilbao proclaimed the impending election a fraud and demanded constitutional reforms. The government responded by proclaiming a state of siege and suppressing the Society of Equality. Regarding these acts as a prelude to an attempt to liquidate the opposition, groups of liberals in Santiago and La Serena rose in revolts that were quickly crushed. Lastarria was exiled; Bilbao and Arcos fled to Argentina. The conservatives easily elected their candidate; like his predecessor, he served two terms (1851–1861). In the wake of the election, however, the liberals again rose in a large-scale revolt that Montt crushed with a heavy loss of life. Montt had

triumphed but immediately took steps to resolve the crisis by granting amnesty to the insurgents; he went on to make concessions to the spirit of the times with two important reforms: the abolition of entails and the tithe.

The abolition of entails, which was designed to encourage the breakup of landed estates among the children of the great landowners, affected a dwindling number of great aristocratic clans. Its effects were less drastic than the anguished cries of the affected parties suggested, for the divided estates were almost invariably acquired by other latifundists, and the condition of the inquilinos who worked the land remained the same. The elimination of the tithe, and Montt's refusal to allow the return of the Jesuits, greatly angered the reactionary clergy. Responding to their attacks, Montt promulgated a new civil code in 1857 that placed education under state control, gave the state jurisdiction over the clergy, and granted non-Catholics the right of civil marriage.

The abolition of entails and the tithe represented a compromise between liberals and conservatives, between the new bourgeoisie and the great landowners. In the process, the bourgeoisie gained little, and the landowners lost almost nothing; the chief loser was the church. Montt's reforms alienated the most reactionary elements of the Conservative party; in Congress these elements combined into a conservative-clerical bloc that formed the right-wing opposition to the government. On the other hand, his reforms gained Montt the support of moderate liberals while he retained the loyalty of the majority of moderate conservatives. In the 1850s, this coalition of moderate liberals and conservatives took the name of the National party. Its motto was the typically positivist slogan "Freedom in Order."

The radical liberals, however, continued to demand the repeal of the constitution of 1833. A leading spokesman for the left wing of the Liberal party was the brilliant historian Benjamin Vicuña Mackenna, who founded a newspaper in 1858 in which he hammered away at the need for drastic political and social change. The government soon shut the newspaper down, however, and Vicuña Mackenna was exiled from the country.

In the last years of his second term, President Montt faced severe economic and political problems. The depression of 1857 caused a sharp fall in the price of copper and reduced Australian and Californian demand for Chilean wheat. The economic decline fed the fires of political discontent. Montt had designated his energetic and influential cabinet minister, Antonio Varas, to succeed him in 1861. But the radical liberals disliked Varas for his stern suppression of dissidents, while clerical conservatives associated him with Montt's attacks on the church's privileges. Agitation against Varas's candidacy erupted into armed revolt in several Chilean cities in January 1859. Montt managed to quell the revolt, but his political position had been seriously weakened. Hoping to avoid new storms, Montt allowed Varas to withdraw his candidacy and supported a new candidate, José Joaquín Pérez, who was acceptable to moderate liberals and many conservatives. He easily won election as the candidate of the National party but formed a coalition government composed of Nationals, conservatives, and liberals. He served the customary two terms (1861–1871).

By 1861 the depression had lifted, and another boom began, creating new fortunes and bringing large shifts of regional influence. A growing stream of settlers, including many Germans, flowed into southern Chile, founding cities and transforming woodlands into farms.

But Chile's true center of economic gravity became the desert north, rich in copper, nitrates, and guano; the last two, in particular, were objects of Europe's insatiable demand for fertilizers. The major nitrate deposits, however, lay in the Bolivian province of Antofagasta and the Peruvian province of Tarapacá. Chilean capital, supplemented by English and German capital, began to pour into these regions and soon dominated the Peruvian and Bolivian nitrate industries. In the north there arose an aggressive mining capitalist class that demanded a place in the sun for itself and its region. A rich mineowner, Pedro León Gallo, abandoned the liberals to form a new party, called Radical, that fought more militantly than the liberals for constitutional changes, religious toleration, and an end to repressive policies. Under Pérez, liberals and Radicals combined to secure reforms that included toleration for non-Catholics, a curtailment of presidential powers, and a ban on immediate presidential reelection.

Liberal Control

The transition of Chile's political life to liberal control, begun under Montt, was completed in 1871 with the election of the first liberal president, Federico Errázuriz Zañartú. Between 1873 and 1875, a coalition of liberals and Radicals pushed through Congress a series of constitutional reforms: reduction of senatorial terms from nine to six years; direct election of senators; and freedom of speech, press, and assembly. These victories for enlightenment also represented a victory of new capitalist groups over the old merchant-landowner oligarchy that traced its beginnings back to colonial times. By 1880, of the fifty-nine Chilean personal fortunes of over 1 million pesos, only twenty-four were of colonial origin; the rest belonged to coal, nitrate, copper, and silver interests or to merchants whose wealth had been formed only in the nineteenth century. But the victories of the new bourgeoisie brought no relief to the Chilean masses, the migrant laborers and tenant farmers on the haciendas, and the young working class in Chile's mines and factories.

BRAZIL

Dom Pedro, Emperor

Brazil took its first major step toward independence in 1808, when the Portuguese crown and court, fleeing before a French invasion of Portugal, arrived in Rio de Janeiro to make it the new capital of the Portuguese Empire. Full national sovereignty came in 1822, when Dom Pedro, who ruled Brazil as regent for his father, João VI, rejected a demand that he return to Portugal and issued the famous Cry of Ipiranga: "Independence or Death!" Dom Pedro acted with the advice and support of the Brazilian aristocracy, which was determined to preserve the autonomy Brazil had enjoyed since 1808. It was equally determined to make a transition to independence without the violence that marked the Spanish-American movement of liberation—a violence that could be infinitely dangerous to a country like Brazil, whose economy and social order rested on a base of black slavery. The Brazilian aristocracy had its wish; Brazil made a transition to independence with comparatively little disruption and bloodshed. But separation from Portugal with a minimum of internal dislocation meant that independent Brazil retained not only monarchy and slavery but such other colonial features as the large landed estate and monoculture; a wasteful, inefficient agricultural system; a highly stratified society; and a free population that was 90 percent illiterate and had a strong prejudice against manual labor.

Dom Pedro had promised to give his subjects a constitution, but the constituent assembly that he summoned in 1823 drafted a document that seemed to the emperor to place excessive limits on his power. He responded by dissolving the assembly and assigning to a hand-picked commission the making of a new constitution, which he approved and promulgated by imperial proclamation. This constitution, under which Brazil was governed until the fall of the monarchy in 1889, concentrated great power in the hands of the monarch. In addition to a Council of State, it provided for a two-chamber parliament, a lifetime senate whose members were chosen by the emperor, and a Chamber of Deputies elected by voters who met property and income requirements. The emperor had the right to appoint and dismiss ministers and summon or dissolve parliament at will. He also appointed the provincial governors or presidents, who were

assisted by elective councils with very little power.

Resentment over Dom Pedro's highhanded dissolution of the constituent assembly and the highly centralist character of the constitution of 1824 was particularly strong in Pernambuco, a center of republican and federalist ferment. Here in 1824 a group of rebels, led by the merchant Manoel de Carvalho, proclaimed the creation of a Confederation of the Equator that would unite the six northern provinces under a republican government. A few leaders voiced antislavery sentiments, which frightened away some sugar planters, but nothing was done to abolish slavery, which deprived the movement of the potential support of a large slave population. Within a year, imperial troops had smashed the revolt, and fifteen of its leaders were executed.

Dom Pedro had won a victory but resentment at his autocratic tendencies continued to smolder, and his popularity steadily waned. The emperor's foreign policies contributed to this growing discontent. In 1826, in return for recognition of Brazilian independence and a trade agreement, Dom Pedro signed a treaty with Great Britain that obligated Brazil to end the slave traffic by 1830. Despite this ban and the efforts of British warships to intercept and seize the slave ships, the trade continued with the full knowledge and approval of the Brazilian government. But British policing practices caused the price of slaves to rise sharply. The prospering coffee growers of Rio de Janeiro, São Paulo, and Minas Gerais could afford to pay high prices for slaves, but the cotton and sugar growers of the depressed north could not compete with them for workers and blamed Dom Pedro for their difficulties.

Another source of discontent was the costly and fruitless war with Argentina (1825–1828) over the Banda Oriental (Uruguay), which the Brazilians called the Cisplatine Province. The war was supported by the ranchers of Rio Grande do Sul, who coveted the rich pasturelands of Uruguay, but it aroused much opposition elsewhere. When it ended, under British pressure, in a compromise that guaranteed the independence of Uruguay, its outcome was regarded as a humiliating defeat for Brazil, and Dom Pedro suffered a further loss of prestige. Two other causes of the emperor's growing unpopularity were the favoritism he showed to the arrogant and corrupt Portuguese courtiers of his entourage and his continued involvement in Portuguese politics, especially his expenditure of much money and effort in upholding the claims of his daughter Maria to the Portuguese throne.

News of the July Revolution of 1830 in France, a revolution that toppled an unpopular, autocratic king, produced rejoicing and violent demonstrations in Brazilian cities. *Exaltados* (radical liberals) placed themselves at the head of the movement of revolt and called for the abolition of the monarchy and the establishment of a federal republic. In the face of the growing crisis, Don Pedro vacillated; first he made concessions to anti-Portuguese sentiment by appointing a new cabinet of Brazilian-born ministers, then he dissolved it and named a new cabinet that included the most hated figures in his Brazilian entourage. In April 1831, mass demonstrations in the streets of the capital were joined by the local garrison. Presented by a delegation of city magistrates with a demand that he reinstate the former ministry, Dom Pedro refused. The next day, April 7, he abdicated in favor of his five-year-old son Pedro, and two weeks later he sailed for Portugal, never to return.

Regency, Revolt, and a Boy Emperor

The revolution had been the work of radical liberals who viewed Dom Pedro's downfall as the first step toward the establishment of a federal republic, but its fruits were garnered by more moderate men. In effect, the radicals had played the game of the monarchist liberals who guided the movement of secession from Portugal and later lost influence at court as a result of Dom Pedro's shift to the right. Dom Pedro's departure was a victory for these moderates, and they hastened to restore their ascendancy over the central government and prevent the revolution from getting out of hand.

As a first step, parliament appointed a three-man regency composed of moderate liberals to govern for the child emperor until he reached the age of eighteen. Another measure created a national guard, recruited from the propertied classes, to repress urban mobs and slave revolts. Simultaneously, the new government began work on a project of constitutional reform designed to appease the strong federalist sentiment. After a three-year debate, parliament approved the Additional Act of 1834, which incorporated a series of constitutional amendments. The act gave the provinces elective legislative assemblies with broad powers, including control over local budgets and taxes. This provision assured the great landowners of a large measure of control over their regions. The Council of State, identified with Dom Pedro's reactionary rule, was abolished. But centralism was not abandoned, for the national government continued to appoint provincial governors with a partial veto over the acts of the provincial assemblies. Centralism was even strengthened by the replacement of the three-man regency with a single regent. To this post parliament named the moderate liberal Diogo Antônio Feijó.

Almost immediately, Feijó had to struggle against a rash of revolts, most numerous in the northern provinces, whose economy suffered from a loss of markets for their staple crops, sugar and cotton. None occurred in the central southern zone (the provinces of Rio de Janeiro, São Paulo, and Minas Gerais), whose coffee economy prospered and whose planter aristocracy had secure control of the central government. These revolts had a variety of local causes. Some were elemental, popular revolts; such was the so-called *cabanagem* (from the word *cabana*, "cabin") of Pará, which originated in the grievances of small tradesmen, farmers, and lower-class elements against the rich Portuguese merchants who monopolized local trade. Others, like the republican and separatist revolt in Bahia (1837–1838), reflected the frustrations of the planter aristocracy of this once-prosperous area over its loss of economic and political power.

Most serious of all was the revolt that broke out in 1835 in the province of Rio Grande do Sul. Although it was dubbed the *Revolução Farroupilha* (Revolution of the Ragamuffins) in contemptuous reference to its supposed lower-class origins, the movement was led by cattle barons who maintained a more or less patriarchal sway over the gauchos who formed the rank-and-file of the rebel armies. An intense regionalism, resentment over taxes and unpopular governors imposed by the central government, and the strength of republican sentiment were major factors in producing the revolt of Rio Grande. The presence of considerable numbers of Italian exiles such as Giuseppe Garibaldi, ardent republicans and antislavery men, gave a special radical tinge to the revolt in Rio Grande. In September 1835, the rebels captured the provincial capital of Pôrto Alegre; one year later they proclaimed Rio Grande an independent republic. For almost a decade, two states—one a republic, the other an empire—existed on Brazilian territory.

The secession of Rio Grande and the inability of imperial troops to quell the revolt further weakened the position of Feijó, whose authoritarian temper and disregard for parliamentary majorities in the choice of ministers had caused much discontent. By now, the political struggle had begun to assume an organized form, with the emergence of a Liberal party, composed chiefly of moderate liberals, which favored concessions to federalism, and a Conservative party, which preferred to strengthen the central government at the expense of the provinces. However, on such essential issues as the monarchy, slavery, and the maintenance of the status quo in general, liberals and conservatives saw eye to eye.

In September 1837, Feijó, weary of political attacks and unable to repress the Rio Grande revolt, resigned and was succeeded as regent by the conservative Pedro de Araújo Lima. Like his predecessor, Araújo Lima concentrated his efforts on putting down the Rio Grande rebellion and other regional revolts in the north. The Rio Grande experiment in republican government and its offer of freedom to all slaves who joined the republic's armed forces posed an especially serious threat to monarchy and slavery. Among both liberals and conservatives, the idea gained favor of calling the young Pedro to rule before his legal majority in order to strengthen the central government in its war against subversive and separatist movements. By the beginning of 1840, the project had won virtual acceptance, liberals and conservatives differing only with respect to timing and other details. On July 22, in what was in effect a parliamentary coup d'état, the two chambers of parliament proclaimed the fourteen-year-old Dom Pedro emperor; he was formally crowned a year later, in July 1841.

In March 1841, after forcing a short-lived liberal ministry to resign, the emperor called the conservatives to power. The new government proceeded to dismantle the federalist reforms, which it blamed for the revolutionary climate in the country, in the Additional Act of 1834. The powers of the provincial assemblies were sharply curtailed; locally elected judges were stripped of their judicial and police powers, which were vested in a new national police; and the Council of State was restored. Having consolidated their position, the conservatives decided to change the balance of forces in the new Chamber of Deputies, where the liberals had won a majority and, charging corruption in the elections, persuaded the emperor to dissolve it.

The liberals of São Paulo and Minas Gerais responded with a revolt (1842) that had little popular support, for it was dictated solely by the desire for the spoils of office. Baron Caxias swiftly crushed the uprising. But the emperor treated the vanquished rebels leniently; indeed, a short time later he called on the liberals to form a new ministry. Once returned to power, the liberals made no effort to repeal the

Dom Pedro II. (Courtesy of the Organization of American States)

conservative revisions of the constitution and made extensive use of the broad police powers vested in the central government for their own ends.

With the unity of the ruling class restored, the government undertook to settle scores with the rebels of Rio Grande. As a result of internal squabbles and the cessation of aid from friendly Uruguay when that country was invaded by Rosas' troops in February 1843, the situation of the republic became extremely difficult. Meanwhile, Baron Caxias advanced with large forces against the rebels and wrested town after town from their troops. Facing defeat, the republican leaders accepted an offer from Rio de Janeiro to negotiate a peace, which was signed in February 1845. The peace treaty extended amnesty to all rebels but annulled all laws of the republican regime. The cattle barons won certain concessions, including the right to nom-

inate their candidate for the post of provincial governor and retention of their military titles.

The last large-scale revolt in the series that shook Brazil in the 1830s and 1840s was the uprising of 1848 in Pernambuco. Centered in the city of Recife, its causes included hostility toward the Portuguese merchants who monopolized local trade, the appointment of an unpopular governor by the conservative government, and hatred for the greatest landowners of the region, the powerful Cavalcanti family. The rebel program called for the removal from Recife of all Portuguese merchants, expansion of provincial autonomy, work for the unemployed, and division of the Cavalcanti lands. Even this radical program, however, contained no reference to the abolition of slavery. The movement collapsed after the capture of Recife by imperial troops in 1849. Many captured leaders were condemned to prison for life, but all were amnestied in 1852.

The Game of Politics and the Crisis of Slavery

By 1850, Brazil was at peace. The emperor presided over a pseudo-parliamentary regime that in reality was a royal dictatorship exercised in the interests of a tiny ruling class. He paid his respects to parliamentary forms by alternately appointing conservative and liberal prime ministers at will; if the new ministry did not command a majority in parliament, one was obtained by holding rigged elections. Since the ruling class was united on essential issues, the only thing at stake in party struggles was the spoils of office. An admirer of Dom Pedro, Joaquim Nabuco, described the operation of the system in his book *O abolicionismo*:

The president of the council lives at the mercy of the crown, from which he derives his power; even the appearance of power is his only when he is regarded as the emperor's lieutenant and is believed to have in his pocket the decree of dissolution—that is, the right to elect a chamber made up of his own henchmen.

Below him are the ministers, who live by the favor of the president of the council; farther down still, on the third plane, are found the deputies, at the mercy of the ministers. The representative system, then, is a graft of parliamentary forms on a patriarchal government, and senators and deputies only take their roles seriously in this parody of democracy because of the personal advantage they derive therefrom. Suppress the subsidies, force them to stop using their positions for personal and family ends, and no one who had anything else to do would waste his time in such shadow boxing.[3]

The surface stability of Brazilian political life in the decades after 1850 rested on the prosperity created by a growing demand and good prices for Brazilian coffee. As the sugar-growing northeast and its plantation society continued to decline because of exhausted soil, archaic techniques, and competition from foreign sugars, the coffee-growing zone of Rio de Janeiro, São Paulo, and Minas Gerais gained new importance.

The crisis of the northeast grew more acute as a result of English pressure on Brazil to enforce the Anglo-Brazilian treaty banning the importation of slaves into Brazil after November 7, 1831. Before 1850 this treaty was never effectively enforced; more than fifty thousand slaves a year were brought to Brazil during the 1840s. In 1849 and 1850, however, the British government instructed its warships to enter Brazilian territorial waters if necessary to seize and destroy Brazilian slave ships. Under British pressure, the Brazilian parliament passed the Queiroz anti-slave-trade law, which was effectively enforced. By the middle 1850s, the importation of slaves had virtually ended.

The ending of the slave trade had major consequences. Because of the high mortality among slaves due to poor food, harsh working conditions, and other negative factors, the slave population could not be maintained by natural reproduction, and the eventual doom of the slave system was assured. The passing of the slave trade created a serious labor shortage, with a large flow of slaves from the north to the south because of the coffee planters' greater capacity to compete for slave labor. This movement aggravated the imbalance between the prosperous south central zone and the declining north. The end of the slave trade had another important result: Large sums formerly expended for the purchase of slaves were now channeled to other uses, partly into coffee agriculture, partly into the building of an infrastructure for the emerging national economy. The first telegraph lines in Brazil were established in 1852; the first railroad line was begun in 1854. In these years, a pioneer of Brazilian capitalism, Irineu Evangelista de Sousa, later the baron Mauá, laid the foundations of a veritable industrial and banking empire.

By the 1860s, a growing number of Brazilians, including some in high places, had become convinced that slavery brought serious discredit to Brazil and must be placed in the way of extinction. The abolition of slavery in the United States as a result of the Civil War, which left Brazil and the Spanish colonies of Cuba and Puerto Rico the only slaveholding areas in the Western Hemisphere, sharpened sensitivity to the problem. The Paraguayan War also promoted the cause of emancipation. In an effort to fill the gaps caused by heavy losses at the front, a decree was issued granting freedom to government-owned slaves who agreed to join the army, and some private slave owners followed the official example. Criticism of slavery was increasingly joined with criticism of the emperor, who was censured for his cautious posture on the slavery problem. The antislavery movement began to merge with the nascent republican movement. In 1869 the left wing of the Liberal party, organized in a Reform Club, issued a manifesto demanding restrictions on the powers of the emperor and the grant of freedom to the newborn children of slaves. The crisis of slavery was fast becoming a crisis of the Brazilian Empire.

[3] Quoted in Benjamin Keen, ed., *Latin American Civilization: The National Era*, vol. 2 (Boston: Houghton Mifflin, 1974), p. 159.

CHAPTER TEN

The Triumph of Neocolonialism

Beginning about 1870, the quickening tempo of the Industrial Revolution in Europe stimulated a more rapid pace of change in the Latin American economy and politics. Responding to a mounting demand for raw materials and foodstuffs, Latin American producers increased their output of those commodities. The growing trade with Europe helped to stabilize political conditions in Latin America, for the new economic system demanded peace and continuity in government.

Encouraged by the increased stability, European capital flowed into Latin America, creating railroads, docks, processing plants, and other facilities needed to expand and modernize production and trade. Latin America became integrated into an international economic system in which it exchanged raw materials and foodstuffs for the factory-made goods of Europe and North America. Gradual adoption of free-trade policies by many Latin American countries, which marked the abandonment of efforts to create a native factory capitalism, hastened the area's integration into this international division of labor.

THE NEW COLONIALISM

The new economic system fastened a new dependency on Latin America, with Great Britain and later the United States replacing Spain and Portugal in the dominant role; it may, therefore, be called "neocolonial." Despite its built-in flaws and local breakdowns, the neocolonial order displayed a certain stability until 1914. By disrupting the markets for Latin America's exports and making it difficult to import the manufactured goods that Latin America required, World War I marked the beginning of a general crisis the area has not yet overcome.

Although the period from 1870 to 1914 saw a rapid overall growth of the Latin American economy, the pace and degree of progress were uneven, with some countries (like Bolivia and Paraguay) joining the advance much later than others. A marked feature of the neocolonial order was its one-sidedness (monoculture). One or a few primary products became the basis of each country's prosperity, making it highly vulnerable to fluctuations in the world demand and price of these products. Thus, Argentina and Uruguay depended on wheat and meat; Brazil on coffee, sugar, and briefly on rubber; Chile on copper and nitrates; Honduras on bananas; Cuba on sugar.

In each country, the modern export sector became an enclave isolated from the rest of the economy; this enclave actually accentuated the backwardness of other sectors by draining off their labor and capital. The export-oriented nature of the modern sector was reflected in the pattern of the national railway systems, which as a rule were not designed to integrate each country's regions but to satisfy the traffic needs of the export industries. In addition, the modern export sector often rested on extremely precarious foundations. Rapid, feverish growth,

punctuated by slumps that sometimes ended in a total collapse, formed part of the neocolonial pattern; such meteoric rise and fall is the story of Peruvian guano, Chilean nitrates, and Brazilian rubber.

Expansion of the Hacienda System

The neocolonial order evolved within the framework of the traditional system of land tenure and labor relations. Indeed, it led to an expansion of the hacienda system on a scale far greater than the colonial period had known. As the growing European demand for Latin American products raised the value of land, the great landowners in country after country launched assaults on the surviving Indian community lands. In Mexico the Reforma laid the legal basis for this attack in the 1850s and 1860s; it reached its climax in the era of Porfirio Díaz.

Seizure of church lands by liberal governments also contributed to the growth of the latifundio. Mexico again offered a model, with its Lerdo Law and the Juárez anticlerical decrees. Following the Mexican example, Colombian liberal governments confiscated church lands in the 1860s, the liberal dictator Antonio Guzmán Blanco seized many church estates in Venezuela in the 1870s, and Ecuadorian liberals expropriated church lands in 1895.

Expansion of the public domain through railway construction and Indian wars also contributed to the growth of great landed estates. Lands taken from the church or wrested from Indian tribes were usually sold to buyers in vast tracts at nominal prices. Concentration of land, reducing the cultivable area available to Indian and mestizo small landowners, was accompanied by a parallel growth of the minifundio—an uneconomical small plot worked with primitive techniques.

The seizure of Indian community lands for immediate use or to hold for a speculative rise in value gave great landowners another advantage by giving them control of the local labor force at a time of increasing demand for labor. Expropriated Indians rarely became true wage earners paid wholly in cash, for such workers were too expensive and independent in spirit. A more widespread labor system was debt peonage, in which workers were paid wholly or in part with vouchers redeemable at the *tienda de raya* (company store), whose inflated prices and often devious bookkeeping created a debt that was passed on from father to son. The courts enforced the obligation of peons to remain on the estate until they had liquidated their debts. Peons who protested low wages or the more intensive style of work demanded by the new order were brought to their senses by the landowner's armed retainers or by local police or military authorities.

In some countries, the period saw a revival of the colonial repartimiento system of draft labor for Indians. In Guatemala, this system— here called *mandamiento*—required able-bodied Indians to work for a specified number of days on haciendas. It was the liberal President Justo Rufino Barrios who issued instructions to local magistrates to see to it "that any Indian who seeks to evade his duty is punished to the full extent of the law, that the farmers are fully protected and that each Indian is forced to do a full day's work while in service."

Slavery survived in some places well beyond mid-century—for example, in Peru until 1855, in Cuba until 1886, in Brazil until 1888. Closely akin to slavery was the system of bondage, under which some ninety thousand Chinese coolies were imported into Peru between 1849 and 1875 to work on the guano islands and in railway construction; they were sold to employers for an average price of 400 pesos a head on eight-year work contracts. The term *slavery* also applies to the system under which political deportees and captured Indian rebels were sent by Mexican authorities to labor in unspeakable conditions on the coffee, tobacco, and henequen plantations of southern Mexico.

More modern systems of agricultural labor

and farm tenantry arose only in such regions as southern Brazil and Argentina, whose critical labor shortage required the offer of greater incentives to the millions of European immigrants who poured into those countries between 1870 and 1910.

Labor conditions were little better in the mining industry and in the factories that arose in some countries after 1890. Typical working conditions were a workday of twelve to fourteen hours, miserable wages frequently paid in vouchers redeemable only at the company store, and arbitrary, abusive treatment by employers and foremen. Latin American law codes usually prohibited strikes and other organized efforts to improve working conditions, and police and the armed forces were commonly employed to break strikes, sometimes with heavy loss of life.

Foreign Control of Resources

The rise of the neocolonial order was accompanied by a steady growth of foreign corporate control over the natural and man-made resources of the continent. The process went through stages; in 1870 foreign investment was still largely concentrated in trade, shipping, railways, public utilities, and government loans. At that date, British capital enjoyed an undisputed hegemony in the Latin American investment field. By 1914 foreign corporate ownership had expanded to include most of the mining industry and had deeply penetrated real estate, ranching, plantation agriculture, and manufacturing. By that date, too, Great Britain's rivals had effectively challenged its domination in Latin America. Of these rivals, the most spectacular advance was made by the United States, whose Latin American investments had risen from a negligible amount in 1870 to over $1.6 billion by the end of 1914 (still well below the nearly $5-billion investment of Great Britain.)

Foreign economic penetration went hand in hand with a growth of political influence and even armed intervention. The youthful American imperialism proved to be the most aggressive of all. In the years after 1898, a combination of "dollar diplomacy" and armed intervention transformed the Caribbean into an "American lake" and reduced Cuba, the Dominican Republic, and several Central American states to the status of dependencies and protectorates.

The Politics of Acquisition

The new economy demanded a new politics. Conservatives and liberals, fascinated by the atmosphere of prosperity created by the export boom, the rise in land values, the flood of foreign loans, and the growth of government revenues, put aside their ideological differences and joined in the pursuit of wealth. In the process, conservatives tended to abandon their paternalist attitudes toward their workers and some of their traditional distaste for entrepreneurial activity; liberals, for their part, lost much of their concern with constitutional methods and civil liberties. The positivist slogan, "Order and Progress," now became the watchword of Latin America's ruling classes. The social Darwinist idea of the struggle for survival of the fittest and Herbert Spencer's doctrine of "inferior races," frequently used to support claims of the inherent inferiority of the Indian, mestizo, and mulatto masses, also entered the upper-class ideological arsenal.

The growing domination of national economies by the export sectors and the development of a consensus between the old landed aristocracy and more capitalist-oriented groups caused political issues like the federalist-centralist conflict and the liberal-conservative cleavage to lose much of their meaning; in some countries, the old party lines dissolved or became extremely tenuous. A new type of "progressive" caudillo—Porfirio Díaz in Mexico, Rafael Núñez in Colombia, Justo Rufino Barrios in Guatemala, Antonio Guzmán Blanco in Venezuela—symbolized the politics of acquisition.

As the century drew to a close, dissatisfied urban middle-class, immigrant, and entrepreneurial groups in some countries combined to form parties, called Radical or Democratic, that challenged the traditional domination of politics by the Creole aristocracy. They demanded political, social, and educational reforms that would give more weight to the new middle sectors. But these middle sectors were in large part a creation of the neocolonial order, depended on it for their livelihood, and as a rule did not question its viability. The small socialist, anarchist, and syndicalist groups that arose in various Latin American countries in the 1890s challenged both capitalism and neocolonialism, but the full significance of these movements lay in the future.

The trends just described lend a certain unity to the history of Mexico, Argentina, Chile, and Brazil in the period from 1870 to 1914. Each country's history, however, presents significant variations on the common theme—variations that reflect that country's specific historical background and conditions.

MEXICAN POLITICS AND ECONOMY

Dictatorship Under Díaz

General Porfirio Díaz seized power in 1876 from President Lerdo de Tejada with the support of disgruntled regional caudillos and military personnel, liberals angered by the political manipulations of the entrenched Lerdo machine, and Indian and mestizo small landholders who believed that Díaz would put an end to land seizures. Having installed himself as president, Díaz paid his respects to the principle of no reelection by allowing a trusted crony, General Manuel González, to succeed him in 1880. However, he returned to the presidential palace in 1884 and continued to occupy it through successive re-elections until his resignation and flight from Mexico in 1911. He got rid of the now-inconvenient issue of no re-election by having the constitution amended in 1887 and

Porfirio Díaz. (Courtesy of the Organization of American States)

1890 to permit his indefinite re-election; in 1904 he obtained an extension of the president's term from four to six years. Thus, Díaz, who had seized power in the name of republican legality, erected one of the longest personal dictatorships in Latin American history.

The construction of the dictatorship, however, was a gradual process. During his first presidential term, Díaz permitted reasonably fair elections, Congress and the judiciary enjoyed a certain independence, and the press, including a vocal radical labor press, was free. The outlines of Díaz's economic and social policies, however, soon became clear. Confronted with an empty treasury, facing pressures from above and below, Díaz decided in favor of the great landowners, moneylenders, and foreign capitalists, whose assistance could insure his political survival. In return, he assured these groups of protection for their property and other interests. Díaz, who had once proclaimed that in the age-old struggle between the people and the haciendas

he was on the side of the people, now sent troops to suppress peasant resistance to land seizures. Before taking power, Díaz had denounced Lerdo for his generous concessions to British capitalists; by 1880, Díaz had granted even more lavish subsidies for railway construction to American companies. Economic development had become for Díaz the great object, the key to the solution of his own problems and those of the nation.

Economic development required political stability; accordingly, Díaz promoted a policy of conciliation that consisted of offering an olive branch and a share of spoils to all influential opponents, no matter what their political past or persuasion—*Lerdistas*, Juaristas, conservatives, clericals, anticlericals. A dog with a bone in its mouth, Díaz cynically observed, neither kills nor steals. In effect, Díaz invited all sections of the upper class and some members of the middle class, including prominent intellectuals and journalists, to join the great Mexican barbecue, from which only the poor and humble were barred. Even bandit chieftains and their followers were offered a place at the feast; from their ranks Díaz recruited a force of mounted police, the *rurales,* distinguished by their picturesque dress. The rurales, says H. B. Parkes, "made Mexico one of the safest countries in the world—for all except Mexicans." Aside from chasing unrepentant bandits, the major function of the rurales was to suppress peasant unrest and break strikes.

There was another side to the policy of conciliation, however, a side described by the formula *pan o palo* (bread or the club). Opponents who refused Díaz's bribes—political offices, monopolies, and the like—suffered swift reprisal. Dissidents were beaten up, murdered, or arrested and sent to the damp underground dungeons of San Juan de Ulúa or the grim Belén prison, a sort of Mexican Bastille. Designed to hold two hundred prisoners, Belén commonly held four to five thousand inmates. One prominent journalist, Filomeno Mata, was jailed thirty-four times.

By such means, Díaz virtually eliminated all effective opposition by the end of his second term (1884–1888). The constitution of 1857 and the liberties it guaranteed existed only on paper. Elections to Congress, in theory the highest organ of government, were a farce; Díaz simply circulated a list of his candidates to local officials, who certified their election. The dictator contemptuously called Congress his *caballada*, his stable of horses. The state governors were appointed by Díaz, usually from the ranks of local great landlords or his generals. In return for their loyalty, he gave them a free hand to enrich themselves and terrorize the local population. Under them were district heads called *jefes políticos*, petty tyrants appointed by the governors with the approval of Díaz; below them were municipal presidents who ran the local administrative units. One feature of the Díaz era was a mushrooming of the administrative and coercive apparatus; government costs during this period soared by 900 percent.

The army, as indispensable to Díaz as it had been to Santa Anna, naturally enjoyed special favor. There was a plethora of officers: an average of one officer to every ten soldiers, a general for every three hundred men. Higher officers were well paid and enjoyed many opportunities for enrichment at the expense of the regions in which they were quartered. The Díaz army, however, was pathetically inadequate for purposes of national defense. Generals and other high officers were appointed not for their ability but for their loyalty to the dictator. Discipline, morale, and training were extremely poor. A considerable part of the rank-and-file were recruited from the dregs of society; the remainder were young Indian conscripts. These soldiers, often used for brutal repression of strikes and agrarian unrest, were themselves harshly treated and miserably paid—the wage of ranks below sergeant was fifty cents a month.

The church became another pillar of the dictatorship. Early in his second term, Díaz reached an accommodation with the hierarchy. The church agreed to support Díaz; in return he allowed the anticlerical Reforma laws to fall into disuse. In disregard of those laws, monasteries and nunneries were restored, church schools established, and wealth again began to accumulate in the hands of the church. Faithful to its bargain, the church turned a deaf ear to the complaints of the masses and taught complete submission to the authorities. As in colonial times, many priests were utterly venal and corrupt. An American visitor, Charles Flandrau, learned "of a powerful bishop whose 'wife' and large family of sons and daughters are complacently taken for granted"; one devout Catholic warned him "never under any circumstances to allow one's American maid servants to converse with a priest or to enter his home on any pretext whatever." Only in the closing years of the dictatorship did the church, sensing the coming storm, begin to advocate modest social reforms.

The Díaz policy of conciliation was directed at prominent intellectuals as well as more wealthy and powerful figures. A group of such intellectuals, professional men, and businessmen made up a closely knit clique of Díaz's advisers. Known as *Científicos*, they were especially influential after 1892. The Científicos accepted the positivist philosophy as expounded by Herbert Spencer; they got their name from their insistence on "scientific" administration of the state. About fifteen men made up the controlling nucleus of the group. Their leader was Díaz's all-powerful father-in-law, Manuel Romero Rubio, and, after his death in 1895, the new minister of finance, José Yves Limantour.

For the Científicos, the economic movement was everything; they believed that Díaz's stern discipline was necessary to create the peace needed for economic advance. Most Científicos accepted the thesis of the inherent inferiority of the Indian and mestizo population and the consequent necessity for relying on the native white elite and on foreigners and their capital to lead Mexico out of its backwardness. In the words of the journalist Francisco G. Cosmes, "the Indian has only the passive force of inferior races, is incapable of actively pursuing the goal of civilization."

But there were differences of opinion within the group. The most distinguished intellectual among the Científicos was the old-time liberal Justo Sierra, a biographer of Juárez who wistfully clung to his libertarian ideas, yet served Díaz, believing that he was preparing Mexico to be free. By contrast with such racists as Francisco Bulnes and José Yves Limantour, Sierra rejected the notion of Indian racial inferiority and argued that education could correct their seeming dullness and apathy.

Some members of the Díaz establishment even harbored doubts about Díaz's policies and methods. Troubled by the immobility of the regime, fearing revolution, some Científicos urged a variety of reforms, including an end to re-election and the introduction of a multiparty system. But their advice was not heeded and, being practical men, most resigned themselves to the more profitable task of enriching themselves.

Thanks to the devoted efforts of educators like Justo Sierra, the Díaz era saw some advances in public education. In 1887, Sierra secured the adoption of a federal law making primary education obligatory. Official figures indicate a growth of schools and students considerably faster than that of population. But much of this progress existed only on paper. Aside from the unreliability of the official data, it appears that on the average only one out of three children between the ages of six and twelve were enrolled. The vast majority of these children probably went only through the first year and remained functionally illiterate. The principal beneficiaries of the educational progress under Díaz were the sons of the rich: For every student enrolled in the primary schools in 1910, the state spent about 7 pesos; for every student in the college preparatory schools, it spent nearly 100 pesos.

In the last analysis, however, apologists for the dictatorship rested their case on the "economic miracle" that Díaz had allegedly worked in Mexico. A survey of the Mexican economy in 1910 reveals how modest that miracle was.

Concentration of Landownership

At the opening of the twentieth century, Mexico was still predominantly an agrarian country; 77 percent of its population of 15 million still lived on the land. The laws of the Reforma had already given impetus to the concentration of landownership, and under Díaz this trend was greatly accelerated. There is some evidence of a link between the rapid advance of railway construction, which increased the possibilities of production for export and therefore stimulated a rise in land values, and the growth of landgrabbing in the Díaz period.

A major piece of land legislation was a law of 1883 that provided for the survey of so-called vacant public lands, *tierras baldías*. The law authorized real estate companies to survey such lands and retain one-third of the surveyed area; the remainder was sold for low fixed prices in vast tracts, usually to Díaz's favorites and their foreign associates. The 1883 law required the surveying companies and purchasers to settle at least one person for each five hundred acres surveyed, but a second law (1894) removed this obligation and deleted the clause restricting the amount of land that one individual could purchase.

The 1883 and 1894 laws opened the way for vast territorial acquisitions. One individual alone obtained nearly 12 million acres in Baja California and other northern states. "By the end of the Díaz period," says Charles Cumberland, "the government had divested itself of an area roughly equal to that of California, or equal to the combined totals of Ohio, Indiana, Illinois, and half of Kentucky; the alienated land constituted nearly one-fifth of the total land area of Mexico."

But the land companies were not satisfied with the acquisition of true vacant lands. The law of 1894 declared that a parcel of land to which a legal title could not be produced might be declared vacant land, opening the door to expropriation of Indian villages and other small landholders whose forebears had tilled their lands from times immemorial but who could not produce the required titles. Since the spoilers dominated the courts, resort to litigation was usually futile. If the victims offered armed resistance, troops were sent against them, and the vanquished rebels were sold like slaves to labor on henequen plantations in Yucatán or sugar plantations in Cuba. This was the fate of the Yaqui Indians of the northwest, defeated after a long, valiant struggle.

Another instrument of land seizure was an 1890 law designed to give effect to older Reforma laws requiring the distribution of Indian village lands among the villagers. The law created enormous confusion. In many cases, land speculators and hacendados cajoled the illiterate Indians into selling their titles for paltry sums. Hacendados also used other means, such as cutting off a village's water supply or simply brute force, to achieve their predatory ends. By 1910 the process of land expropriation was largely complete. More than 90 percent of the Indian villages of the central plateau, the most densely populated region of the country, had lost their communal lands. Only the most tenacious resistance enabled villages that still held their lands to survive the assault of the great landowners. Landless peons and their families made up 9.5 million of a rural population of 12 million.

As a rule, the new owners did not use the land seized from Indian villages or small landholders more efficiently. Hacendados let much of the usurped land lie idle. They waited for a speculative rise in value or for an American buyer. By keeping land out of production, they helped to keep the price of maize and other staples artificially high. The technical level of hacienda agriculture was generally extremely low, with little use of irrigation, machinery, and commercial fertilizer, although some new landowning groups—such as northern cattle raisers and cotton growers, the coffee and rubber growers of Chiapas, and the henequen producers of Yucatán—employed more modern equipment and techniques.

The production of foodstuffs stagnated, barely keeping pace during most of the period with the growth of population, and per capita production of such basic staples as maize and beans actually declined toward the end of the century. This decline culminated in three years of bad harvests, 1907–1910, due principally to drought. As a result, the importation of maize and other foodstuffs from the United States steadily increased in the last years of the Díaz regime. Despite the growth of pastoral industry, per capita consumption of milk and cheese barely kept pace with the growth of population, for a considerable proportion of the cattle sold was destined for the export market.

The only foods whose increase exceeded the growth of population were alcoholic beverages; some idea of the increase in their consumption is given by the fact that the number of bars in Mexico City rose from fifty-one in 1864 to fourteen hundred in 1900. At the end of the century, the Mexican death rate from alcoholism—a common response to intolerable conditions of life and labor—was estimated to be six times that of France. Meanwhile, inflation, rampant during the last part of the Díaz regime, greatly raised the cost of the staples on which the mass of the population depended. Without a corresponding increase in wages, the position of agricultural and industrial laborers deteriorated sharply.

The Economic Advance

While food production for the domestic market declined, production of food and industrial raw materials for the foreign market experienced a vigorous growth. By 1910, Mexico had become the largest producer of henequen, source of a fiber in great demand in the world market. Mexican export production became increasingly geared to the needs of the United States, which was the principal market for sugar, bananas, rubber, and tobacco produced on plantations that were largely foreign-owned. American companies dominated the mining industry, whose output of copper, gold, lead, and tin rose sharply after 1890. A spectacular late development was shown by the oil industry, which was controlled by American and British interests; by 1911, Mexico was third among the world's oil producers. French and Spanish capitalists virtually monopolized the textile industry and other consumer goods industries that had a relatively rapid growth after 1890. Operating behind the protection of tariff walls that excluded foreign competition in cheap goods, they compelled the masses to pay high prices for articles of inferior quality.

Foreign control of key sectors of the economy and the fawning attitude of the Díaz regime toward foreigners gave rise to a popular saying: "Mexico, mother of foreigners and stepmother of Mexicans." The ruling clique of Científicos justified this favoritism by citing the need for a rapid development of Mexico's natural resources and the creation of a strong country capable of defending its political independence and territorial integrity.

Thanks to an influx of foreign capital, some quickening and modernization of economic life did take place under Díaz. The volume of foreign trade greatly increased, a modern banking system arose, and the country acquired a relatively dense network of railways. But these successes were achieved at a very heavy price: a brutal dictatorship, the pauperization of the mass of the population, the stagnation of food agriculture, the strengthening of the inefficient latifundio, and the survival of many feudal or semifeudal vestiges in Mexican economic and social life.

Labor, Agrarian, and Middle-Class Unrest

The survival of feudal vestiges was especially glaring in the area of labor relations. There was some variation in labor conditions from region to region. In 1910 forced labor and outright slavery, as well as older forms of debt peonage, were characteristic of the south (the states of Yucatán, Tabasco, Chiapas, and parts of Oaxaca and Veracruz). The rubber, coffee, tobacco, henequen, and sugar plantations of this region depended heavily on the forced labor of political deportees, captured Indian rebels, and contract workers kidnapped or lured to work in the tropics by a variety of devices.

In central Mexico, where a massive expropriation of Indian village lands had created a large landless Indian proletariat, tenantry, sharecropping, and the use of migratory labor had increased, and living standards had declined. The large labor surplus of this area diminished the need for hacendados to tie their workers to their estates with debt peonage. In the north, the proximity of the United States, with its higher wage scales, and the competition of hacendados with mine owners for labor made wages and sharecropping arrangements somewhat more favorable and weakened debt peonage. In all parts of the country, however, the life of agricultural workers was filled with hardships and abuses of every kind.

Labor conditions in mines and factories were little better than in the countryside. Workers in textile mills labored twelve to fifteen hours daily for a wage ranging from eleven cents for unskilled women and children to seventy-five cents for highly skilled workers. Employers found ways of reducing even these meager wages. Wages were discounted for alleged "carelessness" in the use of of tools or machines or for "defective goods"; workers were usually paid wholly or in part with vouchers good only in company stores, whose prices were higher than in other stores. Federal and state laws banned trade unions and strikes. Hundreds of workers, both men and women, were shot down by troops who broke the great textile strike in the Orizaba (Veracruz) area in 1907, and scores were killed or wounded in putting down the

Striking workers at the Rio Blanco textile works in Mexico in 1909; the business was owned by Spanish and German capital. Troops broke up the strike and much blood was shed. (Brown Brothers)

strike at the American-owned Consolidated Copper Company mine at Cananea (Sonora) in 1906. Despite such repressions, the trade union movement continued to grow in the last years of the Díaz era, and socialist, anarchist, and syndicalist ideas began to influence the still small working class.

The growing wave of strikes and agrarian unrest in the last, decadent phase of the Díaz era indicated an increasingly rebellious mood among ever broader sections of the Mexican people. Alienation spread among teachers, lawyers, journalists, and other professionals, whose opportunities for advancement were sharply limited by the monolithic control of economic, political, and social life by the Cien-

tíficos, their foreign allies, and regional oligarchies. In the United States in 1905 a group of middle-class intellectuals, headed by the Flores Magón brothers, organized the Liberal party, which called for the overthrow of Díaz and advanced a platform whose economic and social provisions anticipated many articles of the constitution of 1917.

Even members of the ruling class began to join the chorus of criticism. These upper-class dissidents included liberal hacendados of a more bourgeois type and national capitalists who resented the competitive advantages enjoyed by foreign companies in Mexico. They also feared that the static, reactionary Díaz policies could provoke the masses to overthrow the capitalist system itself. Fearing revolution, these upper-class critics urged Díaz to end his personal rule, shake up the regime, and institute the reforms needed to preserve the existing economic and social order. When their appeals fell on deaf ears, some of these bourgeois reformers reluctantly prepared to take the road of revolution. Typical of these men was the wealthy hacendado and businessman Francisco Madero, soon to become the Apostle of the Mexican Revolution.

The simultaneous advent of an economic recession and a food crisis sharpened this growing discontent. The depression of 1906–1907, which spread from the United States to Mexico, caused a wave of bankruptcies, layoffs, and wage cuts. At the same time the crop failures of 1907–1910 provoked a dramatic rise in the price of staples like maize and beans. By 1910, Mexico's internal conflicts had reached an explosive stage. The workers' strikes, the agrarian unrest, the agitation of middle-class reformers, the disaffection of some great landowners and capitalists all reflected the disintegration of the dictatorship's social base. Despite its superficial stability and posh splendor, the house of Díaz was rotten from top to bottom. Events proved that only a slight push was needed to send it toppling to the ground.

ARGENTINIAN POLITICS AND ECONOMY

In the presidential contest of 1874, Nicolás Avellaneda, a lawyer from Tucumán who had the support of Domingo Sarmiento and powerful provincial bosses, defeated former president Bartolomé Mitre. Mitre, who believed that Buenos Aires must retain control of the republic if it were to stay on a progressive course, promptly organized a revolt. He was defeated and captured but was soon released and continued to enjoy for many years the position of Argentina's most honored elder statesman.

Avellaneda, however, did not represent provincial backwardness and *caudillismo*. A cultured liberal and a disciple of Sarmiento, in whose

cabinet he had held office, he continued his predecessor's work of promoting education, immigration, and domestic tranquillity. In 1876 he defeated the last of the old-time turbulent caudillos, Ricardo López Jordan; in the same year, he inaugurated railroad service between Buenos Aires and his native city of Tucumán. The new line forged stronger economic and political links between the port city and the remote northwest, contributing to the end of the long quarrel between Buenos Aires and the interior.

Consolidation of the State

One more sharp confrontation, however, proved necessary before the quarrel between Buenos Aires and the interior could be finally laid to rest. For almost two decades, Buenos Aires had been both capital of the province of the same name and provisional capital of the republic. In 1880, Carlos Tejedor, governor of the province of Buenos Aires and a fanatical champion of the city's predominance, became a candidate for the presidency against another *Tucumano*, Julio Roca. Roca was Avellaneda's secretary of war and protégé and was supported by a powerful group of provincial politicans known as the Córdoba League. Tejedor and his supporters responded to Roca's election with a new revolt that government and provincial forces soon crushed.

The victors proceeded to carry out the long-standing pledge to federalize Buenos Aires, which became the capital of the nation, while the provincial capital was moved to the city of La Plata. The interior seemed to have triumphed over Buenos Aires, but that apparent victory was an illusion; the provincial lawyers and politicians who carried the day in 1880 had absorbed the commercial and cultural values of the great city and wished not to diminish but to share in its power. Far from losing influence, Buenos Aires steadily gained in wealth and power until it achieved an overwhelming ascendancy over the rest of the country.

The federalization of Buenos Aires completed the consolidation of the Argentine state. Simultaneously, however, a certain decline appeared in the quality of Argentina's political leadership. The great architects of Argentine national unity—Mitre, Alberdi, Sarmiento—had ardently promoted material progress, which they regarded as the key to the solution of all other problems, but their ultimate goal was a democratic society based on access to land and education for the broad masses. That is why they had sponsored—unsuccessfully—homestead legislation and promoted public education, believing, in the words of Sarmiento, that education would "make the poor gaucho a useful man." Austere idealists, they took pride in their personal integrity; their harshest critics never charged Mitre or Sarmiento with using their high offices to advance their personal fortunes.

With President Roca, a new generation of leaders came to the fore, closely identified with and often recruited from the ruling class of great landowners and wealthy merchants. The "generation of 1880," or the oligarchy, as it was also called, shared the faith of Alberdi and Sarmiento in economic development and the value of the North American and European models, but that faith was now deeply tinged with cynicism, egotism, and a profound distrust for the masses. Positivists and social Darwinists of the Spencerian school, like the Mexican Científicos, these autocratic liberals prized order and progress above freedom. They regarded the gauchos, the Indians, and the mass of illiterate European immigrants flooding Argentina unfit to exercise civic functions—or at least wanted to put off to an indefinite future the time when these lower orders would be ready to assume such functions. Asked to define universal suffrage, a leading oligarch, Eduardo Wilde, replied, "It is the triumph of universal ignorance."

The new rulers identified the national interest with the interest of the great landowners, wealthy merchants, and foreign capitalists. Regarding the apparatus of state as their personal property or as the property of their class, they used their official connections to enrich themselves. Although they maintained the forms of parliamentary government, they were determined not to let power slip from their hands and organized what came to be called the *unicato* (one-party rule), exercised by the National Autonomist party, which they formed. Extreme concentration of power in the executive branch and systematic use of fraud, violence, and bribery were basic features of the system.

There are some obvious political and ideological affinities between Argentina's rulers in the period from 1880 to 1910 and Mexico's ruling clique of Científicos in the same period, but also some important differences. Whereas the Díaz government favored the church, Argentine governments displayed a moderate anticlericalism, as indicated by a law of 1884 that barred the church from taking part in public education. This official anticlericalism could have been a tactical maneuver designed to win for the oligarchy a progressive reputation and allay middle-class discontent with its other policies; it may also have reflected the influence of the strong English colony, interested for its own reasons in the secularization of Argentine life. Argentine governments also seem to have made greater efforts than the Díaz regime in the field of public education. By 1914 the Argentine illiteracy rate had been reduced from more than two-thirds in 1869 to a little over one-third (but this improvement was largely concentrated on the coast and in the cities). Finally, the Argentine oligarchy had a better record than the Mexican dictatorship with respect to civil liberties, although suppression of the press, jailings, and even torture of radical dissidents were far from unknown.

Economic Boom and Inflation

The ominous new trends of the oligarchy emerged in the administration of President Julio Roca (1880–1886) and flowered exuberantly under his political heir and brother-in-law, Miguel Juárez Celman (1886–1890). Roca presided over the beginnings of a great boom that appeared to justify all the optimism of the oligarchy. As secretary of war under Avellaneda, Roca had led a military expedition—the so-called Conquest of the Desert—southward against the pampa Indians in 1879–1880. This conquest added vast new areas to the province of Buenos Aires and to the national public domain. The campaign created a last opportunity for implementing a democratic land policy directed toward the creation of an Argentine small farmer class. Instead, the Roca administration sold off the area in huge tracts for nominal prices to army officers, politicians, and foreign capitalists. The aging Sarmiento, who had seen the defeat of his own effort to acquire and distribute to settlers public land suitable for farming, lamented: "Soon there will not remain a palm of land for distribution to our immigrants."

Coming at a time of steadily mounting European demand for Argentine meat and wheat, the Conquest of the Desert triggered an orgy of land speculation that drove land prices ever higher and caused a prodigious expansion of cattle raising and agriculture. This expansion took place under the sign of the latifundio. Few of the millions of Italian and Spanish immigrants who entered Argentina in this period realized the common dream of becoming independent small landowners.

Some foreign agricultural colonies were founded in the provinces of Santa Fe and Entre Ríos in the 1870s and 1880s. By the mid-1890s, with wheat prices declining and land prices rising, there was a shift from small-scale farming to extensive tenant farming. This was true even in Santa Fe, the heartland of the foreign colonies. Soaring land prices and the traditional unwillingness of the estancieros to sell land forced the majority of would-be independent farmers to become ranch hands, sharecroppers, or tenant farmers. As sharecroppers or tenants, their hold on the land was very precarious; leases were usually limited to one, two, or three years. The immigrant broke the virgin soil, replaced the tough pampa grass with the alfalfa pasturage

needed to fatten cattle, and produced the first wheat harvests but then had to move on, leaving the landowner in possession of all improvements.

As a result, the great majority of new arrivals either remained in Buenos Aires or, having spent some years in the countryside, returned with their small savings to the city, where the rise of meat-salting and meat-packing plants, railroads, public utilities, and many small factories created a growing demand for labor. True, the immigrant workers received very low wages, worked long hours, and lived crowded with their families into one-room apartments in wretched slums; but in the city barrio they lived among their own people, free from the loneliness of the pampa and the arbitrary rule of great landowners, and had some opportunity of rising in the economic and social scale. As a result, the population of Buenos Aires shot up from 500,000 in 1889 to 1,244,000 in 1909. There arose a growing imbalance between the great city and its hinterland, which held the greater portion of the wealth, population, and culture of the nation, and the interior—particularly the northwest—which was impoverished, stagnant, and thinly peopled. Argentina, to use a familiar metaphor, became a giant head set on a dwarf body.

Foreign capital and management played a decisive role in the expansion of the Argentine economy in this period. The Creole elite obtained vast profits from the rise in the price of their land and the increasing volume of exports but showed little interest in plowing those gains into industry or the construction of the infrastructure required by the export economy, preferring a lavish and leisurely lifestyle over entrepreneurial activity. Just as they left to English and Irish managers the task of tending their estates, so they left to English capital the financing of meat-packing plants, railroads, public utilities, and docks and other facilities. As a result, most of these resources remained in British hands. Typical of the oligarchy's policy of surrender to foreign interests was the decision of Congress in 1889 to sell the state-owned Ferrocarril Oeste, the most profitable and best-run railroad in Argentina, to a British company. Service on a growing foreign debt claimed an ever larger portion of the government's receipts.

Meanwhile, imports of iron, coal, machinery, and consumer goods grew much faster than exports. Combined with the unfavorable price ratio of raw materials to finished goods, the result was an unfavorable balance of trade and a steady drain of gold. New loans with burdensome terms brought temporary relief but aggravated the long-range problem. Under President Miguel Juárez Celman, the disappearance of gold and the government's determination to keep the boom going at all costs led to the issue of great quantities of unbacked paper currency and a massive inflation.

The great landowners did not mind, for they were paid for their exports in French francs and English pounds, which they could convert into cheap Argentine pesos for the payment of local costs; besides, inflation caused the price of their lands to rise. The sacrificial victims of the inflation were the urban middle class and the workers, whose income declined in real value.

The Formation of the Radical Party

In 1889–1890, just as the boom was turning into a depression, the accumulated resentment of the urban middle class and some alienated sectors of the elite over the catastrophic inflation, one-party rule, and official corruption produced a protest movement that took the name *Unión Cívica* (Civic Union). Although the new organization had a middle-class base, its leadership united such disparate elements as urban politicians like Leandro Além, its first president, who was at odds with the Roca–Juárez Celman machine; new landowners and descendants of old aristocratic families who felt excluded from office and access to patronage by the same clique; and Catholics outraged by the government's anticlerical legislation. Aside from the demand for effective suffrage, the only thing uniting these heterogeneous elements was a common determination to overthrow the government.

The birth of the new party at a mass meeting in Buenos Aires in 1890 coincided with a financial storm: The stock market collapsed, bankruptcies multiplied, and in April the cabinet resigned. Encouraged by this last development, and counting on support from the army, the leaders of the Unión Cívica planned a revolt against Juárez Celman in July. Three days of sharp fighting ended in defeat for the rebels. This was due in considerable part to the vacillating conduct of their commander, General Manuel Campos, who at a critical moment in the struggle accepted a truce that ended the fighting with a promise of amnesty by the government.

The oligarchy now showed its ability to maneuver and divide its enemies. Juárez Celman was forced to resign with an abject confession of his errors; his place was taken by his vice president, Carlos Pellegrini (1890–1892), who moved to appease disgruntled elements of the elite by revising the system of distribution of jobs. Bartolomé Mitre, among other aristocratic dissidents, took the bait and reached an accommodation with the oligarchy that provided for an electoral accord between the National party and his followers. Simultaneously, Pellegrini took steps to improve economic conditions by a policy of retrenchment that reduced inflation, stabilized the peso, and revived Argentine credit abroad. Thanks to these measures and a gradual recovery from the depression, popular discontent began to subside.

The defection of Mitre and other aristocratic leaders of the Unión Cívica isolated Leandro Além and other dissidents who were excluded from Pellegrini's peacemaking scheme. Denouncing the accord between Mitre and Pellegrini as a sellout, Além and his nephew, Hipólito Yrigoyen, formed a new party committed to a "radical" democracy—the *Unión Cívica Radical*. The party named Bernardo de Yrigoyen as its presidential candidate in 1892 but, knowing that rigged elections made his victory impossible, they also prepared for another revolt—a move that Pellegrini effectively squelched by deporting Além and other Radical leaders until after the election of Luis Sáenz Peña (1892–1895).

On his return from exile, Além organized a new revolt, which began in July 1893. The rebels briefly seized Santa Fe and some other towns, but after two and a half months of fighting, the revolt collapsed for lack of significant popular support. Depressed by his failures and the intrigues of his nephew to seize control of the Radical party, Além committed suicide in 1896.

Between 1896 and 1910, the Radical party, now led by Yrigoyen, proved unable to achieve political reform by peaceful or revolutionary means. The reunited oligarcy continued to win election after election by the traditional methods. The architect of the system of corruption and nepotism, Julio Roca, was re-elected president in 1898 and was succeeded by another oligarch, Manuel Quintana, in 1904; on Quintana's death in 1906, Vice President José Figueroa Alcorta served out the rest of his term. A Radical revolt in 1905 proved to be another dismal fiasco.

In Yrigoyen, however, the Radicals possessed a charismatic personality and a masterful organizer who refused to admit defeat. Yrigoyen was a one-time police superintendent in Buenos Aires, a former minor politician who had maneuvered among various factions in the official party, using his political connections to acquire a considerable wealth, which he invested in land and cattle. As a Radical caudillo, Yrigoyen surrounded himself with an aura of mystery, lived in an ostentatiously modest manner, avoided making speeches, and cultivated a literary style that cloaked the poverty of his thought with turgid rhetoric. "Abstention," refusal to particiapte in rigged elections, and "Revolutionary Intransigence," the determination to resort to revolution until free elections were achieved, were the party's basic slogans.

The vagueness of the Radical program was dictated by the party's need to appeal to very diverse elements and by its wholehearted acceptance of the economic status quo. The Radical

party represented the bourgeoisie, but it was a dependent bourgeoisie that did not champion industrialization, economic diversification, or nationalization of foreign-owned industries. Far from attacking the neocolonial order, the Radical party proposed to strengthen it by promoting cooperation between the landed aristocracy and the urban sectors, which were challenging the Creole elite's monopoly of political power. In all respects, it was much more conservative than the contemporaneous reformist movement of José Batlle y Ordóñez in Uruguay.[1]

The Radical party went into eclipse after the debacles of 1890 and 1893, but gradually revived after 1900, due in part to Yrigoyen's charismatic personality and organizing talent. The most important factor, however, was the steady growth of an urban and rural middle class largely composed of sons of immigrants. The domination of the export sector, which limited the growth of industry and opportunities for entrepreneurial activity, focused middle-class ambitions more and more on government employment and the professions—two fields dominated by the Creole elite. Signs of growing unrest and frustration in the middle class included a series of student strikes in the universities, caused by efforts of Creole governing boards to restrict enrollment of students of immigrant descent.

---

[1] Under the leadership of José Batlle y Ordóñez (1856–1929), president of Uruguay from 1903 to 1907 and again from 1911 to 1915, Uruguay adopted an advanced program of social reform that made it "the chief laboratory for social experimentation in the Americas and a focal point of world interest." The program included the establishment of the eight-hour day, old age pensions, minimum wages, and accident insurance; abolition of capital punishment, separation of church and state, education for women, and recognition of divorce; and a system of state capitalism that gradually brought under public ownership banks, railroads, electric systems, telephone and telegraph companies, street railways, and meat-packing plants. Batlle supported labor in its strikes against foreign-owned enterprises. But his advanced welfare legislation was effective only in the port city of Montevideo. Batlle made no effort to challenge the land monopoly of the great estancieros or to apply his social legislation to their peons.

*Electoral Reform and the Growth of
the Labor Movement*

Meanwhile, a section of the oligarchy, headed by Carlos Pellegrini, had begun to advocate electoral reform. These aristocratic reformers argued that the existing situation created a permanent state of tension and instability; they feared that sooner or later the Radical efforts at revolution would succeed. It would be much better, they believed, to make the concessions demanded by the Radicals, open up the political system, and thereby gain for the ruling party—now generally called Conservative—the popular support and legitimacy it needed to remain in power. Moreover, the conservative reformers were aware of a new threat from the left—from the labor movement and especially its vanguard, the socialists, anarchists, and syndicalists—and hoped to make an alliance with the bourgeoisie against the revolutionary working class.

Pellegrini converted President Figueroa Alcorta to his viewpoint, and Figueroa's disciple and political heir, Roque Sáenz Peña, took office as president in 1910 with a promise that he would satisfy the Radical demands. At his urging, Congress passed a series of measures known collectively as the Sáenz Peña Law (1912). The new law established universal and secret male suffrage for citizens when they reached the age of eighteen. This measure, conceding the Radicals' basic demands, compelled them to abandon their revolutionary posture and operate as a regular party through legal channels. In 1912, having abandoned "Abstention," the Radicals made large gains in congressional and local elections, foreshadowing the victory of Hipólito Yrigoyen in the presidential election of 1916.

The Sáenz Peña Law, "an act of calculated retreat by the ruling class," in the words of David Rock, opened the way for a dependent bourgeoisie to share power and the spoils of office with the landed aristocracy. The principal political vehicle for working-class aspirations was the Socialist party, founded in 1894 as a split-off from the Unión Cívica Radical by the Buenos Aires physician and intellectual Juan B. Justo, who led the party until his death in 1928.

Despite its professed Marxism, the party's socialism was of the parliamentary reformist kind, appealing chiefly to highly skilled native-born workers and the lower middle class. The majority of workers, foreign-born noncitizens who still dreamed of returning someday to their homelands, remained aloof from electoral politics but readily joined trade union organizations. Here the Socialist party competed for influence with the anarchists and syndicalists, who in turn competed with each other for leadership of trade unions and strikes. Between 1902 and 1910 wage scales and working conditions deteriorated as surplus immigrant labor accumulated in Buenos Aires; a series of great strikes was broken by the government with brutal repression and the deportation of so-called "foreign agitators." Despite these defeats and the negative consequences of discord among socialists, anarchists, and syndicalists, the labor movement continued to grow and struggle, winning such initial victories as the ten-hour day and the establishment of Sunday as a compulsory day of rest.

CHILEAN POLITICS AND ECONOMY

Nitrates and War

In 1876 the official Liberal candidate for the presidency, Aníbal Pinto, defeated two rivals, both distinguished historians—Miguel Luis Amunátegui and Benjamin Vicuna Mackenna. From his predecessor, the new president inherited a severe economic crisis (1874–1879). Wheat and copper prices dropped, exports declined, and unemployment grew. The principal offset to these unfavorable developments was the continued growth of nitrate exports from the Atacama Desert as a result of a doubling of nitrate production between 1865 and 1875.

But nitrates, the foundation of Chilean material progress, also became the cause of a major war with dramatic consequences for Chile and her two foes, Bolivia and Peru.

The nitrate deposits exploited by Anglo-Chilean companies lay, it will be recalled, in territories belonging to Bolivia (the province of Antofagasta) and Peru (the province of Tarapacá). In 1866 a treaty between Chile and Bolivia defined their boundary in the Atacama Desert as the twenty-fourth parallel, gave Chilean and Bolivian interests equal rights to exploit the territory between the twenty-third and twenty-fifth parallels, and guaranteed each government half of the tax revenues obtained from the export of minerals from the whole area. Anglo-Chilean capital soon poured into the region, developing a highly efficient mining-industrial complex. By a second treaty of 1874, Chile's northern border with Bolivia was left at the twenty-fourth parallel. Chile relinquished her rights to a share of the taxes from exports north of that boundary but received in return a twenty-five-year guarantee against increase of taxes on Chilean enterprises operating in the Bolivian province of Antofagasta.

Chile had no boundary dispute with Peru, but aggressive Chilean mining interests, aided by British capital, soon extended their operations from Antofagasta into the Peruvian province of Tarapacá. By 1875, Chilean enterprises in Peruvian nitrate fields employed more than ten thousand workers, engineers, and supervisory personnel. At this point, the Peruvian government, on the brink of bankruptcy as a result of a very expensive program of public works, huge European loans, and the depletion of the guano deposits on which it had counted to service those loans, decided to expropriate the foreign companies in Tarapacá and establish a state monopoly over the production and sale of nitrates. Producers were compensated for their properties with certificates redeemable in two years and bearing an interest rate of 8 percent, but since Peru failed to obtain the loan needed to redeem the bonds, they rapidly declined in value. Meanwhile, Peru and Bolivia had negotiated a secret treaty in 1874 providing for a military alliance in the event either power went to war with Chile.

Ejected from Tarapacá, the Anglo-Chilean capitalists intensified their exploitation of the nitrate deposits in Antofagasta. In 1878, Bolivia, counting on her military alliance with Peru, challenged Chile by imposing higher taxes on nitrate exports from Antofagasta, in violation of the treaty of 1874. When the Chilean companies operating in Antofagasta refused to pay the new taxes, the Bolivian government threatened them with confiscation. The agreement of 1874 provided for arbitration of disputes, but the Bolivians twice rejected Chilean offers to submit the dispute to arbitration.

In February 1879, despite Chilean warnings that expropriation of Chilean enterprises would void the treaty of 1874, the Bolivian government ordered the confiscation carried out. On February 14, the day set for the seizure and sale of the Chilean properties, Chilean troops occupied the port of Antofagasta, encountering no resistance, and proceeded to extend Chilean control over the whole province. Totally unprepared for war, Peru made a vain effort to mediate between Chile and Bolivia. Chile, however, having learned of the secret Peruvian-Bolivian alliance, charged Peru with intolerable duplicity and declared war on both Peru and Bolivia on April 5, 1879.

In this war, called the War of the Pacific, Chile faced enemies whose combined population was more than twice its own; one of these powers, Peru, also possessed a respectable naval force. But Chile enjoyed major advantages. By contrast with its neighbors, it possessed a stable central government, a people with a strong sense of national identity, and a disciplined, well-trained army and navy. Although small, the navy included two modern ironclads with revolving turrets and heavy firing power. Chile also enjoyed the advantage of being closer to the theater of operations, since Bolivian troops had to come over the Andes, while the Peruvian army had to cross the Atacama Desert.

All three powers had serious economic problems, but Chile's situation was not as catastrophic as that of its foes. Equally important, Chile had the support of powerful English capitalist interests, who knew that the future of the massive English investment in Chile depended in large part on the outcome of the war. British capitalists, like the house of Antony Gibbs, had invested heavily in the Antofagasta Nitrate and Railway Company, whose dispute with Bolivia had precipitated the war; its British manager, George Hicks, had energetically championed the company before the Bolivian government. The prospect of Chilean acquisition of the valuable nitrate areas of Antofagasta and Tarapacá naturally pleased the British capitalists. British capital was also invested in Bolivia and Peru, but whereas the Chilean government had maintained service on its debt, Bolivia and Peru had suspended payment on their English loans. Besides, the Peruvian nationalization of the nitrate industry in Tarapacá had seriously injured British interests; they held most of the certificates issued by the Peruvian government to pay for the seized properties and had little hope of their redemption by Peru.

The decisive battle of the war took place on the sea on October 8, 1879, when the two Chilean ironclads, recently acquired from England, forced the surrender of the Peruvian ship *Huáscar*, which had done great damage to Chilean coastal traffic and severed communications between Santiago and the Chilean forces operating in the Atacama Desert. Having command of the sea, the Chilean forces resumed operations in the Atacama, and in a short time overran the Peruvian provinces of Tarapacá, Tacna, and Arica. By the middle of 1880, Bolivia had effectively been knocked out of the war. In January 1881, a thirty-thousand-man Chilean army under the command of General Manuel Baquedano overcame tenacious Peruvian resistance and occupied the enemy capital of Lima. Meanwhile, the Chilean navy had sunk the last Peruvian warship, the *Atahualpa*. Although scattered fighting between Chilean occupation forces and

Peruvian guerrillas continued for over two years, Chile had clearly won the war.

By the Treaty of Ancón (October 20, 1883), Peru ceded the province of Tarapacá to Chile in perpetuity. Tacna and Arica would be Chilean for ten years, after which a plebiscite would decide their ultimate fate. But the plebiscite was never held, and Chile continued to administer the two territories until 1929, when Peru recovered Tacna and Arica went to Chile. An armistice signed in April 1884 by Bolivia and Chile assigned the former Bolivian province of Antofagasta to Chile, but for many years no Bolivian government would sign a formal treaty acknowledging that loss. Meanwhile, Chile remained in de facto possession of the port and province of Antofagasta. Finally, in 1904, Bolivia signed a treaty in which Chile agreed to pay an indemnity and to build a railroad connecting the Bolivian capital of La Paz with the port of Arica. That railroad was completed in 1913.

Aftermath of the War of the Pacific

Chile took advantage of the continued mobilization of its armed forces during the negotiations with Peru to settle scores with the Araucanian Indians, whose struggle in defense of their land against encroaching whites had continued since colonial times. After two years of resistance against very unequal odds, the Araucanians were forced to admit defeat and sign a treaty (1883) that resettled the Indians on reservations and permitted them to retain their tribal government and laws. The Araucanian campaign of 1880–1882, which extended the Chilean frontier to the south into a region of mountain and forest, sparked a brisk movement of land speculation and colonization in that area.

From the War of the Pacific, which shattered Peru economically and psychologically and left Bolivia more isolated than before from the outside world, Chile emerged the strongest nation on the west coast, in control of vast deposits of nitrates and copper, the mainstays of its economy. But the greater part of these riches would soon pass into foreign hands. In 1881 the Chilean government made an important decision: It decided to return the nitrate properties of Tarapacá to private ownership, that is, to the holders of the certificates issued by the Peruvian government as compensation for the nationalized properties.

During the war, uncertainty as to how Chile would dispose of those properties had caused the Peruvian certificates to depreciate until they fell to a fraction of their face worth. Speculators, mostly British, had bought up large quantities of these depreciated certificates. Two English businessmen, John Thomas North and Robert Harvey, who may have had prior knowledge of the plans of the Chilean government, were particularly active in buying up these title deeds to the nitrate fields; as a result, almost overnight they became "kings" of the nitrate industry.

In 1878, British capital controlled some 13 percent of the nitrate industry of Tarapacá; by 1890, its share had risen to at least 70 percent. British penetration of the nitrate areas proceeded not only through formation of companies for direct exploitation of nitrate deposits but through the establishment of banks that financed entrepreneurial activity in the nitrate area and the creation of railways and other companies more or less closely linked to the central nitrate industry. An English railway company with a monopoly of transport in Tarapacá, the Nitrate Railways Company, controlled by North, paid dividends of up to 20 and 25 percent, compared with earnings of from 7 to 14 percent for other railway companies in South America.

The Chilean national bourgeoisie, which had pioneered in the establishment of the mining-industrial-railway complex in the Atacama, offered little resistance to the foreign take-over. Lack of strong support from the state, the relative financial weakness of the Chilean bourgeoisie, and the cozy and profitable relationships maintained throughout the nineteenth century between the Chilean elite and British interests facilitated the rapid transfer of Chilean nitrate and railway properties into British hands and the transformation of the Chilean bourgeoisie into a dependent bourgeoisie content with a share in the profits of British companies.

The presidential election of 1881 pitted a conservative military hero of the War of the Pacific, General Manuel Baquedano, against the candidate of a liberal coalition, Domingo Santa María, who won handily. The religious issue, one of the few issues still separating the new bourgeoisie from the landed aristocracy, dominated his administration (1881–1886). A dispute with the Vatican over its refusal to approve the government's nomination of an archbishop of liberal views led to the expulsion of the apostolic delegate, followed by congressional passage of a series of religious reforms: civil marriage, civil registration of births and deaths, and lay control of some cemeteries. However, the church continued to own extensive properties and receive subsidies from the state. More radical proposals to divorce church and state failed to win approval. In 1884 an electoral reform was adopted; the property qualification for voting was replaced with a literacy test. Since the great majority of Chilean males were illiterate *rotos* (seasonal farm workers) and inquilinos, this change did not materially add to the number of voters; as late as 1915, out of a population of about 3.5 million, only 150,000 persons voted.

The official liberal candidate for president in the election of 1886, José Manuel Balmaceda, had a distinguished record of public service as a diplomat and cabinet minister. As minister of the interior in Santa María's cabinet, he had piloted through congress the religious reforms just described. Balmaceda took office with a well-defined program of state-directed economic modernization. By the 1880s, factory capitalism had taken root in Chile. The Chilean Society for Industrial Development, which campaigned for state assistance to industrialization in the form of tariffs, subsidies, and other preferential treatment was founded in 1883. In addition to consumer goods industries—flour mils, breweries, leather factories, furniture factories, and the like—there existed foundries and metal-working enterprises that served the mining industry, railways, and agriculture. Balmaceda proposed to consolidate and expand this native industrial capitalism.

Balmaceda's Nationalistic Policies

Balmaceda came to office when government revenues were at an all-time high (they had risen from about 15 million pesos a year before the War of the Pacific to about 45 million pesos in 1887). The chief source of this government income was the export duty on nitrates. Knowing that the proceeds from this source would taper off as the nitrate deposits diminished, Balmaceda wisely planned to employ those funds for the development of an economic infrastructure that would remain when the nitrate was gone. Hence, public works figured prominently in his program. In 1887 he created a new ministry of industry and public works, which expended large sums on extending and improving the telegraphic and railway systems and on the construction of bridges, roads, and docks. Balmaceda also generously endowed public education, needed to provide skilled workers for Chilean industry. During his presidency, the total enrollment in Chilean schools rose in four years from some 79,000 in 1886 to over 150,000 in 1890. He also favored raising the wages of workers but was inconsistent in his labor policy; yielding to strong pressure from foreign and domestic employers, he sent troops to crush a number of strikes.

Central to Balmaceda's program was his determination to "Chileanize" the nitrate industry. In his inaugural address to Congress, he declared that his government would consider what measures it should take "to nationalize industries which are, at present, chiefly of benefit to foreigners," a clear reference to the nitrate industry. Later, Balmaceda's strategy shifted; he encouraged the entrance of Chilean private capital into nitrate production and exportation to prevent the formation of a foreign-dominated nitrate cartel whose interest in restricting output clashed with the government's interest in maintaining a high level of production in order to collect more export taxes. In November 1888, he scolded the Chilean elite for their lack of entrepreneurial spirit:

Why does the credit and the capital which are brought into play in all kinds of speculations in our great cities hold back and leave the foreigner to establish banks at Iquique and abandon to strangers the exploiting of the nitrate works of Tarapacá? . . . The foreigner exploits these riches and takes the profit of native wealth to give to other lands and unknown people the treasures of our soil, our own property and the riches we require.[2]

Balmaceda waged a determined struggle to end the monopoly of the British-owned Nitrate Railways Company, whose prohibitive freight charges reduced production and export of nitrates. His nationalistic policies inevitably provoked the hostility of English nitrate "kings" like John Thomas North, who had close links with the Chilean elite and employed prominent liberal politicians as their legal advisers.

But Balmaceda had many domestic as well as foreign foes. The clericals remembered his leading role in the religious reforms and noted his plans to further curb the powers of the church. The landed aristocracy resented his public works program because it drew labor from agriculture and pushed up rural wages. The banks, whose uncontrolled emission of notes had fed an inflation whose sole beneficiaries were mortgaged landlords and exporters who received payment in foreign currencies, were angered by his proposal to establish a national bank with a monopoly of note issue. The entire oligarchy, liberals as well as conservatives, opposed his use of the central government as an instrument of progressive economic and social change.

[2] Harold Blakemore, *British Nitrates and Chilean Politics, 1886–1896: Balmaceda and North* (London, 1974), p. 80.

Meanwhile, the government's economic problems multiplied, adding to Balmaceda's political difficulties by narrowing his mass base. By 1890 foreign demand for copper and nitrates had weakened. Prices in an overstocked world market fell, and English nitrate interests responded to the crisis by forming a cartel to reduce production. Reduced production and export of nitrates and copper sharply diminished the flow of export duties into the treasury and caused growing unemployment and wage cuts even as inflation cut into the value of wages. The result was a series of great strikes in Valparaíso and the nitrate zone in 1890. Despite his sympathy with the workers' demands and unwillingness to use force against them, Balmaceda, under pressure from domestic and foreign employers, sent troops to crush the strikes. These repressive measures insured much working-class apathy or even hostility toward the president in the eventual confrontation with his foes.

Indeed, Balmaceda had few firm allies at his side when that crisis came. The industrial capitalist group whose growth he had ardently promoted was still weak. The mining interests, increasingly integrated with or dominated by English capital, joined the bankers, the clericals, and the landed aristocracy in opposition to his nationalist program of economic development and independence.

Since the elections of 1888, Balmaceda had lacked a reliable parliamentary majority, a condition that made for a growing deadlock between president and Congress. In October 1890, Balmaceda dismissed a cabinet imposed upon him by the congressional majority and appointed one acceptable to himself. Instead of summoning Congress, which was dominated by a coalition of anti-Balmaceda forces, to pass the budget for 1891, the president simply announced that the 1890 budget would continue in force for the next year. In effect, Balmaceda abolished the system of parliamentary government and returned to the traditional system of presidential rule established by the constitution of 1833. His

rash act, made without any serious effort to mobilize popular forces, played into the hands of his enemies, who were already preparing for civil war.

On January 7, 1891, congressional leaders proclaimed a revolt against the president in the name of legality and the constitution. The navy, then as now led by officers of aristocratic descent, promptly went over to the rebels, while most army units remained loyal to the president. A junta headed by fleet captain Jorge Montt assumed direction of the revolt. With navy support, the congressionalists seized the ports and customhouses in the north and established their capital at Iquique, the chief port of Tarapacá.

English-owned enterprises actively aided the rebels. Indeed, by the admission of the British minister at Santiago, "our naval officers and the British community of Valparaíso and all along the coast rendered material assistance to the opposition and committed many breaches of neutrality." Many nitrate workers, alienated by Balmaceda's repression of their strike, remained neutral or even joined the rebel army, organized by a German army officer, General Emil Korner. Having gained control of the north and its vast revenues, the congressionalist forces moved south. Victories over Balmaceda's army in the battles of Concón and Placilla opened the way for capture of Valparaíso and Santiago, forcing the president to seek refuge in the Argentine embassy. On September 19, 1891, the day on which his legal term of office came to an end, Balmaceda put a bullet through his head.

The death of Chile's first anti-imperialist president restored the reign of the oligarchy, a coalition of landowners, bankers, merchants, and mining interests closely linked to English capital. A new era began, the era of the so-called Parliamentary Republic. Taught by experience, the oligarchy now preferred to rule through a Congress divided into various factions rather than through a strong executive. Such decentralization of government favored the interests of the rural aristocracy and its allies. A new law of 1892, vesting local governments with the right to supervise elections both for local and national offices, reinforced the power of the landowners, priests, and political bosses who had fought Balmaceda's progressive policies. The presidents of this period, beginning with Jorge Montt (1891–1896), were little more than puppets pulled by strings in the hands of congressional leaders. Corruption, cynicism, and factional intrigue characterized the political life of the Parliamentary Republic. Members of Congress, who received no salaries, paid large sums to secure election, which gave them access to the ample opportunities for graft on the national level.

The Parliamentary Republic, Foreign Economic Domination, and the Growth of the Working Class

The era of the Parliamentary Republic was accompanied by a growing subordination of the Chilean economy to foreign capital, which was reflected in a steady increase in the foreign debt and foreign ownership of the nation's resources. English investments in Chile amounted to 24 million pounds in 1890; they rose to 64 million pounds in 1913. Of this total, 34.6 million pounds formed part of the Chilean public debt. In the same period, American and German capital began to challenge the British hegemony in Chile. England continued to be Chile's principal trade partner, but United States and German trade with Chile grew at a faster rate. German instructors also acquired a strong influence in the Chilean army, and the flow of German immigrants into southern Chile continued, resulting in the formation of compact colonies dominated by a Pan-German ideology.

The revival of the Chilean economy from the depression of the early 1890s brought an increase of nitrate, copper, and agricultural exports and further enriched the ruling classes, but it left inquilinos, miners, and factory workers as desperately poor as before. Meanwhile, the working class grew from 120,000 to 250,000 between 1890 and 1900, and the doctrines of trade unionism, socialism, and anarchism achieved growing popularity in its ranks.

Luis Emilio Recabarren (1876–1924), the father of Chilean socialism and communism, played a decisive role in the social and political awakening of the Chilean proletariat. In 1906, Recabarren was elected to Congress from a mining area but was not allowed to take his seat because he refused to take his oath of office on the Bible. In 1909, he organized the Workers Federation of Chile, the first national trade union movement. Three years later, he led the founding of the Socialist party, a revolutionary Marxist movement, and became its first secretary.

The growing self-consciousness and militancy of the Chilean working class found expression in a mounting wave of strikes. Between 1911 and 1920, almost three hundred strikes, involving more than 300,000 workers, took place. Many were crushed with traditional brutal methods that left hundreds and thousands of workers dead.

BRAZILIAN POLITICS AND ECONOMY

The Antislavery Movement

From the close of the Paraguayan War (1870), the slavery question surged forward, becoming the dominant issue in Brazilian political life. Dom Pedro, personally opposed to slavery, was caught in a crossfire between a growing number of liberal leaders, intellectuals, and urban middle-class groups who demanded emancipation and slave owners determined to postpone the inevitable as long as possible. In 1870, Spain freed all the newborn and aged slaves of Cuba and Puerto Rico, leaving Brazil the only nation in the Americas to retain slavery in its original colonial form. Yielding to pressure, a conservative ministry pushed through parliament the Rio Branco Law in 1871. This measure freed all newborn children of slaves but obligated the masters to care for them until they reached the age of eight. At that time, owners could either release the children to the government in return for an indemnity or retain them as laborers until they reached the age of twenty-one. The law also freed all slaves belonging to the state or Crown and created a fund to be used for the manumission of slaves.

The Rio Branco Law was a tactical retreat designed to put off a final solution of the slavery problem. The imperial government applied the law with ponderous slowness, the compensation fund was never large enough to buy the freedom of many slaves, and few slave owners came forward to redeem the slave children for money. As late as 1884, only 113 had been freed by this means. Given the option of exploiting the labor of these children until they reached the age of twenty-one or exchanging them for government bonds, the great majority of slave owners chose the first course. Regarding them as temporary property, masters often worked these "free" children very hard; even after they reached the age of twenty-one, tradition and lack of education tended to keep them in a condition of semibondage. In effect, the Rio Branco Law gave an indefinite stay of execution to Brazilian slavery. Without later legislation, it would have taken at least half a century at the prevailing rate of manumission for the institution to disappear in Brazil.

Abolitionist leaders denounced the law as a sham and illusion and advanced ever more vigorously the demand for total and immediate emancipation. From 1880 on, the antislavery movement developed great momentum. Concentrated in the cities, it drew strength from the process of economic, social, and intellectual modernization under way there. To the new urban groups, slavery was an anachronism, glaringly incompatible with modernization. Among the slave owners themselves, divisions of opinion appeared. In the north, where slavery had long been dying as a result of the sale of the best slaves south and where many of those who remained were aged or dying, a growing number of planters converted to the use of free labor, drawing on the pool of freedmen made available by the Rio Branco Law and the *sertanejos* (inhabitants of the interior), poor whites and mixed-bloods who lived on the fringes of the plantation economy. Another factor in the decline of the slave population of the Northeast was the great drought of 1877–1879, which caused many of the region's wealthier folk to abandon the area. Some sold their slaves before departing for Rio; others brought slaves with them. In states like Amazonas and Ceará, where black slaves were few and most of the work was done by Indians and mixed-bloods, the move to emancipation was relatively easy; in 1884 both of these states declared the end of slavery within their borders. By contrast, the coffee planters of Rio de Janeiro, São Paulo, and Minas Gerais, joined by northern planters who trafficked in slaves, selling them to the coffee zone, offered the most tenacious resistance to the advance of abolition.

The abolitionist movement produced leaders of remarkable intellectual and moral stature. One was Joaquim Nabuco, son of a distinguished liberal statesman of the empire, whose eloquent dissection and indictment of slavery, *O abolicionismo,* had a profound impact on its readers. Another was a mulatto journalist, José do Patrocinio, a master propagandist noted for his fiery, biting style. Another mulatto, André Rebouças, an engineer and teacher whose intellectual gifts won him the respect and friendship of the emperor, was a leading organizer of the movement. For Nabuco and his comrades-in-arms, the antislavery struggle was the major front in a larger struggle for the transformation of Brazilian society. Abolition, they hoped, would pave the way for the attainment of other goals: land reform, public education, and political democracy. Thus, André Rebouças denounced latifundia, feudal barons, and landlords and demanded a distribution of land to freedmen, a land tax, and laws that would break up the "enormous territorial properties of the nefarious landocratic barons of this Empire."

Yielding to mounting pressure, parliament

Slaves drying coffee on a plantation in Terreiros,
in the state of Rio de Janeiro, about 1882.
(Photograph by Marc Ferrez; courtesy of Gilberto
Ferrez)

adopted another measure on September 28, 1885, that liberated all slaves when they reached the age of sixty but required them to continue to serve their masters for three years and forbade them to leave their place of residence for five years. These conditions, added to the fact that few slaves lived beyond the age of sixty-five, implied little change in the status of the vast majority of slaves. The imperial government also promised to purchase the freedom of the remaining slaves in fourteen years—a promise that few took seriously, in the light of experience with the Rio Branco Law. Convinced that the new law was another tactical maneuver, the abolitionists spurned all compromise solutions and demanded immediate, unconditional emancipation.

By the middle 1880s, the antislavery movement had assumed massive proportions and a more militant character. Large numbers of slaves began to vote for freedom with their feet; they were aided by abolitionists who organized an underground railway that ran from São Paulo to Ceará, where slavery had ended. Efforts to secure the return of fugitive slaves encountered growing resistance. Army officers, organized in a *Club Militar*, protested against the use of the army for the pursuit of fugitive slaves.

In February 1887, São Paulo liberated all slaves in the city with funds raised by popular subscription. Many slave owners, seeing the handwriting on the wall, liberated their slaves on condition that they remain at work for some time longer. By the end of 1887, even the die-hard coffee planters of São Paulo were ready to adjust to new conditions by offering to pay wages to their slaves and improve their working and living conditions; they also increased efforts to induce European immigrants to come to São Paulo. These efforts were highly successful; the flow of immigrants into São Paulo rose from 6,600 in 1885 to over 32,000 in 1887 and to 90,000 in 1888. As a result, coffee production reached record levels. With its labor problem solved, São Paulo was ready to abandon its resistance and even join the abolitionist crusade.

When parliament met on May 3, 1888, to deliberate again on the slavery question, the institution was in its last throes. By overwhelming majorities, both houses of parliament approved a measure whose laconic text read: "Article 1. From the date of this law slavery is declared abolished in Brazil. Article 2. All contrary provisions are revoked." Princess Isabel, ruling as regent for Dom Pedro, who was in Europe for medical treatment, signed the bill on May 13. Contrary to a traditional interpretation, however, the decision of May 1888 was not the climax of a gradual process of slavery's decline and the peaceful acceptance of the inevitable by the slave owners. The total slave population dropped sharply only after 1885, as a result of abolitionist agitation, mass flights of slaves, armed clashes, and other upheavals that appeared to many conservatives to threaten anarchy. In effect, abolition had come not through reform but by revolution.

The aftermath of abolition refuted the dire predictions of its foes. Freed from the burdens of slavery, Brazil made more economic progress in a few years than it had during the almost seven decades of imperial rule. For the former slaves, however, little had changed. The abolitionist demand for the grant of land to the freedmen was forgotten. Relationships between former masters and slaves in many places remained largely unchanged; tradition and the economic and political power of the *fazendeiros* gave them almost absolute control over their former slaves. Denied land and education, victims of prejudices inherited from the days of slavery, the freedmen were assigned the hardest, most poorly paid jobs. Fazendeiros replaced freedmen with immigrants in the coffee plantations; in the cities, black artisans lost their jobs to immigrants.

The Fall of the Monarchy

The fall of slavery dragged down with it its sister institution—the monarchy. The empire had long rested on the support of the planter class, especially the northern planters, who saw in the empire a guarantee of the survival of slavery. Before 1888, the Republican party had its principal base among the coffee interests, who resented the favor shown by the imperial government to the sugar planters and wished to achieve a political power corresponding to their economic power. Now, angered by abolition and embittered by the failure of the Crown to indemnify them for their lost slaves, those planters who had not previously shifted to the use of free labor joined the Republican movement. The monarchy that had served the interest of the regional elites for the previous sixty-seven years had lost its reasons for existence.

Republicanism and a closely allied ideology, positivism, also made many converts in the officer class, disgruntled by what it regarded as neglect and mistreatment of the armed forces by the imperial government. Many of the younger officers came from the new urban middle class or, if of aristocratic descent, were discontented with the ways of their fathers. Positivism, it has been said, became "the gospel of the military academy," where it was brilliantly expounded by a popular young professor of mathematics, Benjamin Constant Botelho de Magalhães, a devoted disciple of Auguste Comte, the doctrine's founder. The positivist doctrine, with its stress on science, its ideal of a dictatorial republic, and its distrust of the masses, fitted the needs of urban middle-class groups, progressive officers, and businessmen-fazendeiros who wanted modernization but without drastic changes in land tenure and class relations.

In June 1889, the liberal ministry headed by the Viscount of Ouro Prêto made a last effort to save the monarchy by proposing a reform program that included extension of the suffrage, autonomy for the provinces, and land reform. It was too late. On November 15, a military revolt organized and headed by Benjamin Constant and Marshal Floriano Peixoto overthrew the government and proclaimed a republic with Marshal Deodoro da Fonseca as provisional chief of state. Like the revolution that gave Brazil its independence, the republican revolution came from above; the coup d'état encountered little resistance but also inspired little enthusiasm. Although the provisional government included some sincere reformers like Ruy Barbosa, a champion of public education and civil liberties, the radical wing of the abolitionist movement was excluded. Power was firmly held by representatives of the business and landed elites and the military.

The new rulers promptly promulgated a series of reforms. On November 15, the same day that Brazil was proclaimed a republic, a decree ended corporal punishment in the army; on November 19, a literacy test replaced property qualifications for voting (since property and literacy usually went together, this measure did not significantly enlarge the electorate); and in January 1891, successive decrees separated church and state and established civil marriage.

The New Republic

In November 1891, two years after the revolt, a constituent assembly met in Rio de Janeiro to draft a constitution for the new republic. The draft offered for approval by the assembly provided for a federal, presidential form of government with the customary three branches—legislative, executive, and judicial. The principal debate was between the partisans of greater autonomy for the states and those who feared the divisive results of an extreme federalism. The coffee interests, which dominated the wealthy south central region, sought to strengthen their position at the expense of the central power. The bourgeois groups, represented in the convention chiefly by lawyers, favored a strong central government that could promote industry, aid the creation of a national market, and offer protection from British competition.

The result was a compromise tilted in favor of federalism. The twenty provinces in effect became self-governing states with popularly elected governors, the exclusive right to tax exports (a profitable privilege for wealthy states like São Paulo and Minas Gerais), and the right to maintain militias. The national government was given control over the tariff and the income from import duties, while the president obtained very large powers: He designated his cabinet ministers and other high officers, he could declare a state of siege, and he could intervene in the states with the federal armed forces in the event of a threat to their political institutions. The constitution proclaimed the sanctity of private property and guaranteed freedom of the press, speech, and assembly.

If these freedoms had some relevance in the cities and hinterlands touched by the movement of modernization, they lacked meaning over the greater part of the national territory. The fazendeiros, former slave owners, virtually monopolized the nation's chief wealth, its land. The land monopoly gave them absolute control over the rural population. Feudal and semifeudal forms of land tenure, accompanied by the obligation of personal and military service on the part of tenants, survived in the backlands, especially in the northeast. Powerful *coronéis* (colonels) maintained armies of *jagunços* (full-time private soldiers) and waged war against each other.[3] Banditry flourished in the interior, the bandits sometimes hiring themselves out to the coronéis, sometimes operating on their own, and occasionally gaining the reputation of modern Robin Hoods who took from the rich to give to the poor.

In this medieval atmosphere of constant insecurity and social disintegration, there arose messianic movements that reflected the aspirations of the oppressed sertanejos for peace and justice. One of the most important of such movements arose in the interior of Bahia, where the principal activity was cattle raising. In this area appeared a messiah called Antônio Conselheiro (Anthony the Counselor), who established a settlement at the abandoned cattle ranch of Canudos. Rejecting private property, Antônio required all who joined his sacred company to give up their goods, but he promised a future of prosperity in his messianic kingdom through the sharing of the treasure of the "lost Sebastian" (the Portuguese king who had disappeared in Africa in 1478 but would return as a redeemer) or through division of the property of hostile landowners.

Despite its religious coloration, the existence of such a focus of social and political unrest was intolerable to the fazendeiros and the state authorities. When the sertanejos easily defeated state forces sent against them in 1896, the governor called on the federal government for aid. Four campaigns, the last a large-scale operation directed by the minister of war in person, were required to break the epic resistance of the men of Canudos. A Brazilian literary masterpiece, *Os sertões* (Rebellion in the Backlands) by Euclides da Cunha (1856–1909), immortalized the heroism of the defenders and the crimes of the victors.

It also revealed to the urban elite another and unfamiliar side of Brazilian reality.

The Economic Revolution

An enormous historical gulf separated the bleak sertão, or interior, in which the tragedy of Canudos was played out from the cities, the scene of a mushrooming growth of banks, stock exchanges, and corporations. With the economic revolution came a revolution in manners. In Rio de Janeiro, writes Pedro Calmon,

barons with recently acquired titles jostled each other in the corridors of the Stock Exchange or in the Rua da Alfandega, buying and selling stocks; the tilburies [light two-wheeled carriages] that filled the length of São Francisco Street were taken by a multitude of millionaires of recent vintage—commercial agents, bustling lawyers, promoters of all kinds, politicians of the new generation, the men of the day.[4]

A few more years and even the physical appearance of some of Brazil's great urban centers would change. These changes were most marked in the federal capital of Rio de Janeiro, which was made into a beautiful and healthful city between 1902 and 1906 through the initiative and efforts of Prefect Pereira Passos, who mercilessly demolished the narrow old streets to permit the construction of broad, modern avenues, and the distinguished scientist Oswaldo Cruz, who waged a victorious struggle to conquer the endemic malaria and yellow fever by filling in swamps and installing adequate water and sewerage systems.

The economic policies of the new republican regime reflected pressures from different quarters: from the planter class, from urban capitalists, from the military. Many planters, left in a difficult position by the abolition of slavery, required subsidies and credits to enable them to convert to the new wage system. The emerging industrial bourgeoisie, convinced that Brazil

---

[3] The title coronel was often honorary and did not necessarily indicate a military command or land-ownership; especially after 1870, a coronel might be simply a political boss or even an influential lawyer or priest.

[4] Quoted in Benjamin Keen, ed., *Latin American Civilization: The National Era*, vol. 2 (Boston: Houghton Mifflin, 1974), p. 313.

must develop an industrial base in order to emerge from backwardness, asked for protective tariffs, the construction of an economic infrastructure, and policies favorable to capital formation. Within the provisional government, these aspirations had a fervent supporter in the minister of finance, Ruy Barbosa, who believed that the factory was the crucible in which an "intelligent and independent democracy" would be forged in Brazil. Finally, the army, whose decisive role in the establishment of the republic had given it great prestige and influence, called for increased appropriations for the armed services. The aggregate of these demands far exceeded the revenue available to the federal and state governments.

The federal government solved this problem by resorting to the printing press and allowing private banks to issue notes backed by little more than faith in the future of Brazil. In two years, the volume of paper money in circulation doubled, and the foreign exchange value of the Brazilian monetary unit, the *milréis*, plummeted disastrously. Since objective economic conditions (the small internal market and the lack of an adequate technological base, among other factors) limited the real potential for Brazilian growth, much of the newly created capital was used for highly speculative purposes, including the creation of fictitious companies.

The great boom collapsed in 1891, bringing ruin to many investors and unemployment to workers even as inflation continued to cut into the real value of their wages. Disputes over methods of coping with the crisis contributed to a clash between President Deodoro da Fonseca and Congress when it assembled for its first session in November 1891. When da Fonseca attempted to dissolve Congress and assume dictatorial power, the army and navy turned against him. Faced with a threat from the navy to bombard Rio, the president resigned and was succeeded by his vice president, Marshal Floriano Peixoto.

Under Peixoto, the urban middle-class sector gained even greater influence in the government,

and inflation continued unchecked, to the dismay of the planters. The rapid fall in the price of coffee expressed in foreign hard currency brought a decline of real income from exports and a rise in the cost of many imported items to almost prohibitive levels. This hurt the planters but stimulated the growth of Brazilian manufactures: The number of such enterprises almost doubled between 1890 and 1895. The discontent of the "outs" sparked a new revolt with strong aristocratic and monarchical overtones in 1893. The movement began in Rio Grande do Sul and was soon joined by the navy, a stronghold of aristocractic prejudice and influence. Peixoto's firm refusal to bow to threats of a naval bombardment of the capital brought a collapse of the fleet revolt and allowed the government to launch an offensive south against the rebels of Rio Grande; by August 1895, the last insurgents had surrendered.

Peixoto's victory, which won him the name of "consolidator of the republic," was largely due to the loyalty and financial and military support of the state of São Paulo. But this support came at a price; the coffee planters were resolved to end the ascendancy of the urban middle classes, whose policies of rapid industrialization they distrusted and held responsible for the inflation and political instability that had plagued the first years of the republic. In 1893 the old planter oligarchies, whose divisions had temporarily enabled the middle classes to gain the upper hand in coalition with the military, reunited to form the Federal Republican party with a program of support for federalism and fiscal responsibility. Since they controlled the electoral machinery, they easily elected Prudente de Morais president in 1894. Morais, the first civilian president of Brazil (1894–1898), initiated an era marked by the domination of the coffee interests and the relegation of urban capitalist groups to a secondary role in political life.

Morais' successor, Manuel Ferraz de Campos Sales (1898–1902), continued and expanded his program of giving primacy to agriculture. Campos Sales fully endorsed the system of the international economic division of labor as it applied to Brazil. "It is time," he proclaimed, "that we take the correct road; to that end we must strive to export all that we can produce better than other countries, and import all that other countries can produce better than we." This formula meant the abandonment of the goal of independent economic development— in other words, the acceptance of neocolonialism. Determined to halt inflation, Campos Sales drastically reduced expenditures on public works, increased taxes, and made every effort to redeem the paper money in order to improve Brazil's international credit and secure new loans, which were vital to the coffee interests.

Coffee was king. Around the monarch were grouped his obedient barons: rubber, cacao, cotton, sugar. Whereas in the period from 1880 to 1889, Brazil produced only 56 percent of the world's coffee output, in the period from 1900 to 1904, it accounted for 76 percent of the total production. Its closest competitor, rubber, supplied only 28 percent of Brazil's exports in 1901. Sugar, once the ruler of the Brazilian economy, now accounted for barely 5 percent of the nation's exports. Minas Gerais and especially São Paulo became the primary coffee regions, while Rio de Janeiro declined in importance. Enjoying immense advantages—the famous rich, porous *terra roxa* (red soil), an abundance of immigrant labor, and closeness to the major port of Santos— the *Paulistas* harvested 60 percent of the national coffee production.

Coffee was king, but from the closing years of the nineteenth century its reign was a troubled one. The classic symptoms of overproduction— falling prices and unsalable stocks—had appeared as early as 1896. The problem arose from a vast increase in plantings of coffee trees (from 220 to 520 million between 1890 and 1900). And foreign competition and speculative activity on the part of middlemen added to the difficulties of the planters. These middlemen (usually agents of foreign banks and merchant houses) bought when the coffee harvest flowed into the ports, forcing prices down, and formed reserves that they doled out in periods of shortage, when prices were high.

Responding to the planters' clamor for help, the government of São Paulo took the first step for the "defense" of coffee in 1902, forbidding new coffee plantings for five years. New steps soon proved necessary. Faced with a bumper crop in 1906, São Paulo launched a coffee price-support scheme to protect the state's economic lifeblood. With financing from British, French, German, and American banks, and the eventual collaboration of the federal government, São Paulo purchased several million bags of coffee and held them off the market in an effort to maintain profitable price levels. Purchases continued into 1907; from that date until World War I the stocks were gradually sold off with little market disruption. The operation's principal gainers were the foreign merchants and bankers who, since they controlled the Coffee Commission formed to liquidate the purchased stocks, gradually disposed of them with a large margin of profit. The problem, temporarily exorcised, was presently to return in even more acute form.

The valorization scheme, which favored the coffee-raising states at the expense of the rest, reflected the coffee planters' political domination. Under President Campos Sales, this ascendancy was institutionalized by the so-called *política dos governadores* (politics of the governors). Its essence was a formula that gave the two richest and most populous states (São Paulo and Minas Gerais) a virtual monopoly of federal politics and the choice of presidents. Thus, the first three civilian presidents from 1894 to 1906 came from São Paulo; the next two, from 1906 to 1910, came from Minas Gerais and Rio de Janeiro, respectively.

In return, the oligarchies of the other states were given almost total freedom of action within their jurisdictions, the central government intervening as a rule only when it suited the local oligarchy's interest. Informal discussions among the state governors determined the choice of president, with his election a foregone conclusion. No official candidate for president lost an election before 1930. In 1910 the distinguished statesman and orator Ruy Barbosa ran for president on a platform of democratic reform and antimilitarism against the official candidate, Hermes da Fonseca, a conservative military man. Barbosa was beaten by almost two to one; out of a population of 22 million, about 360,000 voted. Similar reciprocal arrangements existed on the state level between the governors and the coronéis, urban or rural bosses who rounded up the local vote to elect the governors and were rewarded with a free hand in their respective domains.

Despite the official bias in favor of agriculture, industry continued to grow in the period from 1904 to 1914. By 1908, Brazil could boast of more than three thousand industrial enterprises. Foreign firms dominated the fields of banking, public works, utilities, transportation, and the export and import trade. Manufacturing, on the other hand, was carried on almost exclusively by native Brazilians and permanent immigrants. This national industry was concentrated in the four states of São Paulo, Minas Gerais, Rio de Janeiro, and Rio Grande do Sul. Heavy industry did not exist; over half of the enterprises were textile mills and food-processing plants. Many of these "enterprises" were small workshops employing a few artisans or operated with an archaic technology, and Brazilians in the market economy continued to import most quality products. The quantitative and qualitative development of industry was hampered by the semifeudal conditions prevailing in the countryside, by the extreme poverty of the masses, which sharply limited the internal market, by the lack of a skilled, literate labor force (as late as 1910, Brazil had an enrollment of only 566,000 pupils out of a population of 20 million, and the great majority received less than two years of formal instruction), and by the hostility of most fazendeiros and foreign interests to industry.

Together with industry there arose a working class destined to play a significant role in the life of the country. The Brazilian proletariat was partly recruited from sharecroppers and minifundio peasants fleeing to the cities to escape dismal poverty and the tyranny of coronéis, but above all it was composed of the flood of European immigrants, who arrived at a rate of 100,000 to 150,000 each year. Working and living conditions of the working class were often intolerable. Child labor was common, for children could be legally employed from the age of twelve. The workday ranged from nine hours for some skilled workers to more than sixteen hours for some categories of unskilled workers. Wages were pitifully low and often paid in vouchers redeemable at the company store. There was a total absence of legislation to protect workers against the hazards of unemployment, old age, or industrial accidents.

Among the European immigrants were many militants with socialist, syndicalist, or social-democratic backgrounds who helped to organize the Brazilian labor movement and gave it a radical political orientation. National and religious divisions among workers, widespread illiteracy, and quarrels between socialists and anarcho-syndicalists hampered the rise of a trade union movement and a labor party.

But trade unions grew rapidly after 1900 in response to unsatisfactory working conditions, with immigrant workers often providing the leadership. In 1906 the first national labor congress, representing the majority of the country's trade unions, met and began a struggle for the eight-hour day. One result of the congress was the formation of the first national trade union organization, the Brazilian Labor Confederation, which conducted a number of strikes. Repression was the typical answer of the authorities and employers to labor's demands. Police conducted periodic roundups of labor leaders. Immigrants were deported, while native-born leaders were imprisoned or sent to forced labor on a railroad under construction in distant Mato Grosso. The phrase "the social question is a question for the police" was often used to sum up the labor policy of the Brazilian state.

CHAPTER ELEVEN

Society and Culture

in the Nineteenth

Century

Independence left much of the colonial social
structure intact. This fact was very apparent to
liberal leaders of the postindependence era. "The
war against Spain," declared the Colombian
liberal Ramón Mercado in 1853, "was not a
revolution. . . . Independence only scratched
the surface of the social problem, without
changing its essential nature." A modern historian, Charles C. Griffin, comes to much the
same conclusion. "Only the beginnings of a
basic transformation took place," he writes, "and
there were many ways in which colonial attitudes and institutions carried over into the life
of republican Spanish America."

HOW NEW WAS THE
NEW SOCIETY?

We should not minimize, however, the extent
and importance of the changes that did take
place. Independence produced, if not a major
social upheaval, at least a minor one. It opened

wide fissures within the elite, dividing aristocratic supporters of the old social order from modernizers who wanted a more democratic, bourgeois order. Their struggle is an integral aspect of the first half-century after the end of Spanish and Portuguese rule. Independence also enabled such formerly submerged groups as artisans and gauchos to enter the political arena, although in subordinate roles, and even allowed a few to climb into the ranks of the elite. The opening of Latin American ports to foreign goods also established a relatively free market in ideas, at least in the capitals and other cities. With almost no time lag, such new European doctrines as utopian socialism, romanticism, and positivism entered Latin America and were applied to the solution of the continent's problems. These new winds of doctrine, blowing through what had lately been dusty colonial corridors, contributed to the area's intellectual renovation and promoted further social change.

THE PASSING OF THE SOCIETY OF CASTES

Verbally, at least, the new republican constitutions established the equality of all men before the law, destroying the legal foundations of colonial caste society. Since little change in property relations took place, however, the ethnic and social lines of division remained essentially the same. Wealth, power, and prestige continued to be concentrated in the hands of a ruling class that was mainly white, although in some countries, such as Venezuela, it became more or less heavily tinged with individuals of darker skin who had managed to climb the social ladder through their prowess in war or politics.

The Indians

Of all the groups composing the old society of castes, the status of the Indians changed least of all. The Mexican historian Carlos María Bus-

tamante was one of the few Creole leaders who recognized that independence had not freed the Indians from their yoke. "They still drag the same chains," he wrote, "although they are flattered with the name of freemen." Even Indian tribute and forced labor, abolished during or after the wars of independence, soon reappeared in many countries under other names. What was worse, Indian communal landholding, social organization, and culture, which Spanish law and policy had to some extent protected in colonial times, came under increasing attack, especially from liberals who believed that Indian communal traditions constituted as much of an obstacle to progress as the Spanish system of castes and special privileges.

Until about 1870, however, large, compact Indian populations continued to live under the traditional communal landholding system in Mexico, Central America, and the Andean region. Then, the rapid growth of the export economy, the coming of the railroads, and the resulting rise in land values and demand for labor caused white and mestizo landowners and landowner-dominated governments to launch a massive assault on Indian lands. The expropriation of Indian lands was accompanied, as noted in Chapter 10, by a growth of Indian peonage and tenantry. Employers used a variety of devices, ranging from debt servitude to outright coercion, to attach laborers to their estates. In some areas, there arose a type of Indian serfdom that closely resembled the classic European model. In the Andean region, for example, Indian tenants, in addition to working the master's land, had to render personal service in his household, sometimes at the hacienda, sometimes in the city. During his term of domestic service, the Indian serf could be given or sold to the master's friends. This and other forms of serfdom survived well into the twentieth century.

The master class, aided by the clergy and local magistrates, sought to reinforce the economic subjection of the Indian with psychological subjection. There evolved a pattern of relations and role-playing that assigned to the patrón the role of a benevolent figure who assured his peons or tenants of a livelihood and protected them in all emergencies in return for their absolute obedience. In countries with Indian populations or peasants descended from Indians, the relations between master and peon often included an elaborate ritual that required the Indian to request permission to speak to the patrón, to appear before him with head uncovered and bowed, and to seek his approval for all major personal decisions, including marriage.

The greater freedom of movement that came with independence, the progressive disappearance of Indian communities, and the growth of the hacienda, in which Indians mingled with mestizos, strengthened a trend toward Indian acculturation that had begun in the late colonial period. This acculturation was reflected in a growth of Indian bilingualism: Indians increasingly used Spanish in dealing with whites, reserving their native languages for use among themselves. To the limited extent that the public school entered Indian regions, it contributed to the adoption of Spanish as a second language or, in the case of the rare Indian whose talents and good fortunes elevated him into the ranks of the white and mestizo elite, sometimes led to total abandonment of his native tongue. The Mexican historian Eduardo Ruíz recalled that as a child he spoke only Tarascan but had forgotten it during his twelve years of study at the colegio. "I did not want to remember, I must confess, because I was ashamed of being thought to be an Indian." Some acculturation also occurred in dress, with frequent abandonment of picturesque regional styles in favor of a quasi-European style, sometimes enforced by legislation and fines. Over much of Mexico, for example, the white trousers and shirt of coarse cotton cloth and the broad-brimmed hat became almost an Indian "uniform."

Yet pressures toward Indian acculturation or assimilation failed to achieve the integration into white society that well-meaning liberals had hoped to secure through education, the growth of Indian wants, and the Indian's entrance into the modern world of industry and trade. At the end of the nineteenth century, the processes of acculturation had not significantly reduced the size of the Indian sector in the five countries with the largest native populations: Mexico, Guatemala, Ecuador, Peru, and Bolivia. There were various reasons for this. The economic stagnation and political troubles of the first postrevolutionary decades tended to reinforce the isolation and cultural separateness of Indian communities. When the Latin American economies revived as a result of the expansion of the export sector, this revival was achieved largely at the expense of the Indians and served mainly to accentuate their poverty and backwardness. Their economic marginality, their almost total exclusion from the political process, the intense exploitation to which they were subjected by white and mestizo landowners, priests, and officials, and the barriers of distrust and hatred that separated them from the white world prevented any thoroughgoing acculturation, much less integration.

Indian communities made such concessions to the pressures for assimilation as were necessary but preserved their traditional housing, diet, social organization, and religion—which combined pagan and Christian features. In some regions, the pre-Conquest cults and rituals, including occasional human sacrifice, survived. The existence in a number of countries of large Indian populations, intensely exploited and branded as inferior by the ruling social Darwinist ideology, constituted a major obstacle to the formation of a national consciousness in those lands. With good reason, the pioneer Mexican anthropologist Manuel Gamio wrote in 1916 that Mexico did not constitute a nation in the European sense but was composed of numerous small nations, differing in speech, economy, social organization, and psychology.

A Question of Color

The wars for independence, by throwing "careers open to talents," enabled a few Indians and a larger number of mixed-bloods of humble origins to rise high in the military, political, and social scale. The liberal caudillos Vicente Guerrero and Juan Álvarez in Mexico and such talented leaders as Juan José Flores of Ecuador, Andrés Santa Cruz of Bolivia, and Ramón Castilla of Peru illustrate the ascent of the mixed-bloods.

The rise of these mestizo or mulatto leaders inspired fears in some members of the Creole elite, beginning with Bolívar, who gloomily predicted a race war that would also be a struggle between haves and have-nots. Bolívar revealed his obsessive race prejudice in his description of the valiant and generous Vicente Guerrero as the "vile abortion of a savage Indian and a fierce African." These fears proved groundless; although some mixed-blood leaders, like Guerrero and Álvarez, were loyal to the humble masses from which they had sprung, the majority were soon co-opted by the Creole aristocracy and firmly defended its interests.

On the other hand, Creole politicians of the postrevolutionary era had to take account of the new political weight of the mixed-blood middle and lower classes, especially the artisan groups. The mixed-bloods were exploited politically by white elites who promised to satisfy the aspirations of the masses—promises they failed to fulfill. This happened in Bogotá, where Colombian liberals courted the artisans in their struggle against conservatives; in Buenos Aires, where Rosas demagogically identified himself with the gauchos and urban artisans—who were mixed-bloods in the great majority—against the aristocratic liberal *unitarios*; and in Venezuela, where the liberal Antonio Leocadio Guzmán announced his revolt with the cry "death to the whites!"

After mid-century, the growing influence of European racist ideologies, especially Spencerian biological determinism, led to a heightened sensitivity to color. From Mexico to Chile, members of the white elite and even the middle class claimed to be superior to Indians and mixed-bloods. A dark skin increasingly became an obstacle to social advancement. Typical of the rampant pseudoscientific racism by the turn of the century is the remark of the Argentine Carlos Bunge, son of a German immigrant, that mestizos and mulattos were "impure, atavistically anti-Christian; they are like the two heads of a fabulous hydra that surrounds, constricts, and strangles with its giant spiral a beautiful, pale virgin, Spanish America."

Even before the revolutions, black slavery had declined in various parts of Latin America. This occurred in part because of economic developments that made slavery unprofitable and favored manumission or commutation of slavery to tenantry. An even more significant reason, perhaps, was the frequent flight of slaves to remote jungles and mountains, where they formed self-governing communities. In Venezuela, in about 1800, it was estimated that alongside some eighty-seven thousand slaves there were twenty-four thousand fugitive slaves.

The wars of independence gave a major stimulus to emancipation. Patriot commanders like Bolívar and San Martín and royalist officers often offered slaves freedom in return for military service, and black slaves sometimes formed a majority of the fighting forces on both sides. About a third of San Martín's army in the campaign of the Andes was black. Moreover, the confusion and disorder produced by the fighting often led to a collapse of plantation discipline, easing the flight of slaves and making their recovery difficult if not impossible.

After independence, slavery further declined, partly because of its patent incompatibility with the libertarian ideals proclaimed by the new states but even more as a result of the hostile attitude of Great Britain, which had abolished the slave trade in all its possessions in 1807 and henceforth brought pressure for similar action by all countries still trading in slaves: We have seen that British pressure on Brazil contibuted to the crisis of Brazilian slavery and its ultimate demise.

Emancipation came most easily and quickly in countries where slaves were a negligible element in the labor force; thus, Chile, Mexico, and the Federation of Central America (1823–1839) abolished slavery between 1823 and 1829. In other countries, the slave owners fought a tenacious rear-guard action. In Venezuela a very gradual manumission law was adopted in 1821, but not until 1854 was slavery finally abolished by a liberal government. Slavery was abolished in Peru in 1855 by Ramón Castilla. The Spanish Cortes decreed the end of slavery in Puerto Rico in 1873 and in Cuba in 1880, but in Cuba the institution continued in a disguised form (the patronato) until 1886, when it was finally abolished.

The record of Latin American slavery in the nineteenth century, it should be noted, does not support the thesis of some historians that cultural and religious factors made Hispanic slavery inherently milder than the North American variety. In its two main centers of Cuba and Brazil, under conditions of mounting demand for Brazilian coffee and Cuban sugar and a critical labor shortage, there is ample evidence of systematic brutality with use of the lash to make slaves work longer and harder. The slaves responded with a resistance that varied from slowdowns to flight and open rebellion—a resistance that contributed to the final demise of the institution.

THE PROCESS OF MODERNIZATION

The Landowners

Patriarchal family organization, highly ceremonial conduct, and leisurely lifestyle continued to characterize the landed aristocracy and Latin American elites after independence. The kinship network of the large extended family ruled by a patriarch was further extended by the institution of *compadrazgo*, which established a relationship of patronage and protection on the part of the upper-class godparent toward his lower-status godchild and its parents. They in turn were expected to form part of the godparent's following and to be devoted to his interests.

As in colonial times, great landowners generally resided most of the time in the cities, leaving their estates in the charge of administrators (but it must not be assumed that they neglected to scrutinize account books or were indifferent to considerations of profit and loss). From the same upper class came a small minority of would-be entrepreneurs who challenged the traditional agrarian bias of their society and, in the words of Richard Graham, were "caught up by the idea of capitalism, by the belief in industrialization, and by a faith in work and practicality." Typical of this class was the Brazilian viscount Mauá, who created a banking and industrial empire between 1850 and 1875 against the opposition of traditionalists. Mauá's empire collapsed, however, partly because the objective conditions for capitalist development in Brazil had not fully matured, partly because of official apathy and even disfavor. The day of the entrepreneur had not yet come; the economic history of Latin America in the nineteenth century is strewn with the wrecks of abortive industrial projects. These fiascos also represented defeats for the capitalist mentality and values.

After mid-century, with the gradual rise of a neocolonial order based on the integration of the Latin American economy into the international capitalist system, the ruling class, although retaining certain precapitalist traits, became more receptive to bourgeois values and ideals. An Argentine writer of the 1880s noted that "the latifundist no longer has that semibarbarous, semifeudal air; he has become a scientific administrator, who alternates between his home on the estate, his Buenos Aires man-

The family of an Indian cacique wearing Spanish
dress. (From Carl Nebel, *Voyage Pittoresque et
Archéologique . . . [au] Mexique*, Paris, 1836.
Courtesy of The Newberry Library.)

sion, and his house in Paris." In fact, few estancieros or hacendados became "scientific administrators." They preferred to leave the task
of managing their estates to others, but the
writer accurately pointed to a process of
modernization or Europeanization of elites under
way throughout the continent.

The process began right after independence
but greatly accelerated after mid-century. Within
a decade after independence, marked changes
in manners and consumption patterns had occurred. "Fashions alter," wrote Fanny Calderón
de la Barca, Scottish-born wife of the Spanish
minister to Mexico, who described Mexican upper-class society in the age of Santa Anna in a

series of sprightly letters. "The graceful mantilla
gradually gives place to the ungraceful bonnet.
The old painted coach, moving slowly like a
caravan, with Guido's Aurora painted on its
gaudy panels, is dismissed for the London-built
carriage." Flora Tristan, a visitor to Peru in
1833–1834, made similar observations:

*In the past four or five years great changes have
taken place in Peruvian customs and practices; Parisian
fashions now hold sway there. . . . The clothes of
the upper classes do not differ at all from those of
Europe; women and men dress exactly as in Paris;
women scrupulously follow the dictates of new styles,
save that they do not cover their heads and that*

custom requires that they attend church dressed in black, with the mantilla, in all the severity of the Spanish costume. French dances are replacing the fandango, the bolero, and the native dances, which decency frowns upon. Scores from our operas are sung in the salons and even our novels are read there. A little while longer, and people will not go to mass unless they can hear good music there. The well-to-do pass their time in smoking, reading newspapers, and playing faro. The men ruin themselves at play, the women in buying clothes.[1]

The old yielded much more slowly and grudgingly to the new in drowsy colonial cities like Quito, capital of Ecuador, but yield it did, at least in externals. The American minister to Ecuador in the 1860s, Friedrich Hassaurek, who was harshly critical of Quitonian society and manners, noted that "in spite of the difficulty of transportation, there are about one hundred and twenty pianos in Quito, very indifferently tuned." Another American visitor to Quito in this period, Professor James Orton of Smith College, observed that "the upper class follow *la mode de Paris*, gentlemen adding the classic cloak of Old Spain." He added sourly that "this modern toga fits an Ecuadorian admirably, preventing the arms from doing anything, and covers a multitude of sins, especially pride and poverty."

Under the republic, as in colonial times, dress was an important index of social status. According to Orton, "no gentleman will be seen walking in the streets of Quito under a poncho. Hence citizens are divided into men with ponchos and gentlemen with cloaks." Dress even served to distinguish followers of different political factions or parties. In Buenos Aires under Rosas, the artisans who formed part of the dictator's mass base were called *gente de chaqueta* (wearers of jackets), as opposed to the aristocratic unitarian liberals, who wore dress coats.

By the close of the century, European styles

of dress had triumphed in such great cities as Mexico City and Buenos Aires and among non-Indian sectors of the population generally. But attitudes toward clothes continued to reflect aristocratic values, especially scorn for manual labor; dress still made the man. In Buenos Aires, for example, at the turn of the century, a worker's blouse would bar entrance to its wearer to a bank or the halls of Congress. As a result, according to James Scobie, "everyone sought to hide the link with manual labor," and even workingmen preferred to display the traditional coat and tie.

The Immigrants

After 1880, there was a massive influx of European immigrants into Argentina, Uruguay, and Brazil and of lesser numbers into such countries as Chile and Mexico. Combined with growing urbanization and continued expansion of the export sector, this helped to accelerate the rate of social change. These developments helped to create a small industrial working class of the modern type and swelled the ranks of the middle class and the blue-collar and white-collar workers.

But aside from that minority of the working class that adopted socialist, anarchist, or syndicalist doctrines, the immigrants posed no threat to the existing social structure or the prevailing aristocratic ideology; instead, many were conquered by that ideology. The foreigners who entered the upper class as a rule already belonged to the educated or managerial class. Movement from the middle class of immigrant origin to the upper class was extremely difficult and rare; for the lower-class immigrant it was almost impossible. A few immigrants made their fortunes by commerce or speculation. Their children or grandchildren took care to camouflage the origins of their wealth and to make it respectable by investing it in land. These nouveaux riches regarded Indians and workers with the same contempt as their aristocratic associates.

[1] Flora Tristan, *Pérégrinations d'une Paria (1833–1834)*, 2 vols. (Paris, 1838), 1:369–370.

The Women

Independence did not better the status of women. Indeed, their civil status probably worsened as a result of new bourgeois-style law codes that strengthened husbands' control over their wives' property. More than ever, women were relegated to the four walls of their houses and household duties. Church and parents taught women to be submissive, sweetly clinging, to have no wills of their own. The double standard of sexual conduct prevailed; women were taught to deny their sexuality and believe that procreation was the sole end of sexual intercourse.

The democratic, liberal movements of the first half-century after independence stimulated some developments in favor of women. In Argentina, Sarmiento wrote that "the level of civilization of a people can be judged by the social position of its women"; his educational program envisaged a major role for women as primary-school teachers. In Mexico, the triumph of the Reforma was followed by promulgation of a new school law that called for the establishment of secondary schools for girls and normal schools for the training of women primary-school teachers. In both countries after 1870 there arose small feminist movements, largely composed of schoolteachers, that formed societies, edited journals, and worked for the cultural, economic, and social improvement of women. In the last decades of the century, with the development of industry, women in increasing numbers entered factories and sweatshops, where they often were paid half of what male workers earned, becoming a source of superprofits for capitalist employers. By 1887, according to the census of Buenos Aires, 39 percent of the paid work force of that city was composed of women.

The Church

The church, which had suffered some discredit because of the royalist posture of many clergy during the wars of independence, experienced a further decline in influence as a result of increasing contacts with the outside world and a new and relatively tolerant climate of opinion. In country after country, liberals pressed with varying success for restrictions on the church's monopoly over education, marriage, burials, and the like. Since the church invariably aligned itself with the conservative opposition, liberal victories brought reprisals in the form of heavy attacks on its accumulated wealth and privileges.

The colonial principle of monolithic religious unity was early shattered by the need to allow freedom of worship to the prestigious and powerful British merchants. It was, in fact, the reactionary Rosas, who disliked foreigners and brought the Jesuits back to Argentina, who donated the land on which the first Anglican church in Buenos Aires was built. Despite the efforts of some fanatical clergy to incite the populace against foreign heretics, there gradually evolved a system of peaceful coexistence between Catholics and dissenters, based on reciprocal good will and tact.

The Inquisition, whose excesses had made it odious even to the faithful, disappeared during the wars of independence. In many countries, however, the civil authorities assumed its right to censor or ban subversive or heretical writings. Occasionally, governments exercised this right. In the 1820s, clerical and conservative opposition forced the liberal vice president of Gran Colombia, Francisco de Paula Santander, to authorize the dropping of a textbook by the materialist Jeremy Bentham from law school courses. In Buenos Aires, under Rosas, subversive books and other materials were publicly burned. According to Tulio Halperin-Donghi, however, a reading of the press advertisements of Buenos Aires booksellers suggests that this repression was singularly ineffective. In Santiago in the 1840s, Francisco Bilbao's fiery polemic against Spain and Catholicism was burned by the public hangman. According to Sarmiento, however, it was not the content of Bilbao's book but its violent, strident tone that caused this reaction; Bilbao, he added, had been justly punished for his clumsiness.

After mid-century, with the enthronement of positivism, which glorified science and rejected theology as an approach to truth, efforts to suppress heretical or anticlerical writings diminished or ended completely in many countries. In general, during the last half of the nineteenth century, there existed in Latin America a relatively free market in ideas—free, that is, as long as these ideas were couched in theoretical terms or referred primarily to other parts of the world and were not directed against the incumbent regime. Governments were often quick to suppress and confiscate newspapers and pamphlets whose contents they considered dangerous to their security, but they remained indifferent to the circulation of books containing the most audacious social theories. By way of example, the Díaz dictatorship in Mexico struck at opposition journalists and newspapers but permitted the free sale and distribution of the writings of Marx and the anarchist theoretician Peter Kropotkin.

As a result of the ascendancy of positivism, the church suffered a further decline in influence and power. Conservative victories over liberalism sometimes produced a strong proclerical reaction, typified by Gabriel García Moreno, who ruled Ecuador from 1860 to 1875 and carried his fanaticism to the point of dedicating the republic to the Sacred Heart of Jesus. Rafael Núñez, dictator of Colombia from 1880 to 1894, drafted a concordat with the Vatican that restored to the church most of the rights it had enjoyed in colonial times. But such victories failed to arrest the general decline of the church's social and intellectual influence among the literate classes. Anticlericalism became an integral part of the ideology of most Latin American intellectuals and a large proportion of other upper-class and middle-class males, including many who were faithful churchgoers and observed the outward forms and rituals of the church. However, church influence continued strong among women of all classes, Indians, and the submerged groups generally.

THE ROMANTIC REVOLT

The achievement of political independence did not end Latin American cultural dependence on Spain and Portugal. The effort of Latin American writers to find their own means of self-expression, to create national literatures, fused with the larger effort to liquidate the Hispanic colonial heritage in politics, economics, and social life. Accordingly, Latin American literature was from the first a literature of struggle; the concept of art for art's sake had little meaning for the writers of the first half-century after independence. Many writers were also statesmen and even warriors, alternately using pen and sword in the struggle against tyranny and backwardness. This unity of art and politics is expressed by the famous comment of Ecuadorian essayist and polemicist Juan Montalvo when he learned that the dictator García Moreno had been assassinated: *"Mi pluma lo mató"* ("My pen killed him"). That unity found its most perfect embodiment in the Cuban José Martí, who devoted himself almost from childhood to the struggle against Spanish rule in Cuba and died in 1895 in action against Spanish troops. He also blazed new trails in Latin American poetry and prose.

Latin American writers took the first step toward literary independence by breaking with Hispanic classic traditions and adopting as their models the great French and English poets and novelists of the romantic school. Romanticism, which Sarmiento once defined as "a true literary insurrection, like the political uprising that preceded it," seemed peculiarly appropriate for the achievement of the tasks the revolutionary young writers of Latin America had set themselves.

Victory over classicism, however, did not come without a struggle. In 1842 a famous debate took place in Chile between the Venezuelan Andrés Bello, conservative arbiter of literary taste, and the Argentine Domingo Sarmiento, who upheld a democratic freedom of expression and the superiority of contemporary French literature over all others. Their opposition was by no means absolute, for Bello was not a true reactionary in politics or literature. A distinguished poet, scholar, and educator, he had made major contributions to the development of Hispanic culture. His Spanish grammar, published in 1857, ended the domination of Latin grammatical rules and forms over the language and won acceptance by the Spanish Academy. His poem "The Agriculture of the Torrid Zone," despite its classic form, stimulated the rise of literary Americanism. He was an admirer of Victor Hugo's romantic writings and had himself translated Hugo and Dumas.

But Bello had a conservative's love for order and decorum and regarded himself as a guardian of the purity of the Castilian language. He was shocked when Sarmiento, in a review of a recently published grammar, wrote that "teachers of grammar are useless, for people learn by practical example and general discussion . . . the people are the real creators of a language, while grammarians are only the maintainers of tradition and compilers of dictionaries." Writing in a conservative journal, Bello retorted with praise of linguistic purity and academic standards; it would make as little sense, he wrote, to allow the people to make their own laws as to permit them to dictate the forms of their language. Sarmiento countered with an ardent defense of democracy in language and style. Bello, who disliked polemic, soon withdrew from the fray, but his disciples continued the debate.

Its high point came when a writer in the conservative *Semanario* (Weekly) objected to Victor Hugo's depiction in the play *Ruy Blas* of "a lackey, who had never been anything but a lackey, as madly in love with a queen, and filled with thoughts that would hardly befit one of the haughtiest grandees of Spain." Sarmiento, himself a self-made man, was enraged:

This scribbler takes a lackey for nothing more than

a lackey. He does not see that the lackey is the peon, the worker, the sailor, the tavern-keeper, the roto [farm worker], the man, in fine, who occupies a lowly place in society but may nevertheless be an exceptional individual. . . . He does not know that the majority of men of genius were born lackeys. . . . The Spanish American War of Independence threw up many a Ruy Blas who took advantage of that social upheaval to emerge from the mass, shoulder a rifle, and end the campaign as a general, a governor, a representative of the people. To this day every republic in America has its share of generals and diplomats who began their careers as genuine lackeys.[2]

Before the controversy ended, Sarmiento had silenced his opponents and converted Bello's chief disciple, José Victorino Lastarria, to his own beliefs. Romanticism soon triumphed everywhere, but Latin American romanticism was not a simple carbon copy of the European original; it bore its own vigorous stamp, displayed its own distinctive character. It lacked a number of characteristic elements of European romanticism—its medievalism, to begin with; its introspective Byronic individualism; and its flaunting of bourgeois conventions—elements that would have been completely out of place in a Latin American setting, where bourgeois relations were very weakly developed.

Because of their disapproval of these elements of European romanticism, some Latin American writers even rejected the use of the name to describe the new Latin American literary school. Juan Bautista Alberdi declared that the new art "must discuss the fatherland, humanity, equality, progress, liberty, glory, victory, passions, desires, the national hopes, and not the pearl, the tear, the angel, the moon, the tomb, the dagger, poison, crime, death, hell, the devil, the witch, the hobgoblin, the owl, or any of that hodgepodge vocabulary that constitutes the

[2] Quoted in Benjamin Keen, *Latin American Civilization: The National Era*, vol. 2 (Boston: Houghton Mifflin, 1974), p. 111.

esthetics of Romanticism." And Sarmiento, even as he proclaimed the superiority of French romantic literature over all others, also announced that romanticism had played out its constructive role and had disappeared, giving way to "socialism." This Sarmiento vaguely defined, according to the usage of that pre-Marxian time, as "the ideal of enlisting science, art, and politics in the service of the people, with the sole aim of improving their condition, of fostering liberal tendencies, of combating reactionary prejudices, and of redeeming the people, the mulatto, and all the disinherited."

Romanticism in Argentine Writing

By no coincidence, Esteban Echeverría, the founder of Argentine romanticism, gave the name *Dogma socialista* (*Socialist Teaching*) to his first important writing in which "socialism" stood for a nebulous concept of the primacy of the general interest of society over the individual interests. "Association, progress, liberty, equality, fraternity: these sum up the great social and humanitarian synthesis; these are the divine symbols of the happy future of nations and of humanity." By the time *Dogma socialista* was published in 1839, Echeverría had been forced by the Rosas terror to flee from Buenos Aires to Montevideo, where a group of young exiles combined literary activity with plots to overthrow the Rosas regime.

Echeverría also produced a body of works that gave concrete expression to his artistic theories. Of special importance is his narrative poem "La cautiva" ("The Captive") (1837), which deals with an episode of life in the Argentine pampa, an Indian raid on a frontier village and the efforts of María and her husband Brian to escape from their captors. Echeverría's realistic depiction of the brooding pampa contrasted sharply with the idyllic portrayals by European romantics of American nature as a refuge from corrupt European civilization. Different, too, was Echeverría's attitude toward the Indians. Whereas

European romanticism, rejecting the Industrial Revolution and its fruits, idealized the primitive as a noble savage, Echeverría, who knew the harsh reality of Indian-white conflict on the frontier, portrayed the Indian as a ferocious enemy of civilization. Here his views coincided with those of his archenemy, Rosas.

In his short prose masterpiece, *The Slaughterhouse*, (published posthumously but probably written about 1840), Echeverría rejects another element of European romanticism, its idealized view of the common man. With unsparing realism, he describes the repellent sights and smells of a slaughterhouse that is also a gathering place of the Mazorca, the band of thugs who terrorize the enemies of Rosas. The story is also a political allegory: The slaughterhouse, with its butchers in gaucho dress and the black and mulatto women who carry away entrails, empty stomachs and bladders, and wade in blood, is a symbol of Rosas' Argentina, in which barbarous lower-class elements are given a free hand to torture and kill. The climax of the story comes when the butchers intercept a passing unitarian, a young man who wears stylish European dress and has his beard cut in the shape of a U. They tie him up, taunt him, and prepare to beat him. He scornfully replies to their taunts, breaks loose with a supreme effort, and dies from a hemorrhage before their very eyes. In the words of Arturo Torres-Rioseco, "the whole story is a sombre and terrible vignette, against a background of howling curs, bedraggled Negresses, circling vultures—a slaughterhouse that represents the real *matadero* [slaughterhouse] tyranny of Rosas."

A few years after Echeverría's death in 1851, another Argentine émigré, José Marmol, began to publish in serial form in Montevideo the first Argentine novel, *Amalia*. Again, as in the *The Slaughterhouse*, literature and political attack fuse. The young unitarian, Eduardo Belgrano, tries to escape from his federalist pursuers; he takes refuge in the house of the widowed Amalia, and the two fall deeply in love. But the dictator's secret police discover Eduardo's hiding place and kill the lovers. Despite a stilted style and the artificiality of some of the characters, its intensity of feeling and the vivid descriptions of various social types and life in Buenos Aires lend portions of the book a genuine power.

Another exile from Rosas' Argentina, Domingo Sarmiento, illustrated his artistic theories in his formless masterpiece, *Life of Juan Facundo Quiroga: Civilization and Barbarism* (1845). Sarmiento offers a geographical and sociological interpretation of Argentine history, showing how the pampa had molded the character and lifestyle of the gauchos, the mass base of the Rosas dictatorship and the petty caudillos who ruled under him. From this tough, self-reliant breed of men springs the "hero" of Sarmiento's book, the provincial caudillo Facundo. Facundo was master of the Argentine western provinces and Rosas' lieutenant until the greater tyrant, who brooked no rival, had him ambushed and killed.

The dilemma of Echeverría, the liberal who proclaimed such great words as "democracy," "association," and "equality" but felt scorn and hatred for Indians, blacks, mulattos, and gauchos, reappears in Sarmiento. He was sensitive to the gaucho's admirable qualities. Even the gaucho outlaw, "this white-skinned savage, at war with society and proscribed by the laws, is no more depraved at heart than the inhabitants of the settlements. The reckless outlaw who attacks a whole troop does no harm to the traveler."

Sarmiento recognized the poetry of gaucho life and the gaucho passion for poetry and music, noting that the whisper "he is a poet," dispelled all their prejudice toward a newcomer. But the gaucho was a medieval survival, an obstacle to the progress that the city and the railroad symbolized for Sarmiento. So the gaucho must disappear or be transformed by education. Like Echeverría, Sarmiento mistakenly regarded the gaucho as a cause rather than a victim of the Rosas dictatorship.

The ambiguity of Sarmiento's posture toward the gaucho—condemnation tempered by recognition of his admirable qualities—gave way to total defense and vindication of the gaucho and his values in the climactic work of gaucho literature, the epic poem *The Gaucho Martín Fierro* (1872) of José Hernández. Written some thirty years after Sarmiento's *Facundo*, its poignant, nostalgic mood reflects the uprooting of the old patriarchal estancia, the unfenced pampa, and the free gaucho way of life by the triumphant bourgeois "civilization" championed by Sarmiento. Hernández, a federalist who opposed Mitre and Sarmiento, supported the revolt of the last untamed gaucho chieftain, General López Jordán, and believed that the city, the seat of the central government, was exploiting and strangling the countryside. He portrayed the gaucho as a victim of the forces of "civilization"—judges, recruiting officers, corrupt police. The poem is strongly influenced by the folk songs of the gaucho *payador* (minstrel) and makes restrained but effective use of gaucho dialect words.

It opens as Martín Fierro tunes his guitar and begins his story. He recalls the old easy life on the estancias before the central government came to enforce conscription and frontier garrison duty. Sent to the frontier, he suffers persecution by officers, is denied his pay, and is brutally punished for asking for it. He deserts, returns to find his home in ruins and his family scattered, swears to be revenged, and becomes an outlaw. Wandering over the pampa "like a tiger whose cubs have been stolen from him," he moves about from bar to bar and kills two men in fights in defense of his honor. Pursued by the police, he is ambushed but escapes when a police sergeant, Cruz, a former gaucho outlaw, comes to his aid. The first part of *Martín Fierro* ends with the two men resolved to join the Indians "because the power of the government does not reach there." The second part, published in 1879, tells of Martín's return to civilization and reunion with his sons and the son of Cruz, each of whom has his own story of injustice and mistreatment. The story ends with the gaucho family again dispersing and wandering off in search of work. A work of social protest, it is also a great work of art.

Mexican National Literature

The beginnings of Mexican national literature are linked to the founding in 1836 of the Academy of Letrán, an informal literary circle whose members met to talk of literature or listen to readings of poetry and prose. Here, according to the Mexican literary historian González Peña, "was incubated the generation which later filled half a century of the history of Mexican literature." One of its founders, Guillermo Prieto, wrote that "the great and transcendent significance of the Academy was its decided tendency to 'Mexicanize' our literature, emancipating it from all other literatures and giving it a specifc character." Prieto also noted that the academy "democratized literary studies, recognizing merit without regard to social position, wealth, or any other considerations." The effort to create a Mexican literature was closely linked to the struggle for political and social reform. Most major Mexican literary figures of the first half-century after independence—such men as Guillermo Prieto, Ignacio Altamirano, and Ignacio Ramírez—took an active part in that struggle.

Prieto himself promoted the tendency to Mexicanize and democratize literature with his agile *costumbrista* sketches, which depict life and manners on various social levels in a racy, ironic style. But the most serious effort to create a national Mexican literature was made by the Indian comrade-in-arms of Juárez, Ignacio Altamirano. Believing that Mexican poetry and literature should be as completely original as "are our soil, our mountains, our generation," Altamirano rejected the imitation of foreign models. He attempted to offer an example of such originality in his novel *Clemencia* (1869), set in the period of the French intervention.

However, aside from the originality of making the hero of the novel the dark-skinned officer Fernando Valle and its villain the blond but cowardly Enrique Flores, the novel has little to distinguish it from the conventional romantic novel of the period. More successful, because of its fresh, unpretentious descriptions of life in a small Mexican village, was his *Christmas in the Mountains* (1870).

From the Academy of Letrán also issued a school of romantic poetry whose most remarkable creation was the "Prophecy of Cuauhtemoc" (1839) of Ignacio Rodríguez Galván. The poem sounds some major themes of Mexican romanticism: nationalism, anti-Spanish sentiment, and the glorification of pre-Cortesian Mexico. The poet turns from bitter musings on his own woes to reflect on the sorrows of his country, humiliated by European powers and Texan rebels. Hoping to be heard by "the venerable shades of the kings who ruled Anahuac, today the prize of birds of prey and wolves who tear at its bosom and heart," he invokes Cuauhtemoc, the last Aztec warrior-king. The king appears; in the fire that still plays beneath his feet, the shackles and heavy chains wound about his body, the halter about his neck, the poet recognizes the work of Cortés.

Galván calls on Cuauhtemoc to return, grasp again his powerful lance, and make decrepit kings tremble at his voice. Cuauhtemoc replies: "My age is past: my people will never again raise their dark faces, pressed into filthy mud." He prophesies disaster for Mexico from implacable "English America" and Europe, "the sons of the East." Mexico's day of vengeance will come, not through the hand of man, but through divine intervention. As the first morning light crosses the sky, amid tremblings of the earth and other awesome phenomena, the shade of Cuauhtemoc, transformed into a colossal phantasm, disappears. The magnificent coloring of the poem, its authentic romantic agony, the restless alternation in the poet's mind between thoughts of his personal sorrow and the woes of his people, make it, in the words of Menéndez y Pelayo, "the masterpiece of Mexican romanticism."

Chilean Writers

Chile lagged behind some of the other republics in the development of a national literature, perhaps—as Sarmiento suggested in his duel with Bello—because the absolute sway of Bello's classicist doctrines had created inertia, or, perhaps, because the relative stability of Chilean politics and the upward movement of the Chilean economy deprived its writers of the spur that the more dramatic contrasts of Argentine and Mexican life gave to creative literary activity. But if Chile lacked a Sarmiento or an Echeverría, it produced, in José Victorino Lastarria and Francisco Bilbao, two major writers on sociological topics who in their own way promoted the ideal of Chilean cultural emancipation.

Francisco Bilbao threw a bombshell into staid Santiago society with his essay "The Nature of Chilean Society" (1844), in which he declared: "Slavery, degradation: that is the past. . . . Our past is Spain. Spain is the Middle Ages. The Middle Ages are composed, body and soul, of Catholicism and feudalism." Later (1856), in his *American in Danger*, Bilbao issued a powerful cry of warning to Latin America to unite under a regime of freedom and democracy. He sounded a special alarm against the expansionist designs of the United States in Latin America. In *The American Gospel* (1864), he offered much the same message: Latin America must throw off its Hispanic heritage of repression and obscurantism, and it must adopt rationalism rather than Catholicism as its guide if the Disunited States of Latin America were to achieve the place the United States had gained among the nations of the earth.

Lastarria, more moderate and scholarly than Bilbao, caused a lesser stir with his address, "Investigations of the Social Influence of the Conquest and the Colonial System of the Span-iards in Chile" (1844). Despite an occasional factual error, it remains an effective summary of the liberal case against the Spanish colonial regime. Andrés Bello undertook to review it. Conceding the general correctness of Lastarria's criticism of Spanish policy and work in America, he offered a partial defense that stressed the mildness of Spanish rule and its civilizing mission in the New World. Whereas Bilbao was profoundly influenced by French left-wing republican and utopian socialist ideas, Lastarria's thought reflected the more conservative positivist teachings of the French philosopher Auguste Comte. Like Bilbao, however, Lastarria waged a consistent struggle against the backwardness he identified with Spanish civilization, which he felt was "the principal cause of our political and social disasters. . . . We cannot remedy these disasters except by reacting frankly, openly, and energetically against that civilization, in order to free our minds and adapt our country to the new form, democracy."

Brazilian Romantic Literature

A strong nationalism characterized the Brazilian romantic literature of the first decades after independence. In contrast with the Argentine writers of the same period, Brazilian writers expressed their nationalism in glorification of the Indian past. This Indianism reflected differences in the historical experience of the two countries: The Brazilian Indian had long ceased to pose a serious threat to white society, and Indian blood was widely diffused throughout the Brazilian people. Indianism, moreover, represented an effort to find roots for Brazilian nationalism—roots that could not be found in Portugal or Europe generally. In 1843 the critic Joaquim Norberto stressed the poetic quality of the Indian heritage:

The Indian past is our history, for we have no Middle Ages with the knights, tournaments, legends that nourished the imagination of European poets. But we have our own myths, our own spirits of rivers, lakes, mountains, and valleys. All we lack is pens capable of depicting our own Ossians, Fausts, and Ivanhoes.

The greatest romantic poet of the first generation and the principal exponent of Indianism in poetry was Antônio Gonçalves Dias, in whose veins ran the blood of three races—white, Indian, and black. Basing himself on a careful study of Indian languages and culture, Gonçalves Dias conjured up the image of the defeated Indian with extraordinary emotive power in his *American Poems* (1846) and in the narrative poem "The Timbiras" (1857). He also celebrated the beauty of the Brazilian landscape in poems like the nostalgic "Song of Exile" (1846), which opens with the line: "My land has palm trees where the sabiá sings."

Indianism also found expression in the novels of José de Alencar, whose two most popular novels, *Iracema* (1865) and *The Guarani* (1856), deal with the theme of love between Indian and white. Despite the improbable plots and the sentimentality and artificiality of the dialogue and characters, Alencar's limpid, poetic style successfully evokes, somewhat in the manner of James Fenimore Cooper, the drama of the clash of Indian and white cultures and the grandeur of the Brazilian wilderness, with its majestic rivers, dense forests, and great waterfalls.

After the optimistic nationalism of the first generation of Brazilian romantic poets came the introspection, pessimism, and escapism of the second generation, which perhaps were a reaction to the defeat of the republican revolts of the 1830s and 1840s. In sharp contrast to these second-generation poets, who appeared to be sensitive only to their own sufferings and misfortunes, Antônio de Castro Alves devoted his poetic talent above all to the struggle against slavery. Because of his lofty, impassioned style, he is known as the founder of the *condoreira*, or condor school of poetry. A passage from "The Slave Ship," published posthumously

(1883), suggests the tone of his abolitionist poems:

It was a Dantesque nightmare! The deck, drenched with blood,
Gave a red hue to the reflected glow of the lights;
The irons clanked! The whips whistled!
And legions of men, black as night, horridly danced.

Castro Alves's verses, read at countless abolitionist meetings and frequently published in the abolitionist press, gave a major stimulus to the growth of the abolitionist and republican movements in Brazil.

In 1867, Latin American romanticism, already in decline, produced its finest prose flower, the delicate love story *María* by the Colombian Jorge Isaacs. The story is set in a patriarchal country estate in the Cauca River Valley. Told in a simple, elegiac style, pervaded by a mood of gentle nostalgia, it relates the unfolding of an idyllic romance between a landowner's son and his cousin María. The story ends tragically when María dies during her lover's absence in London.

The Historical Novel

The romantic movement yielded an abundant harvest of historical novels, most of which dealt with episodes from the Spanish Conquest and the colonial era. Often their authors seemed chiefly concerned with exposing Spanish cruelty and the horrors of the Inquisition. Whether or not faithful to the historical facts, they generally lacked originality, talent, and psychological realism.

In 1872, however, Ricardo Palma began to publish his ironic and sparkling evocations of colonial Lima, *The Peruvian Traditions* (1872–1906). With these "traditions," Palma created a new genre: "A short sketch that was not history, anecdote, or satire, but a distillation of all three." Drawing on his immense knowledge of the colonial period (he was director of the National Library of Peru during the latter part of his life), Palma applied his own formula for the traditions: "a little bit, and quite a little bit of lying, a dose of the truth be it ever so infinitesimal, and a great deal of nicety and gloss in the style." From these elements Palma spun a long succession of cheerfully malicious tales that played on the follies and frailties of viceroys, priests, and highborn ladies as well as lesser folk. Palma's "traditions" evoked the past far more successfully than the typical historical novel of this period.

LITERATURE AND SOCIAL CHANGE, 1880–1910

By 1800 the romantic movement in Latin American literature had almost completed its tasks and exhausted its creative possibilities. As a result of the economic and political changes that we have surveyed, a new social reality had arisen. The growth of industry, immigration, and urbanization gave a new face to Latin American society. The ruling classes were increasingly acquisitive, arrogant, and philistine; the condition of the masses had not improved and may even have deteriorated. Latin America had become more European; in the process, it had failed to solve some old problems and had acquired some new ones.

In conformity with the specific conditions of their countries and their own backgrounds, writers responded to the new environment in a variety of ways. Generally speaking, romanticism survived as a vital force only in those countries where the old problems had not been solved. (Examples are Ecuador, the scene of a bitter struggle between liberals and conservatives, and Cuba, whose struggle for independence did not reach its climax until the 1890s).

Poetry and Modernism

In poetry, the most important new phenomenon was the movement called modernism. Because the movement comprises an immense variety of stylistic and ideological tendencies, it is dif-

ficult to define. The common feature of modernist poets, however, was their search for new expressive means, for new stylistic forms, in reaction against the outworn language and forms of romanticism. The artistic creed of many modernist poets included rejection of literature as an instrument of social and political struggle. Turning their backs on "a world they never made," the world of shoddy and unstable prosperity ruled, in Rubén Darío's words, by *el rey burgués* (the bourgeois king), these escapists sought refuge in the ivory tower of art.

Most escapist of all was the prodigiously gifted Nicaraguan Rubén Darío (1867–1916), who defined modernism as the rejection of any explicit message in art; stress on beauty as the highest value (in Darío's poems, the swan is the recurrent symbol of beauty as an end in itself);

Rubén Darío. (Courtesy of the Organization of American States)

and the determination to free verse from the tyranny of traditional forms. Not unexpectedly, in view of their conception of the artist as an outcast from bourgeois society, Bohemianism, alcohol, and drugs were elements in the lifestyle of many escapist poets, and not a few came to tragically early ends.

In their effort to achieve a renovation of poetry (and prose as well), the modernists drew on a variety of foreign sources (French Parnassianism, impressionism, symbolism, Whitman and Poe, Spain's medieval ballads). But they did not imitate; they appropriated these foreign methods for the creation of poetry and prose that were "entirely new, new in form and vocabulary and subject matter and feeling."

Escapism was a major current of modernism but not the only one. Indeed, before the movement had run its course, some of the leading escapist poets had risen to a new awareness of the continent's social and political problems and the writer's responsibility to his people. Darío himself exemplifies this evolution. If in the first, escapist phase of his poetic career he peopled his verses with satyrs, nymphs, centaurs, peacocks, and swans, in its second phase he gave voice to a powerful public poetry that reflected his new Americanism and concern with political and social themes. Darío's Americanism led him to a search for symbols in both the Spanish and the Indian past, regarded as the sources of a Latin American culture threatened by the aggressive expansionism of the United States.

In the poem "To Roosevelt" (1905), Darío flings a challenge to the United States, "future invader of that simple America that has Indian blood, that still prays to Jesus Christ and speaks Spanish." To the America of Theodore Roosevelt, Darío opposes "our America, which has had poets since the old times of Nezahualcoyotl," "the America of the Great Moctezuma and the Inca, the fragrant America of Christopher Columbus, Catholic America, Spanish America, the America where the noble Cuauhtemoc said: 'I am not on a bed of roses.' "

In the poem "Tutecotzimi" (1907), Darío works the vein of poetic material furnished by the legends and history of Ancient America. The poem opens with a striking archaeological image:

Digging into the soil of an ancient city,
the metal point of a pick encounters a golden
  ornament,
a sculptured stone,
an arrow, a fetish, a god of ambiguous form,
or the vast walls of a temple. My pick
is working in the soil of an unknown America.
May my poet's pick make harmonious sounds!
May it turn up gold and opals and fine rich
  stones,
a temple, or a broken statue!
And may the Muse divine the meaning of the
hieroglyphics.[3]

The poem is a superb example of the fusion of modernist poetic technique and social message, with an ancient Mexican legend as its vehicle. Fresh and optimistic, it reveals the Darío who dreamed of a Spanish America free from domestic misrule and foreign aggression.

More often, however, pessimism overcame Darío when he considered the melancholy state of "our America." Then he was inclined to wish that the New World had never been discovered. In his poem to Columbus (1907), Darío sings:

Unhappy admiral! Your poor America,
your lovely and hot-blooded Indian maid,
the pearl of your dreams is now hysterical,
her nerves convulsive and forehead pale.[4]

In a biting commentary on the social reality of "our America," he says:

[3] From *The Aztec Image in Western Thought* by Benjamin Keen, p. 459. Copyright © 1971 by Rutgers University, the State University of New Jersey. Reprinted by permission of Rutgers University Press.
[4] From *The Aztec Image in Western Thought* by Benjamin Keen, p. 461. Copyright © 1971 by Rutgers University, the State University of New Jersey. Reprinted by permission of Rutgers University Press.

Christ, gaunt and feeble, walks through the
streets,
Barabbas wears epaulets and keeps his slaves,
And the land of the Chibcha, Cuzco and
Palenque,
Have seen panthers acclaimed and in their glory.[5]

Darío, in the words of Arturo Torres-Rioseco, "was the complete master of modernism in all its many ramifications. His was the greatest technical skill, the greatest success with metrical innovations. He was the escapist par excellence—and at the same time the poet of that New Worldism which was to make the end of the modernist movement."

Literary critics dispute whether the Cuban José Martí was a precursor of modernism or one of its major figures and creators. Certainly, his spirit was alien to the escapist tendency of many modernist poets. Far from seeking refuge in an ivory tower, he dedicated his life to the struggle for Cuban independence; Cubans of all political faiths still call him "the Apostle." Martí's faith in man and progress reflected his links to Enlightenment thought, to romanticism, and to the optimistic evolutionism of the late nineteenth century. "I have faith," he wrote in the preface to his first book of verse (1882), "in the improvement of man, in the life of the future, in the utility of virtue." In a time of rampant racism, he denounced race prejudice of every kind.

From 1881 to 1895, Martí lived in exile in New York. As a correspondent for various Latin American newspapers, he wrote a vast number of articles in which he subjected political, economic, and cultural developments in the United States to searching analysis. Martí fervently admired Lincoln, Emerson, Mark Twain, and the abolitionist Wendell Phillips but expressed growing concern over the rise of monopolistic and imperialist tendencies. He especially feared and disliked the Republican leader James G.

Blaine, whom he regarded as the chief exponent of American imperialist designs on Latin America. He wrote in 1889: "What is apparent is that the nature of the North American government is changing in its fundamental reality. Under the traditional labels of Republican and Democrat, with no innovation other than the contingent circumstances of place and character, the republic is becoming plutocratic and imperialistic." In 1895 he left the United States to launch the Cuban Revolution. On the day before his death on May 19, 1895, while fighting Spanish troops, he set down his fears concerning American policy toward Cuba: "I know the monster because I have lived in its lair, and my sling is that of David."

Martí's artistic ideas reflected his belief in the organic links between art and society, in the social responsibility of the artist. Art should reflect the joys and sorrows of the masses; in that sense it is a collective product. "Poetry is durable when it is the work of all. Those who understand it are as much its authors as those who make it." Simplicity and directness characterize his poems, but he was capable of using vivid, concrete imagery of great symbolic power. The very simplicity of his verse makes it difficult to render into English. In prose he achieved a genuine stylistic revolution. "The style he achieved," writes Pedro Henríquez-Ureña, "was entirely new to the language. He follows no single rhythmical pattern, but constantly varies it . . . he combines words—and meanings—in many unfamiliar ways. The effect is a constantly varied interplay of light and color. In style, as well as in what lies beyond style and becomes expression, his power of invention was inexhaustible." Darío said of Martí: "He writes more brilliantly than anyone in Spain or America."

The Romantic Revolt Continued: Ecuador and Peru

The fires of romantic revolt continued to burn in two Andean republics where small groups

[5] "A Colón," in *El canto errante* (Buenos Aires, 1948), p. 43.

of intellectuals battled the rule of reactionary landowners, generals, and the church. In Ecuador, the writer Juan Montalvo, exiled by the fanatical dictator Gabriel García Moreno, leveled polemical attacks against him and claimed credit for García Moreno's assassination. Unhappy with the new rulers of Ecuador, Montalvo spent much of his life in exile from his native country. His *Seven Essays* (1882), reflecting a somewhat old-fashioned liberalism, propose the regeneration of Latin America through the formation of a model elite. His curious *Chapters That Cervantes Forgot*, a continuation of *Don Quijote*, published posthumously, display Montalvo's virtuosity in the use of sixteenth-century Castilian and express his ideas on a wide variety of topics.

The Peruvian writer Manuel González Prada advanced more radical ideas. A member of that generation of Peruvian youth that witnessed with feelings of profound humiliation the swift defeat of their country in the War of the Pacific, he initiated a new era of social unrest and intellectual ferment in Peru. He launched his "prose thunderbolts" against all that was sacrosanct in Peruvian society: the army, the church, the state, the Creole aristocracy. In 1886 he founded a *Círculo Literario* (Literary Circle) with the declared aim of creating a nationalistic literature of "propaganda and attack." He proclaimed that "the people must be shown the horror of their degradation and misery; a good autopsy was never made without dissecting the body, and no society can be thoroughly known until its skeleton is laid bare."

González Prada made good his promise of dissecting the Peruvian organism by the ferocity of his attacks. Peru, he wrote, was a great boil: "press down anywhere and the pus comes out." He described the Peruvian congress as a sewer where all the filth of the country had come together. He called for the creation of a vigorous new literature that would deal with national problems; this required writers to reject tradition and forge a new language: "Archaism implies

backwardness: show me an archaic writer and I show you a reactionary thinker."

In contrast to the social content and lavalike flow of González Prada's prose, much of his poetry was introspective, meditative, aristocratic in mood. Yet notes of social revolt occasionally sound in his verses, as in his *Peruvian Ballads*, which deal with the suffering and exploitation of the natives, or in this ironic question to a "profound sociologist":

Oh profound sociologist,
Darling of the bourgeoisie,
You who know the unknowable,
Solve for me this pretty riddle:
Why is it that some must fast
while others feast,
Why should some only eat thin soup
and others cake?[6]

A woman writer who formed part of González Prada's literary circle and shared many of his progressive ideas, Clorinda Matto de Turner (1854–1909), wrote the first Indianist protest novel, *Birds Without a Nest* (1889). Set in an Indian village of the sierra, the novel denounces the abuses committed against the natives by the exploitive trinity of judge, priest, and governor. "We were born Indians," declares an Indian woman, "slaves of the parish priest, slaves of the governor, slaves of the cacique, slaves of all those who hold the rod of authority." However, aside from the lesson of the personal charity and benevolence that well-disposed upper-class whites should show to the Indians, the writer offers no solution for the Indian problem. As the novel ends, the young married couple who sought to protect the Indians return discouraged and defeated to Lima, leaving the Indians in their former state. With all its weaknesses, however, *Birds Without a Nest* was the

---

[6] "O sociólogo profundo . . . ," in Jean Franco, *An Introduction to Spanish-American Literature* (Cambridge, England, 1969), pp. 100–101.

forerunner of a genre, the Indianist novel, that had a great future.

Realism and Naturalism

Schools of literary realism and naturalism first arose in lands like Chile, Argentina, and Brazil, where capitalism and capitalist relations had struck firm roots. The Chilean writer Alberto Blest Gana began writing realist novels between 1860 and 1867. Strongly influenced by French realism—especially by Balzac—Blest Gana made the corrosive power of money on human relations the primary theme of his novels, *Arithmetic in Love* (1860), *Martín Rivas* (1862), and *A Good-for-Nothing's Ideal* (1863). Blest Gana painted broad canvases depicting a Chilean society in which merchants, landowners, army officers, and humble provincials struggled to improve their situation by marriage. In 1860, bestowing a literary award to him for *Arithmetic in Love*, a jury that included José Victorino Lastarria and the historian Miguel Luis Amunátegui praised the novel because "the characters are Chileans, they are very like the people we know, the people we shake hands with and talk to. . . . The novel presents vivid, colorful, and accurate pictures of our national customs." The characters in *Arithmetic in Love* are, with rare exceptions, motivated by greed. Some hunt for wealthy heiresses, others for wealthy husbands, still others impatiently await the death of rich relatives. Thus, by implication, Blest Gana sharply criticized the bourgeois order that had arisen in Chile.

The boom of the 1880s, which transformed Argentine society, inspired the writing of some naturalistic novels whose authors, however, lacked the great talent of Blest Gana. Buenos Aires, with its atmosphere of feverish prosperity and cosmopolitanism, provided the setting for most of these novels. A typical work is *The Bourse* (1890) by José María Miró, which deals with the rise and fall of a financier on the stock exchange. The novel is weakened by poor tech-

nique and naive attacks on gold, Jews, and immigrants, regarded as the chief causes of the materialism that was allegedly destroying Argentina. Similar attacks on materialism and the egotism of the ruling classes characterize the naturalist novels of Eugenio Cambaceres (1843–1888).

In the urban novels of Joaquim María Machado de Assis (1839–1908), a master of ironic realism, Brazilian psychological letters display a precocious maturity. Although Machado, a mulatto, shunned involvement in the abolitionist or republican struggles of his time, his work exposes the stifling atmosphere of a society dominated by racism and the race for wealth; cynicism and disillusionment are the typical attitudes of his characters. In *Dom Casmurro* (1900), the principal character ends his melancholy story by congratulating himself that he had no children of his own and thus "transmitted to no one the legacy of his misery." The last words of the narrator of the story "The Attendant," as he is about to die, are a cynical revision of the Sermon on the Mount: "Blessed are they that *possess*, for they shall be comforted." More explicit criticism of Brazilian society appears in the naturalistic novels of Aluizio Azevedo (1857–1913), notably in *The Mulatto* (1881), in which a scheming priest and the relatives of a white girl plan the murder of her well-educated, cultured mulatto sweetheart.

At the turn of the century (1902) appeared an impressive study of rural Brazil, Euclides da Cunha's *Os sertões* (*Rebellion in the Backlands*), which deals, among other things, with the siege of Canudos in 1896–1897, when a handful of wretched backwoodsmen, led by the mystic Antônio Conselheiro, heroically resisted a federal army of some six thousand men. In his style—now lush and sensuous, now rugged; in his unsparing realism; and in his outspoken but unsentimental sympathy with the semibarbarous folk of the backlands, da Cunha blazed a trail for the regional and social novelists who would soon dominate the Brazilian literary scene.

HISTORY AND THE FORGING OF NATIONALITY

Historians made their own contributions to the process of Latin American cultural emancipation. Their special mission was to promote a sense of nationhood in each of the new states by making its people aware of their common historical experience and awaking pride in its past. Like the literature, Latin American historical writing achieved a maturity that contrasted sharply with Latin American backwardness in other areas. Indeed, the best achievements of Latin American historiography in the nineteenth century compare favorably with the peaks of European and North American historical writing in the same period. Like the poets and novelists, many historians were political activists who took part in revolutions and civil wars and sometimes suffered imprisonment and exile. The following sections briefly survey the historical schools that arose in Mexico, Argentina, Chile, and Brazil in the nineteenth century.

The Mexican Historical Schools

A veteran of the Mexican struggle for independence, the romantic historian Carlos María Bustamante undertook to give the Mexican people, in his own words, some idea of their origins. In addition to editing and publishing many important manuscripts, he wrote a long series of original works on ancient and colonial Mexico. Along with much irrelevancy and display of credulity, these works contain much varied and useful information. Bustamante also published a valuable, lengthy account of the revolution from 1808 to 1821, *Cuadro histórico de la revolutión de la América mexicana* (1823–1832) in the form of letters to an imaginary correspondent.

Two liberal leaders of the reform movement of 1833 offered lucid interpretations of recent and contemporary Mexican history in their works: José María Luis Mora in his *Méjico y sus revoluciones* (1836), and Lorenzo de Zavala in his *Ensayo histórico de las revoluciones de Méjico* (1831–1832). Lucas Alamán, the principal conservative ideologist, offered a skillful defense of the Spanish Conquest and Spain's work in America in his *Disertaciones sobre la historia de la República Mejicana* (1844–1849), a history of the colony. His *Historia de Méjico* (1849–1852), which concentrates on events in the period from 1808 to 1824, displays nostalgia for the supposed tranquillity and prosperity of prerevolutionary Mexico.

In the same period, José Fernando Ramírez, a moderate liberal, laid the foundations of the positivist historical school with his impressive editorial and bibliographical labors. His most important original work is his notes to the second Spanish edition of William H. Prescott's *Conquest of Mexico* (1845). Although generous in his praise of Prescott, Ramírez complains of the author's "instinctive" race prejudice and his efforts to palliate Cortes's crimes. This prejudice, remarks Ramírez, so pervaded Prescott's history that only the most unskilled eye could miss it.

The Reforma was accompanied by the rise of a flaming nationalism that expressed itself, among other ways, in a stock-taking of Mexico's spiritual and natural resources and intensive study of its past. Amid the violence of war and revolution, Mexican scholars continued to lay a documentary base for the study of ancient and colonial Mexico. In 1858, for example, Joaquín García Icazbalceta published the first volume of his important *Coleccíon de documentos para la historia de México*.

The flowering of the positivist, nationalist school, however, came during the Diáz era. Between 1880 and 1881, Manuel Orozco y Berra published his *Historia antigua y de la conquista de México*, an impressive effort to reconstruct Aztec history, society, and the Conquest on the basis of the written sources. To do this Orozco used the positivist, sociological method of Ramírez, which attempted to disclose the natural roots of all historical phenomena.

A major work in the cycle of Mexican positivist historiography was the large collaborative work *México a través de los siglos,* published in five volumes between 1887 and 1889 under the editorship of Vicente Riva Palacio. The great cycle closed with the writings of Justo Sierra, author of the brilliant if worshipful biography *Juárez: Su obra y su tiempo* (1905) and the elegantly written, thoughtful survey of Mexican history, *Evolución política del pueblo mexicano* (1900–1902).

Argentinian Historical Writing

Esteban Echeverría sketched a liberal, romantic interpretation of Argentine history in his *Dogma socilista* (1839), in which he denounces Spanish colonial rule and its legacy of ignorance and superstition. Similar attacks on Spain from a liberal positivist point of view occur in the writings of Domingo Sarmiento and Juan Bautista Alberdi. The flowering of the Argentine positivist historical school, however, had to await the fall of Rosas and the establishment of a unified Argentine state. The two giants of the school are Vicente Fidel López and Bartolomé Mitre, authors of monumental works that retain much of their value to this day.

López wrote a ten-volume *Historia de la República Argentina* (1883–1893), concentrating on the period from about 1800 to 1829. A disciple of the romantic historians Thomas Macaulay and François Guizot, he sought to produce an animated, colorful account of events, to make history come alive. In a famous early debate with Mitre, he wrote: "All that has been said about the value of documents is completely erroneous; the important thing is the value and linkage of events. History does not need to be documented like an account book; it needs to be made correct and natural through the telling of the events and their interconnections." Despite his disparaging reference to documents,

López later made great use of them and even added an appendix of documents to each volume of his work. López wrote from a fervently liberal point of view; he condemned caudillos and religious fanaticism and saw the solution for Argentina's problems in the steady evolution of a democratic state, with education as the principal instrument of social improvement.

Bartolomé Mitre, one of the greatest Latin American historians, wrote the *Historia de Belgrano y la independencia Argentina* (1858–1876) and the *Historia de San Martín y de la emancipación de Sud América* (1887–1890). Each work, in Mitre's words, "is the life of a man and the history of an epoch." These books have a massive documentary base and are written in a flowing, magisterial style. The interpretation is a mix of geographical determinism, the "great man" theory, and Spencerian positivism. Mitre continues the traditional liberal criticism of Spanish rule, but the criticism is muted and qualified. Denouncing the aberrations of Spanish policy, he also praises the conquistadors, who brought "the spirit of independence" to America. Mitre sharply distinguishes the colonial process in Argentina from that which took place elsewhere. Because colonial Argentina lacked the mines and abundant Indian labor that engendered an aristocracy of counts and marquises and a semi-feudal system in Peru and Mexico, it developed an embryonic democracy in which, he claimed, all were equal in fact and in law.

Reflecting the strong influence of Spencer, Mitre claims that of the three races that contributed to the genesis of Argentine society, the European or Caucasian played the active part, with the Indian and black playing auxiliary roles. "From their fusion resulted a new type in which European blood prevailed by reason of its superiority, being constantly regenerated through immigration"; if the mixed-bloods also improved, it was through assimilation of the physical and moral qualities of the superior white race. Mitre's social Darwinism sometimes got in the way of his facts; thus, having described the active role played by blacks and Indians in the struggle for independence, he claims that Indians and blacks were an "inert element" in that process.

The Chilean Positivist School

The early stabilization of Chilean political life under a conservative leadership favorable to education and culture helped to produce a national school of historiography without equal in Latin America. Andrés Bello made an important contribution to the founding of the school by his criticism of the "philosophical" approach to writing history, exemplified by José Victorino Lastarria's essay on the social consequences of Spanish rule in Chile. Bello insisted on the need to establish the facts of Chilean history by careful study and analysis of documents before philosophizing on the subject. His advice was taken to heart by three young future historians, Miguel Amunátegui, Diego Barros Arana, and Benjamin Vicuña Mackenna. They became convinced that a truthful, scientific history of Chile could not be written without archival research.

These young men were also ardent liberals. The most radical was Amunátegui, a sworn foe of great landowners and the church. His works, well documented and written in an attractive style, are based on diligent research in Chilean archives. In 1870–1872, he published *Los precursores de la Independencia*, which glorifies the forerunners of independence and condemns the Spanish colonial system, whose principal aims, he claims, were "supine ignorance, an almost complete segregation from other civilized peoples, and a constant and minute coercive action by the authorities in the most trifling aspects of public and private life." In 1876–1879 appeared his *Crónica de 1810*, a study of that decisive revolutionary year. It, too, drew a somber picture of the Spanish colonial regime. The rich social

material in Amunátegui's works gives them a special interest and value.

Amunátegui, Vicuña Mackenna, and Barros Arana belonged to the same liberal, positivist historiographic tradition. All three were strongly influenced by such contemporary European sociologists and historians as Auguste Comte, John Stuart Mill, Henry Thomas Buckle, and Hippolyte Taine. In 1859 the conservative government exiled Vicuña Mackenna and Barros Arana to Europe for their political misdeeds, giving them the opportunity to begin the search for materials on Chile in European archives.

A prominent public figure, senator, governor, and unsuccessful candidate for president, Vicuña Mackenna was also one of the most prolific of Chilean historians. In 1862 he published a book on the Chilean Inquisition, *Lo que fué la Inquisición en Chile*, which aroused clerical anger and efforts at refutation. Strongly interested in mining and economic history (his own interests included nitrate fields), he published in 1882 a history of Chilean copper mining, *El libro del cobre*, which remains the best work on the subject, and another on the history of silver, *El libro de la plata*.

The immense bibliography of Diego Barros Arana, professor and rector of the University of Chile, contains more than three hundred historical works, but his masterpiece was the monumental *Historia jeneral de Chile*, published in sixteen volumes between 1884 and 1902. The work opens with a description of the Indian tribes inhabiting Chile at the time of the Conquest. Barros Arana deplores Spanish cruelty to the Indians but describes their life and manners in darkest colors, as the "most terrifying barbarism." Sharply critical of the Spanish colonial legacy of backwardness and obscurantism, Barros Arana nevertheless absolves the Spanish kings of deliberately pursuing those ends; it was Spanish civilization itself that was to blame: "Here, as in Spain, the militarist spirit of the majority of the population, the aristocratic disdain for industrial labor, were the causes of backwardness, poverty, and turbulence." Barros Arana had much praise for the reformist efforts of the Bourbon kings and the famous captain general Ambrosio O'Higgins; he believed that O'Higgins's abolition of the encomienda was "a work of humanity worthy on many counts of the respect of posterity." Barros Arana assigned five volumes to the struggle for independence (1808–1822) and another five to events from 1822 to 1833. A notable feature of the work is its broad conception of history, with much attention given to social, economic, and cultural history. Notable, too, is its analytical spirit, which yields many valuable insights.

To the same liberal, positivist tradition belongs José Toribio Medina, whose work spans the last decades of the nineteenth century and the first decades of the twentieth century. In addition to his immense bibliographical achievements, still indispensable to students of the colonial period of Latin American history, Medina wrote important studies of the Inquisition in various Latin American cities and one on Chilean colonial literature.

Brazilian Historiography

Brazilian historical writing of the national period effectively opens with the multivolume *História geral do Brasil antes de sua separação e independencia de Portugal* of Francisco Adolpho de Varnhagen, published between 1854 and 1857. Based on massive archival research, the work traces in a clear, orderly manner the course of Brazilian administrative and diplomatic history during the colonial period. It remains a standard history of the colonial period. At his death, Varnhagen left an important study of the independence period, not published until 1916.

The slavery problem, the major economic and social problem of the empire, found its reflection in Brazilian historiography. In *A escravidão no Brasil* (1866–1867), A. M. Perdigão Malheiro,

a constitutional monarchist who favored gradual emancipation, studied the history of Indian and black slavery and the current position of the Negro in Brazilian society. Joaquim Nabuco's *O abolicionismo* (1883), a book that made history, traces the rise of abolitionism in Brazil and brilliantly exposes the devastating effects of slavery on its social, economic, and political life. Nabuco also wrote a masterful life of his statesman father, *Um estadista do imperio. Nabuco de Araujo, sua vida, suas opiniões, sua epoca* (1897). A fundamental study of the political system of the empire and the role of the planter elite within it, it has been called "the best book ever written on the empire in Brazil."

With the fall of slavery and monarchy, positivist-evolutionist conceptions became dominant in Brazilian historical writing. A major figure of the positivist school was J. F. Rocha Pombo, who proposed to write a scientific history of Brazil that would replace the accounts of kings and wars with the life of the people, their customs, laws, and institutions. In 1905 he published a ten-volume *História do Brasil*, the most extensive general history ever written by a Brazilian.

In the closing years of the century, a giant of Brazilian historiography, José Capistrano de Abreu, began to write his *Capítulos de história colonial, 1500–1800,* not published until 1907. Based on immense research in archival and published sources, the book is a synthesis of a new type. Free from pedantry, written in a simple style, it replaces the traditional lists of dates and names of viceroys with summaries of important economic and social movements and much interesting description of life and manners.

Capistrano de Abreu also published in 1899 a pioneering study of the early penetration and colonization of the Brazilian interior, *Caminhos antigos e povoamento do Brasil;* its influence in Brazil is comparable to that of Frederick Jackson Turner's essay "The Significance of the Frontier in American History" on North American historians. Strongly influenced by Buckle, Capistrano de Abreu stresses the effect of geography on the direction of social development. Influenced also by Spencer, he praises the bravery of the colonial bandeirantes, or slave-hunters, and suggests that the resulting additions to Brazilian territory compensated for the horrors of their slave-raiding activity. Capistrano de Abreu's turning away from the coast to the interior, his praise of the heroism of the mixed-blood bandeirantes, reflected the tendency of the great nineteenth-century Latin American historians to search for native roots, to stress those aspects of each country's historical experience that were peculiarly its own.

PART THREE

LATIN AMERICA IN THE TWENTIETH CENTURY

The complexity of Latin America's political and economic evolution in the twentieth century seems to require an overview of the process that will enable us to comprehend it as a whole. In this section, our survey of Latin American history broadens to include three Andean republics with predominantly Indian populations (Peru, Bolivia, and Ecuador); Cuba, the scene of a socialist revolution with continental repercussions; and three Central American countries where social revolutionary movements have recently triumphed or are in progress (Nicaragua, El Salvador, and Guatemala). In addition we look at Mexico, Argentina, Chile, and Brazil.

The struggle of Latin America's peoples to eliminate neocolonialism and *latifundismo*, the chief obstacles to the achievement of a juster economic and social order, gives meaning and direction to the turbulent flow of modern Latin American history. Viewed in the large, that history appears to form a sequence of stages, each representing a higher level of effort to achieve complete economic and political emancipation. Such an overview inevitably ignores the great differences between the Latin American countries and therefore oversimplifies a complex process. On the other hand, it helps to make clear the general unity of problems and the common direction of movement of all the Latin American states, from little Panama to gigantic Brazil.

1910–1930

The Mexican Revolution of 1910 and the start of World War I offer two points of departure for this period. The Mexican Revolution swiftly developed into the first major effort in Latin American history to uproot the system of great estates and peonage and curb foreign control of the area's natural resources. The famous constitution of 1917 spelled out this social content of the revolution. In the leadership struggle between agrarian and bourgeois revolutionaries, the latter emerged victorious and adopted a program that subordinated the interests of peasants and workers to the goals of rapid capitalist development. Despite the discrepancies between its professed social ideals and its achievements, the Mexican Revolution unleashed creative energies in art, literature, and the social sciences that gave Mexico a leading place in the cultural life of Latin America.

World War I seriously disrupted the markets for Latin America's goods and placed difficulties in the way of importing the manufactured goods that the area required. As a result, some local capital and labor were diverted from agriculture to manufacturing in an effort to supply the needed goods. Although the postwar period saw some revival of the export economy, Latin America's unfavorable terms of trade with industrialized countries encouraged a further growth of manufacturing. However, at the end of this period, industrialization was still almost completely limited to light consumer goods industries.

The United States, which emerged from World War I as the world's principal industrial and financial power, soon replaced Great Britain as the major source of foreign investments in Latin America. Continuing the "big stick" and "dollar diplomacy" policies of their predecessors, both Democratic and Republican administrations used armed intervention and economic pressure to expand United States control over the Caribbean area. By the end of the period, deep Latin American resentment of these strong-arm tactics had forced Republican policy-makers to consider a change of policy in dealing with Latin America.

1930–1945

The Great Depression dramatically exposed the vulnerability of a neocolonial, monocultural economy: The area's foreign markets collapsed, and the prices of its raw materials and foodstuffs fell much more sharply than those of the manufactured goods it had to import. Latin America's unfavorable balance of trade made necessary exchange controls and other trade restrictions that encouraged the growth of industries to produce goods formerly supplied through importation. World War II, which caused a virtual suspension of imports of manufactured goods, gave further stimulus to the movement for Latin American industrialization. In part from sheer economic necessity, in part with the deliberate aim of promoting economic independence, a series of Latin American governments in this period adopted policies of tariff protection, subsidies to industry, and stringent state control over foreign trade that encouraged the growth of native industry.

The nationalist temper of the times also found expression in the formation of state enterprises in such fields as oil exploitation and in efforts to nationalize some foreign-owned utilities and natural resources. The most dramatic example of this trend was the seizure of foreign oil properties in Mexico by President Lázaro Cárdenas in 1938. The new nationalist regimes also made some concessions to labor in the form of social legislation but maintained tight control over working-class organizations.

By 1945 the movement for Latin American industrialization could point to some successes. Consumer goods industries had arisen in all the Latin American republics, and some countries had laid the foundations of heavy industry. Industrial development, however, was everywhere hampered by shortages of capital, lack of advanced technology, and the extremely low purchasing power of the masses. Latin American economists often related these deficiencies to such background conditions as latifundismo and its corollary of wretchedly small farms (*minifundismo*), widespread disease and illiteracy, and absorption of a large part of the area's economic surplus by foreign investors in the form of dividends, interest, and the like. Meanwhile, aside from the massive assault of Lázaro Cárdenas on the Mexican latifundio, little or nothing was done in the way of agrarian reform.

In the same period, the United States, reacting to the diplomatic and economic losses caused by the old-style imperialism and a wave of "anti-Yanqui" feeling throughout the continent,

adopted the Good Neighbor Policy, which proclaimed the principle of nonintervention by one American state in the affairs of another. But the policy represented more of a change in form than in content. Washington's friendly, cooperative relations with such tyrannies as those of Anastasio Somoza in Nicaragua, Rafael Trujillo in the Dominican Republic, and Fulgencio Batista in Cuba insured a continuance of North American hegemony in the Caribbean. For the rest, the immense economic power of the United States in Latin America, exercised through investments and its role as the area's main trading partner, usually sufficed to obtain approval of its policies in most parts of the continent.

1945–1959

In the new postwar era, the Latin American drive to industrialize continued, but after 1950 the pace of advance slowed, and the industrialization process underwent a certain deformation. Perceiving the changes taking place in the Latin American economy, foreign firms began to shift the bulk of their new investments from agricultural and mining activities (which had declined in value because of the depressed price level of raw materials) to manufacturing. This shift allowed them to leap over tariff walls and penetrate the Latin American market. The immensely superior resources of foreign firms and their monopoly of advanced technology gave them a great advantage in competition with national companies. The result was that many small and middle-sized national companies went under or were swallowed up by subsidiaries of foreign firms.

A favorite device of foreign economic penetration was the mixed company, dominated by foreign capital, with native capitalists reduced to the role of junior partners or directors. The huge sums exported annually by foreign companies in profits, dividends, and other types of income led to a process of "decapitalization" that slowed down the rate of Latin American capital accumulation and industrial growth.

The failure to modernize archaic agrarian structures and improve income distribution also held back industrialization. Indeed, the experience of those countries that had the largest growth of capitalism, such as Brazil and Argentina, suggested that the new industrial and financial oligarchies were as fearful of social change, as prone to come to terms with foreign economic interests, as the old landed aristocracy had been. In the 1950s, a number of leading Latin American countries moved to the right. The fall of such champions of national industry as Getúlio Vargas in Brazil and Juan Perón in Argentina and the collapse of the Popular Front government in Chile reflected the conservatism of the new elites and the pressures of the cold war policy of the United States.

A similar rightward swing took place in Mexico, where the conservative successors of President Lázaro Cárdenas pursued policies favorable to big business and large landowners but neglected the peasantry. As a result, a new corporate hacienda arose and soon dominated Mexican agriculture. By the end of the 1950s, the once-fashionable hope that a dynamic entrepreneurial class could lead Latin America out of dependence and underdevelopment had largely faded.

Meanwhile, the discontent of the masses, sharpened by the "revolution of rising expectations," continued to erupt in revolts. In 1952 a spontaneous rising of Bolivian peasants and miners brought agrarian reform, nationalization of mines, and other progressive changes, but the middle-class revolutionaries who assumed leadership of the movement soon braked and partially reversed the process of change. In 1944 a revolution in Guatemala, led by progressive intellectuals and officers, overthrew the tyrant Jorge Ubico and launched an agrarian reform directed especially against the United Fruit Company. An intensive United States effort to isolate Guatemala, combined with large-scale financial and military assistance to an invasion force of right-wing dissidents and mercenaries, brought down the revolutionary government in 1954, but its achievements in democracy and reform made a lasting mark on the country's life. Even more important was the armed struggle begun by Fidel Castro and his comrades against the Cuban dictator Bastista in July 1953. Their long guerrilla war ended with the victorious entry of the rebel army into Havana on January 1, 1959.

1959 TO THE PRESENT

The victory of the Cuban Revolution, soon transformed into a socialist revolution, marks a turning point in Latin American history. The swift, thoroughgoing Cuban agrarian reform and nationalization of foreign enterprises and the revolution's successes in raising the living standards of the masses offered Latin America a radical alternative to development along capitalist lines. The specter of social revolution, which the CIA and the State Department had exorcised in Guatemala, arose anew and grown much larger in Cuba, ninety miles from Miami.

Washington responded to the Cuban threat to the old order in Latin America with a variety of tactics. In 1961, President John F. Kennedy proclaimed the establishment of the Alliance for Progress, which was designed to show that Latin America's social revolution, with United States help, could be achieved peacefully within the framework of capitalism. But within a few years, the failure of the corruption-ridden program to achieve structural change was apparent to all.

Simultaneously, the United States government sought to undermine and destroy the Castro regime, first by economic blockade and political isolation and then by a CIA-sponsored effort by Cuban exiles to invade Cuba (1961)—an effort that met with a swift and humiliating defeat. Responding to clamorous demands in and out of Congress for direct action against the "communist bridgehead" in the Americas, the Soviet Union stepped up its flow of arms to Cuba, which led to the Cuban missile crisis (1962). For a space of ten days, a jittery world lived in the shadow of nuclear war between the United States and the Soviet Union. The crisis ended with a pledge on the part of the United States not to invade Cuba in return for the withdrawal of Soviet missiles from the island.

Forced to retreat in Cuba, the United States redoubled its efforts to prevent a spread of the Cuban "contagion" to other parts of the hemisphere. In these efforts, it had the support of the old and new Latin American elites, increasingly fearful of radical social change. In 1964 a coalition of reactionary Brazilian military, great landowners, and big capitalists overthrew the mildly progressive government of President João Goulart, whose heresies included a modest program of agrarian and electoral reform. It was succeeded by a heavy-handed military dictatorship that offered large incentives to foreign investors and proclaimed its unswerving loyalty to the United States, which responded with generous financial assistance. The next year, proclaiming the Johnson Doctrine, which authorized the United States to intervene to suppress "communist" activity, President Lyndon B. Johnson sent armed forces into the Dominican Republic to crush a popular revolt led by Colonel Francisco Caamaño and other progressive officers.

But the movement for structural social change and economic independence proved irrepressible; suppressed in one area, it burst out with redoubled force in another. As in the Dominican case, nationalist military sometimes played a leading role in these upheavals, disproving the common assumption that the Latin American officer class is one reactionary mass. Thus, the military take-over in Peru in 1968 was quickly followed by nationalization of key foreign-owned industries and land reform that transferred many large estates to peasants and workers, organized into cooperatives. The Peruvian Revolution—a revolution from above, without significant participation by the masses—soon faltered, however, primarily because of its failure to break with the traditional strategy of development based on foreign loans and export expansion.

In 1975 a moderate faction of the military seized power and in 1980 turned it over to a conservative elected civilian government, which attempted to dismantle the major reforms of the previous era.

The struggle against neocolonialism scored a temporary major victory with the triumph of the Marxist presidential candidate Salvador Allende and his Popular Unity coalition in Chile in 1970. In the three short years allotted to the Allende regime, it carried out the nationalization of copper mines and banks and a massive agrarian reform and made significant advances in housing, health, and education. The gains made by the Popular Unity front in successive elections proved its growing popularity.

But the Allende government made serious errors. Most serious was its failure to take preventive action against a coup by reactionary military. In September 1973, military plotters overthrew the Allende government and murdered the president. Published evidence has since confirmed the complicity of the United States in a "destabilization" of the Allende government that prepared the way for the coup. Admitting the existence of a policy of destabilization of left-leaning governments, President Gerald Ford arrogantly claimed the right to continue this policy in the "national interest."

The new fascist junta not only reversed the progressive policies of the Allende regime but transformed Chile into a concentration camp, torturing and killing thousands of opponents. Its economic policies reduced the living standards of the masses to near-starvation levels.

The destruction of Chilean democracy formed part of a general counteroffensive of Latin American reaction and its foreign allies, designed to halt and roll back the movement for structural economic and social change. By mid-1976 a block of authoritarian states—Brazil, Chile, Bolivia, Uruguay, and Paraguay—had taken shape in the center and south of Latin America. Following the deposition of the government of President Isabel Perón by right-wing military in early 1976, they were soon joined by Argentina.

But these regimes, whose policies included the systematic use of torture and assassination against political opponents and the abandonment of the effort to achieve economic independence, offered no solutions for the deepseated problems of their countries. Their most shining success, the "Brazilian miracle" of steady economic growth since 1964, was made possible by reducing wages to the subsistence level, an annual inflation rate of about 20 percent, and massive foreign investments that hastened the foreign conquest of Brazilian industry. By the mid-1970s the "Brazilian miracle" was running down; by 1980, Brazil was in deep recession, with factories closing, unemployment rising, and a balance of payments problem growing steadily worse. By the end of 1982, Brazil's foreign debt stood at about $90 billion, the largest in the Third World. Only a rescue package organized by the International Monetary Fund (IMF) and the U.S. government and bankers saved Brazil from immediate default.

Other military regimes, such as Argentina and Chile, faced similarly grave economic problems. But the crisis was not one of dictatorships alone; it confronted all the countries of the region, whatever their political systems, that pursued a strategy of dependent development based on foreign loans and investments. By 1982, Mexico, a formal democracy, had a foreign debt of about $85 billion—almost the same as Brazil's. Little Costa Rica, one of the few genuine parliamentary democracies of the area, with a foreign debt of over $4 billion, announced in 1981 that it could not make payments on either principal or interest on outstanding debts, thus becoming the first Latin American country ever to declare itself in default. The only Latin American country to reduce its debts to Western banks between 1979 and 1982 was Cuba, whose debts had declined by $795 million or 38 percent.* During the same period Latin America's twelve

main borrowers had increased their indebtedness by $79 billion, or 75 percent.

At the heart of the debt problem lies the unequal exchange between advanced capitalist countries, such as the United States, and the Third World of which Latin America is a part. A major factor in Latin America's balance of payments deficit is the imbalance between the low prices of Latin American export commodities and the high prices of the manufactured goods and oil that most of the countries in the area must buy. Falling commodity prices in recent decades have greatly aggravated the problem. In 1960 a ton of coffee could purchase 37.3 tons of fertilizers; in 1982 the same amount of coffee purchased only 15.8 tons of fertilizers. In 1960 a ton of sugar could purchase 6.3 tons of oil; in 1982 only 0.7 tons of oil could be bought with the same amount of sugar. These unfavorable terms of trade help to explain Latin America's mountainous debt, raised still higher by the usurious interest rates that the United States has maintained in recent years.

Certain recent changes in the Latin American industrialization programs have contributed to the growing gap between Latin American exports and imports. Since about 1955, countries like Brazil and Mexico have increasingly stressed production of consumer durables and capital goods that required the importation of expensive machinery, equipment, and technical licenses from countries like the United States. The result was a growing surplus of imports over exports. The transnational companies' take-over of much of the Latin American manufacturing sector, especially of the most modern or dynamic industries, contributed to the same result. In the 1970s, for every dollar invested in Latin America, transnationals repatriated approximately $2.20 to their home countries. To cover the deficits in their balance of payments, Latin American countries had to borrow from Western bankers at interest rates that reached double digit figures

---

*Cuba's debt to Comecon (the socialist bloc's counterpart of the European Economic Community) is estimated by Western bankers at $7 billion. This debt was renegotiated in the mid-1970s on generous terms:

twenty-five years at zero interest, with a grace period of thirteen years.

by 1980. In 1982, of the total income of $64 billion in interest received by U.S. bankers from abroad, $27 billion came from Latin America.

By 1982, with their national treasuries almost empty of foreign exchange, a number of major Latin American countries faced the prospect of immediate default. This posed immense dangers to the international banking system, for defaults by Mexico and Brazil alone could wipe out 95 percent of the capital of the nine largest U.S. banks. Defaults were averted by emergency aid packages provided by Western governments and bankers in return for agreements by the recipient governments to carry out "austerity" programs that further reduced the living standards of their workers and peasants. Nevertheless the problem has been postponed, not resolved. There is no prospect that even a portion of the huge Latin American debt can be repaid without large write-offs and long delays in payment. Meanwhile the flow of new loans to Latin America—at higher rates of interest because of increased risk—has sharply declined, while the Latin American countries have in turn reduced their imports; Mexico and Brazil are already committed to reducing imports by $12 billion a year.

It seems that the Latin American model of "dependent development"—in reality a new, streamlined form of neocolonialism—has almost exhausted its potential for generating economic growth. Forced to reduce their dependence on foreign loans and investments, Latin American countries will have to adopt more autonomous, inward-directed strategies of development. These solutions will have to be based on more rational exploitation of human and natural resources. They will have to aim at raising the material and cultural level of the masses rather than at enriching tiny landed and industrial elites and foreign investors. Such strategies cannot be implemented, however, without profound changes both in the relations between Latin America and the outside world and in Latin America's economic and social structures, particularly in the areas of land tenure and use, ownership of industry, and income distribution.

As the 1980s opened, there were signs, in fact, that the reactionary tide of the 1970s was receding and that a new era of revolutionary change may have begun. The signs included real or tactical retreats by the military regimes of Brazil and Argentina, which promised transitions to democracy, and the overthrow of a brutal military junta in Bolivia, replaced by a left-wing government that accepted workers' control of the decisive mining industry. Most significant of all, however, was the revolutionary storm that broke over Central America, an area where the problems of latifundismo, repressive rule, and neocolonialism existed in their most concentrated form. The triumph in July 1979 of the radical nationalist *Frente Sandinista de Liberación Nacional* (Sandinist* Front for National Liberation) over the Somoza family dynasty, whose tyrannical rule the United States had supported for more than four decades, had an electrifying effect in the region and throughout Latin America. The originality of the Sandinist regime, with its mix of Marxism and progressive Catholic thought, of socialism and private enterprise, suggested the variety of forms that social revolution could assume in Latin America. The Nicaraguan revolution was swiftly followed by a revolt against a corrupt and repressive ruling junta in El Salvador. This revolution was led by a broad coalition of social and political groups united in a *Frente Democrático Revolucionario* (FDR) whose guerrilla army had government forces on the defensive by the spring of 1983. In Guatemala, meanwhile, where a CIA-organized coup had overthrown a democratic reformist regime in 1954, a guerrilla movement continued to struggle against a barbarous military government that fought "subversion" by a scorched earth policy that included the massacre of peasant men, women, and children. All Latin America watched with fascination the unfolding revolutionary drama in Central America.

*After Augusto César Sandino, legendary leader of a prolonged guerrilla struggle against U.S. interventionist forces in Nicaragua (1927–1933).

CHAPTER TWELVE

The Mexican Revolution—and After

On the eve of the presidential election of 1910, signs of unrest multiplied in Mexico. Peasant risings and workers' strikes became more frequent, and the Mexican Liberal party, founded and led by the exiled revolutionary journalist Ricardo Flores Magón, intensified its conspiratorial activities. Divisions appeared within the oligarchy. Bernardo Reyes, a foe of the Científicos and the powerful governor of Nuevo León whose rule combined iron-fisted repression with reformist trends, announced his candidacy for the post of vice president. Reyes saw this office as a steppingstone to the presidency when Díaz, who was eighty years old in 1910, died or retired.

In an unusual atmosphere of political ferment and debate, there appeared a tract for the times, *The Great National Problems* (1909) by the lawyer Andrés Molina Enríquez. Financed by Reyes, the book combined the customary eulogies of Díaz with incisive criticism of his political system and especially of his agrarian policy. Its denunciation of the latifundio and appeal for land reform anticipated the radical slogans of the coming revolution.

Díaz had contributed to this ferment by announcing in 1908, in an interview with an American journalist, that Mexico was now ready for democracy and that he would welcome the emergence of an opposition party. Francisco Madero, a Coahuila hacendado whose extensive family interests included cattle ranches, wheat farms, vineyards, textile factories, and mines, took Díaz at his word. A member of the elite, Madero was no revolutionary. He feared that continuance of the existing political order would inevitably breed social revolution. In a book published in 1908, *The Presidential Succession in 1910*, he proclaimed the need for democracy in order to preserve social stability, which was threatened by the immobility and absolutism of the Díaz personal dictatorship.

Madero made clear, however, that by democracy he meant control by an elite. "The ignorant public," he wrote, "should take no direct part in determining who should be the candidate for public office." He sought to reassure conservatives by pointing out that even in advanced liberal democracies "the lower classes do not determine who should hold the reins of power. Democratic nations are generally ruled by party leaders drawn from a small number of intellectuals."

Madero criticized Díaz's social policies—his genocidal Indian wars and violent repression of strikes—as counterproductive; in place of those brutal tactics, he proposed a policy of modest concessions to peasants and workers that would reduce mounting tensions and check the growth of radical ideas. Madero regarded democracy as an instrument of social control that would promote the acceptance of capitalism by the masses through the grant of limited political and social reforms, with a large stress on education.

In December 1909, Madero began to tour the country, making speeches in which he explained his reform program. In April 1910, an opposition anti-re-electionist party was formed and announced Madero as its candidate for president. Díaz at first refused to take Madero seriously but soon became alarmed by his growing popularity. In early June he had Madero arrested and charged with preparing an armed insurrection; arrests of many of his supporters followed. In September the election was held, and it was announced that Díaz and his hand-picked vice-presidential candidate, Ramón Corral, had been elected by an almost unanimous vote.

After the election, Díaz no longer considered Madero dangerous and allowed him to be released on bail. Convinced that the dictator could not be removed by peaceful means, Madero prepared to resort to armed struggle. On October 7, he fled across the border to Texas and from there announced the Plan of San Luis Potosí. Declaring the recent elections null and void, Madero assumed the title of provisional president of Mexico but promised to hold general free elections as soon as conditions permitted and turn power over to the elected president. The plan made a vague reference to the return of usurped peasant lands, but most of its articles dealt with political reforms. That Madero was allowed to organize the revolution on American soil with little interference by the authorities suggests the American government's displeasure with Díaz. Fearing that American domination of investments in Mexico threatened Mexican economic and political independence, the dictator had recently favored British over American capitalists in the grant of concessions and had given other indications of an anti-American attitude. The administration of President Taft evidently hoped that Madero would display a more positive attitude toward United States interests.

THE GREAT REVOLUTION, 1910 TO 1920

The revolution got off to a shaky start when Madero, having crossed back into Mexico, found

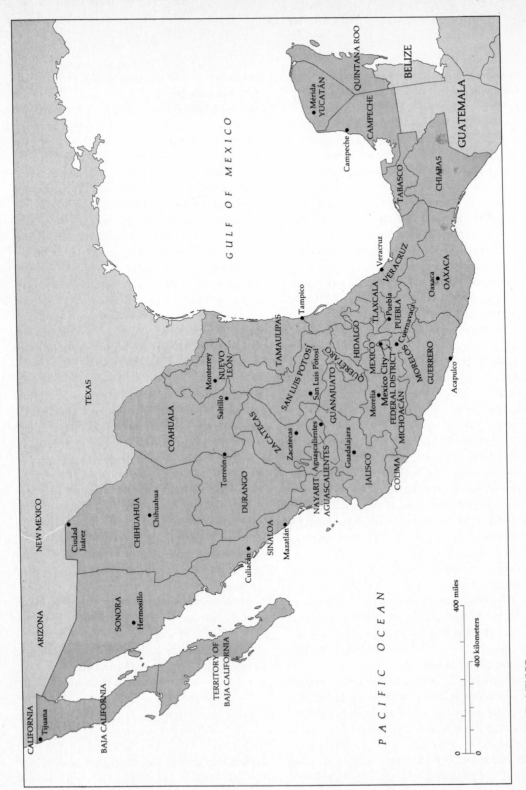

CONTEMPORARY MEXICO

only twenty-five supporters waiting for him and hurriedly returned to Texas. But it soon gathered momentum as two major movements of peasant revolt responded to his call. In the huge northern border state of Chihuahua, where peons and small farmers suffered under the iron rule of the Terrazas-Creel clan, masters of a vast landed empire, the rising began under the leadership of Pascual Orozco, a mule driver, and Pancho Villa, a social bandit with a reputation for taking from the rich to give to the poor. By the end of 1910, guerrilla armies had seized control of most of the state from federal troops.

Another seat of rebellion was the mountainous southern state of Morelos, where Indian communities had long waged a losing struggle against encroaching sugar haciendas. Here the mestizo insurgent leader Emiliano Zapata, attracted by the promise of land reform in the Plan of San Luis Potosí, proclaimed his loyalty to Madero.

In May 1911, the rebels won two decisive victories: In the south, the *Zapatistas* captured Cuautla, the provincial capital and an important railway center; in the north, Pascual Orozco and Pancho Villa captured Ciudad Juárez. Rather than face an invasion of the poorly defended capital by Zapata's dreaded agrarian rebels, Díaz and his advisers decided to reach an agreement with Madero. Disregarding urgent warnings by the left wing of the revolutionary movement against compromises with the Díaz regime; Madero signed the Treaty of Ciudad Juárez on May 21. This treaty provided for the removal of Díaz but left intact all existing institutions. It was completely silent on the subject of social change. On May 25, the aged dictator resigned the presidency and a few days later left for Europe. Francisco León de la Barra, the Mexican ambassador to the United States, assumed the interim presidency.

On June 7, 1911, Madero entered Mexico City in triumph, but the rejoicing of the crowds who thronged into the streets to greet the "apostle

of democracy" was premature. The provisional president, León de la Barra, was closely tied to the old regime and had no sympathy with the revolution. The *Porfirista* aristocracy and its allies had not given up hope of regaining power; they regarded the compromise that made León de la Barra provisional president a tactical retreat, a means of gaining time to allow the revolutionary wave to subside so they could prepare a counterblow. Under the interim president, the huge Díaz bureaucracy remained largely intact. The reactionary officer corps remained in command of the federal army and burned for revenge over the revolutionary peasant armies that had defeated it.

Social conditions throughout the country remained largely unchanged, and the provisional government sought a total restoration of the status quo. Efforts were made to disband the revolutionary troops, and León de la Barra sent federal forces into Morelos to initiate hostilities against the Zapatistas, who had begun to confiscate large estates and distribute land to the villages. Madero's ineffective efforts to halt the fighting and mediate between Zapata and León de la Barra only deepened the hatred of the reactionaries for the visionary meddler who had unleashed anarchy in Mexico. But the revolutionary wave was still running strong, and reaction had to bide its time. In October 1911, Madero and his running mate, José María Pino Suárez, were elected president and vice president by overwhelming majorities.

Madero's Presidency: Inadequacy and Revolt

On November 6, 1911, Madero assumed the presidency from León de la Barra. It soon became evident that the "apostle of democracy" had no fundamental solutions for Mexico's grave social and economic problems. Even on the political plane, Madero's thought was far from advanced. His conception of democracy was a formal democracy that would give the masses the illusion of power and participation in political life but would vest all decision making in the hands of an elite.

In regard to economic and social democracy, his vision was even more limited. Madero allowed workers to organize trade unions and to strike and permitted a national workers' center, the *Casa del Obrero Mundial,* to be formed in Mexico City. But his answer to the agrarian problem was a totally inadequate program of purchase of land from large landowners and recovery of national land for distribution among landless peasants. In fact, Madero, who believed that only large landholdings would permit Mexican agriculture to modernize, was totally opposed to land reform at the expense of the haciendas. Madero's retreat on the land issue led to a break with his most faithful ally, Emiliano Zapata. Zapata urged Madero to carry out the agrarian provisions of the Plan of San Luis Potosí. Madero refused, arguing that the treaties that set up the interim government of León de la Barra obliged him to accept the legality of the legal and administrative decisions of the Díaz regime. Madero also demanded the disarmament of Zapata's peasant troops; in effect, he demanded Zapata's total surrender.

Convinced that Madero did not intend to carry out his pledges to restore land to the villages, Zapata announced his own program on November 28, 1911. The Plan of Ayala proclaimed that "the lands, woods, and waters usurped by the hacendados, Científicos, or caciques through tyranny and venal justice" would be returned to their owners, and Zapata began to put the plan into effect. The Zapatista movement soon spread to other states in central and southern Mexico. Madero followed De la Barra's example and sent a series of generals against Zapata; their campaigns devastated Morelos but failed to crush Zapata and his peasant armies.

As a result of his indecisive policies, Madero fell between two stools. His failure to carry out a genuine agrarian reform lost him the trust and support of the revolutionary peasantry without mollifying the reactionaries, who resented his modest concessions to labor and his efforts to transform Mexico into a bourgeois democracy with freedom of speech and press and the rule of law. They also feared that under pressure from the peasantry and under the influence of urban middle-class reformers like Luis Cabrera, a strong advocate of land reform, Madero might move farther to the left.

The aristocracy, its possessions and influence almost intact, dreamed of restoring the lost paradise of Don Porfirio, when peasants, workers, and Indians knew their place. Almost from the day that Madero took office in November 1911, therefore, counterrevolutionary revolts sprouted in various parts of Mexico. Most serious was a revolt in the north led by Pascual Orozco, who was encouraged and bribed by conservative elements in Chihuahua, especially the Terrazas-Creel clan. Federal troops under General Victoriano Huerta crushed the Orozco revolt in a series of battles, but Huerta's victory, joined with the alienation of Zapata and other of Madero's old revolutionary allies, increased Madero's dependence on an officer corps whose loyalty to his cause was highly dubious.

Abortive revolts succeeded each other throughout the rest of 1912. The danger to Madero increased as it became clear that he had lost the support of the United States. Madero had done nothing to injure foreign economic interests, which continued to dominate the most important branches of the Mexican economy. Indeed, the influx of foreign—especially American—capital increased, and American companies recovered their former dominant position in the oil industry. Madero made clear that he favored foreign investments and guaranteed their security. But he refused to show special favors to American capitalists and warned foreign investors that the crony system that had operated under Díaz was dead. This independent spirit, plus Madero's legalization of trade unions and strikes, which alarmed American companies, and his inability to cope with the peasant revolution and establish the stability demanded by the American government, alienated the United States. American foreign policy, originally favorable to Madero, turned against him.

The American ambassador, Henry Lane Wilson, became increasingly hostile to Madero. In February 1912, a hundred thousand American troops were stationed along the border, and throughout the year Wilson made vehement threats of intervention if the Madero government failed to protect American lives and property. This pressure, coinciding with a wave of revolts against Madero, signified a de facto alliance between domestic reaction and the American ambassador.

Meanwhile, preparations for a coup d'état were under way in the capital. Implicated in the conspiracy were General Huerta, the recent conqueror of Orozco; General Miguel Mondragón, former chief of artillery under Díaz; Bernardo and Rodolfo Reyes, father and son; and Félix Díaz, nephew of the old dictator. Bernardo Reyes and Díaz had been imprisoned for their parts in previous abortive revolts but were treated like honored guests and had every facility for communicating with their fellow conspirators.

The blow fell on February 9, 1913. On that day, the military garrison at Tacubaya "pronounced" against Madero. Joined by cadets from the garrison, they freed Bernardo Reyes and Félix Díaz from prison. Then the rebels marched on the National Palace. Their attack failed, and Bernardo Reyes was killed in an exchange of fire. Díaz then retreated with his troops to the Citadel, a well-fortified army arsenal, and between the rebels and the loyal troops holding the palace there developed a bitter artillery duel. Since the two parties were more than a mile apart, the principal victims of the cannonade were civilians. Meanwhile Huerta, to whom

Madero had entrusted command of military operations, only awaited the right moment to dispose of the president. That is why he limited his operations to a futile bombardment of the Citadel and ordered troops known to be loyal to Madero to storm the Citadel without cover, sending them to certain death.

Meanwhile, the American ambassador, in complete sympathy with the counterrevolutionary revolt, was secretly negotiating with Huerta and Díaz. On February 12, Wilson sent Madero a sharp protest against the conduct of military operations in Mexico City because they threatened American life and property. At his urging, the British, German, and Spanish representatives sent similar demands. As the crisis moved toward a climax, Wilson became feverishly active. On February 14, he demanded that the Mexican government begin negotiations with the other warring parties; otherwise, American marines would be landed in Mexican ports. The same day, Wilson invited other foreign diplomats to a conference at which it was agreed to force Madero to resign. A message to that effect was sent to Madero from the diplomatic corps. Madero firmly rejected the demand. He would rather die, he said, than allow foreign intervention.

Huerta's Dictatorship

Wilson's activities were clearly coordinated with those of the conspirators and encouraged Huerta to strike the long-planned blow. On February 18, a detachment of Huerta's troops entered the palace and arrested the president, his vice president, Pino Suárez, and other members of his government. A dispute between Huerta and Díaz over who should head the new regime was settled through Wilson's mediation. At a meeting at the American embassy, agreement was reached that Huerta should head a provisional government, with Díaz to succeed him as soon as an election could be held. Wilson then called a meeting of foreign diplomats to whom he introduced Huerta as the "savior of Mexico."

To give some semblance of legality to his usurpation, Huerta obtained the "voluntary" resignations of Madero and Pino Suárez in return for the promise that they would then be free to leave Mexico. An intimidated Congress accepted the resignations and recognized Huerta as provisional president, almost without dissent. There remained the question of what should be done with Madero. Asked by Huerta for his advice, the American ambassador replied that he should do "what was best for the country." Despite urgent requests by other members of the diplomatic corps and Madero's wife that he intercede to save Madero's life, Wilson refused. On the evening of February 22, Madero and Pino Suárez were murdered as they were being transferred from the National Palace to the penitentiary; the official explanation was that they had been killed during an attempt by armed men to release them. The two assassins, officers of the rurales, were quickly advanced in rank, one being made a general.

Huerta's seizure of power, which was greeted with rejoicing by the landed aristocracy, the big capitalists, and the church, was an effort to set the Mexican clock back, to restore the Díaz system of personal dictatorship. The promise to Félix Díaz that he would succeed Huerta as president was soon broken, and Díaz was shunted aside by sending him off on a diplomatic mission to Japan. On October 10, 1913, preparing for his own election, Huerta arrested 110 congressmen and dissolved both houses. He then installed a new Congress packed with his military followers. The election held on October 26 under these auspices was so fraudulent, the results so obviously falsified, that Huerta's own Congress, with his approval, nullified it and put off a new election until a future date, with Huerta to continue as provisional president. Meanwhile, political assas-

sinations occurred at a rate unknown in earlier Mexican history.

Hoping to broaden the social base of his dictatorship and conceal its reactionary character as long as possible, Huerta invited some intellectuals sincerely interested in reform to join his cabinet, but their modest reform proposals were turned down by a Huerta-dominated Congress, and the ministers resigned or were dismissed and replaced by military men. For the same reason, Huerta for a time continued Madero's labor policies and even allowed the Casa del Obrero Mundial to hold the first May Day demonstration in Mexican history, but as the terrorist nature of the regime became more apparent and labor more and more allied itself with the anti-Huerta movement, he proceeded to arrest its leaders and eventually closed down the Casa.

The Opposition: Zapata, Villa, Carranza, and Obregón

Huerta had counted on a quick victory over the peasant revolutionaries of the south and favorable reception of his coup d'état by conservative economic and political interests in the north. He miscalculated badly. The revolutionary wave, still running strong, rose even higher in reaction to Madero's brutal murder and the imposition of Huerta's terrorist regime. Zapata, who had offered Madero a thousand men to combat the rebels—an offer that Madero declined—intensified his struggle against local great landowners, Huerta's allies, and federal troops. In the northern border states of Sonora, Chihuahua, and Coahuila, meanwhile, an anti-Huerta coalition of disparate social groups— liberal hacendados, middle classes, miners, industrial workers, cowboys, and peasants—began to take form.

The successive campaigns launched by Huerta against the Zapatistas failed to achieve decisive victories. In mid-1913 the peasant armies laid siege to Cuernavaca, the capital of the state of Morelos, and cut it off from the national capital. Driven from Morelos in the latter part of 1913, they continued to operate in neighboring states. Zapata himself led the struggle in Guerrero, where his forces occupied the major towns and besieged Chilpancingo, the state capital, which fell on March 24, 1914. In April the Zapatistas returned to Morelos and by the end of May had taken all the towns in the state except Cuernavaca. In June they laid siege to Cuernavaca and took it in August 1914.

By forcing Huerta to commit a considerable part of his troops to the campaign in the south, Zapata assured the success of the revolutionary movement that sprang up anew in the north. Pancho Villa assumed leadership of the Constitutionalists, as Huerta's northern opponents called themselves, in Chihuahua (March 1913). Enjoying an immense popularity among the *vaqueros* (cowboys) of the state, he soon recruited an army of three thousand men. He inflicted a series of defeats on federal troops and by the end of the summer had won control of almost all Chihuahua except the large cities. In mid-November he captured Ciudad Juárez and went on to capture the state capital, Chihuahua City. Swift cavalry movements, including daring night raids that took the enemy by surprise, contributed to his military successes.

Master of Chihuahua City, Villa imposed a revolutionary new order on the state capital. He employed his soldiers as a civil militia and administrative staff to restore normal life. Stealing or the sale of liquor to the army was made punishable by death. The army was put to work running the electric light plant, the street railways, the telephone system, the waterworks, and the flour mill once owned by the Terrazas family. Other soldiers were assigned to administer confiscated haciendas and the slaughterhouse. Villa ordered a reduction of meat prices and distributed money, clothing, and other goods to the poor. Education was a passion

with the almost illiterate Villa; according to the American correspondent John Reed, who accompanied him, he established some fifty new schools in Chihuahua City.

Clearly, Villa's social policies were more radical than those implemented by the Constitutionalist leaders in the neighboring states of Sonora and Coahuila. In December 1913, he announced the expropriation without compensation of the holdings of the pro-Huerta oligarchy in Chihuahua. His agrarian program, however, differed in significant ways from that of Zapata. Whereas in the area ruled by Zapata confiscated estates were promptly distributed among the peasants, Villa's decree provided that they should remain under state control until the victory of the revolution. The revenues from these estates would be used to finance the revolutionary struggle and support the widows and orphans of the revolutionary soldiers. Once victory had been achieved, they were to be used to pay pensions to such widows and orphans, to compensate veterans of the revolution, to restore village lands that had been usurped by the hacendados, and to pay taxes left unpaid by the hacendados. Meanwhile Villa turned control of some confiscated haciendas over to his lieutenants; the rest were administered by the state. Cattle were sold in the United States to secure arms and ammunition for Villa's army, and meat was distributed on a large scale to the urban unemployed, to public institutions like orphanages and children's homes, and for sale in the markets. The differences between the agrarian programs of Villa and Zapata may be explained in part by the fact that the economy of the north was based not on agriculture but on cattle raising, which required large economic units. These units had to be administered by the state or on a cooperative basis. In addition, the percentage of peasants in the population was much smaller in the north, and the problem of land hunger much less acute.

In the neighboring state of Coahuila, mean-

Mexican Generals Alvaro Obregón and Pancho
Villa (at left) with U.S. General John J. Pershing,
photographed at a meeting on the International
Bridge between Juarez and El Paso on August 27,
1914. (Aultman Collection, El Paso Public Library)

while, the elderly Venustiano Carranza, a great
landowner who had once served Díaz but joined
Madero in 1911 and was appointed by him governor of the state, raised the standard of revolt
against Huerta. On March 26, 1913, he announced his Plan of Guadalupe, which called
for the overthrow of the dictator Huerta and
the restoration of constitutional government but
did not mention social reforms. Carranza assumed the title of first chief of the Constitutionalist Army. By April he commanded some
forty thousand men. He was soon joined by

Villa, who placed himself under Carranza's
command, but retained much autonomy in
Chihuahua; Villa's troops were renamed the
Northern Division. Carranza gained another
important recruit in the young *ranchero* Alvaro
Obregón, who led the anti-Huerta forces in the
state of Sonora. Named commander of the Army
of the Northwest, he soon proved his large
military gifts by driving the federal troops out
of almost all Sonora; in April the state legislature
recognized Carranza as first chief of the
revolution.

Intervention by the United States

By the beginning of 1914, the Constitutionalist revolt had assumed significant proportions, and Huerta's fall appeared inevitable. Meanwhile, in March 1913, Woodrow Wilson had succeeded Taft as president of the United States. Alone among the great powers, Wilson's government refused to recognize the Huerta regime. Wilson justified his nonrecognition policy with moralistic rhetoric, refusing to recognize a government that had come to power illegally. More important, he was convinced that Huerta could not provide the stable political climate required by American interests in Mexico.

Wilson's concern with a suitable political climate for American investments emerges from a note sent to British officials in November 1913, in which he assured those officials that the United States government "intends not merely to force Huerta from power, but also to exert every influence it can exert to secure Mexico a better government under which all contracts and business concessions will be safer than they have been." On the other hand, Huerta's policy of favoring British capital, especially Lord Cowdray's Anglo-Mexican Petroleum Company, which received new concessions in return for financial assistance, gained him support in that quarter.

By yielding to a British demand for uniform rates for all shipping using the nearly completed Panama Canal, Wilson obtained an end of British support for Huerta by the end of 1913. As a result, Huerta's financial position became increasingly difficult. Seeking to avert a catastrophe, he suspended payment on the interest on the national debt for six months on January 13, 1914. That extraordinary measure only increased Huerta's difficulties, however. Foreign creditors began to demand the seizure of Mexican customhouses, and some even clamored for immediate intervention. By February 1914, having failed to obtain Huerta's resignation by diplomatic pressure, Wilson decided force must be used. After receiving assurances from Carranza's agent in Washington that the Constitutionalists would respect foreign property rights, including "just and equitable concessions," Wilson lifted the existing embargo on arms shipments to the Carranza forces.

Wilson would have preferred to use Carranza as the instrument of Huerta's ouster, but pressure for intervention in Mexico was growing in the United States. Wilson found a pretext for such intervention when a party of American sailors from the cruiser *Dolphin* landed in a restricted area of Tampico and were arrested. They were almost immediately released, with an apology, but the commander of the *Dolphin*, under orders from Washington, demanded a formal disavowal of the action, severe punishment for the responsible Mexican officer, and a twenty-one-gun salute to the American flag. For Huerta to grant these demands might have meant political suicide, and he refused.

Wilson now sent a fleet into the Gulf of Mexico, and on April 21, 1914, learning that a German merchant ship was bound for Veracruz with munitions, he ordered the seizure of the city. When Mexican batteries at the fortress of San Juan de Ulúa attempted to prevent a landing, they were silenced by answering fire from the American ships. Huerta's forces evacuated Veracruz the same day, but the local population and cadets of the naval academy continued a courageous resistance until April 27, when the American flag was raised over Veracruz. The occupation of Veracruz sent a wave of anti-Yankee sentiment rolling through Mexico; protests were also organized in a number of Latin American countries. Meanwhile Carranza, whom Wilson had hoped to control, bitterly denounced the American action and demanded the immediate evacuation of Veracruz.

The rising storm of Mexican anger and Carranza's defiant stand placed Wilson in a quandary. He sought a way out of his difficult sit-

A Mexican revolutionary firing from a mountain
slope. (Aultman Collection, El Paso Public Library)

uation by obtaining an offer from Argentina,
Brazil, and Chile to mediate the dispute between
the United States and Mexico. A conference
was convened at Niagara Falls, Canada, in May
1914. Wilson hoped to do more than reduce
tensions; he intended to use the mediation
as a means of eliminating Huerta and establishing a new provisional Mexican government
that he could control. The American candidate
to head this provisional government was the
moderate Carranza, since the revolutionary
peasant leaders Zapata and Villa were obviously
unacceptable. But Carranza would not rise to

Wilson's bait. The conservative but fiercely nationalist first chief sent representatives to the
Niagara Falls conference but did not give them
official status, and he refused the mediation of
the conference. Mexico, his representatives informed the United States delegates, would settle
its own problems without interference from any
other source.

By this time, the fall of the Huerta regime
was imminent. With the northern tier of states
securely in Constitutionalist hands, Pancho Villa's Northern Division drove south in March
from Chihuahua City toward Torreón, a major

railroad center on the way to Zacatecas and Mexico City. On April 2, Torreón fell to Villa after twelve days of bitter fighting; the fall of Monterrey, Saltillo, and Tampico followed soon after. Having taken Saltillo, Villa advanced on Zacatecas and took the city by storm on June 23. Meanwhile, Obregón's Army of the Northwest was advancing down the Pacific coast into Jalisco; on July 9, he seized the important railroad and industrial center of Guadalajara. Recognizing that his situation had become hopeless, Huerta took flight for Europe on July 15. On August 15, Obregón's troops entered Mexico City.

Huerta's fall deprived the United States of any pretext for continuing its armed intervention, but Wilson delayed the evacuation of Veracruz as long as possible in the hope of securing commitments from Carranza that would have effectively prevented any basic changes in Mexico's social and economic structure. Despite hints that "fatal consequences" might follow, Carranza resolutely rejected these demands and continued to insist on the end of the military intervention. American troops finally evacuated Veracruz on November 23, 1914.

Fighting Among the Victors

As the day of complete victory drew near, differences emerged within the Constitutionalist camp, especially between Carranza and Villa. There were personal factors, such as Carranza's jealousy of Villa as a potential rival, but more important was Carranza's failure to define his position on such fundamental issues as the agrarian question, the role of the church, and the new political order. At a conference held in early July at Torreón between representatives of Villa and Carranza, Villa proposed to incorporate in an agreement a clause drawn up by one of his intellectuals that defined "the present conflict as a struggle of the poor against the abuses of the powerful" and committed the

Constitutionalists "to implant a democratic regime . . . to secure the well-being of the workers; to emancipate the peasants economically, making an equitable distribution of lands or whatever else is needed to solve the agrarian problem." Under pressure from his generals, who recognized the potential dangers of an open break with Villa, Carranza permitted his representatives to sign the agreement containing this radical clause, which he personally found unacceptable. Villa, however, continued to distrust Carranza, and his distrust was confirmed by various of Carranza's actions, notably his unilateral occupation of the capital.

Relations also deteriorated between Carranza and Zapata. Zapata had waged war against Huerta independently of Carranza's forces and refused to recognize his leadership; a Zapatista manifesto proclaimed that the Plan of Ayala must prevail, and all adherents of the old regime must be removed. Efforts by some of Carranza's partisans who were sympathetic to land reform to resolve the dispute ended in failure.

In October 1914, a convention of revolutionary leaders and their delegates met at Aguascalientes to settle the conflict between Carranza and Villa. At the insistence of the *Villistas*, Zapata was invited to attend, and presently a delegation from "the Liberating Army of the South" arrived at Aguascalientes. After an eloquent speech by Antonio Díaz Soto y Gama, Zapata's leading adviser, the convention endorsed the Plan of Ayala. The convention also assumed supreme authority, called for the resignation of Carranza as first chief, and appointed General Eulalio Gutiérrez provisional president of the nation. Gutiérrez was a compromise candidate pushed by delegates equally opposed to Carranza and Villa. Since Aguascalientes swarmed with Villa's troops, Gutiérrez had no choice but to name Villa commander in chief of the Conventionist Army, as the Northern Division now came to be called.

Carranza, however, refused to accept the

decisions of the Aguascalientes Convention, claiming it had no authority to depose him. When he failed to meet the deadline for his resignation, November 10, the armies of Zapata and Villa advanced on the capital and occupied it. Carranza retreated with his depleted forces to Veracruz, which had been evacuated by the Americans shortly before. There he established his Constitutionalist government, while Obregón, who had remained loyal to Carranza, rebuilt his army with the aid of arms and munitions purchased abroad.

On December 4, Villa and Zapata held their first meeting and came to full agreement. But although the peasant revolutionaries controlled the capital and much of the country, they could not consolidate their successes. Unskilled in politics, they entrusted state power to the unreliable provisional president, Gutiérrez, a former general in Carranza's army, who sabotaged the Conventionist war effort and opened secret negotiations with Obregón. Meanwhile a conservative wing in the convention, headed by the influential Felipe Ángeles, one of Villa's ablest generals, strongly opposed land reform, expropriation of foreign properties, and other radical social changes. They argued that such reforms would alienate the United States, on whose support they counted for victory over Carranza. Although Villa's sympathies were with the radicals as regarded land reform, he avoided taking sides in the dispute, probably because he believed that unity was necessary to gain a rapid military victory and recognition by the United States, which he also regarded as essential to his final triumph. For these and other reasons the convention proved unable to forge a clear national program of socioeconomic reforms that could unite the interests of the peasantry, industrial workers, and the middle class. Zapata's Plan of Ayala contained no reference to labor's demands. His later attempts to broaden his program to attract labor, the middle class, and even national capitalists were too little and too late.

The Constitutionalists did not make the same mistake. At the insistence of Obregón and intellectuals like Luis Cabrera, who were aware of the need for broadening the social base of the Constitutionalist movement, the conservative Carranza adopted a program of social reforms designed to win the support of peasants and workers. In December 1914, during the darkest days of the Constitutionalist cause, Carranza issued in Veracruz a decree that promised agrarian reform and improved conditions for the industrial workers. Other decrees followed, the most notable being one of January 6, 1915, which provided for the restoration of lands usurped from the villages and the expropriation of additional needed land from haciendas. (Simultaneously, Carranza secretly promised the hacendados that he would return the haciendas that had been confiscated by revolutionary authorities—promises that in the end he would keep). Carranza's agrarian decrees, combined with the social reforms effectively carried out by some members of Carranza's left wing (Salvador Alvarado in Yucatan, for example, who abolished debt peonage, imposed minimum wages, and compelled hacendados to establish schools), gained him a certain mass base among the peasantry. Carranza also courted labor support by the promise of a minimum wage law applying to all branches of industry and by affirming the right of workers to form trade unions and to strike.

After Obregón's troops reoccupied Mexico City in January 1915, an alliance was formed between the Carranza government and the Casa del Obrero Mundial, which was restored after the fall of Huerta. Members of the Casa agreed to join "the struggle against reaction"—meaning above all the revolutionary peasantry. Six "red battalions" of workers were formed and made an important contribution to the offensive launched by Obregón against Villa and Zapata in January 1915. Inadequate understanding on the part of the peasant and working-class leaders of their common interests and the skillful opportunism of the middle-class politicians in Carranza's camp contributed to this disastrous division between labor and the peasantry.

As a result, the balance of forces shifted sharply in favor of the Constitutionalists. In early 1915, Carranza's forces won significant victories; having captured Puebla, they threatened the capital. President Gutiérrez, who had long wanted to break with Villa, left the city with a group of his ministers, some troops, and 10 million pesos from the national treasury. Shortly afterward, he submitted his resignation. Following Gutiérrez's flight, the Conventionist government, or what remained of it, designated Roque González Garza as president in his place.

Under pressure from Carranza's troops, Villa was forced on January 19 to evacuate Mexico City, which Obregón soon occupied. A series of complicated movements followed, with Constitutionalists and Conventionists successively occupying and abandoning the city. These maneuvers ended with Obregón in possession of the capital. In April 1915, Obregón advanced toward the important railroad center of Celaya, occupied it, and awaited Villa's attack. Obregón had studied accounts of the great war in progress in Europe and had learned that trenches and barbed wire could stop mass attacks. His army received Villa's furious infantry and cavalry assault with a withering fire from machine-gun emplacements and entrenched infantry. For the first time in his military career, Villa suffered a disastrous defeat, with thousands of men killed or taken prisoner. Fighting a series of battles, he retreated northward. In the hour of his defeat (May 1915), Villa issued a comprehensive, well-thought-out agrarian reform law, providing that all estates above a certain size were to be divided among the peasantry, with some indemnity for the owners, and payment by the peasants in small installments, but the program was never implemented. By the end of 1915, he was back in Chihuahua; here, among his own people, on terrain that he knew perfectly, he was invincible. For three more years he carried on

guerrilla warfare but ceased to exist as a major political and military factor. The Constitutionalists had destroyed Villa, whom they regarded as the primary danger.

There remained the Zapatistas, who threatened the capital and temporarily occupied it in July when the defending *Carrancista* general evacuated it to protect Obregón's lines of communication with Veracruz. But Zapata's battered forces could not check the advance of General Pablo González's army. In August the Constitutionalists returned to Mexico City to stay, while González, one of Carranza's ablest generals, pursued the Zapatistas into Morelos in a campaign of devastation and plunder that failed to capture Zapata or destroy his movement.

In October 1915, after unsuccessful efforts to play off the revolutionary chiefs against each other or to achieve a coalition under United States leadership, President Wilson acknowledged Carranza's ascendancy and extended de facto recognition of his regime; equally important, he placed an arms embargo on Carranza's opponents. But the United States had not abandoned its efforts to influence the course of the Mexican Revolution. A memorandum to Carranza dictated the conditions he must meet before he could obtain de jure recognition. They amounted to a claim to determine Mexican policy not only in the area of foreign economic rights but in such internal matters as the role of the church, elections, and the like. These demands were as unacceptable to Carranza in October 1915 as they had been a year before.

In the first months of 1916, relations between the United States and Mexico deteriorated sharply. In part, this resulted from initial efforts by Mexican federal and state authorities to regulate the operations of foreign oil companies. A crisis arose in March when Villa, angered by the arms embargo and wrongly convinced that Carranza had bought United States recognition by agreeing to a plan to convert Mexico into a United States protectorate, raided Columbus,

New Mexico, in an apparent effort to force Carranza to show his hand. The Wilson administration responded by ordering General John Pershing to pursue Villa into Mexico. The United States counted on the enmity between Villa and Carranza to secure the latter's neutrality. Carranza denounced the invasion, demanded the immediate withdrawal of American forces, and began to prepare for war with the United States. In a note to other Latin American nations, the Mexican government declared its belief that the basic reason for the intervention by the United States was its opposition to the Mexican policy of eliminating privileged treatment of foreign capital and affirmed that the "foreign invasion" must be repelled and Mexican sovereignty respected.

The United States had anticipated an easy victory, but Pershing's hot pursuit of the elusive Villa proved a fiasco, and Wilson accepted Carranza's offer to negotiate a settlement of the dispute. Wilson was unsuccessful in his efforts to link the evacuation of American forces with acceptance of the United States formula for Mexican domestic policy. In January 1917, influenced by the troubled international scene and his conviction that a war with Mexico would involve at least half a million men, Wilson decided to liquidate the Mexican venture. On January 28, the War Department formally announced the withdrawal of the punitive expedition. Mexican nationalism had won a major victory over yet another effort to impose American hegemony.

The Constitution of 1917

In the fall of 1916, Carranza issued a call for the election of deputies to a convention that was to frame a new constitution and prepare the way for his election as president (formally, he was still only the first chief). The convention opened in Querétaro on December 1, 1916. Since the call effectively excluded persons who had not sworn loyalty to the Plan of Guadalupe, it seemed likely that the constitution would be what Carranza wanted it to be. At the first session of the convention, Carranza offered a draft of recommendations that showed little in the way of social change. The draft did not contemplate a radical agrarian reform; with regard to labor, it limited itself to proclaiming the "right to work" and the right of workers to form organizations for "lawful purposes" and to hold "peaceful" assemblies.

These abstract proposals were unsatisfactory to a majority of the deputies, who formed the radical, or Jacobin, wing of the convention. These radical deputies—military men for the most part, but there was a sprinkling of workers—reflected the views of Obregón, the secretary of war, who was aware of the ferment among the masses and the need to make concessions to labor and the peasantry. The principal spokesman for this left wing was Francisco J. Múgica, a young general who helped to make the first land distribution of the revolution. The radicals obtained majority approval to create a commission to revise Carranza's project and introduce necessary changes. Múgica himself was largely responsible for Article 3, which struck a heavy blow at church control of education by specifically forbidding "religious corporations" and "ministers of any cult" to establish or conduct schools.

A most important article was Article 123, dealing with the rights of labor. Carranza had asked only that the federal government be empowered to enact labor legislation. The convention went much further. The finished article, a true labor code, provided for the eight-hour day; abolished the tienda de raya, or company store, and debt servitude; guaranteed the right of workers to organize, bargain collectively, and strike; and granted many other rights and privileges, making it the most advanced labor code in the contemporary world.

Article 27, dealing with property rights, had

an equally advanced character. It proclaimed the nation the original owner of all lands, waters, and the subsoil; the state could expropriate them, with compensation to the owners. National ownership of water and the subsoil was inalienable, but individuals and companies could obtain concessions for their exploitation. Foreigners to whom that privilege was granted must agree that they would not invoke the protection of their governments in regard to such concessions. Of prime importance were the same article's agrarian provisions. It declared that all measures passed since 1856 alienating *ejidos* (communal lands) were null and void; if the pueblos needed more land, they could acquire it by expropriation from neighboring haciendas.

These and other provisions of the constitution of 1917 made it the most progressive law code of its time. It laid legal foundations for a massive assault on the latifundio, for weakening the power of the church, and for regulating the operations of foreign capital in Mexico. But the constitution was not anticapitalist. It sanctioned and protected private property; it sought to control rather than eliminate foreign enterprises. By restricting the activity of foreign capital, it created more favorable conditions for the development of national capitalism.

The convention completed its work on January 31, 1917, and Carranza ordered promulgation of the new constitution on February 5, 1917. This date coincided with the withdrawal of the last troops of the American punitive expedition. Carranza expressed some reservations about the new constitution as going in some respects "beyond our social milieu," but promised to uphold it. Then he issued a call for an extraordinary presidential election to be held in March. His election was a foregone conclusion, and on May 1 he was formally installed as president— the first legally elected president since Madero. On inauguration day, Obregón, his secretary of war, resigned and retired to private life. Obregón, who had been moving to the left, dis-

trusted many of the men around Carranza as reactionaries of Porfirista stamp.

Carranza's Presidency

The three remaining years of the Carranza regime were marked by a sharp swing to the right. Carranza soon made it clear that he did not intend to implement the reform articles of the constitution. Only a trifling amount of land was distributed to the villages. Carranza returned many confiscated haciendas to their former owners; others he turned over to his favorite generals. In the words of a Zapatista manifesto, "the old latifundistas have been replaced by modern landowners in epaulets and kepis, with pistols in their belts." Official corruption existed on a massive scale. The working class, whose aid Carranza no longer required, suffered severe repression. When workers in the Federal District struck for higher wages in the face of a rampant inflation that sharply reduced their real wages, Carranza shut down the Casa del Obrero Mundial, arrested the strike leaders, and threatened to shoot all strikers. The constitution's promise of free education was ignored: There were fewer children in school than before. Only in Carranza's foreign policy, marked by a genuine revolutionary nationalism, did the spirit of the constitution live. Carranza staunchly resisted American pressure to give guarantees that Article 27 of the constitution would not be implemented against foreign interests. He also kept Mexico neutral in World War I and insisted on an independent Mexican diplomatic position in the hemisphere—postures that the United States regarded as unfriendly.

Meanwhile, Carranza continued to battle the tenacious Zapatista movement in the south and Villa in the north. Against the Zapatistas, Carranza's favorite general, Pablo González, launched campaign after campaign. Zapata's forces diminished and the territory under his control shrank to the vanishing point, but he remained unconquerable, supported by the affection and loyalty of the peasantry. His fall came through treachery. Invited to confer with a Carrancista officer who claimed to have gone over to his side, Zapata was ambushed and slain on April 10, 1919. But his people continued their struggle for *tierra y libertad* (land and liberty).

Carranza's legal term was due to end in 1920, but the president had no intention of relinquishing power. Barred from running again by the constitutional rule of no re-election, he picked as his successor the ambassador to Washington, Ignacio Bonillas, generally regarded as a nonentity. Meanwhile, Obregón, supported by a Labor party formed to further his interests, announced his candidacy for the presidency. As the campaign proceeded, it became clear that Carranza intended to manipulate the electoral machinery to impose Bonillas on the nation. In April 1920, Obregón and the governor of Sonora, Adolfo de la Huerta, issued a call for the removal of Carranza and the appointment of a provisional government until an election could be held. The swift triumph of the revolt revealed the depth of the unpopularity of the distant, aloof Carranza and his policies. In May 1920, Carranza fled from the capital toward Veracruz, taking with him 5 million pesos in gold and silver from the national treasury. On the night of May 21, the mountain village in which he slept was attacked by local guerrillas, and Carranza was slain.

On May 24, Adolfo de la Huerta, the chief of the Liberal Constitionalist Army, was chosen president at a special session of Congress. He promptly scheduled a presidential election for September 5, with the candidacy and victory of Alvaro Obregón a certain outcome. Under the interim president, pacification was the order of the day. The Zapatistas, who had joined the uprising against Carranza, obtained confirmation of the agrarian reform for which they had so long fought. Villa, who also aided the anti-Carranza movement, was rewarded with a ha-cienda, and other lands were given to his men. Speaking to an American journalist, this complex, contradictory figure summed up the meaning of his ten-year struggle: "I have a principle: I fought . . . so that poor men could live like human beings, have their own land, send their children to school and have human freedom." Villa did not long enjoy his newfound peace and prosperity; he was assassinated in the summer of 1923 under obscure circumstances.

In November 1920, Alvaro Obregón assumed the presidency. At last, peace had come to Mexico, and the work of reconstruction could begin. It would not be an easy task. The great wind that swept Mexico had left a devastated land, with hundreds of thousands dead or missing; the Mexican population had actually declined by 1 million since 1910. The constitution of 1917 offered a blueprint for a new and better social order, but major obstacles to change remained. Not the least were the hundreds of generals thrown up by the great upheaval, men of humble origins who once had nothing and now had an incurable itch for wealth and power. With his characteristic wry humor, Obregón summed up the problem when he said that the days of revolutionary banditry had ended because he had brought all the bandits with him to the capital to keep them out of trouble.

RECONSTRUCTION: THE RULE OF THE MILLIONAIRE SOCIALISTS

Obregón and Reform

With Obregón there came to power a group of northern generals and politicians who began the work of economic and social reconstruction that Madero, Huerta, and Carranza were unable or unwilling to achieve. Of middle-class or even lower-class origins—Obregón had been a mechanic and farmer, his successor Calles, a schoolteacher—products of a border region where American cultural influence was strong, where capitalism and capitalist relations were more highly developed than in any other part of Mexico, theirs was a pragmatic business mentality as far removed from the revolutionary agrarian ideology of Zapata as it was from the aristocratic reformism of Carranza. Quite deliberately, these men set out to lay the economic, political, and ideological foundations of a Mexican national capitalism. Their agrarian, labor, and educational reforms were directed to that end.

Aware that the revolution had radicalized the masses, aware of the appeal of socialism and anti-imperialism to the workers on whose support they counted, Obregón, Calles, and the men about them employed a revolutionary rhetoric designed to mobilize popular support and conceal how modest were the social changes that actually took place. In practice, the Obregonian program was revolutionary only by contrast with the reactionary trend that characterized the last years of Carranza's rule. Far from promoting socialism, Obregón sought accommodation with all elements of Mexican society except the most reactionary clergy and landlords. He allowed exiles of the most varied political tendency to return to Mexico, and radical intellectuals rubbed shoulders with former Científicos in his government. Power was held by a ruling class of wealthy generals, capitalists, and landlords; elections remained a farce; the president was a dictator who kept power by playing regional warlords and various factions against one another. Labor and the peasantry were the government's obedient clienteles, represented by a Labor party and an Agrarian party whose leaders formed part of the establishment and mediated between their clienteles and the all-powerful president.

Regarding agrarian reform as a useful safety valve for peasant discontent, Obregón distributed some land to the pueblos. But the process

proceeded slowly, haltingly, against the intense opposition of the hacendados and the church, which condemned the agrarian reform because it did not take account of the "just rights of the landlords." Litigation by landlords, their use of armed force to resist occupation of expropriated land, and the opposition of the clergy, who threatened peasants who accepted land with the wrath of God, slowed down the pace of the land reform.

Even after a village had received land, its prospect for success was poor, for the government failed to provide the peasants with seeds, implements, and adequate credit facilities or scientific training. Such credit assistance as they received usually came from government rural banks, which exercised close control over land use, intensifying the client status of the peasantry, or from rural loan sharks. The Obregón land reform was neither swift nor thoroughgoing; by the end of his presidency, only some 3 million acres had been distributed among 624 villages, while 320 million acres remained in private hands, chiefly those of a few thousand wealthy hacendados.

Obregón also encouraged labor to organize, for he regarded trade unions as useful for stabilizing labor-capitalist relations and as an important bulwark of his regime. The principal trade union organization was the *Confederación Regional Obrera Mexicana* (CROM), formed in 1918. Despite the rhetoric of its leaders about "class struggle" and freedom from the "tyranny of capitalism," CROM was about as radical as the American Federation of Labor, with which it maintained close ties. Its perpetual boss was Luis Morones, a former electrical worker who rose to become an important politician and ally of Obregón and became known for his flashy dress, diamonds, and limousines. As the only labor organization sponsored and protected by the government, CROM had virtually official status. Boards of arbitration representing labor, capital, and government, with the deciding vote cast by the government representative, invariably found CROM strikes legal and those of its rivals illegal. Despite this official protection, Morones's method of personal negotiation with employers yielded scanty benefits to labor; wages barely kept pace with the rising cost of living.

Perhaps the most solid achievements of the Obregón regime were in the areas of education and culture. The creation of a native Mexican capitalism demanded the development of a national consciousness, which meant the integration of the Indian masses—still forming so many small nations—into the national market and the new society. From this point of view, the Indians were the key problem of Mexican reconstruction. Because incorporating them into the modern world required a thorough understanding of the Indians' past and their present conditions of life, the revolutionary regimes encouraged the scientific study of the Indians. Under Obregón, Manuel Gamio, appointed director of the first government office of anthropology in the Americas in 1917, fused the methods and goals of archaeology and applied anthropology in his famous pilot study of Teotihuacán. Gamio sought not only to preserve and restore a precious cultural heritage but to amass the data needed for a sound plan of economic and social recovery for this area.

An integral part of the new cult of *indigenismo* was a reassessment of the Indian cultural heritage that the arbiters of artistic taste under the Porfiriato had regarded with scorn. To insist on the greatness of the old Indian arts was one way of asserting the value of one's own, of revolting against the tyranny of the pallid, lifeless French and Spanish academicism over Mexican art during the last decades of the Diáz era.

From Europe returned two future giants of the Mexican artistic renaissance, Diego Rivera and David Alfaro Siqueiros, to join another gifted artist, José Clemente Orozco, in creating a militant new art that drew much of its inspiration from the Indians and their ancient art. Believing

Cuauhtemoc, as painted by David Alfaro Siqueiros—an imaginary portrait of the last Aztec king. (Collection of Dr. Alvar Carrillo Gil, Mexico D. F.)

that "a heroic art could fortify the will to reconstruction," Obregón's brilliant young secretary of education, José Vasconcelos, offered the walls of public buildings for the painting of murals that glorified the Indians, past and present.

The Indianist cult had great political significance. The foes of the revolution, unregenerate Porfiristas, clericals, and reactionaries of all stripes, looked back to Spain as the sole source of enduring values in Mexican life and regarded Cortés as the creator of Mexican nationality; partisans of the revolution tended to idealize Aztec Mexico (sometimes beyond recognition) and elevated the last Aztec warrior-king, Cuauhtemoc, to the status of a demigod.

Convinced that the school was the most important instrument for unifying the nation, that "to educate was to redeem," Vasconcelos, with ample budgetary support from Obregón, launched an imaginative program of cultural missions designed to bring literacy and health to primitive Indian villages. Hundreds of young, idealistic teachers went out to bring the gospel of sanitation and literacy to remote pueblos. Vasconcelos also founded teacher-training colleges, agricultural schools, and other specialized schools. An achievement in which he took special pride was the publication of hundreds of classic works in cheap editions for free distribution in the schools.

The new secular, nationalist school, with its Deweyite stress on preparing the child for life and on struggle against superstition and fanaticism, provoked clerical anger, for it threatened to replace the priest with the teacher as the guiding force of the Indian community and to substitute the religious world outlook taught by the Catholic church with a scientific world outlook. The church fought back with all the means at its disposal. Some priests denounced secular education from their pulpits and threatened parents who sent their children to state schools with excommunication. As a result of this campaign, many teachers were attacked and some killed by fanatical villagers. Despite this campaign, Obregón made no effort to implement Article 3 of the constitution, which banned religious primary schools, for he believed that in the absence of enough resources on the part of the state it was better that Mexican children receive instruction from priests rather than remain illiterate.

The Catholic issue joined with other issues to cause Obregón difficulties in his relations with the United States. For three years, the United States government withheld diplomatic recognition from Obregón in an effort to force him to recognize that Article 27 of the constitution should not apply to mineral concessions obtained by foreigners before 1917. Like Carranza, Obregón was willing to respect the principle of nonretroactivity but refused to formalize it in a treaty, which he considered humiliating.

However, in 1923, with a growing threat of a counterrevolutionary coup to prevent the victory of Obregón's hand-picked successor, Plutarco Elías Calles, Obregón decided to compromise; for its part, the Harding administration adopted more flexible tactics. Mexican diplomats signed the Bucareli Agreement (not a formal treaty), which confirmed that Article 27 was not retroactive, and agreed to pay compensation for damages to American property during the revolution. The United States promptly extended formal recognition to Obregón in August 1923. When the expected revolt broke out in December 1923, the United States allowed Obregón to procure large quantities of war materiel. Together with the help of the organized labor and peasant movements, this aid enabled Obregón to crush the uprising, which was supported by reactionary landowners, clergy, and military. On November 30, 1924, Calles assumed the presidency of Mexico.

Calles's Regime

In and out of office, as legal president or de facto dictator, Calles dominated the next decade of Mexican politics. Building on the foundations Obregón had laid, he continued his work with much the same methods. His radical phraseology tended to conceal the pragmatic essence of his policy, which was to promote the rapid growth of Mexican national capitalism, whose infrastructure he helped to establish. To strengthen the fiscal and monetary system he created the Bank of Mexico, the only bank permitted to issue money. A national road commission was organized, and a national electricity code was enacted to aid the electric power industry. These measures stimulated the growth of construction and consumer goods industries, in which members of Calles's official family—or the "revolutionary family," as the ruling elite came to be called—were heavily involved. Protective tariffs, subsidies, and other forms of aid were generously extended to industry, both foreign and domestic. In 1925 an assembly plant of the Ford Motor Company began operations in Mexico after Calles and the company negotiated an agreement providing for concessions in freight rates, custom duties, and taxes; the company also received assurances that there would be no problems with labor.

Calles showed more enthusiasm for land reform than Obregón, and the tempo of land distribution increased sharply during his presidency. Like Obregón, Calles regarded land reform as a safety valve for peasant unrest. "It is my ambition," he declared, "to see the peasants own the land on which they work. For to make every peasant a proprietor is the best way of avoiding revolution and political unrest." During the four years of his term, Calles distributed about twice as much land as Obregón; by 1930 over four thousand villages with a population of about 2 million people had received more than 8 million hectares of lands.

But of that amount less than 2 million hectares consisted of arable land, for Calles did not require the hacendados to surrender productive land, and most of the land given up came from pasture or forest lands, or even land that was completely barren. Nor did Calles make a serious effort to provide the peasantry with irrigation, fertilizer, implements, or seed. He established a government bank that was supposed to lend money to the ejidos, promote modern farming techniques, and act as agents for the sale of their produce. But four-fifths of the bank's resources were loaned not to ejidos but to hacendados with much superior credit ratings, and many of the bank's agents took advantage of their position to enrich themselves at the expense of the peasants.

Under these conditions, it is no wonder that the land reform soon appeared to be a failure. By 1930 grain production had fallen below the levels of 1910, and Calles, concluding that peas-

ant proprietorship was economically undesirable, announced the abandonment of land distribution. Meanwhile, on his own large estates Calles introduced machinery and other modern agricultural techniques and advised other large landowners to do the same.

Like Obregón, Calles regarded labor unions as desirable because they helped to stabilize labor–capitalist relations and avert radical social change. In 1927 he declared that trade unions served a twofold purpose: "They keep the growing power of capitalism in check, on the one hand; and serve as a barricade in the event of an attack being launched on the capitalist ranks, on the other hand. The trade unions stand or fall with capitalism." Luis Morones, the flamboyant boss of CROM, made similar statements. By the end of the *Callista* decade, however, Mexican labor, disillusioned with a corrupt leadership that kept wages at or below the subsistence level, had begun to break away from CROM and form independent unions.

Calles continued the Carranza and Obregón policies of asserting Mexico's right to regulate the conditions under which foreign capital could exploit its natural resources, but he was far from hostile to foreign capital. Indeed, he stressed that there could be "no rapid development of the material factors of life and the standards of living without foreign capital to develop natural resources" and gave assurances that "the government will do everything in its power to safeguard the interests of foreign capitalists who invest money in Mexico."

However, a serious dispute with the United States arose in 1925 when the Mexican Congress passed laws to implement Article 27 of the constitution. The most important of these measures required owners of oil leases to exchange their titles for fifty-year concessions dating from the time of acquisition, to be followed, if necessary, by a thirty-year renewal, with the possibility of yet another extension if needed. No Mexican oil well had ever lasted more than eighty years. Far from injuring the foreign oil companies, the law eliminated the vagueness of their status under Article 27, gave them firm titles emanating from the government, and served to quiet more radical demands for outright nationalization. However, a number of American oil companies denounced the law as confiscatory and threatened to continue drilling operations without confirmatory concessions, in defiance of the Mexican government.

The State Department vigorously protested the restrictive legislation, and the American ambassador, James R. Sheffield, who complained that "there is very little white blood" in Calles's cabinet, pursued a hard-line, uncompromising policy. By late 1926 the United States appeared to be moving toward war with Mexico. Secretary of State Frank Kellogg contributed to the war talk by sending the Senate a memorandum on "Bolshevik aims in Mexico and Latin America."

Fortunately, the interventionist policy came under severe attack from Progressive Republican senators like William Borah of Idaho, George Norris of Nebraska, and Robert La Follette of Wisconsin and from the press, church groups, and the academic world. President Coolidge and Kellogg, realizing that war with Mexico would have little national support, sought a way out of the impasse; they were aided by American international bankers, who had a clearer understanding of Mexican policies and intentions. The appointment of Dwight Morrow, a partner in the financial firm of J. P. Morgan, as ambassador to Mexico in September 1927 marked a turning point in the crisis. Morrow managed to persuade Calles that portions of the oil law had the potential for injuring foreign property rights, with the result that the Mexican Supreme Court found unconstitutional that portion of the law setting a time period on concessions. As rewritten, however, the law still provided for confirmatory concessions and reaffirmed national ownership of the subsoil.

In addition, a serious domestic dispute arose as a result of the growing opposition of the church to the whole modernizing thrust of the revolution as embodied in the constitution of 1917. Under Calles, this opposition assumed the proportions of a civil war. In January 1926, the church hierarchy signed a letter declaring that the constitution of 1917 "wounds the most sacred rights of the Catholic Church" and disavowed the document. Calles responded by enforcing the anticlerical clauses of the constitution, which had lain dormant. The Calles Law, as it was called, ordered the registration of priests with the civil authorities and the closing of religious primary schools. The church struck back by suspending church services throughout Mexico, a powerful weapon in a country so overwhelmingly Catholic.

But neither this strike nor the boycott organized by the church, which urged the faithful to buy no goods or services except absolute necessities, brought the government to its knees. By the end of 1926, militant Catholics, in frequent alliance with local hacendados, had taken to arms. Guerrilla groups were formed, with the mountainous backcountry of Jalisco the principal focus of their activity. Government schools and young teachers sent into remote areas were frequent objects of clerical fury; many teachers were tortured and killed. The total number of Catholic guerrillas, known as *Cristeros* from their slogan, *Viva Cristo Rey* (Long Live Christ the King), was small, but federal commanders helped to keep the insurrection alive by the brutality of their repressions, often accompanied by systematic looting of the affected regions. By the summer of 1927, however, the revolt had largely burned itself out, and Calles could turn his attention to the forthcoming presidential election in July 1928.

In an apparent deal between Calles and Obregón, the latter's supporters in Congress amended the constitution to allow a former president to be re-elected after one term, and the presidential term was extended from four to six years. The plan was for Obregón to succeed Calles and Calles to succeed Obregón. Angered by this arrangement, two frustrated presidential hopefuls, General Francisco Serrano and Arnulfo Gómez, began to conspire against Obregón and Calles. Calles acted decisively; the plotters were seized and shot, and Obregón remained the only candidate. In July, Obregón was duly elected, but three weeks later a fanatical Cristero assassinated him in a Mexico City restaurant.

With the passing of the formidable Obregón, Calles became the *jefe máximo,* the maximum chief of the revolution. The presidents who successively held office during what was to have been Obregón's six-year term—Emilio Portes Gil, Pascual Ortiz Rubio, and Abelardo Rodríguez—were Calles's stooges and obediently resigned when they incurred his displeasure. In 1929, after crushing a rebellion that proved to be almost the last hurrah of the regional military caudillos, Calles organized the National Revolutionary party (PNR) as an instrument for pacifying the country and institutionalizing the rule of the "revolutionary family," the military leaders and politicians who had ruled the country since 1920.

The PNR was an amalgam of local political machines. Calles managed to make the generals see that only the creation of a political party that would represent their interests and mediate their conflicts could avoid further rebellions and assure their joint political control of Mexico. Their growing wealth—four of the top generals of Mexico between 1929 and 1935 were millionaires—made the prospect of an enduring peace more attractive to them. Under different names and with leaderships of differing composition, the party formed by Calles has been the ruling party of Mexico since 1929. The official party's candidates for president have never lost an election.

As the "revolutionary family" consolidated its power and its wealth increased, its members became more conservative. Their humble beginnings disposed the revolutionary generals to become even more corrupt and predatory than the old Porfirista aristocracy. "You want

us to have the honesty of angels?" says a former general in Carlos Fuentes's novel *Where the Air Is Clear.* "Because we were born in dirt-floored shacks we have the right to live in mansions with high ceilings and stone walls, with a Rolls-Royce at the door." As large landowners, they were naturally hostile to agrarian reform; as owners of construction firms and factories, they were naturally hostile to strikes and unions.

Calles and his cronies had never been committed to a radical reconstruction of Mexican society. After 1928, however, they retreated from their own modest reform program. To camouflage their shift to the right and validate their revolutionary credentials they indulged freely in anticlerical demagoguery and excesses. Their acts blew new life into the dying Cristero movement, causing a brief but bitter new conflict that took many lives.

This rightward shift of the Callista regime coincided with the beginning in 1929 of the Great Depression, which exposed the bankruptcy of capitalist economics and added to the misery of Mexican peasants and workers. Their growing unrest created fears of a new revolutionary explosion. Rumblings of protest were heard even within the ruling party. A new generation of young, middle-class reformers demanded vigorous implementation of the Constitution of 1917. Some were intellectuals influenced by Marxism and the success of the Soviet example, especially by its concept of economic planning, but their basic message was the need to resume the struggle against the latifundio, peonage, and economic and cultural backwardness, that is, to resume the advance of the bourgeois revolution, stalled by the corruption, cynicism, and conservatism of the Callistas.

By 1933 the growing influence of the progressive wing within the PNR had led to a partial reform of the agrarian laws that transferred land distribution from the states to the federal government and to the beginnings of a school reform under the direction of the brilliant

Narciso Bassols during his brief tenure as secretary of education under Abelardo Rodríguez.

The acknowledged leader of the reform group within the PNR was General Lázaro Cárdenas, governor of Michoacán. As governor, Cárdenas had established an enviable record for honesty, compassion, and concern for the common man. He had spent almost 50 percent of his budget on education, doubling the number of schools in the state. Despite his progessive ideas, he was close to the inner circle of the "revolutionary family," and the jefe máximo regarded him as a loyal lieutenant. In October 1930, he was chosen chairman of the PNR, a post that made him one of its most powerful figures.

The 1934 presidential elections approached. Aware of the growing strength of the left wing in the PNR, Calles decided to make concessions to the reformers that would leave him in control of the government. With Calles's blessing, Cárdenas was nominated for president at the PNR convention in December 1933. With Calles's approval, the convention also drafted a Six-Year Plan (in obvious imitation of the Soviet model) that would give life to the ideals and promises of the constitution of 1917. Although there was no doubt that he would be elected, Cárdenas campaigned vigorously, visiting the most remote areas of the country, patiently explaining to workers and peasants the Six-Year Plan and the need to strengthen the ejidos, build modern schools, and develop workers' cooperatives. In July 1934, he was elected and took office in November with a cabinet hand-picked for him by Calles. The jefe máximo was confident that the loyal Cárdenas would carry out his orders as the puppet presidents who preceded him had done.

THE YEARS OF CÁRDENAS

Under Cárdenas, the Mexican Revolution resumed its advance. Land distribution to the villages on a massive scale was accompanied by a many-sided effort to raise agricultural productivity and improve the quality of rural life. In addition, labor was encouraged to replace the old, corrupt leadership with militant leaders and to struggle for improved conditions. A spirit of service began to pervade at least a part of the governmental bureaucracy. Cárdenas set an example to subordinates by the democratic simplicity of his manners, by cutting his own salary in half, and by making himself available to the delegations of Indians and workers who thronged the waiting rooms of the National Palace.

These and other policies of the new president—such as the closing down of illegal gambling houses, most of which were owned by wealthy Callistas—angered the jefe máximo, who began to make threatening noises. In June 1935, Calles summoned a number of senators to Cuernavaca, denounced the labor movement and its alleged radicalism, and ominously recalled the brief tenure of President Ortiz Rubio. Cárdenas responded by requesting the resignation of all his cabinet members; then he proceeded to form a new cabinet dominated by the left wing but representing a broad coalition of anti-Callista elements, from right to left. There followed a purge of reactionary state governors, acclaimed by peasants' and workers' demonstrations. By the end of 1935, Cárdenas was the undisputed master of Mexico. In April 1936, amid indications that Calles was planning a coup with the aid of a fascist organization, the Gold Shirts, and other reactionary groups, Cárdenas ordered his immediate deportation to the United States.

Land Reform

Having consolidated his political control, Cárdenas proceeded to implement his reform program. Land distribution he regarded as being of prime importance. Land was distributed to the peasantry in a variety of ways, according to the climatic and soil conditions of the different regions. The principal form was the ejido, the communal landholding system under which land could not be mortgaged or alienated (except under very special conditions), with each *ejidatario* entitled to use a parcel of community land. The ejido was the focal point of the agrarian reform. But Cárdenas also distributed land in the form of the *rancho*, the individual small holding widely prevalent in the northern Mexican states. Finally, in regions where natural conditions favored large-scale cultivation of such commercial crops as sugar, cotton, coffee, rice, and henequen, large cooperative farms (collective ejidos) were organized on a profit-sharing basis. The first experiment in collective farming was made in the cotton-growing Laguna district in Coahuila and Durango, an area with unusually fertile soil. The government generously endowed these enterprises with seeds, machinery, and credit from the *Banco de Crédito Ejidal*.

During the Cárdenas years, some 45 million acres of land were distributed to almost twelve thousand villages. The Cárdenas distribution program struck a heavy blow at the traditional, semifeudal hacienda and peonage, satisfied the land hunger of the Mexican peasantry for the time being, and promoted a general modernization of Mexican life and society. By 1940, thanks to the land reform, supplemented by the provision of villages with schools, medical care, roads, and other facilities, the standard of living of the peasantry had risen, if only modestly. These progressive changes in turn contributed to the growth of the internal market and therefore of Mexican industry. The land reform also justified itself in terms of productivity; average agricultural production during the three-year period from 1939 to 1941 was higher than it had been at any time since the beginning of the revolution.

Granted these benefits and Cárdenas's excellent intentions, the fact remains that the land reform suffered from the first from certain structural defects. To begin with, it was basically conceived as a means of satisfying land hunger rather than as an instrument of dynamic agricultural development. Seeking to satisfy land hunger by the grant or restitution of land to the villages, government agencies overlooked the need to establish agricultural units that would be viable from an economic point of view. In many cases, the *ejidal* parcel, especially in areas of very dense population, was so small as to form a minifundio. Much of the distributed land was of poor quality (the agrarian law always allowed the landowner to retain a portion of his estate, and naturally he kept the best portion for himself), and aid in the form of seeds, technical assistance, and credit was frequently inadequate (the collective ejidos fared better in this respect).

In addition, the peasant received his land from the government and was tied to it through the operations of the *Departamiento Agrario*, the Banco de Crédito Ejidal, and the officially organized Peasant Leagues; thus, he was increasingly dependent on the public authorities. Under Cárdenas, officials of these agencies often worked in a spirit of disinterested service and sought to develop peasant collective initiative and democracy; under his successors in the presidency, they tended to become corrupt and self-seeking, to enmesh the peasantry and its organizations in a bureaucratic network that manipulated them to satisfy its own interests. After 1940, moreover, Mexican governments increasingly favored the large private property and neglected the ejido. In concert with the structural defects of the land reform, this tendency produced a gradual decline of the ejido system and a parallel growth of the large landed property, leading to the emergence of a new latifundio.

Labor Reform

Under Cárdenas, the labor movement was revitalized. Aware of the sympathetic attitude of the new regime, workers struck in unprecedented numbers for higher wages and better working conditions; in 1935 there were 642 strikes, more than twice the number in the preceding six years. In 1936 the young radical intellectual Vicente Lombardo Toledano organized a new labor federation, the *Confederación de Trabajadores Mexicanos* (CTM), to replace the dying and discredited CROM. Labor supported and in turn was supported by the Cárdenas government.

Labor, the peasantry, and the army became the three main pillars of the official party, reorganized in 1938 and renamed the Party of the Mexican Revolution (PRM). The power of the generals was weakened by a policy of raising wages and improving the morale of the rank and file and by the distribution of weapons to the peasantry, formed into a militia. The last important regional caudillo, General Saturnino Cedillo of San Luis Potosí, a foe of Cárdenas's agrarian policy who was linked to the fascist Gold Shirts, launched a revolt in 1938. It was promptly smashed, and Cedillo was killed in a skirmish with federal troops.

Like the land reform, the labor reform had structural flaws that created serious problems for the future. In return for concessions from a paternal government, labor, like the peasantry, was invited to incorporate itself into the official apparatus and to give automatic and obligatory support to a government that in the last analysis represented the interests of the national bourgeoisie. In the domestic and international situation of the 1930s, which was dominated by a struggle between profascist and antifascist forces, the interests of that bourgeoisie and Mexican labor largely coincided, but in the changed conditions after 1940, labor's loss of independence and the meshing of its organizations with the official apparatus led to a revival of corruption and reactionary control of the trade unions.

Economic Reform

Although Cárdenas was sympathetic to labor's demands for better conditions, he was no foe of private enterprise, despite efforts by his foes to link him to socialism and communism. As Cárdenas himself asserted emphatically, "No one can show me a single line in which I proclaimed that communism was my doctrine or inspired my policies." In fact, industrial capitalism made significant strides under Cárdenas. If Cárdenas supported labor's efforts to raise wages where the financial condition of an enterpise warranted it, he also favored Mexican industry with government loans and protective tariffs that insured the creation of a captive market for high-priced consumer goods. In 1934 the Cárdenas government established the *Nacional Financiera,* a government bank and investment corporation that used funds supplied by the federal government and domestic investors to make industrial loans, finance public welfare projects, and issue its own securities. The coming of World War II, which sharply reduced the availability of imports, greatly stimulated the movement toward industrialization and import substitution.

Mexico's struggle for economic sovereignty reached a high point under Cárdenas. In 1937 a dispute between American and British oil companies and the unions erupted into a strike, followed by legal battles between the contending parties. When the oil companies refused to accept a much-scaled-down arbitration-tribunal wage finding in favor of the workers, Cárdenas intervened. On March 18, 1938—a date celebrated by Mexicans as marking their declaration of economic independence—the president announced in a radio speech that the properties of the oil companies had been expropriated in the public interest. With support from virtually all strata of the population, Cárdenas was able to ride out the storm caused by economic sanctions against Mexico on the part of the United States, England, and the oil companies. The oil nationalization was a major victory for Mexican nationalism. It provided cheap, plentiful fuel for Mexican industry, and the needs of the nationalized oil industries further stimulated industrialization. But the oil nationalization did not set a precedent; some 90 percent of Mexico's mining industry remained in foreign hands.

The Cárdenas government gave firm support to governments resisting the advance of fascism. Mexico and the Soviet Union were the only countries to give significant amounts of aid to the Spanish Republicans during the civil war of 1936–1939. After the Fascist victory, Mexico opened its doors to Loyalist refugees, including many talented professionals who made a significant contribution to Mexican culture and economic life. It steadfastly refused to recognize the legality of the Franco regime.

Cárdenas's Growing Moderation and the Election of 1940

Education, especially the rural school system, made considerable progress under Cárdenas, but in the last years of his presidency, in apparent deference to clerical and conservative opposition, he soft-pedaled the so-called socialist character of Mexican education. Himself a Tarascan Indian, Cárdenas also displayed much concern for Indian welfare. He created a *Departamiento de Asuntos Indígenas* to serve and protect Indian interests and encouraged the study of Indian culture, past and present, by founding the *Instituto Nacional de Antropología de México*. Under Cárdenas, Mexico played host to the congress that established the *Instituto Indigenista Interamericano* (1940), which was directed by Manuel Gamio until his death.

Right-wing opposition to Cárdenas's progressive policies grew in the closing years of his presidency. Reactionary groups encouraged and financed by German agents and the Spanish fascist Falange attacked the regime for its supposed communist tendencies. In apparent response to conservative pressure, Cárdenas slowed down the pace of land distribution during the last years of his presidency and displayed a conciliatory attitude toward the entrepreneurial class, assuring its members that he regarded them as part of the *fuerzas vivas* (vital forces) of the country and that they need not fear the safety of their investments.

On the eve of the presidential election of 1940, right-wingers organized a campaign in favor of General Juan Andreu Almazán, a veteran revolutionary who was now a wealthy industrialist of Monterrey. The left wing of the PRM advanced the candidacy of General Francisco Múgica, author of some of the most advanced provisions of the constitution of 1917 and Cárdenas's close friend and mentor. No man was better qualified to carry out the promises of the second Six-Year Plan, which proposed to continue the rapid pace of agrarian reform; provide the ejidos with cheap credit, irrigation, and roads; and intensify collectivization of ejidos. But the official party was an amalgam of social forces, including increasingly conservative and influential industrialists. Evidently fearing that the nomination of the radical Múgica would be a signal for a rightist revolt, Cárdenas gave him no support, and he soon withdrew his candidacy. Another radical candidate, the labor leader Vicente Lombardo Toledano, also withdrew in the interests of unity. Supported by the powerful CTM, the party gave its nomination to General Manuel Ávila Camacho, who was loyal to Cárdenas but a devout Catholic and a man of generally conservative views; he was elected with almost 99 percent of the vote.

The defeated Almazán fled to Texas, proclaiming fraud. For a time, it seemed that a revolt would break out, but Almazán soon returned to Mexico and private life. Meanwhile, Ávila Camacho was making statements designed to reassure foreign and domestic capital. He dissociated himself from the radical leadership of the unions, expressed a flexible attitude toward the question of whether the ejido or the small private property was the best form of agrarian organization, and assured the Catholics that he was a *creyente* (believer). In December 1940, Ávila Camacho assumed the presidency without any serious disturbances.

THE BIG BOURGEOISIE IN POWER, 1940–1976

Erosion of Reform

The Cárdenas era was the high-water mark of the struggle to achieve the social goals of the revolution. Under his successors, there began an erosion of the social conquests of the Cárdenas years. During those years, the material and cultural condition of the masses had improved, if only modestly; peasants and workers managed to secure a somewhat larger share of the total national income. After 1940 these trends were reversed. The new rulers of Mexico favored a development strategy that sharply restricted trade union activity, slowed the tempo of agrarian reform, and reduced the relative share of total income of the bottom two-thirds of the Mexican population.

Ávila Camacho presided over the first phase (1940–1946) of this reversal of policy. Regarding unlimited private profit as the driving force of economic progress, he proposed to create a favorable climate for private enterprise. In practice, this meant the freezing of wages, the repression of strikes, and the use of a new weapon against dissidents in the form of a vaguely worded law dealing with the "crime of social dissolution."

Meanwhile, World War II stimulated both the export of Mexican raw materials and import substitution through industrialization. Significant advances were made in food processing, textiles, and other consumer goods industries, and the capital goods industry, centering in the north, was considerably expanded. Steel production increased, with Monterrey Steel and other companies producing structural and rolled steel for buildings, hotels, highways, and steel hardware. The Nacional Financiera played a leading role in this process of growth through loans to industry for plant construction and expansion. In view of this spontaneous economic growth, the concept of planning was forgotten; the second Six-Year Plan remained on paper. Indeed, a characteristic of the economic expansion was its unplanned character. No effort was made to produce a balanced development of the Mexican regions; most of the development took place in the Federal District and the surrounding area. Meanwhile, land distribution was sharply reduced, and a conservative spirit began to pervade the educational system.

In 1946 the official party changed its name from PRM to the PRI (Partido Revolucionario Institucional), and Ávila Camacho was succeeded as president by the lawyer Miguel Alemán (1946–1952). Alemán continued the policies of his predecessor. He made every effort to encourage private investment through tariff protection, import licensing, subsidies, and government loans. A rapid rate of inflation, while wages were virtually frozen by official repression of strikes, supported by corrupt labor leaders, naturally encouraged investment. These policies produced the desired results; during the period from 1940 to 1950, real wages fell in both agricultural and nonagricultural activities, while the real incomes of entrepreneurs rose swiftly. This favorable economic climate attracted not only domestic but foreign investors looking for outlets for their surplus capital after World War II. A characteristic of the new foreign capital investment was that it flowed primarily into manufacturing rather than the traditional extractive industries.

Under Alemán, land distribution and efforts to increase the productivity of the ejidos were neglected in favor of the large private landholding. To provide an incentive to capitalist entrepreneurs, Alemán had Article 27 of the constitution amended. This "reform" consisted in the grant of certificates of "inaffectibility" to landowners, which exempted them from further expropriation for holdings up to 100 hectares of irrigated land or 200 hectares of land with seasonal rainfall. For the production of certain specified crops, the size of inaffectible holdings was made even larger: 150 hectares for cotton and up to 300 hectares for such crops as coffee, sugar cane, and henequen.

There was also introduced the right of *amparo* (injunction) for farmers whose property had been declared "affectible"; in the judicial climate of Mexico after 1940, the right of amparo proved an effective barrier to expropriation. A massive program of irrigation also contributed to the explosion of capitalist agriculture that began in this period. The irrigation projects were concentrated in northern and northwestern Mexico, where much of the land was owned directly or indirectly by prominent Mexican politicians, their friends, and relatives. Alemán presided over a great boom in public works construction, accompanied by an orgy of plunder of the public treasury by entrepreneurs and officials; his was probably the most corrupt administration in recent Mexican history.

Alemán's successor, Adolfo Ruiz Cortines (1952–1958), had to cope with a financial crisis brought on by Alemán's extravagant fiscal policies and the recession imported from the United States. He responded by reducing public spending, which caused a further contraction of the economy. Faced with a steadily deteriorating balance of trade, his administration decided to devaluate the peso in 1954, setting its exchange value at 12.50 to the dollar.

In general, Ruiz Cortines's economic and social policies resembled those of his predecessors. The pace of land distribution was further reduced, and the ejidos suffered a neglect that contributed to the low productivity for which they were criticized. Irrigation works continued to be concentrated in areas dominated by large private landholdings.

Thanks to the new laws of "inaffectibility" and the varied ruses employed by large landowners to violate the agrarian laws, concentration of landownership continued to grow. There arose a new hacienda, technically efficient and often arrayed in modern corporate guise, that soon accounted for the bulk of Mexico's commercial agricultural production and shared its profits with processing plants that were usu-

ally subsidiaries of foreign firms. By 1961, fifty years after the revolution began, less than 1 percent of all farms possessed 50 percent of all agricultural land. Meanwhile, increasing numbers of small landholders, starved for credit and lacking machinery, had to abandon their parcels of land and become peons on the new haciendas or emigrate to the cities in search of work in the new factories.

Industry continued to grow but was increasingly penetrated and dominated by foreign capital. Direct foreign investments, averaging $26 million a year in the 1940s, rose to an average of $102 million a year in the 1950s. A favorite device for foreign penetration of Mexican industry was the mixed, or joint, company, which had a number of advantages. It satisfied the requirement of Mexican law that Mexican nationals hold 51 percent of most companies operating in Mexico; it camouflaged actual domination of such enterprises by the foreign partners through control of patents, licensing agreements, and other sources of technological and financial dependence; and it formed strong ties between foreign capitalists and the native industrial and financial bourgeoisie.

President Adolfo López Mateos (1958–1964) declared early in his administration that he belonged to the "extreme left within the Constitution," but his social and economic policies did not differ significantly from those of his predecessors. To allay mounting unrest among landless peasants who began to seize uncultivated hacienda lands in different parts of the country, he distributed a large amount of land, but most of it was of inferior quality. He continued the repressive labor policies of his predecessors; thus, he broke a general railroad strike with federal troops and had its leaders arrested and jailed for years. When the world-famous mural artist David Alfaro Siqueiros denounced his repressive policies, López Mateos had him charged with the crime of "social dissolution" and sent to prison for four years. More creditable to López Mateos was his initiative in commencing construction of the magnificent National Museum of Anthropology in Mexico City. An imposing complex of marble and glass, fountains and gardens, with excerpts from Aztec poems and speeches engraved on its walls, the museum opened in 1964.

The colorless, small-minded lawyer Gustavo Díaz Ordaz succeeded López Mateos as president in 1964. During his term of office (1964–1970), discontent among workers mounted as their real income shrank as a result of chronic inflation, a virtual freeze on wages, and official control of trade union organizations. Student unrest also grew in reaction to police brutality against student protestors and violations of the constitutional autonomy of the national university. The student protest broadened into a nationwide movement demanding democratization of Mexican economic and political life. The government responded with a savage assault by army troops on a peaceful assembly of students and others in the Plaza of Three Cultures in Mexico City (October 2, 1968), leaving a toll of dead and wounded running into the hundreds.

The economic strategy of the Díaz Ordaz administration, like that of his predecessors, centered on providing the greatest possible incentives to private investment, foreign and domestic. These included the traditional incentives of tariff protection, government loans, low wages, and a regressive tax system that placed the main burden on the lowest income groups, thanks to a multitude of omissions and exemptions that favored income from capital over income from labor.

The foreign debt grew alarmingly under Díaz Ordaz, with the volume of foreign loans reaching a figure four times that of the Ruiz Cortines era. By 1970 reliance on foreign borrowing to finance Mexico's public-sector investment had reached a point where amortization and interest payments on foreign loans to the Mexican government came close to 30 percent of Mexico's annual export earnings. This heavy influx of loans increased the dependent character of the Mexican economy.

In his foreign policies, however, Díaz Ordaz continued the traditional Mexican posture of diplomatic independence. Despite objections from the United States, Mexico maintained diplomatic relations with revolutionary Cuba, expressed disapproval of American intervention in Cuba (the Bay of Pigs affair), and opposed President Lyndon Johnson's intervention in the Dominican Republic. This independent foreign policy reflected both popular anti-imperialist sentiment and a striving on the part of the Mexican ruling class to achieve a partial independence from Washington.

The official presidential candidate in 1970, Luis Echeverría, took office amid deepening political, social, and economic storm clouds. Violence increased in the countryside as great landowners, aided by police and federal troops, resisted the efforts of landless peasants and agricultural workers to seize uncultivated tracts of land. Workers, faced with an annual inflation rate of about 20 percent in the 1970s, increasingly resorted to strikes and sought to replace corrupt trade union bosses linked with the government with democratically chosen leaders.

On taking office, Echeverría signaled a tactical shift when he released a large number of students and intellectuals imprisoned after the 1968 student disturbances, promised to struggle against colonialism and corruption, and condemned the unjust distribution of income in Mexico. Impressed by Echeverría's apparent commitment to reform, some of the bitterest academic critics of the regime accepted jobs in his administration—a form of co-optation of political dissenters known in Mexico since the time of Porfirio Díaz.

Echeverría's foreign policies gave some credibility to his liberal image: He hosted a visit by Marxist President Salvador Allende of Chile, opened Mexico's doors wide to Chilean refugees after the fascist seizure of power in Chile, and urged Cuba's full re-entry into the inter-American community. These actions gave Echeverría a reputation for radicalism in certain quarters, especially in the United States.

There seems little doubt that Echeverría began his administration with a genuine desire to achieve reform, to reduce dependency, to spread the fruits of development more widely, and to create a somewhat more open, democratic political system. Conservative Mexican capitalists, closely linked with foreign capital, struck back by withholding investment funds from the market, setting off a serious recession. Under intense pressure from the right, Echeverría retreated. During his last three years in office he reverted to traditional policies and methods, poorly concealed by a populist rhetoric. After an initial thaw in its dealings with labor, his government once again repressed strikes and gave full support to corrupt trade union leaders. Despite his promise to achieve a more equitable distribution of income, Echeverría rejected a progressive tax on corporate profits on the grounds that such a measure might discourage private investment. He publicly denounced colonialism and multinational corporations, but his government did its utmost to attract foreign investments, especially from the United States. With the investments came growing foreign penetration and domination of Mexican industry, especially of its most strategic sectors. By the mid-seventies, 70 percent of earnings from the capital goods industry went to foreign capital, leaving 20 percent for public firms and 10 percent for national private companies. The share of multinational enterprises in the sale of manufactured goods rose from 38 percent in 1962 to 45 percent in 1970; by 1972 they controlled half the capital in manufacturing. This meant that foreign companies had a significant degree of control over decisions with respect to Mexican development.

As the investments increased, so did Mexico's indebtedness and the drain of its capital in the form of dividends, interest, and other returns on foreign investment. In 1974, profits from foreign direct investment and payments of interest on the foreign debt came to $1,222 million; in 1975, $1,549 million; in 1976, $1,839 million. By June 1976, Mexico's foreign debt had reached $25 billion. Mexico and Brazil shared the distinction of having the highest foreign debts among Third World countries. By September of that year the growing trade deficit had forced the government to order a 60 percent devaluation of the peso, causing a sharp rise in inflation and greater hardship for the masses. The 1976 devaluation, says Peter Evans, "signaled the failure of control over inflation, which had been the hallmark of Mexico's growth in the fifties and sixties." It may be useful at this point to assess the social costs of a quarter-century of Mexican dependent development.

According to official government figures, the poorest tenth of the population in 1950 received 2.43 percent of the disposable family income; that share fell to 1.42 percent in 1970 and to 0.35 percent in 1975. The richest tenth received 45.3 percent of the disposable income in 1950; 38.8 percent in 1970; 43.4 percent in 1975. Thus its share of the national income remained remarkably stable throughout the period. Unemployment in the mid-seventies ranged between 10 and 15 percent, with another 40 percent underemployed—condemned to a marginal existence of unskilled, part-time work.

An official government publication, *Comercio Exterior*, presented this somber picture of living conditions in the countryside:

Over the course of the 25 years from 1950 to 1975, 40% of the population at the poorest end suffered a 38% drop in real income. 12 million inhabitants in the rural areas live in conditions of extreme poverty. . . . More than 20 million inhabitants in rural areas lack any health service; in 1973, almost 14 million had no running water; only 55% of children between the ages of 6 and 14 enjoyed access to basic education. . . . Malnutrition is virtually the general condition in the countryside, but it is above all the children that are most affected.

In March 1978, Dr. Adolfo Chavez of the National Nutrition Institute expressed alarm over the rising infant mortality rate in both rural and urban areas: "In some really depressed rural communities, few children born since 1974 have survived. We have what we call generational holes. But infant mortality is also growing in slum areas of the cities."

When he came to office in 1970, Echeverría promised to provide the ejidos with irrigated land and other aid; in fact, little aid was given. When he left the presidency six years later, the problem of landlessness or inadequate land and rural unemployment and underemployment remained as stubborn as ever. Some 6 million peasants were landless, but in the state of Sinaloa, to take perhaps an extreme example, fifty wealthy families possessed 300,000 hectares of the best irrigated land. Perhaps the most oppressed, miserable group in Mexican society were the Indians. Numbering some 7 to 12 million, they suffered from especially severe forms of discrimination, exploitation, and physical aggression at the hands of white and mestizo landowners, merchants, and officials. Their situation has been aptly described as "internal colonialism."

In 1976, prospects for the solution of Mexico's urgent problems through the electoral process appeared dim, at least for the near future, because the PRI, dominated by the industrial and financial oligarchy, had an unshakable grip on power. That power rested in the last analysis on a system of institutionalized coercion and fraud. Generally, when the PRI suffered defeat in local elections, either the elections were annulled for one or another technicality by an administrative tribunal, which then ordered new

elections to be held, or the elected officials were subjected to severe harassment. But fraud, force, and threat of force were not the only means used by the government and the ruling party to retain control. Other methods included the co-optation of dissidents into the state apparatus; the provision of greater access to medical services, schools, low-cost housing, and other benefits to such strategic groups as state employees, professionals, and organized workers; the paternalistic distribution of goods and services to the urban poor; and a populist rhetoric that identified the ruling party with the great ideals of the Revolution. These policies did little to reduce mass poverty or the growing inequalities of income in Mexican society, but they provided a precarious popular base and legitimacy for the PRI's monopoly of political power. By the mid-seventies, both popularity and legitimacy were threatened by rampant inflation and a stagnant economy.

At the time of the 1976 election, bleak economic conditions might have been expected to produce a major challenge to the ruling party. Discouragement on the part of other parties, however, was so great that the official party candidate, José López Portillo, ran without opposition other than that of an unregistered (that is, officially unrecognized) Communist party candidate. The PRI rolled up the usual huge majority.

López Portillo was reputed to be more conservative than Echeverría, and it seemed unlikely that his administration would break with the long-established policy of favoring the country's elites. In fact, López Portillo soon made it clear that he was opposed to further large-scale land distribution and would not touch efficiently run large estates even if their size exceeded legal limits. In the ironic words of one Mexican weekly, "the constitution is to protect peasants wearing collars and ties, and not those wearing rope sandals."

On the other hand, López Portillo, like Echeverría, appeared to recognize the need to provide a safety valve for growing political dissent and to modernize the monolithic political structure created by Calles in 1929. In October 1977, he offered a constitutional reform bill that eased the requirements for registration of minority political parties and created a system of partial proportional representation designed to insure the presence of opposition elements in Congress. Under the plan the chamber of deputies was expanded from 300 to 400 seats, with the additional seats apportioned to minority parties on the basis of their vote. Nothing in the so-called reform bill, however, threatened the PRI's control over the electoral machinery and its continued domination of the government.

FROM OIL BOOM TO BUST, 1977–1983

López Portillo took office on December 1, 1976 amid growing optimism over Mexico's economic prospects as a result of the recent discovery of vast new oil and gas deposits on Mexico's east coast. Figures for the country's estimated and proven oil reserves steadily rose; by January 1980 they were put at 200 billion barrels, and Mexico ranked among the world's major oil producers. With oil prices increasing steeply, government planners counted on the oil and gas bonanza to alleviate Mexico's balance-of-payments problem and to finance the purchase of the goods needed for further development and the creation of new jobs. The resulting expansion of production, however, was largely concentrated in capital-intensive industries— petrochemical factories, steel mills, and the like— that generated relatively few jobs. In agriculture, too, the main growth was in capital-intensive, export-oriented agribusiness operations that created little employment and diverted labor and acreage from staple food production. Indeed, staple food production actually declined during the 1970s. The acreage of maize dropped an annual average of 4.8 percent during the

decade; by 1980, one-third of the maize consumed in Mexico came from the United States. In 1979, with the oil boom under way, the output of maize and beans fell by 18 and 32 percent, respectively, and the price of tortillas nearly doubled. The rise in the cost of these staples, even in the government-controlled stores established in the countryside, reduced their consumption by a large part of the population.

The cost of the imported equipment and technology required to expand oil production came very high and had to be covered by new loans. Despite increasing revenues from oil and gas exports, Mexico's trade deficit rose from $1.4 billion in 1977 to over $2 billion in 1978, and $3 billion in 1979. Inflation again moved upward; Mexican workers lost 20 percent of their purchasing power between 1977 and 1979. Despite these troubling signs, the international bankers appeared eager to lend more, advancing Mexico $10 billion in 1980. Who could question the credit of a country that seemed to float on a sea of oil?

The oil boom and the massive infusions of foreign loans gave a new dimension to the familiar problem of corruption in Mexican political life.[1] One of its signs was a wave of monumental private construction. General Durazo, Mexico City police chief and "one of the most spectacularly corrupt men in the country," according to the French journal *Le Monde Diplomatique*, built near Acapulco a gigantic Greek palace of white marble, estimated to be worth $7 million, on land expropriated without compensation. Asked about the origins of his colossal fortune, Durazo frankly admitted that it did not come from his official salary. "If I had to live on my policeman's salary," he said, "I would already have died from hunger." Another PRI notable, Carlos Hank González, departing mayor of

---

[1] One Mexican news magazine, *Proceso*, estimated that officials of López Portillo's administration had misused or stolen $3 billion of public funds.

Mexico City, purchased a magnificent Tudor-style country-house worth $1,275,000 in New Canaan, Connecticut. And President López Portillo, a severe critic of official corruption, built palatial homes for himself and his children in the hills of Vista Hermosa, a fashionable quarter of Mexico City, leading a Communist deputy to ask the president to explain why he used federal funds for the construction of these homes.

But "the dance of the billions" was drawing to a close. In the first months of 1981, responding to weakening demand and a developing world oil glut, oil prices fell sharply. This development threw the government into confusion. When the director of Pemex (the national oil industry) cut oil prices $4 a barrel to bring them into line with world prices, he was dismissed, and the new director raised the price. When buyers cancelled contracts, the government lowered prices again; these maneuvers cost the government a loss of $6 to $7 billion in 1981. Mexico's projected earnings in 1982 from oil and gas exports, source of 75 percent of Mexico's foreign exchange, fell from $27 billion to under $14 billion. Instead of reducing expenses and the rate of growth of the economy, which had been growing at an annual rate of 8 percent, the government continued to borrow abroad and tried to maintain the overvalued peso's value against the dollar. But rising interest rates strained Mexico's ability to meet its debt obligations, and some smaller banks, skeptical of Mexico's ability to repay, refused to roll over (refinance) its short-term debts. Many wealthy Mexicans, losing confidence in their currency, hurried to buy dollars and deposit them in U.S. banks. In February 1982, with the government's foreign exchange reserves dwindling at an alarming rate, López Portillo allowed the peso to fall by 60 percent. Fear of further devaluations provoked another flight of dollars; by mid-year some $14 billion had left for the shelter of U.S. banks; another $25 billion had been invested in real estate in the United States. The growing shortage of dollars, vitally needed fuel for Mexican industry, caused a widening recession and unemployment. In April, Mexico's largest industrial conglomerate, Grupo Industrial Alfa, announced that it could not pay part of the interest on its $2.4 billion debt and soon afterward laid off 8,500 employees.

In July, Mexicans went to the polls to elect a new president. The PRI, operating with its usual efficiency, gave the official candidate, Harvard-trained economist Miguel De la Madrid, some 74 percent of the vote; the main opposition parties, the Christian Democratic *Partido de Acción Nacional* (PAN) and a coalition of leftist forces, the *Partido Socialista Unificado de México* (PSUM), were allotted 14 percent and 6 percent of the vote, respectively. On the local level there was evidence of growing resistance to efforts to impose official candidates. Yielding to popular pressure, the regime accepted the victory of opposition candidates in a number of towns.

President-elect De la Madrid was not to take office until December 1, and López Portillo had to cope with the growing economic crisis. The peso continued its steady decline, falling to the rate of 95 pesos to one dollar by the end of August, while the cost of imported goods rose sharply. Bankruptcies and closings multiplied as more and more businesses lacked the dollars needed to obtain imported parts and raw materials or to pay debts contracted in dollars. With the Banco de México almost drained of reserves, López Portillo took a dramatic step. On September 1, in his last annual message to Congress, he announced the nationalization of all private (but not foreign) banks and the establishment of stringent exchange controls. In his message he declared that in the last two years a group of Mexicans, aided and advised by the private banks, had "taken more money out of the country than the empires that have exploited us since the beginning of our history." The bank nationalization, the most radical measure taken by a Mexican president since the "Mexicanization" of the oil industry by Cárdenas in 1938, was greeted with cries of protest from the private banking sector and great demonstrations of support by the PRI and its client organizations, the trade unions, and the parties of the left.

In Washington, usually so allergic to all measures smacking of collectivism or socialism, the bank nationalization did not arouse the hostility that might have been expected, probably because even conservative United States officials regarded it as a necessary step, given the circumstances. The prime concern of the Reagan administration was to save Mexico, the third largest trading partner of the United States, from a default that could wreck the international banking system and bring down the great American banks to which Mexico owed $25.8 billion—almost a third of its foreign debt. Since July, consultations had been taking place between Mexican finance minister Jesús Silva Herzog and United States officials concerning the details of the rescue operation. The final plan provided for United States aid of $2.9 billion for Mexico's current-account problem; a seven-month freeze on the repayment of principal due to American, Western European, and Japanese bankers; and an eventual IMF (International Monetary Fund) loan of $3.9 billion, which could initiate a new cycle of commercial bank loans to Mexico. The IMF loan was, of course, subject to the usual conditions: Mexico must accept certain austerity measures—reduction of subsidies, restraints on wage increases, and other economies that were bound to hit Mexico's poor the hardest.

Even before he took office on December 1, 1982, President-elect De la Madrid had indicated his approval of the strong financial medicine prescribed by the IMF. To his cabinet he appointed figures praised by the *Wall Street Journal* as "conservative young technocrats . . . inclined to take politically unpalatable steps." These

"politically unpalatable steps," it turned out, included price increases of 100 percent and 50 percent on gasoline and natural gas, respectively, and the lifting of price controls and subsidies for consumer items ranging from shoes to television sets. Some three hundred essential items remained under partial control, but even at the controlled prices many were out of reach of a large part of the population—and it was uncertain how long the remaining controls would continue. Another measure was a new devaluation of the peso that was expected to stimulate exports. It would, however, also make imports more costly, increase the burden of foreign debt service, and reduce real wages. By the spring of 1983 the peso had declined to the rate of about 150 to the dollar. Finally, accepting the bank nationalization as "irreversible," De la Madrid clearly indicated that he would not use nationalization to control private credit and investment. He even sent Congress a bill that partially "denationalized" the banks by allowing private investors to purchase 34 percent of their shares.

The solution for the Mexican crisis devised in Washington and accepted by the Mexican political leadership consisted, in essence, of adding new debts to old ones, without the slightest prospect that the huge foreign debt of some $85 billion could ever be paid or even significantly reduced without a large write-off, and of imposing heavy new burdens on already impoverished groups of the Mexican population—a policy that could lead to sharp confrontations with the Mexican working class, peasantry, and even the middle class. Hopes for the success of the recovery plan rested on two doubtful premises: (1) that the recession now gripping the capitalist world would soon end; and (2) that oil prices would soon rise again or at least remain stable. For the rest, the plan appeared to ignore the lessons of Mexico's long experience with the model of dependent development that collapsed so ingloriously in

1982. "Like Brazil," wrote Peter Evans, "Mexico has found that dependent development requires a mass of imported inputs even larger than the exports it generates, and that even when the multinationals cooperate in the promotion of local accumulation they still ship more capital back to the center than they bring in. Mexico's newly discovered oil reserves may alleviate its balance of payments, but Mexico still reinforces the lessons of Brazil. Dependent development does not correct the imbalances in semi-peripheral relations with the center; it replaces old imbalances with new ones."[2]

[2] Peter Evans, *Dependent Development: The Alliance of Multinational, State, and Local Capital in Brazil* (Princeton, N.J.: Princeton University Press, 1979), p. 307.

CHAPTER THIRTEEN

Argentina:
The Failure of
Democracy

After thirty years of explosive economic growth and sustained political stability, Argentina seemed ready to take a place among the developed nations by the first decade of the twentieth century. Argentines could proudly point out that their nation was the world's greatest exporter of grain and one of the most important exporters of meat; they could boast of a railroad network unsurpassed outside western Europe and the United States and of a capital, Buenos Aires, that ranked among the world's most beautiful and cultured cities. Argentines were seemingly prosperous, relatively well educated, and increasingly urban. The burgeoning population (nearly 8 million in 1910) and transportation system promised to create an internal market that would stimulate the rise of native manufacturing and elevate Argentina to the position of one of the world's modern industrialized countries.

The full flowering of democracy, too, seemed close at hand. With the passage of the Saenz

Peña reforms in 1912, providing for universal suffrage and the secret ballot, the landed oligarchy, which had long monopolized Argentine politics, at last appeared ready to recognize the aspirations of other social groups and even to share political power with the middle class.

The appearance of prosperity and emerging democracy, however, proved illusory. Stagnation, interspersed with periods of depression and runaway inflation, marked the Argentine economy during the succeeding seven decades. Military coups, disorder, and brutal repression afflicted the nation's politics. At the base of these problems lay Argentina's structural dependence on foreign markets and capital, a dependence that placed the country's economy at the mercy of foreign events and decisions made abroad and helped to perpetuate a deformed social and political system.

THE EXPORT ECONOMY

Argentina's dynamic economic development during the latter quarter of the nineteenth century and the early twentieth century was due to three factors: the appearance of a large market in Europe for its products—wool, mutton, beef, and wheat; the inflow of millions of immigrants, who provided cheap labor for the expanding agricultural sector; and finally, the influx of large quantities of foreign investment capital, which went to construct railroads, to put more land under cultivation, and to establish food (mainly meat) processing plants. The nation's prosperity depended on its ability to export huge amounts of agricultural commodities, to import the manufactured goods it required, and to attract a steady stream of large-scale foreign investment.

Consequently, Argentina was critically vulnerable to fluctuations in international market and finance conditions. Any reduction in overseas trade reverberated disastrously throughout the economy. Because Argentines usually imported more than they exported—a tendency made worse by the fact that the market price

for raw materials remained steady or declined while the prices of manufactured goods rose— the country suffered from large deficits in its balance of payments. To make up the difference, the nation relied heavily on foreign investment.

Foreign investment reached enormous proportions in the first decades of the twentieth century. During the years 1900 to 1929, foreigners came to control between 30 and 40 percent of the nation's fixed investments. Argentina absorbed nearly 10 percent of all foreign investment carried out by capital-exporting nations, one-third of all the foreign investment in Latin America, and more than 40 percent of the total foreign investment of Great Britain, the world's leading capitalist power. Investment was concentrated in railroads and government bonds, the proceeds from which were used to subsidize the construction of railroads and public works.

Although foreign investment unquestionably helped fuel economic development, it simultaneously created immense economic difficulties. Huge interest payments on foreign debts and the profit remittances of foreign-owned companies, often representing between 30 and 50 percent of the value of Argentina's exports, produced serious balance of payments problems. Because government bodies owed much of the foreign debt, a substantial portion of government revenue went to service payments. Rigid interest rates and repayment schedules meant that the burden remained the same, even when state revenues declined because of adverse economic conditions, and that revenues earmarked for debt service could not be diverted to other areas.

Every sector of the Argentine economy depended on exports. Agriculture and livestock raising employed 35 percent of the work force. The nation's greatest agricultural area, the pampas, exported 70 percent of its production. Argentine industry centered on food processing, mainly meat packing. As late as 1935, foodstuff processing accounted for 47 percent of all industrial production, and textiles for another 20 percent. The transportation industry—railroads and coastal shipping—handled mostly export commodities.

Rich and poor alike relied on the export economy for their livelihood. The ruling elite was composed of large landowners, who produced almost entirely for the export trade. Their income and their political power rested squarely on the export economy. In addition to large numbers of farm laborers, many urban and industrial workers depended on exports for their jobs. The major trade and industrial unions in Argentina arose in those industries—coastal shipping, railroads, dock work, and packinghouses—whose workers owed their well-being to overseas trade. Because the government relied on revenues derived from import taxes, significant numbers of white-collar workers and professionals employed by the government also were intimately tied to the export economy.

Foreign control and influence permeated the economy. Most of the large merchant houses, which carried on the all-important export-import trade, were either owned by or closely affiliated with foreign houses. The major shipping lines (both intercoastal and interoceanic), the railroads, and the *frigoríficos* (meat-packing plants) were owned and operated by British or American companies.

The export economy brought indisputable benefits to Argentina, but those benefits were unequally distributed. There were, for example, sharp differences in economic development among regions. While the pampas and Buenos Aires boomed, most of the interior provinces stagnated. Mendoza and Tucumán with their wine and sugar made some headway, but all the other central and northwestern provinces—Jujuy, La Rioja, Santiago del Estero, and Salta—experienced social and economic decline.

The inequalities of property and income between the various classes were equally glaring. The rich were very rich and growing richer; the poor grew poorer. In the countryside, the estancieros, masters of thousands of acres of rich land, built palaces, while the majority of foreign-born immigrant sharecroppers eked out a miserable living. In Buenos Aires, wealthy landowners, merchants, and lawyers gathered at the sumptuous Jockey Club, while laborers struggled to make ends meet as inflation eroded their already insufficient paychecks.

Argentina's greatest treasure was its land, but only a few Argentines owned sizable portions of it. In 1914, farm units larger than 2,500 acres accounted for only 8.2 percent of the total number of farms but held 80 percent of the nation's farm area. Farms larger than 125,000 acres accounted for only 1.7 percent of the total number of farms, but they encompassed nearly one-half of the nation's farmland. Over 40 percent of farms were worked by tenants, most on terms that were less than favorable. In 1937, 94.8 percent of the active working population in rural areas were landless workers, tenant farmers, sharecroppers, and smallholders. A mere 1 percent of the active rural population owned properties larger than 5,000 acres, but these landowners controlled over 70 percent of Argentina's farmland, much of which they left idle. Yet the land was fertile and suitable for intensive agriculture, unlike the large estates of arid northern Mexico before the revolution of 1910. Thousands of immigrants came to Argentina in search of land only to discover that virtually all had long since been taken up by the estanciero oligarchy.

Income distribution followed the same pattern. Less than 5 percent of the active population garnered 70 percent of the gross income derived from agriculture. Not only did workers and rural laborers receive little benefit from the export system, but the operation of the system's finances and taxation eroded what little return they did receive for their labor. Faced with chronic deficits in the balance of payments and unwilling or unable to tax the land or income of the landed elite, the government had no alternative but to resort to the printing press to finance its costs. The result was inflation.

Exporters also demanded a fluctuating currency exchange rate, which had an adverse effect on wage earners. Finally, the tax structure placed its burden squarely on the mass of consumers through such indirect taxes as those on imports.

ARGENTINE SOCIETY

Argentine society divided roughly into three classes—upper, middle, and lower. The upper class acquired its wealth and prestige through its ability to capitalize on the opportunities presented by the export economy. Large landholders even before the export boom of the last quarter of the nineteenth century, the upper class used the boom to solidify and enhance its power. The most powerful group within the elite was the cattle fatteners, who supplied beef for both the domestic and the foreign market. This inner circle was composed of approximately four hundred families who were closely allied through social clubs and business associations. Geographically, most of the wealth was located in the cattle and cereal regions of the pampas near Buenos Aires. From 1880 to 1912, the elite class that controlled the nation's land and wealth also controlled its politics. It used its control over the government to promote meat and grain exports, to guarantee easy credit for its members, and to provide favorable taxation and currency policies. The other great institutions of Argentine society, the military and the church, also reflected the views of the elite.

As the nation grew more urban, its class structure became more complex. An urban middle class arose, which David Rock divides into three categories: rentier (landlords), bureaucratic, and professional groups; entrepreneurs and proprietors; and salaried employees in the private sector. Rock maintains that the urban middle class (unlike its counterparts in the industrialized West) did not challenge the agrarian sector for primacy because its origins lay in the international commercial and service sectors. The middle class, heavily concentrated in the bureaucracy and professions, depended on the export economy. Rock points out that this dependent sector of the middle class almost equaled in numbers the entrepreneurial and white-collar sectors together. It was this dependent group that attached itself to the Radical party. Many members of the entrepreneurial sector were foreign born and thus disfranchised.

The lower class divided into two groups, workers and urban marginals. Most members of the working class lived in Buenos Aires. They labored in small factories, where Argentina's industrial expansion was concentrated until 1914. (The primary exceptions to the predominance of small industries were the frigoríficos.) A considerable number of workers were employed by the railroads and urban tramways and in the Port of Buenos Aires.

Although the Socialist party, born during the 1890s, professed to represent the working class, it failed to achieve a position of leadership because its roots and leaders were mainly middle class. The working class did, nevertheless, organize into unions. The most important unions were those of the railroad workers (*La Fraternidad*) and the dock workers. Numerous strikes occurred after the turn of the century and throughout the first Radical regime (1916–1922). The labor movement, however, was weakened by diverse viewpoints on political activity and by internecine rivalries among Socialists, Anarchists, and Syndicalists, all of whom claimed its allegiance.

THE MILITARY

In the first decade of the twentieth century, the Argentine military underwent two important transformations: It was professionalized, and it became a national institution. By 1910 seniority and merit were firmly entrenched as the criteria for promotion. The Superior School was established in 1901 to train officers in modern warfare. Also in 1910 a law of conscription was instituted; this greatly expanded the size of the armed

CONTEMPORARY SOUTH AMERICA

forces and required the expansion of the officer corps. As a result, the social make-up of the officer corps changed. In time, men of the middle class, mostly the sons of immigrants, replaced the old officer groups, and the oligarchy gradually lost its predominance. Military personnel developed considerable pride and independence. They resisted political tampering and demanded modern weapons and better pay from the government. As cohesion grew, the military became an important political force. In 1916 it favored the transfer of power from the oligarchy to the Radical party.

THE RADICAL ERA, 1916–1930

The Rise of the Radical Party

Amid growing unrest among the urban middle class, university students, and small groups of junior military officers, the Radicals staged their third unsuccessful attempt to overthrow the oligarchy by force in February 1905. Despite their failure, the Radicals attracted growing popular support in the decade that followed. Local party organizations, formed before the February coup, expanded rapidly, drawing heavily from university-educated sons of immigrants. After the adoption of the Saenz Peña Law in 1912, the Radicals abondoned the sterile policy of electoral abstention and began to organize the urban middle class from the grassroots level, especially in Buenos Aires. Members of the middle class, many of whom were university graduates and professionals who lacked the necessary social credentials for prestigious and remunerative employment, increasingly sought to acquire stature and wealth through politics. The party tried to fulfill these aspirations.

Radical party strength rested on twin pillars: its local urban organization, which acted to meet the needs of the middle class, and its leader, Hipólito Yrigoyen. Precinct and ward committees, headed by local bosses, dispensed patronage and favors in return for votes. They provided housing, extended loans to businessmen, and helped constituents in minor scrapes with the police. The committees' activities peaked at election time, when they took on the trappings of little social service agencies. In Buenos Aires, before the presidential election of 1916, local committees provided children's concerts and movies, gave away Christmas presents, set up medical and legal aid centers, and sometimes even distributed inexpensive food.

The Radical party was by no means a unified or homogeneous organization, however. Although the party drew most of its popular support and intermediate leadership from the middle class, large landowners dominated its hierarchy. In addition, there were important regional rivalries, most prominently between the provinces and Buenos Aires. Such diverse elements as rural hacendado-caudillos, who brought in the docile peasant vote, urban sons of immigrants, and university-educated professionals joined together under the Radical umbrella. They could come together in part because the Radical program was vague enough to satisfy widely disparate groups and also because of the manipulative skills of Hipólito Yrigoyen.

Yrigoyen played a dual role as the titular head of the Radical party. First, he was the great mediator who managed to reconcile the often conflicting interests of the middle class and large landowners who made up his political coalition. Second, although inarticulate and a recluse, Yrigoyen managed to project an austere democratic image that made him the party's charismatic leader. This clever deal maker and manipulator symbolized for the middle class the Radical dedication to democracy. Despite a checkered past that included shady business deals, he furnished the party with much of its moral appeal.

The Radical propaganda effectively presented the party as a national party, transcending the narrow regional and class interests that had previously governed Argentine politics. The

Radical program was purposely vague. It straddled the line between its two major constituencies, the middle class and the landed elite. The Radicals (reflecting the views of both the landowners and the dependent middle class) never challenged the basic premises of the export economy. The party advocated neither land reform nor industrialization.

From 1912 to 1916, the Conservatives failed to construct the broad-based national political party they had hoped would arise as a result of the passage of the Saenz Peña Law. Regional differences and conflicts of interest between cattle fatteners and cattle breeders made such a party impossible. Itself divided, the oligarchy proved incapable of developing a program that would appeal to urban middle groups.

The Socialist party also failed to become a party of national scope. Like the Radicals, the Socialists suffered from a political split personality. The bulk of the party's support came from the working class, but the leaders of the party were middle-class intellectuals. Unlike the Radicals, the Socialists kept party membership small and the lines of authority centralized. Their reformist program appealed to the lower middle class in white-collar jobs in transportation, commerce, and industry. The most serious weakness of the Socialists was their propensity for ruinous bickering that split the party. For the most part, the Socialists could never extend their influence beyond Buenos Aires, nor could they get the group for whom the party had the greatest attraction, the foreign-born workers, to register to vote. The party was, however, strong among skilled workers, particularly those on the railroad.

The Socialists had competition for working-class and union support. Anarchists gained the allegiance of dock workers and of many workers in small industrial and service occupations. They played an important role in the rise of Argentine unions from the 1890s. After 1906, Syndicalists increasingly influenced the unions. The Syndicalists, who shared the Anarchist ideal of abolishing the state, stressed economic struggle and powerful unions as a means of attaining that goal. They won support among larger workers' groups, such as the coastal shipping workers and railway shop workmen. Syndicalists were younger, more apt to be native born, and skilled, while Anarchists were older, immigrants, and skilled. The growing importance of the Syndicalists after 1906 reflected the changes that were taking place in the composition of the working class.

Having the advantages of a finely tuned grassroots political organization and a well-known and astute leader as their presidential candidate and untroubled by an ideology or specific program other than the vaguely defined "class harmony," the Radicals won the 1916 presidential elections with 46.5 percent of the vote. Although it was necessary for Yrigoyen to put together a backroom political deal in order to acquire a majority of the electoral college, the Radicals had clearly won a great victory. The Progessive Democrats, their nearest rivals, managed to win only 13 percent of the popular vote.

The First Radical Government: Yrigoyen, 1916–1922

The characters of the first and subsequent Radical administrations were determined by the delicate relations between the Radicals and the conservative landowner elite. The elite controlled the military and the major agricultural lobbying groups and had close contacts with the powerful foreign business interests. Yrigoyen continually walked an unsteady tightrope between the middle class, which was clamoring for a piece of the governmental pie, and the oligarchy, which was still wary of the party that had rebelled three times in three decades and that had won an election campaigning against the selfish interests of that oligarchy. He could not push too hard too fast, or the oligarchy would surely overthrow him.

The operating mechanism of the Radical government was a conservative fiscal policy and political stability, in return for which the oligarchy was to allow the middle class wider access to the governmental bureaucracy and the professions. Yrigoyen had little room to maneuver, for there were inherent difficulties in the operation of this arrangement. First, expansion of access to government employment meant that government expenditures necessarily had to increase. But this violated the tenet of fiscal conservatism, unless the economy continued to expand at a rapid rate. Second, Yrigoyen had to maintain the fragile alliance of landowners and members of the middle class within his own party. In sum, the key to the Radicals' staying in power was Yrigoyen's ability to distribute the fruits of Argentine economic development to the middle class without antagonizing the oligarchy.

Nonetheless, the most pressing political problem was that the Radicals did not have control over the government. Although they had won the 1916 election for the presidency, they did not control most of the provinces and were a minority in Congress. Not until 1918 did they win a majority in the Chamber of Deputies. Because Senate terms were for nine years, they did not control that body until 1922. Without complete political control, Yrigoyen faced an impossible task in attempting to meet the conflicting requirements of the elite and the middle class. His first cabinet reflected both the make-up of his party and his eagerness to win the goodwill of the ruling elite; it was composed entirely of members of the landed oligarchy.

Yrigoyen's balancing act became even more difficult with the emergence of labor agitation for improved wages and working conditions. Wartime demand for Argentine exports had brought on inflation, and as a result, the purchasing power of wages was seriously eroded. Yrigoyen had to move cautiously in attempting to alleviate labor's plight, for the oligarchy might look upon such moves as interference in their economic domain. The problem was complicated by the fact that much of the labor agitation was directed against foreign-owned companies with close ties to the elite. There was growing discontent on the part of the middle class, too, because the decline in government revenues from imports meant fewer government jobs for its members.

From 1913 to 1917, Argentina experienced a serious depression. The prospect of war dried up foreign investment in 1913 and 1914, and the war itself caused a shortage of shipping for export commodities and of imported goods, both of which were critical in an economy based on the export of foodstuffs (bulk commodities) and the import of manufactured goods. To make matters worse, the 1913 harvest failed.

Between 1917 and 1921, however, Argentina again prospered as a result of an export boom. The distribution of the benefits of the new prosperity were decidedly uneven, however, and Yrigoyen again found himself under pressure from his rival constituencies. Europe's mounting demand for cereals and meat exports forced prices for domestically consumed food to rise rapidly. Food prices rose 40 percent, and the cost of living in the cities rose 65 percent. The Radical government was squeezed between the urban community's need for lower prices (wages had not kept pace) and the interests of the landed elite, which insisted on keeping the prices of its products high. The best way to satisfy both constituent groups was to expand job opportunities in government, but this expansion required an increase in government spending, which was severely limited because sources of revenue were limited and the oligarchy was opposed to it. In 1918 the Radicals proposed a modest income tax and a tax on exports, but these proposals met defeat at the hands of a conservative Congress. Some relief came in 1919, when revenues again started to increase.

In the first years after the electoral reforms of 1912, the Radical party made a considerable effort to win labor support through close relations with the labor unions. The party attempted to win labor support primarily because it feared the Socialist party, which had won impressive victories in the Buenos Aires elections in 1912, 1913, and 1914. The Socialists made inroads not only into the working class but into the middle class as well. Although the Socialist challenge ran aground in 1915 after the party suffered another of its debilitating internal splits, the Radicals continued to woo union support.

After becoming president, Yrigoyen sought to broaden his support by making some overtures to the working class. But he had little success, for his fear of antagonizing the landed elite severely limited the concessions he could offer the workers. The use of patronage—a tactic eminently successful with the middle class— failed when applied to the working class. The middle class possessed a low degree of class identity and was more or less isolated from community feeling. Its members were more concerned with their own upward mobility and aspirations than with the welfare of their fellows. Labor, on the other hand, had developed a sense of class consciousness and, unlike the middle class, was organized along occupational lines. When the strategy of attaching the rank-and-file of the workers to the local Radical political machine failed, Yrigoyen sought to form individual links with the leadership of the trade unions, which at this time were under strong Socialist influence.

From 1916 to the early 1920s, however, Yrigoyen's efforts to form an alliance with organized labor clashed with the Radicals' obligations to the oligarchy, which regarded such an alliance as prejudicial to its interests. Confronted with the bitter opposition of the ruling elite, Yrigoyen backed down and abandoned the workers.

From 1916 to 1919, Yrigoyen had to deal with a wave of large, sometimes violent strikes. Radical policy toward these struggles was clearly determined by expediency and, in the last analysis, by the degree of pressure exerted by the landed elite. The major strikes occurred against foreign-owned companies engaged in export-related enterprises. The workers sought higher wages to compensate for the erosion of their wages by wartime inflation.

Since Argentine governments often sent in the police and armed forces to break strikes, the attitude of the Yrigoyen regime was decisive. The Maritime Workers' Federation struck twice, in 1916 and 1917, for higher wages. The first strike was timed to coincide with harvest shipments. In both instances the union gained access to Yrigoyen, the government kept out of the dispute, and the union won. The Federation of Railroad Workers (La Fraternidad) struck in 1917 and, despite outbreaks of violence, the government at first supported the strikers. But in late 1917, the government abandoned the unions when a general strike began to jeopardize export interests. With the strike threatening the entire harvest, the British government and the elite brought joint pressure on Yrigoyen to intervene, and troops were used. The strike collapsed. The frigorífico strike of 1917–1918 met the same fate when the government sent in marines to subdue the strikers.

The climactic episode came in January 1919 and is known in Argentine history as the *Semana Trágica* (Tragic Week) in reference to the heavy loss of life that followed when Yrigoyen, apparently fearing intervention by the army to topple his government, abandoned his original conciliatory position and sent police and armed forces to break a general strike that had grown out of a strike in a metal works. This violence was accompanied by a wave of brutal pogroms against Russian Jewish immigrants by members of the elite and the middle class, organized in an Argentine Patriotic League. Instead of denouncing the anti-"communist" witch hunt, the Radical government added its voice to the right-wing cry that the strike was a revolutionary conspiracy and even encouraged party members to joint the vigilante bands. From that time, the Yrigoyen government gave up efforts to achieve a reconciliation with the workers. Henceforth, it concentrated on catering to its middle-class constituency through the use of patronage and on strengthening Yrigoyen's popular, electoral base. The last three years of Yrigoyen's term were a struggle merely to survive.

The Argentine university reform of 1918, which had continental reverberations, reflected Yrigoyen's desire to cater to his middle-class constituency. The series of events leading to this famous reform began with a student strike at the University of Córdoba; the students demanded, among other changes, simplification of the entrance requirements and secularization of the curriculum. When the strike deteriorated into violence, Yrigoyen intervened and acceded to the student demands. But he went further, establishing a series of new universities that increased middle-class access to the professions and the government jobs for which so many middle-class aspirants hungered.

The government also sought to strengthen its electoral position through intervention in the provinces, removing provincial governors on the pretext that they had violated the federal constitution. These interventions were aimed at gaining a majority for the Radicals in the Argentine Senate, for the outcome of elections to the Senate depended on control of the strategic provincial governorships. The government also strove to enhance its popularity by expanding the patronage system.

By 1921 the boom unleashed by the war had ended, and depression followed. The union movement disintegrated. Layoffs eroded union membership, and internal bickering rendered the unions ineffective. The Radicals actually experienced some success in recruiting among the workers during the depression, because their local committees were able to provide charitable services.

The Second Radical Government: Alvear, 1922–1928

Despite adverse economic conditions, the Radicals won the election of 1922. With 48 percent of the vote, Marcelo de Alvear, Yrigoyen's hand-picked successor, became president. Immediately, however, the party began to come apart. Although couched in personal terms—Alvear against Yrigoyen—the division more accurately reflected the growing split between the middle-class and elite sectors of the party. The conflict arose from the fact that the government was not meeting expenses through revenues but rather through a large number of short-term loans from local and overseas banks. Yrigoyen had increased the floating government debt to a staggering 1 billion pesos by 1922, a tenfold increase during his term.

Alvear cut the payroll to trim expenses and hiked tariff rates to increase revenue. The tariff increase was also aimed at reducing imports and alleviating the balance of payments problem. A balanced budget directly contradicted middle-class demands for even more government employment opportunities. In 1924 the Radicals split into two factions. The Radical party's Anti-Personalist wing separated under the leadership of Alvear.

Yrigoyen's Second Term, 1928–1930

Four years later, Yrigoyen made a smashing comeback, winning his second presidential term with an overwhelming 57 percent of the vote. Nonetheless, his political situation was greatly weakened. His local organization had deteriorated during the Alvear years from lack of patronage. In some cases, the local bosses had become gangsters. Yrigoyen set about reviving the patronage system in order to strengthen his underpinnings in the middle class. He also moved to eliminate opposition, and he stepped up intervention in the provinces to assure a majority in the Senate. When grumbling arose in the military, he tried to place loyalists in powerful positions. A Radical paramilitary organization was formed and clashed with its right-wing counterpart.

In October 1929, the depression hit Argentina. The Radicals, whose strength had been increasing, suffered a mortal blow. Exports dropped

40 percent; foreign investment stopped. Unemployment was widespread. Government efforts to spark a recovery served only to induce inflation. The decline in imports severely undermined the goverment's fiscal position, since it relied on import duties for most of its revenue.

The government incurred a huge deficit, which it tried to cover by borrowing. As a result, it found itself in the position of competing for increasingly scarce credit resources with the landed elite, which desperately needed money to ride out the decline in the export market. Yrigoyen's policy threatened the interests of the landed elite, and he became expendable. Further, his meddling with the military had seriously undercut his standing with that powerful institution. Finally, the depression destroyed his personal popularity in the middle class, his main base.

Yrigoyen became the scapegoat. His enemies pictured him as senile and corrupt, incapable of ruling the nation in a time of crisis. The depression ruined the party apparatus, for there was no patronage to dispense. The political situation continued to disintegrate, and violence increased. Yrigoyen was overthrown by the military on September 6, 1930.

THE "INFAMOUS DECADE," 1930–1943: THE CONSERVATIVE RESTORATION

The coup marked the end of Argentina's short experiment with democracy and the entry of the military into the nation's politics; it ushered in a period of harsh repression and corruption, which came to be known as the "infamous decade." Lieutenant General José F. Uriburu, who had led the group of conspirators that overthrew Yrigoyen, became the head of a coalition of widely diverse elements, including traditional Conservatives, right-wing nationalist-facists, and such center and left parties as the Progressive Democrats, Independent Socialists, and Socialists. There strange bedfellows had agreed

on the elimination of Yrigoyen, but little else. Consequently, the loosely built alliance soon fell apart. The military was also divided. One faction, led by Uriburu, sought to establish a regime patterned on the Italian corporate state. A second faction, led by General Agustín P. Justo, desired only a return to the pre-1916 political arrangements. The split was exacerbated by the long-standing and bitter personal rivalry between Uriburu and Justo.

In the months following the coup, Uriburu conducted a campaign of brutal repression against opponents of his provisional government. At the beginning of 1931, he felt that the opposition was sufficiently cowed and—in the case of the Yrigoyen Radicals—sufficiently discredited to call elections for Buenos Aires Province. The result of the elections was a tremendous victory for the Yrigoyen Radicals. Uriburu quickly annulled the elections. The Conservatives scrambled to find allies and at last found a partner in the Anti-Personalist wing of the Radicals. They formed a coalition known as the *Concordancia*. Their agreement called for the Anti-Personalists to provide a presidential candidate, while the Conservatives would furnish a running mate and control government finances. The alliance soon crumbled when Uriburu refused to permit the ex-president, Alvear, to head the ticket. Alvear took most of his party with him, and the Radicals adopted a policy of electoral abstention until 1935.

What remained of the Concordancia, the conservative National Democratic party and some Anti-Personalists, chose General Justo as their presidential candidate. With the help of fraud, the intimidation tactics of goon squads and gangsters, and the general apathy of an embittered and cynical electorate, Justo won easily. The Concordancia had a very narrow popular base, but its main potential opposition, the Radical party, was deeply fragmented and unable to cooperate with other opposition groups. The regime used its patronage power and benefited from the upturn in the economy after 1934 to consolidate its hold on power.

The Radicals staged several unsuccessful rebellions in the provinces during the early 1930s. Yrigoyen died in 1933, but not before he had been reconciled with Alvear and passed on the mantle of Radical leadership to his old rival. In 1935, Alvear rejoined the main Radical party and led it back into the political arena. In 1937, he opposed the Concordancia ticket composed of the Radical Roberto M. Ortiz for president and the right-wing Conservative Ramón S. Castillo for vice president. With the aid of widespread vote fraud, Ortiz won.

Hoping to broaden the political base of the Concordancia, Ortiz set about restoring some semblance of free and honest elections. He intervened in provincial elections whenever corruption and coercion appeared excessive. In March 1940, Ortiz overturned the Buenos Aires provincial elections, among the most corrupt of all time. As a result, the Radicals and other opposition parties won a majority in Congress. Unfortunately for Argentine democracy, however, Ortiz was a diabetic who was rapidly losing his vision. He therefore had to take an extended leave of absence, handing over the reins of government to Castillo in 1940. Castillo was an archconservative who attempted to undo Ortiz's reforms. The two men fought publicly until Ortiz died in 1942, and Castillo became president. For three years, he maintained an almost constant state of siege and ruled by decree.

Despite his narrowing base of support, Castillo insisted on naming as his successor the unpopular Conservative Robustiano Patrón Costas, a millionaire sugar planter from Salta who was notorious for mistreatment of his Indian laborers. Castillo's arbitrary ways had won him enemies on all sides, but the oligarchy and the Radical party were divided, the labor movement was weak and divided, and the public, disillusioned by a decade of fraud and corruption, was cynical and apathetic. Into the resulting vacuum moved the army. On June 4, 1943, a coup organized by the secret officers' lodge known as the Group of United Officers (GOU) overthrew Castillo and established a ruling junta. Its first head,

General Arturo Rawson, lasted only two days; he was followed by General Pedro P. Ramírez, who fell in his turn in 1944; his successor, General Edelmiro Farrell, ruled from 1944 until the elections of 1946.

Before leaving the "Infamous Decade," we should take note of the economic policies pursued by the Conservative administrations. It is an irony of Argentine history that the organizers of the 1930 coup, who proposed to restore the golden age of pre-1916 Argentina, not only failed to prevent far-reaching change in Argentine society but themselves had to abandon the free-trade, laissez-faire economic doctrines on which the prewar export economy was based. Conservative economic policy of the 1930s established state intervention as a decisive factor in the economy. For the most part, the Conservative policies and administration were successful. The men who conducted fiscal matters were extremely competent, sometimes brilliant. The basic aim of their policy was to protect the nation from the effects of the cyclical nature of the world capitalist economy. To accomplish this, they sought to protect their main foreign market, Great Britain, limit production of farm commodities, and restrict imports through indirect methods, such as the establishment of a currency exchange system that discriminated against non-British imports. They also sought to establish new import-substitution industries primarily through foreign investment.

In this period, finding that they could not export manufactured goods to Argentina on a competitive basis because of high tariffs and the discriminatory exchange system, United States manufacturers established plants in Argentina. As a result, foreign capital played an increasingly important role in the economy during the 1930s, accounting for 50 percent of the total capital invested in Argentine industry. Foreign companies virtually monopolized the meat-packing, electric power, cement, automobile, rubber, petroleum, pharmaceutical, and several other industries.

The British market for beef and grain was

critical for the Argentine export economy. During the late 1920s and early 1930s, the British government was under constant pressure to reduce Argentine imports in order to protect producers within the empire. The result of Argentine efforts to secure the British market was the controversial Roca-Runciman Treaty of 1933. By this treaty, Britain guaranteed Argentina a fixed, though somewhat reduced, share of the chilled beef market. It also promised to eliminate tariffs on cereals. Argentina, in return, lowered or eliminated tariffs on British manufactures. It also agreed to spend its earnings from the British market on British goods to be imported into Argentina.

To some analysts, the Roca-Runciman treaty has symbolized the Concordancia's surrender of national interests in favor of the landed elite and foreigners. It has been argued that Argentina had little choice but to protect its major market, especially when the United States refused Argentine beef except in cans. Nonetheless, the oligarchy made precious little effort to find other alternatives, such as seeking out new markets or attracting capital into industry.

Be that as it may, the Conservatives managed the Argentine economy quite successfully, reforming the fiscal system, balancing the budget most years, and reforming the banking and credit system. The government used the considerable profits from its exchange controls to repay its foreign debt and invest in transportation facilities and other public works. These projects helped to alleviate unemployment.

The economy improved after 1934, and by 1936 the crisis had passed. Cereal prices rose gradually on the world market until 1937, when they again dropped. Meat prices rose until 1936 and then remained steady. Industrial investment reached predepression levels. Although real wages declined, unemployment fell sharply as a result of public works and industrial investment. In general, Argentines were relatively well off during the 1930s. Consumption of consumer goods and food rose considerably.

The nature of Argentine industrialization during the 1930s remains a matter of some controversy. Some historians depict the decade as one of intense expansion of import-substitution manufacturing. However, recent findings suggest that industrial growth did not accelerate during the 1930s but continued to grow at approximately the same rate as previously. In fact, it appears that more industrialization took place during the 1920s than in the 1930s. What did change was the type of products manufactured. Increased foreign investment stimulated the growth of new, technologically more advanced industries, which produced chemicals and electrical and metal products.

The process of industrialization was accompanied by a growth of the native industrialist class and a parallel increase in the size of the working class and its organizations. In 1930 the General Confederation of Labor (CGT) arose from the merger of two large unions. During the first half of the decade, the growth of the trade union movement was seriously hampered by large-scale unemployment and the hostility of employers and the government, which used right-wing thugs to harass the workers. By 1935, however, a degree of recovery had strengthened the workers' bargaining power. Strikes led by the Communist party erupted, and the unions began to grow again. The construction workers, for example, organized and joined the CGT. In 1942 differences over policy and tactics split the CGT, leading to the rise of two organizations, one dominated by Syndicalists, the other by Socialists and Communists. Nevertheless, by 1943 the membership of the trade union movement was estimated to be between three hundred and three hundred and fifty thousand.

The growth of the Argentine industrial bourgeoisie, a class profoundly dissatisfied with the economic policies of the landed oligarchy, and of the working class, still relatively small and unorganized but gaining in self-consciousness and developing new social and political aspirations, heightened the tensions within Argentine society. The military coup of 1943 represented an effort to resolve the gathering crisis.

THE PERÓN ERA, 1943–1955

Perón's Rise to Power

The military coup that overthrew Castillo in 1943 had deep and tangled roots. The fraud and corruption that tainted both Conservative and Radical politics in the "Infamous Decade" no doubt offended military sensibilities, and Castillo's choice of the pro-Ally Patrón Costas as his successor also angered some of the military, who were divided in their attitude toward the belligerents in World War II. But the coup of 1943 had deeper causes. During the 1930s, the officer corps of the Argentine armed forces, predominantly middle class in its social origins, developed an ardent nationalism that saw the solution for Argentina's problems in industrialization and all-around technical modernization. The interest of the military in industrialization was closely linked to its desire to create a powerful war machine capable of creating a Greater Argentina that could exercise hegemony in a new South American bloc. To industrialize it was necessary to end Argentina's neocolonial status, to free it from dependence on foreign markets. The pro-German attitude of many officers stemmed in part from the German military instruction that they had received and from their admiration for the supposed successes of the Nazi New Order, but even more, perhaps, from the conviction that England and the United States had conspired to keep Argentina a rural economic colony. Their pro-German attitude was not translated into a desire to enter the war on Germany's side but rather into the wish to keep Argentina neutral in the great conflict.

As concerned domestic policy, the military proposed a massive speedup of industrialization and technical modernization, even though it feared the social changes and forces that such transformations might unleash. In particular, it feared the revolutionary potential of the working class. In effect, the military proposed to build Argentine industrial capitalism with a thoroughly cowed, docile working class. As a result, one of the first acts of the military regime was to launch an offensive against organized labor. The government took over the unions, suppressed newspapers, and jailed opposition leaders. This policy of direct confrontation and collision with labor had disastrous results and threatened to wreck the industrialization program. The military was saved from itself by an astute young colonel, Juan Domingo Perón, who took over the Department of Labor in October, 1943 and promptly raised it to the status of the Ministry of Labor and Welfare.

Born in 1895, the son of immigrant and Creole parents of somewhat marginal economic status (his father was a farmer), Perón entered the military college at sixteen and very slowly rose in rank to captain in 1930. He played a minor role in the coup of that year. During the next decade, he spent several years in Europe, where he was much impressed by the German and Italian dictatorships. In 1941, Perón joined the Group of United Officers, although only a junior colonel, and quickly rose to its leadership ranks. He was prominent in the colonels' clique that replaced the GOU in power in 1944. Beginning with a subcabinet post as secretary of labor and welfare, Perón became the indispensable man in the Ramírez government. He subsequently became vice president and minister of war, in addition to secretary of labor and welfare.

Perón's genius lay in his recognition of the potential of the organized and unorganized working class and the need to broaden the social base of the nationalist revolution. He became the patron of the urban proletariat. Workers were not only encouraged to organize but favored in bargaining negotiations, in which his department participated. As a result, workers' wages not only rose in absolute terms but their share of the national income grew. This, of course, increased mass purchasing power and thereby promoted the process of industrialization. Perón also created a state system of pensions and health benefits, with the result that employers' contributions for pensions, insurance, and other benefits rose steadily until the year of Perón's fall (1955). In return for these real gains, however, the unions lost their independence and became part of a state-controlled apparatus in Perón's hands. Meanwhile, Perón was strengthening his position within the military. In February 1944, he led a group of officers in forcing the resignation of President Ramírez, who, as noted previously, was replaced by General Farrell.

Not all of the military was happy with Perón's prolabor policies or with his meteoric rise to power. The end of the war in 1945 also provoked civilian demands for an end to military rule and the restoration of the constitution. In October 1945, Perón's military and civilian foes staged a coup that resulted in his ouster and imprisonment. But the organizers of the coup were divided and unclear about their objectives, and Perón's followers mobilized rapidly. Loyal labor leaders organized the Buenos Aires working class for massive street demonstrations to protest Perón's jailing. The workers virtually took over the city, without opposition from the armed forces. The bewildered conspirators released Perón from prison. Thereupon, he resigned from his various government posts, retired from the army, and began his campaign for the presidency in the 1946 elections.[1]

In preparation for the election of 1946, Perón, taking due account of the defeat of fascism in Europe, cast himself in the role of a democrat ready to abide by the result of a free election. He created a Labor party to mobilize the working class, the principal component in a class alliance whose other major elements were the national industrial bourgeoisie and the army. Perón's chief opponent was José Tamborini, candidate of the *Unión Democrática* (Democratic Union), a heterogeneous coalition of conservative landed elite, the bureaucratic and professional middle class that traditionally supported the Radical party, and even the Socialist and Communist parties. Perón defeated Tamborini, by 300,000 votes out of 2.7 million. He was helped in the election by the blundering foreign policy of the United States, whose State Department issued a Blue Book blasting Perón for his fascist ties. Perón countered by circulating a Blue and White Book (blue and white were Argentina's national colors) that stressed the theme of Yankee imperialism.

Postwar Economics

The postwar boom enabled Perón to keep his coalition together. The export sector produced large surpluses in the balance of payments, making available funds for industrialization, mainly in labor-intensive manufactures. Between 1945 and 1948, real wages for industrial workers rose 20 percent. Personal consumption also rose. Since there was only a slight decline in the share of the national income that went to profits, the redistribution of income to the working class did not come at the expense of any other segment of the alliance. Industrialists kept profits up and benefited from increased domestic consumption, which provided a growing market for their products. The only sector of the economy that was slighted was agriculture.

Perón managed to win over a considerable sector of the dependent middle class through his use of government patronage, just as Yrigoyen had done before. He kept the military happy by his commitment to industrialization, an important aspect of its desire for national self-sufficiency and by providing it with generous salaries and the latest equipment for modern warfare.

---

[1] Myth has it that Perón's mistress (later his wife) Eva Duarte almost singlehandedly mobilized the *descamisados* to rescue him from prison. She in fact had little influence. Perón's supporters in organized labor brought him back.

Juan and Evita Perón, 1952. (United Press
International Photo)

One of Perón's greatest assets was his beautiful and stylish wife Eva Duarte de Perón, known affectionately by Argentines as "Evita," who acted as his liaison to the working class. Evita, a former dance hall girl and radio and movie star, headed a huge charitable network that dispensed tremendous amounts of money and patronage. So beloved was she that when she died in 1952 at the age of thirty-two, Perón led a movement to get the Catholic Church to canonize her. The president's popularity with the working class suffered after her death. Evita strongly advocated women's suffrage, which was granted in 1947. Consequently, women supported Perón in large numbers.

After 1948, however, the economic picture changed drastically. With the exception of a short-lived recovery during the Korean War (1950–1951), Argentina entered a period of severe recession, which included several drought-induced bad harvests. The late 1940s brought the first signs that Argentina would face serious long-term economic difficulties. Its export commodities began to confront increased competition from the United States and from revitalized Western European agriculture. Later, the advent of the Common Market worsened Argentina's position. Balance of payments deficits replaced the large surpluses that had financed the nation's import-substitution industrialization. Industrial production fell, as did per capita income. Real wages dropped 20 percent from the 1949 level in 1952–1953. It was in this decline that Perón's political failure was rooted.

There are two schools of opinion regarding Perón's economic policy. The first, typified by the English scholar H. S. Ferns, is highly critical. According to this analysis, Perón's policies were disastrous in the long run. In the first place, he drained the export agricultural sector to the point where farmers had no incentive to expand acreage or modernize production. Farm production dropped precipitously (although this was in part due to bad weather during the early 1950s). Furthermore, higher real wages increased internal consumption of Argentine foodstuffs, thus lessening the amount of food commodities available for export.

In addition, the critics hold that the major portion of government expenditures was ill-advised. Perón's economic policy revolved around two essential points: government intervention in the economy on a large scale and re-establishment of Argentine control of its own economy. The president nationalized the Central Bank, the railroads, the gas industry, much of the electric power industry, the merchant marine, and the air transport, insurance, and communications industries. The government controlled prices on consumer goods and rents. Mismanagement and corruption permeated these state enterprises, and this siphoned off much of the utility and profits of these operations. The critics also claim that Perón paid inflated prices for these nationalized enterprises, leaving no money for capital improvements. The problem was especially acute with the state railroads, which desperately needed new equipment and repairs. But Perón had paid the British an enormous sum for the railroads and had nothing left for improvements. In some cases, the Argentine government paid off bonds at par years ahead of maturity, although the bonds were selling on the stock exchanges in Europe for 60 to 70 percent of par, and they

paid low interest. Paying off such debts, it is claimed, was financial madness.

A second school of opinion, led by Jorge Fodor, defends Perón. This analysis maintains that the dictator's maneuvering room was severely limited by world financial and market conditions, especially in Britain and the United States. Argentina's alternatives were governed by four crucial factors. First, much of the nation's export surplus was tied up in Great Britain and virtually unavailable, because Britain was in the midst of an economic crisis. Perón paid a high price for the railroads and perhaps for some bonds because the British used the enormous sum of Argentine money locked in their country as a bargaining device.

Second, the amount of Argentina's gains during the world war was vastly exaggerated. It was true that Argentina received high prices for its farm commodities during and after the war, but these prices were deceiving, for Argentina, through its trading monopoly, the Argentine Institute for Trade Promotion (IAPI), had to extend credit to enable Europe to buy its products. This meant that Perón did not have as much capital to spend as his critics have maintained. His money was tied up in England or on the Continent in credit.

Third, even if Perón had possessed these huge sums, he had no place to spend them. He has been attacked for not sinking money into much needed public works, especially railroads and roads, and into heavy industry. The fact is, however, that neither England nor the Continent could supply these products, and the United States was unable and unwilling to supply them. Argentine neutrality during the war meant that the United States would not export capital goods and other industrial commodities to Argentina.

Fourth and finally, Argentina's own economic forecasts predicted that its future as an exporter of foodstuffs was bleak, given the economic condition of Europe and the specter of growing competition. Perón, therefore, acted rationally when he shortchanged agriculture in favor of industry. When the market conditions for agricultural exports improved, Perón put money into this sector.

The critics appear to be on solid ground when they point to the enormous funds spent on the military and on impractical military schemes for industrial self-sufficiency, such as nuclear energy projects. Perón's defenders would underline that he had a very limited area for maneuver and did the best he could.

Furthermore, many of Perón's moves were made to counteract or eliminate undue foreign influence in Argentina's economy. He nationalized the Central Bank, not only because he wanted to extend government control over fiscal policy, but because the Central Bank was controlled by foreign banks. The establishment of the IAPI was also designed to counteract foreign influence. During the war, the Allies established a joint purchasing agency; this meant that Argentina, in effect, had only one market for its products. The IAPI, the sole seller of the nation's commodities, had more bargaining power than individual producers could have had. It played an important role in the rise of Argentine industry through its monopoly of the export of cereals. Buying the cereals at low prices and selling them on the world market at high prices, it channeled the surplus into industrial development. But in the early 1950s, with world prices for cereals falling, the IAPI gradually lost its capacity for financing industry.

Whatever one may think of Perón's economics, the fact remains that he solved none of the country's major economic problems. The main roadblocks remained. Transportation continued to be inadequate and obsolete, and a scarcity of electric power stood in the way of industrial modernization. Argentina did not produce enough fuel to meet domestic needs, and this created an enormous drain on the balance of payments. The nation's industry remained limited for the most part to import-substitution light industry. Despite his anti-imperialist rhetoric, Perón did not nationalize such key foreign-owned industries as meat packing and sugar refining. Most serious of all, Perón did nothing to break the hold of the latifundio on the land. As a result, agriculture was marked by inefficient land use, which impeded long-range development.

Perón's Downfall

After his re-election in 1952 and in response to the economic crisis of the early 1950s, Perón formulated a new plan (the Second Five-Year Plan, 1953–1957) that, to a great extent, reversed his previous strategy. He tried to expand agricultural production by paying higher prices to farmers for their produce and by buying capital equipment for this sector (tractors and reapers). He sought to increase the agricultural production available for export by means of a wage freeze, which he hoped would restrict domestic consumption. Although real wages declined, workers did not suffer proportionately more than other groups. But the industrial bourgeoisie was unhappy, for labor productivity declined while the regime's prolabor policies propped up wages. The industrialists, supported by a considerable portion of the army, wanted deregulation of the economy so they could push down wages. But the major problem of the industrial sector was lack of capital, since the agricultural sector no longer generated a large surplus.

In order to solve the capital shortage, Perón abandoned his previously ultranationalistic stand and actively solicited foreign investment. In 1953 the government reached an agreement with a North American company, the Standard Oil Company of California, for exploration, drilling, refining, and distribution rights in Argentina. Perón hoped thereby to reduce the adverse effect oil purchases abroad had on the balance of payments. The following year, the government entered into a partnership with H. J. Kaiser, an American businessman, to produce automobiles. Argentina's aviation industry, a pet project of the military, was converted to auto production. Foreign capital used the most modern technology and machines, which required fewer workers and, therefore, tended to create unemployment in the affected industrial sectors.

In order to maintain government expenditures and a bloated bureaucracy in the face of declining revenues, Perón printed more money. The amount in circulation increased from 6 to 45 billion pesos during his two terms. By 1954 he had had some success in stabilizing the economy; he achieved a balance of payments surplus, and capital accumulation showed an upward curve. But his new economic strategy had alienated key elements of his coalition of workers, industrialists, and the armed forces. Perón then sought to divert attention from economic issues—with disastrous results.

Perón adopted two new strategies. First, he attempted to enhance his moral and ideological appeal. Second, he began to employ greater coercion to suppress a growing opposition. The vehicle for his ideological and moral appeal was *justicialismo*, Perón's ideal of justice for all—a third route to development that was neither communist nor capitalist.

Perón's strategy included attacking the church. Starting in 1951, the regime grew more repressive. The government suppressed and took over Argentina's most famous newspaper, *La Prensa* (1951). Further, Perón used his National Liberating Alliance, a private army of thugs, and the thirty-five-thousand-man federal police force to intimidate the political opposition. Torture, imprisonment, censorship, purges, and exile became the order of the day. After 1954, even the General Confederation of Labor became a coercive force, whose prime function seemed to be to suppress opposition within the labor movement.

Perón's reluctance to go along with the industrialists' desire to push down wages and increase productivity alienated that group; the industrial bourgeoisie then joined forces with the agrarian interests, which had long and bit-

terly opposed Perón. This desertion ended Perón's once highly successful coalition. Inevitably, Perón's hold on the working class loosened as the wage freeze and inflation reduced the value of their wages. The death of Eva Perón in 1952 contributed to the deterioration in the relations between Perón and the working class. She had served as her husband's ambassador to the workers. With Evita (little Eva) no longer at the head of the Social Aid Foundation, a vast philanthropic organization that distributed food, clothing, and money to the needy, Perón's relations with labor did not go so smoothly.

Despite economic adversity, Perón could not have been overthrown had not the military abandoned him. For the better part of a decade, he had masterfully balanced, divided, and bribed the military. Most of the senior officers owed him both their rank and their prosperity. The army was heavily involved in industrial production, and this provided an excellent means to become rich. In addition, to win its allegiance, Perón had showered the military with expensive military hardware and excellent wages. However, his relations with the armed forces began to disintegrate when he altered his economic policy to lessen emphasis on industrialization and self-sufficiency. On this score, his concession to Standard Oil in 1953 was the last straw for the nationalist military. The military was also affronted by the dictator's personal behavior (he had an affair with a teenage girl), and it objected to his virulent attacks on the Catholic church, a pillar of traditionalism, during 1954 and 1955. It also resented Perón's efforts to indoctrinate the military in the tenets of justicialismo.

Thus, in struggling to extricate the nation from an economic quagmire, Perón undermined the multiclass coalition that had brought him to power and sustained him there. When the final successful revolt took place in September 1955, after a failure in June, enough of the working class was alienated to assure the military's success. Perón briefly threatened to arm his working class supporters, the *descamisados* (the shirtless ones), but instead fled into exile.

THE SHADOW OF PERÓN, 1955–1973

Economic Stagnation

Chronic, sometimes violent, economic fluctuations characterized the post-1955 period. At the base of these difficulties lay continuous balance of payments deficits, which were caused by the decline in agricultural production. The nation could not earn enough from its exports to pay for the large expenditures necessary to fuel domestic industry. Periods of rapid economic growth were invariably followed by acute depressions, which wiped out all previous gains. Runaway inflation accompanied these cyclical conditions. Between 1958 and 1967, retail prices increased on the average of 27 percent a year. From 1958 to 1962, the cost of living in Buenos Aires rose 323 percent. (It rose 100 percent between 1961 and 1963). Inflation, of course, redistributed income away from the urban working class. The prevailing economic conditions meant the end to Perón's brand of populist politics. Such politics were predicated on the ability of the economy to expand, which then permitted distribution of benefits to several groups at the same time. This enabled multiclass alliances to form.

Outright class conflict was avoided because the unions were able to beat back repeated attempts by the government to suppress working-class organizations, and the upper and middle classes soon divided over divergent economic interests. The military, too, was divided over whether or not it should rule or should return the reins of government to civilians. Agrarian and industrial groups were the first to split, for they disagreed over government actions concerning currency, credit, and taxation. Furthermore, the industrialist sector split into two groups—old, traditional industrialists and the newer import-substitution industrialists. The latter opposed the inflow of foreign investment as a development strategy.

Development initiated by foreign investment had severe drawbacks (which were experienced by virtualy all noncommunist underdeveloped nations). Foreign companies tended to monopolize credit opportunities, certain key industries became concentrated in foreign hands, and profits earned by foreign subsidiaries and remitted to the home company added to the balance of payments deficits. Finally, foreign investment was usually technologically intensive and therefore created unemployment. It was during the post-Perón era of development spurred by foreign capital that Argentina saw the emergence of large numbers of underemployed and unemployed urban workers.

At various times during the period, the Argentine government had dealings with the International Monetary Fund (IMF), an agency that was supposed to help nations overcome their economic difficulties through advice and loans. The IMF's main concern was to control inflation. Its recommended stabilization programs invariably led to downturns in the business cycle, and unemployment and business failures ensued at an awesome rate. Such austerity programs were politically unpalatable because they held down real wages and therefore elicited labor opposition. During the presidential term of Arturo Frondizi (1958–1962), the IMF had a great deal of influence, and the result was disastrous. Inflation proved unconquerable, and the fund's economic "medicine" was too bad-tasting for Argentines to tolerate.

The Military in Politics

The major political contradiction of the period from 1955 to 1973 was the position of the army regarding Perónism. To win the presidency and a majority in Congress, it was necessary to garner working-class support. The Peronists controlled much of the working-class vote, but the army was unwilling to permit any of the civilian political parties to dicker with either Perón or his best-known henchmen.

General Eduardo Lonardi succeeded Perón. He favored conciliation with the Peronists, but his attempt to implement this policy ran afoul of a large segment of the army, which overthrew him in November 1955, after a tenure of scarcely two months. General Pedro Aramburu replaced Lonardi and set about to sweep away the vestiges of Perón, destroy the power of the trade unions, and deregulate the economy. The government took over the Peronist-led unions and arrested their leaders. Aramburu also eliminated Perón's subsidy of foodstuffs. These blows against the working class had an effect exactly opposite of what was intended. The severely fractured working class found new solidarity in common adversity, and the exiled Perón regained his popularity. The effort to destroy Peronism in the unions failed, and the period from 1956 to 1958 was marked by numerous strikes, accompanied by violence.

Politics became fragmented to an almost incomprehensible degree. The provisional government tried in 1957 to hold a constitutional convention to modernize the 1853 constitution. No fewer than forty parties ran candidates. This did not include the Peronists, who abstained. The convention was a shambles.

Facing rampant inflation, labor unrest, and political fragmentation, the military permitted a return to the game of electoral politics and again stepped into the background. In February 1958, Arturo Frondizi, the head of the Radical party's Intransigent wing and long an adamant opponent of Perón, became president, capturing 45 percent of the vote. The Intransigents also won a wide majority in Congress. Frondizi at first advocated an anti-Perón, anticlerical, anti–foreign investment program that favored economic nationalism and state intervention.

During the election campaign, however, he struck an agreement with Perón, promising to deal leniently with the Peronists in return for their support. His first move was to grant labor a 60 percent wage increase. Then, although he had campaigned as an economic nationalist, Frondizi proceeded to borrow vast sums from various foreign governments and the IMF. Frondizi, who had denounced Perón's Standard Oil contract, also signed oil contracts with eight oil companies, provoking a general strike in protest, and opened the doors wide to foreign capital, removing all restrictions on profit remittances. Seeking to stimulate business and agriculture, he removed controls on the economy. Finally, he embarked on a program of trimming the government bureaucracy and the excess labor force, especially in government-owned enterprises like the railroads.

Frondizi, however, proved unable to solve Argentina's most pressing problems—inflation and unemployment. In one year, 1959, the retail price index rose over 130 percent. Workers suffered immensely from the loss of real wages. Despite an upturn in 1960 and 1961, unemployment remained very high. His failure to revive the economy meant that his political strategy was bound to fail as well, since he could not hope to attract wide-based support without an expanding economy. From the beginning, he had been unable to achieve a political consensus and was forced to rule by decree or by proclaiming a state of siege. In the face of escalating violence, his inability to retain high-level government officials, and repeated coup attempts (there were thirty-five during his term), it is a wonder that Frondizi managed to survive as long as he did. Finally, he alienated the military by allowing Peronist participation in elections. The Peronists won a large bloc of seats in the Congress and ten governorships in the spring 1962 elections. The armed forces demanded that Frondizi annul the results, but he consented to cancel only some and was soon overthrown.

During the next year, José Mario Guido

headed a provisional government that was a front for the military. Guido ruled by decree, and his term coincided with another depression. The period was tumultuous because the armed services were badly split over whether or not to hold elections and return to civilian rule. In September the dispute became so intense that civil war erupted. In April 1963, the navy revolted. Nevertheless, new elections were held in June. The Peronists, now called the *Unión Popular* (Popular Union) were permitted to run candidates for Congress and provincial congresses only.

Arturo Illia and his Popular Radical party won the presidency, but with a weak 25 percent of the vote. Illia was on shaky ground; not only had he failed to gain anything near to a majority of the popular vote, but he had to share Congress with no fewer than twenty-four different parties. His primary strategy was to unite anti-Peronist groups among the urban middle class and the rural sector. He continued extensive government intervention in the economy and sought to find new markets for Argentine exports. He also tried to divide the labor unions with a policy of rewarding cooperative unions. On all fronts, his program failed. Although the economy did improve during his first two years, inflation continued its upward spiral and agricultural production declined. His only economic measure of importance, and his only popular move, was the cancellation of foreign oil concessions in 1963.

Illia's liberalism was of the Yrigoyen brand, cautious and conciliatory toward the oligarchy, but it was enough to arouse disquiet among the hard-liners of the military. They were discontented with his failure to crack down on Peronists and left-wingers and with his reluctance to support the intervention by the United States in the Dominican Republic and proposals for an inter-American peace force to cope with hemispheric subversion. They were alarmed most of all by the sweeping victory of the Pe-

ronist Popular Union in the congressional elections of March 1965, which opened up the frightening possibility of a Peronist victory in the presidential election of 1969.

Determined to prevent such an outcome, the military ousted Illia in June 1966 and installed General Juan Carlos Onganía as president. This time it appeared that the military had come to stay. The government abolished political parties and purged the universities of left and center elements. The trade union movement, meanwhile, suffered from internal divisions owing to differences in policy and personal rivalries over the successor to Perón after his anticipated death. This split enabled Onganía to crack down on the militant wing of the labor movement with the cooperation of its moderate wing.

As minister of the economy Onganía appointed Adalbert Krieger Vaseña, who presided over a program of spurring foreign investment to revive the lagging economy. To attract foreign capital, Krieger Vaseña removed all restrictions on profit remittances; he also stimulated the process of industrial denationalization by devaluating the peso by 40 percent. Devaluation of the peso meant that many local companies could no longer afford expensive capital imports and royalty payments to owners of foreign technology. These local companies disappeared, leaving their share of the market to the remaining firms. In this way, Coca Cola and Pepsi gained control of 75 percent of the soft-drink market. Bankruptcies grew from 1,647 in 1968 to 2,982 in 1970. In other cases, devaluation encouraged the process of acquisition of national companies by foreign firms, a process that had grown almost uninterruptedly since Frondizi's time. Between 1963 and 1971, foreign interests bought out fifty-three Argentine companies representing almost every industrial sector, particularly the automotive, chemical, petrochemical, metallurgical, and tobacco industries. Meanwhile, wages were frozen, although prices continued their steady rise.

Growing outrage on the part of workers and students over the government's economic program, especially its policy of industrial denationalization and the wage freeze, erupted into violence in the interior in the spring of 1969. Major riots took place in Rosario, Corrientes, and Córdoba. In Córdoba, the most industrialized city of Argentina, workers and students rose in revolt, occupying major sectors of the city until they were ousted by troops. At the same time, there was an upsurge of urban guerrilla activity by a number of groups, of which the most important was the Montoneros, who represented the left wing of the Peronist movement. Their tactics included raids on police stations, assassinations, and robberies. In May 1970, the Montoneros kidnaped and later killed former President Aramburu.

Onganía's failure to cope with the mounting wave of guerrilla activity precipitated the military coup of June 1970, which deposed him and installed General Roberto M. Levingston as president. An expert in military intelligence and counterinsurgency, Levingston decreed the death penalty for terrorist acts and kidnapings; his repressive decrees were answered with fresh acts of violence by the guerrillas. Meanwhile, to make things worse, the economy, after some recovery under Ongania, turned down again in 1970–1971. Industrial production declined and unemployment increased.

THE RETURN OF PERÓN

Displeased with a resurgence of labor unrest, the military ousted Levingston in March 1971. His replacement, General Alejandro Lanusse, carried out a dual policy combining brutal repression of leftist guerrillas with a general liberalization of the political climate. In effect admitting the military's failure to renovate Argentine politics, Lanusse undertook negotiations that led to the restoration of political activity and the return of the Peronists to full electoral participation for the first time since 1955.

The military briefly held out hope that the moderate political parties would unite to stand against the Peronists, but the latter's superior organization and their leader's unchallenged popularity assured their victory. The Peronists formed the FREJULI party (*Frente Justicialista de Liberación* or Justicialist Liberation Front) which nominated Héctor J. Cámpora, a leader of the Peronist left wing, as its presidential candidate. Cámpora handily won the March 1973 election with 50 percent of the vote against 21 percent for Radical party candidate Ricardo Balbín. In a series of fast-moving events during the spring and summer, Cámpora took office in May, Juan Perón returned from exile in June, Cámpora resigned in July to pave the way for Perón. Perón, with his wife Isabel Martínez de Perón as his running mate, was overwhelmingly elected president in September.

At the heart of the Peronist program were formal agreements with labor and industry that pledged compliance with a wage and price freeze. (These included the so-called Social Contract, or *Pacto Social,* with the labor unions and the *Acto Compromiso del Campo* with industrialists.) This cooperation lasted for about a year, while the Argentine economy, buoyed by high world market prices for beef and grain, boomed. The agreements disintegrated in mid-1974 with the onset of renewed inflation brought on by a huge increase in international oil prices.

Even before these economic arrangements ended, the Peronist movement had begun to disintegrate, divided between left and right wings. By the time Perón died in July 1974, the regime had already veered rightward. With the rise of Welfare Minister José López Rega during the first months of President Isabel Perón's administration, the shift to the right quickened. The level of violence increased. (In 1975 left- and right-wing thugs reportedly killed 1,100 people.) Rightist "death squads" roamed the streets. Left-wing terrorists staged spectacular kidnappings. In the face of escalating violence and economic chaos, the military stepped in again, overthrowing Isabel Perón in March 1976 and installing General Jorge Rafael Videla as president of a three-man junta composed of the three commanders of the armed forces.

MILITARY RULE

In the ensuing years, the military presided over a roller-coaster economy that has torn the guts out of Argentine industry and a reign of terror unprecedented in the nation's history. The Videla government managed to reduce inflation from over 300 percent in both 1975 and 1976 to an average of 170 percent from 1977 to 1979 and 100 percent in 1980. By the summer of 1982, however, the annual rate of inflation shot up to a catastrophic 500 percent, the highest in the world. Economic growth fluctuated wildly: the gross domestic product (the total of all the goods and services produced) grew in 1977 and 1979 and fell in 1978 and 1980. During the first six months of 1982, the GDP fell a dismaying 7 percent. Worst of all, the free market policies of finance minister José Alfredo Martínez de Hoz led to record numbers of bankruptcies and bank failures. By eliminating tariffs on imported industrial goods and reducing government involvement in the economy, Martínez de Hoz presided over the destruction of many of Argentina's largest corporations. The real wages of Argentine workers plummeted 40 percent between 1976 and 1979, before recovering in 1980 and falling again in the severe crisis of 1982. The Catholic church set up soup kitchens in order to feed the needy in Buenos Aires. Many professionals, desperate for work, drive taxis or sell gum on the streets. More than 800,000 Argentines have left their country in search of economic opportunity since the military junta took power in 1976.

Unlike in its previous coups of 1955 and 1966, the military for the first five years of its dictatorship seemed determined to maintain itself in power in order to effect a "Process of National Reorganization." To this end the junta banned all normal political activity and embarked on a "dirty war" against the left. Since 1976, an estimated 6,000 to 15,000 (some calculate as high as 24,000) Argentines have disappeared (they are called *desaparecidos* or disappeared ones), many victims of illegal rightist death squads. Argentines came to fear the knock on the door at midnight, after which unknown kidnappers would take family and friends, who were never to be heard from again. Those lucky enough to survive inprisonment have recounted terrifying tales of torture and mistreatment.

Retired Major General Roberto Viola succeeded Videla as president in October 1980. He was unable to manage the growing economic crisis and deepening criticism from landowners and industrialists, who had ranked among the regime's firmest backers. With the "dirty war" won by 1980, the military itself was split into hard-liners (*duros*) and moderates (*blandos*) over whether or not to ease repression.

In response to intensifying criticism, Viola opened his cabinet to representatives of critical groups. This came too late, however. The military ousted Viola in November 1981, replacing him with the commander-in-chief of the army, General Leopoldo Galtieri.

The unpopularity of the military widened as the economy continued to deteriorate and the full extent of its butchery was gradually revealed to the Argentine people. The persistent marches of mothers of the *desaparecidos* in Buenos Aires and the revelations of newspaper editor Jacobo Timmerman brought the junta international notoriety.[2]

THE MALVINAS WAR

In April 1982, Galtieri took a desperate gamble to divert the nation from its economic woes and unite Argentines behind the regime. He

---

[2] Timmerman was imprisoned and tortured. His memoirs *Prisoner Without a Name, Cell Without a Number* accused the junta of virulent anti-Semitism.

Argentines rally in support of the war for the
Malvinas (Falklands). (United Press International
Photo)

sent Argentine forces to capture the Malvinas
Islands (known also as the Falklands) in the
South Atlantic three hundred miles off the coast.
Argentina and Great Britain had both claimed
the islands for 150 years. For the previous 17
years the two nations had conducted on-and-
off negotiations to turn them over to Argentina,
but each time agreement seemed imminent talks
had broken off. On April 2, Galtieri sent 9,000
troops to settle the matter once and for all.

The invasion was the culmination of a series
of colossal miscalculations by the Argentine
military. First, Galtieri had not expected Britain
to fight to retain the islands. The British, however, sensitive to their position as a declining
world power, chose to fight as a matter of na-

tional honor. The Argentines also misjudged
the position of the United States. They believed
that the Americans, who had recently made a
number of friendly overtures, would remain
neutral in the conflict. Instead, after an initial
period during which it tried to mediate a peaceful
agreement, the United States actively supported
the British.

The war was a disaster for Argentina. Although the Air Force acquitted itself well, inflicting heavy casualties on the British, the Navy
stayed in port after the tragic loss of the *Belgrano*
(300 men died) and, most importantly, the Army
disgraced itself. Poorly trained, atrociously led
Argentine troops offered little resistance to the
British. Some Argentine commanders actually

abandoned their soldiers. In the ten-week war the British recaptured the islands and took the Argentine army prisoner. There were nearly 2,000 casualties in all, and 600 Argentines died.

In addition to the devastating loss on the battlefield, the military lost credibility by misleading Argentines with false reports of victory. In the aftermath of the war, Argentina faced a political and economic crisis of unprecedented proportions. Galtieri was forced out, replaced by another retired general Reynaldo Benito Antonio Bignone in July. He promised new congressional elections by the end of 1983 and an end to military rule by the end of 1984. The main sticking point in returning to civilian rule was the growing popular pressure for the military to account for the "missing ones." The

military feared retribution for the crimes of the dirty war. One report issued by the government that tried to whitewash the problem of the *desaparecidos* was met with widespread cynicism. As agitation for democracy increased in 1983, the regime stepped up its repression and the death squads resumed their activities against protestors.

Although the restoration of democratic rule was all but inevitable, Argentina faced profound problems. The political and economic dislocations resulting from the years of military rule would certainly take years to repair. The political alignments that produced the vicious cycle of military coups had changed little, if at all. By 1983 Argentina remained a nation of promise unfulfilled.

CHAPTER FOURTEEN

The Chilean Way

For a century and a half, Chile set a high standard of political behavior on a continent notorious for its turmoil and dictatorships. Compared to its neighbors, Peru, Bolivia, and Argentina, Chile was a model of domestic tranquillity, rarely disturbed by popular unrest, regional conflicts, or a petulant and meddlesome military. The nation seemed for the most part to have escaped the harsh class and ideological confrontations that had led other Latin American countries to flirt with fascism during the 1930s and fall under the rule of extreme right-wing military regimes during the 1960s. Chilean democracy appeared so firmly rooted that it permitted the election and installation of a Marxist head of state, President Salvador Allende Gossens, in 1970. Only three years later, however, amid growing economic and political chaos, military rebels overthrew Chile's legitimate government, killed President Allende, and established a right-wing dictatorship whose rule was characterized by brutal oppression.

How could Chile maintain its parliamentary democracy so long when the rest of Latin America could not? Why, after almost a hundred and fifty years of respect for parliamentary democracy, did it crumble so swiftly? The answers to these questions lie in the nature of the Chilean political process and its socioeconomic underpinnings. In retrospect, the bounds of Chilean democracy were narrowly drawn; the elite never allowed political freedom and the practice of politics to endanger its basic interests. Instead of seeking to solve the nation's desperate economic and social problems, successive governments merely evaded them. When, finally, a coalition government headed by Chile's working-class parties came to power in 1970 and inaugurated structural reforms that threatened oligarchical privilege, the elite responded by calling in the army, abolishing parliamentary democracy, and establishing a reactionary dictatorship.

AN ECONOMIC HISTORY, 1900–1970

The Export Sector in the Twentieth Century

The export sector played a crucial and basically detrimental role in Chilean history. Raw material exports generated enormous profits, but relatively few benefits flowed to the nation as a whole. Instead of stimulating balanced economic growth, the lucrative export sector tended to stunt the country's social and political development. Like the "banana republics" of Central America and the sugar islands of the Caribbean, Chile relied for its revenues on one export commodity, first nitrate and then copper, making it extremely vulnerable to cyclical world market demands for its products. Moreover, the copper industry, which produced the nation's major export in the twentieth century, was operated as an enclave, almost totally isolated from the rest of the economy. Finally, and most importantly, the presence of an export sector that

produced sufficient revenue to operate the government and provide employment for a growing middle class enabled the Chilean oligarchy to retain political power and maintain an obsolete system of land tenure and use; these conditions severely hampered the growth of democracy and economic development.

Until World War I, nitrate was Chile's primary export, but after the war a cheaper, synthetic product displaced it on the world market; copper then became Chile's leading export. Initially, small-scale, low-technology operations mined most of Chile's copper, but shortly after 1900 a downturn in copper prices forced many of these producers to close. At the same time, the introduction of improved methods for the extraction of low-grade ore and the lower transportation costs promised by the opening of the Panama Canal attracted large North American companies, which soon came to dominate the industry.

From 1904 to 1923 giant United States–based corporations such as Guggenheim, Kennecott, Anaconda, and Braden purchased the largest and most productive copper mines, including the three mines of the *Gran Minería*.

In 1960 the three great mines of the Gran Minería, all owned by the foreign giants Anaconda and Kennecott, accounted for 11 percent of the country's gross national product, 50 percent of its exports, and 20 percent of government revenues. They pumped from $150 to $200 million a year into the economy. But these millions of dollars in sales, profits, and tax revenues generated by copper mining provided little stimulus for Chilean commerce and industry. Copper extraction was capital-intensive and required relatively few employees. The Gran Minería, for example, employed only seventeen thousand workers in 1960 (including miners and white-collar staff). Employment in the mines declined steadily in the post–World War II era, and the surplus of miners made it possible for the companies to pay the largely unskilled labor force relatively low wages. Until the 1950s, machinery, equipment, and technical skills were imported entirely from abroad.

The copper companies earned huge profits, which they remitted to their parent corporations in the United States, adding to the outflow of capital from the country. Chile's modest share in copper's riches took the form of taxes, wages, and other limited economic linkages. Until 1925, however, tax revenue was meager. The Braden Company, for example, paid only $1 million in taxes from 1913 to 1924 on sales of $135 million. The Chilean government did not impose an income tax on profits until 1925, when the levy was set at 6 percent. Subsequently, the tax rate was raised to 18 percent in 1931, to 33 percent in 1938, and to 60 percent in 1953.

A brief history of the copper industry since 1929 illustrates Chile's vulnerability to world market cycles. In 1929, the price of copper dropped precipitously. The value of the production of the Gran Minería fell, in the period from 1929 to 1931, from $111 million to $33 million, as the price of copper dropped from 17.5 cents per pound to 7 cents. Since the government relied heavily on copper taxes for revenue, the depression forced it to curtail daily operations severely and default on its large foreign debt. In 1932, the United States, Chile's main market for copper, adopted a high tariff on copper imports, which caused mine closings and severe unemployment.

Copper prices recovered in 1935, however, and by 1937 copper production exceeded the predepression level. World War II brought a new copper boom, although profits and revenues were limited by price ceilings imposed by the United States. After the war, with the elimination of controls, prices skyrocketed. The Korean war (1950–1953) brought new price controls by the United States, but on somewhat better terms for Chile. In 1953, world market prices again plummeted, and Chile was rescued only by the United States government's purchase of a hundred thousand tons of copper for its military reserve. By the mid-1950s, copper boomed

again, and the boom continued through the 1960s. A new down cycle, however, occurred during the last two years of the Allende administration (1971–1973).

The revenues generated from copper taxes enabled the government to avoid taxing large landholdings. Without the spur of equitable taxes, latifundists continued to leave vast tracts of fertile land uncultivated or underutilized. Although it had the potential to feed its own people, Chile had to import foodstuffs—a policy that drained the nation of foreign exchange that would have been better used to purchase capital goods for industrialization or to build roads and harbors.

An equitable tax on idle or underutilized land might have led to the breakup of the latifundia, the modernization of agriculture, and the emergence of a class of small peasant proprietors. Thanks to government policy in favor of the latifundia, however, none of these things happened. Chilean agriculture remained relatively backward and inefficient (per capita production in agriculture actually declined by about 5 percent between 1940 and 1970), and such commercialization of agriculture as occurred resulted in further proletarianization of the peasantry.

With its coffers swelled by revenue from the export sector, the Chilean government expanded its role in the economy. A large bureaucracy developed, staffed by an emerging middle class. As the government became the major employer of the middle class and the nation's most important venture capitalist, Chile grew ever more dependent for its economic development on external factors beyond its control.

Foreign Domination of the Chilean Economy

After World War I, the United States replaced Great Britain as the major foreign investor in Chile. By 1920, North American investors had placed $250 million in direct investment in the country, with an additional $100 million in loans and portfolio investments. By 1930 it had risen to more than $1 billion. Guggenheim and Anaconda accounted for better than 80 percent of the copper production, Bethlehem monopolized iron ore, and Guggenheim held 70 percent of the nitrate industry through its *Compañía de Salitres de Chile* (Chilean Nitrate Company, or COSACH).

Although depression and war slowed the inflow, foreign capital surged into Chile in the postwar period—not only into the extractive sector but into manufacturing and commerce as well. From 1954 to 1970, foreigners invested $1.67 billion in Chile, mostly during the period from 1962 to 1970. U.S. companies continued to dominate copper, nitrate, and iodine production. Foreign companies also dominated the import trade, conducting approximately half the nation's wholesale trade. Foreign companies monopolized the telephone and telegraph industries and had important stakes in electric utilities and banking. Even the major advertising agencies were foreign subsidiaries or affiliates.

Foreigners owned 20 percent of the stock of Chile's manufacturing companies in 1969; in the most important growth industries, such as chemicals, transport equipment, and rubber and electrical products, holdings were higher, ranging from 33 to 60 percent. Foreign investment centered in the largest companies, controlling the administration of forty of the one hundred largest Chilean corporations and substantial blocks of stock in twenty-one others.

Chile depended not only on direct investment from abroad but on loans as well. Payment of interest and amortization on the national debt consumed an increasing share of its revenue from the export sector. In addition, foreign investors financed 30 percent of all private investments in Chile. The country also relied on foreign sources for industrial technology.

Because most foreign investment, like the copper enclave, was capital-intensive, it provided little employment and few linkages to the rest of the economy. The benefits to Chile's long-range economic development were minimal.

Without doubt, Chile was not the master of its own economic fate. This fact became particularly evident when the nation embarked on its socialist experiment in 1970.

The Concentration of Land and Wealth

In 1964, on the eve of the first serious effort in Chile's history to reform its agrarian structure, there was an extreme concentration of landownership, the condition of rural laborers was wretched, and the inefficient great landed estates were clearly incapable of providing enough food to feed Chile's growing urban centers. By contrast with the situation in most underdeveloped nations, Chile's agricultural sector played only a small role in the economy. It accounted for less than 10 percent of the gross national product and employed less than 25 percent of the work force. The inability of agriculture to provide employment, on the one hand, and sufficient food, on the other, resulted in an overurbanized, underemployed, and undernourished population.

The statistics for landholding indicate that there was little change in these patterns between 1930 and 1970. In 1930, holdings of over 2,500 acres composed only 2 percent of the total number of farms but comprised 78 percent of the cultivable land. Eighty-two percent of all farms were under 125 acres but held only 4 percent of the land. By the 1960s, 11,000 units, accounting for 4.2 percent of the farms, composed 79 percent of the land. Farms under 100 acres—77 percent of all farms—held 10.6 percent of the land. Over 700,000 people, the majority of the rural labor force, had no land at all. The living and working conditions of agricultural laborers were appalling—and getting worse. Agricultural wages had consistently declined since the 1940s, falling 23 percent from 1953 to 1964. The average annual per capita income of small farmers and farm laborers was a mere $100.

Government credit and tax policies before

1964 assured that the maldistribution of land and agricultural income would continue. Small landholders, having no access to bank or government loans, had to rely on moneylenders or store owners, who charged outrageous interest. Smallholders and agricultural laborers also bore a disproportionate burden of taxes. The Chilean tax structure was such that taxes on sales and other transactions (turnover taxes) exacted a higher toll from lower-income groups, because most of their transactions involved the purchase of foodstuffs. Taxes on land, capital, income, and inheritance, on the other hand, were light. The large estates, especially those that were not farmed, went virtually untaxed.

Despite unused land and plentiful manpower, production of food did not keep pace with population growth from the mid-1930s. The deficit had to be made up by imports, which aggravated the balance of payments problem and contributed to Chile's chronic inflation. Livestock production, for example, remained stagnant during this period, while the population nearly doubled. As a result, the poor were undernourished, and even large portions of the middle class suffered from inadequate diet.

Land was not the only sector of the Chilean economy concentrated in a very few hands. A few powerful clans controlled a wide variety of industrial and financial enterprises and thus exerted a decisive influence on the national economy as a whole. Typically, each sector of the economy was controlled by one, two, or three large companies; this, as noted previously, was especially true of sectors dominated by foreign companies. In 1967, 12 companies out of 2,600 transacted nearly half the total wholesale business in the country. One bank, Banco de Chile, furnished 32 percent of the nation's private bank credit; the five largest banks furnished 57.4 percent.

These facts, however, tell only part of the story, for control of the economy was even more concentrated. According to Stefan De Vylder, fifteen large economic groups controlled the Chilean economy. The most powerful of the clans, the Edwards family, controlled one commercial bank, seven financial and investment corporations, five insurance companies, thirteen industries, and two publishing houses and was closely associated with North American companies active in the country. The family's newspaper chain accounted for over half the circulation of daily newspapers in Chile; together with another publishing house, it virtually controlled the entire market for periodicals.

A POLITICAL HISTORY, 1891–1970

The Parliamentary Republic, 1891–1920

The defeat and suicide of President José Manuel Balmaceda during the civil war of 1891 ushered in the era of the so-called Parliamentary Republic. It was a time of political stagnation, in sharp contrast to the rapid social change. The contradiction between an immobile political structure and a rapidly changing society became increasingly apparent in the first two decades of the twentieth century. The dominant political parties, the Liberal and Conservative parties, represented the great landowners of the Central Valley and supplied the nation's presidents and congressmen. The six presidents who served during the period of the Parliamentary Republic were little more than puppets manipulated by congressional leaders.[1]

A third major party, the Radicals, founded in 1861 by dissident Liberals, enjoyed the support of low-level professionals, bureaucrats, teachers, artisans, and other middle-class groups, as well as that of large landowners on the southern frontier around Concepción, northern mine owners from the Copiapó region, and businessmen from Santiago, the capital. A

---

[1] Jorge Montt (1891–1896), Federico Errázuriz Echaurren (1896–1901), Germán Riesco (1901–1906), Pedro Montt (1906–1910), Ramón Barros Luco (1910–1915), and Juan Luis Sanfuentes (1915–1920).

fourth party, the Democrats, had some base in the lower middle class and among workers.

The only issue separating the major parties was the role of the church in education. The chief concerns of the parties appeared to be the preservation of the status quo and the distribution of the spoils of office. Corruption and inefficiency pervaded the political life of the era.

While politics stagnated in an atmosphere of fraud and apathy, Chilean society underwent profound transformation. The nation grew increasingly urbanized and industrialized, and new classes emerged from these processes. An industrial working class rose in the mining regions of the north, first in the nitrate fields and then in the copper mines. Although their wages were higher than elsewhere in the country, the miners suffered from low pay, inadequate housing, the tyranny of company stores, and unsafe working conditions. In the cities, where wages were even lower, workers lived in wretched slums and were periodically battered by epidemic disease.

After the turn of the century, workers began to struggle against these dismal conditions. The first major strike broke out in Iquique in the northern mining region in 1901 and lasted for two months. Workers of the South American Steamship Line struck in 1903 and again in 1905 in Valparaíso, Chile's major port. In 1907 the nitrate workers of Iquique again struck against inhuman living and working conditions; the government responded by sending in troops that slaughtered two thousand workers. The wave of strikes continued, with a notable upsurge during World War I. Unrest increased at the war's end, for the nitrate industry collapsed, leaving thousands of miners unemployed and plunging the entire country into a severe depression. In 1919, faced with growing unrest, the government declared a state of siege (suspending civil liberties) in the mining areas.

Labor had meantime begun to organize in the effort to achieve better conditions. Luis Em-ilio Recabarren played a leading part in establishing the Workers' Federation of Chile (*Federación de Obreros de Chile*, or FOCH) in 1909. Three years later he founded the first workers' party, the Socialist, or Socialist Labor, party. In 1922 it became the Communist party and joined the Third (Communist) International. By contrast with the Argentine Socialist party, with its large middle-class base, Chile's first working-class party grew directly out of the labor movement.

In the same period, the middle class became larger and more diverse. The growth of industry and commerce and the expansion of the state created many new white-collar jobs. This growing middle class displayed few of the entrepreneurial traits commonly associated with the North American and European middle classes. The domination of decisive sectors of the economy by large-scale enterprise effectively barred small and medium-size entrepreneurs from playing an important role in economic life. The inflationary policies pursued by oligarchical governments, which eroded the savings needed to finance middle-class business, further discouraged such ventures. Aristocratic control of choice government jobs through clientele and kinship ties also restricted the sphere of middle-class activity. As the twentieth century opened, the middle class began to agitate for a place in the sun.

Meanwhile, the composition of the oligarchy was also changing, for it began to incorporate new elements from among industrialists and businessmen. More completely than elsewhere in Latin America, the Chilean landed elite fused with the new urban upper and upper-middle classes. They intermarried, and the urban rich acquired land, adopting the values of the traditional elite. This elite, instead of investing its wealth from the land in industry, often preferred to spend it on conspicuous consumption. The ability of the state to provide salaried jobs to many members of the middle class, and the elite's policy of forming kinship and social ties with the new industrialist and business class, meant that conflicts between the oligarchy and the bourgeoisie were kept to a minimum, save in times of serious economic crisis. This was a serious impediment to reform. Missing in Chile, too, were the large number of immigrants who in some measure challenged the values and hegemony of the elite in Argentina. The relatively few immigrants who came to Chile preferred to emulate rather than challenge the oligarchy.

Alessandri, the Military Radicals, and Reform

By 1920, even sections of the oligarchy were aware that they could no longer ignore the needs of the rest of Chilean society. It was apparent that some concessions to the working and middle classes had to be made, but the elite appeared incapable of devising a solution for the country's grave economic and social problems. In 1918 the Liberal Alliance, which included Radicals, Liberals, Democrats, and *Balmacedists*, achieved control of the Chamber of Deputies in the election of that year, and in 1920 it offered a possible "savior" of the country, nicknamed the "Lion of Tarapacá," Arturo Alessandri, as its candidate for president.

A former corporation lawyer turned populist politician, Alessandri appealed to the lower and middle classes with promises to reform the constitution and relieve the bleakness of working-class life. He promised a social security system, a labor code, cheap housing, educational reform, women's rights, and state control of banks and insurance companies. With considerable support from sections of the oligarchy, which hoped that he could placate the restless masses with a minimum of effective social change, Alessandri defeated the candidate of the conservative National Union in the close presidential election of 1920.

During the first four years of Alessandri's term, he proved unable to make good his campaign pledges. The Liberal Alliance, which had

Chilean President Arturo Alessandri. (United Press International)

supported his election, split and failed to give him the support he needed in Congress. Moreover, although the Liberal Alliance controlled the Chamber of Deputies, it did not control the Senate, where conservative opposition blocked passage of reform legislation. The postwar depression also forced Alessandri to lay aside reform projects while he wrestled with economic problems. Widespread unemployment in Santiago and Valparaíso caused general strikes to erupt in those cities, bringing them to a standstill. Strikes and lockouts plagued the economy. The president issued ever more paper currency to pay unemployment benefits; the result was runaway inflation. In 1925 the peso was worth only half its 1920 value. The only reform measures secured by Alessandri were a minimum wage law and a trifling tax reform.

Congress, representing entrenched oligarchical interests, stood squarely in the way of any meaningful social and political reforms. Accordingly, Alessandri urged the passage of laws that would restore the balance of power between Congress and the executive branch—a balance destroyed after the civil war of 1891. He wanted an end to congressional censure of cabinet members, a practice that had toppled successive cabinets and kept Chilean governments in turmoil for three decades. He also sought such social reforms as a shorter workday, labor laws to protect women and children, the right of workers to strike, and health insurance. These modest proposals certainly did not threaten the status quo, but they would require money. In view of the catastrophic decline of the nitrate industry, this money could be raised only by taxing the oligarchy's land and income—a solution the elite found unthinkable. As a result of the parliamentary deadlock, the Chilean government could not cope with the mounting economic and social crisis.

The Liberal Alliance won a majority in both houses of Congress in 1924, but the new Congress, ignoring the pressing need for reform legislation, proceeded to vote themselves salaries for the first time in Chilean history. The innovation was entirely proper, for congressmen no longer came exclusively from the oligarchy and needed salaries to support themselves, but in a time of depression, when many public employees had not been paid for many weeks, it gave great offense.

The Chilean military, predominantly of middle-class origins, had observed the unfolding crisis with growing impatience and resentment. Many junior and middle-grade officers favored the enactment of Alessandri's social and political reform program; they also felt that Congress had neglected the needs of the armed forces. For these officers, the salary episode was the last straw. Organized in a military junta, they staged a coup on September 5, 1924, and compelled Congress to enact in rapid succession all of Alessandri's reform proposals and, in addition, to raise the size of the army and its pay

scale. Alessandri, however, refused to share power with the military and left the country.

Growing tension between progressive junior and middle-grade officers on the one hand and conservative generals on the other produced another coup in January 1925, which brought to power a reform-minded group of officers, led by Carlos Ibáñez del Campo and Marmaduke Grove. The new junta promptly invited Alessandri to return, which he did in March.

On his return, Alessandri set about accomplishing the political reforms for which he had campaigned. The result was the constitution of 1925, which ended the Parliamentary Republic and restored the balance of power between Congress and the president. It provided that the president would be elected by direct vote, serve a six-year term, be ineligible for immediate re-election, and have control over his cabinet and government finance. The constitution proclaimed the inviolable right of private property but stated that this right could be limited in the interest of social needs. Other measures included a new and extensive labor code, the grant of the vote to literate males over twenty-one, the establishment of an electoral registry to reduce electoral fraud, a nominal income tax on income over ten thousand pesos a year, and the establishment of a central bank.

In September, a plebiscite approved the constitution, although Conservatives and Radicals abstained from voting. Soon thereafter, Alessandri again resigned, citing unbearable military pressure. The ensuing election brought to the presidency the weak and colorless Emilio Figueroa Larrain. However, Ibáñez, who became interior minister in the new administration, gradually emerged as a strong man. Blaming the country's problems on communism, Congress, and the leadership of all political parties, he proceeded to jail or deport Communists and key members of Congress who dared to challenge his power. On May 5, 1927, placed in an untenable position by Ibáñez's inroads on his authority, President Figueroa resigned the presidency. Less than two weeks later, Ibáñez, running unopposed, was elected president in a special election.

Ibáñez and the Great Depression

The military reform movement of 1924, which for a time appeared to be forging an alliance with the working and middle classes for the achievement of structural reforms, ended in the military dictatorship of Ibáñez (1927–1931). The only fruits of that movement for social change were the social legislation adopted since 1924 and provided for in the constitution of 1925.

To implement that legislation and secure the position of state employees, which was necessary to maintain political stability, Ibáñez needed substantial amounts of money; his program of welfare, public works, and modernization was based above all on huge loans from foreign bankers. Between 1927 and 1931, the government borrowed and spent approximately $250 million on public works and government projects. The armed forces were a special beneficiary of government largesse, obtaining generous promotions and salary increases.

The so-called Ibáñez land reform involved efforts at colonization of some state-owned lands, the improvement of credit facilities in underdeveloped areas, and the breaking up of a few large estates. Ibáñez spent large sums on education—five times as much as had been spent in 1920—and the number of schools, teachers, and students increased steadily from 1924 to 1931. Educational reform failed, however, because too few teachers were available and because Ibáñez saw education primarily as a propaganda tool. Meanwhile, all opposition was suppressed, political foes were jailed or deported, and efforts were made to split the Communist-led labor movement by the sponsorship of government-backed unions.

Aided by a temporary revival of copper and nitrate sales and massive foreign loans, the Chilean economy prospered for the first two years of Ibáñez's rule. But the Wall Street crash of 1929 cut off the all-important flow of capital and loans, and by the following year the nitrate and copper markets had both collapsed. Unemployment spread throughout the nation. In a vain effort to find a solution for the economic crisis, the government chartered the Chilean Nitrate Company (COSACH), dominated by the Guggenheim interests, which tried to maintain a price level by restricting the amount sold at given times. Ibáñez trimmed social services and his public works program and hiked taxes, but the financial situation grew increasingly desperate.

In July 1931, confronted by a general strike that involved not only workers but professionals, white-collar employees, and students and faced with growing doubts about the army's loyalty to him, Ibáñez resigned and went into exile in Argentina. The next seventeen months brought a succession of military coups. One such coup, led by Marmaduke Grove, commander of the air force, led to the proclamation of a Socialist Republic of Chile, which lasted barely twelve days before it was overthrown by a new military revolt. The socialist republic was the last gasp of a small group of officers who had been radicalized by the crisis of the 1920s. Ironically, the program of the socialist republic was not socialist; it proposed, rather, to create jobs through public works financed by the issue of paper money.

Finally in September 1932, a new coup led by General Bartolomé Blanche installed a caretaker regime that presided over new elections and a return to civilian government. In the presidential election, Arturo Alessandri, supported by Radicals, Liberals, Democrats, and even some Conservatives, defeated five rivals, including the Socialist Grove.

The Return of Alessandri

Alessandri began his second term in the depths of the depression, with a hundred and sixty thousand people unemployed in Santiago alone, while a typhoid epidemic ravaged the country. Income from nitrates was one-twentieth the 1927 figure; public employees, including soldiers and policemen, had not been paid for months. In the succeeding five years, 1932 to 1937, the president and his finance minister, Gustavo Ross, presided over an economic recovery that reflected a partial revival and stabilization of the world market. Exports more than tripled, nitrate and industrial production rose, unemployment was eliminated, and the budget was balanced. During the last years of Alessandri's term, the government actually had a budget surplus. In 1933, Alessandri replaced the COS-ACH nitrate monopoly, in which the Guggenheim interests had the largest share with the Chilean Nitrate and Iodine Corporation, earmarking one-fourth of its profits for the government. However, he avoided interference with the American-controlled copper industry. As the economy revived, government revenues increased, and Alessandri had more money to implement social legislation already on the books.

But Alessandri had no greater success in solving Chile's structural problems in the 1930s than he did in the 1920s. Foreign capital controlled the lucrative mining sector of the economy, and the inefficient latifundio continued to dominate Chilean agriculture. The urban and rural working class received few benefits from the economic revival; those social reforms that touched urban areas did nothing for Chile's tenant farmers and farm laborers. The government's devaluation of the peso, designed to stimulate exports, sharply increased the cost of living while wages remained stable. Workers' strikes for better wages and living conditions were often brutally suppressed.

Middle-class critics of the regime fared little better. Following the example of Ibáñez, Alessandri closed down hostile newspapers, exiled political critics, and dealt highhandedly with Congress. Against the background of the rise

and expansion of fascism in Europe, Alessandri's autocratic methods appeared to threaten a similar fate for Chile. These conditions produced a major new effort to mobilize workers, peasants, and the urban middle sector to defend democracy and promote social progress. This effort was called the Chilean Popular Front.

The Rise of the Left and the Popular Front

The Chilean left had its roots in the Socialist Labor party, founded by Luis Emilio Recabarren in 1912; ten years later, it joined the Third (Communist) International and became the Communist party. During the 1920s, the Communists won considerable support among organized labor, particularly the railroad workers' union and the Confederation of Chilean Workers (FOCH), which claimed two hundred thousand members. Later, however, the Communists suffered a series of severe setbacks. Recabarren killed himself in 1924, apparently from despair over the military dictatorship that replaced Alessandri. Although they had had a part in framing the constitution of 1925, Communist leaders were imprisoned and exiled during the Ibáñez regime. After the fall of Ibáñez in 1931, however, the party began to revive under the leadership of Carlos Contreras Labarca, and it gained considerable popularity among both workers and intellectuals.

The communists' principal rival on the left was the Socialist party. Its predominantly middle-class leadership, though it advocated a leftist program that included revolution, was highly opportunistic, especially the charismatic Marmaduke Grove, who repeatedly left and re-entered the party. From the first, the party was an uneasy alliance of left and right wings. In general, it was not as firmly rooted in the industrial working class as the Communist party.

Despite the economic recovery during Alessandri's second term, Chile in the 1930s was fertile ground for the growth of left-wing parties and ideologies. Only the upper class benefited from the economic revival. Inflation eroded the living standards of the working class, which responded with strikes for better wages and living conditions. In February 1936, ten thousand railroad workers struck, and many other workers went out in sympathy strikes. Alessandri countered with repression: He declared a state of siege, dissolved Congress, and closed down the opposition press.

Alessandri's repressive policies and a severe depression helped give rise to the Chilean Popular Front between 1935 and 1937. International developments also played a part in its formation, for the Third International, alarmed by German, Italian, and Japanese imperialism and the growing threat of fascism, called on Communist parties in 1935 to form broad-based popular fronts with all supporters of democracy, including the progressive and democratic bourgeoisie. The Chilean Communist party quickly adopted this program. It suggested the formation of a popular front uniting itself, the Socialists, and the Radical party, which represented the middle class and sections of the bourgeoisie, to contest the presidential election of 1938 with a common candidate and platform. The Socialist party agreed in March 1937 to enter the Popular Front. Losses in the congressional elections of 1937 convinced the Radicals that only an alliance with the left-wing parties could win them the presidential election the following year; the hesitant Radicals joined the front.

The Popular Front nominated Radical Pedro Aguirre Cerda as its presidential candidate in 1938. The Popular Front's electoral platform called for the restoration of constitutional rule and civil liberties and basic social reforms, summed up in the slogan *pan, techo, y abrigo* (bread, clothing, and a roof). Despite the advantages enjoyed by Alessandri's candidate, Gustavo Ross, including control of the electoral machinery and the support of the large state bureaucracy, Aguirre Cerda gained a razor-thin victory, receiving 50.3 percent of the vote.

The short, stormy life of the Popular Front—it officially ended in 1941 when first the Socialists and then the Radicals withdrew, but was reformed in 1942 as a "Democratic Alliance" of Communists, Radicals, and miscellaneous groups that lasted until 1947—yielded some achievements. In 1938 the State Development Agency, CORFO, was formed to foster industrialization. Aided by a virtual cessation of imports as a result of World War II and by governmental policies of subsidies, low taxes, and protective tariffs on imported consumer goods, native manufacturing made steady progress between 1940 and 1945.

The policy of state-supported industrialization also promoted the growth of the Chilean industrial working class; between 1940 and 1952, the number of workers employed in manufacturing rose from 298,000 to 408,000—from 15 percent of the work force to 19 percent. The industrialization process was accompanied, at least until 1945, by an improvement in the workers' economic position: Workers' real purchasing power rose 20 percent between 1940 and 1945, while that of white-collar workers increased 25 percent. After 1945, as the incumbent Radical administrations moved to the right and the basis of the Popular Front strategy disintegrated, the working class's relative share of the national income declined sharply.

Aside from accelerated industrialization and the accompanying growth of the industrial working class, the Popular Front era produced no structural changes in the Chilean economy and society. Popular Front governments were unable to institute basic economic and social reforms because the members of the coalition had irreconcilable differences over domestic and foreign policy. During Aguirre Cerda's administration (1938–1941), the Communists and Socialists favored neutrality in World War II, while the Radicals sided with the Allies. This issue disappeared when Germany attacked the Soviet Union. Under Aguirre Cerda's successor, the Radical Juan Antonio Rios (1942–1946), the government's harsh suppression of a strike in the nitrate fields split the left.

The next Radical president, Gabriel González Videla (1946–1952), won election with the support of the Communist party, while the Socialist party ran its own candidate. González Videla's first Cabinet was a curious mix of three Radicals, three Communists, and three members of the Liberal party (actually a small conservative party that played a decisive role in González Videla's election by Congress after he had failed to get a majority of votes in the election). Soon, responding to the pressures of the cold war, González Videla moved to the right, ousted the Communist members of his Cabinet, broke a strike of Communist-led coal miners (with Socialist support), and the following year pushed through the Law for the Defense of Democracy, known unofficially as the *Ley Maldita*, or the Accursed Law, which outlawed the Communist party and eliminated Communists from Congress. González Videla also established a concentration camp for Communist party members and other left-wing militants in an abandoned mining camp in the northern desert. By now the Socialist party had officially split into two, the Socialist party of Chile, which endorsed González Videla's repressive measures, and the Popular Socialist party, which denounced the president's anticommunist drive.

Massive discontent with skyrocketing inflation, the freezing of workers' wages, and González Videla's repressive policies paved the way for a comeback by the old ex-dictator Carlos Ibáñez del Campo in 1952. Offering repeal of the Ley Maldita, a minimum salary, a family allowance for workers, and a sympathetic hearing for just wage demands, Ibáñez defeated several rival candidates, including Salvador Allende Gossens of the Socialist party, who had Communist support. But the decline in Chilean copper revenues following the end of the Korean war made it impossible for Ibáñez to make good on his populist promises. To stabilize the economy he sought loans from North American banks and the International Monetary Fund; meanwhile, he sought to force the working class to absorb inflation through cuts in real wages. Threatened with labor unrest, Ibáñez embarked on a course of harsh repression. By the end of his term, he had alienated all sectors of the Chilean people.

New Alignments: The Emergence of Christian Democracy

Between 1953 and the presidential election year of 1958, the parties of the left restored their unity by forming the *Frente de Acción Popular* (Popular Action Front, or FRAP), which included both wings of the reunited Socialist party and the Communists. Simultaneously, a new party emerged from the fusion in 1957 of the National Falange with the small Social Christian party. This party, the Christian Democratic party, led by Eduardo Frei, appealed to Catholic workers, especially white-collar sectors, with a vague ideology that claimed to be neither capitalist nor socialist. In its first try for office in 1958, it emerged as an important electoral force.

Four major candidates contested the presidency in 1958. They were the Conservative Jorge Alessandri, a son of the former president and a leading industrialist; Eduardo Frei, a Christian Democrat; Salvador Allende, of FRAP; and Luis Bossay, a Radical. Surprisingly Alessandri beat Allende by a threadbare margin of only 33,500 votes, and Allende would probably have won if an obscure minor-party candidate had not drawn away some slum and rural poor votes.

Alessandri had no more success than his predecessors in coping with Chile's problems of inflation and economic stagnation. His formula for recovery was to restore the free market, end state intervention in the economy, and employ foreign loans and investment as the basis for economic development. Between 1958 and 1964, Chile's foreign debt (public and private) climbed from $569 million to $1,896 million, with most of the loans coming from the United

States. In effect, Alessandri's policy was a replay of Ibáñez's effort between 1927 and 1932 to solve Chile's economic problems through an endless cycle of loans and repayments. By 1962, however, the injections of foreign capital had lost their capacity to stimulate the nation's economy. A serious balance of payments problem arose, and inflation began to increase again.

Politics in Chile during the early 1960s were profoundly affected by changes in United States policy in response to the Cuban Revolution (1959). The United States sought to bolster reform movements throughout Latin America as an alternative to social revolution. As part of this policy, it covertly financed the Christian Democrats. Combined with the backing of the conservative parties, which were badly scared by Allende's near-election six years earlier, U.S. support enabled Frei to win the 1964 election with 56 percent of the vote.

Frei and Christian Democracy, 1964–1970: A "Revolution in Freedom" Unfulfilled

Eduardo Frei came to the presidency with promises of a "revolution in freedom" that would correct the extreme inequities of Chilean society without a violent class struggle. The problems he faced were familiar ones: inflation and stagnation, a domestic market too narrow to support an efficient mass industry, and an industry and an agriculture incapable of supplying the basic needs of the population. In order to create the market needed for a modern mass industry, Frei proposed agrarian reform, tax reform, and other measures to redistribute income to the lower classes. Agrarian reform was bound to anger the traditional landed elite, but Frei counted on support from progressive industrialists, who understood that cheap production of food could hold down wage increases. He also counted on massive foreign economic aid from the United States.

Frei's plan for the Chileanization of the copper industry was designed both to appease widespread nationalist sentiment and to obtain new government revenue through increased copper production. The plan required the government to buy 51 percent of the shares in the foreign-owned mines. In return for a promise to increase production and refine more ore in Chile, the foreign companies retained control of management and obtained new concessions with respect to taxation and repatriation of profits. The agreement proved quite profitable for the companies concerned; in 1969 the Anaconda Copper Company drew 80 percent of all its profits from Chile. However, the plan failed to expand production significantly or to increase government revenues.

Frei's program of agrarian reform also had mixed results. He began by attempting to improve conditions in rural areas by increasing wages, establishing peasant unions, and instituting a more equitable system of taxation; he also redistributed some land to the peasants. However, inflation eroded wage gains, and land redistribution fell far short of what was promised. As a gradualist, Frei shied away from precipitous or widespread expropriations. Peasants who received land faced a difficult time, for the government did not provide them with credit needed to start off as independent farmers. In July 1967, the Christian Democrats pushed through a fundamental land reform law empowering the government to expropriate landholdings of over 80 hectares (approximately 190 acres) in fertile areas and the equivalent elsewhere, but Frei never implemented the law.

Frei lost labor support when he adopted a tough line toward strikes and wage demands and tried to undermine the country's major labor federation. Increased worker militancy made Socialist and Communist union leadership more influential.

As early as 1965, the president had decided on an economic policy that would attract foreign and domestic investors; as a result, he abandoned the redistributive efforts of his first year and froze wages. During 1966, the government reacted harshly to strikes in the copper mines, at one point sending in troops.

The need to appease his political constituency and the economic decline after 1966 defeated Frei's efforts at reform. Upper-class Catholic intellectuals had founded and provided the leadership of the Christian Democratic party. Its membership was overwhelmingly middle class, including urban professionals, white-collar workers—especially from the public sector—skilled workers, and managers—groups that had emerged during the preceding two decades as the Chilean economy diversified. The party did well in the larger towns, among urban slum dwellers, and among women. In 1964, Frei got considerable support from industrialists and bankers who feared the election of Allende. These were hardly the elements of a revolutionary party. Like the Argentine Radical party under Yrigoyen, the Christian Democrats could not risk alienating their main constituency in an attempt to better the condition of the working class. Their program of reform depended entirely on a healthy, expanding economy that would enable the government to distribute benefits to the lower class without injuring the middle class or altering the basic economic and social structures.

When Frei came to office in 1964, the economy was expanding rapidly, for the Vietnam war kept copper prices high. Frei's moderate reform goals insured good relations with the United States and a resulting flow of loans and private investment. Even Chile's chronic inflation slowed.[2] Two good years, however, were followed by four bad ones. After 1967 the economy stagnated while inflation surged again. From 1967 to 1970, inflation rose steadily, averaging almost 30 percent a year. Income inequalities increased, and living standards declined sharply. Frei's rhetoric brought hope to Chileans, but he fulfilled few of his promises. During his term, the working class grew increasingly restive. Groups like *pobladores* (urban slum dwellers) and rural workers organized for the first time. As the Christian Democrats proved less and less capable of dealing with Chile's economic woes, these newly organized groups and the trade unions moved further to the left. Inflation, wage and salary controls, rising taxes, shortages of consumer goods, and the costly but unsuccessful and unpopular copper policy further eroded Christian Democratic support and pushed the electorate leftward.

This leftward move was reflected within the Christian Democratic party itself. In 1969 disillusioned progressives split off to form the Movement for United Popular Action (MAPU), which later joined the Popular Unity Coalition. This break left Frei the leader of the right wing of the party and Radomiro Tomic the head of what remained of the left wing after the succession of MAPU. Since Frei was ineligible to run again under the constitution, and the party could not risk further erosion of its social base by running a hard-liner, it advanced Tomic as its presidential candidate in 1970. He ran on a platform almost indistinguishable from that of Allende, the candidate of the left coalition, *Unidad Popular* (Popular Unity, or UP), whose main elements were the Socialist, Communist, and Radical parties.

The right backed ex-President Jorge Alessandri, the standard-bearer of the National party (formed in 1966 through the merger of the Conservative and Liberal parties). The right, already alienated by Frei's agrarian reform, found Tomic totally unacceptable and refused to join forces with the Christian Democrats as it had in 1964. Allende won the election with 36 percent of the vote, while Alessandri got 35 percent and Tomic 28 percent. Since Allende failed to receive

[2] Inflation was 25.9 percent in 1965, 17 percent in 1966, 21.9 percent in 1967, 27.9 percent in 1968, 29.3 percent in 1969, and 34.3 percent in 1970.

Salvador Allende. (Ingeborg Lipmann/Magnum
Photos, Inc.)

a majority, the election went to Congress which,
after much-publicized maneuvering, approved
Allende as president.

THE CHILEAN ROAD
TO SOCIALISM

The Opposition

When Allende took office in 1970, political conditions appeared favorable to his program for
the achievement of socialism in Chile within a

framework of legality and nonviolence. The assassination in October 1970 of General René
Schneider, the commander in chief of the army,
who had kept the army neutral during the period
after the election just before Allende assumed
the presidency, had discredited the right. Prospects were excellent that the Popular Unity
would receive the cooperation of the left wing
of the Christian Democratic party in Congress.
For the time being, the UP coalition remained
united behind a program that called for the
progressive take-over of large foreign companies

and monopolies in the fields of commerce, industry, and land distribution and expropriation of all landholdings over 80 hectares.

Nonetheless, the array of forces against the UP was formidable. It did not have a majority in Congress. Both the judiciary and the *Contolaría General* (the government's fiscal arm) opposed Allende's policies. The entire domestic economic establishment, foreign interests (the most prominent of which was the International Telephone and Telegraph Company), much of the officer corps of the military and national police, and the Catholic church were also aligned against the UP. The anti-UP political coalition, the *Confederación Democrática* (Democratic Confederation) controlled virtually all of the nation's media—two of the three television stations, 95 percent of the radio stations, 90 percent of the newspaper circulation, and all of the weekly magazines.

On its side, the UP had 36.3 percent of the voters, who made up the best-organized and most politically active sector of the electorate. However, most of the labor force was unorganized (only 2 percent belonged to unions) and unsympathetic with the left. Wide disparities in the economic conditions of various sectors of the working class made it difficult to construct a program that would satisfy all interests. White-collar workers were much better off than blue-collar workers and therefore tended toward conservatism, seeking to maintain what they had. There were sharp differences among blue-collar workers also. For example, copper miners were among the most highly paid workers, while coal and nitrate miners received very low wages. Similar differentials existed in the various industrial and craft unions. The UP also had trouble organizing in the countryside, for most campesinos were firmly attached to the Christian Democrats, who still controlled the state bureaucracy that dealt with agrarian affairs.

A lack of internal cohesion also hindered the UP. At the moment of victory, its leadership was not fully prepared for the task of governing.

Many had doubted that it could win the election. Later, a schism arose within the coalition when the Leftist Revolutionary Movement (*Movimiento Izquierdista Revolucionario,* or MIR) demanded a more radical land program. This split reflected the variety of viewpoints within the UP on the strategy and tactics of the transition to socialism. The old problem of how to satisfy the claims of both the working class—even more militant than during the Popular Front days—and the middle sectors—who worried that their interests were being threatened by the structural reforms undertaken by the UP—was never fully resolved.

The First Year, 1971

The UP's immediate problems were to better the living standard of the working class and get the economy moving. The government accomplished this goal by bringing about an enormous increase in purchasing power, which in turn stimulated demand and industrial production. During the first year of Allende's term, worker income rose a startling 50 percent. The government instituted a massive program of public spending, especially for labor-intensive projects such as housing, education, sanitation, and health, all of which filled desperate social needs. Since Congress refused to accept an increase in taxes to help pay for this program, Allende had to borrow heavily from the Central Bank. At the same time, the government established price controls, which were backed up by local, housewife-operated price and supply committees. The rate of inflation fell to 22.1 percent in 1971 from 34.9 percent in 1970 and, as a result, real income rose 30 percent.

The short-term policies of the UP government, which aimed to stimulate the dormant economy, alleviate unemployment, improve living standards, and increase popular support for a minority regime, were highly successful—a success reflected in the municipal elections of April 1971, in which the Popular Unity won over 50 percent of the vote. In the long run, however, the depletion of stocks, the outflow of foreign exchange to pay for the import of consumer goods, and the fall of profits in what was still basically a market economy proved very damaging to the government's economic program.

For the first year, middle-class businessmen, industrialists, and peasants fared very well and cooperated with the Allende regime. There were scattered cases of larger owners sabotaging their own property but, for the most part, business was not hostile. The government also employed coercion to gain cooperation from industry, threatening companies with intervention if they did not agree to increase production. Coercion and increased demand combined to bring about an expansion of industrial production and employment.

Allende's first problems arose when copper prices declined sharply, leading to an imbalance in the terms of trade and the depletion of foreign exchange reserves. In addition, the expropriation of the Gran Mineria in July 1971 virtually halted the flow of private investment capital from the United States and put an end to the extensive credit that had been forthcoming from such agencies as Agency for International Development (AID), the Export-Import Bank, the Inter-American Development Bank, and the World Bank. The Soviet bloc, Western European nations, and other Latin American countries provided credit, but not enough to compensate for the loss of American loans. The fall of copper prices and the resulting deficit in the balance of payments led Allende to stop servicing the national debt. He eventually managed to reach satisfactory agreements with all of Chile's creditors except the United States, whose continued opposition posed a serious impediment to economic development.

The Left's Old Dilemma: Caught in the Middle, 1972–1973

After the gains of 1971, stagnation and inflation again set in. While Allende's popularity re-

mained high at the polls, he was increasingly unable to cope with the delicate balancing act needed to reconcile the interests of the working class and the middle sectors. The UP program tried to separate the so-called nonmonoply segment of the bourgeoisie from the monopoly sector (the great family groups and corporations). However, as economic conditions worsened, medium-size businessmen and farmers became less and less willing to cooperate as they had in 1971; eventually, UP policies and right-wing pressure turned them against the UP.

From 1972 on, despite official price controls, Chile suffered rampant inflation and widespread scarcities. Nonetheless, real wages stayed up, and unemployment did not rise.

Allende's economic policies reflected the dilemma of the contradiction between his desire to restructure the Chilean economy by land expropriation and redistribution, elimination of sectoral monopolies, eradication of foreign domination of key industries, and improvement of working-class living conditions, on the one hand, and his desire to maintain the support of the middle class, on the other. The intent of Allende's nationalization program was to leave small and medium-size businesses alone, although they were to be subject to supervision. But there were serious difficulties in determining what businesses fit into what category. Because the UP could get none of its reform measures through Congress, the president relied on laws passed under previous administrations. Two laws passed during the Grove regime in 1932 made it possible to expropriate almost any concern. Using one of these, the government expropriated both the Ford Motor Company and International Telephone and Telegraph. The government, however, had no long-range plans or criteria for the implementation of these laws.

Expropriation of large companies did little for the great majority of workers who were employed by small and medium-size firms and were the worst off. To increase the scope of expropriations threatened widespread conflict with small and medium-size capitalists. As a result, 80 percent of the working population was left out of the socialist economy. In many cases, the workers took matters into their own hands by occupying and operating factories. State mismanagement of expropriated businesses also damaged the economy. Expenses rose sharply, especially the cost of fringe benefits such as housing and medical care.

A backward, inefficient agriculture, incapable of absorbing the large pool of rural labor or supplying enough food for the growing urban centers, was perhaps the most serious impediment to Chilean development. The result was an undernourished population and an unending exodus of people from the countryside. Land reform was badly needed to put idle land into use and create jobs for campesinos. A succession of governments had failed to alleviate agrarian problems, and agrarian workers' wages fell 23 percent in real terms from 1953 to 1964. The Frei administration had begun an agrarian reform, but the process had been slow and compensation for the landowners expensive.

Allende's inability to push new laws through a hostile Congress forced him to operate with the reform law he had inherited from the Frei administration, which permitted the expropriation of all latifundia. By the end of 1972, the government had completed its expropriation program; the latifundio system had effectively been liquidated. (The expropriation process was accompanied by frequent land seizures by impatient campesinos; since about half the land seizures were on farms of less than 200 acres, they raised questions of legality and of the government's attitude toward medium-size landowners.) The organizational form favored by the Popular Unity was the *Centro de Reforma Agraria* (Agrarian Reform Center), which united a number of farms into large-scale production units; farms of a more industrial nature, such as animal breeding and forestry, were organized as state farms, with technicians and agricultural workers both paid a fixed daily wage.

The 1972–1973 harvest was poor. The inevitable disruption involved in expropriation and redistribution, as well as landowner resistance to the Allende regime, caused the acreage under cultivation to drop by 20 percent. Bad weather and land seizures accounted for part of this decline; strikes in the transportation sector also hurt agricultural output and marketing. In the face of increased demand for food, domestic production actually fell in 1973. The Chilean experience, like that of Cuba, showed that major land reforms, however successful in the long run, may lead to declines in production during the period of reform.

By the fall of 1972, the Allende administration faced a full-fledged economic and political crisis. This crisis was not due solely to the disruptions inevitable in any revolutionary process, the mistakes and shortcomings of the UP government, and conflicts within the governing coalition (between the MIR, pressing for accelerated land seizures and factory takeovers, and the more moderate Allende, supported by the Communists and a section of the Socialists). The spreading chaos was in a significant degree engineered by large-scale Chilean capitalists in actions synchronized with those of their North American allies.[3]

The bourgeoisie had lost much of its economic base through the nationalization of large industries and the expropriation of latifundia, but it retained enormous assets: control of much of the mass media, the judiciary, a majority of Congress and, as a reserve striking force to be used if all other means of taming or toppling UP failed, the armed forces. Most important of all, perhaps, it retained a large cultural and

[3] The United States was deeply involved in Chilean politics. We know from the testimony of William Colby, the director of the Central Intelligence Agency (CIA), before a U.S. Senate subcommittee that the CIA spent $11 million between 1962 and 1970 to help prevent Allende from being elected president and that the CIA, with authorization from Secretary of State Henry Kissinger, spent $8 million between 1970 and 1973 to "destabilize" the Chilean economy.

psychological influence over the urban middle sectors, which were traditionally hostile to socialism and suffering from a soaring inflation against whose consequences they could not defend themselves as well as the better-organized industrial workers could. All of Allende's efforts to reassure and win over the middle class failed to gain the loyalty of its majority. This middle class provided the mass base for the coup that eventually overthrew the Popular Unity.

Allende's opponents took advantage of the growing economic crisis in late 1972 to embark on a program of sabotage and direct action that included an employers' strike in October, a strike of truck drivers (subsidized by the CIA), which developed into a full-scale lockout by a majority of Chilean capitalists: Factories closed, stores shut their doors, and transportation was halted by lack of gas. Meanwhile, hoodlums of the Fatherland and Freedom organization roamed the streets, trying to coerce shopkeepers who remained open to join the strike.

The strike ended when Allende made major concessions to his opponents, guaranteeing the security of small and medium-size industries and promising that industries that did not form part of the monopoly area would be returned to their owners. He also agreed to the inclusion of generals in his cabinet to insure law and order and to supervise the congressional election scheduled for March 1973. The opposition hoped to gain a sweeping victory in that election, a victory that would give it the two-thirds majority needed to impeach Allende and legally oust his government. Instead, the UP vote rose from 36 percent (in 1970) to 44 percent—proof that its policies of full employment, redistribution of income, and advance toward socialism had substantially increased its support among the working class and peasantry. However, the opposition still commanded a majority in Congress and it redoubled efforts to create economic and political chaos by disruptive strikes, the organization of terrorist bands, and calls on the armed forces to intervene.

When Popular Unity came to power in 1970, the Chilean officer class was divided into two factions: a sizable conservative wing and a moderate wing sympathetic to reform of the kind advocated by the Christian Democrats. General René Schneider, commander in chief of the Chilean army, who was assassinated by reactionary military in 1970, and General Carlos Prats, who succeeded Schneider and held various cabinet posts in the Allende government, were among the moderates. Unquestionably, the Chilean military was greatly influenced by the United States military. Many Chilean officers had undergone counterinsurgency training in the United States or the Panama Canal Zone. Throughout the Allende presidency, even after the United States had cut off all forms of economic aid to Chile and successfully exerted pressure on international banks to cut off loans, U.S. military aid continued. The United States even doubled its usual contribution in 1973. Chile and Venezuela were the principal beneficiaries of U.S. military aid in Latin American. The rigid anti-Communist stance of much of the military was bolstered significantly by material support from the United States, which enabled them to maintain their intransigent opposition to Allende.

By the spring of 1973, the balance of forces within the military had clearly shifted in favor of the conservative wing, and preparations for a coup were well advanced. On June 29 a premature coup was swiftly put down by loyal troops under the direction of General Prats. Following the defeat of the coup, workers called for occupation of the factories and distribution of arms among them. Instead, Allende renewed his efforts to achieve a compromise with the Christian Democrats, relying on the armed forces to maintain law and order. The armed forces raided factories in search of illegal weapons, while making no effort to disarm the increasingly aggressive rightist paramilitary groups. Control of many localities effectively passed from the UP administration to the armed forces. In the face of the growing danger from the right-wing military, the government seemed paralyzed. In August, General Prats, under great pressure from his colleagues, resigned from the Cabinet and as commander in chief; Allende, acceding to the requests of the generals, appointed General Augusto Pinochet as Prats's successor.

The coup began on September 10, 1973. The next morning, after Allende rejected a demand by the armed forces that he resign, the army and the air force attacked the presidential palace; Allende was killed. Despite scattered resistance, the left was crushed within a week.

THE JUNTA

After the coup, Chileans endured the most brutal and large-scale repression in Latin American history. The four-man military junta headed by General Augusto Pinochet set about to "regenerate" Chilean society. To this end they abolished civil liberties, dissolved the national congress, banned union activities, prohibited strikes and collective bargaining, and erased the Allende administration's agrarian and economic reforms. It jailed, tortured, and put to death thousands of Chileans. Some sources estimate that the junta killed between eighteen and thirty thousand people in its first two years. The dreaded secret police, DINA (*Dirección de Inteligencia Nacional*)—with guidance from Colonel Walter Rauff, a former Nazi who supervised the extermination of Jews at Auschwitz—spread its network of terror throughout Chile and carried out assassinations abroad. The junta also set up at least six concentration camps. It is estimated that one of every one hundred Chileans has been arrested at least once since the coup.

The dictatorship outlawed or suspended left and center political parties and suspended dissident labor and peasant leaders and clergymen. Eduardo Frei and other Christian Democratic leaders initially supported the coup. Later, they assumed the role of a loyal opposition to the military rulers, but soon lost most of their in-

fluence. Meanwhile, left-wing Christian Democratic leaders like Radomiro Tomic were jailed or forced into exile. The church, which at first expressed its gratitude to the armed forces for saving the country from the danger of a "Marxist dictatorship," became increasingly critical of the regime's social and economic policies.

The junta's efforts to restore the free market economy created extreme hardship for the Chilean people. The regime's wage controls did not abate the world's highest rate of inflation; between September 1973 and October 1975, the consumer price index rose a total of 3,367 percent. Exhange rate depreciations and cutbacks in government spending produced a depression that set the economy back ten years. Industrial and agricultural production declined. Massive unemployment, estimated at 25 percent in 1977 (it was only 3 percent in 1972), and inflation eroded the living standard of workers and many members of the middle class to subsistence levels.

In the meantime, the rich grew richer. While the upper 5 percent of the population received 25 percent of the total national income in 1972, it received 50 percent in 1975. Wage and salary earners got 64 percent of the national income in 1972 but only 38 percent at the beginning of 1977. The junta's economic program pushed large numbers of Chileans to or over the edge of starvation. Malnutrition affected half of the nation's children, and 60 percent of the population could not afford the minimum amount of protein and calories per day. Infant mortality increased sharply. Beggars flooded the streets.

The junta's economics also ruined the Chilean small business class. Decreased demand, lack of credit, and monopolies produced by the regime pushed many small and medium-size enterprises into bankruptcy. The curtailment of government expenditures created widespread white-collar and professional unemployment. The middle class began to rue its early support of the junta but appeared reluctant to join the working class in resistance to the regime.

Chilean soldier guarding prisoners after the 1973
coup. (Naul A. Ojeda/Magnum Photos, Inc.)

The junta relied on the army, the police, the oligarchy, huge foreign corporations, and foreign loans to maintain itself. Many military men grew rich from the opportunities created by the coup. As a whole, the armed services received generous salary increases and new equipment. The oligarchy recovered most of its lost industrial and agricultural holdings, for the junta sold to private buyers most of the industries expropriated by the Popular Unity government. This policy created monopolies and produced widespread speculation. Large foreign banks received millions of dollars in repayments of interest and principal from the junta; in return, they loaned the government millions more. Foreign multinational corporations such as International Telephone and Telegraph, Dow Chemical, and Firestone, all expropriated by Allende, returned.

After the deep recession of 1975–1976, the economy experienced a boomlet until 1980, with annual growth rates averaging 8 percent. The inflation rate plunged to 30 percent in 1980 and 10 percent in 1981. The Chilean "economic miracle" was superficial and short-lived. Based on speculation, its benefits concentrated only among the very rich, and heavily reliant on huge foreign loans, the upsurge collapsed in 1980. By the end of 1981 the government, in violation of its own free market principles, was forced to step in to take over the nation's largest banks in order to forestall economic calamity. Bankruptcies multiplied; the country's second largest insurance company, for example, failed. Production declined sharply. Unemployment rose to 20 percent by the end of 1982; and the gross national product actually declined in that year. Inflation rose again to nearly 50 percent.

In January 1978, the military dictatorship held a plebiscite, which—unsurprisingly—overwhelmingly approved General Pinochet, who subsequently proclaimed that there would be no further elections for ten years. Although the regime remains largely impervious to the outcry from abroad against its repression, international pressure, including protests from the United States against human rights violations, has produced some substantive results. Pinochet has released some political prisoners and permitted a few political exiles to return home. Pinochet has also seen his personal power base and credibility erode because of disagreements with high-ranking Air Force officers and the adverse publicity surrounding assassinations carried out abroad by DINA. But the worsening economic crisis created political unrest, especially among the middle classes, whose small businesses were undermined or ruined by the government's policies, and professionals who had suffered from government's withdrawal from educational and health services.

In September 1980 Chileans, faced with little choice, overwhelmingly endorsed a new constitution that will keep Pinochet in power at least until 1987 and perhaps to 1997. The military is to choose a new president and elect a legislature in 1989.

The Pinochet regime has a very narrow political base, drawing support from the military (which has doubled in size since the coup), far-right-wing groups, and the small number of oligarchs who have benefited from the government's economic policies. This became clear in 1983, when as the economic situation worsened, the clamor for the return to democracy increased. Popular demonstrations erupted throughout the nation. Copper miners in the north struck, despite the government's arrest of their union's leaders and strikers. The same middle class women in the cities who had clanged their cooking pots from their windows to protest during the Allende years did the same in protest against the Pinochet regime. The dictator tried to meet this challenge by alternating concessions with repression, but the protests continued. After a decade of military rule, unprecedented in its brutality, in which Chile had actually gone backwards economically, Chileans sought, ever more boldly and bravely, to restore democracy.

CHAPTER FIFTEEN

Republican Brazil

On the eve of World War I, Brazil's economic, political, and social structures showed growing strain and instability. Between 1910 and 1914, the Amazonian rubber boom began to fade as a result of competition from the new and more efficient plantations of the Far East. The approaching end of the rubber cycle revealed the vulnerability of Brazil's monocultural economy to external factors beyond its control and heightened its dependence on coffee. The coffee industry was itself plagued by recurrent crises of overproduction that required periodic resort to valorization—governmental intervention to maintain coffee prices by withholding stocks from the market or restricting plantings.

Violence was endemic over large areas of the country. In the backcountry, feudal *coronéis* (colonels) with private armies recruited from dependents and *jagunços* (hired gunmen) maintained a patriarchal but frequently tyrannical rule over the peasantry. Over large areas of the country, the peasants lived in feudal bondage, obligated to give one or more days per week of free labor as homage to the landowners. Lacking written contracts, they could be evicted at any moment, and could find work elsewhere only on the same conditions. The interior was also the scene of mystical or messianic movements that sometimes assumed the character of peasant revolts. Banditry, especially widespread in the northeast, was another response to the tyranny of rural coronéis and the impotence of officials. A few *cangaceiros* (outlaws) were true social bandits who took the part of the peasantry against their oppressors; most, however, served as mercenaries in the coronéis's private wars.

Violence was not confined to the countryside. Even in the growing cities, proud of their European culture and appearance, popular anger at the arbitrary rule of local oligarchies, or divisions within those oligarchies, sometimes flared up into civil war. Intervention by the federal government in these armed struggles on the side of its local allies greatly enlarged the scale of violence.

DECLINE AND FALL OF THE OLD REPUBLIC, 1914–1930

Economic Impact of World War I

The outbreak of World War I in August 1914 had a negative initial impact on Brazil. Exports of coffee, a nonessential product, declined, and in 1917 the government came to the rescue of the planters with a new valorization (price maintenance) program. However, the growing demand of the Allies for sugar, beans, and other staples had by 1915 sparked a revival that turned into a boom. Brazil's expanding trade with the Allies exposed its shipping to German reprisals, and in October 1917, after German submarines had torpedoed a number of Brazilian merchant ships, Brazil declared war on Germany. Brazil's

major contribution to the Allied war effort continued to be the supply of goods, but its navy assisted an English squadron in patrolling south Atlantic waters.

The war accelerated some changes under way in Brazilian economic life. It weakened British capitalism and therefore strengthened the American challenge to British financial and commercial pre-eminence in Brazil. The virtual cessation of imports of manufactured goods also gave a strong stimulus to Brazilian industrialization. Profits derived from coffee, an industry protected by the state, provided a large part of the resources needed for industrialization. Favored by its wealth, large immigrant population, and rich natural resources, the state of São Paulo led the movement, replacing Rio de Janeiro as the foremost industrial region. Brazil doubled its industrial production during the war, and the number of enterprises (which stood at about 3,000 in 1908) grew by 5,940 between 1915 and 1918. But these increases were concentrated in light industry, especially food processing and textiles, and most of the new enterprises were small shops.

The advance of industry and urbanization enlarged and strengthened both the industrial bourgeoisie and the working class. In response to wartime inflation that eroded the value of workers' wages, the trade union movement grew, and strikes became more frequent. In 1917 a general strike—the first in Brazilian history—gripped the city and state of São Paulo. The strikers' demands included a wage increase of 30 percent, the eight-hour day, improved working conditions, and the release of political prisoners. The strike brought the city of São Paulo to a standstill. The federal government sent troops to crush the strike but recalled them when the soldiers refused to fire on the workers. Although the strike wave of the years 1917–1920 forced many employers to grant higher wages, the living conditions of most workers did not permanently improve. The labor movement, composed largely of foreign-born workers, remained small and weak, without ties with the peasantry, who formed the overwhelming majority of the Brazilian people.

Postwar Industry and Labor

Industrialization and urbanization weakened the foundations of the neocolonial order, which was based on the primacy of agriculture and dependence on foreign markets and loans, but it emerged from the war essentially intact, although its stabilization proved temporary and precarious. A chronically adverse balance of trade and a declining rate of exchange against foreign currencies gave Brazilian industry a competitive advantage in goods of popular consumption. It continued to grow, but it had little support from a central government dominated by the coffee interests. Bitter debates between the friends and foes of tariff protection for industry marked the political life of the 1920s.

As that decade opened, Brazil remained an overwhelmingly rural country. A few export products—coffee, sugar, cotton—dominated Brazilian agriculture; food production was so neglected that the country had to import four-fifths of its grain needs. There was an exteme concentration of landownership: 461 great landowners held more than 27 million hectares of land, while 464,000 small and medium-sized farms occupied only 15.7 million hectares. Archaic techniques prevailed in agriculture: The hoe was still the principal farming instrument, and the wasteful slash-and-burn method the favored way of clearing the soil. Even relatively progressive coffee planters gave little attention to the care of the soil, selection of varieties, and other improvements. As a result, the productivity of plantations rapidly declined, even in regions of superior soil.

In the cities, most workers toiled and lived under conditions that recalled those of the early Industrial Revolution in Europe. In 1920 the average industrial worker in São Paulo earned about 4 milréis (60 cents) a day; for this wage he worked ten to twelve hours, six days a week. A system of fines for "imperfect" work further reduced this miserable wage, and the need for advances kept many workers in perpetual debt to employers. About one-third of the work force was female, and child labor was widespread, with half of all workers under eighteen. Since a budget for a family of seven prepared by a government agency in 1919 assigned four times as much for food alone as the average worker earned in São Paulo, it was common for whole families to go to work, but women and children were paid less than men for the same tasks. Rural laborers were somewhat worse off: In the 1920s, workers in the sugar plantations of Pernambuco toiled from dawn to dusk for 2½ to 4½ milréis a day.

Malnutrition, parasitic diseases, and lack of medical facilities limited the average life span in 1920 to twenty-eight years. In the same year, more than 64 percent of the population over the age of fifteen was illiterate. Since literacy was a requirement for voting, the general lack of schools kept the masses not only ignorant but politically powerless. Some of the poorer states had virtually no public schools. The peasantry, vegetating in poverty and ignorance, could not initiate a struggle to transform Brazilian society.

Political Unrest

The task of transforming society fell to the rapidly growing urban bourgeois groups, and especially to the middle class, which began to voice ever more strongly its discontent with the rule of corrupt rural oligarchies. In the early 1920s, there arose a many-faceted movement for the renovation of Brazilian society and culture. Intellectuals, artists, junior military officers, professional men, and a small minority of radical workers participated in this movement. But they had no common program and did not comprehend the convergence of their aims and work.

Three seemingly unrelated events of 1922 illustrate the diverse forms that the ferment of the times assumed. First, in February of that year, the intellectuals of São Paulo organized a Modern Art Week to commemorate the centenary of Brazilian independence. The young poets, painters, and composers who presented their works there laid a common stress on independence from old forms and content, on the need to develop an indigenous Brazilian culture. Then, in March, after the appearance of Marxist groups in a number of cities, the Brazilian Communist party was founded at a congress in Rio de Janeiro and began a struggle against the anarcho-syndicalist doctrines that still dominated much of the small labor movement. Last, in July, *tenentes* (junior officers) at the Copacabana garrison in Rio de Janeiro rose to prevent the seating of Artur da Silva Bernardes, who had been elected president according to the agreement between the two dominant states of São Paulo and Minas Gerais. The rebel program denounced the rule of the coffee oligarchy, political corruption, and electoral fraud. Government forces easily crushed the revolt, but it left a legend when a handful of insurgents refused to surrender and fought to the death against overwhelming odds.

The officers' revolt signaled the beginning of a struggle by the Brazilian bourgeoisie to seize power from the rural oligarchy. Given the closed political system, it inevitably assumed the character of an armed struggle; that is why its spearhead was the nationalist young officer group, mostly of middle-class origins, which called for democratic elections, equal justice, and similar political reforms.

President Bernardes (1922–1926) took office amid growing economic and political turmoil. As a result of a massive increase in coffee plantings between 1918 and 1924, the industry again suffered from overproduction and falling prices.

Bernardes added to his unpopularity by an armed intervention in the state of Rio de Janeiro, the political base of Nilo Peçanha, his opponent in the 1922 election; by his insistence on trying and punishing the young officers who had rebelled against him; and by his severe repression of strikers and leftists.

In 1924 another military revolt, headed by retired General Isidro Dias Lopes, broke out in São Paulo. It was again organized by junior officers whose program called for the restoration of constitutional liberties and curbs on the executive power but made no reference to economic and social reform. The large working class of São Paulo was sympathetic to the revolt, but its conservative leaders rejected the workers' request for arms.

The rebels held the city for twenty-two days before evacuating it under pressure from greatly superior numbers of government troops. Meanwhile, the revolt had spread to other states. Another group of rebels in Rio Grande do Sul, led by Captain Luís Carlos Prestes, moved north to join the insurgents from São Paulo, and their combined forces, known in history as the Prestes column, began a prodigious march through the interior. The tenentes hoped to enlist the peasantry in their struggle against Bernardes. But they knew little of the peasants' problems and offered no program of agrarian reform. The peasants, for their part, had no interest in fighting the "tyrant" Bernardes in distant Rio de Janeiro. Beating off or eluding attacks by government forces and bands of cangaceiros in the government's employ, the Prestes column covered fourteen thousand miles before reaching Bolivia, where the rebels dispersed.

The long march had much educational value for the officers who took part in it. For the first time in their lives, many of these young men came face to face with the reality of rural Brazil and began to reflect on its problems. As a result, the tenente reform program acquired an economic and social content. It began to speak of the need for economic development and social legislation, including agrarian reform as well as minimum wages and maximum working hours.

Bernardes had survived a second military crisis, but he continued to be plagued by economic problems, with the coffee problem paramount. Bernardes applied the now orthodox remedy of valorization, but gave it a decentralized form. The central government turned over the supervision of the scheme to the individual coffee-producing states. The state of São Paulo established an agency, the Coffee Institute, which undertook to control the export trade in coffee by regulating market offerings to maintain a balance between supply and demand. This was done by withdrawing unlimited stocks of coffee, storing them in warehouses, and releasing them according to the needs of the export trade. The plan required financing the producers whose coffee was withheld from the market. An official bank of the state of São Paulo offered planters loans of up to 30 percent of the value of the withdrawn stocks. A group of English and American bankers advanced the necessary resources. To cover the costs of the plan and service of the foreign debt a new coffee tax was imposed on each bag. The program appeared to work, for prices rose and remained stable until 1929. But the burdens of valorization steadily grew, for high prices stimulated production, requiring new withdrawals and new loans to finance the unsold output. To make matters worse, Brazil's competitors—especially Colombia—were attracted by the high prices and expanded their own output.

Economic Crisis

In 1926, Bernardes turned over the presidency to the Paulista Washington Luís Sousa de Pereira (1926–1930). He had been elected, without opposition, according to the agreement that usually rotated the presidency between São Paulo and Minas Gerais. During his administration, a series of new loans was made to support the valorization program. As a result, Brazil's foreign debt had risen to $1,181 million by 1930, and debt service in that year amounted to $200 million—one-third of the national budget. By 1930, American investment in Brazil had reached a figure of $400 million, considerably larger than the British total, and the United States had supplanted England as Brazil's chief trading partner.

Brazil's heavy dependence on foreign markets and loans made it extremely vulnerable to the crisis that shook the capitalist world after the New York stock market collapsed in October 1929. Coffee quotations at once fell 30 percent, and the subsequent decline was even sharper; between 1929 and 1931, coffee prices fell from 22.5 to 8 cents a pound, and immense stocks of coffee piled up in the warehouses. By the end of 1930, Brazil's gold reserves had disappeared, and the exchange rate plummeted to a new low. As foreign credit dried up, it became impossible to continue the financing of withheld coffee, and the valorization program collapsed, leaving behind a mountain of debt.

The presidential campaign and election of 1930 took place against a background of economic crisis whose principal burdens—unemployment, wage cuts, and inflation—fell chiefly on the working classes. But the crisis sharpened all class and regional antagonisms, especially the conflict between the coffee oligarchy and the urban bourgeois groups, who regarded the depression as proof of the bankruptcy of the old order. A rift even appeared within the coffee oligarchy, and the traditional alliance of São Paulo and Minas Gerais fell apart as a result of the selection by Washington Luís of another Paulista, Júlio Prestes, governor of São Paulo, as his successor. Angered by this violation of the agreement to rotate the presidency between the two states, many politicians from Minas Gerais joined the opposition to the official candidate.

As a result of these alignments and realignments, two coalitions took shape and confronted each other in the election of 1930. One united the coffee planters of São Paulo, their rural allies in other areas, and the commercial bourgeoisie engaged in the export-import trade. The other coalition, called the Liberal Alliance, joined the bulk of the urban groups, groups of great landowners—like the ranchers of Rio Grande do Sul, who resented São Paulo's dominant position—and disaffected politicians from Minas Gerais and other states. The conservative coalition nominated the Paulista Júlio Prestes for president; the Liberal Alliance named Getúlio Vargas (1883–1954), a wealthy rancher and politician from Rio Grande do Sul, as its candidate.

The working class was not a participant in the Liberal Alliance, but many workers sympathized with its program. The most ardent supporters of Vargas were the veterans of the revolt of 1924, but their former leader, Luís Carlos Prestes, an exile in Buenos Aires, would not endorse Vargas or his program. Prestes, now a Marxist, issued a manifesto in May 1930 in which he proclaimed that the chief task before the Brazilian people was to struggle against the latifundio and Anglo-American imperialism. A few years later, he would join the Communist party and become its leader.

During the campaign, both candidates made vague promises and statements, but Júlio Prestes clearly represented the latifundist and neocolonial interests. "The fazendeiro," declared Prestes, "is the representative type of the Brazilian nationality, and the fazenda is the hearth of Brazilian life. . . . Brazil rests on a social base composed of fazendas." Vargas, although careful not to give offense to his latifundist supporters, spoke of the need to develop industry, including heavy industry, advocated high tariffs to protect Brazilian industry using local raw materials, and called on Brazilians to "perfect our manufactures to the point where it will become unpatriotic to feed or clothe ourselves with imported goods." Reflecting the influence of the tenentes,

he advanced a program of social welfare legislation and political, judicial, and educational reform. He even made a cautious pledge of "action with a view to the progressive extinction of the latifundio, without violence, and support for the organization of small landed property through the transfer of small parcels of land to agricultural laborers."

In any event, Prestes defeated Vargas in the election of March 1930 by a supposed margin of some three hundred thousand votes. Since both sides cheated on a large scale, the outcome merely proved that the government and its rural allies had control of the electoral machinery in decisive areas. In May, Congress, which was dominated by the administration, refused to seat opposition deputies from Minas Gerais and Paraíba. Political tension ran high and reached the explosive point in July with the murder of Vargas's running mate, João Pessoa, a deed regarded by the opposition as a political assassination.

Vargas's lieutenants now convinced him of the need to overthrow the Washington Luís government. The uprising began simultaneously in Rio Grande do Sul, Minas Gerais, and Paraíba on October 3. Insurgent forces led by veterans of the 1922 and 1924 revolts were soon joined by army units commanded by other tenentes, and their combined forces seized a series of state capitals. Perceiving that the collapse of the discredited regime was probably inevitable, senior army officers deposed Washington Luís on October 24, formed a ruling junta, and ordered the army to lay down its arms; one week later, they turned their power over to Getúlio Vargas as head of the provisional government. The Old Republic, born in 1889 and dominated since 1894 by the coffee oligarchy, was dead. A new era had begun that may with fair accuracy be called the era of the bourgeois revolution. The political career of its chieftain, Getúlio Vargas, faithfully mirrored its advances, retreats, and ultimate defeat.

VARGAS AND THE BOURGEOIS REVOLUTION, 1930–1954

The liberal revolution of 1930, whatever the motives of its participants, represented a victory for the urban bourgeois groups who favored industrialization and the modernization of Brazil's economic, political, and social structures. But the bourgeoisie had gained that victory with the aid of allies whose interests had to be taken into account. Getúlio Vargas presided over a heterogeneous coalition that included conservative fazendeiros—who had joined the revolution from jealousy of the overweening Paulista power but feared radical social change—and intellectuals and tenentes who called for agrarian reform, the formation of cooperatives, and the nationalization of mines. On the sidelines was the working class, vital to the development of Brazilian capitalism but a potential threat to its very existence. Finally, Vargas had to take account of foreign capitalist interests, temporarily weakened but capable of applying great pressure on the Brazilian economy when the capitalist world emerged from the depths of the Great Depression. Vargas's strategy of attempting to balance and reconcile these conflicting interests—that is, to reconcile the irreconcilable—helps to explain the contradictions and abrupt shifts of course that marked his career.

Brazilian President Getúlio Vargas (center) during a press interview. (Pictorial Parade)

Vargas's Economic and Political Measures

The most pressing problem facing the new government was to find some way out of the economic crisis. Vargas did not abandon the coffee industry, the base of his political enemies, to its fate; he attempted to revive it by such classic valorization measures as the restriction of plantings and the purchase of surplus stocks and the more drastic expedient of burning the excess coffee. By 1940 some 60 million bags of coffee had been destroyed. Despite these efforts, the level of coffee exports and prices remained low throughout the 1930s. The government had more success with efforts to diversify agriculture. Production of cotton, in particular, grew with the aid of capital and labor released by the depressed coffee industry, and cotton exports rose steadily until 1940, when the outbreak of war interrupted their advance. But diversification of agriculture could not compensate for the steep decline in Brazil's import capacity, which was even lower in 1937 than in 1929. The key to recovery was found in import substitution through industrialization.

The Great Depression did not create Brazilian industrialization, but it created the conditions for a new advance. Beginning as a spontaneous response to the loss of import capacity that resulted from the catastrophic decline of exports and a falling rate of exchange, industrialization received a fresh impetus from the Vargas policies. He encouraged industry through exchange controls, import quotas, tax incentives, lowered duties on imported machinery and raw materials, and long-term loans at low interest rates. Thanks to the combination of favorable background conditions and the Vargas policy of state intervention, Brazilian industrialization, based entirely on production for the home market, made notable strides in a few years: Industrial production doubled between 1931 and 1936. As early as 1933, when the United States was still in a deep depression, Brazil's national income had begun to increase; this indicated that for the moment, at least, the economy no longer depended, as had traditionally been the case, on external factors but on internal ones.

Meanwhile, Vargas pursued an uncertain political course that now appeared to favor the left wing of the revolutionary coalition, the tenentes, and now its conservative fazendeiro wing. The tenentes appeared to have considerable influence over Vargas during the first two years of the provisional government; he used them as his political lieutenants in various capacities, especially as interventors, or temporary administrators, in the states, replacing unreliable elected governors. Believing that a strong centralized government was needed to carry out the necessary structural reforms and fearing that premature elections would enable the oligarchies to frustrate those reforms, the tenentes urged Vargas to remain in power indefinitely. Some tenentes alarmed conservatives by their radical innovations; thus João Alberto, named by Vargas as interventor in place of the elected governor of São Paulo, angered the Paulista elite by decreeing a 5 percent wage increase for workers and distributing some land to participants in the revolution.

The Paulistas demanded the removal of João Alberto, but they wanted more; supported by oligarchical elements in other states, they asked for a return to constitutional government through immediate elections, preferably under the old federal constitution of 1891, which would most likely enable them to regain power in their own state. Vargas sought to appease the Paulistas with concessions: He replaced João Alberto with a civilian from São Paulo, appointed a conservative banker from the same state as his first minister of finance, and announced a date for the holding of a constituent assembly.

Emboldened rather than appeased, the Paulistas launched a counterrevolutionary "constitutionalist revolt" in July 1932. Lacking popular support either in São Paulo or in other parts of the country, it collapsed after three months of halfhearted combat. But Vargas neither punished nor humiliated the vanquished rebels. Determined to maintain and strengthen his ties with the São Paulo establishment, he made new concessions to it: He pardoned 50 percent of the bank debts of the coffee planters and ordered the Bank of Brazil to take over the war bonds issued by the rebel government. After mid-1932 the influence of the tenente group over Vargas rapidly waned, although individual tenentes of moderate tendency continued to hold important positions in the regime.

In February 1932, Vargas had promulgated an electoral code that established the secret ballot, one of the major planks in the revolutionary program, lowered the voting age from twenty-one to eighteen, and extended the vote to working women. The code, however, still denied the vote to illiterates, who formed the majority of the adult population. A constituent assembly elected under this code drafted a new constitution, which was promulgated on July 16, 1934. This document retained the federal system but considerably strengthened the powers of the executive. The president was to serve for four years but could not succeed himself. The assembly, constituting itself the first Chamber of Deputies, elected Vargas president for a term that was to extend until January 1938. A novel feature of the new constitution, reflecting the influence of European corporatist doctrines, was the provision for the election of fifty representatives of various classes and professions to the Chamber of Deputies, in addition to two hundred and fifty representatives of areas and populations.

The section of the constitution on the "economic and social order" stressed the government's responsibility for economic development. Article 119 declared that "the law will regulate the progressive nationalization of mines, mineral deposits, and waterfalls or other sources of energy, as well as of the industries considered as basic or essential to the economic and military defense of the country."

The section on the rights and duties of labor revealed the importance Vargas attached to the imposition of a tutelage over the working class, a class to be courted through concessions but denied independence of action. One of the first acts of the provisional government (November 1930) had been to create a Ministry of Labor, which served as the government's agency in dealing with labor. Another decree (March 1931) authorized the ministry to organize the workers into new unions, to operate under strict government control. The constitution of 1934 established a labor tribunal system, gave the government power to fix minimum wages, and guaranteed the right to strike. Subsequent decrees set the working day at eight hours in commerce and industry, fixed minimum wages throughout the country, and created an elaborate social security system that provided for pensions, paid vacations, safety and health standards, and employment security.

In exchange for these gains, obtained without struggle, the working class lost its freedom of action. The trade unions, formerly subject to harsh repression, but militant and jealous of their autonomy, became official agencies controlled by the Ministry of Labor. The workers had no voice in the drafting of labor legislation.

Police and security agencies brutally repressed strikes not approved by the government.

The labor and social legislation, moreover, was unevenly enforced, and employers frequently took advantage of their employees' ignorance of the law. The legislation did not apply at all to the great majority of agricultural workers, who comprised some 85 percent of the labor force. Determined to maintain his alliance with the fazendeiro wing of his coalition, Vargas left intact the system of patrimonial servitude that governed labor relations in the countryside, just as he left intact the latifundio. The promises of agrarian reform made during the campaign of 1930 and right after the revolution were forgotten.

Vargas's concessions to the Paulista oligarchy and the ouster of reformist tenentes from positions of power formed part of a rightward shift that grew more pronounced in 1934. This growing conservatism lost Vargas support among liberal tenentes, intellectuals, and radical workers and drew especially sharp criticism from the Communist party. Founded in 1922, the party had dismissed the revolution of 1930 as a struggle between two factions of the bourgeoisie. The party gained growing influence after 1930 as a result of its anti-imperialist policies and the prestige of its most famous recruit, Luís Carlos Prestes. Prestes had refused to take advantage of the amnesty for political exiles proclaimed after the revolution but returned in 1934 to join the Communist party and become honorary president of the *Aliança Nacional Libertadora* (National Liberation Alliance, or ANL), a popular front movement that attracted middle-class as well as working-class support with its slogans of liquidation of the latifundio, nationalization of large foreign companies, and cancellation of imperialist debts. The ANL was also sharply critical of the inadequacies of Vargas's labor and social legislation. Meanwhile, on the right there had arisen a fascist movement (*Integralismo*, or Integralism), complete with the trappings of its European models, including colored shirts (green), special salutes, and an ideology that denounced democrats, Communists, Masons, and Jews as "enemies of the state."

While tolerant of the Integralist movement, Vargas and an increasingly conservative Congress harassed the leftist opposition as "subversive." In March 1935, Congress enacted a National Security Act, which gave the government special powers to suppress "subversive" activities. Denounced by the ANL as a "monstrous law," it was clearly directed at the left. In July, on the anniversary of the tenente revolt at Copacabana in 1922, Prestes made a speech in which he attacked Vargas's failure to implement the tenente ideals and called for the creation of a truly "revolutionary and anti-imperialist government." Vargas responded by banning the ANL and ordering the arrest of many leftist leaders.

With the legal avenues of opposition for the left disappearing, the ANL and one wing of the Communist party began an armed uprising in November. Despite some initial successes, it was quickly crushed by government forces and followed by a savage repression. There were some fifteen thousand arrests, and many prisoners were tortured, some to death. Prestes and other leaders of the revolt were captured, tried, and sentenced to many years in prison. The Communist party was banned and went underground for a decade.

Vargas as Dictator

The repression of the left paved the way for the establishment of Vargas's personal dictatorship. A presidential election was scheduled for January 1938, but under the new constitution Vargas was barred from succeeding himself. He allowed candidates to emerge and campaign but meanwhile carefully prepared for the coming coup by strategic "interventions" in the states

and transfers in the army that filled key posts with reliable commanders. His war minister, General Eurico Dutra, and the army chief of staff, General Goes Monteiro, played key roles in planning and carrying out the coup.

On September 29, 1937, armed with the Cohen Plan, a crude forgery concocted by the Integralists that set out a detailed plan for a Communist revolution, Dutra went on the radio and demanded the imposition of a state of siege. He had set the stage for the scrapping of what remained of constitutional processes. On November 10, Vargas made a broadcast in which he canceled the presidential elections, dissolved Congress as an "inadequate and costly apparatus," and assumed dictatorial power under a new constitution patterned on European fascist models. On December 2, all political parties were abolished.

The new regime, baptized the *Estado Novo* (New State), copied not only the constitutional forms of the fascist regimes but their repressive tactics. Strict press censorship was established, and prisons filled with workers, teachers, military officers, and others suspected of subversion. The apparatus of repression included a special police force for hunting down dissidents; its methods included torture. Yet there was little organized resistance to the regime. Labor, its most likely opponent, was neutralized by a paternalist social legislation and doped by populist rhetoric, and it remained passive or even supported Vargas.

The affinity between the Estado Novo and the European police states suggested to some observers that it was merely a Brazilian variant of the Continental fascist model. Such pronouncements by Vargas as "the decadence of liberal and individualistic democracy represents an incontrovertible fact" appeared to support this point of view. Brazil's growing trade and increasingly friendly relations with Germany and Italy also led to fears that the country was moving into the fascist orbit. Between 1933 and

1938, Germany became the chief market for Brazilian cotton and the second largest buyer of its coffee and cacao. German penetration of the Brazilian economy also increased, and the German Bank for South America established three hundred branches in Brazil.

But Brazil's economic rapprochement with Germany and Italy did not reflect sympathy with the expansionist goals of the fascist bloc; Vargas, the great realist, sought only to open up new markets for Brazil and to strengthen his hand in bargaining with the United States. Nor was there any true likeness between the internal structures and aims of the Estado Novo and the European fascist systems, which arose in response to very different economic and social conditions. Despite its authoritarian, repressive aspects, the Estado Novo continued the struggle against neocolonialism and the effort to achieve economic independence and modernization.

Indeed, under the new regime the state intervened more actively than before to encourage the growth of industry and provide it with the necessary economic infrastructure. The constitution of 1937 repeated the restrictions of the 1934 constitution on foreign exploitation of natural resources. Rejecting laissez faire, the Estado Novo pursued a policy of planning and direct investment for the creation of important industrial complexes in the basic sectors of mining, oil, steel, electric power, and chemicals. In 1940 the government announced a Five-Year Plan whose goals included the expansion of heavy industry, the creation of new sources of hydroelectric power, and the expansion of the railway network. In 1942 the government established the *Companhia Vale do Rio Doce* to exploit the rich iron-ore deposits of Itabira; in 1944 it created a company for the production of materials needed by the chemical industry; and in 1946 the National Motor Company began the production of trucks. In the same year, Vargas saw the realization of one of his cherished dreams: The National Steel Company began

production at the Volta Redonda plant between Rio de Janeiro and São Paulo. Aware of the need of modern industry for abundant sources of power, Vargas created the National Petroleum Company in 1938 to press the search for oil.

By 1941, Brazil had 44,100 plants employing 944,000 workers; the comparable figure for 1920 was 13,336 plants with about 300,000 workers. Aside from some export of textiles, the manufacturing industries served the domestic market almost exclusively. State and mixed public-private companies dominated the heavy and infrastructural industries and private Brazilian capital predominated in manufacturing, but the 1930s also saw a significant growth of direct foreign investment as foreign corporations sought to enlarge their share of the internal market and overcome tariff barriers and exchange problems by establishing branch plants in Brazil. By 1940 foreign capital represented 44 percent of the total investment in Brazilian stock companies. Vargas made no effort to check the influx of foreign capital, perhaps because he believed that the growth of Brazilian state and private capitalism would keep the foreign sector in a subordinate status.

The Estado Novo banned strikes and lockouts but retained and even expanded the body of protective social and labor legislation. In 1942 the labor laws were consolidated into a labor code, regarded as one of the most advanced in the world. But, as noted previously, it was unevenly enforced and brought no benefits to the great mass of agricultural workers. Moreover, spiraling inflation created a growing gap between wages and prices; prices rose 86 percent between 1940 and 1944, whereas between 1929 and 1939, they had risen only 31 percent. In effect, inflation, by transferring income from wages to capitalists, provided much of the financing for the rapid economic growth of the 1940s.

World War II accelerated that growth through the new stimulus it gave to industrialization.

Brazil exported vast quantities of foodstuffs and raw materials, but the industrialized countries, whose economies were geared to war, could not pay for their purchases with machinery or consumer goods. As a result, Brazil built up large foreign exchange reserves, amounting to $707 million in 1945. Most of the economic advance of the war years was due to expansion and more intensive exploitation of existing plants or to the technical contributions of Brazilian engineers and scientists.

However, Vargas adroitly exploited Great Power rivalries to secure financial and technical assistance from the United States for the construction of the huge state-owned integrated iron and steel plant at Volta Redonda. U.S. companies and government agencies were notably cool to requests for aid for establishing heavy industry in Latin America. But Vargas's hints that he might have to turn for help to Germany removed all obstacles. A series of loans from the Export-Import Bank made possible the completion of the Volta Redonda plant by 1946. By 1955 it was producing 646,000 tons of steel, a major contribution to Brazil's industrial growth. Volta Redonda was a great victory for the Vargas policies of economic nationalism and state intervention in economic life. In return for American assistance, Vargas allowed the United States to lease air bases in northern Brazil even before it entered the war against the Axis. In August 1942, after German submarines had sunk a number of Brazilian merchantmen, Brazil declared war on Germany and Italy. A Brazilian expeditionary force of some twenty-five thousand men participated in the Allied invasion of Italy in 1944 and suffered relatively heavy losses in the fighting.

The paradox of Brazil's participation in an antifascist war under an authoritarian regime was not lost on Brazilians; the demands for an end to the Estado Novo grew stronger as the defeat of the Axis drew near. Ever sensitive to changes in the political climate and the balance of forces, Vargas responded by promising a new postwar era of liberty. In January 1945, he announced an amnesty for political prisoners, promulgated a law allowing political parties to function openly, and set December 2 as the date for presidential and congressional elections.

A number of new parties were formed to fight the coming elections. Two were created by Vargas himself. They were the *Partido Social Democrático* (Social Democratic Party, or PSD) and the *Partido Trabalhista Brasileiro* (Brazilian Labor Party, or PTB). The PSD, the largest of the new parties, united pro-Vargas industrialists and rural machines, above all. The PTB had its base in the government-controlled trade unions and appealed to workers with a populist rhetoric proclaiming Vargas the "Father of the Poor." The *União Democrática Nacional* (National Democratic Party, or UDN) was the most conservative and chiefly represented neocolonial agrarian and commercial interests; it was strongly pro-American. Its position with respect to economic policy was that "it is necessary to call on foreign capital for the exploitation of our idle natural resources, assure it just treatment, and allow it to repatriate its proceeds." Of the other national parties, the most important was the Communist party, led by Prestes, which emerged from the underground with considerable prestige and strength.

A Military Coup

Vargas announced that he would not run for president but set the stage for a well-organized campaign by his supporters, called *queremistas* (from the Portuguese verb *querer*, "to want"), who wanted Vargas to declare himself a candidate in the forthcoming election. Soon after issuing the decrees restoring political freedom, Vargas moved to the left in economic policy. In June he authorized the expropriation of any organization whose practices were harmful to the national interest; the decree specifically named "national or foreign enterprises known to be connected with associations, trusts, or cartels.''

The authorization decree, which was aimed at keeping down the cost of living, inspired alarm in conservative foreign and domestic circles. The American ambassador, Adolph A. Berle, Jr., made no effort to conceal his suspicion of Vargas's aims. Senior military officers also regarded Vargas's political manuevers and leftward move with growing uneasiness. The wartime alliance with the United States had accentuated their inherent conservatism and made them ready to accept the gospel of free enterprise and American leadership in the cold war against the Soviet Union and world communism.

On October 29, 1945, Generals Goes Monteiro and Eurico Dutra staged a coup, forced Vargas to resign, and entrusted the government to José Linhares, chief justice of the Supreme Court, until after the election. The new government promptly indicated its tendency by repealing Vargas's antitrust decree and launching a suppression of the Communist party. Ostensibly, the military had acted to defend democracy by preventing Vargas from seizing power as he had done in 1937. But its democratic credentials were more than dubious; Goes Monteiro and Dutra were, after Vargas, the chief architects of Estado Novo and had supported Vargas's most repressive measures. Vargas, says Richard Bourne, ''was right to suspect that behind the concern for democracy there was also a hostility to state economic intervention of the sort that was building the Volta Redonda steel plant and a lack of sympathy for his labor and welfare policies.''

The military coup insured that Brazil would return to the parliamentary system under conservative auspices, with two generals as the major presidential candidates, Eurico Dutra for the PSD and Eduardo Gomes for the UDN. Dutra won, while Vargas had the satisfaction of winning election as senator from two states and congressman from six states and the Federal

District. The newly elected Congress, sitting as a constituent assembly, framed a new constitution that retained both the federal system and the powerful executive created by Vargas and guaranteed civil liberties and free elections, but it still denied the vote to illiterates and enlisted men in the armed forces—more than half the adult population.

Under the mediocre, colorless President Eurico Dutra (1946–1951), neocolonial interests regained much of the influence they had lost under Vargas. In his foreign and domestic policies, Dutra displayed a blind loyalty to the anticommunist creed propounded by Washington. Vargas, wishing to broaden Brazil's economic and diplomatic contacts, had resumed diplomatic relations with the Soviet Union; Dutra found a pretext for severing those relations. Alarmed by the growing electoral strength of the Communist party, Dutra outlawed the party, and Congress followed his lead by expelling the party's elected representatives, seventeen congressmen and one senator. Dutra exploited the resulting witch hunt to smash the independent, left-led labor movement; the Workers' Federation, organized in 1946, was declared illegal, and the government intervened in a large number of unions to eliminate "extremist elements." The imposition of a wage freeze and the failure to raise the officially decreed minimum wage caused the real income of workers to drop sharply.

With respect to economic development, Dutra pursued a laissez-faire policy that meant the virtual abandonment of the Vargas strategy of a state-directed movement toward economic independence. Dutra's finance minister, Correia e Castro, openly declared the government's bias in favor of the old neocolonial relationship when he described Brazil as "essentially an agrarian country," adding the "the essence of the Latin American economy, and Brazil is an integral part of this area, is a certain concentration of effort in the export of primary products and foodstuffs, as well as in the import of a wide variety of manufactured goods and processed foodstuffs." In conformity with this point of view, the Dutra government removed all import and exchange controls and allowed the large foreign exchange reserves accumulated during the war—reserves that Vargas had proposed to use for re-equipping Brazilian industry—to be dissipated on imported consumer goods, luxury goods in large part.

Attracted by the new economic climate, foreign capital flowed into Brazil. Direct investments by the United States rose from $323 million in 1946 to $803 million in 1951. Meanwhile, seeking to curb inflation according to the prescription of American advisers, the government pursued a restrictive credit policy harmful to Brazilian entrepreneurs and industrial growth. In 1947, after the negative results of these policies had become apparent and the foreign exchange reserves had almost disappeared, the Dutra government set up a new system of import licensing, with a scale of import priorities according to need, and adopted an easier credit policy. Thanks to these measures, the last two years of the Dutra regime saw a revival of economic growth.

Vargas's Return to Power

In 1950, having assured himself of the neutrality of the armed forces, Vargas ran for president with the support of the PTB and a broad coalition of workers, industrialists, and members of the urban middle class. His campaign concentrated on the need to accelerate industrialization and expand and strengthen social welfare legislation. Defending his past record, Vargas affirmed that his whole effort had been to "transform into an industrial nation" a country "paralyzed by the myopia of rulers wedded to the existing monoculture and to the simple extraction of primary materials." Riding a wave of discontent with the economic and social policies of the

Dutra regime, Vargas easily defeated his two opponents.

Vargas inherited a difficult economic situation. After a brief boom in coffee exports and prices in 1949–1951, the balance of trade again turned unfavorable, and the inflation rate increased. In the absence of other major sources of financing for his developmental program, Vargas had to rely largely on a massive increase in the money supply, with all its inevitable social consequences. Meanwhile, his national program of state-directed industrialization, using state corporations as its major instrument, encountered increasing hostility from neocolonial interests at home and abroad. In the United States, the Eisenhower administration decided that the Vargas government had not created the proper climate for private investment and terminated the Joint United States–Brazilian Economic Commission. Within Brazil, despite his sweeping victory in the election of 1950, Vargas's program faced sabotage at the hands of the rural forces that continued to dominate the majority of state governments and Congress. This hardening of attitudes signified that Vargas's options and his capacity for maneuvering between different social groups were greatly reduced.

In December 1951, Vargas asked Congress to approve a bill creating a mixed public-private petroleum corporation to be called *Petrobrás*, which would give the state a monopoly on the drilling of oil and new refineries. Petrobrás illustrated Vargas's belief that the state must own the commanding heights of the economy; it also represented an attempt to reduce the balance of payments deficit by substituting domestic sources of oil for imported oil. Vargas sought to appease domestic and foreign opponents by leaving the distribution of oil in private hands and allowing existing refineries to remain privately owned, but almost two years passed before Congress, under great popular pressure, passed the law creating Petrobrás in October 1953. However, Vargas's proposal to create a similar agency for electric power—to be called *Electrobrás*—which would supplement the power production of foreign-owned public utilities, remained bottled up in Congress. The depth of nationalist feeling aroused by the debate over Petrobrás and Electrobrás convinced foreign and domestic conservatives that Vargas was traveling a dangerous road.

Vargas's labor policy became another political battleground. Under Vargas, labor regained much of the freedom of action that it had lost during the Dutra years. In December 1951, the government decreed a new minimum wage that only compensated for the most recent price rises. In 1953, three hundred thousand workers went on strike for higher wages and other benefits. In June of that year, Vargas appointed a young protégé, João Goulart, minister of labor. Goulart, a populist in the Vargas tradition, was sympathetic with labor's demands. In January 1954, observing that "it is not wages which raise the cost of living; on the contrary it is the cost of living which requires higher wages," Goulart recommended to Vargas a doubling of the minimum wage. This recommendation evoked a violent "manifesto of the colonels," in which a group of officers charged that the government was penetrated by communism and corruption, that the armed forces were being neglected, and that the recommended new minimum wage would demoralize the badly underpaid officer class. Under military pressure, Vargas dismissed Goulart, but in a May Day speech to workers he announced that the increased minimum wage would be enacted and even praised the fallen minister of labor.

The battle lines between Vargas and his foes were being drawn ever more sharply. In speeches to Congress, Vargas attacked foreign investors for aggravating Brazil's balance of payments problem by their massive remittances of profits and claimed that invoicing frauds had cost Brazil at least $250 million over an eighteen-month period. Meanwhile, attacks on him by the conservative-dominated press and radio grew even more bitter; especially vituperative were the editorials of Carlos Lacerda, editor of the ultraconservative *Tribuna da Imprensa.*

An effort to silence Lacerda presented Vargas's enemies with a golden opportunity to destroy him. Unknown to Vargas, the chief of the president's personal guard arranged for a gunman to assassinate Lacerda. The plot miscarried, for Lacerda was only slightly wounded, but one of his bodyguards, an air force major, was killed. The resulting investigation revealed the complicity of palace officials and uncovered the existence of large-scale corruption in the presidential staff. The chorus of demands for Vargas's resignation was joined by the military, which informed him on August 24 that he must resign or be deposed. Isolated, betrayed by the men he had trusted, the seventy-two-year-old Vargas found the way out of his dilemma by suicide. But he left a message that was also his political testament. It ended with the words:

I fought against the looting of Brazil. I fought against the looting of the people. I have fought bare-breasted. Hatred, infamy, and calumny did not beat down my spirit. I gave you my life. Now I offer my death. Nothing remains. Serenely I take the first step on the road to eternity and I leave life to enter history.

REFORM AND REACTION, 1954–1964

The death of Vargas foreshadowed the demise of the nationalist, populist model of independent capitalist development over which he had presided for the better part of a quarter-century. That model, based on a strategy of maneuver and compromise, of reconciling the clashing interests of the national bourgeoisie, fazendeiros, foreign capitalists, and the working class, of avoiding such structural changes as agrarian reform, had about exhausted its possibilities.

Two options remained. One was for Vargas's

political heirs to mobilize the working class and the peasantry for the realization of a program of structural changes, including agrarian reform, that could impart a new dynamic to Brazilian national capitalism. The alternative was for Vargas's political enemies to impose a streamlined neocolonial model based on the denationalization and modernization of Brazilian industry, on its transformation into an extension of the industrial park of the great capitalist powers, accompanied by a shift in emphasis from the export of raw materials to the export of manufactured goods. Since such a course entailed immense sacrifices for the Brazilian people, it also required the imposition of a dictatorship of the most repressive kind. The balance of forces in 1954 already favored the second option. For a decade, however, Brazil would sway uncertainly between the two alternatives.

The right-wing military and civilian conspirators who spearheaded the movement for Vargas's removal had hoped to use it as a springboard for the establishment of a right-wing dictatorship. But the massive outpouring of grief and protest caused by Vargas's death and suicide message frustrated their plans. Vice president João Café Filho was allowed to serve Vargas's unexpired term. A conservative without sympathy for Vargas's economic nationalist policies, he pursued a course designed to attract foreign capital. One of his decrees exempted foreign firms in Brazil from the need to provide foreign exchange cover for importing machinery. The decree, which discriminated against national companies without foreign links, aroused the anger of nationalists.

The Kubitschek Era

The presidential election of 1955 took place under the watchful gaze of the military. The UDN nominated the conservative General Juarez Távora for president; the PSD and PTB jointly nominated Juscelino Kubitschek, governor of Minas Gerais, with João Goulart as his running mate. Their platform stressed the defense of democracy and the acceleration of economic growth. Kubitschek was not an economic nationalist in the Vargas mold, but the nationalist and reformist groups, knowing the limits of military tolerance, gave him their support. As the campaign progressed, there grew a clamor on the right for a coup to prevent the victory of Kubitschek and Goulart.

However, they won the election in October, with the popular Goulart polling more votes than the president-elect. One month later, a crisis arose when Café Filho, hospitalized by a heart attack, turned over his office to Carlos Luz, the president of the Chamber of Deputies, an enemy of Kubitschek and Goulart who could be expected to deny them the posts to which they had been elected. At this point, centrist senior generals, led by war minister Henrique Teixeira Lott, staged a preventive coup of their own, deposing Luz in order to insure the inauguration of Kubitschek and Goulart.

Kubitschek took office in January 1956 with a promise of "fifty years of progress in five." But this progress was to be achieved with the aid of massive foreign investments, to which Kubitschek offered most generous incentives. These included assurances concerning profit remittances, low taxes, donations of land, and special privileges for the importation of machinery. Eugenio Gudin, an economist favorable to foreign investment, calculated that through this last item alone Brazil donated $1 billion to foreign enterprises. Attracted by these incentives, foreign capital flowed into Brazil; the total inflow between 1955 and 1961 amounted to $2.3 billion. The bulk came from the United States, whose investments in Brazil reached the figure of $1.5 billion in 1960.

This influx of capital, which benefited from advantages denied to Brazilian enterprises, promoted a rapid foreign conquest of Brazilian national industry. In the process, the native entrepreneurs were frequently transformed into directors or partners of the foreign-controlled firms. The take-over concentrated on the most modern and fastest-growing industries (chemical, metallurgy, electrical, communications, and automotive). By way of example, foreign companies controlled 69 percent of the automotive industry by 1960, 62 percent of the chemical industry, 28 percent of plastics production, and 22 percent of the cellulose industry. In the same year, foreign investment accounted for 70 percent of the capital invested in the 34 largest companies and more than 30 percent in the 650 corporations with capital of a million dollars or more. A study of the great economic groups of Brazil in this period revealed that among the conglomerates with a capita of more than 4 billion *cruzeiros*, more than half were foreign, mostly North American; of the groups with a capital of more than 10 billion cruzeiros, twelve were foreign, only five Brazilian. Of the ten conglomerates enjoying a virtual monopoly or leadership in their fields, eight were affiliates of great U.S. corporations.

The Kubitschek era was a heady time of unprecedented economic growth, with an average annual growth rate of 7 percent for the period from 1957 to 1961. By 1960, Brazil had been transformed from an agrarian country into an agrarian-industrial country with a base of heavy industry, for it could boast that it produced half its heavy-industry needs. Construction of a series of great dams provided much of the power needed by Brazil's growing industry. Kubitschek's decision to build a new capital, Brasilia, in the state of Goias, six hundred miles from the coast in an area still roamed by Indians, reflected his exuberant optimism about Brazil's future. Completed in three years, the new capital was inaugurated on April 21, 1960. A network of "highways of national unity" was constructed to link Brasilia with the rest of the country.

But these triumphs of development had to be paid for, and their cost was high. A major source of financing was foreign loans, which swelled Brazil's already large foreign debt from $1.6 billion in 1954 to $2.7 billion in 1961. Service of the foreign debt took an ever-increasing share of the national budget, rising from $180 million to $515 million (more than half the value of Brazil's exports) in the same period. But this source of financing had its limits; by 1959 the International Monetary Fund threatened to withhold loans if Brazil did not adopt a stabilization program and live within its means. Kubitschek responded by breaking off negotiations with the IMF and increasing the money supply; the amount of cruzeiros in circulation rose from 60 billion in 1956 to about 200 billion in 1961. The result was an unprecedented inflation rate and a catastrophic decline in the value of the cruzeiro, whose exchange rate for the dollar fell from 70 to 210 between 1955 and 1961. This in turn greatly diminished the value of Brazil's exports. In 1959, Brazil exported 4,290 million tons of goods and received $1,550 million in payment; in 1961, it exported 10 million tons, two and a half times more, but received in return only $1,260 million. Inflation, like foreign loans, appeared to have reached the limits of its possibilities as a source of financing Brazilian development.

The Quadros Regime

The election of 1960 took place amid growing social unrest and intense debate over domestic and foreign policy. Inflation, corruption, and foreign control of the economy were major campaign issues. The campaign oratory and programs of all the principal candidates reflected the ascendancy that the nationalist, populist ideology had gained over public opinion. Even the conservative UDN recognized this fact by nominating as its candidate the flamboyant Jânio da Silva Quadros, former governor of São Paulo, whose campaign symbol was a broom with which he promised to "sweep out of the government the corrupt elements, the thieves and exploiters of the people." Although Quadros endorsed a balanced budget and stressed the need for a favorable climate for foreign investment, he also opposed the participation of foreign firms in Brazilian oil production, and he showed his independence in foreign policy by paying a visit to revolutionary Cuba at a time when the United States was bringing pressure on Latin American governments to sever diplomatic relations with Cuba.

Quadros's chief opponent was Marshal Henrique Teixeira Lott, who was endorsed by the UDN and the PTB, with João Goulart as his running mate. Less colorful than Quadros, but a more authentic economic nationalist, Lott favored sharply limiting profit remittances sent abroad by foreign firms and supported giving illiterates the vote. Quadros won the election in October 1960, but João Goulart was re-elected vice president.

The short-lived Quadros administration was marked by a mixture of orthodox and unorthodox policies, by an essentially conservative posture in economic affairs and an independent posture in foreign policy. Without breaking with the traditional dependence on the capitalist countries for markets and loans, Quadros sought to reduce that dependence by developing new trade and diplomatic relations with the socialist countries and the Third World. Accordingly, he initiated negotiations for the resumption of diplomatic relations with the Soviet Union, sent a trade mission to the People's Republic of China, and denounced the CIA-backed invasion of Cuba in April 1961. Although he stressed the need for foreign investments and guaranteed their security, Quadros proposed to modify the "laws and regulations which place the Brazilian company in an inferior position" and to restrict the remittance of profits abroad.

However moderate, Quadros's foreign and domestic policies aroused the hostility of military and civilian conservatives. Carlos Lacerda, now governor of the new state of Guanabara (the former Federal District of Rio de Janeiro) launched against him vitriolic attacks of the kind that had helped to destroy Vargas. Quadros's problems were compounded by an increasingly recalcitrant Congress, in which the eighteen rural states, dominated by conservative fazendeiros, were overrepresented. Determined to break the legislative deadlock by some dramatic act. Quadros submitted his resignation on August 25, 1961, after only seven months of rule. His resignation message recalled Vargas's suicide note in its fervent nationalist tone and its claim that hostile foreign forces had obstructed his program of Brazil for the Brazilians. Convinced, it seems, that the military would not permit the prolabor Vice President Goulart to succeed him, Quadros evidently believed that public clamor for his return would bring him back to office with the ample powers he needed to govern.

But he had miscalculated. His resignation caused great public excitement and perplexity, but the clamor that went up was not for his return but for a constitutional solution to the problem: the elevation of Goulart to the presidency. When the constitutional crisis broke out, Goulart was in China on a trade mission. The military cabinet officers, headed by war minister Odílio Denys, regarded Goulart, a wealthy rancher, as a dangerous demagogue and radical and announced that they considered his return to Brazil inadmissible for reasons of "national security."

A grave split developed within the military; in Goulart's home state of Rio Grande do Sul the commander of the Third Army announced his total support for Goulart, and the governor of the state rallied the population to defend the constitution and insure Goulart's elevation to the presidency. The threat of civil war loomed, but the military ministers, facing divisions within the armed forces and feeling the pressure of public opinion, agreed to a compromise. Goulart was permitted to take office, but a constitutional amendment was adopted that replaced the presidential system of government with a parliamentary one. Under this system, the president would share power with a council of ministers named by him, but drawn from and responsible to the legislature.

Goulart's Presidency

The right-wing military and its civilian allies had grudgingly accepted Goulart as president, but on probation. Taking office in September 1961, he began by steering a cautious course designed to allay conservative suspicions at home and abroad. In April 1962, he paid a visit to Washington. Addressing a joint session of Congress, he announced his opposition to the Castro regime and promised reasonable treatment of foreign-owned utilities in Brazil. The United States provided $131 million in aid for the depressed northeast, but the International Monetary Fund, whose approval was a condition for the cooperation of private bankers, remained skeptical of Goulart's intentions.

At the same time that he courted foreign capital, Goulart continued Quadros's independent foreign policy of expanding Brazil's trade and diplomatic contacts with the socialist countries and the Third World. Goulart's refusal to join the United States in imposing sanctions against Castro's Cuba especially angered the right; Congress showed its displeasure with Goulart's able foreign minister, San Tiago Dantas, by refusing to approve his nomination as prime minister.

The first one and a half years of Goulart's rule under the parliamentary system showed few major legislative achievements. One was the passage of a long-delayed law establishing Electrobrás, the national agency proposed by Vargas for the control of the production and distribution of electric power. The other was a law requiring foreign capital to be registered

with the Brazilian government and barring profit remittances abroad in excess of 10 percent of invested capital—certainly not a radical measure. Yet it produced a sharp drop in foreign investments, from $91 million in 1961 to $18 million in 1962. Lacking other sources for financing development, Goulart had to resort to the Kubitschek formula of a massive increase of the money supply. The new inflationary spiral brought the collapse of the cruzeiro and a wave of strikes and food riots, accompanied by a growing radicalization of labor and sections of the peasantry. But the economic slowdown apparent since 1961 continued. Import substitution as a stimulus to industrialization appeared to have reached its limits, and further advance was blocked by the small domestic market, the inequities of Brazilian income distribution, and the drain of capital through debt repayment and profit remittances (amounting to $564 million, or 45 percent of the value of Brazil's exports, in 1962).

With the advice of the brilliant young economist Celso Furtado, who had directed an ambitious effort to develop Brazil's backward, poverty-ridden northeast, Goulart drafted a program of structural reforms that was intended to impart a new dynamism to Brazil's faltering economy. The major proposed reforms were in the areas of land tenure, tax structure, and voting. Reform of the archaic land tenure system would expand the domestic market and increase agricultural production. Tax reform would reduce the inequities of income distribution and provide funds needed for public education and other social welfare purposes. The grant of votes to the illiterates would, it was hoped, drastically reduce the power of the rural oligarchy in the national and state legislatures.

To implement these changes, however, the legislative deadlock in Congress had to be broken. Accordingly, in mid-1962 Goulart launched a campaign for a plebiscite to let the people choose between presidential and parliamentary government. Under great public pressure, Congress agreed to the plebiscite; and on January 1, 1963, more than 12 million voters decided by a three to one majority to restore to Goulart his full presidential powers under the constitution of 1946.

But Goulart's victory did not change the balance of forces in Congress, which repeatedly voted down his reform proposals. Meanwhile, there was a growing polarization of opinion in the country, with the bourgeoisie and the middle class joining the landed oligarchy in opposition to Goulart's domestic program. Goulart's moderate reform proposals in reality favored the industrial bourgeoisie and should have enjoyed its support. But the dynamic industrialist class that had arisen and thrived under Vargas no longer represented a significant social force. The progressive foreign conquest of Brazilian industry had greatly reduced that class's influence as more and more national entrepreneurs gave up an unequal struggle and solved their personal problems by becoming directors or associates of foreign-owned firms. This dependent bourgeoisie shared the fears of social change of its foreign and rural allies. Those fears were also shared by the large urban middle class, battered by inflation and injected by the media with a virulent anticommunist prejudice.

The apprehension of these groups increased as a result of the extravagant rhetoric indulged in by the radical populists and by the spread of radical populism, hitherto confined to the cities, to the countryside. Under the leadership of the lawyer Francisco Julião, peasants in the bleak northeast, afflicted by drought, famine, and oppressive land tenure and labor systems, began to join groups known as Peasant Leagues and agricultural unions and invade fazendas. Their activities seemed to threaten the existence of the latifundio, which was also threatened by Goulart's proposal to give the vote to illiterates and enact agrarian reform.

By the end of 1963, the forces on the right—the fazendeiros, the big bourgeoisie, the military, and their foreign allies—had begun to mobilize against the threat from the left. The military was especially angered by Goulart's proposal to give the vote and the right to hold office to enlisted men, regarding it as a fatal blow to the principle of hierarchy and discipline. The press, radio, and television launched a powerful, orchestrated attack on Goulart, seeking to convince the uneasy, frustrated middle class that he was an agent of the international communist conspiracy and urging the military to intervene in order to safeguard "democracy" and "freedom." As the year 1964 opened, Governors Adhemar de Barros of São Paulo and Carlos Lacerda of Guanabara announced the imminent intervention of the military to check what they called the "advance of communism and anarchy."

Defeated in his efforts to secure passage of his legislative program and under strong pressure from the impatient radical populists, Goulart moved to the left. Appearing at a mass rally in Rio de Janeiro on March 13, 1964, he signed two decrees. One nationalized all private oil refineries. The other made liable to expropriation all large and "underutilized" estates close to federal highways or railways and lands of over seventy acres near federal dams, irrigation works, or drainage projects. At the same meeting, Goulart announced that he would shortly issue a decree on rent control. Three days later, in a message to Congress, he declared, "I have chosen to fight the privileged and take the initiative for basic reforms," and he asked Congress to pass reforms that included tax reform, the vote for illiterates and enlisted men, an amendment to the constitution providing for land expropriation without immediate compensation, and legalization of the Communist party.

By the middle of March, the military-civilian conspiracy for Goulart's overthrow was well advanced. The governors of a number of important states met with a view to transferring

Congress to São Paulo, where a "legalist government" would be installed. An emissary returned from the United States with assurances from the State Department that the United States would immediately recognize the new government. Then, if it became necessary, the "legalist government" would solicit aid from the United States, and the dispatch of American troops would not constitute intervention but a response to a legitimate government's request for aid to suppress communism and subversion.

On March 31, the governor of Minas Gerais announced that he no longer accepted the president's authority. The same day, army units in Minas, soon joined by units from São Paulo, began to march on Rio de Janeiro. The American ambassador to Brazil, Lincoln Gordon, was well informed of the progress of the conspiracy; five days before the coup he cabled Secretary of State Dean Rusk naming General Humberto de Alencar Castelo Branco as the probable head of the new military junta. Recently published documents also show that the United States was prepared to give aid, if needed, to the rebels. A United States naval force with an aircraft carrier, a helicopter carrier, six destroyers, and oil tankers was ordered to take position off the Brazilian coast and await orders from Ambassador Gordon. But Operation Uncle Sam (its code name) proved unnecessary; the Goulart regime fell almost without a struggle on April 1, and the president fled into exile in Uruguay.

The ease with which the Goulart government was overthrown reflected the change in the alignment of forces in Brazil since 1945, and especially the movement of the Brazilian bourgeoisie and middle class into the camp of reaction, but it also revealed the weaknesses and divisions within the camp of Goulart's supporters. The working class, most of which was politically immature and accustomed to passively receiving favors and instructions from populist chieftains, failed to respond to Goulart's appeal for aid. The mass of the peasantry was still under the control of rural coronéis, while the

Peasant Leagues and unions were weak and distant from the main theater of events. The left was badly split ideologically; there was little unity of program or coordinated direction of the groups making up the populist coalition.

Another cause of the passivity with which many received the coup was the widespread belief that it was simply another in a long series of military interventions; sooner rather than later the military would return to its barracks and political life would return to normal. Events proved the error of this opinion. As the military regime consolidated its power, it became clear that the generals had come to stay. They had come to install the alternative to the nationalist economic model. That alternative was a streamlined neocolonial model based on the thorough integration of a dependent Brazilian economy into the international capitalist economy and the rapid modernization of Brazilian industry and agriculture without regard to its social consequences. Because of the regime's combination of brutally repressive policies with primary economic and political dependence on the United States, the Brazilian scholar Hélio Jaguaribe has aptly called it "colonial fascism."

BRAZIL'S "COLONIAL FASCISM"

The first acts of the military leaders of the self-proclaimed "democratic revolution" on April 1964 revealed their long-range intentions. On April 9, the Supreme Revolutionary Command issued the First Institutional Act, permitting the president to rule by decree, declare a state of siege, and deprive any citizen of his civil rights for a period of ten years. A docile Congress approved the military's choice for president, General Humberto de Alencar Castelo Branco. Like many of his colleagues, Castelo Branco was a product of the *Escola Superior de Guerra* (School of Higher Military Studies), dominated in recent years by advocates of a *linha dura* (hard line), whose main tenets were fanatical anticommunism, favorable treatment of foreign capital, and acceptance of the leadership of the United States in foreign affairs.

Encouragement of Foreign Capital and Repression of Labor

It was in the area of economic policy that the new government most clearly defined its character and long-range aims. Roberto Campos, minister of planning, worked out a program for stimulating the entry of foreign capital by incentives that included the free export of profits, reduced taxes on the income of foreign firms, and a special type of exchange for the payment of external financing in case of devaluation. At the same time, internal credit was severely reduced in compliance with the anti-inflationary prescriptions of the International Monetary Fund, while the level of consumption of the domestic market fell as a result of a wage freeze and the decline in the real value of wages. These policies, placing Brazilian-owned companies in an unfavorable position, caused many to go under; 440 went bankrupt in 1966, 550 in 1967. Roberto Campos justified this state of affairs in Spencerian language:

Obviously men are not equal. Some are born intelligent, others fools. Some are born athletes, others paralyzed. The world is composed of large and small enterprises. Some die early, in the flower of life; others drag themselves criminally through a long, useless life. There is a basic, fundamental inequality in human nature, in the nature of things. The mechanism of credit is not exempt from this condition. To ask that Brazilian enterprises should have the same access to foreign credit as foreign enterprises is simply not to know the basic realities of economic life.

The new government's economic policies accelerated the foreign take-over of Brazilian industry. By 1968, according to the findings of a commission of the Brazilian Congress, foreign capital controlled 40 percent of the capital market of Brazil, 62 percent of its foreign trade, 82 percent of its maritime transport, 77 percent of its overseas air transport, 100 percent of its motor vehicle production, 100 percent of its tire production, more than 80 percent of its pharmaceutical industry, and 90 percent of its cement industry. The United States led, with about half of the total foreign investment, followed by Germany, Britain, France, and Switzerland.

To insure foreign and domestic capital of an abundant supply of cheap labor, the government froze wages and banned strikes, with the result that workers' living standards fell sharply. In 1968 the minister of labor estimated that the real value of wages had fallen between 15 and 30 percent in the past four years. Labor was further shackled by the appointment of military interventors to oversee more than two thousand of the country's leading industrial unions.

Further, the government suppressed dissent in all areas of Brazilian life. It suspended the political rights of thousands of so-called extremists, including such world-famous scholars as the economist Celso Furtado and the nutritionist Josué de Castro. Three former presidents, Kubitschek, Quadros, and Goulart, also lost their political rights for ten years. Thousands of federal employees were fired, and hundreds of nationalist military officers were arbitrarily retired or dismissed. The government shut down the Brazilian Institute of Higher Studies, a major center of nationalist economic theory, suppressed the National Student Union, and outlawed the Peasant Leagues.

Meanwhile, the military government unswervingly followed the lead of the United States in foreign policy: It broke off diplomatic relations with Cuba, opposed the seating of the People's Republic of China in the United Nations, participated in the U.S. military intervention in the Dominican Republic, and actively supported the American military effort in Vietnam.

In October 1965, after the government's candidates had suffered humiliating defeat in a series of local elections, President Castelo Branco issued the Second Institutional Act, which dissolved all political parties and instituted indirect elections of the president and vice president. The Third Institutional Act (February 1966) ended the popular election of governors of states and mayors of state capitals.

Yet for various reasons, probably including the wish to avoid embarrassing their principal patron, the United States, Brazil's military rulers chose to maintain a façade of democracy and representative government. They established two official parties, the *Aliança Renovadora Nacional* (National Renovating Alliance, called Arena) and a legal opposition party, *Movimento Democrático Brasileiro* (Brazilian Democratic Movement, or MDB). Since the ranks of the MDB were carefully screened to exclude subversives and its elected representatives held their mandates at the pleasure of the military, with ouster and arrest the likely fate of legislators who displayed an excessive independence, it had little or no impact on policy and legislation. However, it was the only legal channel for expressing and mobilizing dissent, and the vote for the MDB offered a measure of the growing discontent with the dictatorship.

Costa e Silva and a New Constitution

In March 1967, Castelo Branco turned over the presidency to Marshal Artur da Costa e Silva, who had been nominated by the military to succeed him and was duly elected by an obedient, purged Congress. On the day he assumed office, the government gave Brazil a new constitution, the sixth in its history, which incorporated the successive institutional acts. In general, Costa e Silva continued the policies of his predecessor but allowed a certain thaw in the climate of repression; this encouraged a revival of opposition activity and demands for changes in policy. Nationalists inside and outside the armed forces called for a return to the na-

tionalist model of economic development, workers for an end to the wage freeze, intellectuals and students for an end to censorship and a return to academic freedom. A portion of the clergy, headed by the courageous archbishop of Recife and Olinda, Helder Câmara, added their voices to the general cry for social, political, and economic reforms.

Heartened by this show of popular resistance to the dictatorship, two branches of government, Congress and the Supreme Court, gave signs of wanting to reassert their independence. The Supreme Court defied the military by granting a writ of habeas corpus for three student leaders who had been imprisoned for three months. Congress, after months of heated debate, rejected the government's demand that it lift the immunity of a deputy who had bitterly criticized the military for its brutal treatment of political prisoners and student dissenters.

These acts of defiance precipitated a governmental crisis and brought into the open a struggle within the regime between adherents of the hard line and a group of military officers who proposed to reduce foreign economic influence, pursue a more independent foreign policy, and make some concessions to the clamor for social and political reform. The hard-liners won out; under their pressure, Costa e Silva issued a Fifth Institutional Act in December 1968 that dissolved Congress, imposed censorship, suspended the constitution, and granted the president dictatorial powers. One result of the defeat of the moderates was the resignation in January 1969 of Minister of the Interior Afonso de Albuquerque Lima, who favored strengthening national industry and advocated agrarian reform.

The "coup within a coup" of December 1968 was accompanied by an increase in the use of terrorist tactics by a variety of police forces, local and national, against real or suspected opponents of the regime. The official security forces were joined by vigilante groups, sporting such names as "The Communist-Hunting

Command," "The Death Squadron," and "Operation Bandeirante" and operating with the covert approval of the government. The systematic use of torture by special units of the military police and the "death squads" reached a level without precedent in Brazilian history. The victims included intellectuals, students, workers and even priests and nuns, as well as common criminals.

This intensified campaign of repression convinced some elements of the Brazilian left that there was no alternative to armed struggle against the dictatorship. There arose some half-dozen guerrilla groups whose activities included attacks on banks and armories, reprisal killings of notorious torturers, and kidnaping of diplomats and other prominent figures to secure the release of political prisoners. Their most sensational victory was the kidnaping in September 1969 of United States Ambassador Charles Burke Elbrick, who was later released in return for the freeing of fifteen political prisoners and the publication of an antigovernment manifesto by the press, radio, and TV.

But the guerrilla movement never achieved a mass character. Its tactics were rejected by the most powerful force on the left, the underground Communist party, which held that under existing conditions "our principal tactical task consists in mobilizing, uniting, and organizing the working class and the other patriotic forces for the struggle against the dictatorial regime, for its defeat and the conquest of democratic liberties." The death of the most prominent guerrilla leader, Carlos Marighella, who was slain in an ambush by members of the Death Squadron in November 1969, dealt a heavy blow to the movement, which gradually declined until it ceased to pose a serious problem for the regime.

In August 1969, a stroke incapacitated President Costa e Silva. Disregarding the constitutional provision that made Vice President Pedro Aleixo his successor, the three military ministers seized power in October and formed a triumvirate. When it became apparent that the ailing Costa e Silva could not return to his duties, they designated General Emílio Garrastazú Médici as his successor, and Congress confirmed their choice on October 22. A great landowner and former head of the secret police, Garrastazú Médici was completely identified with the hard line.

At the same time, the military junta presented the country with a new constitution. This document provided that the president would henceforth be chosen indirectly by an electoral college composed of Congress and delegates from state legislatures; it also weakened Congress by stripping its members of immunity against charges of libel or slander and making them liable to prosecution on the vague charge of endangering the public security. The junta also announced that instead of merely serving out the unexpired term of Costa e Silva, the new president was to have a full term of office, serving until March 15, 1974.

President Garrastazú Médici (1969–1974) was succeeded by General Ernesto Geisel (1974–1978), who continued in all essential respects his hard-line policies. Geisel proclaimed his desire for a détente with opposition elements and allegedly attempted to stop torture and arbitrary arrests, but Brazil remained a police state: Torture was routinely used against arrested political dissidents or suspects, who sometimes mysteriously disappeared or committed "suicide," and Geisel himself freely used the Fifth Institutional Act to strip elected representatives of the MDB of their political rights.

The Economy and Denationalization

More significant changes took place in the Brazilian economy. By 1970 the denationalization of key sectors of Brazilian industry was almost complete. One or a few giant multinational firms dominated each major industry. The automotive industry, which was dominated by three firms—Volkswagen, General Motors, and Ford—typified the concentration of industrial ownership and production. The military champions of free enterprise did not dismantle the state sector, however, as one might expect. Instead they assigned it the function of providing cheap steel, power, and raw materials to the profitable foreign-owned enterprises.

A counterpart of the concentration of production was the concentration of income. According to the economist Cyro Kurtz, writing in 1970,

more than 80 percent of the population live on the margins of the market for industrial products. They live on the subsistence level. . . . Capacity to consume industrial products is effectively concentrated in that 5 percent of the population who absorb approximately 45 percent of the national income. This immense purchasing power is not translated into a quantitative increase of consumption but into an ever more sophisticated consumption.

Brazil's gross national product grew at an average annual rate of 8 percent, one of the highest in the world, but there was no parallel growth of mass capacity to consume.

The contradiction between a highly productive, technologically advanced industrial plant and an extremely small domestic market had to be resolved somehow. The regime's economic planners found the answer by programming a vast increase in Brazil's exports. Primary products continued to dominate the export trade, but exports of manufactured goods increased at a rate of about 12 percent between 1968 and 1972. Most Brazilians lacked shoes and were poorly clad, but Brazil became a major exporter of shoes and textiles. Increasingly, however, primacy was placed on the export of durable consumer and capital goods (cars, electrical products, machine tools, and the like).

Government planners hoped that exports would help to solve the problem of the balance of payments, a problem that grew ever more acute. But even as the volume of exports increased, so did the annual trade deficit: It was $237 million in 1967, $1.29 billion in 1971, and $4.7 billion in 1974. Meanwhile, the foreign debt, which stood at $12.5 billion in 1973, climbed to $17.6 billion in 1974 and stood at about $30 billion by the end of 1976. Service on this foreign debt, an important component of which was the increased cost of imported oil, amounted to nearly the total value of Brazil's exports in 1977. The problem was compounded by the heavy drain of interest and dividends in amounts considerably greater than the foreign investments that generated them; the total foreign investment for the period from 1964 to 1971 was $670 million, but remittances abroad were $2.319 billion. The deficits in the balance of payments contributed to a steep fall in the exchange value of the cruzeiro and an inflationary spiral that reached a rate of about 46 percent in 1976.

The recession that spread throughout the capitalist world in 1973–1974, combined with much higher oil prices, added to Brazil's economic difficulties. The passage of "antidumping" laws[1] in various countries, including the United States, cut into Brazil's exports of manufactured goods, creating overproduction and unemployment in various industries. By the mid-1970s, the bloom was off Brazil's "economic miracle." Official figures showed that the average indebtedness of Brazil's biggest five hundred companies had risen from 50 percent of net assets in 1971 to 63 percent in 1975, suggesting that many of these major companies were dangerously overextended. The contraction in mass purchasing power as a result of the government's wage policies caused concern even

[1] These laws imposed duties designed to prevent the sale of goods in international trade at below-market prices.

Favelas (slums) ring Rio de Janeiro. (Paul Conklin)

Modern São Paulo. (Bruno Barbey/Magnum Photos, Inc.)

in conservative capitalist circles. In November 1976, the influential weekly *Business Trends*, noting that inflation had been running ahead of wage increases and that real purchasing power was below its 1962 level, rejected the government view that rising wages were the prime cause of inflation.

The government's own figures documented the devastating effect of the "economic miracle" on the general welfare. By 1974, those figures revealed, the minimum wage was only half the minimum income required to buy food for sub-

sistence. When the costs of rent, clothing, and transportation were added, a worker needed four times the minimum wage. Official data revealed an intolerable situation with respect to public health. Nearly half the population over the age of twenty suffered from tuberculosis and about 150,000 people died every year from the disease; about 42 million suffered from parasitic diseases that caused general debility and reduced working capacity. The great majority of Brazilian homes lacked running water and sanitary facilities, a condition that contributed to the prevalence of parasitic disease. According to the president of the National Institute of Nutrition, 12 million preschool children—70 percent of all children in that category—suffered from malnutrition in 1973.

These conditions prevailed not only in rural areas but in São Paulo, the hub of the "economic miracle." Infant mortality in the city increased between 1964 and 1974 and published studies linked this increase to the low income of workers. In rural areas, infant mortality reached a level of 168 deaths per 1,000 births. The situation was no better with respect to primary education. Of every 1,000 students who entered the first grade in 1968, only 301 finished the fourth grade in 1971.

In February 1969, the government announced a program of agrarian reform. Latifundia that had not been exploited for four years were to be expropriated, with compensation to the owners in cash or government bonds, and divided among the landless. It soon became clear that the "agrarian reform" was primarily directed at prodding and assisting semifeudal great landowners to transform their estates into agribusinesses at the expense of their tenants. The stress on "voluntary" adherence gave landowners time for delay and circumvention of the law by dividing the land among relatives or forming it into commercial enterprises exempt from the law's provisions. Thus, its principal result was to stimulate the development of capitalist large-scale agriculture, accelerating a process that had been under way since the 1930s.

Sociologists warned that the so-called agrarian reform was spurring a new wave of rural emigration, throwing a new mass of cheap labor on an overstocked urban labor market. The expansion of capitalist agriculture, wrote the sociologist Bongiovanni Saffioti in 1975,

involves two lamentable social processes: (1) loss by the small agricultural producer of the means of production that assured him of a livelihood under the system of subsistence agriculture or simple commodity production; (2) the transformation of a man who was only formally free, but was protected under the system of "patrimonial servitude," into a temporary wage laborer, deprived of the rights established by labor legislation.

Again, instead of correcting the profound regional contrasts of the Brazilian economy, the government had accentuated them. No serious effort was made to channel investment into the poorer areas of the north and northeast, and private investments naturally flowed into the developed south-central areas, widening the gap between the developed and the "submerged" zones. But official public investment policy also sharpened the tendency toward regional concentration of industry: In 1973 the Council for Industrial Development assigned about 90 percent of its resources to the southeast (of which 77 percent went to São Paulo), and only 3 percent to the northeast.

The Opposition and the Struggle for Rights

Ruled by a brutal military dictatorship, the Brazilian people expressed their dissent and discontent through the few available channels. In September 1974, in a massive repudiation of the regime, the voters gave 62 percent of their votes to the legal opposition party, the MDB, which secured 16 out of 22 seats in the Senate and 170 out of 364 seats in the Chamber of Deputies. The MDB also won majorities in the state assemblies of four of the largest states. Its program called for immediate amnesty for political prisoners, abolition of censorship, and reinstatement of habeas corpus and other traditional liberties, but its victory had little more than symbolic value, since the national legislature had been reduced to a "talking shop" without the power to influence official action. Nevertheless, the system offered a forum for guarded criticism of the government, and the size of the opposition vote provided some index of the government's unpopularity. In 1976, the MDB elected the mayors and gained control of the municipal councils in fifty-nine of the largest urban centers, compared with thirty-one in 1972, when the last local elections were held. In the fifteen cities with populations of more than half a million, the MDB won in ten. The military government, however, continued to appoint the mayors of state capitals.

The Brazilian church occupied a leading place in the struggle for human rights and social justice in Brazil in the 1970s. A substantial minority of the hierarchy, led by Archbishop Helder Câmara, openly opposed capitalism and neocolonialism. In a document dated May 1, 1973, twenty-one bishops and religious superiors of the northeast proclaimed that

the socio-economic structures in Brazil are built on injustice and oppression which stem from a capitalism dependent on international power centers. Within this country, a minority, accomplices of international capitalism and its services, have determined to use all the means at its disposal to preserve the situation created in its favor. In this way it has created structures which are inhuman and, for that reason, un-Christian.

A similar statement, entitled "A Cry from the Church," was issued by the bishops of the east-central regions. Forbidden to publish these documents, the bishops had to print them without indication of the printers or place of publication. Such radical pronouncements by members of a hierarchy that once was among the most conservative in Latin America suggested the depth of mass discontent with the military regime. By 1975, Cardinal Paulo Evaristo Arns of São Paulo, a supporter of Christian grassroots socialism, had become the most visible and influential spokesman of the church against official repression and violence.

As the year 1978—the fourteenth year of the

dictatorship—opened amid preparations for the election of a new president and a new Congress, there were many signs of an upsurge of democratic sentiment and resistance to the regime. With the government in firm control of the electoral college, the candidate of the MDB, retired General Euler Bentes Monteiro—who had played a major role in the coup of 1964 and now campaigned on a platform of immediate return to democracy—had virtually no chance to win against President Geisel's hand-picked successor, General João Baptista Figueiredo, former head of the secret police. But the campaign gave the opposition another means of agitation for change. Despite continuing though less frequent repression, including arrests, torture, and beatings of suspected "subversives," it made the most of its opportunities. Especially significant was the growing strength of a dissident group within the military, including high-ranking officers like General Hugo Abreu, a former member of the presidential entourage, who was jailed for sending letters in which he charged that the regime was pervaded by corruption and called for an end to military rule. Even some big businessmen who in the past had supported and financed political repression sensed the explosive potential of the rising popular discontent and joined the chorus for democratization. In September, thirty-three unions issued a manifesto demanding the right to strike, freedom to organize, and political amnesty. When all was said and done the official candidate was chosen president by the electoral college on October 15.

The next test of strength between the government and its opponents came in November, with the election of a new Congress. Once again, despite a new law that barred the opposition from using television and radio, the MDB made sweeping gains, with the biggest advances in the more developed southern parts of the country. Equally significant was the clear preference shown by the electorate for the more radical candidates of the MDB. Thanks to a bag of political tricks that included the selection of one-third of the senators by government-controlled electoral colleges and a gerrymander that reduced the representation of the more populous states in the Chamber of Deputies, the government retained a narrow control of the Congress. But the elections reflected the immense discontent of Brazilians with the economic and social results of fourteen years of dictatorial rule and the growing strength of an opposition that united ever wider sections of the population.

The Dictatorship in Crisis, 1978–1983

There have been three major developments on the Brazilian scene since 1978: (1) A weak recovery from the recession of 1974–1975 soon gave way to an even more severe recession, culminating in a balance of payments crisis that brought Brazil to the verge of national bankruptcy. (2) The living standards of the masses continued to decline as a result of mounting unemployment, skyrocketing inflation, and the government's austerity measures, causing increased discontent and resistance on the part of the working class and the peasantry. At the same time, opposition to the military regime grew among the middle class and sections of the capitalist class. (3) In an effort to defuse the growing opposition, the regime applied the policy of abertura, or "opening toward democracy." This policy of limited political concessions left real power in the hands of the military and allowed it to continue the economic and social policies that have brought Brazil to its present plight. Taken together, these developments defined a general crisis of the Brazilian model of dependent development.

Brazil's recovery from the recession of 1974–1975 was not strong or lasting. Between 1976 and 1979 the industrial growth rate hovered about 5 or 6 percent, compared with an average growth rate of 13 percent between 1967 and 1974. By 1980 Brazil had relapsed into an even more severe slump; as 1983 opened, that slump continued with no relief in sight. Many feared that it might deepen into a major depression. Despite the downturn, inflation reached an unprecedented annual rate of 120 percent in mid-1981 and was running at about 95 percent at the end of 1982. By then many companies, including some of Brazil's biggest firms, had failed. Even the powerful multinational companies suffered losses, but some were able to strengthen their hold over the economy by the acquisition of national companies in trouble. Particularly hard hit was the recently created capital goods sector. It was working at only about 50 percent of capacity and suffered as a result of large cuts in the budgets of the state companies that provided a large proportion of its orders. Adding to the difficulties of the sector was the balance of payments problem, which forced the government to accept "financial packages" that linked loans to the purchase of foreign equipment even where it could be manufactured locally. As a result, the share of Brazilian-made equipment in large new projects was expected to fall from 70 percent in 1979 to 40 percent over the next few years. In 1981, under pressure from foreign creditors to reduce public spending, the government announced a plan to sell many of the country's 564 state-owned companies to the private sector. Since local capital was insufficient to buy more than a few of these companies, the program was likely to strengthen the hold of multinationals on the economy.

The economic crisis resulted from the interplay of domestic and external factors. An important cause was the inability of the domestic market to absorb the growing output of Brazilian industry. For almost two decades, the dictatorship had pursued a policy of promoting the growth of profits and capital by keeping wage increases below the cost of living; this policy sharply limited the purchasing power of the masses. The economic downturn of the 1970s and the 1980s, however, also reduced the purchasing power of the middle classes, who provided a major part of the market for cars, television sets, and other durable consumer goods. In 1981, for example, the domestic market for cars collapsed, bringing losses to all four leading manufacturers (Fiat had begun large-scale production just before the slowdown).

The most direct cause of the crisis, however, was an unmanageable balance of payments and debt service problem. By 1980, Brazil had a foreign debt of $55 billion, largest in the Third World, and service of the debt absorbed 40 percent of the nation's export earnings. President Figueiredo complained that, because of the drain of interest, Brazil had "nothing left over for development." The size of that drain is suggested by the 1979 annual report of New York City–based Citicorp, which showed that 20 percent of all its profits—more than was generated in the United States—came from Brazil. The high interest rates caused by the monetarist tight money policies of the Reagan administration added to Brazil's debt service burden. The export of a considerable part of the profits made by multinational companies in Brazil also increased Brazil's trade deficit. By 1980 these companies controlled 40 percent of the major industrial and mining enterprises of the country and were sending home 55 percent of their profits.

The military planners had counted on a great increase in exports, especially of durable consumer and capital goods, to help solve the balance of payments problem. But each increase in exports was accompanied by an even greater increase in the imports of goods needed to maintain the export drive. In 1980, exports increased 24 percent, but imports grew by 50 percent. Brazilian exports also suffered from protectionist measures taken by the governments of industrialized countries under pressure from manufacturers' lobbies and trade unions worried about unemployment. Brazil's relations with the United States, in particular, have deteriorated in recent years as a result of differences over trade. Meeting with Brazil's planning minister in July 1982, the United States special trade representative demanded that Brazil completely end export subsidies by March 1983 or face reprisals in the form of countervailing duties on such Brazilian exports as steel, light aircraft, and footwear.

This trade conflict, adding to the resentment caused by the earlier Carter administration's criticism of Brazilian violations of human rights, its ban on the shipment of arms to Brazil, and its refusal to sell Brazil nuclear reactors, reinforced a tendency on the part of Brazil to go its own way in foreign policy. Seeking to expand and diversify its markets, Brazil widened its ties with black Africa, including Marxist states like Angola and Mozambique, with the Arab world, and especially with the Soviet Union. More recently, Brazil has distanced itself from the Central American policy of the United States by maintaining friendly relations with the Sandinist government of Nicaragua, a special target of United States destabilization efforts.

By early December 1982, the balance of payments problem had reached a critical point. Brazil had almost run out of the foreign exchange it needed to meet its financial obligations. The foreign debt stood at about $89 billion, and many of the approximately 1,400 banks that had lent money to Brazil, grown suddenly nervous, were refusing to renew outstanding loans to Brazilian entities. A Brazilian default, however, could send shock waves that might topple the international banking system. Once more, as in the similar Mexican emergency, the self-interest of the Western financial community dictated a rescue operation. The plan was organized by the IMF, with strong support from the United States government and major United States banks, Brazil's biggest creditors. Brazil would receive a total of $6 billion from the IMF, an emergency credit of over $1 billion from the United States, and pressure would be brought on the uneasy private bankers to restore reductions in outstanding credit and make new loans to Brazil. Having reached agreement with the IMF, on December 20 Brazil asked the country's main creditors for a rescheduling of its debts. The rescheduling plan called for Brazil to pay the interest due in 1983, some $10 billion, but to make no amortization payments. Brazil had gained a momentary respite, but the social costs of the relief operation to Brazil were high. The IMF's insistence on removal of subsidies meant that the price of gasoline, bread, wheat, and sugar would rise substantially. Small and medium-sized companies and farmers would be required to pay higher interest rates on their loans. Cuts in government spending were certain to swell unemployment and increase bankruptcies. The new loans would give Brazil a breathing space, but the balance of payments problem remained as intractable as ever, and it was doubtful that the financial juggling act of 1982 could be indefinitely repeated.

The austerity program imposed by the IMF was a new blow at popular living standards that had sharply declined since the establishment of the military dictatorship in 1964. In mid-1978, one study concluded that at least 70 percent of the population lived below the officially calculated economic survival level. The state-decreed minimum wage lagged substantially behind inflation levels. In 1982 the minimum monthly wage was 23,000 cruzeiros, about $95.00. According to Brazilian sociologists, however, a family of five needed three times that amount to survive. In 1950 only one member of the average family needed to work; in 1982 three had to join the work force to provide a subsistence wage. The superexploitation of Brazilian workers took its heaviest toll on the weakest group of the population—its children. "For tens of millions of children in this country of 122 million," wrote a correspondent in the Los Angeles *Times* (December 20, 1982), "the business of economic survival begins at age 5, sometimes younger. Statistics, academic studies, and experiences reported by children give strong support to the conclusion that life for most ordinary Brazilian children is one of work, exploitation, degradation, and sometimes virtual slavery." A partial census taken in 1982 indicated that half of all Brazilian children over 10 worked.

Despite the official ban on strikes, with the threat of long prison sentences and other severe penalties for strike organizers, Brazilian unions have waged many strike struggles in recent years and have wrested partial gains from employers, especially for the skilled sectors of the work force. A rash of strikes in the spring of 1979 met with a conciliatory attitude on the part of the new Figueiredo government, which approved settlements granting workers large wage increases, assurances against reprisals, and recognition of elected strike leaders. There was a return to hard-line policies in 1981 when a military court in São Paulo, invoking the National Security Law, sentenced the popular labor leader Luis Inacio da Silva (Lula) and ten other metalworkers to prison for having led the 1980 metalworkers' strike in the highly industrialized region around São Paulo. In April 1982, however, Brazil's Supreme Military Tribunal, hearing an appeal from the decision, accepted the defense's argument that the strike could not be considered a matter of national security and ruled itself incompetent to hear the case. This has set a precedent for other National Security Law indictments of union leaders for strike activities. In another landmark case in 1982, a military court found a military policeman guilty of shooting a union activist and sentenced him to six years in prison. The severe slump of 1980, accompanied by growing unemployment, made it more difficult for unions to back up their demands with the threat of strike action, but the trade union movement has consolidated its position and is now a major force in the struggle against the dictatorship and for social progress.

If the level of violence and repression has declined in industrial labor conflicts, the same is not true of the situation in rural areas, especially in the northeast and the Amazon. The number of violent land conflicts has increased in recent years. A survey made at the end of 1981 by the Catholic church's Land Commission recorded 915 cases of conflict involving 1.5 million people and about 37.2 million hectares (1 hectare = 2.47 acres), an area the size of Italy. The same report found that over thirty months, 47 peasant leaders and their supporters had been murdered by landowners or their gunmen. None of these crimes had resulted in an indictment or trial.

A major cause of these conflicts is the explosion of land concentration and land-grabbing in recent decades. A 1975 survey found that the 0.8 percent of farms over 1000 hectares in size occupy 43 percent of the land, whereas the 52 percent of farms less than 10 hectares occupy only 2.8 percent of the land area. In part this process of land concentration reflects the growth of capitalist, mechanized agriculture producing such crops as soya beans or sugar cane[2] on land formerly devoted to coffee or subsistence crops. In part it is due to the pattern of occupation of the new lands opened up for settlement in the Amazon by the construction of the Transamazonian Highway and other roads. Instead of taking advantage of the new agricultural frontier to settle thousands of landless peasant families, as recommended by the church's Land Commission, the Amazon development agency has given big companies large sums of money to set up vast cattle ranches. As a result, some 95 percent of the new landholdings in the Am-

azon are of 10,000 hectares or more. Unlike coffee plantations, the large new soya bean and sugar cane farms and cattle estates employ little labor. Many of the dispossessed or discharged tenants and rural laborers have migrated to the cities, swelling the ranks of the unemployed and underemployed and aggravating all the urban social problems. Thousands of others drifted to the Amazon frontier, becoming *posseiros* (squatters) who raise subsistence crops of rice, cassava, and maize on their small plots. They enjoy considerable rights under Brazilian law, but these rights have little value on the violent frontier. The posseiros are frequently threatened with eviction by powerful land-grabbers, who arrive with their gunmen and sometimes enjoy the open or covert support of the local military or other officials. The posseiros have responded by organizing rural unions and defending their land by all the means at their disposal; they have found allies in courageous Catholic clergy who have on occasion been arrested, tortured, and even murdered for their humanitarian activities. Because the countryside is a major remaining bastion of reactionary forces, the struggle for land and human rights in the rural areas is crucial for the future of Brazil.

Discredited and isolated on account of its failed economic policies and corruption, in recent years the military regime has sought a way out of its impasse by a strategy of détente with the opposition. This policy was begun under President Geisel as *distensão*, or "decompression," and expanded under President Figueiredo as abertura. Its successive steps included the lifting of most censorship; an amnesty that permitted the return of political exiles and the restoration of their political rights; and an overhaul of the political system that allowed the formation of new parties in addition to the two official government and opposition parties. The process was capped in 1980 by a congressional measure, approved by President Figueiredo, that provided for the direct election of all municipal officials,

[2]A major factor in the expansion of sugar cane cultivation is the success of Brazil's program for developing alcohol as a fuel. This fuel is now used in one-third of the country's large vehicle fleet.

state governors, and members of the federal Congress. This meant that in the general election of 1982, for the first time since 1967, all members of the federal Congress and state and municipal officials would be elected directly by the voters.

These concessions were certainly not without significance, but their limited, calculated character must be understood. They were hedged about by constitutional amendments, replaced or added as the political situation required. These amendments were designed to ensure the continuation of military rule. In preparation for the election of 1982, the government introduced two such provisions. One banned party coalitions, thus severely limiting the possibilities of unity among the opposition parties. Another, designed to compensate for the expected loss of the larger industrial states by the government party, changed the electoral college that would elect the new president; under the new rules, a vote cast in a remote, sparsely settled Amazonian state would have as much weight as 22 votes cast in São Paulo![3]

Yet the election of November 15, 1982, in which 55 million Brazilians participated, was a major event, a plebiscite that rendered a decisive verdict on the military regime. The major opposition party was the Brazilian Democratic Movement party (PMDB), an informal coalition of bourgeois liberal and left-wing groups supported by many capitalists, at one end of the political spectrum, and by the still illegal Communist party, at the other end. Avoiding controversial issues that might divide its followers, its program stressed the need to carry the process of democratization to its logical conclusion. Two labor parties—one led by the trade union leader known as Lula, the other by the veteran populist leader of the Vargas-Goulart era, Leonel Brizola—also took part in the elections. Despite

all the legal and illegal maneuvers of the regime, including widespread tampering with ballots, the opposition took 62 percent of the vote and won the governorships of ten of the twenty-three states, including all of the industrialized southern states except Santa Catarina. A major surprise was the election of Brizola as governor in the state of Rio de Janeiro. The opposition gained control of the lower house of Congress, but the government party (the Democratic Social party, an outgrowth of the old Arena) retained control of the senate, only one-third of whose membership was up for election, and had a comfortable majority in the electoral college that would elect President Figueiredo's successor in January 1985.

The opposition had made large gains, but it was doubtful whether it could soon translate its electoral victories into concrete economic and social benefits for the long-suffering Brazilian masses. Under the constitution imposed by the military, the all-powerful president controlled both the federal budget and the operating funds of the states. Even before the election, the government was preparing changes in the tax collection system that would limit even further the power of the state governments. It seemed certain that a military man or a nominee of the military would be the next president of Brazil.

Thus the prospects for an early change in economic and social policy seemed poor. Yet pressures for change were building up and might prove irresistible. Paradoxically, the industrialization program of the military regime, so disastrous in social costs, had transformed Brazilian society in ways that powerfully reinforced the groups that must lead the movement for the construction of a new Brazil. In 1964 Brazil was half urban, half rural; by 1982 it was 70 percent urban, 30 percent rural. The industrial working class had greatly increased in size, doubling every ten years, and it was a more mature and independent working class than that of 1964. In the same period the number of college stu-

[3] "An electoral trick which worked" is the way the *Latin American Regional Report: Brazil* described the amendment.

dents, so hostile to the military regime that their national union was still proscribed, had risen from about 400,000 to about 1 million. Large numbers of women had joined the work force, and many were active in politics and social movements. Even the peasantry, traditionally unorganized, passive, and dominated by coronéis and government officials, had begun to display a new spirit of militancy and independence. Against this background of growing social awareness and ferment, it was possible that the elections of 1982 might ultimately prove, as the sociologist Fernando Henrique Cardoso suggested, if not a social revolution, at least a point of transition from the old to the new Brazil.

CHAPTER SIXTEEN

Storm over the Andes: Peru's Ambiguous Revolution

In the second half of the twentieth century, revolutionary change came at last to three countries whose economic and social structures were among the most archaic in Latin America, the Andean republics of Peru, Bolivia, and Ecuador. Here, as elsewhere on the continent, the movement for reconstruction fused the effort to modernize with the struggle for greater social justice for the masses: Economic sovereignty, industrialization, and land reform were the main slogans of the Andean revolutions. But the presence of large, compact Indian-speaking groups, ranging from some 70 percent of the population of Bolivia to about 40 percent of the populations of Peru and Ecuador, gave a distinctive character to the nationalist, reformist movements in these countries.

THREE ANDEAN REVOLUTIONS

Landlocked Bolivia, the most Indian of the three lands, a country where as late as 1976 only a minority of the population were monolingual speakers of Spanish, was the scene of the first true Andean social revolution. In 1952 the middle-class National Revolutionary Movement (MNR), led by Victor Paz Estenssoro, overthrew the rule of the great landlords and tin barons with the support of armed Indian miners and peasants. The Bolivian land reform, begun by the spontaneous rising of the peasantry and legitimized by the revolutionary government of President Paz Estenssoro, broke the back of the latifundio system in Bolivia. Like the Mexican land reform, however, the Bolivian reform created some new problems even as it solved some old ones. The former latifundia were usually parceled out into very small farms—true minifundia—and the new peasant proprietors received little aid from the government in the form of credit and technical assistance. Yet despite its shortcomings, the Bolivian land reform brought indisputable benefits: some expansion of the internal market, some rise in peasant living standards and, in the words of Richard W. Patch, "the transformation of a dependent and passive population into an independent and active population."

The new government also nationalized the principal tin mines, most of which were controlled by three large companies, and recognized its debt to the armed miners by placing the mines under joint labor-government management. It also abolished the literacy qualification for voting and thus enfranchised the Indian masses. But the new regime inherited a costly, run-down tin industry, while the initial disruptive effect of the agrarian reform on food production added to its economic problems.

Under strong pressure from the United States, which made vitally needed economic aid to the revolutionary government conditional on the adoption of conservative policies, the MNR leadership gradually moved to the right. The government of Paz Estenssoro offered generous compensation to the former owners of expropriated mines, invited new foreign investment

on favorable terms, ended labor participation in the management of the government tin company, and reduced welfare benefits to the miners. Equally important, it agreed to the restoration of a powerful American-trained national army to offset the strength of the peasant and worker militias. These retreats broke up the worker–middle class alliance formed during the revolution and facilitated the seizure of power in 1964 by right-wing generals.

In the violent ebb and flow of Bolivian politics since 1964, governments have risen and fallen, but a persistent theme has been the conflict between radical workers, students, and nationalist military, on the one hand, and a coalition uniting remnants of the old landowning aristocracy, a new elite of businessmen and politicians grown wealthy through U.S. aid, and conservative military, on the other. The peasantry, neutralized by the land reform that satisfied its land hunger, initially remained passive or even sided with the government in its struggles with labor, but later peasant unrest began to grow as a result of deteriorating economic conditions. There was a brief revival of social revolutionary and nationalist trends under President Juan José Torres (1970–1971), who nationalized various foreign-owned enterprises and sought to promote Bolivia's economic independence by expanding economic ties with the Soviet Union and other socialist states. But in August 1971, his government was overthrown by a rightist army coup led by Colonel Hugo Banzer Suárez, whose dictatorial regime threw Bolivia's doors wide open to foreign investors and brutally repressed all dissidents. Massive financial aid from the United States enabled the Banzer government to survive despite growing popular opposition.

In July 1978, after a presidential election tainted by large-scale fraud in favor of Banzer's chosen successor, General Juan Pereda Asbun, Pereda seized power and proclaimed a government of "democratic transformation," promising new elections in 1980. Significantly, the peasantry, the regime's former ally, had voted heavily in favor of the presidential candidate of the united left parties. In an atmosphere of revival and mobilization of trade union, student, and other opposition movements, Pereda repealed various pieces of repressive legislation, yielded to the demands of various striking unions, and reopened the universities, closed arbitrarily by the Banzer regime. But a continuing wave of strikes and demonstrations revealed the fragility of Pereda's hold on power. In November a new military coup ousted Pereda and installed General David Padilla as president. Padilla continued the dismantling of Banzer's repressive system and promised a return to civilian rule, with elections scheduled for July 1979.

Elections were duly held in July 1979, but produced no clear winner. Congress decided to hold new elections the next year, appointing a caretaker president to preside over the government pending their outcome. In November a military junta overthrew the provisional government, but itself fell within a few short weeks as a result of a general strike by the powerful Bolivian labor confederation and protests by students, the civilian parties, and virtually all sections of the population. Congress now elected a new caretaker president, Lydia Gueiler Tejada, the first woman president in Bolivian history. In June 1980, general elections gave victory to Hernán Siles Zuazo, presidential candidate of a coalition of leftist forces, the UDP (*Unidad Democrática Popular*), and a highly respected veteran of Bolivian politics. But Siles Zuazo was prevented from taking office when a group of military hard-liners, led by General Luis García Meza, seized power in July and established a regime probably unprecedented in Bolivian history for brutality, corruption, and inefficiency. Contributing to the regime's discredit at home and abroad were its close links to the international drug traffic; under García Meza cocaine production became a major crop of the Bolivian

economy, with prices for coca leaves rising from $50 to a reported $15,000 a ton in less than a year. Meeting stubborn resistance from the labor movement, the peasantry, all civilian parties, and even a section of the military, in August 1981 García Meza yielded power to another military junta, which then decided to convene Congress so that it might certify Siles Zuazo's election as president. In October 1982, Siles Zuazo took office amid large popular demonstrations of support in La Paz, which had become "the democratic capital of South America," while many officials of the previous regime, fearing punishment for their corruption and other crimes, took flight for right-wing havens in Paraguay and Argentina.

The new government faced a desperate economic situation. Tin prices were at their lowest level in twenty years and still falling. The peso had lost 90 percent of its value since February 1982, inflation stood at over 150 percent for the year, and 75 percent of the work force were unemployed or underemployed. In addition, 70 percent of Bolivia's income from exports went to service the foreign debt of $3.9 billion. The political turmoil of recent years, especially the strikes against the military juntas, had drastically reduced production levels. Mistakes by previous regimes in the allocation of government investments in development projects had caused the country to be oversupplied with smelters and refineries, while production of hydrocarbons and tin faced declines because of inadequate exploration for new sources. To achieve even a modest recovery and begin the transition to a more balanced and independent development required cooperation and sacrifice from the masses, who had defeated the reactionary military and expected much from the new government.

The Siles Zuazo team's first task was to achieve control over a galloping inflation. This necessitated raising food prices for such staples as sugar, beef, and rice, but the government showed its desire to favor the poorer sectors by setting lower rates for electricity and cooking oil in working-class districts. In addition to granting small wage increases, the government implemented its promise to give labor representation on the boards of state companies by appointing three workers' delegates to the boards of the state mining corporation and the state oil company. In the Cabinet, the ministries of labor and mining were assigned to members of the Communist party, strongly supported by the miners' union. The new government also displayed its nationalist temper by announcing plans to take over the U.S. and Canadian-owned *Electricidad de La Paz* (Bolivian Power Company). Foreign policy reflected the leftward shift, with the resumption of diplomatic relations with Cuba and the expansion of diplomatic and commercial relations with other socialist countries.

Perhaps recalling the experience of President Allende in Chile, Siles Zuazo dismissed the entire military command in October 1982 and replaced it with reliable officers who supported democratic government. The "sudden Bolivian spring" had begun; whether it would continue largely depended on unity among the parties composing the ruling leftist coalition and its progress in the solution of Bolivia's formidable economic and social problems.

Ecuador, the smallest of the Andean republics, experienced the beginnings of a social revolution in 1972, when a group of nationalist military headed by General Guillermo Rodríguez Lara ousted the aging, demagogic President José María Velasco Ibarra, who had dominated Ecuadorean politics for the past four decades. The new military junta promised social reform, including radical land reform, and offered a program of rapid economic development that stressed industrialization and the modernization of agriculture. It also promised to reverse the previous official policy of surrender of the country's rich oil resources in the Oriente, the

Amazonian lowlands, to foreign companies. The new government counted on revenue from oil to finance the planned reforms and program of economic development.

Five years later, the advance of the Ecuadorean Revolution appeared to be stalled. Opposition from the still-powerful hacendado class had almost completely paralyzed agrarian and tax reform. Some land had been distributed to the peasants, but big landowners still controlled 80 percent of the cultivated area. The military government appeared virtually to have abandoned land redistribution in favor of cooperating with the hacendados to increase production and revenues by mechanization, greater concentration of landownership, and the ouster of peasants from the land. The result was growing peasant agitation for true land reform, accompanied by invasions of estates and clashes between peasants and security forces.

Industrialization continued the advance begun in the 1960s, but it was a dependent industrialization based on massive importation of foreign capital and goods. By the early 1970s, foreign interests controlled some 35 percent of all industrial enterprises, nearly 60 percent of all commercial enterprises, and half of all banking assets in Ecuador. Under pressure from foreign oil companies for lower taxes and wider profit margins—a pressure exerted through a boycott on oil exports—the military regime retreated from its insistence on tight control over prices, profits, and the volume and rate of oil production. These concessions represented a defeat for the nationalist left wing of the military junta and sharpened the divisions within it.

In Ecuador, as in other Latin American countries under military control, the late 1970s saw a growing movement for a return to civilian rule. Aware of their economic failures and especially their failure to relieve the dismal poverty of the Ecuadorean masses—official figures showed that the wage earners' share of the national income had declined from 53 percent in 1960 to less than 46 percent in 1973 and that 7 percent of the population received more than 50 percent of the national income—the military appeared quite willing to abandon the burden of governing the country. In July 1978, Jaime Roldós, the populist candidate of the Concentration of Popular Forces, handily won the first round of a presidential contest presided over by the armed forces. During the campaign, the young, energetic Roldós promised a new deal that would include a revived agrarian reform and an end to foreign economic control. In April 1979, his victory was confirmed by the second round of the presidential elections. But a conflict with the congressional leader of his own party, who consistently blocked legislation proposed by Roldós, prevented him from implementing his program until May 1980, when he was assured of the support of a majority in Congress.

Central to that program was the use of large amounts of Ecuador's oil earnings to modernize agriculture, promote industrialization, and construct a network of roads to expand the internal market. Roldós's Five-Year Plan called for investment of $800 million in rural development that would bring some 3 million acres of coastal, highland, and Amazonian farmland into new production. The pace of agrarian reform was to be accelerated, with almost 2 million acres to be distributed to landless peasants by 1984. Roldós's foreign policy stressed greater independence of the United States, reflected in his maintenance of friendly relations with Cuba, expansion of diplomatic and commercial ties with socialist countries, and support for Central American revolutionary movements. But Roldós's ambitious reform and development program had hardly begun when he was killed in a plane crash in May 1981. He was immediately succeeded by Vice-President Oswaldo Hurtado Larrea of *Democracia Popular,* a Christian Democratic party.

This transition took place amid deteriorating economic conditions as a result of a developing recession and declining prices for Ecuadorian oil. Hurtado, more conservative than Roldós, reversed his foreign policy, abandoned much of his reform and development program, and adopted austerity measures, including the removal of subsidies on wheat and gasoline. Such moves were designed to ease the burdens of servicing a massive $4.7 billion foreign debt and to compensate for declining revenues from oil exports. These measures, it was hoped, would pave the way for an IMF loan. But the austerity program encountered intense opposition from the trade unions, who responded with strikes. In Congress Roldós's Concentration of Popular Forces secured votes of censure against the oil minister and the finance minister, who were forced to resign. While the stalemate between Congress and the president continued, the economic situation steadily deteriorated. By the end of 1982, the foreign debt stood at around $5.5 billion, and payments took 25 percent of the budget. Especially alarming was the rapid decline in Ecuador's oil reserves, fallen by early 1982 to as low as 650 million barrels, according to some estimates; unless new reserves were discovered in the country's Amazonian region, it was predicted, her oil wealth and chief exchange earner would be gone in a decade.

The economic slump sharpened the social problems created by advances in industrialization and the modernization of agriculture. From 1970 to 1980 the proportion of peasants in the population had fallen from 68 percent to 52 percent. The agrarian reform, stressing mechanization and concentration of landownership rather than distribution of land to the landless, had ended semiservile relations in the countryside but actually aggravated the problem of landlessness and rural unemployment. The result was to swell the number of rural people fleeing to the cities in search of work that only few found. By the early 1980s the great port city of Guayaquil had a population of 1 million; an estimated two-thirds of its inhabitants were unemployed or underemployed and lacked adequate shelter, food, or medical care. Thus, in an atmosphere of economic and political crisis, social problems and tension accumulated with little prospect that solutions would soon be found.

A revolution of a unique kind began in Peru in October 1968. Developments in that country between 1968 and 1975 exposed the fallacy of the common assumption that the Latin American military constitutes one reactionary mass. Moving with greater speed and vigor than any civilian reformist regime in Latin American history, a military junta headed by General Juan Velasco Alvarado decreed the nationalization of key industries and natural resources, a land reform that transferred great estates to peasant and worker cooperatives, and the creation of novel new forms of economic organization that should be "neither capitalist nor communist." In 1975 the Peruvian Revolution halted its advance and began to retreat; today even its major conquests—the agrarian reform and the great nationalizations—are threatened with erosion and even destruction. Yet it must rank among the more serious recent Latin American efforts to achieve a breakthrough in the struggle against backwardness and dependency. Despite its mistakes and failures, it has already made an indelible mark on Peruvian society. The study of those mistakes and failures will help Peruvians as they search for new approaches to the solution of their country's great national problems.

Peru's "ambiguous revolution" poses some intriguing questions. Why should a group of military officers, a class commonly regarded as the staunchest defenders of the old order in Latin America, launch a major attack on that order in Peru? What economic and social interests did the Peruvian military reformers represent? In the last analysis, was the Peruvian Revolution a "bourgeois revolution" designed to promote the rise of an autonomous native capitalism? If the military reformers failed to make a clean break with the past, with the model of dependent development and the problems it generates, what were the reasons for that failure? An attempt to answer these questions requires an examination not only of the revolution itself but of its remote origins, going back to the establishment of an independent Peru.

PERU: FROM INDEPENDENCE TO THE WAR OF THE PACIFIC

The liberation of Peru from Spanish rule came from without, for the Creole aristocracy, whose wealth was derived from the forced labor of Indians and black slaves in mines, workshops, and haciendas, rightly feared that revolution might set fire to this combustible social material. The elite, although eager for the economic and political benefits of self-rule, would have preferred a peaceful settlement through negotiation and the grant of autonomy within a reformed Spanish Empire. The process of Peruvian liberation began when an army of Argentinians and Chileans under General José de San Martín landed on the coast near Lima in 1820 and occupied the capital. It ended when Bolívar's lieutenant, General Antonio José de Sucre, at the head of a mainly Colombian army, accepted the surrender of José de la Serna, the last Spanish viceroy on the American continent, on the field of Ayacucho in December 1824.

The liberators, San Martín and Bolívar, attempted to reform the social and economic institutions of the newly created Peruvian state. San Martín decreed a ban on the importation of slaves, the automatic emancipation of all children born of slaves in Peru, and the abolition of Indian tribute, the mita, and all other kinds of Indian forced labor; he also proclaimed that all inhabitants of Peru, whether Indians or Creoles, were Peruvians. Since these reforms did not conform to the interests of the Creole elite, they remained on paper. When Bolívar assumed power in Peru in 1823, he enacted reforms reflecting the same liberal ideology. Wishing to create a class of independent smallholders, he decreed the dissolution of the Indian communities and ordered the division of the communal lands into parcels of land; each family was to hold its plot as private property, with the surplus to become part of the public domain. While attacking communal property, Bolívar left alone feudal property, the great haciendas inhabited by Indian sharecroppers or serfs (*yanaconas, colonos*) who had to pay their landlords a rent that amounted to as much as 50 to 90 percent of the value of their crops, in addition to free personal service (*pongueaje*).

The well-intentioned Bolivian land reform played into the hands of hacendados, public officials, and merchants who took advantage of Indian weakness and ignorance to build up vast estates at the expense of Indian communal lands; the process began slowly but gathered momentum as the century advanced. Bolívar's efforts to abolish Indian tribute had no greater success. After he left Peru in 1826, the Peruvian government reinstituted the tribute for the Indians of the sierra under the name *contribución de indígenas,* and for good measure reintroduced the *contribución de castas* for the mestizo population of the coast.

The heavy dependence of the new government on Indian tribute as a source of revenue reflected the stagnant condition of the Peruvian economy. The revolution completed the ruin of the mining industry and coastal plantation agriculture, both declining since the close of the eighteenth century, and the scanty volume of exports could not pay for the much larger volume of imports of manufactured goods from Britain. As a result, the new state, already burdened with large wartime debts to English capitalists, developed a massive deficit in trade with Great Britain, its largest trading partner. There was some growth of export of wool from the sierra after 1836, and in 1840 a new economic era opened on the coast with the beginnings of exploitation of guano (bird droppings used as fertilizer), but in its first stage the guano cycle failed to provide the capital accumulation needed to revive the coastal agriculture.

The Military Caudillos

The backward, stagnant state of the Peruvian economy, the profound cleavage between the sierra and the coast, and the absence of a governing class (such as arose in Chile) capable of giving firm and intelligent leadership to the state produced chronic political turbulence and civil wars. Under these conditions, military caudillos, sometimes men of plebeian origin who had risen from the ranks during the wars of independence, came to play a decisive role in the political life of the new state. Some were more than selfish careerists or instruments of aristocratic Creole cliques. For example, the mestizo general Andrés Santa Cruz had a vision of Peru and Bolivia united into a powerful modern state; as president of the Peruvian-Bolivian Confederation from 1836 to 1839, he made a serious effort to reform its institutions.

The ablest and most enlightened of the military caudillos was the mestizo general Ramón Castilla, who served as president of Peru from 1845 to 1851 and again from 1855 to 1862. Castilla presided over an advance of the Peruvian economy based on the rapid growth of guano exports. This export trade was dominated by British capitalists who obtained the right to sell guano to specified regions of the world in return for loans to the Peruvian government (secured by guano shipments). Exorbitant interest and commission rates swelled their profits. Although Castilla gave some thought to direct government exploitation of some guano deposits, to setting controls over the amount and price of guano to be sold, and to plowing guano revenues into development projects, he did nothing to implement these ideas. However, the guano boom stimulated some growth of native Peruvian commerce and banking and created the nucleus of a national capitalist class. Many of the guano producers were also landlords on the coast and utilized profits from guano to restore their plantations, and some Peruvian firms also participated in the guano trade as exporters. Guano prosperity also financed the beginnings of a modern infrastructure; thus, in 1851 the first railway line began to operate between Lima and its port of Callao.

The rise of guano revenues enabled Castilla to carry out a series of social reforms that also contributed to the process of modernization. In 1854 he abolished the Indian tribute, relieving the natives of a heavy fiscal burden, and that same year he freed the remaining black slaves, numbering some twenty thousand, with compensation to the owners of up to 40 percent of their value. Abolition had an initial disruptive effect on coastal agriculture, but in the long run it was very advantageous to the planter aristocracy. With the indemnities for their freed slaves, planters could buy seeds, plants, and Chinese coolies brought to Peru on a contract basis that made them virtually slaves. Meanwhile, the freed slaves often became sharecroppers who lived on the margins of the hacienda and supplied a convenient unpaid labor force and a source of rent. Stimulated by these developments, cotton, sugar cane, and grain production expanded on the coast. Highland economic life also quickened, though on a smaller scale, with the rise of extensive cattle breeding for the export of wool and leather through Arequipa and Lima.

The upward movement of the Peruvian economy after 1850 was briefly interrupted in the 1860s by two crises, one foreign, the other domestic. In 1864, Spain, which had not totally abandoned its imperial ambitions, seized the Chincha Islands, Peru's richest guano area, in a dispute caused by alleged mistreatment of Spanish immigrants by the Peruvian govern-

ment. There followed a short war that ended with Spanish surrender of the islands and final recognition of Peru's independence. In 1865 a liberal revolt broke out, reflecting the discontent of the new commercial and planter aristocracy with the rule of conservative military caudillos. This revolt merged with a great Indian uprising in the sierra, caused by ruthless exploitation of the Indians by local gobernadores, who compelled the natives to exchange their wool for poor-quality manufactured goods sold at vastly inflated prices. Both revolts ended in failure, and the conservative military was again in full control by 1868.

Freed from these crises, the Peruvian economy resumed its advance. Aided by such favorable factors as the temporary dislocation of the cotton industry of the American South and large inflows of foreign capital, exports of cotton and sugar increased sharply. The coastal latifundia continued to expand at the expense of sharecroppers and tenants, who were expelled from their lands, and of the remaining Indian communal lands. This process was accompanied by the modernization of coastal agriculture by the introduction of cotton gins, boilers, refinery equipment for sugar, and steam-driven tractors.

While profits from the agricultural sector enabled the commercial and landed aristocracy of Lima to live in luxury, the Peruvian state sank even deeper into debt. The guano deposits, Peru's collateral for its foreign borrowings, were being depleted at an ever-accelerating rate, and the bulk of the proceeds from these loans went to pay interest on old and new debts. In 1868, during the administration of the military caudillo José Balta, his minister of the treasury, Nicolás de Piérola, devised a plan for extricating Peru from its difficulties and providing funds for development. The project eliminated the numerous consignees to whom guano had been sold and awarded a monopoly of guano sales in Europe to the French firm of Dreyfus and Company. In return, the Dreyfus firm agreed to make Peru a loan that would tide it over immediate difficulties and in addition to service its foreign debt. The contract initiated a new flow of loans that helped to create a boundless euphoria, an invincible optimism, about the country's future.

An American adventurer and entrepreneur, Henry Meiggs, who had made a reputation as a railway builder in Chile, easily convinced Balta and Piérola that they should support the construction of a railway system to tap the mineral wealth of the sierra. As a result, much of the money obtained under the Dreyfus contract, and a large part of the proceeds of the dwindling guano reserves, were poured into railway projects that could not show a profit in the foreseeable future.

Pardo and the Civilianist Party

The good fortune of Dreyfus and Company displeased the native commercial and banking bourgeoisie that had arisen in Lima. A group of these men—including former guano consignees who had been eliminated by the Dreyfus contracts—headed by the millionaire businessman Manuel Pardo, challenged the legality of the contract before the Supreme Court, arguing that assignment of guano sales to a corporation of native consignees that they proposed to form would be more beneficial to Peru's economic development. The native bourgeoisie suffered defeat, but in 1871 they organized the *Civilista*, or Civilianist party (in reference to their opposition to military caudillos), which ran Manuel Pardo as its candidate for president. An amalgam of "an old aristocracy and a newly emerging capitalist class," the Civilianist party opposed clerical and military influence in politics and advocated a large directing role for the state in economic development. Pardo won handily over two rivals and took office in 1872 after defeating with popular support an effort by military rebels to prevent his inauguration.

Pardo presided over a continuing agricultural boom, with exports reaching a peak in 1876. Foreign capital poured into the country. In those years, an Irish immigrant, W. R. Grace, began to establish an industrial empire that included textile mills, a shipping line, vast sugar estates, and Peru's first large-scale sugar-refining plants. While private industry prospered, the government sank ever deeper into a quagmire of debts and deficits. The guano cycle was nearing its end, with revenues steadily declining as a result of falling prices, depletion of guano beds, and competition from an important new source of fertilizer, nitrates, being exploited by Anglo-Chilean capitalists in the southern Peruvian province of Tarapacá. In 1875, wishing to control the nitrate industry and make it a dependable source of government income, Pardo expropriated the foreign companies in Tarapacá and established a state monopoly over the production and sale of nitrates. This measure angered the Anglo-Chilean entrepreneurs whose holdings had been nationalized and who were indemnified with bonds of dubious value. Meanwhile, due to unsatisfactory market conditions in Europe, the nationalization measure failed to yield the anticipated economic benefits.

In 1876, Peru felt the full force of a worldwide economic storm. In a few months, all the banks of Lima had to close; by the following year, the government had to suspend payments on its foreign debt and issue unbacked paper money. The economic collapse was followed by a military disaster: the War of the Pacific. Despite heroic resistance, Peru suffered a crushing defeat at the hands of a Chilean state that enjoyed a more advanced economic organization, political stability, and the support of British capitalists. The war completed the work of economic ruin begun by the depression. The Chileans occupied and ravaged the economically advanced coastal area; they levied taxes on the hacendados and dismantled equipment from the haciendas and sent it to Chile; they also sent troops into the sierra to exact payment from hacendados, towns, and villages. Their extortions infuriated the Indian peasantry. Led by General Andrés Cáceres, those Indians began to wage an effective guerrilla war of attrition against the Chilean occupiers. The war was finally ended by the Treaty of Ancón (1883).

NEOCOLONIAL PERU: THE ENGLISH AND NORTH AMERICAN CONNECTIONS, 1883–1968

The war left a heritage of political and social turbulence as well as economic ruin. Military and civilian leaders disputed one another's claims to be the legitimate president and mobilized bands of guerrillas and outlaws (*montoneros*) for their armed struggles. In some areas, the Indian peasantry, having acquired arms during the war with Chile, rose in revolt against oppressive hacendados and local officials. Banditry was rife in parts of the sierra; on the coast, conflicts took place between bands armed by landowners or their agents for control of irrigation canals or over property boundaries.

From the struggle for power the militarists once again emerged victorious: In 1884 the guerrilla leader General Andrés Cáceres battled his way into Lima and seized the National Palace. Two years later, he was elected president for a four-year term. Under Cáceres, a slow, painful process of economic recovery began. His first concern was the huge foreign debt. In 1886 the Peruvian government negotiated the so-called Grace Contract with British bondholders. This agreement created a Peruvian Corporation, controlled by the British bondholders, that assumed the servicing of Peru's foreign debt and received in exchange Peru's railways for a period of sixty-six years. The agreement confirmed British financial domination of Peru but also initiated a new flow of investments that hastened the country's economic recovery. Particularly important was the resulting rehabilitation of the railways and their extension to important mining centers, especially into La Oroya, whose rich silver mines began

to be exploited and contributed to the economic revival.

Economic recovery strengthened the political hand of the planter aristocracy and the commercial bourgeoisie, who were increasingly impatient with the arbitrary ways of the military caudillos. Their leader was the flamboyant Nicolás de Piérola, founder of the Democractic party, which united various *Civilista* factions in an effort to bring the military under civilian control. In 1895, Piérola led a successful revolt against Cáceres when that guerrilla fighter sought to impose himself as president for a second time. The same year, Piérola, running unopposed, was elected president and presided over four years of rapid economic recovery. On the coast, the sugar plantations expanded at the expense of small landholders and Indian communities and underwent intensive modernization. In the Andes, the economic revival spurred a renewed drive by hacendados to acquire Indian communal lands, a drive extended to regions hitherto free from land-grabbing. A new law (1893) that in effect re-enacted Bolívar's decree concerning the division and distribution of communal lands facilitated the process of land acquisition. In this period there also arose a new contract labor system, the *enganche,* designed to solve the labor problem of coastal landlords now that Chinese contract labor was no longer easily available. By this system, Indians from the sierra were recruited for prolonged periods of labor on coastal haciendas, sometimes under conditions of virtual serfdom.

The Indian Problem

Yet the postwar period also saw the birth of a new sensitivity to the Indian problem and a movement in behalf of the Indians. The rise of this indigenismo was closely connected with the crisis of conscience caused by the disastrous War of the Pacific. By exposing the incompetence and irresponsibility of a Creole elite that had totally failed to prepare Peru materially and morally for its greatest ordeal, the war led many intellectuals to turn to the Indian peasantry as a possible source of national regeneration. At the University of San Marcos in Lima there arose a generation of teachers who rejected the traditional positivist tendency to brand Indians as inherently inferior. The apathy, inertia, and alcoholism of the Indians, these scholars claimed, resulted from the narrow, dwarfed world in which they were forced to live. However, as a rule these bourgeois reformers ignored the economic aspect of the Indian problem and focused on a program of education and uplift that would teach Indians Western work habits and other good customs and thus enable them to enter the new capitalist society.

The great iconoclast Manuel González Prada (1848–1918) rejected this gradual, reformist approach to the Indian problem. "To him who preaches the school," he wrote, "let the answer be *school* and *bread*. The Indian question is an economic and social question rather than one of pedagogy." Schools and well-intentioned laws could not change a feudal reality based on the economic and political power of the great landowners, or *gamonales*, lords of all they surveyed:

If on the coast there appears some glimmer of legal guarantees under a semblance of republican government, in the sierra the violation of all rights under a true feudal regime appears in all its nakedness. There neither law codes nor law courts prevail, because the landowners and gamonales decide everything, arrogating to themselves the roles of judges and executors of their verdicts.

Elimination of the hacienda system, therefore, was a prerequisite for the solution of the Indian problem. But that change would never come through the benevolence of the ruling class: "The Indian must achieve his redemption through his own efforts, not through the humanity of his oppressors." And González Prada advised Indians to spend on rifles and cartridges the money they now wasted on drink and fies-tas. "Do not preach humility and resignation to the Indian; rather teach him pride and rebellion."

Splendid on the attack, sound in his general diagnosis of the Indian problem, González Prada proved incapable of working out a well-defined political and economic program for its solution. But his powerful indictment of the oppressors of the Indians, his faith in the creative capacity of the Indian masses, and his rebellious spirit, expressed in prose that flowed like molten lava, profoundly influenced the next generation of intellectuals, who revered the master but went beyond his unsystematic radicalism in their search for solutions to Peru's problems.

The Return of Pardo

The Indian question was Peru's gravest social problem, but the rapid economic advance that began under Piérola produced the emergence of a working class whose demands also threatened the peace and security of the ruling class. By 1904 an organized labor movement had arisen, and strikes broke out in Lima's textile mills and other factories. Guillermo Billinghurst, a self-made millionaire and leader of the Democratic party who won election as president in 1912, was convinced that the stubborn refusal of employers to make reasonable concessions to the workers threatened the very existence of capitalism. Accordingly, as president he decreed the eight-hour day for some worker groups, legalized strikes, and pushed through Congress a law requiring collective bargaining between workers and management in individual plants. But Billinghurst's reform proposals and his tactic of mobilizing the workers in support of his program antagonized conservative interests, and in 1914 he was overthrown by an army coup. The next year, elections organized by a military junta again gave the presidency to the former president, Manuel Pardo.

Pardo's second term spanned the years of World War I. Although Peru remained neutral, the conflict had a large impact on the country's economy. After an initial brief recession, a boom developed as the belligerents sharply increased their demand for Peruvian oil, copper, cotton, rubber, and guano. Since the importation of consumer goods virtually came to a halt, there was a mushrooming growth of light industry. The profits of planters, mine owners, and merchants swelled, but a catastrophic inflation imposed great hardships on workers; food prices, in particular, soared as landowners abandoned food production in favor of such export commodities as cotton and sugar.

In 1918 miners, port workers, and textile workers went out on strike. Armed clashes took place between the strikers and the troops sent out to disperse them, and many strikers were arrested. News of the success of the Russian Revolution contributed to the workers' militancy. The strike movement culminated in a three-day general strike in January 1919; the workers demanded the implementation of currently unenforced social legislation, the reduction of food prices, and the imposition of the eight-hour day. Under pressure from the workers, Pardo granted part of their demands, including the eight-hour day for the manufacturing and extractive industries. The labor struggles of that stormy year merged with the struggle of university students, especially at the University of San Marcos, for the reform of an archaic system of higher education that made the university the preserve of a privileged few and denied students any voice in determining policies and faculty appointments.

As his turbulent term drew to a close, Pardo designated a conservative landowner, Antero Aspillaga, as his political heir. But sections of the oligarchy were convinced that the new and unstable political and social atmosphere required a new way of ruling. An astute businessman and politician, Augusto B. Leguía, who had served as minister of finance in the early 1900s and as president from 1908 to 1912, offered a new political model that could be called Cae-

sarist: It combined unswerving fidelity to the dominant domestic and foreign interests with severe repression of dissidents and a demogogic program of nationalism and social reform designed to disarm the workers and achieve class peace. Charging that Aspillaga was a reactionary who did not understand the needs of the masses, Leguía presented himself as a candidate for president and easily defeated Aspillaga in the election of May 1919. Instead of waiting to be formally installed in office, he seized power in July, sent his predecessor Pardo into exile, and established a personal dictatorship that lasted eleven years (1919–1930).

The Leguía Regime: American Investment and Peruvian Disillusionment

Leguía encouraged by every means at his disposal the influx of foreign—especially American—capital: This was the cornerstone of his economic policies. Oil and copper were major fields of American investment in Peru in this period. By 1930, American investment amounted to $220 million, by comparison with a British total of $150 million. The fruits of Leguía's policy of opening the doors wide to foreign capital soon became evident; in 1927 a vice president of the First National City Bank wrote that "Peru's principal sources of wealth, the mines and oil-wells, are nearly all foreign-owned, and excepting for wages and taxes, no part of the value of their production remains in the country. . . . As a whole, I have no great faith in any material betterment of Peru's economic condition in the near future." Perhaps the most scandalous example of Leguía's policy of giving away Peru's natural resources was his cession of the oil-rich La Brea–Pariñas fields near the northern coastal town of Talara to the International Petroleum Company, or IPC (a subsidiary of Standard Oil of New Jersey) in return for a minimal tax of about 71 cents a ton. This cession and a 1922 arbitral award confirming the dubious claims to the area in question of an English oil company, whose rights had passed to the IPC, became an abiding source of Peruvian nationalist resentment.

Peru under Leguía received a plentiful infusion of American bond loans, amounting to about $130 million. The bankers were aware of the risks involved, but the prospects of extremely large profits (Peru received only 85 to 90 percent of the face value of the loans) made these transactions extremely attractive. A trail of corruption, involving Leguía's own family, followed these deals; Leguía's son Juan, acting as agent for Peru, received more than half a million dollars in commissions.

Leguía used the proceeds of these loans and the taxes on foreign trade and foreign investment operations for a massive public works program (including a large road-building program carried out with forced Indian labor) that contributed to the boom of the 1920s. During those years, Lima was largely rebuilt, provided with modern drinking water and sanitation facilities, and embellished with new parks, avenues, bank buildings, a racetrack, and a military casino. But these amenities did not improve the living conditions of Andean Indians or dwellers in the wretched shantytowns (*barriadas*) that began to ring Lima.

However, convinced that the threat of communism required some concessions to the masses, Leguía did make some gestures in the direction of reform. The constitution of 1920, framed at his bidding by a congress summoned for that purpose, had some striking resemblances to the Mexican constitution of 1917. It declared the right of the state to limit property rights in the interest of the nation, vested ownership of natural resources in the state, and committed the state to the construction of hospitals, asylums, and clinics. It empowered the government to set the hours of labor and to insure adequate compensation and safe and sanitary conditions of work. It also offered corporate recognition of the Indian communities, proclaimed the right of the Indians to land, and promised primary education to their children. But these and other provisions of the constitution were, in the words of Fredrick Pike, a "model for the Peru that never was."

What actually happened in the sierra illustrates the gap between Leguía's promises and his performance. After seizing power, Leguía set up a Bureau of Indian Affairs in the Ministry of Development to demonstrate his interest in the Indian problem. He also appointed a commission of specialists in Indian affairs to study the causes of their growing unrest. However, when this commission submitted to Congress a legislative code designed to provide protection and education to the Indians, alarmed landowners protested to Leguía, who promptly dissolved the commission. Their hopes of relief frustrated, the Indians of the sierra rose in revolt. Leguía sent troops to inflict a bloody repression on the rebels, and by 1923 order had been restored in the area.

The same contrast between promises and performance marked Leguía's labor policy. During his campaign for the presidency, he denounced "reactionaries" and made lavish promises to the workers. Indeed, on seizing power in July 1919 he immediately freed the labor leaders imprisoned under Pardo. He also permitted a congress of workers to meet in Lima in 1921 and form a Federation of Workers of Lima and Callao. However, when the labor movement began to display excessive independence, he intervened to crush it. A second workers' congress, organized in 1927, was abruptly ended by repression, its leaders arrested, and the federation itself dissolved. Workers were forced to accept token reforms and a program of government- and church-sponsored paternalism, crumbs from the well-laden table of the wealthy.

Leguía's performance was especially disillusioning to the university students. Impressed by his promises of educational reform, they had proclaimed Leguía "Mentor of the Youth" and supported his presidential campaign in 1919.

Once in power, however, he sought to drive a wedge between students and workers, jailing such student leaders and prominent future politicians as Raúl Haya de la Torre, Luis Alberto Sánchez, and Manuel Seoane, and outlawing the Popular University of González Prada, organized by the students to provide the workers with political education. Frequent jailings and deportations of dissident journalists and professors brought Leguía into chronic confrontation with the students and faculty, who often went on strike, while the University of San Marcos was repeatedly closed down by the government.

Indianism and Socialism

The surrender to the dictator of what remained of the traditional oligarchical parties, the Democrats and the Civilistas, and the weakness and immaturity of the young Peruvian working class meant that the leadership of the movement of opposition to Leguía fell to middle- and lower-middle-class intellectuals who sought to mobilize the peasantry and the workers for the achievement of their revolutionary aims. Socialism, anti-imperialism, and Indianism provided the ideological content of the movement that issued from the struggles of the turbulent year of 1919, but Indianism was the most important ingredient.

From the writings of the revered González Prada, these intellectuals had obtained a somewhat idealized conception of Indians and had learned that the revolution that would regenerate Peru must come from the sierra, from the Andean Indians, who would destroy age-old systems of oppression and unify Peru again, restoring the grandeur that had been the Inca Empire. Common to most of the indigenistas was the belief that the Inca Empire had been a model of primitive socialist organization (a thesis rejected by modern scholars) and that the Indian community had been and still was the "indestructible backbone of Peruvian collectivity" (in fact, by the 1920s almost all land in Peru was individually owned and worked). The mission of the intellectuals, they believed, was to blow life into the coals of Indian rebellion and link the Indian revolution to the urban revolution of students and workers.

An influential indigenista of this period was Luis E. Valcarcel, author of the widely read *Tempest in the Andes* (1927). In ecstatic prose, Valcarcel hailed the Indian revolts of the sierra as portents of the coming purifying revolution. "Culture will again come down from the Andes. . . . The Race . . . will appear splendidly, crowned with the eternal values, with firm step toward a future of certain glories. . . . It is the avatar which marks the reappearance of the Andean peoples on the scene of civilization." For Valcarcel, the Indians only awaited their Lenin.

A more important and systematic thinker, José Carlos Mariátegui (1895–1930), attempted the task of wedding Indianism to the scientific socialism of Marx and Engels. His major work was the *Seven Interpretive Essays on Peruvian Reality* (1928). In a style "as precise as an engineer's, aseptic as a physician's," in the words of José Basadre, Mariátegui "introduced to Peru a serious and methodical approach to national affairs that disdained pedantry, excessive details, and rhetoric." The *Seven Essays* apply the Marxist method to the Indian and land problems, public education, the religious factor, regionalism, and literature. Basing his theory on Indian communal practices and traditions, on the revolutionary experience of other lands, and on his study of history and economics, Mariátegui concluded that socialism offered the only true solution for the Indian problem: "Socialism preaches solidarity with redemption of the working classes. Four-fifths of Peru's working classes consist of Andean Indians. Therefore, socialism means the redemption of those Indians."

Like other Indianists of his time, Mariátegui idealized the Inca Empire, which he regarded as the "most advanced primitive communist organization which history records." But he

Religious festival in the Andean village of
Urubamba in Peru. (Paul Conklin)

opposed a "romantic and anti-historical tendency of reconstruction or re-creation of Inca socialism," for only its habits of cooperation and corporate life should be retained by modern scientific socialism. Moreover, he stressed that the coming revolution must be led by the urban proletariat. Before his untimely death, Mariátegui founded in 1929 the Peruvian Communist party, which affiliated the next year with the Communist International. Despite recent efforts to save Mariátegui from himself by stressing his tactical differences with the Communist International, it is clear that he was in basic agreement with its policies, admired the Soviet achievements, and did not change his positions before his death.

Indianism was a major plank in the program of the *Alianza Popular Revolucionaria Americana,* or APRA, as it is more commonly known, a party founded in Mexico in May 1924 by Víctor Raúl Haya de la Torre, a student leader who had been exiled by Leguía. Haya de la Torre proclaimed that it was the mission of APRA to lead the Indian and proletarian masses of Peru and all "Indo-America" in the coming socialist, anti-imperialist revolution. Despite the high-sounding rhetoric of *Aprista* propaganda, the party's first concern was and remained Peru's middle sectors—artisans, small landowners, professionals, and small capitalists. These groups' opportunities for development diminished as a result of the growing concentration of economic power in Peru by foreign firms and a dependent big bourgeoisie.

In a revealing statement in the mid-1920s, Haya de la Torre declared that the Peruvian working class, whether rural or urban, lacked the class consciousness and maturity needed to qualify it for the leadership of the coming revolution. He assigned that role to the middle class: "It is this middle group that is being pushed toward ruination by the process of imperialism. . . . The great foreign firms extract our wealth and then sell it outside of our country. Consequently there is no opportunity for our middle class. This, then, is the abused class that will lead the revolution." To this opinion Haya de la Torre joined a belief in the mission of the great man (himself) who "interprets, intuits, and directs the vague and imprecise aspirations of the multitude."

Haya de la Torre early assumed an ambiguous position on imperialism. Standing on its head Lenin's theory that imperialism was the last stage of capitalism, he argued that in weak, underdeveloped countries like Peru, imperialism was not the last but the first stage of capitalism, for there it provided the capital needed to create industry, a powerful working class, and the middle class that would lead the nation in a socialist revolution. From this to the position that imperialism must be encouraged and defended was an easy step, one that Haya de la Torre eventually took. Mariátegui, who was associated with Haya de la Torre in the student and labor struggles of the early 1920s, soon perceived the inconsistencies and ambiguities of his position and assailed APRA for its "bluff and lies" and its personalism. Despite or precisely because of its opportunism and the vagueness of its ideology, APRA managed to win over an important section of the Peruvian middle class, especially the students, during the three decades after 1920 and to gain great influence over groups of peasantry and urban workers, whom it organized into unions that were its main political base.

APRA versus the Military

The onset of a world economic crisis in 1929, which caused a serious decline of Peruvian exports and dried up the influx of loans, brought the collapse of the Leguía dictatorship. However, neither the small Communist party nor the stronger APRA movement was able to take political advantage of Leguía's downfall. An army officer of *cholo* (Indian) background, Luis Sánchez Cerro, seized power and became the dominant figure in a ruling military junta. In 1931, Sánchez Cerro ran for president on a populist platform that proclaimed the primacy of the Indian problem, the need for agrarian reform through expropriation of uncultivated lands, and the aim of regulating foreign investments in the national interest. In effect, Sánchez Cerro had stolen much of APRA's thunder, to the annoyance of Haya de la Torre, who had returned from exile to run for president; his campaign featured demagogic attacks on capitalism, the church, and the aristocracy but was vague with regard to specifics.

Sánchez Cerro was pronounced the winner, but the Apristas refused to accept the election results and prepared a revolt; in July 1932 they launched the revolt, seizing the garrison and town of Trujillo. Before the arrival of government reinforcements forced them to flee, the Aprista leaders ordered the execution of some sixty officers and soldiers who had been held as hostages. On breaking into the city, the government forces took summary vengeance, sending perhaps a thousand residents of Trujillo before firing squads. On April 30, 1933, in apparent retaliation, an Aprista assassin shot down Sánchez Cerro. This chain of events created a vendetta between the army and APRA that helps to explain the stubborn opposition of the Peruvian armed forces to APRA's assumption of power, whether by force or peaceful means.

Congress chose Oscar Benavides, a representative of the financial and landed oligarchy, to fill Sánchez Cerro's unexpired term; in 1936, when an Aprista-backed candidate for president appeared to have won the election, the government canceled the election and announced that Benavides would rule for a full six years from the time he had taken power. Under Benavides, the economy gradually emerged from the depths of the depression; his term of office was also marked by some attempts to provide housing projects and other social services to the workers and by an intensive effort to suppress APRA, which continued to operate underground and organized several abortive coups.

In 1939, Benavides was succeeded by his political heir, the banker Manuel Prado, who had run virtually unopposed; at the same time, the voters approved a constitutional amendment extending the presidential term to six years. Prado presided over a boom based on growing wartime demand and high prices for Peru's exports. Prosperity and Peru's alignment on the side of the democracies in World War II (Peru broke off relations with the Axis countries in 1942 and declared war on them in 1945) helped to achieve a thaw in the repressive climate created by Benavides; in particular, Prado made overtures to APRA, which began to change its policies. Without abandoning their drive for exclusive power, the movement's leaders apparently had determined that they could better achieve this end through negotiation and integration with the militarist-oligarchical establishment than through revolution. Certain shifts in Aprista ideology reflected this change of strategy. The notion that imperialism was the first rather than the last stage of Peruvian capitalism now assumed a new prominence in Aprista theory, and capitalism itself came in for praise, while the perspective of a socialist revolution receded into an increasingly dim and distant future.

Prado left office in 1945, immensely popular as a result of a victorious short war with Ecuador, followed by the signing of a treaty in 1945 that confirmed Peruvian claims to most of a disputed area of some 120,000 square miles. Prado's successor, the law professor José Luis Bustamante y Rivero, was elected as the candidate of a broadly based National Democratic Front that took in the outlawed Communist party and even APRA, renamed the Party of the People. Bustamante accelerated the process of liberalization that had begun under Prado. He expanded civil rights, legalized the Communist party, and attempted to institute some social reforms.

But he confronted immense political and economic problems. The Apristas, commanding a majority in Congress, accepted posts in Bustamante's cabinet but soon made clear that their first loyalty was to Haya de la Torre and that they expected Bustamante to function as a figurehead. Bustamante wished to cooperate with the newly legalized APRA movement but refused to become its puppet. When he resisted their demands, the Apristas increasingly resorted to violence, and when the press criticized their acts of terrorism, the APRA majority in Congress introduced a law calling for press censorship. Meanwhile, although Haya de la Torre and his party had championed land reform for decades, they failed to initiate any significant agrarian reform legislation or any other fundamental economic reform.

To add to Bustamante's woes, the country fell into a postwar slump characterized by sharp declines in the prices and exports of copper, cotton, lead, and wool, while a serious food shortage sent food prices soaring. Searching for new sources of revenue, Bustamante signed a contract with the International Petroleum Company that turned over to the company oil lands that had been set aside as a national reserve. The contract had the support of the Apristas, who had become warm friends of the United States and even supported a measure for compensation of American investors for the worthless bonds they had bought in the 1920s. At this time, the State Department decided that APRA was its favorite Peruvian party. The oil contract encountered strong opposition from nationalist businessmen and officers, however, and was defeated in the Senate.

Odría: A Shift to the Right

By 1948, in a stormy atmosphere of Aprista rioting, abortive revolts, and economic crisis, the oligarchy and the military decided that they had had enough of Bustamante. In October a "restorative revolution" overthrew him and proclaimed General Manuel A. Odría its leader. Two years later, having suppressed all opposition from APRA, the left, and Bustamante's followers, Odría organized his own unopposed election to the presidency. Thus, he stayed in power for eight years (1948–1956).

The "restorative revolution" produced a sharp shift to the right. The movement of rural unionization, which had assumed great strength under Bustamante, was forcibly halted; unions under APRA or leftist control were liquidated or taken over by Odría's supporters, strikes were broken with the use of troops, and a Law of Internal Security empowered the government to use whatever means were judged necessary to maintain public order. Meanwhile, foreign investors were treated with a generosity that recalled the days of Leguía. Their taxes were lowered, and exchange controls were removed. In mining, the total tax burden was lowered from 35 percent of gross profits to about 20 percent in the early 1950s. *Fortune*, a journal reflecting the viewpoint of American businessmen, congratulated Peru on its "scrupulous respect for private property and the principle of free markets and convertibility."

Gradually, thanks in part to the stimulus of the Korean war, Peru emerged from its recession and even experienced a boom. Again imitating Leguía, Odría used part of the increased government revenues for a vast public works program and for a paternalistic program of social assistance to urban workers that recalled the similar program of Juan Domingo Perón in Argentina. With the ending of the Korean war, however, exports and revenues once more declined, and Odría found it increasingly difficult to continue his ambitious public works program. In 1954–1955, with unemployment and inflation both rising, strikes and unrest grew, and Odría even came under hostile criticism from oligarchical elements who were displeased with his arbitrary methods of rule. Under strong pressure for a return to democratic processes, Odría consented to repeal of the Law of Internal Security and promised free elections in 1956.

The two main contenders for the presidency in that year were former president Manuel Prado, who was supported by a coalition of conservatives and APRA, which he promised to legalize, and Fernando Belaúnde Terry, candidate of the National Front of Democratic Youth, a middle-class group that included many disillusioned Apristas and had taken over much of the APRA's program, especially its promise of agrarian reform and incorporation of Indians into national life. The victorious Prado proceeded to restore civil rights and trade unions and allowed the technically illegal Communist party as well as APRA to operate quite freely. In the economic sphere, however, Prado and his conservative finance minister, Pedro Beltrán, continued the policies of Odría: laissez faire; reduction of taxes on business, foreign and domestic; and promotion of foreign investments. The net result was that by the end of Prado's second term, the inequities of Peru's income distribution had markedly increased. In regard to the agrarian problem, Prado and Beltrán limited themselves to setting up commissions to study means of fostering small and medium-sized private property in the countryside, which meant that nothing was done.

As a result, the agrarian problem in the sierra had reached an acute stage by 1960, with unrest spreading like wildfire. Collisions between the hacendados and increasingly militant and well-organized peasants became ever more frequent. In some cases, peasants were revolting against precapitalist labor systems (like the yanacona system, which often required free personal service); in others, violence arose as a result of the efforts of landowners to evict their tenants and sheep in favor of wage labor and cash rent systems. These evictions increased landlessness and population pressure in the Indian communities and accelerated the flow of emigrants to the coast, swelling the population of city slums and shantytowns.

The election of 1962, then, took place against a background of growing social unrest in both the cities and the countryside. The three major candidates were Haya de la Torre, supported by the Prado administration as the "sort of conservative we need in Peru"; Belaúnde, supported by a middle-class party called *Acción Popular* (Popular Action); and Odría, candidate of another new party called the *Odrista* National Union, hastily created for the occasion.

None of the three candidates obtained the required one-third of the votes cast, which meant that Congress had to choose among them. Amid loud charges of Aprista electoral fraud, Haya de la Torre negotiated a deal with Odría, the former persecutor of Apristas, that, in the words of Fredrick Pike, "shocked and disgusted even the most sophisticated and cynical of the Peruvian electorate." Knowing that the military would most likely bar his own assumption of the presidency, Haya de la Torre formed an alliance with Odría that provided for his election as president and the seating of a large bloc of Aprista senators and deputies; Odría was to serve as a figurehead, with real power vested in the Aprista congressional group in alliance with other groups.

But the armed forces spoiled Haya de la Torre's game. Proclaiming that the elections were tainted with fraud, they intervened to nullify them, assuring that truly honest and free elections would be held in one year. During that year, the military government headed by Genral Ricardo Pérez Godoy initiated a number of reform measures that suggested some change in the military mentality. They included an institute for economic planning, a housing agency for slum-clearance projects, and some pilot land reform projects.

Belaúnde: Broken Promises

In June 1963, elections organized by the military gave the presidency to the Popular Action candidate, Fernando Belaúnde, whose campaign had a decided indigenista tinge. Visiting the remotest Andean villages, Belaúnde extolled the Inca grandeur, called on the natives to emulate the energy and hard work of their ancestors, and proclaimed the right of the landless peasantry to land. But his performance in the field of agrarian reform did not match his promises. The agrarian law that issued from Congress the following year stressed technical improvement rather than expropriation and division of latifundia, with the hope that hacendados would adopt modern methods to improve production. As amended in Congress by a coalition of Apristas and rightist followers of Odría, the law exempted from expropriation the highly productive coastal estates, whose workers had been unionized by APRA, reserving for land distribution the archaic haciendas of the sierra. But the loopholes or exceptions were so numerous (the law authorized exemption of all farms of 5,000 hectares or less) that the results of the law were very modest.

Meanwhile, Belaúnde's election after an indigenista campaign of lavish promises to the peasantry had given great impetus to peasant land invasions. By October 1963, invasions had multiplied in the central highlands and were spreading to the whole southern part of the sierra. The land-invasion movement also changed its character; whereas before the peasants had seized only uncultivated lands, they now occupied cultivated lands, whether sown or fallow, arguing that they had paid for it with their unpaid or poorly paid labor of several generations. Militant peasant unions under radical leadership appeared, and a guerrilla movement arose in parts of the sierra. Meanwhile, a wave of strikes broke out in the cities, and workers occupied a number of enterprises in Lima and Callao.

These outbreaks took the Belaúnde administration by surprise. The extreme right, supported by APRA, demanded the use of the armed forces to repress the peasant movement. Indeed, APRA—once so "revolutionary"—called for the harshest treatment of the rebellious peasants. At the end of 1963, after some vacillation, the Belaúnde government decided to crush the peasant movement by force—a task that the armed forces apparently assumed with reluctance, preferring "civic action" programs of a reformist type. By 1966 the peasant and guerrilla movements had been suppressed. According to one estimate, the repression left 8,000 peasants dead and 3,500 prisoner, 14,000 hectares of land burned with fire and napalm, and 19,000 peasants forced to abandon their homes. Among the military, the conviction grew that only radical, structural reforms could definitively end the rural climate of revolutionary violence.

Belaúnde had failed to solve the agrarian problem. He also failed to keep his promise to settle in ninety days after his inauguration the old controversy between Peru and the International Petroleum Company over the La Brea–Pariñas oil fields, claimed by Peru to have been illegally exploited for some forty years. Finally, under strong pressure from United States interests, who delayed large, planned investments in Peru, Belaúnde's government signed a pact that represented a massive surrender to the IPC. Peru regained the now almost exhausted La Brea–Pariñas oil fields, but in return agreed to the cancellation of claims for back taxes and illegal profits amounting to almost $700 million. IPC also received a concession to exploit a vast area in the Amazon region and was allowed to retain the refinery of Talara, to which the government agreed to sell all the oil produced from the wells it had regained at a fixed price. A scandal rocked the country when the government, forced to publish the document, claimed to have "lost" the page setting the price that the IPC must pay the state oil company for its crude oil. As public indignation grew, the armed forces issued a statement denouncing the agreement. Opposition parties demanded annulment of the pact, and even the Catholic church joined the chorus of disapproval. As a result, Belaúnde's Popular Action party and its APRA allies were completely isolated.

For Peru's military leaders, the pact, known as the Pact of Talara, was the last straw. For some years, those leaders had engaged in intense soul-searching over the past and future of their country; now they were convinced that Belaúnde's government and the social forces that supported it were incapable of solving the great national problems. On October 3, 1968, the armed forces seized the presidential palace, sent Belaúnde into exile, and established a military governing junta that began a swift transformation of Peru's economic and social structures.

THE PERUVIAN REVOLUTION, 1968 TO THE PRESENT

The Military About-Face

The first impression of the news of the military seizure of power in October 1968 was that it was but one more in a long series of military coups that punctuate the history of Peru and other Latin American countries—coups that change the occupant of the presidential palace but leave the existing order intact. Typical of this initial reaction was the Communist party statement that the coup had been hatched in Washington to protect vested United States interests. The error of this opinion became evident as the self-proclaimed "Revolutionary Government of the Armed Forces," under the leadership of General and President Juan Velasco Alvarado, decreed in rapid succession the nationalization of oil, a sweeping agrarian reform law, and a law providing for workers' participation in the ownership and management of industrial concerns.

Observers found these events as startling, in the words of Fidel Castro, "as if a fire had started in the firehouse," for the Latin American military had traditionally been regarded as loyal servants of the area's oligarchies. In Peru, however, a social and ideological gulf had been developing between the military and civilian elites for decades. The typical army officer came from a military family or from the lower middle class (as was the case with General Velasco);

very few officers had links with latifundistas or big business.

Faced with growing evidence of the incapacity of the bourgeois APRA and Popular Action parties to solve the great national problems during the 1950s and 1960s, the leadership of the armed forces undertook intensive study of those questions. At the Center for Advanced Military Studies, founded in 1952, emphasis was placed on economics, sociology, and research techniques. Officers studied topics ranging from the agrarian problem in a sierra valley to the development of the Amazonian jungle area. The dominant ideology at the center reflected the developmentalist theories of the United Nations Economic Commission for Latin America; it stressed the need for planning, industrialization, land reform, and an expanded directing role for the state. Disillusionment with civilian politicians and the electoral system appears in one center document, which asserts that the "sad and desperate truth is that in Peru the real powers are not the Executive, the Legislative, the Judicial, or the Electoral, but the latifundistas, the exporters, the bankers, and the American investors." The Pact of Talara, regarded by the military as a sellout of Peruvian national interests, appeared to give decisive proof of the incompetence or corruption of the civilian politicians and triggered the coup of October 3, 1968. Within a week, the Velasco junta had nationalized the IPC's oil fields and its refinery at Talara, and soon after it seized all its other assets. Having settled the IPC question, the junta went on to tackle the country's most burning economic and social questions.

Land Reform and Nationalization of Resources

Land reform was the key problem: Peru could not achieve economic independence, modernization, and greater social democracy without liquidating the inefficient, semifeudal latifundio system, the *gamonal* political system that was its corollary, and the coastal enclaves of foreign oligarchical power. Major specific objectives were to expand agricultural production, both for export and for domestic consumption, and to generate capital for investment in the industrial sector; thus landowners were to be compensated for expropriated lands with bonds that could be used as investment capital in industry or mining. On June 24, 1969, President Velasco announced an agrarian reform designed to end the "unjust social and economic structures" of the past. The program deviated from orthodox Latin American reform policies in two respects: First, it did not retain the homestead or family-sized farm as its ideal; second, it did not exempt large estates from expropriation on account of their efficiency and productivity. Indeed, the first lands to be expropriated were the big coastal sugar plantations, largely foreign-owned and constituting highly mechanized agro-industrial complexes. These enterprises were transferred to cooperatives of farm laborers and refinery workers.

Next came the turn of the haciendas of the sierra. The reform applied to most highland estates above 35 to 55 hectares, but delays in implementing the law allowed many landowners to evade it by parcelling their holdings among family members and others. The initial aim was to encourage division of estates into small or medium-sized commercial farms, but this would have reduced the number of potential beneficiaries. Under pressure from militant, unionized peasants, who were demanding employment and the formation of cooperatives, the junta moved from parcellation toward cooperative forms of organization. Eventually fully 76 percent of the expropriated lands were organized into cooperatives, the remainder was distributed in individual plots. As noted above, expropriated estates were compensated with bonds that could be used as collateral for industrial development; the recipients of land were required to pay the purchase price over twenty years.

Observers agree that the agrarian reform produced some undeniable immediate and long-range benefits. To begin with, it ended the various forms of serfdom that still survived in the sierra in 1968. Second, food production increased, though not substantially or to the level required by Peru's growing population. Third, according to a recent field study of the agrarian reform, it "proved a major economic and political benefit to a significant sector of the peasantry," at least in the case of cooperatives with an adequate capital endowment. "In such cooperatives, members' wages and quality of life improved, often dramatically."[1]

But these gains were offset by the failure of the agrarian reform to raise the general material and political level of the Peruvian peasantry—a failure stemming from incorrect planning and methods on the part of the well-meaning military reformers.

First, the reform was neither as swift nor as thorough as the dimensions of the problem required. As noted above, delays in implementing the program and the ruses employed by landowners meant that a considerable amount of land escaped expropriation. By June 1976, when the agrarian reform was officially declared to have ended, only some 7 million hectares out of a total of about 19 million hectares subject to expropriation had been divided among some 270,000 families, a small fraction of an agricultural work force estimated to number over 1.5 million in 1972. As a result, the reform made only a slight impact on the problem of landlessness and rural unemployment and underemployment, especially in the sierra.

Second, the military reformers lacked a coherent strategy for the general development of the agricultural sector within an overall plan of balanced, inwardly directed national development. Basically, the agricultural sector was viewed as a means of pumping out food and

capital to promote development in the urban-industrial area. This was reflected in the military government's food-pricing policy, which was to keep food prices low in order to check inflation and keep the urban working class and middle class content. In the absence of compensating subsidies for small farmers, this policy "served to perpetuate the long-run unfavorable trend of the rural-urban terms of trade." Within the agricultural sector, the allocation of resources and credit was skewed in favor of the already well endowed and efficient coastal estates producing for export, with the bulk of agricultural investment going into large-scale irrigation projects. The needs of highland small farmers for small-scale irrigation works, fertilizer, and technical assistance were neglected. As a result, the coastal sugar, cotton, and coffee cooperatives tended to become "islands of relative privilege in a sea of peasant poverty and unemployment."

The same lack of a coherent strategy for the development of the agricultural sector as a whole was reflected in the method of distributing hacienda lands. The land was generally transferred to the workers who had been employed full time on the estates. They alone were eligible to be members of the new cooperatives. This left out the temporary laborers and the neighboring peasant villagers who eked out subsistence livings from tiny plots and small herds of sheep. This often led to serious tension and conflict, with the cooperatives defending their privileges and land against invasions by the peasant villagers (comuneros). Combined with the failure to distribute all the land subject to expropriation, this pattern of distribution contributed to the continuing flight of campesinos to the coastal cities where they swelled the ranks of a large unemployed or underemployed population.

Finally, a major flaw of the agrarian reform was that it was a "revolution from above," with little input from below. Despite lip service to participatory ideology and the creation of a National System of Support for Social Mobilization

---

[1] Cynthia McClintock, "Post-Revolutionary Agrarian Politics in Peru," in Stephen M. Gorman, Post-Revolutionary Peru: The Politics of Transformation (Boulder, Colo.: Westview Press, 1982), p. 135.

(SINAMOS), which was supposed to form links between the armed forces and the masses, the military technocrats made the final decisions with respect to work conditions, income policy, crop selection, and the like. Since the government's economic policy tended to subordinate peasant interests to the drive for rapid industrial growth, many peasants became disillusioned with the cooperative model. In some cases, particularly after 1975 when the nationalist reformist Velasco wing of the military was ousted from power by a conservative group stressing private enterprise and a free market, this disillusionment led to peasant demands for dismantling of the cooperatives and parcelling out of the land.

After land reform, the nationalization of key foreign-owned natural resources and enterprises and of domestic monopolies that the military regarded as obstacles to development was the most important objective of the junta's program. When the revolution began, foreign firms controlled the commanding heights of the Peruvian economy. Eight years later, state enterprises had taken over most of these firms. The process began with the nationalization of the IPC, whose assets passed into the control of *Petroperu*, the state-owned oil company. Later, the national telephone system, the railroads (the Peruvian Corporation), and Peru's international airline came under state ownership. The cement, chemical, and paper industries, defined as basic and reserved to the state, were taken over. The important fishmeal industry, in which large amounts of foreign capital were invested, was nationalized. The sugar industry, in large part controlled by the Grace interests, and the cotton industry, dominated by the American firm of Anderson, Clayton, were seized under the agrarian reform law. After the failure of efforts to prod the foreign-owned mining companies into making new investments and developing their unworked concessions, the government decided to enter the field for itself. Nationalization of the giant United States–owned mining complex of Cerro de Pasco in 1974 gave the state ownership of four thousand concessions and vested control of the bulk of mining and refining of copper, lead, and zinc in two state companies, *Minoperu* and *Centrominperu;* nationalization of Marcona Mining in 1975 gave the state control of iron ore and steel. In addition to the take-over of these primarily extractive and manufacturing firms, state companies obtained marketing monopolies of all major commodity exports and most food distribution. Through stock purchases, the government nationalized most of the banking and insurance industries. Thus the state came to control decisive sectors of the Peruvian economy.

The great nationalizations were accompanied by the development of new forms of economic organization—the industrial community and social property—that were conceived by President Velasco and his aides. They were to lay the foundations for a new society that would be "neither capitalist nor communist." The industrial community was a profit-sharing scheme designed to harmonize the interests of employers and workers and stimulate production. The law creating the new system required every industrial firm with six or more workers to allocate 15 percent of its gross earnings annually to the industrial community (comprising all employees, including management). These funds would be used to buy shares in the firm until the industrial community had acquired 50 percent of the stock. Another 10 percent of gross earnings was to be paid out to employees in cash. In addition, the industrial community was to be represented on the board of directors in proportion to the size of the shares it controlled. By 1975 there were 3,446 industrial communities with approximately 200,000 members, representing less than 4.3 percent of Peru's economically active population.

The social property program was viewed by President Velasco as the first step toward a unique Peruvian socialism. According to the law establishing this economic form, a social property firm consisted exclusively of workers, who participated fully in the direction, management, and economic benefits of the firm. However, the firm belonged not to the workers of a given enterprise but to the workers of the social property sector as a whole. Part of the income produced by the firm went into wages, new housing, and other benefits, but part was to be used for expansion and investment in other industries—in other words, for the benefit of society as a whole. This program had barely begun when it was virtually scrapped in the conservative "Second Phase" of the revolution that began in 1975.

The original intent of the military reformers was not to substitute the state for local private capital but to promote its formation by removing such impediments as the latifundio and foreign monopolistic firms and by the creation of an industrial infrastructure to be financed through the export of minerals and agricultural exports. But the radical rhetoric of the nationalistic military only frightened the local bourgeoisie, who in general were satisfied with their technological and financial dependence on foreign capital, and they failed to respond to the incentives for industrial investment (tariff protection and easing of credit restrictions) provided by the government. As a result the government itself had to assume the role of the economy's main investor. "From the original aim of a mixed economy with a strong private sector, the Peruvian economy moved rapidly towards state capitalism." By 1972 the state sector accounted for more than half the total investment in the economy.

But the cost of this investment, added to the large sums expended for compensation for expropriated estates and foreign enterprises, came very high. Tax reform offered one possibility of mobilizing considerable amounts of previously untouched wealth. Such a move, however, would have antagonized the local bourgeoisie, whom the military was wooing, and the middle class, which formed its principal mass base. Because of disputes over expropriation, Peru could not apply for loans to the United States and the multinational agencies it controlled. Accordingly Peru had to turn to foreign private banks. Encouraged by the high price of copper and other Peruvian exports and by the prospect of rich oil strikes in the Amazon Basin, the banks willingly complied with Peru's requests for loans. They lent $147 million in 1972 and $734 million in 1973, making Peru the largest borrower among Third World countries.

By early 1975, a new cyclical crisis had begun to ravage the capitalist world. Rising prices for oil and imported equipment and technology, combined with falling prices for Peru's raw material exports, undermined the fragile prosperity that had made President Velasco's reforms possible. These circumstances created unmanageable balance of trade and debt service problems. The model of development based on export expansion and foreign borrowing had again revealed its inherent contradictions.

Two British economists have offered a perceptive analysis of the reasons for the failure of the Peruvian Revolution to achieve genuine autonomous development. Their analysis stresses the lack of "any constant political or ideological stance"—a trait satirized by a Lima journal that reported a major policy speech by President Velasco under the headline: "Neither Left, Right, nor Center." Thorp and Bertram write:

By refusing to move to the left, the Military lost their opportunity to mobilize mass support among the traditional-sector labor force [the peasantry], and to use major redistributive policies to promote a more inward-directed development strategy. At the same time, by attacking business interests and the Right, the Military lost the confidence and support of local capitalists and alienated foreign interests. As pressures from both sides mounted, a choice of direction was forced on the government by its need for financial resources. A shift to the Left would have extended the state sector into the profitable consumer-goods sector which the Government had refrained from

touching, and might have improved the internal mo-
bilization of resources by taxation, but would have
brought severe problems in the internal sector. A
shift to the Right could bring in more foreign capital
and open the way to a 'solution' in terms of orthodox
economic management and the abandonment of social
goals.[2]

It was the latter course, we shall see, that
was chosen. The experience of the Peruvian
Revolution shows the difficulty of escaping from
dependent development without radical structural changes in class and property relationships
and income distribution. Like the Mexican Revolution, Peru's experience suggests that the revolution that does not advance risks stagnation
and loss of whatever gains have been made.

The Revolution Under Attack, 1975–1983

The economic crisis of 1975 provoked a sharp
struggle within the military between radical nationalists, grouped around the ailing President
Velasco, who proposed to extend the social and
economic reforms, and centrists and conservatives, who called for a halt to the reforms
and for measures that would win the confidence
of native and foreign capitalists, thereby making
possible a revival of private investments and
the foreign loans needed to refinance existing
debts. In August 1975, a peaceful coup replaced
President Velasco with his conservative prime
minister, Francisco Morales Bermúdez; this was
followed by a gradual purge of radical nationalists from the government and the forced resignation of leftist officers from the armed forces.
The so-called "First Phase" of the revolution
had ended. To appease foreign and domestic
capitalists, the new government introduced a
package of severe austerity measures that called
for sharp reductions in government investments

[2] Rosemary Thorp and Geoffrey Bertram, *Peru 1890–
1977: Growth and Policy in An Open Economy* (London:
Macmillan & Co., 1978), p. 319.

in state enterprises, steep increases in consumer
prices, and a 44 percent devaluation of the currency, only partly offset by wage increases of
from 10 to 14 percent. These measures provoked
widespread strikes and rioting, which were
crushed by the government with a full-scale
military operation.

By mid-1976, the process of liquidating the
revolutionary changes of the "First Phase" was
in full swing. In June the government announced
that the agrarian reform was at an end, although
only about one-third of the land subject to expropriation had been distributed. Implementation of the industrial community and social
property programs, created by President Velasco
and his planners in the heady springtime of
the revolution, was abandoned for all intents
and purposes. The industrial community program, seriously undermined by changes made
in 1977 by the Morales Bermúdez government
that deemphasized the law's collective aspect,
barely held its own after that date. Students of
the program agree that it had little redistributive
effect and did not significantly increase production or reduce labor strife. The social property
program, bitterly opposed by the private sector
and denied government support, languished
after 1975. In 1979 there were only fifty-seven
social property enterprises, employing 7,573
workers.

In early 1978, after long negotiations, the Morales Bermúdez government capitulated to the
IMF and accepted its conditions for a new loan:
They included reduction of the state economic
sector, heavy cuts in budgets and subsidies,
large price increases, and severe restraints on
wage increases. When the workers again protested with strikes and demonstrations, the
government sent troops to break strikes, crush
demonstrations, and jail strikers and political
dissidents. The armed forces, writes Stephen
F. Gorman, devoted their last three years of
rule "to brutalizing the popular classes in whose
name they assumed power in 1968."

For the thoroughly discredited military junta,

the prime concern was how to make a smooth transfer of power to a civilian regime that could be trusted to continue its conservative policies. In July 1977, President Morales Bermúdez announced that a constituent assembly would be elected in June 1978 to frame a new constitution to replace the 1933 constitution. This would be the first step toward a restoration of constitutional civilian rule. An electoral law published in November 1977 provided that all citizens who had reached the age of eighteen and could read and write should have the right to vote in the election of the constituent assembly, to be composed of one hundred members chosen by proportional representation from lists presented by different parties. Preparations for the election immediately got under way, with heavy campaigning by parties on the right and the left.

The election, held in June 1978, reflected widespread discontent with the economic policies of the military junta. APRA, the self-proclaimed party of the "democratic left" with an essentially conservative record, gained the largest number of seats, followed by the right-wing *Partido Popular Cristiano* (PPC); together, these two parties had a working majority in the assembly. The leftist parties, operating under difficult conditions because of government harassment and repression, with many of their leaders in jail or in exile, held the balance of the hundred seats in the assembly and formed a strong opposition. The Popular Action party of former President Belaúnde, whom the military had deposed and sent into exile in 1968, boycotted the election to the constituent assembly to symbolize its opposition to the military seizure of power.

The document that emerged from the constituent assembly differed little from the constitution of 1933. It established a bicameral Congress, consisting of a Senate and a Chamber of Deputies, both elected, like the president, for five years. Rejecting efforts by the left to incorporate in the section on the economy such

reforms of the First Phase as the social property enterprise, the APRA-PPC coalition secured the adoption of language ensuring that the foundations of the Peruvian economy would be the free market and the primacy of the private sector. The constitution guaranteed the right to strike and collective bargaining—but those rights were subject to the limitations of law, that is, to parliamentary regulation. The biggest novelty was the grant of the right to vote to illiterates.

Even before the assembly had completed its work, the political parties had begun to campaign for the elections scheduled for May 19, 1980. The biggest surprise of their outcome was the relatively poor showing of APRA, which won only 27 percent of the vote, an 8 percent decline from the 1978 level. The result was attributed to divisions in the party between a conservative and a populist wing, the leadership problem created by the illness of Haya de la Torre (he died August 2), and the hostility engendered by its use of violence against other parties during the campaign. But APRA's losses did not benefit the left, which was fragmented into many small groups and hopelessly divided over doctrinal and tactical issues; its vote fell from one-third of the total in 1978 to less than 21 percent in 1980. The big winner was *Acción Popular* (AP), or Popular Action party, whose presidential candidate, Fernando Belaúnde Terry, a master of populist rhetoric who was surrounded by an aura of martyrdom thanks to his ouster by the military in 1968, obtained over 45 percent of the vote. On July 28, 1980, Belaúnde for a second time was inaugurated president of Peru. On the same day the major daily newspapers of Lima, controlled by oligarchical interests and expropriated in 1974 because of their bitter opposition to the reform program, were formally returned to their original owners.

It soon became clear that Belaúnde and Manuel Ulloa, who served as his prime minister and finance minister, intended to continue and extend the "counter-reformation" begun by the Morales Bermúdez government of the "Second

Fernando Belaúnde Terry (saluting), president of
Peru since 1980, on a visit to Bolivia in the 1950s.
On Belaúnde's right is Galo Plaza, former
president of Ecuador. (Courtesy of the
Organization of American States)

Phase." Export expansion and debt repayment
were the great priorities, to be achieved with
the familiar arsenal of austerity measures and
devaluation, combined with wage freezes. The
resulting decline in living standards caused an
unprecedented popular protest; in January 1981,
for the first time in Peruvian history, all the
major labor groups joined in a general strike.
Despite these austerity measures, the economic
situation continued to deteriorate in 1981–1982
as the prices and demand for Peru's exports
fell while imports rose as a percentage of the
GNP. By the end of 1982 Peru's foreign debt
which stood at about $9 billion when Belaúnde
took office, had risen to $11 billion, and the
government vainly struggled to contain a grow-

ing balance of payments problem. Inflation at
this time was running at an annual rate of 70
percent, and the currency had lost about 80
percent of its value during the year. It was
clear, wrote a correspondent of *Le Monde Diplomatique* in January 1983, that the economy
was sick and that the remedies applied by prime
minister Ulloa, following the prescriptions of
the IMF, had failed to cure the patient.

Meanwhile the Belaunde government had
begun to dismantle the major reforms of the
Velasco era. A major objective was to restore
a free market in agricultural land, frozen by
Velasco, through the dissolution of the cooperative system. A new agricultural promotion
and development law gave the government the

power to divide cooperative land into small individual plots and turn them over to cooperative members. The plots could then be bought, sold, or mortgaged. The law was condemned by the major peasant federations, which feared that it would lead to the reconcentration of land in a few hands. At the same time, despite much rhetoric about the priority of agriculture, its share of the budget fell sharply from 1980 to 1981.

Other legislation, proposed but not yet become law at the end of 1982, would empower the government to sell off many state-owned companies and increase private participation in many publicly owned firms, including the state airline and the state copper mining enterprise, through stock issues and other programs. The government's legislative program also included a law banning general and sympathy strikes, and a 1983 budget that featured drastic reductions in public works and the phasing out of subsidies on basic foods and fuel. These proposals caused bitter wrangling in parliament between the government and the opposition parties; indeed, they provoked rifts within the ruling AP-PPC coalition. In late December 1982, reflecting the disarray within the government's ranks and its failure to cope with the country's grave economic and political problems, Prime Minister Ulloa and his cabinet resigned. A new Cabinet representing the same political forces was soon formed; it gave no indication of a change in policy.

Thus, fifteen years after the military seized power in Peru, the country again faced a crisis of unprecedented proportions. Unemployment climbed to new heights; strikes succeeded each other in industry, the railroads, and the banks; and the rural exodus continued to swell the population of the barriadas, or shantytowns, that ringed Lima. An ominous development in late 1982 and 1983 was a rapid expansion of a guerrilla movement known as the *Sendero Luminoso* (Shining Path), of Maoist inspiration, in the central highlands. In 1982, as he had done in 1963, Belaúnde sent the armed forces to crush an uprising in the Andes. Some observers saw a parallel between the economic and political disarray of Peru in 1983 and the conditions that provoked the military to seize power in 1968. More likely than a new military takeover, however, was the prospect of a realignment in Peruvian politics that might unite nationalist-reformist military, increasingly unhappy with the failed Belaúnde policies, and liberal and leftist parties in a renewed effort to achieve autonomous development and social progress—an effort that would profit by learning from the mistakes and successes of the Peruvian Revolution of 1968.

CHAPTER SEVENTEEN

The Cuban Revolution

In 1959 the island of Cuba—ninety miles from Key West, permeated by North American capital and culture, and long ruled by one of the region's most firmly entrenched dictatorships—became the scene of perhaps the first and certainly the most successful social revolution in Latin America during the twentieth century. Under the banner of Marxism and with the firm military, economic, and political support of the Soviet Union, the revolutionary government led by Fidel Castro has made great progress toward the elimination of such problems as illiteracy, mass unemployment, and unequal distribution of income and wealth in the two decades since taking power.

It is a historical irony that the first socialist state in the Americas has arisen in Cuba, a country bound by the strongest economic and political ties to the United States. In preserving their hard-won gains against the opposition of the United States, the Cuban revolutionaries have survived a CIA-backed invasion, diplomatic isolation, and an economic embargo; they have also overcome the consequences of their own serious miscalculations and inefficiency. In its third decade, the Cuban revolution has, despite economic setbacks, improved the living standard of its people and remains strong.

CUBA UNDER SPANISH RULE

Cuba's development differed markedly from that of most other Latin American countries. For three centuries after its discovery by Christopher Columbus in 1492, the island served primarily as a strategic stopover for the Spanish treasure fleet. Without precious metals or a large indigenous population to exploit, Cuba remained a neglected, sparsely populated outpost of the empire. The island's inhabitants engaged, for the most part, in small-scale farming for domestic consumption. Unlike the other sugar-producing islands of the Caribbean, at the end of the seventeenth century, Cuba had few slaves (its colored population of 40,000 was only one-tenth that of Haiti), many of whom worked in nonagricultural occupations, often as skilled craftsmen. Due to the absence of the harsh plantation system, slaves were frequently able to purchase their freedom.

Economic and Social Change

The second half of the eighteenth century, however, brought profound economic and social change. Spurred by the short-lived British occupation of Havana in 1762 and further stimulated by United States independence in 1783, the island experienced a commercial awakening. Most importantly, Cuba developed into a major sugar producer and slave importer in the aftermath of the Haitian Revolution of the 1790s, which ruined that island as a sugar producer. During the next half-century, sugar production in Cuba skyrocketed, and nearly 600,000 African slaves arrived on its shores. From 1774 to 1861, the island's population leaped from 171,620 to 1,396,530. Havana and Santiago de Cuba became large, busy urban centers and ports, and no

fewer than eight other cities attained populations exceeding 10,000. New immigrants from Santo Domingo and Spain brought an infusion of new technology and capital to the sugar industry. Perceiving new opportunities in agriculture, the Creole landowning class began to construct a latifundio-based economy.

The expansion and diversification of trade and the introduction of large-scale sugar production created a fantastic economic boom and delayed the development of the spirit of rebellion against Spanish rule that swept the rest of Spanish America. Cuba stayed loyal to Spain during the Spanish-American wars of independence, for its Creole leaders saw no reason to tamper with their new-found prosperity. Discontent grew among the slaves and free blacks, however, as a result of tensions caused by the rise of an increasingly harsh plantation system; major slave rebellions, led by free blacks, erupted in 1810, 1812, and 1844. Meanwhile, the wealthy Creoles became increasingly resentful of the arbitrary ways of the corrupt Spanish officialdom, which was determined to enforce continued obedience by Spain's last and richest colony in the New World.

As the colony grew increasingly dissatisfied with repressive Spanish rule, it became less dependent economically on the mother country. By 1776 the British colonies already provided one-third of the island's imports and purchased about one-half of its exports; after the achievement of American independence, Cuba turned more and more toward the United States as a market for its products and a source of needed imports. As a result of these growing economic ties, schemes for the annexation of Cuba to the United States emerged both in the island and in some North American circles. In Cuba, conservative Creole planters saw in annexation an insurance policy against the abolition of slavery; in the United States, some proslavery groups regarded annexation as a means of gaining a vast new area of the expansion of plantation slavery. Some of these groups even dreamed

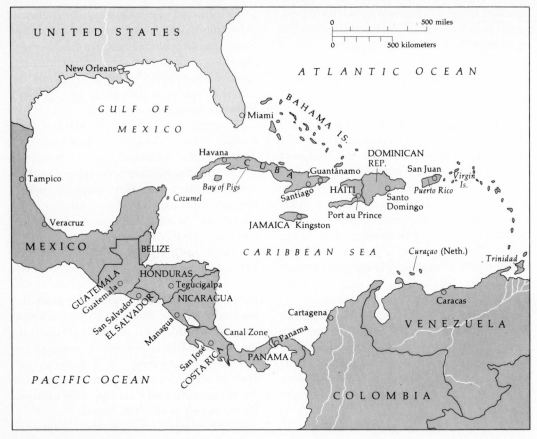

CONTEMPORARY CARIBBEAN

of carving Cuba up into three or five states that would give the South increased power in the national government. The Civil War put an end to these projects.

During the 1860s, Creole discontent grew, heightened by a developing national and class consciousness. The Creole elite rejected various reform proposals offered by a weak Spanish government that was battered by internal dissension and economic difficulties. It became increasingly clear to the Creoles that Spanish economic and political policies were severely restricting Cuban development—a feeling sharpened by a serious economic downturn in the 1860s. On October 10, 1868, in the small town of Yara in Oriente Province, a group of landowners proclaimed Cuban independence

and initiated a struggle that was to continue for ten years.

The Ten Years' War

The Ten Years' War, a long, bitter, devastating guerrilla struggle, ended in 1878, when the Cubans accepted a peace that granted them some concessions but withheld independence. (The Spanish Crown, desperate to retain the last vestige of its American empire, sent ten times as many troops to quell the Cuban insurrection as it sent to all of South America from 1810 to 1828.) The Pact of Zanjón ended hostilities, but some rebel leaders, like the Negro revolutionary Antonio Maceo, the "Bronze Titan," rejected the settlement because it did not achieve the main goals of the revolution—independence and the abolition of slavery. Ironically, the Spanish government, hoping to win the loyalty of the black population, abolished slavery in 1880, with provision for an eight-year *patronato,* or period of apprenticeship for the liberated slaves. The abolition of slavery removed the last major factor tending to keep Creole planters loyal to Spain. Thereafter, the prospect of independence, offering free, unlimited trade with the United States, became increasingly attractive to this class.

The Ten Years' War had a far-reaching impact on the development of Cuban society. It decimated the Creole landowning class, hindering the formation of a traditional Latin American landed elite on the island. Entrepreneurs from the United States came to fill the vacuum created by the ruin of the Creole aristocracy and the bankruptcy of Spanish interests by the war. Thousands of Americans accompanied their investment dollars to the island to run the sugar mills and merchant houses. The McKinley Tariff Act of 1890, which abolished import duties on raw sugar and molasses, greatly increased American trade with and economic influence in Cuba. By 1896, American interests had invested $50 million in Cuba and controlled the sugar industry. By the early 1890s, Cuba supplied one-tenth of all products imported into the United States, ranking third behind Britain and Germany. The United States purchased 87 percent of Cuba's exports. American investment also brought an increasing concentration of sugar production, a trend signaled by the entry of the "Sugar Trust" (the American Sugar Refining Company of Henry Q. Havemeyer) into the island in 1888.

INDEPENDENCE AND THE SPANISH-CUBAN-AMERICAN WAR

The Revolutionary Movement

By the early 1890s, the movement for independence had revived, partly as a result of a worldwide depression that struck heavy blows at the Cuban economy. The spiritual, intellectual, and organizational leader of the revolutionary movement was José Martí (1853–1895). As a lad of sixteen, Martí was arrested on a charge of supporting the 1868 revolt and sentenced to six years in prison at hard labor, but in 1871 he was sent into exile. In 1880, Martí came to New York, his home for the next fourteen years. In the United States, he earned his living in brilliant journalistic and literary activity that won him fame throughout Latin America. A profound student of the American scene, Martí greatly admired Lincoln, the abolitionists, and poets like Walt Whitman but became increasingly alarmed by the emerging power of plutocracy and imperialism.

Meanwhile, Martí worked tirelessly to establish and unite Cuban émigré revolutionary groups. In 1892 he founded *El Partido Revolucionario Cubano* (the Cuban Revolutionary party), which proposed to obtain, "with the united effort of all men of good will, the absolute independence of the island of Cuba, and to foment and aid that of Puerto Rico." He then set about recruiting such military veterans of 1868 as Máximo Gómez and Antonio Maceo, in preparation for an invasion of the island. In April 1895, Martí himself landed on a Cuban beach with a group of insurgents; a little more than a month later, he was killed in a skirmish with a Spanish patrol. In an unfinished letter written on the eve of his death, Martí sounded a recurring note in his writings, fear of American imperialism: "It is my duty . . . to prevent, through the independence of Cuba, the United States from spreading over the West Indies and falling with added weight upon other lands of Our America."

Despite the loss of its ablest, most charismatic leader, the revolution spread and achieved major successes with the aid of time-proven guerrilla tactics. At the beginning of 1896, a new Spanish commander, General Valeriano Weyler, instituted counterinsurgency measures of the type that would later be employed against twentieth-century rebels in the Philippines, Algeria, and Vietnam. He set up population concentration centers and free-fire zones, which resulted in enormous hardships and losses to the peasantry. But his successes were transient and counterproductive, serving mostly to intensify popular hatred for Spanish rule, and whole provinces remained under the absolute control of the liberating army. The failure of Weyler's military policies and growing pressure from the United States led Spain to make a promise of autonomy to Cuba in late 1897.

Involvement by the United States

As the rebellion spread over the land, it became an increasingly volatile issue in the United States. Inevitably, American property was destroyed or damaged in the fighting, and this brought complaints from powerful businessmen and financiers with interests in Cuba. In addition, the Cuban struggle for independence struck a sympathetic chord with the American people, particularly among the working class. William Randolph Hearst and Joseph Pulitzer, then engaged in a newspaper circulation war in New York City, helped to keep popular interest high by running lurid stories of Spanish brutality.

Meanwhile, within the McKinley administration as well as among enthusiastic expansionists like Theodore Roosevelt there was a growing feeling that the Cuban situation was getting out of control, that the autonomy proposal sponsored by the United States was failing, and that if the United States did not intervene an unmanageable Cuban revolutionary government might take over from the collapsing Spanish regime. In the midst of this ferment, the U.S.S. *Maine* blew up in Havana Harbor on February 15, 1898, with a heavy loss of life. This incident helped spur McKinley to a more belligerent stance; he demanded that Spain terminate the concentration camp policy, offer an armistice to the rebels, and accept the United States as a final arbiter between the parties. There was no mention of Cuban independence.

General Calixto Garcia, shown with his staff during the Spanish-American War. (Courtesy of the National Archives)

When Spain delayed its response to American demands, McKinley sent a message to Congress asking it to authorize military intervention by the United States in Cuba. Congress, after considerable debate, adopted a joint-resolution to that effect. It should be noted in passing that almost every major Cuban revolutionary figure— José Martí, Antonio Maceo, Máximo Gómez— opposed American entry into the war, fearing that it would result in direct or indirect American political and economic control of Cuba. All they sought from the United States was recognition of Cuban belligerency and the right to purchase arms in the United States. They believed that the war might drag on for an indefinite period, but time was on the side of the revolution, and the Cubans were bound to win.

The ensuing war was short and nasty. American commanders ignored their Cuban counterparts, excluding Cuban generals from decision making and relegating Cuban soldiers to sentry and cleanup duties. Incompetence was the dominant feature of both the Spanish and American war effort. American military actions were incredibly ill prepared and badly led. The only major land battle of the war, the famous charge up San Juan Hill, which helped to catapult Theodore Roosevelt to national prominence, was very nearly a catastrophic defeat for the United States. Spain, to some extent, defeated itself, for its generals believed the war lost from the beginning and sought above all to minimize their losses. Thus, in a bizzare little war, the United States Army—wretchedly led, scandalously provisioned, and ravaged by tropical disease—swiftly defeated a demoralized, dispirited Spanish army and snatched the fruits of victory from the *mambises*, the Cuban guerrilla fighters who had fought gallantly in a struggle of three years' duration. The exclusion of Cuban leaders from both war councils and peace negotiations foreshadowed the course of Cuban-American relations for the next sixty years.

The First United States Occupation, 1899–1902

The United States Army occupied Cuba from January 1899 to May 1902. The occupation had three basic goals. First, the United States sought to make Cuba into a self-governing protectorate, an arrangement designed to achieve political stability without the administrative burdens and costs of an outright colonial occupation. To this end, the American military sought to pacify the island without serious conflict with the Cuban army, which was still intact and in control of much of rural Cuba. The revolutionary army, however, did not resist the American take-over, as did Emilio Aguinaldo and his insurgent forces in the Philippines at the same time. Cuban passivity in part reflected the fact that the years of struggle had taken their toll—the leading Cuban generals, such as Calixto García and Máximo Gómez, were tired old men, and many of the younger men who could have led a resistance movement had died in battle. In addition, the Americans bought off the army by

offering to purchase its arms, an offer that hungry, unemployed soldiers found difficult to refuse. They also offered key rebel leaders well-paid positions. At the same time, the occupation government established a Rural Guard, not only to eradicate banditry but, in the words of General Leonard Wood, to put down the "agitators who began to grow restive at the presence of the Americans."

After political stability, necessary to attract American capital ("When the people ask me what I mean by stable government," wrote Wood, "I tell them 'money at six per cent' "), the second major American goal was to repair the destruction wrought by the war and provide the sanitation and other services needed for economic recovery. General Leonard Wood, appointed governor general in 1899, launched a program of public works and sanitation that led to a major achievement of the occupation— the conquest of yellow fever. Taking its lead from a Cuban doctor, Carlos Finlay, whose theory correctly attributed the transmission of the dread disease to the mosquito, the American Sanitary Commission succeeded in eliminating it. Another major accomplishment of the Wood administration was the creation of a Cuban national education system, vastly superior to what had existed under Spain but designed to inculcate American principles; even the textbooks were translations of American textbooks. All these programs and reforms, as well as the expenses of the United States troops, were paid for from the Cuban treasury.

Ruling with arbitrary methods and largely ignoring the former revolutionaries in favor of Spaniards and conservative planters who had opposed independence, Wood presided over the election of a convention to frame a constitution for Cuba. The convention, elected in June 1899, began its work in November and after several months of bitter debate adopted a document that, under intense American pressure, included the so-called Platt Amendment. This amendment limited the ability of independent Cuba to conduct foreign policy and to borrow money abroad, gave the United States the right to maintain a naval base at Guantánamo Bay and, most importantly, gave the United States the right to intervene in Cuba for the "preservation of Cuban independence" and for the "maintenance of a government adequate for the protection of life, property, and individual liberty."

The third goal of the occupation was to absorb Cuba into the economic sphere of influence of the United States. Since the Platt Amendment assured American businessmen of protection and a generally favorable investment climate on the island, capital poured into sugar and railroad construction. A reciprocal trade agreement signed by the two nations in 1903 was the final step in bringing Cuba under American hegemony. This treaty cut by 20 percent the tariff on Cuban sugar exported to the United States; in return, Cuba reduced by a similar or higher amount the duties on imported American goods.

THE POLITICS OF CORRUPTION, 1902–1953

Instability and Intervention, 1902–1924

Cuba's political life, afflicted by its status as a United States protectorate and suffering from interventions, had a weak and stunted growth. At the end of 1901, Tomás Estrada Palma was elected the first president of Cuba, and the Americans left the following May. Although he had not lived in Cuba for twenty-five years, Estrada, who headed the Cuban government-in-exile after the Ten Years' War, began his presidency with considerable popularity. However, his administration produced only scandals; public works projects, for example, became major sources of enrichment for politicians.

The 1904 elections to Congress were fraudulent and marked by sporadic violence. Local government was even more turbulent and corruption-ridden. The Estrada presidency established the pattern of Cuban politics for the next fifty years.

In 1905, Estrada, with his adherents in control of the electoral machinery and the opposition boycotting the election, ran for re-election and won. In the summer of 1906, the Liberal party, led by José Miguel Gómez, rose in revolt against the Estrada regime. Unable to suppress the rebellion, the president called for American intervention and left Cuba.

President William Howard Taft responded by sending in the marines, and shortly afterward appointed Charles Magoon, a judge from Minnesota, to preside over an American provisional government. Magoon's solution for the problem of factional violence was to divide the patronage among contending Cuban groups. As a result, the corruption that had emerged during the Estrada regime was institutionalized with the apparent blessing of the United States. The provisional government also took the first steps toward creating a permanent standing army, whose presence, it was hoped, would prevent insurrections of the kind that had toppled Estrada. During the second occupation, Cuban resistance to American domination virtually disappeared. The decline of national consciousness and protest against foreign control was due in large part to the workings of the system of instituionalized corruption, which united all sections of the elite in the eager pursuit of American favor and protection.

Two parties contested the presidential election of 1908, the Conservative party, made up of former supporters of Estrada, and the Liberal party, which had rebelled in 1906. There were no real ideological differences between the parties; the only issue was who should enjoy the spoils of office. The Liberal José Miguel Gómez won and took over the reins of government from Magoon; the United States withdrew its troops on April 1, 1909. Reestablishment of the lottery and legalization of cockfighting were among the highlights of Gómez's presidency.

The Conservative General Mario Menocal succeeded Gómez in 1912 and won re-election in 1916. Menocal continued the tradition of gross political corruption; a millionaire when he took office, he reportedly accumulated $40 million during his two terms. Having formerly managed one of the gigantic American-owned *centrales* (sugar mills), he was closely linked to U.S. economic interests in the island. In the spring of 1917, the Liberals again rebelled, this time in protest against Menocal's re-election. The revolt failed because the United States would not permit disruption of Cuban sugar production during World War I. United States troops landed and remained until 1923.

In 1920, Alfredo Zayas, a former Liberal who had participated in the unsuccessful revolt of 1917, won the presidency with Conservative support. Troubled over the crash of sugar prices in the second half of 1920 and the resulting political unrest in Cuba, President Warren Harding sent General Enoch Crowder to Cuba in January 1921 as his special representative. In effect, Crowder ruled Cuba from his headquarters on board the battleship *Minnesota* until 1923, when he became United States ambassador. In response to promises of fiscal and political reform, Zayas secured a $50 million loan from U.S. bankers in 1923; hardly had the loan become final when he embarked on an unrestrained spending spree of which he was a principal beneficiary. Cuban politics remained a morass of corruption.

The sad pattern of corruption dominated Cuban politics from 1902 to 1924. Control of graft and patronage was the goal of all factions; party labels meant nothing. Four times during this period (1908, 1917, 1919, 1921), the losers of presidential elections staged or threatened revolts, alleging fraud (with good reason). In each instance, and in 1912, when there was minor black rebellion in Oriente Province, United States troops landed to restore order and prevent property damage.

In the last two years of the Zayas administration, Cuban nationalism revived. Crowder's blatant meddling in Cuban politics and the postwar collapse of Cuban sugar, which caused mill closings, mass unemployment, and growing misery, revealed the disastrous consequences of foreign domination and monoculture. Searching for solutions for these problems, Cuban university students entered the political arena in the postwar period. Believing that to change society they must first change the university, they directed their first attacks against inept and corrupt professors and administrators; in 1922 students at the University of Havana demonstrated for reforms along the lines of the recent university reform in Argentina. Students would henceforth play an important role in Cuban politics until the fall of Batista in 1959.

Machado, 1925–1933

Taking advantage of growing nationalistic sentiment, Gerardo Machado y Morales emerged as the Liberal candidate in the presidential election of 1924. Running against the corruption of Zayas, on a platform of national regeneration, he defeated ex-president Menocal. Despite his nationalistic declarations, Machado had very close links to American economic interests, for he had been until his election vice president of an American-owned utility in Havana. Even before he took office, Machado visited the United States to assure President Calvin Coolidge of his government's good intentions.

Machado began his term auspiciously. He embarked on an ambitious program of public works and attempted to institute a system of controls for sugar production designed to protect small and medium-size producers against severe price declines. He also tried to encourage the diversification of agriculture by raising the tariffs on fruits, rice, and cacao; this program effectively increased production of these crops. Machado took steps to institute a merit system for the public bureaucracy and established new technical and commercial schools. He even sought, with little success, to reform the prostitutes of Havana. Thanks to these efforts, Machado enjoyed unparalleled popularity and faced virtually no opposition for two years.

Already, however, there were disturbing signs of tyranny. The number of political assassinations increased alarmingly. A wave of strikes during 1925 was broken by police shooting down strikers. The nation's most prominent Communist leader, Juan Antonio Mella, was murdered in his Mexican exile by a Machado gunman in 1929. Machado's secret police routinely eliminated his opponents by throwing them to the sharks in Havana Harbor.

Machado secured his re-election in 1928 by the simple expedient of outlawing the party of his main rival, Carlos Mendieta. Until the onset of the world depression in 1930, Machado maintained an iron grip on Cuba, despite mounting opposition from university students, the Communists, labor unions, and many old-line politicians led by Mendieta. The economic crisis had particularly catastrophic consequences for Cuba because of its heavy reliance on exports. Machado responded to the growing political unrest engendered by the economic conditions with increasingly harsh repression. A general strike failed in May 1930. In September, after the killing of a student leader, students at the University of Havana organized a large demonstration, which was followed by the firing of hundreds of teachers and the closing of the university.

In August 1931, Mendieta led a group of old-line politicians in an unsuccessful revolt, a last effort to revive the old strategies and leadership of Cuban politics. Late in 1931, a new secret organization, the ABC, sprang up among young members of the middle class and intellectuals as a moderate alternative to the more radical university students' group, the Student Directory. Machado answered these challenges with tightened censorship and stepped-up terror tactics on the part of his secret police, the *Porra*.

By the beginning of 1933, the United States government had become seriously concerned by the spreading violence, which appeared to threaten U.S. economic interests. In April, incoming President Franklin Roosevelt dispatched Sumner Welles as ambassador to attempt to negotiate some sort of understanding between Machado and his opponents. For several months, Welles unsuccessfully tried to mediate between Machado and the opposition, but Machado would not compromise, while the opposition was disunited and unable to agree on a course of action.

In the summer, a bus drivers' strike in Havana mushroomed into a general strike that nearly paralyzed the city. After the police massacred several demonstrators in August, Machado's position seriously deteriorated, for he had lost the support of Ambassador Welles and the army. On August 12, Machado resigned and fled into exile.

The Revolution of 1933

For the next three weeks, a provisional government headed by Carlos Manuel de Cespedes struggled unsuccessfully to end the escalating violence. On September 4, a group of army sergeants, one of whom was Fulgencio Batista, overthrew the government. The Student Directory immediately allied itself with the sergeants, and together they formed a revolutionary junta, a five-man committee known as the Pentarchy.

The new junta had no organized political backing, and its two main components, the noncommissioned officers and the Student Directory, had sharply divergent aims. The sergeants were concerned only with defending their newly won dominent position against any challenge. The students, on the other hand, sought genuine reforms but were unsure just how to achieve them. Within a week after taking control, the junta turned over the reins of government to Dr. Ramón Grau San Martín, a well-known physician and long-time opponent of Machado. Grau, Antonio Guiteras Holmes, a leader of the Student Directory, and Batista were dominant figures in the new alignment.

The first move of the new government was to abrogate the onerous Platt Amendment. A flurry of decrees produced more social legislation than all the previous history of independent

Cuba: an eight-hour day for labor, a labor department, an end to the importation of cheap labor from other islands in the Caribbean, and greater access for children from lower-income groups to the university. There were also measures to redistribute land to peasants, eliminate usury, and give women the vote.

Ultimately, the Grau government was caught in the classic bind of the reformer: the left was dissatisfied because the reforms were not of sufficient scope, and the right opposed all reform. Grau also alienated American financial and agricultural interests when he suspended repayment of several loans owed to the Chase National Bank of New York and seized two mills of the Cuban-American Sugar Company. Consequently, the United States government adamantly refused to recognize the Grau government.

The revolutionary coalition disintegrated. The ABC would not cooperate with Grau, because his program had become too radical. He had earlier lost the support of the more radical elements of the Student Directory, and the Communists attacked him as a "petty bourgeois."

The behavior of Sumner Welles throughout the Grau interregnum was extraordinarily similar to the conduct of U.S. Ambassador Henry Lane Wilson in Mexico during the Madero administration. Welles persistently falsified reports and misrepresented the Cuban government to Secretary of State Cordell Hull and President Roosevelt. As Wilson had befriended Huerta and helped him to power, so Welles allied himself with Fulgencio Batista. Eventually (in November 1933), Welles was recalled, but he had seriously undermined the position of the provisional government. As the economic and political situation worsened, Welles's successor as ambassador, Jefferson Caffery, maneuvered with Batista to form a new government acceptable to the United States. In January 1934, Grau, unable to rule effectively in the face of American opposition, went into exile and was replaced by Carlos Mendieta.

The Era of Batista, 1934–1944

Fulgencio Batista y Zaldivar, the sergeant-stenographer, mulatto son of a sugar worker, dominated Cuban politics for the next decade, ruling the island through puppet presidents from 1934 to 1940 and as elected president from 1940 to 1944. Although Batista alienated many of the "respectable" elements of the middle and upper classes, he was extremely popular among the masses. During the first two years after his successful coup, he presided over a mild reform program with some effort at land redistribution. In 1937, he moved leftward and openly courted the support of labor unions and the Communists. The Communist party, which endorsed the Popular Front strategy recently adopted by the Third (Communist) International, was eager to cooperate.

The Auténtico Interlude, 1944–1952

At the end of 1939, Batista permitted the election of a constituent assembly to draft the constitution of 1940. Grau and his Cuban Revolutionary, or Auténtico party (founded in 1934) and other moderate parties won the election and produced a liberal document with provisions for the protection of labor and limitations on the right of property when it conflicted with the public good. It was Batista, however, who won the presidential election of 1940.

Choosing for reasons of his own to observe the constitutional provision that the president should not succeed himself, Batista, to the general surprise, allowed honest elections to take place in 1944. As a result, Grau defeated Batista's hand-picked choice. Grau, who earlier had been the symbol of Cuban regeneration and democracy, presided over an unparalleled reign of corruption. Violence accompanied the corruption, and the University of Havana became a nest of political gangsterism. True, the Grau government initiated some minor reforms—housing for workers, a rural school program, and road improvement—but it made no attack on such key problems as agrarian reform and monoculture.

In 1947, a charismatic populist leader, Eddie Chibás, launched a new campaign against government oppression and corruption. A former ardent supporter of the Auténticos, Chibás had become disillusioned and formed his own Cuban People's, or *Ortodoxo*, party, which featured a mild program of social reform and clean politics, in the spring of 1947. Extremely popular, he posed a serious threat to the Auténticos. In 1948, Chibás opposed the Auténtico presidential candidate, Carlos Prío Socorrás, former leader of the Student Directory. Prío, who won easily because he controlled the election machinery and had the advantage of four years of economic prosperity, became another in a long line of Cuban country club presidents. He spent much of his time serving his guests daiquiris at his opulent farm in the suburbs of Havana. There was no letup in the corruption, gangsterism, and spoils system characteristic of his predecessor's regime. As under Grau, the prosperity brought on by high sugar prices concealed the mismanagement of the Prío administration.

Chibás was the leading candidate for the presidency for the upcoming election when Batista reappeared in Cuba after a long retirement to announce that he would be a candidate for president in 1952. Cuban politics were thrown into complete disarray when Chibás, in an apparent effort to awake the Cuban public to the extent of political corruption, killed himself on a nationwide radio broadcast in August 1951. In any event, in March 1952, before the election could take place, Batista headed a conspiracy of low-ranking army officers that overthrew Prío. Thoroughly disillusioned with politics, the Cuban people offered little protest.

The Return of Batista as Dictator, 1952–1959

Batista ruled Cuba for the second time until he was overthrown by Fidel Castro in 1959. Like his contemporaries, Carlos Ibañez in Chile, Ge-

túlio Vargas in Brazil, and Juan Perón in Argentina, Batista found the second time around more difficult than the first. A new generation of revolutionaries rose to replace the discredited leaders of 1933. Unlike Grau or Prío, they would not be bought off or collaborate with the dictator. Several groups opposed Batista, including the Auténticos, who plotted from their havens in Florida; the 26th of July Movement led by Fidel Castro, which unsuccessfully tried to overthrow the government in 1953 by assaulting the Moncada army barracks; and the Federation of University Students (FEU). Despite the activities of the students and Castro's guerrilla group, which in 1956 renewed its fight in the Sierra Maestra mountains in Oriente Province, the dictator seemed to be firmly entrenched. The endemic instability and corruption of the Cuban political system was matched in its ill effects by the structural weakness of the economy, produced by reliance on a single crop, sugar.

THE EXPORT ECONOMY: SUGAR AS KING

Cuba is a classic case of monoculture—a nation dependent on the production and export of a single crop for its economic livelihood. Like the other Latin American nations we have examined (Argentina, Brazil, Chile, and Mexico), Cuba has suffered from the cyclical nature of world market demand for its product. Moreover, Cuba suffered the additional burden of almost total economic domination by the United States.

The Early History of Sugar

The Cuban sugar industry dates from the early 1790s, when revolution wrecked the sugar production of Haiti, then the world's leading sugar exporter. At the same time, the United States won its independence from Great Britain, thereby furnishing a ready nearby market for Cuban sugar. Cuban agriculturalists took immediate advantage of their opportunity to shift

Ingenio (sugar mill) in Cuba. (Courtesy of the
Organization of American States)

to sugar and to import cheap slave labor from
Africa.

Initially, the transfer to sugar did not stimulate
the creation of the latifundio; first, because much
of the land converted to sugar was the under-
used acreage of large cattle haciendas, and second, because many farmers did not change over
to sugar, preferring instead to produce coffee
and tobacco, which then enjoyed high prices
resulting from the abolishment of the royal monopoly on these commodities. Furthermore, the
sugar mills themselves stimulated demand for
livestock (to turn the mills) and food crops for
the slaves. During the first decades of the nineteenth century, the number of farm proprietors
increased markedly, and from their ranks came
the leaders of Cuban society for the next century.

The boom that followed the destruction of
Haiti ended by the turn of the century because
other Caribbean islands expanded and initiated
production in response to the same stimuli,
thereby creating an enormous glut on the market. Just as the industry recovered from this
setback, diplomatic maneuvering during the
Napoleonic wars closed U.S. ports. Shortly
thereafter, two new challenges to the Cuban
economy arose: the introduction of beet sugar
in Europe and the British campaign to end the
slave trade. (England forced Spain to end the
trade in 1821.) Further impediments resulted
from the restrictions imposed by Spanish hegemony: high tariffs, scarce and expensive credit,
and the disruptions brought on by the Spanish-
American wars of independence.

By 1820 the first of a series of technological innovations began to transform the character of the sugar industry in Cuba. Millowners had to invest heavily in steam-operated machinery in order to compete with beet sugar. Modern machinery allowed the mills to expand in size, but they could do so only gradually because of the limited transportation facilities that were available. Since railroads were enormously expensive, and in any case there was not sufficient capital on the island or in Spain for large projects of this type, they did not become important until much later.[1] The mills also carried a huge overhead, much of it unused during the off-season. Slaves and livestock had to be fed and sheltered even when the harvest was completed. The problem of fuel for the mills also slowed their expansion. The forests close to the mills were quickly consumed, and transport of wood to the mills proved prohibitively costly. As a result, sugar production was expanded in the first half of the century by increasing the number of mills. In 1827 there were 1,000 mills, by 1846 there were 1,442, and by 1860 there were 2,000.

The Development of the Latifundio

Large plantations developed in Cuba in response to the necessity of building bigger and bigger mills. Sugar technology was continually improving, and Cuban mills had to expend huge sums to remain competitive. The larger the mill the more sugar it could process, the more fuel it consumed, and the more employees it needed. Smaller and less efficient mills were at a severe competitive disadvantage. Many of these were destroyed during the Ten Years' War.

Sugar production was set up in one of two ways: The land might be cultivated by resident or temporary labor, or the land might be parcelled out to farmers, known as colonos, who would work the land for a salary or a share of the crop. The landowners, in either situation, might or might not also be the millowners. As

the number of mills grew smaller, the colonos became the main suppliers of sugar to the mills. They planted and harvested the cane and brought it to the mill to be processed. They paid for the processing in sugar. By the 1870s, sugar production was specialized into these components, colonos and mills (centrales). The number of large plantations did not increase; instead, the number of colonos gradually rose.

The shake-out of mills during the war, the financial crisis of 1885–1890, and the expansion of the island's railroad network combined to stimulate the spread of the latifundio. As the mills grew, they required more cane and sought it over a wider geographic area than previously. At the same time, the introduction of cheap rails spurred railroad construction in Cuba (and all over the world). In their quest for more cane, centrales began to lay their own track in an effort to draw it from a greater area. Competition between centrales for cane, a condition previously unknown because of transportation limitations, resulted.

The centrales confronted the necessity of guaranteeing enough cane at the lowest possible prices for the harvest (zafra). They could do this either by reducing the independence of the colonos or by acquiring their own cane land. The first method transformed the once-free farmers into satellites of the giant mills. The second led to the creation of latifundia. Small and medium-size growers fell by the way, to be replaced by tenants or day labor. The colonos managed to hold their own until independence, after which time the massive influx of foreign capital into the sugar mills overwhelmed them. With their lesser financial resources, they were doomed.

The end of Spanish rule and the American occupation removed the final obstacles to the development of the latifundio in Cuba. The island, at peace at last, could repair the damage done by forty years of guerrilla warfare. The United States military and the new Cuban Rural Guard would prevent new revolutionary outbreaks, and the Platt Amendment guaranteed

[1] The first railroad in Cuba was built in 1836.

a favorable climate for investment. The elimination of yellow fever allowed foreigners to live on the island without fear for their health. The successive occupation governments and their Cuban successors furnished subsidies and other inducements for railroad construction and utilities. At a time when antitrust laws began to restrict industry in the United States, Cuba had no such inhibitions. Finally, Cuban sugar was an attractive investment because the United States was a close and growing market in which it had a competitive advantage because of the reciprocal trade treaty of 1903, which cut the tariff on Cuban sugar by 20 percent.

Two processes worked hand in hand in the following decades: the concentration of land and mills and the proletarianization of the sugar workers. The two wars of independence had devastated small mills: The total number fell from 2,000 in 1861 to 1,000 in 1877 to only 200 in 1899. The rapid and huge influx of foreign—mostly American—investment into sugar enabled the larger mills to buy up surrounding cane land. The colono was reduced to circumstances close to slavery. Ramiro Guerra y Sánchez has estimated that in some provinces, like Oriente and Matanzas, the great mills owned 25 percent of the total land. He further estimates that the mills owned perhaps 20 percent of the island's area in 1927. A quarter of all the land owned by the mills was owned by four companies. Guerra y Sánchez calculates that as much as 40 percent of Cuba's land may have fallen under the control of the latifundia. Cuba was reduced to a "large sugar plantation producing sugar for the benefit of foreign consumers."

The expansion of the latifundio impoverished the rural masses of the island. The colonos were kept at subsistence levels, deeply indebted to the mill and in constant fear of eviction. The wages of rural workers were kept low because the mills imported cheap labor from other Caribbean islands. As a result, a considerable reserve pool of labor was available; even those lucky enough to get work worked only four months of the year during the harvest period. Displaced

farmers had two choices. They could remain and work for small wages on a seasonal basis for the centrales, or they could emigrate to the cities, where jobs were also scarce. Small independent growers were at a severe disadvantage, for the mills squeezed the price paid for their cane to a minimum. In addition, the mills controlled the transportation network.

The ruin of the small mills and farmers and the low wages paid rural labor, which reduced the purchasing power of the masses, sharply limited the domestic market for manufactured goods and commercial services. As a result, there was little Cuban industrialization. Sugar companies monopolized the railroads and operated them solely for their own benefit, often without regard to the public interest. Although Cuba's railroad network exceeded that of most Latin American nations, it was inadequate to develop an internal market.

American companies poured money into Cuban sugar during the first occupation. By 1913, Americans had invested $200 million in Cuba, predominantly in sugar. This accounted for nearly one-fifth the total U.S. investment in all of Latin America.

World War I and the Dance of the Millions

Cuba's greatest sugar boom and bust took place as a consequence of World War I. The fighting in Europe, which disrupted sugar production on the Continent, from the first caused large price increases: Prices nearly doubled in the first two months alone. Eventually, the Allies became totally dependent on Cuban sugar production, since they were fighting their major former supplier, Austria-Hungary. This demand spurred further expansion of Cuban sugar production, with planters moving into previously uncultivated land. The last great surge of mill construction also occurred. As production spread into virgin land, centrales were built and new towns sprang up.

The Allies attempted to keep commodity prices

from skyrocketing by establishing purchasing committees to handle the acquisition of raw materials and food. Nonetheless, Cuban production rose in 1916 to 3 million tons at an average price of 4 cents a pound. Expansion created a severe labor shortage on the island, and laborers were imported from Jamaica and other Caribbean islands to fill the void. The colonos staged a comeback, and a few actually prospered.

The war accelerated the trend toward the concentration of the industry in American hands. By 1919 approximately half the island's mills were owned by U.S. companies, and these controlled more than half the total production. The boom also led to the integration of sugar mills and plantations with distributors and companies that were large sugar users. Giants such as Coca Cola, Hershey (chocolate), and Hires (root beer) bought up producers in order to guarantee their supplies. Producers in turn purchased distributors and refiners.

The postwar years of 1918 to 1920 brought unprecedented prosperity to Cuba, as sugar prices soared and eastern European sugar areas were slow to recover from the war. After the Allied committee deregulated prices in 1920, they began an incredible upward spiral called the "Dance of the Millions." In February 1920, the price of sugar stood at 9⅛ cents per pound. By mid-May, the price had climbed to 22½ cents. Soon, however, prices collapsed as a result of a worldwide depression and Europe's agricultural recovery; by December the Cubans were getting 3¾ cents per pound, which was the prewar price level.

The precipitous rise and equally sudden collapse of sugar prices caused chaos in the Cuban economy. Mills had contracts to buy large quantities of sugar at high prices, prices that were now far higher than the world market. Producers and processors had taken out loans to expand—loans based on anticipated high prices. Banks began to call in these loans. In April 1921, the island's largest bank, the *Banco Nacional*, closed, and others throughout the

country followed suit. Simultaneously, the United States raised its tariff on sugar by one cent, thereby inflicting another blow on the already devastated industry. In 1921 the First National City Bank of New York—long heavily involved with American sugar interests in Cuba—took over nearly sixty bankrupt mills. The harvest reached 4 million tons in 1922, but prices stayed low. The following year, prices rose to 5 cents a pound as a result of the crisis over the French invasion of the Rhineland. Prices were not to reach that level again for three decades.

An Industry in Decline

During the 1920s, the sugar industry entered a long period of stagnation and decline, which lasted until the Castro revolution in 1959. It became clear that the Cuban economy was painfully vulnerable not only to world market fluctuations but to political conditions in the United States. During this decade, Cuba lost much of its U.S. market because it encountered the powerful interests of the sugar beet farmers of the American West. To make matters worse, sugar consumption stayed constant as competition grew more intense. In absolute terms, sugar consumption rose as the population rose, but per capita consumption, which had increased enormously since the 1890s, actually declined over the next forty years (from the 1920s). In part, the decrease resulted from dentists' concern about sugar's effect on the teeth.

In 1926 the harvest reached nearly 5 million tons but brought only an average of 2.2 cents per pound. That same year, the last sugar mill was built in Cuba. For the rest of the decade, the price of sugar stayed below 3.0 cents. After 1928 sugar became a major issue in the U.S. Congress; as a result, the Hawley-Smoot Tariff Act levied a duty of 2.0 cents per pound on Cuban imports two years later. In 1929, Cuban sugar sold for 1.79 cents, and the tariff therefore doubled the price! From then on, Cuba's share of the U.S. market shrank steadily, from 49.4

percent in 1930 to 25.3 percent in 1933. By 1931 the price for sugar was barely a penny a pound, and the next year it fell to 0.72 cents. Mills closed, and people were thrown out of work all over the island.

In 1937 the world's sugar-producing nations met in London to try to reach an agreement that would divide up the market and limit production. They formed an International Sugar Council, which allotted Cuba 29 percent of the U.S. market, half its share in 1929. It should be noted that the bulk of the profits generated by Cuba's sugar economy continued to flow out of the country because foreign companies accounted for 80 percent of Cuban production (American companies controlled 56 percent), while Cubans owned barely 20 percent.

World War II brought on another boom. In 1944 production reached its highest level since the depression. In 1946, as part of its efforts to aid European recovery, the United States agreed to purchase the entire harvest for 3.7 cents a pound. During the Korean war, the price of sugar soared to 5.0 cents. Inevitably, however, Cuba's competitors, especially the Philippines, expanded production. The market soon became glutted with sugar, and prices fell.

Thus, on the eve of the revolution, Cuba's sugar industry had stagnated for the better part of thirty years, and its malaise spread throughout the economy. Agriculture did not become diversified because the land was concentrated in a very few hands—twenty-two companies held one-fifth the island's farmland. Much of the land was kept idle in case sugar prices should ever boom. Industry was almost nonexistent, for a series of reciprocal trade agreements with the United States—which guaranteed Cuba's sugar market—made it impossible to compete with American imports. These same treaties also stunted agriculture by permitting a flow of agricultural products from the United States whose low prices barred potential Cuban competition. Because of its stagnant economy and the peculiar nature of the sugar industry, Cuba suffered from structural unemployment and

underemployment. Most sugar workers were needed only during the harvest; even if well paid during this four-month period, they went jobless and often hungry during the other eight months. It was these structural deficiencies and the economic injustices created by them that helped lay the foundation of the Cuban Revolution.

THE REVOLUTION: THE ODYSSEY OF FIDEL CASTRO

The Cuban Revolution was deeply rooted in the history of the island, for the movement headed by Fidel Castro continued the revolutionary traditions of 1868, 1898, and 1933. By no coincidence, both before and after gaining power, Castro often cited the ideals of José Martí and the principles of the liberal constitution of 1940. Yet profound disillusionment accompanied those traditions, for Cuba's past revolutions had invariably failed—either its leaders had succumbed to the temptations of great wealth, or the United States had intervened to thwart their programs. In large part, the complex development of the Cuban Revolution reflected a combination of loyalty to those liberal traditions and a fear of falling into their errors. Castro desperately sought to avoid past mistakes. This fact helps to explain his tendency toward searching self-criticism and the shifting course of his policies.

Fidel Castro Ruz, the son of a wealthy Spanish farmer in northwest Cuba, was born in 1927. His father's estate extended over ten thousand acres and employed five hundred men. Young Fidel knew little of the hardships of the depression. He attended the famous Jesuit school of Belén in Havana and acquired a reputation as a fine athlete. In 1945 he went off to the University of Havana, where he soon became involved in the frequently violent politics that then plagued the university. In 1947 he participated in an ill-fated invasion of the Dominican Republic, sponsored by student political groups that sought to overthrow dictator Rafael Trujillo. After several hair-raising adventures in Cuba and Colombia, he apparently settled down, married, and became a follower of Eddie Chibás, to whose Ortodoxo party he belonged from 1947 to 1952.

In 1953, Castro headed a small band of lower-middle-class and working-class rebels that attacked the Moncada army barracks near Santiago de Cuba on July 26 in the hope of sparking a rebellion against the Batista dictatorship. Their program called for a return to the constitution of 1940, land reform, educational reform, and an end to the vast waste caused by government corruption and large weapons expenditures. The attack failed, and most of the attackers were killed or captured and tortured. Castro himself was captured several days after the disaster and later put on trial. Although the assault failed, with heavy casualties, the drastic acts of repression the government carried out in its wake, and Castro's eloquent defense speech at his trial ("History Will Absolve Me") made him a national hero.

Fidel spent the next nineteen months in prison on the Isle of Pines, where he read, wrote, and continued to plan the overthrow of Batista. During this period, his *History Will Absolve Me* appeared clandestinely and enhanced his reputation. He also grew increasingly dissatisfied with the programs of the groups then opposing the dictator. Batista's general amnesty freed him in 1955 and shortly thereafter, finding Havana's political climate not to his liking, he went to Mexico to organize a new attack on the dictatorship. While in Mexico, Castro's group received support from ex-president Prío and Venezuelan exile Rómulo Betancourt (later president of Venezuela). Late in 1955, Fidel met Ernesto ("Che") Guevara, who was to become the revolution's second-in-command and its greatest martyr.

In 1956 there was a great increase in the level of violence in Cuba, and Castro was determined to return to the island to renew the struggle. He purchased the yacht *Granma*, and he and his band left Mexico City in November. The *Granma* sailed from Mexico with eighty-two persons aboard. Among them were Guevara, Raúl Castro (Fidel's brother), and Juan Almeida, all of whom were to become major figures in the revolution.

Originally, Castro had planned to coordinate the *Granma's* landing in Oriente Province with an uprising in Santiago. As happened with the Moncada attack, however, the landing encountered logistical and scheduling problems, and Castro and his followers were betrayed. He and a small group of other survivors barely escaped to the Sierra Maestra. From the mountains, Castro and his rebels carried out guerrilla raids, beating off attacks by vastly superior forces and sometimes enduring great hardship.

In February 1957, Castro granted an interview in his mountain hide-out to Herbert Matthews, a well-known reporter for the *New York Times*. Matthews was very favorably impressed, and his articles gave Castro credibility in the United States. The interview also gave notice to the Cuban people that Castro was still alive, despite government claims to the contrary, and that opposition to the regime existed in the mountains. The articles overstated the numerical strength and success of the movement and thereby helped to win adherents to the rebel cause all over the island. The guerrillas continued to conduct raids throughout the spring of 1957, picking up recruits and gaining increased sympathy and support from the peasants of Oriente, who rendered invaluable assistance in the form of supplies and intelligence information about government forces.

By mid-1957, violence, especially in Havana, had become endemic as various groups, most unaffiliated with Castro's 26th of July Movement, attacked the regime and met with brutal retaliation. Life in Santiago and Oriente Province was completely disrupted by terrorism and strikes. The island was increasingly gripped by civil war. In the fall, there was an abortive uprising of junior naval officers at Cienfuegos. Batista used bombers and other military equip-

Fidel Castro and his troops. (Bob Henriques/
Magnum Photos, Inc.)

ment to crush the revolt; this alienated some
of his American support, because the terms of
Cuba's military assistance agreement with the
United States expressly forbade using this
equipment for domestic purposes.

After the New Year, the trend of events began
to turn decisively against Batista. The United
States, foreseeing the shape of things to come,
suspended arms shipments to the Cuban government in March 1958. The rebels suffered a
minor setback in April when a planned general
strike met with little response, but Castro continued to gain support as Batista's situation
worsened. Some elements of the church actively
supported Castro (there had been several priests
in the mountains with him for months). The
middle class abandoned the dictator. In May,
Batista launched a major effort to dislodge Castro

from his base in the Sierra Maestra, and the
resulting defeat doomed his regime. Rebel forces
inflicted heavy losses on the government troops.
Withered by corruption and led by incompetent
cronies of Batista, the army was no match for
the guerrillas.

In August the rebels began their final push.
Three columns led by Castro, Guevara, and
Camilo Cienfuegos set out to cut the island in
two. In the meantime, Castro dispatched emissaries to the various anti-Batista groups, seeking particularly the cooperation of the Communists and the labor unions they controlled.

As Batista's plight grew desperate, frantic negotiations involving the U.S. embassy began
with a view to staving off Castro's victory by
the creation, through a coup or fraudulent elections, of a new government, which the United

States government would recognize and give military assistance to. Batista actually held presidential elections, printing up filled-in ballots in advance, and readied a president to take office in February 1959. But the strong drive of the rebel forces frustrated these maneuvers; by the end of December 1958, the *barbudos* (bearded ones) were on the outskirts of Havana. On January 1, abandoned by his American allies, Batista and his closest aides fled to the safety of Miami. The remaining threat to the *Fidelistas* came from the remnants of the old army. Colonel Ramón Barquín, who had unsuccessfully attempted a coup in 1956 and had been released from prison soon after Batista fled, surfaced as a possible alternative to Castro. Barquín, however, retreated when he realized the overwhelming superiority of the 26th of July Movement and its armed forces. On January 1 and 2, 1959, Guevara and Cienfuegos entered Havana and occupied key military points. The same day, Castro called for a general strike in support of the revolution. He arrived in the capital a week later amid the cheers of its inhabitants.

Thus, a rebel band, numbering fewer than three hundred until mid-1958 and scarcely three thousand when the old regime fell, won a great victory. The rebels won because they were persistent and disciplined and gained the sympathy of all the people—peasants, workers, and the middle class—and because they faced an army wracked by favoritism and incompetence, led by a dictator who preferred to play canasta rather than plan antiguerrilla strategy. The rebels had conscientious, competent commanders and were motivated both by idealism and the knowledge that capture meant torture and death. Batista's army, put to the test, proved capable of terrorizing unarmed citizens but disintegrated when confronted with a formidable insurgency.

THE REVOLUTION IN POWER, 1959–1983

During its first four years (1959–1962), the revolution consolidated its domestic political po-sition, began the socialization of the economy, and established a new pattern of foreign relations. In 1959, Castro and his lieutenants made a series of decisions that determined the course of the revolution for the next decade. First, they concluded that parliamentary democracy was inappropriate for Cuba at that time. The Fundamental Law of the Republic, decreed in February 1959, concentrated legislative power in the executive. As prime minister and, later, as first secretary of the Communist party, Castro held the decisive posts in the government and the ruling party of the Cuban state. Within eighteen months, the revolutionary regime had suppressed the right of free press and the centuries-old autonomy of the University of Havana. The revolutionaries conducted public trials of former *Batistianos*, and a large number of Batista's henchmen, found guilty of torture, killing of students, rape, and similar crimes, were executed.

Second, Castro moved the revolution leftward in order to accomplish his economic goals—land reform, income redistribution, agricultural diversification, and the winning of economic independence from the United States. The radicalism of his economic program and the concentration of political power in the hands of the close-knit 26th of July Movement alienated much of his middle-class support. President Manuel Urrutia, who fell into this category, resigned in July 1959, and was replaced by Osvaldo Dorticós. In October, Major Hubert Matos, one of the foremost military leaders of the revolution and a violent anticommunist, was charged with treason and imprisoned; his case symbolized the moderate-radical split. At the same time, Castro moved toward an alliance with the Popular Socialist (Communist) party, seeking its help in administering the country and the economy.

In January 1960, Castro purged the moderate elements from the leadership of Cuban labor unions. He had long foreseen that conflict with the United States was inevitable and viewed the Soviet Union as Cuba's most logical potential ally and protector. The Soviet Union's deputy premier, Anastas Mikoyan, visited Cuba in January and agreed that his government would purchase 425,000 tons of Cuban sugar in 1960 and 1 million tons the next year. In May, Cuba resumed diplomatic relations with the Soviet Union.

United States–Cuban Relations

Meanwhile, Cuban relations with the United States, already suffering from the unfavorable publicity brought by the trials and the expropriation of large estates, reached a crisis in May 1960. The Cuban government requested that the major petroleum refineries, owned by Texaco, Standard Oil, and Royal Dutch Shell, process Soviet crude oil, which the Cubans had obtained at a lower price than the three companies charged for their oil. At the urging of the U.S. State Department, the companies refused. At the end of June, Castro expropriated the refineries. In response, President Dwight Eisenhower withdrew the Cuban sugar quota. Castro, in turn expropriated numerous American-owned properties.[2] In October, Eisenhower banned all U.S. exports to Cuba—an embargo that has not yet been lifted. This action set off a new wave of expropriations of American property, including Sears, Roebuck, Coca-Cola, and the enormous U.S. government-owned nickel deposits at Moa Bay.

As relations between the two nations deteriorated, the Central Intelligence Agency began to funnel money to various exile groups for arms and training. During the summer of 1960, the CIA set up a training camp in Guatemala for an invasion force. On January 3, 1961, the outgoing Eisenhower administration severed diplomatic relations with Cuba. Three months later, President John F. Kennedy gave the go-ahead to the exile expeditionary force, which landed at the Bay of Pigs beginning on April

15. The revolutionary army swiftly crushed the invasion. Poorly planned and executed, the invasion was based on the false assumption that the Cuban people would rise in revolt as soon as they heard the exiles had landed. The Bay of Pigs fiasco immeasurably increased Castro's prestige and gave new impetus to the movement for radical reconstruction of the Cuban economy and society.

This process was accompanied by ideological changes. What had begun as a program of social and political reform within a framework of constitutional democracy and capitalism swiftly evolved into a Marxist revolution. One month after the Bay of Pigs, Castro proclaimed allegiance to socialism.

In the wake of the Bay of Pigs disaster, the Soviet Union pledged to defend Cuba in the event of an attack by the United States and stepped up its flow of arms to the island. These included missile emplacements and aircraft capable of delivering atomic weapons throughout most of North and South America. The United States claimed that these were offensive weapons; Cuba and the Soviet Union argued that they had a defensive, or deterrent, character. On October 22, 1962, President Kennedy ordered a quarantine on all offensive military equipment bound for Cuba and demanded the dismantling of the missile sites. After several days, during which the world came close to nuclear war, the two powers reached a compromise by which the Soviet Union agreed to remove its missiles from Cuba in return for a pledge from the United States not to invade Cuba. However, efforts by the United States to subvert and harass the Cuban Revolution with the aid of counterrevolutionary Cuban exiles continued: They included CIA-sponsored raids against refineries and ports, infiltration of enemy agents, and even some bizarre attempts to assassinate Castro.

Revolutionary Economics

The Cuban Revolution benefited from advantages few other socialist revolutions have

---

[2] The government had previously taken over only the operation of these properties.

enjoyed. The guerrilla war (in contrast to that of China or Vietnam) was relatively short and caused little destruction of human life or property. Moreover, Cuba possessed well-developed communications and transportation systems, including an extensive railroad network and excellent primary roads. The character of Cuba's rural population promised to make the process of socialist land reform easier than it had been in Russia, for example. Since the sugar industry had proletarianized much of the agricultural work force, farm workers did not demand their own land but rather sought improved working conditions and wages. Cuba also had considerable unused land and industrial capacity, which could be quickly employed to raise living standards and increase productivity. Finally, by 1959 there existed a number of developed socialist states that could offer Cuba substantial assistance, thus offsetting the severe negative effects of the U.S. embargo on exports.

But the revolution also faced serious problems. To begin with, the revolutionaries, inexperienced in economic affairs, made mistakes. The socialist reorientation of the economy inevitably caused disruptions, and the American embargo caused crippling shortages of parts and other difficulties, which the development of new patterns of trade with countries in the socialist camp (and with some capitalist countries) only gradually overcame. Also, many of Cuba's ablest technicians joined the first wave of refugees that fled to the United States. Finally, Castro and his chief aide, Ernesto Guevara, initially spurned material incentives, endorsed by more traditional Marxists as the best spur to production, in favor of moral incentives which would give rise to the "new socialist man." Application of this theory caused considerable economic damage before it was replaced in 1969 by a more pragmatic mix of material and moral incentives.

The first goal of the revolutionary government was to redistribute income to the rural and urban working class. During the first three years, it met with considerable success, raising wages 40 percent and overall purchasing power 20

percent. Unemployment was virtually wiped out. These benefits accrued predominantly to areas outside Havana, for the revolutionaries were determined to reverse the trend toward superurbanization, characteristic of most of Latin America.[3]

Castro decreed the first Law of Agrarian Reform in May 1959. This law restricted the size of landholdings and gave the government the right to expropriate private holdings in excess of stated limits; the owners would be indemnified with twenty-year bonds at 4.5 percent interest. Payment depended on the assessed value of the property for tax purposes (which had invariably undervalued the land). The government distributed the expropriated land in small plots or established cooperatives, which the Institute of Agrarian Reform (INRA) administered. Much of the land redistribution, not surprisingly, took place in Oriente Province, where the peasants had provided early and crucial support for the 26th of July Movement. Eighty-five percent of all Cuban farms fell under the jurisdiction of the reform law, because landownership was so highly concentrated under the old regime.

The land reform began slowly, but its tempo accelerated in response to domestic and foreign pressures. The estates of Batistiano government officials were taken over immediately, followed by intervention of the great cattle estates when their owners resisted Castro's policies. The timing of the expropriation of the American-owned sugar lands was in obvious response to the elimination of Cuba's sugar quota from the American market (1960).

Industrial reforms also began slowly; the government at first took over the management of only one major foreign company, the extremely unpopular telephone company. But conflict with the United States over the initial interventions, the abrogation of the sugar quota,

---

[3] *Superurbanization* is used to describe the vast expansion through internal migration and concentrated industrialization of one city, usually the capital.

and the refusal of the American oil refineries to process Russian oil led to sweeping expropriations of American-owned refineries, factories, utilities, and sugar mills. Next, the government took over the banking system and most urban housing. Finally, the revolutionary regime began to expropriate native-owned businesses.

During the first year of its rule, the Cuban government experimented with three types of agrarian holdings: agricultural cooperatives, INRA-administered farms, and sugar-cane cooperatives, none of which proved successful. Eventually, all became *granjas del pueblo* (state farms). Because of the large-scale character of Cuban agriculture, which was dominated by big ranches and sugar plantations, state farms were considered the most efficient form. Administered by INRA, they usually employed the same workers who had toiled on them before the revolution but paid better wages and offered improved working conditions.

The redistribution of income to workers and peasants resulted in some long-range problems. With more money to spend, Cubans demanded more food, especially meat, consumption of which rose 100 percent. This rising demand led to the overkilling of cattle, which seriously damaged the ability of the government to supply meat in later years. The government lowered rents and utility rates and supplied many services free of charge, which increased disposable income even more. Inevitably, shortages arose, because Cuba no longer imported consumer goods and foodstuffs. The government began rationing in March 1962. The revolutionaries also poured large sums into rural housing, roads, and other improvements, but poor planning wasted scarce resources.

Two other important programs had mixed success during the first three years: agricultural diversification and industrialization. The revolutionary government sought to become more self-sufficient by transferring cane land and idle fields to the production of cotton, vegetable oils, rice, soybeans, and peanuts, which would save badly needed foreign exchange on these previously imported commodities. Industrialization proved too difficult, and the program was officially put off in 1963.

The revolutionaries encountered serious problems in agriculture after 1961, because of their inability to organize, plan, and administer the economy. Although Castro set up a central planning agency, JUCEPLAN, in February 1961, more often than not he ignored or circumvented it with his personal "special" plans. For a long time, the government also ignored the private agricultural sector, a critical oversight because more than half the farmland remained in private hands. In early 1961, in an effort to overcome this neglect, the government established the National Association of Small Farmers (ANAP), which tried to coordinate the production of small farms with national goals. It also furnished credit, set up stores, and organized various associations.

From 1962 to 1970, Cuba put a remarkable portion of its gross national product into investment, but that achievement was largely wasted through inefficient administration and poor planning. Many projects were abandoned unfinished, and those that were completed were often improperly maintained and rendered useless.

The Return to Sugar, 1963–1970: The Ten-Million-Ton Harvest

Experience had shown that Cuba lacked the resources and the administrative and technical expertise to industrialize. As a consequence, Castro decided in 1963 to re-emphasize agriculture and return to intensive sugar production, while continuing the diversification program. Increased agricultural production, it was hoped, would generate large earnings and eventually underwrite future industrialization.

The symbol of this effort was the goal: 10 million tons of sugar to be harvested in 1970. Unfortunately, agriculture, especially sugar, had suffered enormously from well-intentioned but short-sighted policies. The sugar harvests of

1960 and 1961 were extraordinarily successful because they benefited from very favorable weather and because the island's cane was at the age of peak yield. Also, for the first time in a decade, the entire crop was harvested. The sugar harvest of 1962 was the worst since 1955, and subsequent harvests continued to be disappointing. The essential problem was that the revolutionaries, in their fervor to diversify, had ripped up some of the best cane land. They had not replanted cane in two years, and as a result most Cuban cane was well past its peak yield. Moreover, equipment and manpower were badly administered. Transportation and distribution were in chaos.

Sugar mills were damaged and left unrepaired for years. The great effort of the 1970 "ten-million-ton harvest" proved too much for many mills. They were old and mostly American-built; the usable facilities were capable of producing perhaps 6 million tons. Furthermore, in 1968 there were only one-fifth the number of professional cane cutters that there had been a decade before. From 1962 to 1969, agricultural production fell 7 percent. After a slight recovery in 1970, a new slump followed.

The government made considerable efforts to correct the situation. The regime decreed the second Agrarian Law in October 1963; under this law, it expropriated thousands of medium-size farms. State farms became the dominent form of agriculture, controlling 70 percent of the land and taking responsibility for all the major export crops. The government also forced those small farmers who remained to sell their crops to it at low cost.

From 1965 to 1967, Castro launched a new campaign of socialization that centralized the administration of the economy and stressed moral incentives to increase productivity. In effect, the campaign sought not only to achieve economic objectives but also, as mentioned previously, to create a "new socialist man," an ideal communist society. Part of this strategy involved increased aid from the Soviet Union.

In 1963 and 1964, Castro visited Moscow and came away with important trade agreements. The Soviets subsidized the Cuban economy by absorbing over $1 billion in trade deficits between 1961 and 1967.

Cuba and Latin American Guerrilla Movements

During the mid-1960s, the Cuban government, proclaiming its unity with other revolutionary struggles, launched a campaign of support for guerrilla warfare against those Latin American regimes it regarded as reactionary and pro-imperialist. The Cuban government gave much verbal and whatever material support it could to guerrilla fighters throughout the continent. The policy of exporting revolution elsewhere came to an end when Castro's chief aide, Che Guevara was hunted down and killed by U.S.-trained counterinsurgency forces while trying to establish a guerrilla movement in Bolivia in October 1967.

Failure and Reassessment, 1970–1975

The ballyhooed "ten-million-ton harvest" of 1970 failed to reach its acclaimed goal and in the process did extensive damage to the Cuban economy as a whole. To get the 8.5 million tons they eventually harvested, the revolutionaries virtually ruined the sugar industry, and subsequent harvests were generally poor. Resources and manpower were siphoned off from other sectors, causing considerable disruption and turmoil.

The failure of the harvest was the most severe setback suffered by the revolution, and Fidel Castro, whose personal decision it had been, lost some of his prestige. On July 26, 1970, however, he addressed his countrymen and admitted his failure. "We are paying dearly for our ignorance," he said. And he vowed that changes would be made. Castro re-emphasized that sacrifice and hardship lay ahead, but the revolution would go on.

During the next five years, Castro depersonalized the government and institutionalized the revolution. He delegated authority to a new executive committee of the Council of Ministers and gave the bureaucracy wider scope of action and more influence. President Osvaldo Dorticós and Carlos Rafael Rodríguez, a veteran Communist who had fought with Castro in the Sierra Maestra, took charge of Cuba's economic development. Castro reorganized the government so as to draw clear lines of separation between the armed forces, the bureaucracy, and the Communist party. The militia was disbanded and merged into the army. The military was restructured along traditional hierarchical lines, and Cuba got its first revolutionary generals. The judicial system was revamped. In addition, an attempt was made to broaden the popular base of the regime and to strengthen the Communist party. The labor movement was revitalized, a larger role was assigned to the trade unions and the workers' tribunals that saw to the enforcement of labor laws and workers' rights. Steps were taken to involve the workers more actively in the formulation of production goals and plans.

The Cuban leadership also drastically overhauled the revolution's policy of economic development. Sophisticated computerized planning techniques were introduced, and a system of material incentives for workers and managers was inaugurated. After a survey that indicated the 25 to 50 percent of the Cuban working day was wasted because of poor supervision or featherbedding, a work quota system was implemented between 1971 and 1973. It resulted in a 20 percent increase in productivity in just one year (1972). The government also began to differentiate between jobs for pay purposes. No longer were people paid according to their need but rather according to the productivity and complexity of their job. These and other economic reforms led to a dramatic rise in pro-ductivity. For the period from 1971 to 1975, the gross national product grew at an annual rate of more than 10 percent, compared with an annual growth rate of 3.9 percent for the period from 1966 to 1970.

The Institutionalized Revolution

The first Communist party congress in December 1975 ushered in a new era, completing the formal institutionalization of the revolution. The congress adopted Cuba's first socialist constitution, which was approved by nationwide referendum in February 1976. The constitution, which was an attempt to depersonalize government and make it more responsive to the people, provides for a pyramid of elected bodies. At the bottom are popularly elected members of municipal assemblies, who elect delegates to provincial assemblies and to the National Assembly of People's Power. Most of these representatives are Communist party members. Fidel Castro remains entrenched at the top as president of the Council of State (elected from the National Assembly), First Secretary of the Communist party, and Head of Government. The second congress of the Communist party reaffirmed him in these offices in 1980.

Despite (or perhaps because of) its institutionalization, the revolution has encountered severe economic difficulties. Inefficiency and low productivity have proven intractable problems. Cuba, moreover, continues to be heavily dependent on sugar for its economic well-being. From 1976 to 1980 the economic growth rate averaged a disappointing 4 percent a year. At the root of the problem were the lack of professional management, quality control, and labor discipline, all of which added up to poor productivity. One survey, for example, indicated that heavy construction equipment in Cuba was "on line" only 39 percent of the time. Also indicative is the statement by an official in the Ministry of Light Industry in 1981 that "the bulk of clothing now being offered for sale in retail stores was made in 1977." Everything from shoes to televisions is poorly manufactured.

Cuba depends on sugar to as great an extent in the 1980s as at any time in its history. Consequently, the government has spent large sums modernizing the industry. Most sugar cane is harvested by machine; the number of sugar workers has declined sharply since 1959. The first new mills in decades were built. Sugar output reached 8.2 million tons in 1982, second only to the disastrous harvest of 1970. The persistent decline of sugar prices from a high of 60 cents a pound in 1974 to 7 cents in 1982 (actually below Cuban production cost) has wreaked havoc on the economy. In order to maintain its program of development and consumer consumption, Cuba has borrowed heavily abroad (its debt was more than $3 billion in 1983), but the plunge in sugar revenues put the nation in danger of defaulting. To make matters worse the economy suffered from a series of natural disasters in 1980: African swine fever, an outbreak of sugar fungus which destroyed a quarter of the crop, and an infestation of tobacco rust that destroyed the entire crop. Although the economy bounced back in 1981 to grow by 10 percent, it fell again in 1982 to a growth rate of 3.5 percent.

Persistent economic problems led to a massive emigration of Cubans, primarily to the United States, from April to September 1980. The so-called "Mariel exodus" began when Fidel Castro, angered at the Peruvian Embassy's refusal to turn over six Cubans who had taken refuge there, declared that anyone who wanted to leave the island was free to go. He ordered the Cuban guards from the embassy grounds. Within days 10,000 people crowded into its grounds. Various nations in the region, including the United States, offered to take the refugees. More than 125,000 Cubans left, mostly through the port of Mariel. Many sailed aboard dangerously overcrowded, leaky boats.

Achievements

Despite its mixed economic record, the revolution's achievements in the areas of employment, equitable distribution of income, public health, and education are remarkable. Although underemployment is still a problem, unemployment has been virtually eliminated. Cuba has the lowest rate of joblessness in Latin America. Inequalities in the standard of living have been dramatically reduced from the days of Batista; the lower classes in particular have benefited from government policies: rents are controlled, limited to no more than 10 percent of income, as are staple commodities' prices. The regime has occasionally resorted to rationing some food products, the latest was meat in 1977, but it has carried it out fairly. Rural income which was $100 per year in 1959 jumped to between $550 and $850 in 1977. Agricultural workers on state farms get furnished houses with televisions and community recreational centers. Cuban city streets have virtually no beggars and sidewalk vendors, which sets them apart from their Latin American counterparts. Hunger and starvation do not exist; slums are almost wiped out; and the government provides free medical care and education. Cuba has the lowest doctors-to-patient ratio in Latin America. The educational budget amounts to 7 percent of the nation's GNP, the highest in Latin America. The population averages a sixth-grade education; and literacy rates are high. Undoubtedly, most Cubans have benefited from the revolution.

Cuba and the World

From its early years, the Cuban revolutionary government has sent military aid to other Third World countries. It helped the Algerian independence movement and guerrilla groups in Zaire, the Portuguese African colonies, and Tanzania during the 1960s. With the capture of Che Guevara and the economic disasters of the late 1960s, this activity lessened. During the 1970s, as the danger of U.S. invasion diminished and the economy improved, Cuba again took an important role in Africa. It also sent troops to the Middle East and, to a lesser extent, to Southeast Asia. By 1978 Cuba had nearly 40,000 troops in Africa, although the total shrank somewhat thereafter. Most Cubans were stationed in Angola, where they played a key part in the triumph of the current Marxist regime. They have also fought extensively in Ethiopia against Somalia.

Castro has sponsored civilian aid programs in thirty-seven countries, this help following closely Cuban military involvement. By 1980 there were more than 20,000 Cubans abroad in these missions. In 1978 there were 8,500 in Angola alone. Civilian aid consists primarily of medical assistance, education, and construction. Construction has been the Cubans' largest and most ambitious undertaking. They have built major public works projects all over the Third World. Education is next in importance. There are, for example, 2,300 Cuban teachers abroad, half in Nicaragua helping the literacy campaign. Approximately 10 percent of Cuba's doctors and nurses were abroad in 1980.

There are two reasons for these forays abroad. The Cuban government is genuinely committed to the support of international liberation movements. This has been a consistent aspect of the revolution since its initial victory. Its activities have only been limited by lack of means to carry them out. Cubans (and there is a rare general consensus about this) are most definitely not acting as Soviet puppets in their foreign incursions and programs. The policies of the two nations do, however, for the most part, coincide. Increased Cuban activities abroad during the 1970s had more to do with its own domestic situation and the accurrence of op-

portunities in Africa than with Soviet directions. Cuba no longer feared the United States, its economy was improving, its armed forces had been upgraded and professionalized. The prolonged campaign to train professionals and technicians yielded a surplus of personnel for use overseas. Moreover, at the same time, Africa erupted as the Portuguese empire fell apart. Secondly, the Cuban government has used the civilian missions as a way of acquiring much needed foreign exchange. It charges modest amounts for medical and educational aid and substantial sums for construction projects. The latter is a major earner.

What Lies Ahead?

Cuba is overwhelmingly dependent on the Socialist bloc. Nearly 80 percent of its trade is with the Soviet Union alone. Over 60 percent of its imports come from the Soviets. Cuba owes the Soviet Union nearly $5 billion, and there is little likelihood that it will repay this sum any time soon. The Soviet Union has, in addition, probably sunk another $8 billion into various subsidies of the island's economy. The Soviets buy Cuban sugar and nickel at prices above the world market and sell oil to Cuba at below market price. The Soviet share of Cuba's economy has risen steadily since 1975. There is every indication that Cuba will remain heavily reliant on the Soviets.

At the same time, Cuba cannot escape the fluctuations of world market conditions. It must sell sugar to the West, because the socialist countries cannot provide the imports it needs. Because measures taken to diversify its exports have met limited success, Cuba will continue at the mercy of world sugar prices.

In spite of mixed economic prospects, the revolution and its leader Fidel Castro will be secure.

CHAPTER EIGHTEEN

Revolution in Central America: Twilight of the Tyrants?

The July 1979 victory of the *Frente Sandinista de Liberación Nacional* (Sandinist Front for National Liberation) over one of Latin America's oldest tyrannies—the Somoza family dynasty of Nicaragua—was an extraordinary event that reverberated throughout Latin America. Like the Cuban Revolution of 1959, it challenged the geopolitical doctrine that the United States would not allow the success of a social, anti-imperialist revolution in its Caribbean backyard, a part of the world that for almost a century had been its own secure preserve. In Washington, the Sandinist triumph caused gloom and disarray as to how to deal with the new Nicaragua and prevent the spread of the revolutionary virus to its Central American neighbors. It heartened Latin American revolutionaries, their supporters, and all the democratic forces of the region, ending the discouragement caused by a long series of defeats for radical and progressive causes— from the Brazilian counterrevolution of 1964 to the destruction of Chilean democracy in 1973.

Some unique aspects of the Nicaraguan revolution—its blend of Marxism and progressive Catholic thought, its effort to maintain a mix of state and private enterprise—gave food for thought to all who were concerned with the problem of achieving social change in Latin America.

The Carter administration tried to come to terms with the Sandinista regime in the hope of moderating its policies. These efforts ended following the election of Ronald Reagan to the presidency in November 1980. The Reagan administration adopted a posture of fixed hostility toward the Nicaraguan government, accompanied by efforts to isolate and destabilize it. Neighboring Honduras, the poorest and most backward country in Central America, was a typical "banana republic" dominated by the military. It became a base for CIA-organized destabilization activities and armed incursions into Nicaragua by former soldiers of Somoza's National Guard. The Reagan administration also attempted to draw Costa Rica, Central America's only long-standing parliamentary democracy, into the anti-Nicaraguan coalition, which already included Guatemala and El Salvador.

In El Salvador, meanwhile, guerrilla activities against a repressive military-civilian junta had developed into a full-scale civil war by the spring of 1980. The guerrillas had created a revolutionary government (the *Frente Democrático Revolucionario*) with its own army, the *Frente Farabundo Martí de Liberación Nacional*. By the spring of 1983, despite massive infusions of U.S. military and economic aid (over $1 billion) to the Salvadoran government, the rebel forces held about one-fifth of the country and threatened to advance from the thinly populated northern region into its most productive and populous areas. Many observers believed that, short of direct U.S. military intervention, a rebel victory over the poorly led and demoralized government forces was inevitable. Like the Nicaraguan revolution, the struggle in El Salvador had become entangled in international dispute. A growing number of countries supported the insurgent proposals that the conflict be settled by negotiation, but the United States continued to favor a military solution.

Guerrilla movements had risen and waned in Guatemala since 1954, when a counter-revolutionary coup organized and armed by the CIA overthrew a reformist regime and the social changes that it had instituted. The guerrilla struggle gained in intensity and popular support in the late 1970s, even as the level of violence on the part of government security forces and death squads reached new heights. After the Guatemalan military government adopted a scorched earth policy, accompanied by massacres of Indian villagers supposed to support the guerrillas, the guerrillas faded into the mountains and jungles, but the roots of revolution—massive poverty, injustice, and repression—were unchanged and ensured that the revolutionary struggle would revive.

Why should Central America, a region so richly endowed by nature—where United States economic, political, and cultural influence has been so strong—be such a violent land and present such immense contrasts of wealth and poverty? An attempt to answer this question requires a review of the historical background of the area and a more detailed survey of the history of three countries, Guatemala, Nicaragua, and El Salvador, where revolutionary movements have come to power or are in progress.

INDEPENDENCE AND THE FAILURE OF UNION, 1810–1865

On the eve of independence, the five republics—Guatemala, El Salvador, Honduras, Nicaragua, and Costa Rica—that are traditionally included in the region called Central America,[1] were

---

[1] For descriptive convenience, Belize, Panama, and the Panama Canal Zone are usually included in Central America.

CONTEMPORARY CENTRAL AMERICA

provinces of the captaincy general of Guatemala, with its capital at Guatemala City. Under the captain general and his audiencia, a small group of wealthy Creole merchants, organized in a powerful consulado (merchant guild), dominated the economic, social, and political life of the late colony. The guild ruled over trade in Central America, and a tribunal named by the consulado settled all commercial disputes. Through their control of credit, goods, and the system of fairs to which farmers and cattle raisers had to bring their wares, the merchants forced the producers of indigo—the area's most important export—and other staples to sell to them at low prices. Farmers, ranchers, and miners depended on the merchants to supply credit for production

and to export their goods to foreign markets. As a result, they fell into debt, and when prices declined—as indigo prices did between 1800 and independence—many went bankrupt. Tied into the dependency network of Guatemala City and the world, producers concentrated on export products, neglecting subsistence crops, so that food had to be imported. Resentment of this dependent relationship engendered bitter hostility on the part of the other provinces toward Guatemala and its dominant merchant clique.

The large Indian (chiefly Maya) population came under increasing pressure during the Bourbon period to enter the money economy. Tribute in kind was no longer acceptable. Tribute had to be paid in money, and new taxes were assessed. The need to pay tribute in coin forced many Indians to become hacienda peons or migrant laborers, wandering from estate to estate. The Crown also sought to solve its chronic money problems by tapping Indian community or religious brotherhood (cofradía) funds, which the Indians had used in time of trouble to pay tribute; having lost these defenses, the Indians often had to resort to hacienda labor or debt peonage to meet their obligations. Despite the Bourbon dislike for repartimiento and efforts to reduce its use, forced labor drafts were freely used when needed to make Indians and the *castas* (mixed-bloods) work in haciendas, obrajes (workshops), and mines and on public works.

Spain's hold over her American colonies weakened after 1800 as a result of her involvement in European wars, the resulting disruption of trade, and growing political turmoil at home. Central America drifted toward independence. When Mexico declared its independence in 1821, Central America followed suit. City after city declared its independence, not only from Spain, but from Guatemala and rival cities and towns. The captaincy general dissolved into a multitude of autonomous cabildo governments. The transition to independence was complicated by the efforts of Agustín de Iturbide to incorporate Central America into his Mexican empire, efforts that were supported by Central American conservatives and opposed by many liberals. In 1822 a majority of cabildos voted in favor of union with Mexico, but Iturbide's overthrow the next year permanently ended the Mexican connection.

Despite provincial rivalries and resentment against Guatemalan domination, a tradition of Central American unity remained and attempts were made to restore that unity. In 1823 a constituent assembly met and created the federal republic of Central America out of the five former provinces: Guatemala, Honduras, Nicaragua, Costa Rica, and El Salvador. The form of government provoked much debate, with the Guatemalan merchant oligarchy favoring a centralized political structure and representatives of the other provinces demanding a loose federal system. The compromise provided for a federal government with state governments that were "free and independent in their internal government and administration." The constitution had a strong liberal tinge: It abolished slavery and the special privileges of the clergy and established the principles of laissez faire, free trade, and free contract of labor. The next year a Salvadoran liberal, Manuel José Arce, was elected as first president of the republic. Meanwhile the states were forming their own governments. On the state as on the federal level, conservatives and liberals struggled for power: Conservatism—the ideology of the old monopolistic merchant clique, many great landowners, and the church—had its base in Guatemala; liberalism was the dominant doctrine among many large and small landowners of the other states and the small middle class of artisans, professionals, and intellectuals. Behind the façade of elections and universal suffrage, power throughout the area was held by great landowning and mercantile families who often mobilized their private armies of retainers and tenants in a struggle for control of regions and states.

The superficial unity of Central America soon dissolved as it became clear that the states were neither willing nor able to finance both their own governments and the federal government in Guatemala City. Efforts by the federal government to assert its prerogatives by the establishment of a strong army and the collection of taxes to finance its needs led to a destructive civil war between 1826 and 1829. The struggle ended with the defeat of the national government and its conservative leadership by liberal forces headed by the talented Francisco Morazán and the reorganization of the union on a basis of liberal hegemony.

Morazán, elected president of the federal republic and commander of its armed forces, both based in San Salvador, defended it against conservative plots and attacks. At the same time, a former conservative turned liberal, Mariano Gálvez, governor of Guatemala, launched a program for the economic and social reconstruction of his state. "Everything new, everything Republican," proclaimed Gálvez, "nothing of the colonial monarchical system. This is my belief. We must be innovators, because if we are not, independence has done nothing more than change the names of things." The program included the establishment of civil marriage and divorce and secular schools on all levels, anticlerical measures that allowed nuns to leave their orders and reduced the number of church holidays, large land concessions to British companies that were to colonize the land with foreign immigrants and provide it with an infrastructure, and even an agrarian reform that allowed squatters to buy land for half its value and permitted Indians to settle on vacant land. Gálvez also sought to reform Guatemala's judicial system by basing it on the Livingston Code,[2] which provided for trial by jury and habeas corpus and vested power to appoint all judges in the governor of the state. This last feature alienated powerful landed interests who often served as jefes políticos, local officals who combined judicial and administrative functions and were permitted to keep a share of tax collections for themselves.

The loss of the support of local landed interests combined with the ravages of a cholera epidemic that spread over Central America in 1837 to bring down the Gálvez regime and its ambitious reform program. Stirred up by local clergy who proclaimed the epidemic divine retribution for the heresies of civil marriage and divorce, the Indian and mixed-blood masses rose in revolt against Gálvez's radical innovations in law and taxation and the sanitary measures instituted to prevent the spread of disease. The principal

revolt was led by the mestizo Rafael Carrera. In February 1838, at the head of an army of Indians and mixed-bloods whose cry was "Long live religion and death to all foreigners!" Carrera took Guatemala City. In return for a bribe of money for himself and his followers, he agreed to leave but soon threatened to return and sack the city again. The Guatemalans now called on Morazán and the federal army to protect them. Through 1838 and 1839 Morazán continued to battle and defeat Carrera, who retreated into the mountains to prepare for a new attack on the capital. Amid the chaos, the federation of Central America expired. In 1839 Carrera again occupied Guatemala City, this time for good. Morazán, defeated in a last effort to oust him, was forced to flee. He finally found refuge in Peru. Two years later Morazán returned to Central America with a plan to restore the federation, briefly took over Costa Rica, but was captured by his enemies and put to death (1842).

From 1839 until his death in 1865 Carrera dominated Guatemala, either as dictator-president or through his puppets. In 1854, dispensing with the formality of elections, he had Congress name him president for life. Until his death he tried to dominate the rest of Central America, installing conservative puppet presidents in El Salvador and Honduras and generally meddling in the affairs of the other republics. In Guatemala, meanwhile, he implemented a reactionary social revolution that revived the authority of the church, returned church and Indian communal properties to their original owners, brought back Indian forced labor, and even changed the title of local officials from jefe político to the old colonial title of corregidor. What had begun as a lower-class protest against radical innovations, however, was soon taken over by the conservative merchant oligarchy who provided the taxes Carrera needed to pay his army and foreign loans. Conservative ministers drawn from the elite surrounded the dictator. A representative of the great merchant house of Ay-

[2]An influential code of legal and penal reform completed by the American lawyer and statesman Edward Livingston in 1824.

cinena was appointed corregidor of the valley of Guatemala; he controlled the distribution of Indian labor for the cochineal plantations and the city. Alongside the traditional labor arrangements, however, there existed free labor and a money economy, with landless Indians and mestizos working, sometimes under debt peonage, on the plantations.

Similar trends prevailed throughout Central America in the age of Carrera, although labor was freer in most of the area than it was in Guatemala. By the 1850s, a rising world demand for coffee stimulated expansion of the crop (it had been grown on a large scale in Costa Rica since the 1830s), and spurred attacks on Indian communal lands and individual peasant plots. Coffee in Costa Rica, indigo and coffee in El Salvador, made for relative political stability in those countries. In the more backward republics of Nicaragua and Honduras, where cattle barons warred with each other, using their ranch hands as private armies, little centralized authority existed.

Foreign interventions and territorial claims added to the instability created by economic backwardness and political turbulence. In Nicaragua, the British laid claim to the Atlantic Mosquitia coast. In 1848 they disembarked in San Juan del Norte to burn the Nicaraguan flag. The discovery of gold in California gave a new importance to Central America as a transoceanic transit route and sharpened the rivalry of the United States and Great Britain in the area. The threat to the sovereignty and territorial integrity of the Central American republics grew acute as a result of the folly of Nicaraguan liberals, who in 1855 invited the American adventurer William Walker to help them overthrow a conservative regime. Having brought the liberals to power, Walker, supported by a band of some three hundred Americans, staged a coup, proclaimed himself president, legalized slavery, and made English the official language. By mid-1856, in a rare display of unity, Nicaraguan

liberals and conservatives, joined by all the other Central American republics, had combined in a National War against the Yankee intruders, but the Central American army opposing Walker was essentially a conservative army. Defeated in 1857, Walker returned to the United States. He nevertheless made two other attempts to conquer Central America, the last ending in his death before a Honduran firing squad in 1860.

The National War revived the moribund movement for Central American unity. The liberal Gerardo Barrios, who became president of El Salvador in 1859, was a leading advocate of federation. His efforts to realize Morazán's dream provoked Carrera, who was determined to maintain conservative domination over Central America, to send troops into El Salvador and its ally Honduras. The war ended with Barrios's defeat and exile; there were conservative regimes in every Central American republic. In 1865 Barrios attempted to make a comeback but was captured and executed by his enemies. Carrera died in the same year. With his death the violence-filled formative period of Central American history came to an end.

In the last third of the nineteenth century, the three countries we have selected for special study—Guatemala, Nicaragua, and El Salvador—underwent major economic changes in response to the growing world demand for two products that the area was ideally fitted to produce: coffee and bananas. The changes included a "liberal" reform that sought to modernize economic and social structures but left intact the existing class and property relations; the rise of a new dependency based on the export of one or two products, foreign control of key natural resources and much of the infrastructure, and acceptance of U.S. political hegemony. Because these changes were accompanied by concentration of landownership in very few hands, intensified exploitation of labor, and a growing gulf between the rich and the poor, they planted the seeds of today's Central American revolutions.

GUATEMALA

Liberal Reform and A New Dependency, 1865–1944

Carrera's death in 1865 was followed by six years of continuous political and military challenge to conservative rule. The liberals who opposed them were more responsive to changes in the world economy, in particular to the mounting foreign demand for coffee, and the adjustments this required in Guatemala's economic and social structures. In 1871, the liberals seized power; two years later, the energetic Justo Rufino Barrios became president and launched a many-sided reform program. Although a hard, dictatorial man, Barrios had a genuine passion for reform and was an apostle of Central American unity; he died in battle in 1885 in an attempt to unify Central America by force. Under his successors the liberal tradition rapidly lost whatever redeeming qualities it originally possessed. The liberal leaders grew increasingly cynical, corrupt, and repressive, and their professions of faith sounded thin and hollow. Manuel Estrada Cabrera, who held power from 1898 to 1920, became famous for his cruelty. (Miguel Ángel Asturias's novel, *El Señor Presidente*, communicates the nightmarish quality of his reign.) He was finally removed by the expedient of having Congress declare him insane. After eleven years of instability, another strongman, Jorge Ubico, seized power and held it until he, too, was overthrown in 1934.

The liberal reform program included major economic, social, and ideological changes. The ideological reform involved the rejection of clerical and metaphysical doctrine in favor of a firm faith in science and material progress. This called for the secularization and expansion of education at all levels. The shortage of public funds, however, greatly limited public education; as late as 1921 the Guatemalan illiteracy rate was still over 86 percent. Seeking to reduce the power and authority of the church, the liberal governments nationalized its lands, ended its special privileges, and established freedom of religion and civil marriage.

The economic transformation encompassed three major areas: land tenure, labor, and infrastructure. A change in land tenure was necessary for the creation of the new economic order. The old staples of Guatemalan agriculture, indigo and cochineal, were grown by thousands of small and medium-sized producers; coffee, on the other hand, required large expanses of land concentrated in relatively few hands. Under Barrios, there began an "agrarian reform" designed to make such land available to the coffee growers. Church and monastery lands, confiscated by Barrios, were the first target. Next came uncultivated state holdings, which were divided and sold cheaply or granted to private interests, and Indian communal lands. Legislation requiring titles to private property provided the legal basis for expropriation of Indian lands. The principal native beneficiaries of this process were small and medium-sized coffee growers who could purchase or otherwise obtain land from the government. But foreign immigrants, warmly welcomed by the liberal regimes, also benefited by the new legislation. By 1914, foreign-owned (chiefly German) lands produced almost half of Guatemala's coffee. By 1926, concentration of landownership had reached a point where only 7.3 percent of the population owned land.

The land reform in turn helped achieve another objective of the liberal program—the supply of a mass of cheap labor to the new group of native and foreign coffee growers. Many highland Indians who had lost their land migrated to the new coffee-growing areas near the coast. Before Ubico, the most common labor system was debt peonage—legal under Guatemalan law—in which Indians were tied to the *fincas* (plantations) by hereditary debts. Debt peonage was supplemented by the recruitment of Indians who came down from the mountains to work as seasonal laborers on haciendas and plantations to add to their meager income from their own tiny landholdings. Under Barrios, there was also revived the colonial system of mandamientos, under which Indians were required to accept offers of work from planters. The registers of Indians maintained by local officials for this purpose were also used to conscript Indians for military service and public works. Indians who could not pay the 2-peso head tax—the great majority—were required to work two weeks a year (later one month) on road construction.

In 1934 Ubico abolished debt peonage, replacing it with a vagrancy law that required all persons owning less than a stipulated amount of land to carry cards showing that they had worked at least 150 days a year on the haciendas. Indians who failed to comply with this obligation to do "useful work" were jailed.

A third necessity for the new economic order was an infrastructure, particularly road and port facilities for transporting and shipping coffee. Although begun and initially financed with Guatemalan resources, the financing and construction contracts for this infrastructure soon passed into the hands of foreign, predominantly American, companies. The nation's electrical facilities, constructed by German interests and nationalized during World War I under U.S. supervision, were taken over by the American company Electric Bond and Share. Another American firm, International Railways of Central America (IRCA), which was linked to the United Fruit Company through interlocking directors, acquired monopolistic control over land transport in Guatemala and virtual ownership of the major Atlantic port of Puerto Barrios. For its part, the Boston-based United Fruit Company (UFCO) secured a contract in 1901 to carry Guatemalan mail from Puerto Barrios to the United States in its "Great White Fleet" and to carry

bananas, obtained from producers at fixed prices, to the American market. In time the company acquired vast banana holdings of its own on very favorable terms from the Guatemalan government. In the words of Susan Jonas:

The vertical integration, monopolistic at every stage, was complete: from banana lands (and all the necessary installations for company towns), to the IRCA lines, the port facilities, the shipping fleet, and the Fruit Dispatch Company for banana transport and distribution with the U.S. In fact, the Company diversified far beyond what was needed for its banana operations; other subsidiaries included the Tropical Radio and Telegraph Co. (initially constructed by Guatemalans and operated by the government), other transport and shipping lines and numerous (non-banana) food industries. It was, in short, an incipient conglomerate.[3]

The enormous U.S. economic influence based on direct investments, loans, and control over Guatemala's chief foreign market was translated into a growing U.S. tutelage over Guatemala. After World War I, the American embassy became in effect a branch of the Guatemalan government; American ambassadors were approached for favors (support of a president's reelection, for example) in return for cooperation with American corporations.

The 1929 crash in the United States, followed by the long depression of the 1930s, created a crisis for the monocultural economy of Guatemala. During the 1930s, coffee prices declined to less than half the 1929 level. By cutting off European markets, World War II deepened dependence on the United States market and further depressed coffee prices. The crisis in foreign trade led to rising unemployment, wage cuts, and business failure for many small producers.

---

[3] Susanne Jonas, "Guatemala: Land of Eternal Struggle," in R. H. Chilcote and J. C. Edelstein, *Latin America: The Struggle with Dependency and Beyond* (New York: John Wiley & Sons, 1974), p. 143.

Other Latin American countries, particularly the larger ones, took advantage of the crisis of the 1930s and the 1940s to try to reduce their dependence on the advanced capitalist countries by programs of import-substitution industrialization and expansion of the domestic market. For the Guatemalan planter oligarchy and associated export-import interests, closely linked to U.S. enterprises, this did not represent a practical option. Their response to the crisis was to make the masses pay for the depression through wage cuts, intensified exploitation, and reduced government expenditures. Throughout the 1930s, the level of official repression rose; in 1933 alone the government executed some one hundred labor leaders, students, and political dissidents.

The fall of the detested Ubico regime came as a result of the anti-fascist climate of opinion created by United States and Latin American participation in the war against the Axis powers. Although Guatemala, under American pressure, had declared war on the Axis in December 1941, Ubico's pro-fascist views and the ties of many of his close advisers and ministers to German interests were well known. In June 1944 a general strike and antigovernment demonstrations forced Ubico to resign. His efforts to install a puppet president, Federico Ponce, failed when armed workers and students joined rebellious junior military in ousting Ponce. A triumvirate of two army officers and a civilian took over and organized congressional and presidential elections to be held in December 1944. The overwhelming victory of Juan José Arévalo, a prominent educator and scholar who had spent many years in exile, confirmed the demand of the Guatemalan people for the establishment of a government pledged to democracy and social progress.

Revolution and Counterrevolutions
1944–1983

The Guatemalan democratic revolution of 1944 was largely the work of a coalition of urban middle-class groups and discontented junior military, with the small working class as junior partner and the peasantry in a marginal role. The revolutionary leadership favored a capitalist course of development and was friendly to the United States. The program of the Arévalo administration (1945–1951) reflected its desire for a capitalist modernization. An ambitious social welfare program was launched that stressed construction of schools, hospitals, and housing as well as a national literacy campaign. The 1945 constitution abolished all forms of forced labor, and the 1947 labor code established workers' rights to decent working conditions, to social security coverage, and to collective bargaining through trade unions of their own choosing; it also provided for compulsory labor-management contracts. These reforms spurred a rapid organizing drive among urban, banana, and railroad workers, who made a number of limited gains. Labor organization made slower progress in the countryside, and despite appeals from the rural labor confederation, Arévalo made no move toward agrarian reform.

Following the example of many Latin American governments in this period, Arévalo began a program of industrial development and diversification, employing the newly created state bank and other agencies for this purpose. As for the existing foreign economic enclaves (chiefly UFCO and IRCA), Arévalo's policy was not to nationalize but to regulate their operations in the national interest. The government insisted, for example, that UFCO submit wage disputes to arbitration. New laws stipulated that in the future the state or predominantly national companies should exploit natural resources; in industry, foreign investors could operate on the same terms as nationals.

Arévalo's agrarian program was equally moderate. Government programs offered state support to cooperatives and provided agricultural credit and technical assistance. A new law protected tenants from arbitrary ouster by landlords, but the latifundia remained intact, although the constitution of 1945 permitted expropriation of private property in the public interest. As one American observer wrote in 1950, the Arévalo reforms were "not as radical as those of the New Deal in the U.S., or the Labor government in Great Britain."

The pace of reform quickened with the election of Major Jacobo Arbenz to the presidency in 1950. Arbenz defined his objectives thus: "To convert Guatemala from a dependent nation with a semi-colonial economy to an economically independent country; second, to transform our nation from a backward nation with a predominantly feudal economy to a modern capitalist country; and, third, to accomplish this transformation in a manner that brings the greatest possible elevation of the living standard of the great masses of the people."

Arbenz's major strategy to achieve these objectives was import-substitution industrialization, to be accomplished by private enterprise. But the creation of a modern capitalist economy was impossible without an expansion of the internal market—of mass purchasing power—through agrarian reform. The 1952 agrarian reform law provided for the expropriation of holdings over 223 acres, especially idle lands, and their distribution to the landless. Compensation would be made through twenty-five-year bonds at 3 percent interest, with the value determined by the owners' valuations for tax purposes. By June 1954, approximately 100,000 peasant families had received land, together with credit and technical assistance from new state agencies. The agrarian reform inevitably affected UFCO. No more than 15 percent of its holdings of over 550,000 acres were cultivated; the company claimed that it needed these large reserves against the day when its producing lands were worn out or ruined by banana diseases. The land expropriation, coming on top of a series of clashes between the government and UFCO over its labor and wage policies, brought their relations to the breaking point.

The moderate Arévalo had already been attacked in the U.S. media as procommunist. Arbenz's deepening of the revolution, threatening

the profits and properties of UFCO, evoked a much angrier reaction in the United States and caused UFCO's friends in high places to prepare for direct action against Guatemala. By August 1953, President Eisenhower had approved a CIA–State Department plan for the removal of Arbenz. He was to be replaced by the rightist Colonel Carlos Castillo Armas, exiled to Honduras in 1950 for his part in a right-wing coup attempt. Deeply involved in the conspiracy against Guatemala were Secretary of State John Foster Dulles and his brother, CIA director Allen Dulles (both former partners in UFCO's legal counsel), United Nations Ambassador Henry Cabot Lodge, and Assistant Secretary of State for Latin America John Moors Cabot, both UFCO stockholders. A CIA official served as field commander for the operation. With a fund of $6 million and an army of one hundred agents, he set up headquarters in Miami and funneled guns and ammunition through a dummy armaments firm to Castillo Armas's "Liberation Army" of Central American mercenaries. The "Liberation Air Force" consisted of U.S. pilots flying CIA planes. The man in charge of psychological warfare was E. Howard Hunt, later of Watergate fame. His tasks included leaflet barrages, misinformation, subversion of the Guatemalan army, and other activities designed to produce "a spontaneous popular rising."

The arrival in Guatemala of a shipment of Czech arms in May 1954 (the United States had imposed an arms embargo against Guatemala and United States military attachés warned Guatemalan army officers that it would be maintained until they deposed Arbenz) provided a pretext for implementing "Operation Success." In June, Castillo Armas advanced six miles from the Honduras border into Guatemala and waited for his American allies to do the rest. While CIA planes dropped propaganda leaflets and incendiary bombs on the capital, the Guatemalan army remained passive, refusing to turn over arms to the workers and peasants who wanted to defend the revolution. Under intense pressure from his military colleagues, Arbenz resigned and turned over the government to a three-man junta, but the United States ambassador to Guatemala, John E. Peurifoy (designated "theater commander" of "Operation Success" by John Foster Dulles) insisted on the installation of Castillo Armas, the CIA candidate, as president. On July 3, Castillo Armas arrived in the capital in a U.S. embassy plane. Assuming the presidency, he promptly launched a campaign of terror against supporters of the revolution. According to one estimate, eight thousand persons were executed. The land reform of 1952 was revoked, and UFCO and other landowners regained holdings that had been expropriated. Meanwhile Castillo Armas surrounded himself with an entourage that has been described as a gang of "grafters and cutthroats."

The counterrevolution returned power and property to its traditional holders, the landed oligarchy and their foreign allies. The process of land reform was not only checked but reversed; since 1954 the size of the average peasant landholding has decreased, while the percentage of land devoted to commercial farming has increased. But the Guatemalan economy has not stood still since 1954. Two important developments have been the rise of a small dependent industry and some major shifts in the composition of agricultural exports.

Like the Arévalo and Arbenz governments, post-1954 Guatemalan regimes advocated industrialization as a solution to the problems caused by falling prices for coffee and increased competition for the U.S. market from even less developed countries. But there were fundamental differences between the two industrialization programs. The revolutionary governments sought an industrialization based on expansion of the domestic market through agrarian reform and other redistributive reforms and on safeguards against foreign penetration and domination of the national industry. The policy of the counterrevolutionary governments was to industrialize without such reforms or safeguards. The 1961 treaty among Guatemala,

Honduras, El Salvador, and Costa Rica that established the Central American Common Market, combining the upper- and middle-class markets of the area, appeared to provide an adequate consumer base. During the 1960s, in the hopeful climate of the Alliance for Progress, American officials and advisers supported the industrialization program and the Common Market idea, believing that they would promote economic and political stability in the area.

In the absence of controls over the composition of capital and the remittance of profits, however, the net result of the program was a dramatic foreign take-over of Guatemalan industry. By 1968, more than 62 percent of all major manufacturing establishments were controlled by foreigners. Moreover, since much of the new industry is capital- rather than labor-intensive, it has contributed very little to solving the acute problem of unemployment. Thus, although the contribution of manufacturing to the gross national product rose from 10 percent in 1950 to 16.3 percent in 1979, industrial employment as a percentage of overall employment remained almost stable during that period, rising from 11.5 to 12 percent. The shift of foreign investment to manufacturing reflects a general tendency of foreign corporations to eliminate the risks involved in direct investment in agriculture, transport, and utilities, whose visibility made them easy targets of nationalist resentment. The new strategy was illustrated by UFCO's 1958 decision to divest itself gradually of its banana lands (while retaining control over the marketing of bananas).

Since 1954 Guatemala's small industrial working class has been subjected to chronic governmental repression as well as to intimidation and violence by employers using gunmen and private armies. In 1976 some eighty thousands workers were organized, far below the more than one hundred thousand who belonged to unions in 1953. "To be a union leader or active member of a trade union in Guatemala today," declares Amnesty International, "means risking one's life," and many union organizers and trade union activists have lost their lives at the hands of security forces and private gunmen. Although almost all strikes have been declared illegal, workers have struck and they have occasionally won concessions.

Despite a modest advance of industry, Guatemala remains basically a producer of foodstuffs and raw materials. Nevertheless, the composition of its exports has changed considerably as a result of declining coffee prices. Coffee was still the leading export in 1980, but cotton, sugar, and cardamon (used as a spice) ranked second, third, and fourth, respectively, in value. While commercial agriculture has gained, the production of basic grains (wheat and maize) has declined to the point where they have to be imported from the United States. This reflects the continuing concentration of the best lands in the hands of latifundistas, often by usurpation of the plots of mestizo and Indian smallholders, with army and security forces present to prevent armed resistance. The expropriated smallholders must then move onto poor or marginal land or enter the labor force. Since peasant unions are forbidden by law and the minimum wage laws ignored, extremely low wages ($1.12 a day in most jobs in the 1970s) are the rule. A system of debt contracting, similar to that abolished by Ubico, turns many peasants into temporary slaves; the contractor, often assisted by army and police units, rounds up indebted peasants and sells their labor for the harvest to sugar, coffee, or cotton plantations.

Under prodding from the United States, the counterrevolutionary governments have periodically announced programs of "agrarian transformation" (the subversive term "reform" is carefully avoided). Such programs would distribute uncultivated state-owned lands and provide credit and technical assistance to landless peasants. The areas selected for these resettlement programs have usually been inaccessible jungle lands of poor quality, and sometimes the programs have resulted in increased spo-

liation of Indian and mestizo smallholders. This was the case with the major project, begun under President Kjell Laugerud (1974–1978), to cut an east-west road from the Atlantic coast to the Mexican state of Chiapas. This *Carretera del Norte* was expected to open up large tracts of land for peasant resettlement. As the project advanced, high army officers systematically took over the land along the road; the great estates they established were sardonically described by local inhabitants as "the mattresses of the generals." One of the atrocities committed in the course of this "opening up" of the interior filtered to the outside world: the massacre of Panzós in the province of Quiché on May 29, 1978. In this case, reported by qualified observers, Indian peasants who came to assert their title to the land were machine-gunned and more than one hundred men, women, and children were killed. Atrocities of this kind have changed the attitude of the Maya peasantry toward the guerrilla movements; whereas in the 1960s the Indians generally avoided cooperation with the guerrillas, in the 1970s a growing number joined them.

The narrow social base of the post-1954 regimes and the fact that they owe their existence to a flagrant foreign intervention explains their militaristic, repressive character. In the almost three decades since 1954, there has been only one civilian president—Mario Méndez Montenegro, who was elected in 1966—and he was allowed to take office only after he had assured the military that he would not interfere with them and would appoint their nominee as defense minister. It was under Méndez, in fact, that repression and counterinsurgency operations directed as much against peasants as guerrillas reached a climax. In charge of the counterinsurgency was Colonel Carlos Arana, a former military attaché in Washington. Aided by United States military advisers, Arana's "Operation Guatemala" slaughtered an estimated fifteen thousand persons in the department of Zacapa alone between 1966 and 1968.

Some one thousand Green Berets accompanied the counterinsurgency sweeps; U.S. pilots, flying U.S. planes, dropped napalm on peasants; and a U.S. military attaché, Colonel John Webber, promoted the formation of paramilitary groups of great landowners who collaborated with the army in hunting down "subversive peasants." These groups were the prototypes of *La Mano Blanca,* the White Hand, a vigilante organization responsible for many deaths, and other right-wing terrorist groups.

Despite the crushing blows inflicted by this and subsequent counter-insurgency campaigns, the guerrilla movements survived and reached a new height of activity in the mid-1970s, with the formation of the Guerrilla Army of the Poor (*Ejercito Guerrillero de los Pobres*), which scored large gains in an offensive in the heavily Indian department of Quiché in 1976–1977. The resurgence of guerrilla activity was marked by growing cooperation between the guerrilla movements and trade union and peasant organizations. Another significant development was a cleavage in the church between the conservative Archbishop Mario Casariego, firmly loyal to the regime, and many working clergy and some bishops who are sympathetic to "liberation theology" and active in the Catholic *comunidades de base* (grass-roots communities). Their involvement in the daily struggles of the poor brought charges of subversion and attacks by government and paramilitary forces against them; in 1981 alone, twelve priests were killed and many others, including some bishops, were threatened with death. So serious did the situation become that the bishop of Quiché, Monsignor Juan Gerardi, ordered the departure of all his clergy from the diocese as a protest against the killing of clergy and laity. A not unrelated development, perhaps, was a large increase of missionary activity in Guatemala by U.S. Protestant fundamentalist ministers strenuously opposed to the revolutionary movements.

The guerrilla struggle achieved a high point of organizational unity in 1981 following the decision of the three major guerrilla organizations and the Guatemalan Communist party to form a unified command to coordinate their military operations. By the end of 1981 they had scored considerable successes. In many parts of the country public and private transport had virtually ceased; in order to continue operating, many bus-owners were paying "war taxes" to the guerrillas. Army convoys were repeatedly ambushed on country roads. The widespread violence and the growing power of the guerrillas intensified the flight of capital, adding to the economic gloom brought on by low commodity prices and declining industrial activity.

The guerrilla advances produced discord among the military. One group of officers favored a more defensive strategy, controlling what was feasible; others favored an aggressive policy, including "scorched earth" tactics against the areas that were supposed to support the guerrillas. The latter group gained the upper hand in March 1982 when a military coup nullified the presidential election held that month. Claiming that the victorious official candidate had won by fraud, the rebels installed General Efraín Ríos Montt as head of a new three-man junta. Ríos Montt, a born-again fundamentalist Protestant, implemented a "scorched earth" policy against the guerrillas. As explained by the *Latin America Weekly Report* (May 1982), its aim was to clear the mainly Indian population out of the guerrillas' support areas: "Troops and militias move into the villages, shoot, burn, or behead the inhabitants they catch; the survivors are machine-gunned from helicopters as they flee. Any survivors are later rounded up and taken to special camps where Church and aid agencies cope as best they can." American church and humanitarian agencies have recently gathered and published abundant information concerning these genocidal practices. Such information did not deter the Reagan administration from informing Congress that the human rights situation in Guatemala had improved and that therefore he would renew military aid and arms sales to its government.

The experience of Vietnam, Nicaragua, and other countries proves that such counterinsurgency methods, whatever their short-run advantages, in the long run are ineffective and indeed counterproductive. They kill many peasants but few guerrillas. They intensify the hatred of the peasantry for the military murderers and torturers and help to recruit new fighters for the guerrilla forces. The barbaric tactics of the Ríos Montt regime reveal the desperation with which the Guatemalan oligarchy struggles to retain its land and power. It is not too early to say that its effort is bound to fail.

NICARAGUA

Modernization, American Intervention, and Sandino, 1857–1934

The history of Nicaragua for two decades after the collapse of the Central American federation in 1838 was dominated by a struggle between liberals and conservatives. Their responsibility for inviting the American adventurer William Walker to assist them, followed by Walker's attempt to establish his personal empire in Central America, so discredited the liberals that the conservatives were able to rule Nicaragua with very little opposition for more than three decades (1857–1893).

Although coffee was grown commercially as early as 1848, the principal economic activities in Nicaragua until about 1870 were cattle ranching and subsistence agriculture. Indian communities still owned much land, there existed a class of independent small farmers who lived on public land, and peonage was rare. The sudden growth of the world market for coffee created a demand by some members of the elite for land suitable for coffee growing and for a supply of cheap labor. Beginning in 1877, a series of laws required the Indian villages to sell their communal lands; these laws also put the national lands up for sale. These laws effectively drove the Indian and mestizo peasants off their land, gradually transforming them into a class of dependent peons or share-croppers. The passage of vagrancy laws and laws permitting the conscription of natives for agricultural and public labor also ensured the supply of cheap labor needed by the coffee growers. These oppressive laws provoked a major Indian revolt. the War of the Comuneros (1881); its defeat was followed by a ferocious repression that took five thousand lives.

The new class, made up of coffee planters, was impatient with the traditional ways of the conservative cattle raisers who had held power in Nicaragua since 1857. In 1893 the planters staged a revolt that brought the liberal José Santos Zelaya to the presidency. A modernizer in the tradition of Justo Rufino Barrios of Guatemala, Zelaya ruled for the next seventeen years as dictator-president. He undertook to provide the infrastructure needed by the new economic order through the construction of roads, railroads, port facilities, and telegraphic communications. He reorganized the military, separated church and state, and promoted public education. Like other Latin American liberal leaders of his time, he believed that foreign investment was necessary for rapid economic progress, and he granted large concessions to foreign capitalists, especially American firms. By 1909 Americans controlled much of the production of coffee, gold, lumber, and bananas—the principal sources of Nicaragua's wealth.

But Zelaya was an ardent nationalist: He successfully asserted Nicaragua's claim to sovereignty over the Atlantic Mosquitia coast, where the British exercised a protectorate from 1678 to 1894; he was a champion of Central American federation; and he angered the United States by turning down its canal treaty proposal and negotiating with other countries for construction of a Nicaraguan canal that would have competed with the United States–controlled route at Panama. Like Porfirio Díaz in Mexico in the same period, Zelaya had become alarmed over the extent of American economic influence in his country; he sought to reduce that influence by granting concessions to nationals of other countries. Thus, in January 1909 he turned down the offer of a large loan from American bankers in favor of one from a London banking syndicate.

These signs of independence convinced the United States, where imperialist attitudes and policies had flowered since 1898, that Zelaya must go. With American encouragement, a conservative revolt broke out in 1909. American marines were landed at Bluefields on the Atlantic coast, protected the conservative forces there against government attack, and turned over the collectorship of customs to the conservatives. Under military and diplomatic pressure from the United States, Zelaya resigned and in 1910 the conservatives came to power. Their triumph represented a victory for the traditional landed oligarchy and a defeat for its progressive wing, who sought a capitalist modernization.

The conservatives installed Adolfo Díaz, an obscure bookkeeper in an American mining firm in eastern Nicaragua, as president of a puppet regime that hastened to satisfy all the American demands. An American banking firm, Brown Brothers and Seligman, made loans to the Nicaraguan government, receiving as security a controlling interest in the national bank and state railways and the revenues from the customhouse.

The servility and unpopularity of Díaz and his puppet regime provoked a liberal revolt in 1912, led by the young liberal Benjamín Zeledón. The rebels were on the brink of victory when American marines were again sent in at the request of the conservative government. They subjected the city of Masaya, the provisional capital of the rebel government, to an intense bombardment. Ordered by U.S. officials to end his revolt, Zeledón fought on, warning the U.S.

commander that he and his country would bear "a tremendous responsibility and eternal infamy before history . . . for having employed your arms against the weak who have been struggling to reconquer the sacred rights of their fatherland." Zeledón, fighting to the last, suffered defeat and was executed by the conservatives with the apparent approval of the United States. There followed the first U.S. occupation of Nicaragua, with the United States ruling the country through a series of puppet presidents from 1912 to 1925. In return for American protection, the conservative regimes made a number of important concessions, notably the Bryan-Chamorro treaty of 1916, which gave the United States the exclusive right to construct an interoceanic canal across Nicaragua (since the Panama Canal already existed, its real purpose was to prevent any other country from doing the same).

In August 1925, convinced that the conservatives could maintain themselves in power without American assistance, the United States withdrew the marines. Two months later fighting again broke out, and in 1926 the marines returned, ostensibly to protect American and other foreign property. This time they stayed until 1933. The new American strategy was to arrange a peace settlement between cooperative conservative and liberal politicians that would give the latter an opportunity to share in the political spoils. With Henry L. Stimson, President Coolidge's personal representative, as mediator, such a settlement was reached in 1927. Under American supervision, presidential elections held in 1928 and 1932 gave victory to the liberals. But real power remained in American hands; as historian Ralph L. Woodward remarks about the first elected liberal president, José María Moncada: "The United States controlled his regime from a number of points: The American Embassy, the Marines . . .; the Guardia Nacional, with its United States Army officers; the High Commissioner of Customs; the Director of the Railway; and the National Bank."

Only one liberal officer, Augusto César Sandino, refused to accept the U.S.-sponsored peace treaty of 1927. The mestizo son of a moderately well-to-do, ardently liberal landowner and an Indian servant girl, Sandino had worked as a mechanic and had lived in postrevolutionary Mexico between 1923 and 1926. There he was exposed to radical nationalist and social revolutionary ideas. He returned to Nicaragua in 1926 to join the liberal struggle against a conservative puppet regime. He met with a cool reception from José María Moncada, the head of the liberal army; Moncada later claimed that he immediately distrusted Sandino because he heard him speak of "the necessity for the workers to struggle against the rich and other things that are the principles of communism." In fact, although no Marxist, Sandino had profound sympathy with all the disinherited and planned to make far-reaching social and economic changes after achieving his primary goal of the departure of American troops. "Our Army," he wrote in 1932, "is preparing to take the reins of political power to proceed with the organization of large cooperatives of Nicaraguan workers and peasants, who will exploit our own natural resources for the benefit of the Nicaraguan family in general."[4] He also began to set up agricultural cooperatives in the territory under his control; these were destroyed after his death.

Unable to convince the liberal leaders that he should be given an independent command, Sandino organized his own force, consisting mainly of miners, peasants, workers, and Indians. From the first, Sandino regarded the American proposals with suspicion. He refused the bribe of a governorship of a province and other rewards offered by Moncada if he accepted the American plan calling for the rebels to lay

down their arms and accept an American-supervised election. "I decided," he wrote, "to fight, understanding that I was the one called to protest the betrayal of the Fatherland."

For seven years (1927–1933), Sandino's guerrilla army waged war against the United States Marines and the U.S.-trained and equipped Nicaraguan National Guard. It was "one of the first modern examples of what a guerrilla army with mass popular support could do against a technologically superior invader." Learning from early defeats and heavy losses when he attempted to meet the enemy in frontal combat, Sandino developed a new kind of warfare based on hit-and-run attacks, ambushes, temporary occupation of localities and, most important of all, close ties with the peasantry, who provided a supply base for the guerrillas and gave them accurate information about enemy movements and other assistance.

In the United States, meanwhile, the war was growing increasingly unpopular, and eventually Congress cut off all funding for it. It became clear to the new Hoover administration that an American victory in Nicaragua was impossible without large-scale commitment of American forces, and this, at a time when the United States was suffering from a severe depression, would be politically disastrous. The administration decided, therefore, to extricate itself from the Nicaraguan quagmire—but without loss of control. The instrument of that control should be a powerful National Guard, created by the marines in 1927 and trained and equipped by them. In February 1932, Secretary of State Stimson announced the withdrawal of one thousand of the marines in Nicaragua. The rest were to be recalled after the American-supervised presidential election in November 1932. In that election the conservative Adolfo Díaz, widely regarded as an American puppet, was pitted against Juan B. Sacasa, generally regarded as a more independent and genuine liberal than his predecessor Moncada. The election results gave Sacasa a substantial majority, and on Jan-

---

[4] Cited in Harry E. Vanden, "The Ideology of the Insurrection," in Thomas W. Walker, ed., *Nicaragua in Revolution* (New York: Praeger Publishers, 1982), p. 46.

General Sandino (third from left) and his staff. To his right is Salvadoran Agustín Farabundo Martí. (Courtesy of the National Archives)

uary 1, 1933, he was sworn in as president. In the meantime, the U.S. minister to Nicaragua, Matthew Hanna, had personally picked a new director of the National Guard to replace its American head. That replacement was Anastasio Somoza García, a liberal general who had links to the prominent Moncada and Sacasa clans. Somoza had served as foreign minister and in other official capacities under Moncada and had lived in the United States. He spoke fluent English. "The Minister and his wife," we are told, "were impressed by Somoza's absolute mastery of the English language and were captivated by his effervescent personality. Mrs. Hanna thought Tacho Somoza a smooth tango and rumba dancer."

Soon after Sacasa's election, he wrote Sandino proposing a peace conference. The election and postelection developments created a dilemma for Sandino. He had promised to lay down his arms after the marines left, and the last marines left on January 2, 1934. But he profoundly mistrusted Sacasa's entourage, and especially Anastasio Somoza, who demanded that Sacasa order the total disarmament of the *Sandinistas*. In February 1934, Sacasa invited Sandino to Managua for negotiations, giving assurances for his security. In these negotiations Sandino demanded that the National Guard be disbanded— a demand that angered Somoza—but as the talks ended the president and Sandino appeared to be moving toward agreement. On February

21, the president held a farewell dinner, but as Sandino, his brother, and two Sandinist officers were leaving they were arrested by Somoza's officers, taken to the airfield, and shot. Questioned by Sacasa, Somoza protested his innocence; he later assumed full responsibility for the murders. It was his first step toward the establishment of a tyranny that would oppress the Nicaraguan people for well over four decades.

The Somoza Era

Following the assassination of Sandino, Somoza gradually consolidated his political power, more and more openly defying President Sacasa. With the aid of a fascist-type paramilitary force known as the Blue Shirts, Somoza easily secured election to the presidency as the liberal candidate in 1936, taking care to combine the post with that of director of the National Guard. Since the Guard not only represented the military power of the country but controlled its communications and many other vital services, "it was hardly an exaggeration to say that the Guardia was official Nicaragua." With such means at his disposal, Somoza had no difficulty extending his term of office indefinitely, ruling directly as president or indirectly through puppet presidents until 1956, when he was assassinated, or *ajusticiado* (brought to justice) as Nicaraguans see it, by the young poet Rigoberto López Pérez, who was killed on the spot. Thoroughly cynical and self-seeking, Somoza represented the total degeneration of the liberal ideology that had inspired the progressive acts of a Barrios or Zelaya. Always obsequiously pro-American, he cut his ideas to fit the prevailing American style; a warm admirer of Hitler and Mussolini, he became a great friend of democracy when the United States moved toward war with the Axis powers in the 1930s. President Franklin D. Roosevelt in turn professed admiration for Somoza's democratic and progressive ideas and received him with all honors when he visited the United

States in 1939. The saying ascribed to Roosevelt, "Somoza is a S.O.B but he is our S.O.B" may be apocryphal, but it accurately sums up the American official posture toward the Nicaraguan despot. American friendship for Somoza brought him loans from the Export-Import Bank and other U.S. agencies as well as assistance in establishing a military academy to turn out officers for the National Guard. Graduates of the school usually spent their senior year at the School of the Americas, the United States military training center in Panama.

Following Somoza's assassination in 1956, his elder legitimate son and vice-president, Luis Somoza Debayle, took over. Somoza's younger son, Anastasio Somoza, Jr., a West Point graduate, assumed the post of director of the National Guard. Luis was president from 1956 to 1963, then allowed puppet presidents to rule from 1963 to 1967, when he died. In that year Anastasio Somoza, Jr. had himself elected president for a term that was to have lasted until 1971. Once in office, however, he amended the constitution to allow himself another year, then retired for two years while a puppet junta presided over the writing of a constitution that permitted him to be re-elected for another term, which was supposed to run until 1981.

Students of the Somozas found differences in style among them; Luis was regarded as more easygoing and less rapacious than his father or brother. These differences, however, were probably less a matter of personality than adaptations to the changing phases of U.S. Latin American policy. The relative mildness of Luis's rule appeared to reflect the reformist and developmentalist stress of the Alliance for Progress of the 1960s. In fact, all three dictators ruled Nicaragua as a personal estate for their benefit and that of their domestic and foreign allies. By 1970 the Somoza family controlled about 25 percent of the agricultural production of the country and a large proportion of its industry; the total wealth of the family was estimated to be $500 million. American firms also enjoyed profitable investment opportunities in the food-processing industry and mining. Both foreign and domestic employers benefited from the repressive labor policies of the regime, but native capitalists grew increasingly unhappy with the monopolistic propensities of the Somoza family. The church, originally aligned with the Conservative party, shifted its support to the first Somoza and generally remained loyal to the family until the 1960s, when it joined the Christian Democratic party in opposition to Anastasio Jr.'s plans for his perpetual reelection. From first to last, however, the ultimate foundation of the family's power was the National Guard, whose top command always remained in the hands of a Somoza. Its loyalty was cemented by a deliberate policy of allowing the Guard to become "a sort of Mafia in uniform," engaged in a large variety of rackets, legal and illegal. The Guard knew very well that the downfall of the Somozas would spell its ruin as well.

While the dynasty and its allies prospered, the economic and social condition of the Nicaraguan people steadily worsened as a result of the unchecked exploitation of rural and urban labor and the developmental programs of the Somoza era. Responding to growing world demand for new products, especially cotton, the Somozas opened up new lands to the planter class, primarily in the Pacific lowlands. Once again, as during the coffee boom a century earlier, many peasant families were driven from the land and forced to migrate to the cities. The 1960s saw some advance of industry within the framework of the Central American Common Market and regional integration, but this capital-intensive industry provided relatively little new employment, and a rapid rate of urbanization, without a corresponding increase in employment, greatly aggravated all the social problems. Nicaragua under the Somozas had one of the worst income distributions in Latin America; in 1978 the lower 50 percent of the population had an annual per capita income of $256.

Resistance to the Somoza dictatorship had

begun in the 1950s, with a series of unsuccessful revolts led by the irrepressible Pedro Joaquín Chamorro, publisher of the highly respected *La Prensa* and son of parents from two of the most powerful conservative clans—a fact that explains why he was pardoned and allowed to return to Managua after each revolt. A more serious threat to the dictatorship arose with the formation in 1961 of the Sandinist Front for National Liberation (FSLN) founded by Carlos Fonseca, Silvio Mayorga, and Tomás Borge and composed largely of students. Its initial efforts to organize guerrilla warfare in the mountains met with defeat, for the guerrillas had made the mistake of "moving into the zone without first undertaking preparatory political work, without knowing the terrain, and without creating supply lines." However, the rebels gradually improved their tactics and their organizational structure and attracted a growing number of recruits, especially among students in the cities.

A turning point in the recent history of Nicaragua was the devastating earthquake of December 1972, which killed 10,000 Nicaraguans and reduced the entire center of Managua to rubble, wiping out almost all businesses. There was immense public indignation over the shameless behavior of the Somozas, who diverted large amounts of foreign international aid into their own pockets and those of the National Guard. The center of Managua remained "an unreconstructed moonscape" until the Sandinista victory, for Somoza and his cronies had bought large parcels of land on the periphery of the city where they built new houses and shops after the quake, profiting from the disaster.

In December 1974, the FSLN scored a major political and propaganda coup when a group of Sandinistas stormed a party in Managua attended by leading figures of the regime and seized forty of the guests. They were held as hostages until the Sandinistas obtained a ransom of $5 million, freedom for fifteen political prisoners, and a flight to Havana. Somoza responded by declaring a state of siege and launching a brutal repression in the rural areas where the FSLN was believed to be operating. In November 1976 the FSLN suffered a heavy loss when the Guard ambushed and killed its founder and principal ideologist, Carlos Fonseca.

In January 1978 the Somozas committed an act of folly that largely contributed to their downfall. Stung by a series of articles in *La Prensa* about the commercial blood-plasma operation through which Somoza sold the blood of his people in the United States, the family or one of its members gave orders for Pedro Joaquín Chamorro's liquidation. Two cars filled with professional gunmen approached the car Chamorro was driving through the ruins of old Managua and fired several blasts of buckshot at him point blank. The murder of a much loved and courageous journalist provoked an effective general strike that only ended after considerable violence and repression by the National Guard, but its repercussions continued. The crime alienated from the regime sections of the elite who could tolerate the murder, jailing, and torture of peasants and Sandinistas, but who were shocked at the killing of a member of an old privileged family like Chamorro. "If Pedro Joaquín Chamorro could be killed," writes Professor Thomas Anderson, "then everyone was in danger, and the Somozas would have to go. This became the thinking of the Nicaraguan elite."

The Chamorro affair, the general strike, and a brutal National Guard attack on an Indian community that was commemorating the forty-fourth anniversary of Sandino's assassination with a Catholic celebration strengthened the FSLN and contributed to a general broadening of the resistance movement. Against this background, publication of a letter from President Jimmy Carter to Somoza, congratulating him on his "concern to improve human rights in Nicaragua," created astonishment and anger. In August 1978 the Sandinistas launched their most audacious operation to date. Invading the National Palace, twenty-five guerrillas seized as hostages most of the members of the Chamber of Deputies and some 2,000 public employees. After frantic negotiations, Somoza agreed to most of the Sandinist demands: release of 59 Sandinista prisoners, a huge ransom, and a safe flight for the guerrillas and released prisoners to Panama. This development was soon followed by another prolonged general strike and a spontaneous uprising in the city of Matagalpa by *muchachos* (youngsters), who forced the National Guard to retreat to their barracks and held out for two weeks. On September 8, the FSLN launched uprisings in four cities, León, Masaya, Chinandega, and Managua; these were joined the next day by Estelí. With their headquarters surrounded by civilian and FSLN combatants, the Guard called in Somoza's air force for a ferocious bombing of the cities before the ground forces retook them one at a time. This was followed by a house-to-house search in a genocidal "Operation Cleanup," with a death toll of some 5,000 persons.

Alarmed by the September uprisings, the United States attempted to mediate a compromise between Somoza and his traditional elite opponents through a committee of the Organization of American States (OAS). In Nicaragua, it tried to work through the Broad Opposition Front (FAO), an anti-Somoza coalition of businessmen, liberals, and some trade unions. The U.S. initiative was frustrated by Somoza's obstinate refusal to resign and the withdrawal of liberal factions from the mediation process, charging that the OAS commission wanted "*Somocismo* without Somoza." Meanwhile, the FSLN, overcoming the differences over insurrectionary tactics of three groups within it, created a nine-man directorate.

The September uprisings were followed by a mobilization of both sides for a final struggle. Somoza prepared for the worst by liquidating his vast assets and shipping his capital abroad. Meanwhile the FSLN, aided by the Social Democratic parties of Western Europe and governments as diverse as those of Costa Rica, Panama, Venezuela, and Cuba, restocked its arms supply with weapons purchased on the international arms market. The regular FSLN army expanded from a few hundred to several thousand men. Throughout the country the network of neighborhood defense committees established after the September revolts worked feverishly to prepare for the coming struggle by stockpiling food and medical supplies. Comunidades de base (Catholic grass-roots organizations) took an active part in these preparations; a few priests even joined the FSLN.

In June 1979 the FSLN announced a general strike and the launching of a final offensive. Barricades were erected in working-class urban neighborhoods, and the FSLN began attacks in all parts of the country. On June 8, having infiltrated Managua, the Sandinistas launched their offensive in the capital, occupying barrios on both sides of the central zone. Somoza, retreating into his recently constructed bunker, in the fortress of La Loma, ordered a counterattack that included a massive air and artillery bombardment of the city. "The devastation of June 1979 finished what the earthquake had spared," writes Professor Thomas Anderson. "Driving along the Carretera del Norte, early in June 1979, this writer was reminded of photos of the destruction of Hiroshima. Ruined factories with twisted girders, burnt-out machinery, and parts of vehicles lay everywhere."

On June 27, the Sandinistas made an orderly retreat of some 12 miles to Masaya in what proved to be a very successful tactical maneuver. From Masaya they fanned out to encircle the capital, pinning the Guard against Lake Managua. The encirclement was completed on July 5, leaving only one way out of the capital, via the airport six miles east of the city. The Sandinistas could have taken in at will but allowed it to remain in the government's hands, perhaps to give the Somozas and their entourage an

opportunity to leave the capital and thus avoid another bombardment and battle. With victory in sight, the Sandinist directorate named a provisional government, a five-member junta that included three Sandinistas; Alfonso Robelo, the leader of the businessmen's opposition to Somoza; and the widow of the martyred Pedro Joaquín Chamorro.

Meanwhile the United States made last-minute efforts to avoid the coming to power of a radical revolutionary regime. It called on the Organization of American States to send a "peacekeeping" force to Managua but was unanimously rebuffed by the OAS. Then it sent a special representative to Nicaragua to try to persuade the FSLN to broaden the base of the new junta. But the Sandinistas pointed out that they had already made a large concession by including the conservative Robelo and the moderate Violeta Chamorro in the junta; inclusion of the persons nominated by the United States—one was a general of the National Guard and another a personal friend of Somoza's—would ensure the preservation of "*Somocismo* without Somoza."

Under intense pressure from Archbishop Miguel Obando y Bravo and other influential quarters to accept his inevitable defeat and to spare the capital a new assault, Somoza agreed on July 16 to go into exile in Florida with his entourage, including his mistress and his son Anastasio III ("Tachito"). The next day he drove to the airport and left Nicaragua forever. Two days later the FSLN and its government entered Managua.

The Sandinistas in Power

The cost of the Sandinist victory in lives and material destruction was enormous. Estimates of the dead ranged up to fifty thousand, or a loss of 2 percent of Nicaragua's population; as Professor Thomas Walker points out, an equivalent figure for the United States would be around 4.5 million people, or over 75 times the U.S. death toll in the Vietnam war. The material damage was estimated at $1.3 billion; the national debt, a large part of which represented sums that Somoza had diverted into his foreign bank accounts, stood at $1.6 billion.

The government that presided over the immense task of national reconstruction consisted of four parts. The official government included the five-member junta, its Cabinet or Ministries of State, and the Council of State, a legislative and consultative assembly in which a broad variety of mass and economic organizations were represented. The composition of these bodies reflected the sincere desire of the Sandinist leaders to maintain a pluralistic system and approach to the solution of the country's problems. In the first Cabinet, in addition to Marxists like Tomás Borge, minister of the interior, and Jaime Wheelock Román, minister of agriculture, sat two bankers and two Catholic priests, the Maryknoll Father Miguel D'Escoto, minister of foreign relations, and the Trappist monk Ernesto Cardenal, minister of culture, "making Nicaragua probably the only country in the world with Catholic priests in the cabinet." From the first, however, it was understood that these formal organs of government were responsible to the nine-member directorate of the FSLN that had created them. The directorate had direct control of the Sandinist armed forces and police. Elections have been repeatedly promised for 1985, but the virtual state of war in which Nicaragua soon found itself as a result of CIA-organized efforts to destabilize and overthrow the Sandinist regime may delay their holding.

Economic problems dominated the agenda of the new government. One immediate problem was that of repairing the ravages of war and the earthquake of 1972: shattered houses, water lines, communications, and the like. This task was mainly entrusted to the municipalities and the Sandinist Defense Committees. It was completed with such speed that visitors to Nicaragua

in the fall of 1979 marveled at the relatively normal appearance of the country. Food shortages were another serious problem and required the importation of great quantities of foodstuffs, mostly financed with foreign donations. Meanwhile emergency food crops were sown so that domestic supplies of food would be available by the middle of 1980. The work of repair was combined with food-for-work schemes to provide a temporary solution for the vast unemployment that was a legacy of the war.

What to do about the national debt was a vexing question for the new government, for it knew well that many of the more recent loans had served only to swell the bank accounts of Somoza and his cronies. It decided, however, to agree to pay all the loans, even the corrupt ones, for both economic and political reasons. The Sandinistas wanted to retain access to Western loans and technology; they also wished to disprove the charge that the new Nicaragua was a Soviet or Cuban "puppet," solely dependent on the socialist bloc for economic and political support. The socialist countries, particularly the Soviet Union and Cuba, in fact gave considerable aid in the form of food shipments and other supplies. Cuba also sent large numbers of teachers and doctors to assist in the work of reconstruction.

The international lending agencies and Western governments, for their part, hoped that financial aid to Nicaragua would enable the private sector of the country to survive and keep the economy pluralistic. Negotiations with the bankers resulted in agreements to stretch out payments and scale down interest rates on the old loans and for the banks to make new emergency loans to Nicaragua. The principal difficulty in renegotiation arose with the United States. The Carter administration agreed to make a new loan of $75 million, chiefly for aid to the private sector. When Ronald Reagan came to the presidency, however, he froze the remaining $15 million of the loan, alleging that Nicaragua was sending arms to the rebels in El Salvador. Thereafter Nicaragua had to rely for aid on the socialist countries, friendly social democratic governments of Western Europe, and Third World countries, including Brazil.

The Sandinist government was avowedly socialist, but it recognized that private enterprise had a vital role to play in the reconstruction of the national economy. The state, however, became the most decisive and the most dynamic element in the economy and in the provision of social services, particularly health, education, housing, and the like. The strengthening of the state sector was a direct result of the take-over of the enormous properties of the Somoza dynasty and its allies. These properties became the basis of the People's Property Area: They included half of the large farms over 500 hectares, a quarter of all industry, large construction firms, hotels, real estate, an airline, a fishing fleet, and so on. All in all, the expropriation of the holdings of Somoza and his supporters placed approximately 40 percent of the gross national product in the hands of the state. The banking system and foreign trade were completely nationalized.

These expropriations, however, left 60 percent of the GNP in the hands of the Nicaraguan capitalist class. They continued to control 80 percent of agricultural production and 75 percent of manufacturing. The policy of the Sandinist government was to avoid radical changes that might cause a rupture with the "patriotic bourgeoisie," the results of which would be disastrous for the economy. At the same time the government insisted on safeguards with respect to working conditions, wages, hours, and the like that would at least modestly improve the life of Nicaraguan workers. It also encouraged the trade unions to watch over the proper functioning of factories so as to prevent decapitalization, slowdowns in production, and other sabotage by capitalists hostile to the revolution. The result was a built-in tension between the government and a section of the bourgeoisie.

Partly because of this tension, partly because of objective conditions—lack of foreign exchange to buy inputs, obsolete machinery, and other problems—private businessmen began dropping out of manufacturing or failing to invest. In 1982, forty-four firms shut their doors or effectively stopped operations, with a loss of 2,800 jobs. In the same year, the output of the private sector in industry declined 11.7 percent, while that of the state sector (which now accounts for one-third of the total investment in industry) rose by 4.1 percent. Some progress is being made in import substitution through the rebuilding of obsolete machinery and the construction of new machinery that does not require imported spare parts.

The growth of the public sector has been most marked in agriculture. Land reform was placed under the *Instituto de Reforma Agraria* (INRA), which by the end of 1979 had confiscated without compensation over one-fifth of Nicaragua's cultivable land. This land belonged to persons or corporations affiliated with the Somoza regime. The government proposed to maintain these estates as productive units rather than to divide them into small parcels. Most of these lands were large farms that had been operated as capital-intensive enterprises, so parcelization would have resulted in heavy production losses. The decision was made to convert many of these estates into state farms, combined into 170 productive complexes, which in turn formed 27 agricultural enterprises. Others were organized as production cooperatives, called Sandinist Agricultural Communes. In late 1980 there were about 1,327 of these cooperatives. INRA simultaneously tried to improve the living conditions of state-sector workers through the establishment of clinics, schools, and housing projects. In 1980 more than fifty thousand workers worked full time in the state sector. In 1979–1980 the state sector accounted for 20 percent of the production of coffee, 15 percent of cotton production, and 15 percent of livestock production.

Although the government favored state farms and production cooperatives as basic agricultural units, small independent farmers were not neglected. Agricultural credit for small producers was greatly expanded, and they were encouraged to form credit and service cooperatives. In 1979–1980, there were 1,200 of these coops organized; they received over 50 percent of the agricultural credit extended by the government in the same period. In 1979–1980, small farmers accounted for 87.2 percent of the production of maize, 79.1 percent of beans, 73 percent of livestock, 30 percent of coffee, and 18 percent of cotton.

Even after the confiscation of the estates of the Somozas and their supporters, large commercial farms producing such crops as cotton, coffee, cattle, and sugar still held 66.5 percent of Nicaragua's cultivable land. The relationship between this private agricultural sector and the revolutionary government is an uneasy one. Most of the large landowners despised the Somozas, resented their hoggish propensities, and welcomed their overthrow. But the rules of the game have changed, and the new rules are not always to their liking. Landowners can no longer mistreat their workers; they must comply with reform legislation defining the rights of tenants and workers. Despite the government's assurances that it wants to preserve a private sector, large landowners are understandably nervous about their future. The commercial farmers and cattle ranchers defend their interests through their own associations, which negotiate with the government over prices, acreage quotas, and the like. The commercial farmers have access to credit at low interest rates, and a coffee stabilization fund was established to protect growers against fluctuations in the world market. The economic importance of this sector is evident from the fact that in 1979–1980 it accounted for 62 percent of the production of cotton and 55 percent of the production of coffee.

The current difficulties of Nicaraguan agriculture are not due primarily to inadequate volume of production. 1982 saw a record coffee crop, with a yield 100,000 quintals (10 million kilograms) more than predicted. Nicaragua's problems stem above all from falling world prices for its major export crops. Sugar, which sold for 24 cents a pound in 1981, sells for 9 cents in 1983. Natural disasters also hurt production of staple foods in 1982. In May flooding destroyed 20,000 acres of just-planted basic grain crops, destroyed $3.6 million in stored grains, and caused $350 million in damage to the national economic infrastructure according to a United Nations survey. A drought in July and August caused estimated losses of $47 million. Finally, the greatly increased scale of CIA-organized counterrevolutionary activity since 1981, diverting manpower and resources to military purposes, has caused serious damage to Nicaraguan agriculture and to the economy in general—probably a major aim of the U.S. destabilization program.

The implacable pressure of the Reagan administration on Nicaragua represents a threat not only to its economy but to the existence of the revolutionary government. Although the Carter administration's policy was "more than a little schizophrenic," once the FSLN was firmly in power it made a serious effort to come to terms with the revolution, hoping thereby to enable capitalism to survive in Nicaragua. With the election of Ronald Reagan to the presidency, the U.S. attitude changed drastically. Even earlier, a "get-the-Sandinistas" plan was outlined in the pre-election "Santa Fe Document." *Newsweek* (November 8, 1982), quotes an insider as reporting that the driving forces behind the operation were Alexander Haig, Reagan's secretary of state, and Thomas Enders, then assistant secretary of state for Latin America. To further the plan, General Vernon Walters, Haig's ambassador at large, was sent to discuss possible joint operations with conservative Latin American governments, including Argentina, Guatemala, and Honduras.

The Reagan administration authorized formation of a paramilitary force of ex-National Guardsmen, with an acknowledged budget of $19 million. In a move recalling the 1954 coup against Guatemala, Honduras was converted into a staging area for the Nicaraguan operation. Beginning in 1981, Argentine and U.S. advisers trained the *Somocistas* and assisted them in making raids into Nicaragua, killing hundreds of Nicaraguan soldiers and civilians and destroying bridges and construction equipment.

The "secret war" against Nicaragua quickened its pace when Ambassador John Negroponte, a veteran of Vietnam and an Enders protégé, arrived in Honduras in 1982. *Newsweek* quotes a Washington insider as remarking: "Negroponte was sent down there by Haig and Enders to carry out the operation without any qualms of conscience." Although Honduras formally returned to civilian rule in January 1982 when liberal President Roberto Suazo Córdova assumed office after nine years of military rule, real power is held by General Gustavo Adolfo Álvarez, who in turn takes his orders from Negroponte. With Negroponte masterminding the operation, the CIA station in Honduras has grown to an admitted fifty employees, plus a large number of secret agents, including many Vietnam veterans who are now mercenaries under contract to the CIA. United States military aid to Honduras, under $2 million in 1980, grew to $10 million in 1981. According to some sources, American aid will reach as high as $144 million in 1982–1983, with some of it coming from a hidden budget.

In March 1983, the operation moved into high gear when several thousand *Somocistas* and other mercenaries, supported by Honduran troops, invaded Nicaragua at several points on its northern border with Honduras. Simultaneously, in a gesture of "gunboat diplomacy" that must have evoked unpleasant memories in Nicaragua, several U.S. warships were sent to Nicaragua's Pacific coast, ostensibly to monitor suspected movements of arms from Nicaragua to rebels in El Salvador. By the end of March,

despite claims of victory from the invaders' radio, the Nicaraguan armed forces and militia had crushed the counterrevolutionary attacks, although the *contras*, as they were familiarly called by both sides, continued to make raids, mostly of the hit-and-run variety. Meanwhile, in a U.N. Security Council meeting called at Nicaragua's request, representatives of the Sandinist government denounced the attacks, charged the United States with responsibility for them, and proposed direct negotiations between Nicaragua, the United States, and Honduras to settle their disputes peacefully. Inside and outside the United Nations, the Nicaraguan position was supported by a large majority of the international community. In Honduras, public opinion strongly opposed Honduran participation in the CIA-organized operation, and fears were expressed that it might drag Honduras into a disastrous war with its neighbor. In the United States Congress there were calls for an investigation to determine whether the CIA was involved in efforts to destabilize the Nicaraguan government in violation of U.S. law.

By mid-July 1983, it appeared that what some called the Reagan administration's Bay of Pigs had aborted. The Sandinistas had driven the major counterrevolutionary force, the so-called *Fuerza Democrática Nicaraguense* (FDN) back into its Honduran sanctuaries, and probably only the wish to avert an open war with Honduras, with all its incalculable consequences, prevented their pursuit and total rout of the contras. A smaller group of guerrillas operating from the south along Nicaragua's border with Costa Rica, headed by the former Sandinist commander Edén Pastora, announced that it was ceasing its activities. A *Time* (July 4, 1983) correspondent with the contras on the Honduran border found that an atmosphere of discouragement had "replaced the euphoria of early spring."

The international reaction to the March crisis reflected the fact that, despite the U.S. efforts to isolate Nicaragua economically and politically, its international prestige had steadily grown.

In October 1982, for example, Nicaragua won a major diplomatic victory with its election to the U.N. Security Council as representative of the Latin American area. Nicaragua received 104 votes, while the U.S. candidate—the Dominican Republic—received 50. None of the other Central American republics voted for Nicaragua, but the great majority of the South American states voted in its favor. Some observers commented that the vote was an international plebiscite on the Nicaraguan Revolution.

Within Nicaragua, the American intervention served to unify the people around their government as never before. Father Martín Mateo, director of the Agricultural School in Estelí, explained: "While the truth is that Nicaragua's problems are caused by three things: American pressure, government inexperience, and the international financial crisis, the government can pass off their part of the blame on the U.S. because of the intervention. The Sandinistas have never been stronger."

In July 1983, the Nicaraguan Revolution completed its fourth year. When the Sandinistas came to power they found an economy in shambles. Despite the constraints imposed by their limited resources and the disruption caused by American intervention, despite the mistakes that inevitably accompany inexperience, the Sandinist government had laid the foundations of a new model of independent economic development and had achieved at least a modest improvement in the living standards of the Nicaraguan people. Overall food consumption was up 40 percent over the prerevolutionary level. The urban reform law slashed the rents paid by low-income groups as much as 50 percent. Progress was especially marked in the fields of education and health. In 1980, the government received the UNESCO prize for a literacy campaign that had reduced adult illiteracy from 50.3 percent to 12 percent. Since 1979 school enrollment has doubled to 1 million students in a population of 2.7 million; a quarter of these students are adults who are learning to read and write for the first time. Medical and dental care are now free, and infant mortality has declined 28.7 percent since 1979. Of equal significance, the working people of Nicaragua have gained a new dignity and sense of power, of control over their destinies through participation in their mass organizations and trade unions.

The Sandinist government has combined these achievements with a commitment to the protection of individual liberties, the preservation of a responsible private economic sector, and the maintenance of good relations with as many countries as possible—including the United States. Perhaps Nicaragua's most original contribution to the theory and practice of social change in Latin America is its integration of the church into the revolutionary process. In Nicaragua, for the first time in Latin American history, at least a segment of the church, transformed by the participation of many clergy and the mass of the faithful in the popular struggle, walks hand in hand with revolution.

EL SALVADOR

The Coffee Cycle and Peasant Revolts, 1850–1932

The history of El Salvador, the smallest and most densely populated country in Central America, presents in exaggerated form all the economic and social problems of the area: an extreme dependence on a single crop, making the economy very vulnerable to fluctuations in price and the demand of outside markets; a marked concentration of land and wealth in a few hands; and intolerable exploitation of the peasantry, accompanied by ferocious repression of all attempts at protest or revolt.

By the mid-nineteenth century, El Salvador had already passed through two economic cycles. The first was dominated by cacao, whose prosperity collapsed in the seventeenth century; the second by indigo, which entered a sharp decline in the latter half of the nineteenth century, first as a result of competition from other producing areas and then as a result of the development of synthetic dyes. The search for a new export crop led to the enthronement of coffee. Coffee cultivation began about the time of independence but it did not expand rapidly until the 1860s. As elsewhere in Central America, the rise of coffee was marked by expropriation and usurpation of Indian lands—carried out in the name of private property and material progress—since most of the land best suited to coffee cultivation was held by Indian communities. Unlike indigo, which was planted and harvested every year, coffee trees did not produce for three years. Producers, therefore, had to have capital or credit, and the persons who had capital or access to credit were the hacendados who had prospered from the growing of indigo. To help these hacendados in their search for land, a government decree of 1856 declared that if two-thirds of a pueblo's communal lands were not planted in coffee, ownership would pass into the hands of the state. This pressure was replaced by a more direct attack on Indian landholdings: An 1881 law ordered that all communal lands be divided among the co-owners (which opened the way for their acquisition by legal or illegal means by the expanding coffee growers); and thirteen months later a decree abolished all communal land tenure. The new legislation harmed not only the Indian communities but *ladino* (mestizo) small farmers as well. These farmers often relied on municipal *tierras comunes* (the free pasture and woodlot where they could graze their stock) for an important part of their subsistence.

The result of this new legislation was a rapid concentration of landownership in the hands of a landed oligarchy often referred to as "the Fourteen Families." This number, while not an exact figure, expresses symbolically the reality of the tiny elite that dominated the Salvadoran economy and state. As late as September 1979, 0.85 percent of the landowners held 77.3 percent of the cultivable land, while 99.15 percent of the landowners owned 22.7 percent of the land.

The state that arose with the enthronement of coffee was founded on the same "liberal" principles that Justo Rufino Barrios and José Santos Zelaya attempted to implement in Guatemala and in Nicaragua. These principles stressed an ardent positivist faith in science and material progress; the need for internal improvements (railroads, roads, port facilities) to provide an infrastructure for the coffee economy; and the mobilization of labor for the coffee haciendas through vagrancy laws and other coercive labor legislation that accompanied the attack on Indian communal lands. The result was a series of popular uprisings between 1872 and 1898 in the coffee-growing areas.

Throughout most of the nineteenth century the great landowners used their own private armies to deal with the problem of recalcitrant peasants. Governmental decrees of 1884 and 1889 made these private armed forces the basis of the public Rural Police, later renamed the National Police. 1912 saw the establishment of the National Guard (*Guardia Nacional*), modeled after the Spanish National Guard. Like the National Police, the National Guard patrolled the countryside and offered police protection to haciendas. The national army, created in the 1850s, did not become an instrument of repression until the late twentieth century.

For the rural poor, the social consequences of the coffee boom were disastrous. A few of the dispossessed peasants were permitted to remain on the new estates, or fincas, as colonos—peons who were given a place to live and a milpa, or garden plot, where they could raise subsistence crops. Unlike the old indigo or sugar latifundia, however, which required a large permanent labor force, the need for labor on the coffee plantations was so seasonal that for the most part they relied on hired hands. This circumstance determined the pattern of life of the typical Salvadoran campesino (peasant). He might farm a small plot as a squatter or a colono on a plantation, but his tiny plot did not as a rule provide subsistence for his family. He would therefore tend to follow the harvests, working on coffee fincas during the harvest season, moving on to cut sugar cane or harvest cotton during August and September, and finally returning to his milpa, hopeful that the maize had ripened. This unstable migratory pattern created many social problems. Family life tended to be extremely impermanent, with a very high rate of births outside marriage: 59 percent in El Salvador in the 1920s, compared with 24 percent in Costa Rica. Another index of social maladjustment was the very high rate of alcoholism: The sale of liquor produced 25 percent of El Salvador's public revenue in 1918.

The economic and social problems generated by the coffee monoculture became more acute with the advent of the Great Depression in 1929. Campesinos who made 50 cents a day before the depression had their wages reduced to 20 cents a day. The price of coffee was cut in half between July 1929 and the end of the year, ruining many small producers who were forced to go out of business and sell their lands to some three hundred fifty large growers. High unemployment and below-subsistence-level wages added to the discontent caused by harsh treatment by overseers and frauds practiced by company stores.

Even before the depression, there had been scattered peasant revolts in the twentieth century; they were always put down by the National Guard. In the 1920s urban workers and some of the peasantry began to form unions. In 1925 a small Communist party began to operate underground; its leader was Agustín Farabundo Martí, who had been introduced to Marxism at the national university. Expelled from El Salvador in 1927 for his radical activities, Martí joined Augusto César Sandino, who was fighting the marines in Nicaragua. Martí returned to El Salvador in 1930 and again plunged into political activity. Aided by a small group of youths, mostly university students, he carried on propaganda and organizational activity among peasants in the central and western parts of the country. He was soon jailed but was released after going on a hunger strike.

Against this background of depression and growing left-wing agitation, a presidential election, perhaps the first free election in Salvadoran history, was held. The winner was the wealthy reformer Arturo Araujo, who had formed his own Labor party (he was a great admirer of the British Labor party and its policies). This event caused great disquiet among the coffee planters and the military. The new president immediately ran into storms: Teachers and other public servants clamored for back pay, peasants demanded land and other reforms, while the coffee oligarchy and the military pressed him to make no concessions. On December 21, 1931, a military coup ousted Araujo and installed his vice president, General Maximiliano Hernández Martínez, as president. The coup signified the end of direct rule by the oligarchy and the beginning of a long era of military domination of politics.

The fall of the liberal Araujo and the rise of Hernández Martínez to power closed the door to popular participation in politics. Convinced that the new regime had no intention of allowing reforms or free elections, Martí and other radical leaders decided on insurrection. Simultaneous uprisings were set to take place in several towns and barracks on January 22, 1932. But the authorities got wind of the plot several days in advance, and Martí and two of his aides were seized. Other rebel leaders then tried to call off the revolt, but communications had broken down, and the revolt began without its leadership.

In town after town, the campesinos, including many full-blooded Indians, rose up, often armed only with machetes. Having taken over much of the western area of the country, they attacked the regional center of Sonsonate. The unequal combat between peasants armed with machetes and the garrison, supported by the Guard and other police units, all armed with modern weapons, ended in total defeat for the insurgents. In a few days the captured towns were retaken. Then the oligarchy began to take its revenge, relentlessly hunting down the "communists," defined as any peasant who was not vouched for by a landowner as not having taken part in the revolt. "Men were taken in big batches, tied together by their thumbs and lined up along the roadside or against the walls of cuarteles [barracks] or churches. There they were machine-gunned and their bodies hauled off by oxcart to makeshift mass graves, often the drainage ditches along the roadsides. The extermination was so great that they could not be burned fast enough, and a great stench of rotting flesh permeated the air of western El Salvador."[5] Estimates as to the number of killed range from ten thousand to forty thousand. The commonly accepted figure is thirty thousand. Ferocious repression was the oligarchy's way of teaching the peasantry a lesson, of ensuring that there would be no repetition of the revolt. The history of El Salvador since 1932 shows how vain was that expectation.

Oligarchs and Generals, 1932–1979

The coup that installed General Hernández Martínez in the presidency marked a turning point in modern Salvadoran history. Terrified by the peasant uprising of 1932, the oligarchy in effect struck a bargain with the military. That bargain allowed the military to hold the reins of government while the oligarchy directed the economic life of the country. A network of corruption that permitted the officer class—especially its higher echelons—to share in the oligarchy's wealth cemented the alliance between the two groups. Nevertheless, the persistence of reformist tendencies among junior officers

periodically produced strains and tensions within the alliance that threatened its existence.

General Hernández Martínez, known as *El Brujo* (the Witch Doctor) because of his dabbling in the occult, maintained a tight rule over the country through his control of the army and the National Guard until 1944. Notoriously friendly to the Axis powers, his position weakened in the face of Roosevelt's propaganda espousing the Four Freedoms and the general rise of democratic ideology following the entrance of the United States into World War II. In addition, power and access to wealth were concentrated in a clique of Hernández Martínez's cronies. The discontent that this engendered in many junior officers, combined with the political and ideological ferment of the war years, led to his overthrow in 1944. Between that year and 1961, governments came and went. Juntas of reformist junior military and liberal civilians, on the one hand, alternated with governments dominated by conservative military and oligarchs, on the other. In 1961 the friendly posture of the military-civilian junta toward the Cuban Revolution as well as its reformist program earned it the distrust of the oligarchy, the conservative military, and the U.S. embassy. Fabio Castillo, a member of the liberal junta, later testified before the United States Congress that the U.S. chargé d'affaires objected to its plans to educate the people, saying: "Don't you know that educated people will ask for bread?" The coup that ousted the junta was led by Colonel Julio Adalberto Rivera, who promptly announced that his revolution was anticommunist and anti-Cuban.

Rivera established a system, patterned on the Mexican idea of a single dominant party that would perpetuate itself in power, holding elections every five years and employing fraud, coercion, and cooptation to maintain control. On this basis, Colonel Rivera was suceeded as president in 1967 by Colonel Fidel Sánchez Hernández, who was replaced by Colonel Armando Molina in 1972, and he in turn by General

---

[5] Thomas P. Anderson, *The War of the Dispossessed: Honduras and El Salvador, 1969* (Lincoln: University of Nebraska Press, 1981), p. 24.

Carlos Humberto Romero in 1977. While maintaining his control of the political system, Rivera allowed a number of opposition parties to exist. The most important were the Christian Democratic party, *Partido Demócrata Cristiano* (PDC), headed by José Napoleon Duarte, mayor of San Salvador from 1964 to 1970; a Social Democratic party, *Movimiento Nacional Revolucionario* (MNR), led by Guillermo Manuel Ungo; and the *Unión Democrátic Nacionalista* (UDN), a front for the Communist party, which had been illegal since 1932. In the first phase of the system, opposition parties were allowed to win some mayoral contests and even a number of seats in the National Assembly.

As the economic difficulties of the country multiplied during the 1960s and 1970s, however, the strains within the system grew and it became increasingly unworkable. The roots of the problem lay in the monoculture that made the country dependent on a world market over which it had no control and a system of land tenure and use that progressively reduced the land area available to small landowners and staple food production. Beginning under General Hernández Martínez, efforts were made to reduce dependency by agricultural diversification. It was hoped that cotton and sugar could be substituted for coffee. Cotton growing had a rapid expansion from 1940 to the mid-1960s at the expense of woodlands, cattle ranching, and tenants and squatters; in 1964 it accounted for 24 percent of the country's exports. By the end of the decade, however, the rapid soil exhaustion characteristic of cotton and the high costs of fertilizer had reduced the cotton acreage to half that of 1965. As cotton declined in the 1960s, sugar replaced it as the country's second most important export crop. But sugar's external markets were limited; as an export, it ranked far below coffee in value. Like cotton, sugar expanded at the expense of tenant farmers and squatters who were pushed off land that had formerly produced subsistence crops—maize, beans, and rice. As the acreage devoted to cotton

and sugar was reduced, the area used for subsistence crops increased; because of overuse of the soil and the inefficient production techniques characteristic of minifundio farmers, however, production actually declined and the country continued to import maize.

Land monopoly and the prevailing system of land use led to population pressure on land, a problem that was greatly aggravated by the population explosion. Thanks to the eradication of yellow fever and malaria and to the successes of preventive medicine, the population shot up from 1,443,000 in 1930 to 2,500,000 in 1961 and 3,549,000 in 1969. By 1970 the population density was about 400 per square mile. The swelling population put great pressure on wage levels: The average daily wage for a field hand in the early 1960s was about 62 cents a day; for an overseer or mayordomo, a little over a dollar a day. Since labor on coffee plantations was seasonal and a peon was lucky to get 150 days of work a year, the labor of an entire family for that period might yield a total yearly cash income of $300 by 1964. In response to Colonel Rivera's attempt to raise the minimum wage for day laborers to a little over one dollar a day in 1965, the oligarchy laid off as many workers as possible, forbade workers to farm the small plots they had used on the estate, and dropped the traditional daily noon meal of one tortilla and a portion of beans. These economies produced a sharp rise in rural unemployment.

With land reform ruled out as a solution for land hunger and population pressure, Rivera attempted another remedy: industrialization and economic integration through the creation of the Central American Common Market in 1961. The underlying reasoning was that the unrestricted flow of goods and capital throughout the area would stimulate an expansion of markets and industrialization, relieving population pressure and unemployment. The CACM in fact gave a marked impetus to industrialization, with the value added to the industrial sector growing at an annual rate of almost 12 percent between 1962 and 1967. Unfortunately this industrial expansion took place without a corresponding growth in employment, for the new industries were capital-intensive and required relatively few workers. Also, much of the new industry was foreign-owned and geared to exports; much of it was designed to assemble imported components. U.S.-based companies in El Salvador like Texas Instruments and Maidenform could greatly enlarge their profit margins because the U.S. tariff law assessed duty only on the "value added" to the product—that is, the cost of labor. Since salaries in El Salvador averaged $4 a day, these companies' exports to the United States grew from a value of $12 million in 1975 to a value of about $26 million four years later.

The problem of population pressure on the land grew much more acute as a result of a bitter dispute between El Salvador and Honduras that culminated in the so-called "Soccer War" between the two countries in 1969—a war that took several thousand lives and left at least 100,000 Salvadorans homeless. Called the Soccer War because it followed a series of hotly contested games between teams representing the two countries in the qualifying rounds of the 1969 World Cup, the conflict had more pragmatic causes. One was a border dispute of long standing. Another was Honduran resentment over the marked imbalance of trade between the two countries as a result of the operations of CACM, to which both countries belonged. Honduras, an extremely underdeveloped country whose economy was largely based on bananas, lumber, and cattle, felt that it was subsidizing the industrial development of El Salvador. The third and decisive cause of the war was the presence in Honduras of some three hundred thousand illegal Salvadoran settlers. In April 1969, following adoption of an agrarian reform law, Honduras ordered the departure of some of the settlers within thirty days; eventually about eighty thousand were expelled. El Salvador retaliated in July 1969 by invading Honduras and destroying most of its air force on the ground. The war was over in five days, largely due to U.S. pressure on El Salvador in the form of threatened economic sanctions. The war, which was very popular in El Salvador, momentarily diverted popular attention from its great problems, but the effects on the country were entirely negative: El Salvador lost the Honduran market for its manufactures for over a decade, and the exodus of Salvadorans from Honduras swelled the number of landless and homeless peasants.

These developments contributed to the ever-growing economic and social crisis of the 1970s. Population growth continued to outstrip the food supply; among the Latin American countries, only Haiti's people had a lower caloric intake than El Salvador's. By the early 1970s, unemployment was running at 20 percent and underemployment at 40 percent; in 1974 the annual inflation rate reached 60 percent. The calamitous economic situation gave the opposition parties hope for victory in the presidential election of 1972; in September of that year the Christian Democratic party, the *Movimiento Nacional Revolucionario*, and the Communist UDN formed a united front, the *Unión Nacional Opositora* (UNO). Its candidate for president was José Napoleón Duarte. Although Duarte had clearly won the election by some 72,000 votes, the electoral commission found that the official candidate, Colonel Molina, had won by about 100,000 votes. The flagrant electoral fraud provoked a revolt by reformist junior military, and for a few days it appeared to have succeeded. But the National Guard and the air force remained loyal to the regime, and by the end of March the rebels had been forced to surrender. Duarte, the candidate of the united opposition, was arrested, tortured, and exiled to Venezuela.

The Molina government continued the oscillation between concession and repression that had characterized military rule since 1932. In 1975, hoping to promote the emerging tourist industry, Molina decided that El Salvador should play host to the 1975 "Miss Universe" pageant and spent about $30 million on the show. In a country with so many unfilled social needs, this impressed many Salvadorans as a scandalous extravagance. Units of the National Guard—without any provocation—fired on students attending a protest rally in San Salvador. At least thirty-seven died and an unknown number of others "disappeared." The massacre was part of a pattern of growing violence—from the right and from the left. With increasing frequency, guerrilla organizations that had sprung up since 1970 kidnapped and held members of the oligarchy for ransom. In the countryside, the National Guard, aided by right-wing paramilitary organizations like ORDEN (*Organización Democrática Nacionalista*), conducted sweeps against "subversive" peasants, surrounding and destroying villages, killing many villagers, and abducting others who "disappeared."

In an effort to quiet peasant unrest, President Molina announced a modest land reform in 1976 that would have distributed some 60,000 hectares, mostly pasture or land planted in cotton, to about twelve thousand families. The program drew a strong protest from the oligarchy, and Defense Minister Carlos Humberto Romero, Molina's designated successor, threatened a coup if the plan went forward. Under this pressure, Molina retreated and the program was effectively shelved.

Although convinced that the familiar pattern of fraud would be repeated in the 1977 presidential election, the UNO decided to run a symbolic candidate, a hero of the Honduran war, Colonel Ernesto Claramount Rozeville. The election was in fact marked by widespread fraud, with rampant stuffing of the ballot boxes for Romero and armed ORDEN thugs on hand to discourage close scrutiny by the opposition at the polls. The outcome was never in doubt. A massive protest demonstration held on February 15 in the main square of San Salvador and addressed by Claramount and other speakers was attacked by army and police units and by members of ORDEN. More than two hundred people were killed by machine-gun fire. Claramount and other leaders sought sanctuary in the cathedral; later Claramount was permitted to go into exile. As he departed for the airport he uttered a prophetic comment: "This is not the end, it is only the beginning."

The fraudulent election of 1977, ending all hope of reform via the electoral process, and the spiral of violence that followed it marked the opening of a new phase that may be called the prerevolutionary stage of development in Salvadoran politics. On the left, the revolutionary organizations that had sprung up since 1970 began to mobilize their forces and attempted to overcome their ideological and tactical differences. All these groups robbed banks, seized radio stations in order to broadcast propaganda, kidnapped oligarchs for ransom, and assassinated persons identified with official or unofficial repression. There was a rapid growth of labor and peasant unions and other mass movements, known collectively as *Fuerzas Populares* (Popular Forces), and of umbrella organizations, such as FAPU (Front for United Popular Action), which united many groups for joint action against the government. On the right, meanwhile, there was increased repressive activity by the National Guard, the National Police, and other security forces as well as by the death squads of ORDEN and another terrorist organization, the White Warrior Union.

A major development of this period was the changing posture of the church toward the Salvadoran crisis. Prior to the Second Vatican Council and the Medellín Bishops' Conference, the church in El Salvador—as elsewhere in Latin America—supported the regime and the oligarchy. Although most of the hierarchy maintained that position, Archbishop Luis Chávez y González and his successor Oscar Romero, with Vatican II and Medellín as their guides, committed themselves to what Romero called "the preferential option for the poor." A considerable number of young priests assumed an even more radical stance, deciding to "use the analysis of Marxism because it is objective and scientific. But we are not Marxists. We are not able to understand Marx as a religion because we are Christians." One result of this ferment in the church was the formation in a few short years of hundreds of Comunidades de base, which combined Bible study with attention to the economic and social problems of their localities. Between 1970 and 1980, seven centers trained approximately fifteen thousand persons who had been selected by the groups to be catechists and leaders. The message the priests brought to their parishioners was that God is "a God of justice and love who acts on the side of the poor and oppressed," that the people "have a basic human right to organize in order to begin taking control of their own lives." Their social activism inevitably marked the priests as targets of right-wing death squads and security forces. The Jesuit Father Rutilio Grande was murdered by a death squad of the White Warrior Union in March 1977, and three other Jesuits who had been working with him were expelled from the country. By May 1977, leaflets urging Salvadorans to "Be a Patriot! Kill a Priest!" were circulating in San Salvador. Altogether, seven priests were killed by death squads or security forces between 1977 and 1979. The death of Father Grande, three weeks after Romero was installed as archbishop, contributed to what the archbishop referred to as his "transformation." "Once you pose the question of the defense of the poor in El Salvador," he said in 1977, "you call the whole thing into question. That is why they have no other recourse than to call us subversives—that is what we are." From then on, during his three years and one month as archbishop, Romero used his position to denounce the regime's human rights violations and to plead for social justice. His sermons, transmitted via radio to almost every part of the country, "became the single most listened-to program in the nation."

As the crisis deepened month after month,

a differentiation also began to take place within the military. A group of reformist junior military watched with profound anxiety the revolutionary course of events in Nicaragua in July–August 1979; they became convinced that a coup offered the only alternative to a solution of the Nicaraguan type. "The Nicaraguan Revolution, more than any other event, galvanized the feeling within the Young Military that there was a need for change." Planning for a coup began in July 1979, with regular consultations with Archbishop Romero and representatives of the Christian Democratic party as well as contacts with the American embassy, which indicated it would not oppose such an action. On October 15 the coup went off almost without a hitch, with virtually no resistance from any garrison, and President Romero meekly accepted exile. A five-man military-civilian junta was formed. The civilians included two moderate leftists, Román Mayorga Quiroz, rector of the Central American University, and the Social Democrat Guillermo Ungo; the military representatives were the authentically democratic Colonel Adolfo Majano and the rightist Colonel Jaime Abdul Gutiérrez, head of the Military School, who owed his inclusion to U.S. pressure. The junta's program called for dissolution of the terrorist ORDEN organization, respect for human rights, agrarian reform, freedom for the Popular Forces to operate, and improvement of relations with Nicaragua.

Although Gutiérrez gave his nominal approval to the program, he decided, without consulting his colleagues, to change the balance of forces in the government by appointing another conservative, Colonel José Guillermo García, as defense minister in the Cabinet that was to assist the junta. It was a fateful decision.

The left and the Popular Forces, meanwhile, regarded the junta with an intense suspicion that time was to justify. On October 28, a demonstration by several organizations demanding to know the fate of the many persons who had "disappeared" was met with gunfire by the

National Guard, leaving twenty-five people dead. In fact, the October 15 coup did not end repression by the security forces; more people were killed by them in the three weeks after the coup than had died in any similar period under Romero. Efforts by civilian junta members Román Mayorga and Guillermo Ungo to restrain the official violence were totally ineffective, for the armed forces listened to no one but Defense Minister García. A meeting of the junta and the Cabinet with the chiefs of the various armed forces was futile. "We have been running this country for fifty years, and we are quite prepared to keep on running it," the chief of the National Guard is said to have arrogantly declared. Popular humor referred to the junta as the *junta de chompipes*, a junta of turkeys that would be cooked and served up by Christmas.

The fall of the junta in fact occurred not at Christmas but at New Year's. It followed demands by liberal members of the junta and Cabinet that the military recognize the supremacy of the junta and carry out its orders. Failing to receive such assurances, Mayorga and Ungo resigned; all the Cabinet, except Defense Minister García, followed their example. After three days of turmoil and street clashes between the military and the Popular Forces, a new government was announced, the product of a secret deal between the military and the Christian Democratic party. Two Christian Democrats replaced Mayorga and Ungo. The military committed itself to a program of agrarian reform, and nationalization of the banks; all repression would cease; and the armed forces would open a dialogue with the Popular Forces. Barely one week after accepting these conditions, the security forces fired on a massive demonstration of the Popular Forces, the largest in Salvadoran history, killing about twenty persons. This and similar repressive acts, demonstrating the bad faith of the military, caused a split in the Christian Democratic party. One of its representatives, Héctor Dada, resigned from the junta and was replaced by José Napoleón Duarte. At least 60

percent of its membership resigned from the party by November 1981. To add to the junta's problems, a rightist coup led by Roberto d'Aubuisson, head of the White Warrior Union, was barely averted by Defense Minister García and other high military officers. The agrarian reform promulgated with dramatic suddenness by the junta in March 1980 resulted from intense pressure by the United States, eager to give a reformist face to its protégé, even as James Cheek, the American chargé d'affaires, advised the junta to conduct a "clean counter-insurgency war." Typical of its strategy of reform combined with repression, the junta announced a state of siege on the same day that it promulgated the agrarian reform.

The agrarian reform was to be implemented in three stages. Phase I, promulgated in March 1980, nationalized 376 estates of more than 500 hectares, belonging to 244 owners and largely consisting of pasture and cotton land. The owners were to be compensated with thirty-year bonds, and the estates were to be converted into cooperatives with 29,755 peasant members. As of January 1, 1983, only 22 cooperatives had received final title, although 130 of the owners had been paid for their farms; it has been charged that they were overpaid on the strength of forged statements of assessed value and taxes paid over the years. In January 1983, President Alvaro Magaña admitted to the *New York Times* that the Institute of Agrarian Reform that supervises Phase I was "run by people who do not like the reforms." Phase II, which would have affected about 200 farms of between 100 and 500 hectares, including most of the coffee *fincas*, "died before it was born," postponed for an indefinite period.

Phase III, called "land to the tiller," promulgated in April 1980, allowed peasants who rented up to 42 hectares of land to buy it from the owner. As of January 1983, 58,152 applications had been received, roughly half of the number that were possible under Phase III provisions. By June 1982, no permanent titles had been issued to applicants; the number rose to 251 in August of that year, and to 1,050 by January 1983. The Salvadoran Peasants' Union charged that the increase resulted from the need to provide the Reagan administration with proof for certifying to the U.S. Congress that El Salvador was making progress in essential economic reform and had therefore fulfilled the requirements for continued economic and military aid.

This curious land reform was accompanied by a wave of repression directed above all against the peasantry. Responsibility for seizure and distribution of land was assigned to the army and the security forces, who used their authority in several ways. Often they distributed land to members of the terrorist ORDEN organization whether or not they were entitled to it. They also used ORDEN members to identify peasants who belonged to the Popular Forces or to the guerrilla movements; these peasants were then killed by the military. Sometimes they collaborated with landowners who evicted tenants from lands they had recently acquired under land reform provisions. In January 1981, the head of the Salvadoran Institute of Agrarian Reform and two U.S. advisers were gunned down in the restaurant of the Sheraton Hotel in San Salvador by two masked gunmen, who then strolled calmly out of the hotel. In December 1981 the Peasants' Union reported to junta President José Napoleón Duarte (he had been named president in a leadership reshuffle in November 1980) that the "failure of the agrarian reform is an immediate and imminent danger." The union claimed that at least ninety of its officials and "a large number of beneficiaries" of the agrarian reform had died during 1981 at the hands of ex-landlords and their allies, who were often members of the local security forces. The report also charged that twenty-five thousand former *aparceros,* or sharecroppers, had been evicted from their plots, "in the majority of cases with the assistance of members of the military forces," before they could obtain pro-

visional titles. Duarte's inability to carry out the agrarian reform or to check the terror in the countryside proved that the junta was in fact "a rightist military regime with a civilian facade"; it also showed that Duarte himself was an "ornament," in the words of one observer, needed by the United States to maintain the reformist image of the junta, and accepted by the military in order to pacify the U.S. State Department.[6]

The most prominent victim of the terror that accompanied the promulgation of the agrarian reform was Monsignor Oscar Romero, archbishop of San Salvador. For years his attacks on the military and the security forces for their violations of human rights had been a thorn in the government's side. Increasingly disillusioned with the role of the Christian Democractic party in the junta, he gradually moved toward supporting armed struggle as the only remaining resort. In a sermon on February 2, 1980, he proclaimed: "When all peacful means have been exhausted, the church considers insurrection moral and justified." On March 23, responding to the repression that accompanied the land reform, he appealed to soldiers not to turn their guns on unarmed civilians. The next day, as he celebrated mass in a chapel in San Salvador, he was gunned down, probably by a military officer. The National Guard celebrated his death with a savage attack on his hometown of Ciudad Barrios that left ten dead. According to the judge appointed to investigate his death—who made these revelations after he had fled for his life to Costa Rica—the assassination was planned by General José Alberto Medrano, founder of ORDEN, and Major Roberto d'Aubuisson, head of the White Warrior Union. Robert White, former U.S. ambassador to El Salvador, informed a congressional committee that there was "compelling" evidence that d'Aubuisson was

[6] William M. LeoGrande, "Drawing the Line in El Salvador," in Stanford Central America Action Network, ed., *Revolution in Central America* (Boulder, Colo.: Westview Press, 1983), p. 104.

involved in the killing.[7] Romero's martyrdom was to have profound political and military repercussions.

The Salvadoran Revolution, 1980–1983

"If I am killed," Archbishop Romero had prophesied shortly before his death, "I shall rise again in the struggle of the Salvadoran people." His death, in fact, served as a powerful catalyst for the growth of that struggle. In particular, it hastened the breakup of the Christian Democratic party and the unification of its center and left wings with Social Democratic and Marxist-led groups in opposition to the junta. In April 1980, a broad coalition of political parties, professional associations, trade unions, and revolutionary groups formed the *Frente Democrático Revolucionario* (Democratic Revolutionary Front). In January 1981, the FDR set up a kind of government-in-exile, called a "political commission," headed by the Social Democratic leader Guillermo Ungo.

Launching a campaign to secure international support, the FDR sent missions to Europe and Latin America and soon obtained endorsements from four European Social Democratic governments and from the Socialist International at its meeting in June 1980. Strong support also came from Mexico, whose President José López Portillo allowed the FDR to establish political offices in that country. In August 1981, in an implied rebuke to the U.S. position of full support for the junta, the governments of Mexico and France issued a joint declaration recognizing the FDR as a "representative political force" that must be directly involved in any political

settlement. Since then, the FDR's international position has grown even stronger; United States policy in El Salvador received another blow in January 1983, when a meeting of the foreign ministers of Mexico, Venezuela, Colombia, and Panama endorsed various peace initiatives, including the FDR's unconditional offer of dialogue and negotiation with the junta.

As important as achieving the political unity of the opposition was the unification of the various guerrilla movements. By mid-summer of 1980 the five major guerrilla groups had united in a single command, which was given the name *Frente Farabundo Martí de Liberación Nacional* (FMLN), in honor of the leader of the abortive 1932 revolt. In January 1981, the FMLN launched its first general offensive and achieved significant successes: The commander and garrison of Santa Ana, the nation's second largest city, went over to the rebels, who also occupied a number of provincial capitals and captured large quantities of heavy weapons. Eventually, however, the offensive ran out of steam and the guerrillas were forced to retreat to their bases in the thinly populated northern part of El Salvador. FMLN commanders attributed the failure of this "final offensive" to strategic and tactical errors, including lack of a unified war plan, poor coordination among the commanders, and failure to cut the enemy's supply lines.

The ensuing military stalemate ended in the middle of 1982, when the scales began to tip in favor of the insurgents. A turning point was the battle of Mt. El Escandón (June 5), where the army massed 4,000 troops, supported by Honduran troops who crossed into Salvadoran territory, in an effort to encircle and destroy a guerrilla force. Despite intense bombardment and shelling of the rebel positions, the guerrillas succeeded in putting an elite battalion of government troops out of action and captured the army's chief of staff, Colonel Francisco Adolfo Castillo, whose helicopter was shot down. Since October 1982 a series of FMLN offensives, accompanied by systematic destruction of bridges,

---

[7] A copyrighted report in the *Albuquerque* (N.M.) *Journal* (April 15, 1983) offers additional evidence of d'Aubuisson's leading role in the plot to assassinate the archbishop. The report cites two classified cables sent by the U.S. embassy in San Salvador to the Department of State in 1980 and 1981. One cable described a meeting, chaired by d'Aubuisson, at which lots were drawn by military officers for the honor of assassinating the archbishop.

Guerrilla in El Salvador, 1983. (Susan Meiselas/
Magnum Photos, Inc.)

power lines, trucks, and other elements of the infrastructure, have greatly weakened the government's military and economic potential. Defense Minister García put the army's troop losses in 1982 at 3,700 officers and men; he estimated guerrilla losses in the same period at 600–700 men. Whereas the rebels have shown growing mastery of strategy and tactics, the same is not true of the government forces, despite the presence of American advisers. Thus, in April 1983, in "a textbook example of the wrong way to fight experienced guerrillas," two companies of the elite Belloso battalion were virtually destroyed in guerrilla ambushes; 150 men were killed, wounded, or taken prisoner, while the battalion's American advisers, forbidden to enter combat zones, "followed the disaster on radio, furious and close to tears."

The almost uninterrupted series of government defeats provides an answer to the much disputed question of the source of the FMLN's arms. Contrary to the Reagan administration's claim, based largely on fabricated or dubious data, that the bulk of these arms came from Cuba, Nicaragua, or other external sources, the evidence seems overwhelming that the most important source of weapons was the capture of U.S.-supplied government arms. This explains why the U.S.-supplied M-16s virtually became the FMLN's standard weapon. Between June and October 1982 alone the rebels captured six hundred fifty firearms, over twenty guns, mortars, and heavy machine guns, and about eighty thousand rounds of ammunition. One guerrilla commander told a visiting American journalist that the more arms the United States sent, the more the FMLN recovered. "We want to thank the U.S. government for sending us so many weapons." In May 1983, in the square of the little village of San Agustín, a woman guerrilla gave a correspondent of the English newspaper *The Guardian* a similar message for President Reagan. "Tell him to come down here and see how we move all around the country as we please. Say we are preparing for a big attack by the government and that we're grateful for the new equipment America is sending us." Secondary sources of the rebel arms have been the international arms market and corrupt army officers. According to one report, in May 1983 an M-16 rifle sold for around $2,000 on the Salvadoran black market.

Although the guerrillas invariably evacuated the large population centers captured in their offensives, by the spring of 1983 they had considerably expanded the zones of their control. They dominated areas inhabited by some two hundred thousand people; in these areas, political power was based on a self-governing system called the *Poder Popular Local* (PPL). While guerrilla self-assurance and confidence in victory grew, the morale of government troops, poorly led and lacking conviction in the justice of what seemed increasingly a lost cause, continued to decline. In particular, the FMLN's policy of handing over prisoners to the Red Cross has undermined the army's will to fight. Desertions have become more frequent, and more and more soldiers surrender as soon as the first shots are fired. This is true even of the elite "immediate reaction battalions" expensively trained and equipped by the United States. In May 1983, the first of these battalions, the Atlacatl, was reported by military sources to be suffering a 10 percent desertion rate. What was worse, 80

percent of the battalion's strength was likely to be lost in the next six months as the soldiers' contracts expired. To fill the gaps in its ranks, the army increasingly resorted to forcible conscription of youths, some as young as twelve.

The rebel successes sowed dissension within the officers' ranks and spurred demands for the removal of Defense Minister García by critics who wanted a more aggressive conduct of the war. The crisis within the military broke out into the open in January 1983 with a mutiny by a field commander who refused to obey García's orders and demanded his resignation. The dispute was patched up, but broke out afresh in April when the head of the air force threatened to mutiny. This time García agreed to step down, and Provisional President Alvaro Magaña immediately appointed General Carlos Vides Casanova, former head of the National Guard, as his successor. The move pleased hardliners and American military advisers, impatient with García's inept direction of the war. On the other hand, Vides Casanova's association with the National Guard, notorious for its brutality and murder of civilians—the rape and murder of four American churchwomen by National Guardsmen in December 1980 still goes unpunished—could strengthen congressional opposition to President Reagan's program of increased military aid to the Salvadoran government.

Increased military aid was one pillar of Reagan's Salvadoran policy; the other was a plan to improve the image of the regime by holding elections that would legitimize it, giving it a "democratic" face. The elections, it was assumed, would give victory to the Christian Democratic party and its leader José Napoleón Duarte. He would then preside over a modest reform and civic action program that would win "hearts and minds" for the government; Duarte's reforms, combined with expanded military aid, should lead to a speedy pacification of the country. In compliance with American wishes, elections for a sixty-member Constituent Assembly were held in El Salvador in March 1982. Boycotted by the left and the guerrillas, who pointed out that there was no possibility of fair elections under existing conditions (the army had recently published a hit list marking leaders of the FDR and the FMLN for death) the elections were largely organized and dominated by the right-wing parties and the military. Leaving aside the possibility of fraud, the most likely reason for the large reported turnout of 1.55 million voters was fear. As a parish priest in San Salvador described the situation to the American writer Joan Didion: "The army had a truck going around to get out the vote . . . , so they went out and voted. They wanted that stamp on their identity cards to show they voted. The stamp was the proof of their good will. Whether or not they wanted to vote is hard to say. I guess you'd have to say they were more scared of the army than of the guerrillas, so they voted." Two weeks before the election, Defense Minister García drove home the implications of abstention by declaring that anyone who did not vote was committing an act of treason.

In any event, the outcome of the elections did not conform to the expectations of the Reagan administration. With only 35 percent of the vote, Duarte and the Christian Democrats proved unable to form a majority government. The fascist Nationalist Republican Alliance (ARENA) of Roberto d'Aubuisson, implicated in the murder of Archbishop Romero and other death squad activities, garnered one-fourth of the vote and pressed for a coalition with other right-wing parties that would leave the Christian Democrats out in the cold. Thus, instead of legitimating Duarte and the Christian Democrats, as projected in the Reagan administration scenario, the elections appeared to legitimate d'Aubuisson and ARENA. The chagrin of the Washington policy makers can be imagined. Finally, by applying immense pressure, in August 1982 the United States managed to convince the three major parties—ARENA, the right-wing Party of National Conciliation, and the Christian

Democrats—to sign a pact for cooperation in the transition to a new constitutional government. As part of the deal, the U.S.-supported "moderate" banker Alvaro Magaña was elected provisional president of the republic and d'Aubuisson president of the Constituent Assembly. "Nothing is more symbolic of our current predicament in El Salvador," wrote former ambassador Robert White, commenting on these events, "than the administration's bizarre attempt to recast d'Aubuisson in a more favorable light."

The compromise between the fascist ARENA and the Christian Democrats, instead of forging political unity, caused bitter splits within all the major parties. This has led to the formation of seven new parties since the March elections. A major factor in these splits is resentment at the heavy-handed U.S. intervention and arm-twisting to secure political decisions. The municipal and presidential elections scheduled for December 1983 are not likely to improve matters. With the FMLN holding the military initiative and extending its control over larger areas of the country, elections may well prove meaningless.

If elections are held at all, they will almost certainly take place against a background of economic as well as military crisis. In April 1982 the International Monetary Fund reported that the government was "practically bankrupt." The flight of capital has reached catastrophic proportions; for each dollar of U.S. aid received, one and a half dollars has fled abroad. Purchasing power dropped by half in the 1980–1982 period; by mid-1982 about 40 percent of the economically active population had no permanent income. In 1982, two hundred thirty-five enterprises closed, with a loss of twenty-five thousand jobs. The economy survives only thanks to U.S. loans.

Under these conditions, the FDR has called for dialogue and negotiation with the government without any preconditions in order to achieve peace in El Salvador. This call, endorsed by Archbishop Arturo Rivera y Damas, has had some impact on sections of the government and the military. According to the *Central America Report* (May 6, 1983), The Christian Democrats, the party with the largest popular vote in last year's election, now support dialogue or negotiations with the FMLN-FDR. According to the same source, many junior officers in the army favor a negotiated settlement that would replace the top command with both younger officers and FMLN commanders. Significantly, recent FMLN propaganda has assumed a more conciliatory stand toward the army, depicting it as an institution corrupted by reactionary, power-hungry men like former Defense Minister García and his successor.

The prospect of a government military collapse or, alternatively, of a political change in San Salvador that would prepare the ground for a negotiated settlement with the rebels must give policy planners in Washington nightmares. What would they do if either of these contingencies came to pass: Would they opt for a U.S. armed intervention to prevent the rise of a "new Cuba" or a "new Nicaragua," or would they sensibly decide to cut their losses, withdraw the military advisers and trainers, and allow the Salvadorans to decide their own destinies?

CHAPTER NINETEEN

Latin American Society

in Transition

By the early 1980s, Latin America's economic, social, and political problems had reached explosive proportions. The signs of crisis were everywhere, but the imbalance between the area's burgeoning population and the sluggish rate of growth or even decline of staple food production in most Latin American countries was especially disquieting.

CRISES IN THE TWENTIETH CENTURY

Economic Problems

By 1979 the population of Latin America was estimated to be 379 million; it was growing at a rate of almost 3 percent a year and was likely to exceed 600 million by the end of the century. In order to achieve even a modest improvement in Latin American living standards, per capita staple food production should grow considerably faster than population. In fact, Latin American agricultural production in absolute terms has greatly increased in recent decades, due to the expansion of acreage and the "green revolution," which has dramatically raised crop yields through increased use of tractors, fertilizers, and new hybrids. Between 1970 and 1977, agricultural production increased by 30 percent, and the index number for per capita food production, taking 1969–1972 as 100, rose to 108 in 1980. But these figures are misleading. The bulk of this increase is accounted for by increased production of such export crops as sugar, coffee, and soybeans. In the same period the importation of grains (wheat, maize, and rice) has grown at a rate of about 9 percent a year. Today only three Latin American countries—Argentina, Uruguay, and Guyana—are grain exporters. The dependence of all other countries on food imports has grown considerably. Countries that once were self-sufficient now suffer from food shortages. Mexico, which as late as 1969–1971 was a net exporter of grain, had to import 13 percent of its needs in 1978. In the same year, the share of imports in national food consumption rose to 21 percent for Brazil, 75 percent for the Caribbean area, almost 50 percent for Chile. The dependence on food imports is reflected in the price of staple foods, which has risen more rapidly than wages in eighteen of the twenty-one Latin American countries. At least half of the Latin American population cannot satisfy its basic food needs.

Writing about conditions in the northeastern state of Pernambuco, the Brazilian nutritionist Nelson Chaves has vividly described the food problem and its causes.

Hunger is the disease that should cause us the most concern. 70 percent of the children in the state of Pernambuco suffer from malnutrition. . . . The situation was better during the colonial period. Then the slaves received a good diet because the masters were interested in maintaining their labor power. . . . But since the coming of the great sugarmills

and sugar monoculture, the plague of food monotony has afflicted the population. Now we find sugarcane grown even in the towns, and the peasants see no other food than black beans, manioc, and dried meat once in a while. No fish, no milk, no vitamins. . . . The average stature of the peasants is declining. We will soon have a generation of dwarfs.

Chile, whose military dictatorship liquidated the agrarian reforms instituted by previous regimes, offers another example of a dramatic decline in nutritional standards. In 1977–1979, food consumption of the population was 13 percent below the 1971–1973 level, while the poorest portion of the population (40 percent) consumed less than 1,900 calories a day, though the indispensable minimum is 2,318 calories. The consumption of foods of high nutritive content has declined in recent years in some of the most favored countries of the area, such as Argentina and Uruguay.

Population pressure on limited land resources is not a major cause of the food problem. In 1970 the population density of the area was only about 15 persons per square kilometer, and large arable areas remain uncultivated or inadequately exploited. A major cause of the food crisis is an agricultural strategy that emphasizes export crops at the expense of internal consumption. According to the United Nations' Food and Agriculture Organization, if Latin America converted the coffee, cotton, sugar, and banana plantations—many owned by multinational companies—to food production for internal consumption, it could double its wheat yield or increase its rice crop by 250 percent. A closely related cause of the problem is an unjust system of land tenure and use, the latifundio. The new capitalist, highly-mechanized type of latifundio in particular sharply limits employment opportunities and absorbs, by legal or illegal means, many small plots previously devoted to staple food cultivation.

The income disparities of the region are

growing instead of diminishing. Some of the preceding chapters on individual countries have already provided information on this point. It should be noted that high national per capita income figures may be deceptive, concealing a very skewed income distribution. In Venezuela, the country with the highest per capita figure in Latin America, 67 percent of all nonagricultural employees in 1974 received wages insufficient to provide a subsistence family income. It is interesting to note that the political system of a Latin American country, whether a dictatorship of the Brazilian type or a formal democracy of the Mexican or Venezuelan type, seems to have little bearing on the pattern of income distribution. The percentage of the national income received about 1975 by the poorest 20 percent of the population of Chile, Brazil, and Venezuela, was 5 percent, 5 percent, and 2 percent, respectively. For the area as a whole, the share of the total income received by the poorest 40 percent of the population fell from 8.7 to 7.7 percent between 1960 and 1975.

Social Problems

Housing is one of the area's gravest social problems. In Argentina the housing deficit rose from 1.5 million to 2.63 million between 1960 and 1969; in Chile it increased from 375,000 to 630,000 in the same period. Throughout the area, much of the housing is improvised and lacks proper sanitary facilities. Often a whole family is crowded into a single room. In 1973 only 50.2 percent of all housing units had electricity; less than 40 percent had sewage facilities. The absence of adequate drinking water and sewage services contributes to a high incidence of parasitic and infectious diseases. Improvements in preventive medicine and health care have brought a sharp drop in mortality rates, but the infant mortality rate is still much higher than in Europe or North America. In 1974 the infant mortality rate was 63.3 per 1,000 live

births in Chile, 93.8 in Colombia, 119.6 in Honduras, and 149.6 in Haiti. The corresponding figure for the United States (1975) was 16.1 per 1,000 live births.

The region suffers from a tremendous shortage of educational facilities. In Brazil, for example, a majority of school-age children do not attend school because there are not enough schools and teachers or because the poverty of their parents forces them to join the work force. Almost everywhere the dropout rate is very high. Although official figures show that the illiteracy rate among persons fifteen years of age or over declined from 45 to 27 percent between 1950 and 1970, the number of illiterates actually increased by 13 million in those years because of the rapid population growth. In 1977, the illiteracy rates for Mexico, Brazil, and Peru were 35 percent, 33 percent, and 55 percent, respectively. Only socialist Cuba and more recently Nicaragua showed dramatic improvement in this area; Cuba's nationwide campaign to wipe out illiteracy had achieved its goal by 1982. The inadequacy of the area's educational system is reflected in the low technical level of its work force; approximately 90 percent of the work force was classified as unskilled or semiskilled about 1970.

An accelerated urbanization, caused by a massive migration of rural dwellers to the city, has sharpened all these problems. This rural exodus results from the interplay of two forces: the "pull" of the city, which attracts rural people with the frequently illusory prospect of factory work and a better life, and the "push" of the countryside, where concentration of land and mechanization of agriculture are expelling millions of peasants from their farms and jobs. In 1959, 39 percent of the population lived in towns and cities; by 1960 the figure had risen to 47 percent, by 1970 to 54 percent, and by 1975 to an estimated 58 percent. The urban population is increasing at more than twice the rate of the population as a whole. A United Nations es-

Slum dwellers in Rio de Janeiro, Brazil. (Paul Conklin)

timate foresaw that by the year 2000 the urban population ("urban" here refers to a settlement of more than 2,000 people) would form some 80 percent of the total population of the area.

Most striking, however, has been the growth in the number of cities with over 1 million inhabitants. Between 1950 and 1970 the number of such cities rose from six to seventeen, and their total population increased from 15 to 55 million. If present trends continue, in the year 2000 these cities will contain about 220 million inhabitants, or about 37 percent of the total Latin American population at that time.

Industrialization and the rural exodus have produced the phenomenon of hyperurbanization—the rise of vast urban agglomerations or zones of urban sprawl. About 80 percent of Brazil's industrial production is located in the metropolitan zones of São Paulo, Rio de Janeiro, and Belo Horizonte. Two-thirds of Argentine production is concentrated in the area between Buenos Aires and Rosario. More than half of the industrial production of Chile and Peru is located in the metropolitan zones of Santiago and Lima-Callao, respectively; Caracas accounts for 40 percent of the industrial production of

Venezuela. Between 25 and 50 percent of the populations of Uruguay, Argentina, and Mexico now live in the capitals of those countries.

As these vast urban concentrations increase, life becomes more and more difficult for their inhabitants. All the urban problems: food, housing, transportation, schools, drinking water, and sanitation, are immensely aggravated. Mexico City is a case in point. In 1930 the city had 1 million inhabitants and extended over an area of 200 square kilometers; it reached 2.8 million inhabitants in 1950; by 1982 it had a population of 14 million persons spread over an area of 800 square kilometers. At the present rate of growth, the population will be 32 million by the end of the century. In 1950 the city accounted for 22 percent of the country's gross national product, 44 percent in 1975, and nearly 50 percent in 1982. The pollution caused by toxic agents generated by industry and the automobile (Mexico City has more than 2 million cars) has been denounced by medical specialists as a major danger to health and life. Shantytowns cover almost 40 percent of the urban area and house at least 4 million inhabitants, a large proportion of whom are unemployed or underemployed; in 1978, 1.2 million persons lacked potable water. With some variations, most large cities of Latin America have similar slum areas— called *favelas* in Brazil, *callampas* in Chile, *villas miseria* in Argentina—that present the same spectacle of extreme want and squalor.

In Europe and North America, urbanization, industry, and the demand for labor grew at a fairly even pace. In Latin America, however, industrial growth and demand for labor lag far behind the explosive growth of the urban population. Much of the new industry, especially its foreign-owned sector, is highly mechanized and automated; it therefore generates relatively little new employment, as shown by the low rate of growth of the industrial work force (2.7 percent in the period from 1950 to 1974). In such a traditional Latin American industry as textiles, mechanization has actually produced a net loss of jobs. The low purchasing power of the masses also hinders the creation of new jobs, for the market for goods is quickly saturated, and industry chronically operates below capacity. Finally, many of the rural migrants are illiterate and lack the skills required by modern industry. As a result, an immense "reserve army" of labor has arisen both in the city and the countryside. According to the United Nations Economic Commission for Latin America, 40 percent of the area's labor force is completely or partly unemployed.

Industry's inability to absorb the supply of labor has produced an exaggerated growth of the so-called service sector. The growth of this sector considerably exceeds that of the industrial labor force, which grew less than 2 percent during the period from 1945 to 1962, while employment in the service industries rose more than 5 percent. The service sector includes a great number of poorly paid domestic servants and a mass of individuals who eke out a precarious living as lottery ticket vendors, car watchers and washers, shoeshiners, and street peddlers of all kinds.

Cuba alone has made a serious effort to check and reverse the hypertrophy of the city. On the eve of the revolution, Cuba's urban-rural structure closely resembled that of the rest of Latin America. One-fifth of the country's population and almost 53 percent of its industrial production were concentrated in Havana; there was an enormous economic, social, and cultural imbalance between the capital and the countryside. Almost from the day it took power, the revolutionary government undertook to redress the balance by shifting the bulk of its investments to the countryside and by raising rural living standards through the provision of adequate medical, educational, and social services; a more rational geographic distribution of the economic infrastructure; and the creation of planned new cities. Thanks to these policies, aided by the departure of thousands of middle-class dissidents for the United States, the growth of Havana's population had begun to decline by 1965, and a reverse current of migration began from the capital into a countryside that was itself becoming urbanized.

THE NEW CLASS STRUCTURE

Industrialization, urbanization, and the commercialization of agriculture have significantly altered the Latin American social structure and the relative weight of the various classes. These changes include a partial transformation of the old landed elite into a new latifundista class with a capitalist character, the emergence of a big industrial and financial bourgeoisie with close ties to foreign capital, an enormous growth of the so-called urban middle sectors, and the rise of a small but increasingly class-conscious factory working class. A survey of these and other developments suggests the complexity of modern Latin American class alignments and the possible direction of future social and political change.

The Great Landowners

Although they have had to yield first place economically and politically to the big bourgeoisie, the great landowners, Latin America's oldest ruling class, retain immense power, thanks to their control over the land and water resources of the area. In 1970, there were about 105,000 latifundia (estates of more than 1,000 hectares) in Latin America, or 1.4 percent of all landholdings. Much smaller still was the number of truly vast landholdings (of more than 5,000 hectares), but they formed the backbone of the latifundio system in Latin America.

Over the last few decades, as some earlier chapters show, there has been a major expansion of the latifundia, especially of the new type, which produces industrial and export crops with the use of improved technology and wage labor. This expansion was stimulated by rising prices for land, crops, and livestock; by the desire to forestall peasant claims to land under future land reform legislation; and by the prodding of governments that saw modernization as an alternative to radical land reform from below. The movement is gaining momentum throughout the continent and spreading even in countries like Mexico and Bolivia, which had experienced radical but not socialist land reforms. In 1974, the sociologist Rodolfo Stavenhagen described the fruits of this process in Mexico as

the considerable polarization of agricultural development; acute inequality in the distribution of land tenure; the renewed concentration of wealth and resources in the hands of a small minority on the land; and the consequent pauperization and increasing misery of the large masses of the peasant population: the ejidatarios, the small landowners, and the agricultural laborer.

The traditional hacendado described by Manuel González Prada, with his high, wide-brimmed hat, poncho, and spurs, who "exercizes over his peons the authority of a Norman baron," is a vanishing breed. His successor is often a cosmopolitan, university-trained type who combines agribusiness with industrial and financial interests. But the arbitrary and predatory spirit of the old hacendados survives in the new latifundistas. The great landowners continue to be the most reactionary class in Latin American society. The recent history of the area offers many examples of their usurpations and aggressions against the peasantry and their readiness to unleash violence in defense of their vested interests.

The New Bourgeoisie

A native commercial bourgeoisie arose in Latin America after independence and consolidated its position with the rise of the neocolonial order after mid-century. In the second half of the nineteenth century, an industrialist class, largely of immigrant stock, appeared in response to the demand of a growing urban population for consumer goods. World War I further stimulated the movement for import-substitution industrialization. But the day of the industrial entrepreneur did not arrive until the great economic crisis of 1930 disrupted the trading patterns of the area. Aided by favorable international and domestic background conditions and massive state intervention, the native industrial bourgeoisie quickly gained strength and in many countries displaced the landed elite as the dominant social and economic force. However, as a rule, the new bourgeoisie avoided frontal collision with the latifundistas, preferring to form bonds of kinship and interest with the landed elite; in Chile in 1964, a survey of big businessmen revealed that almost half of them owned landed estates or had relatives who owned estates.

Meanwhile, foreign capital, attracted by the potential of the growing Latin American market, began to pour into the area, particularly after 1945. Possessing immensely superior capital and technological resources, foreign firms absorbed many small and middle-sized national companies and came to dominate key sectors of the economy of the host countries. Aware, however, that the survival of a native bourgeoisie was essential to their own security, foreign capitalists endeavored to form close ties with the largest, most powerful national firms through the formation of mixed companies and other devices. This dependence on and linkage with foreign corporations explains why the Latin American big bourgeoisie lacks nationalist sentiment, although it occasionally quarrels with its foreign allies.

Latin American big business, like its foreign counterparts, displays a clear tendency toward monopoly. The typical form of business organization in most countries is the family firm. In Brazil in the 1960s, six large family companies—Matarazzo, Morais Filho, Jafet, Abdalla, Klabin, and Simonsen—dominated the native private industrial sector. The Matarazzo family controlled more than three hundred enterprises (textiles, food, chemical, cellulose, construction, and oil, among others) with a labor force of over thirty thousand persons and an annual turnover of more than $300 million. In Argentina, the giant Bunge y Born firm employed more than seventeen thousand workers in its eighty-two enterprises and had an annual turnover of more than $350 million. The large Tornquist family, which was active in cattle ranching, sugar refining, and industry, illustrated the fusion of industrial and latifundist interests in Argentina. In Chile, the Alessandri, Yarur, Matte, and Edwards families dominated the industrial scene. Here, too, three large holding groups—Banco de Chile, Banco Sud Americano, and the Edwards group—controlled about 70 percent of all capital in business corporations. Similar processes of concentration of capital were visible in Mexico, Colombia, and other countries of the region.

In its youth, some sections of the Latin American national bourgeoisie supported the efforts of such nationalist, populist chieftains as Cárdenas, Perón, and Vargas to restrict foreign economic influence and accepted, though with misgivings, their concessions to labor. Today, grown prematurely old, the big bourgeoisie shares the hostility of its foreign allies to restrictions on foreign capital and independent trade unionism and, with rare exceptions, has supported repressive military regimes in such countries as Brazil, Uruguay, and Chile.

The bourgeoisie, however, is not a monolithic bloc. Alongside the small group of big capitalists there exists in each country a much greater number of small and middle-sized firms that tend to favor state action to restrict foreign economic and political influence. Typical of the

Latin American parties predominantly representing the interests of the petty and middle bourgeoisie is *Acción Democrática* (Democratic Action) in Venezuela. Following its electoral victory in 1974, the Venezuelan government, headed by President Carlos Andrés Pérez, nationalized the foreign-owned oil industry and iron ore mines and began to broaden trade and diplomatic relations with the socialist countries and the Third World. But the commitment of the petty and middle bourgeoisie to nationalist economic policies is far from being firm and consistent; moreover, it tends to share the anti-working-class sentiments of the big capitalists.

The Urban Middle Sectors

The urban middle sectors are that great mass of urban dwellers who occupy an intermediate position between the bourgeoisie and the landed elite, on the one hand, and the peasantry and industrial working class, on the other. The boundaries of this intermediate group with other classes are vague and overlapping. At one end, for example, the group includes highly paid business managers whose lifestyle and attitudes identify them with the big bourgeoisie; at the other, it takes in store clerks and lower-echelon government servants, whose incomes are often lower than those of skilled workers.

The oldest urban middle sector consists of self-employed craftsmen, shopkeepers, and owners of innumerable small enterprises. The great number of small workshops in which the owner both works and employs other workers (90 to 95 percent of all enterprises) suggests the importance of this sector.

White-collar employees form another large urban intermediate sector. Urbanization, the growth of commercial capitalism, and the vast expansion of the state sector in recent decades have contributed to an inflation of both public and private bureaucracies. Public employees make up about one-fifth of the economically active population of the area. About 1970, they numbered about 1.5 million in Argentina, 1.4 million in Mexico, and 500,000 in Chile.

University students compose a sizable urban middle sector. Between 1950 and 1970, their number rose from 250,000 to over 1 million. The great majority (some 90 percent) come from middle-class backgrounds, and many must combine work and study. Student discontent with inadequate curricula and teaching methods and the injustices of the social and political order have made the university a focal point of dissidence and protest. However, the students are in the end transients; in Latin America, as elsewhere, their radical or reformist zeal often subsides after they enter a professional career.

Because of their great size, the ideology of the urban middle sectors and their actual and potential role in social change are issues of crucial importance. Following World War II, many foreign experts on Latin America, especially in the United States, pinned great hopes on the "emerging middle sectors" (to which they assigned the new industrialist class) as agents of progressive social and economic change. In the sardonic words of Ignacio Sotelo, the formula of these experts appeared to be: "Tell me the size of your middle class and I will tell you the level of economic development and political stability that you have attained." The history of the last few decades has not confirmed those expectations. The urban middle sectors have mushroomed, but with the exception of many students and intellectual workers—teachers, writers, scientists—they have not been a force for social change.

The error of the foreign experts consisted in confusing the Latin American middle sectors with their counterparts in Europe and North America. Unlike the European and North American middle classes, the Latin American middle sectors did not arise from a process of dynamic industrial development. They arose in the protective shadow of a neocolonial export-import economy that was gradually transformed into a dependent, deformed capitalism with strong ties to the latifundia. Very few self-made men have come from their ranks. Their ideology mirrors that of the ruling class, whose lifestyle they try to copy by keeping one or two servants and in other ways. They regard manual labor as degrading, resent forced contact with the lower orders in buses or trolleys, and look down on Indians and blacks. Confused and misinformed on economic and political issues, they are easy prey to rightist demagogy and anticommunist propaganda. These groups provided the mass base for the right-wing military coups in Brazil and Chile. However, the urban middle sectors should not be written off as hopeless reactionaries. By their very intermediate nature, they are capable of strong political oscillations, especially in response to the movement of the economy. There is evidence, for example, that in Chile they have begun to reappraise their attitude toward the Popular Unity government and its program.

The Peasantry

The term "peasantry" refers here to all small landowners, tenants, and landless rural laborers. As noted previously, the current expansion of the new type of latifundio is creating an unparalleled crisis for the Latin American peasantry. The increased use of tractors and other mechanized farm equipment has already displaced millions of farm workers, and the process is accelerating. The growing surplus of labor, inflation, and the weakening of rural labor organizations by repressive military regimes are contributing to the decline of peasants' real income from wages and other forms of labor. The majority of the "land reforms" of Latin American governments have not checked the trend toward concentration of land and agricultural income in the hands of a small elite. Out of a Latin American rural labor force of some 32 million,

about 20 million are already landless. Lacking access to agricultural credits, machinery, and soil-improving inputs, the small farmer appears doomed. Foreseeing a time when "practically all the available capital other than land and an increasing share of the output will . . . be controlled by the traditional and modernized latifundios," the agricultural sociologist Ernest Feder concludes that the day may not be far off "when Latin America will see poverty as abject as, say, India."

An exaggerated individualism, political apathy, and religious fanaticism are traits commonly attributed to the Latin American peasantry, but these are stereotypes that most anthropological and sociological studies seem to disprove. The supposed attachment of the peasantry to private landownership is especially open to question. When given an option, as in Cuba, Peru, and Chile, campesinos have usually preferred collective or cooperative farming over small, private landholdings. The failure of capitalist agricultural models to solve the problems of rural poverty, employment, and food production makes it likely that the future of Latin American agriculture belongs in the main to a variety of socialist and cooperative forms of land tenure.

The Industrial Working Class

The rapid growth of capitalism in Latin America in recent decades has been accompanied by a parallel growth of the industrial working class. Between 1917 and 1970, the size of the industrial labor force increased eight times, from 5 to 40 million. Although miners and factory workers formed the best-organized and most class-conscious detachments of the army of labor, they were a small minority of the labor force. Artisans, self-employed or working in shops employing less than five persons, constituted the largest group (47.3 percent). In Brazil factory workers numbered only 1.5 to 2 million out of

Contrasting statuses of Bolivian women: two peasants flank a middle-class shopper. (Paul Conklin)

an industrial labor force of 10 million; in Argentina they numbered only about 600,000 to 800,000, 10 to 15 percent of the total. The predominance of the artisan shop, whose labor relations are marked by paternalism and individual bargaining, hinders the development of workers' class consciousness and solidarity.

The recent peasant origins of great numbers of workers have also had a negative influence on the development of the labor movement, for rural migrants often bring with them traditions of dependence on and deference to the patrón and a general social and cultural backwardness. This backwardness made the new factory workers susceptible to the populist demagogy of leaders like Perón and Vargas, who offered them limited concessions in return for the abandonment of independent trade unionism and class struggle. Even more susceptible to such demagogy and marginal concessions are the large slum populations, composed of rural migrants who are often unemployed or irregularly employed.

These problems of growth delay but do not prevent the development of working-class consciousness, organization, and independence. The collapse of the nationalist-populist model of economic and social reform in countries like

Argentina and Brazil and the equal failure of the Christian Democratic reformist model in Chile and elsewhere have tended to radicalize the Latin American labor movement. Today, socialism is probably the most influential ideology among the factory workers of such key countries as Chile, Argentina, and Brazil, and its authority appears to be increasing.

The industrial working class has played a key role in major recent movements for social and political democracy in Latin America. Armed Bolivian tin miners helped to achieve the victory of the 1952 revolution and its program of land reform and nationalization of mines. Cuban workers gave decisive support to the guerrilla struggle against the Batista dictatorship. Their general strike in 1959 helped to topple it. The working class of Buenos Aires intervened at a critical moment (October 1945) to save Juan Perón from being overthrown by a reactionary coup, and its pressure broadened his reform program. In Chile the working class led the Popular Unity coalition that brought Salvador Allende to the presidency, ushering in a three-year effort (1970–1973) to achieve socialism by peaceful means.

These advances—especially the Cuban and Chilean revolutions—provoked a counterrevolutionary reaction that until recently was still ascendant. In the many countries under military and personal dictatorships, all working-class parties were banned and trade unions abolished or placed under strict government control. In countries such as Chile, where those conditions still prevail, the workers' struggle continues, under difficult conditions, but they are gaining new allies. In the past, reactionary elites were able to play the peasantry against the working class, as happened in Bolivia in the 1950s, or the urban middle sectors against the peasantry and the working class, as occurred in Brazil in 1964 and in Chile in 1973. The price of this disunity appears to have been learned, and new interclass coalitions are being forged in which

the working class will certainly play a large role. Bolivia, Brazil, Chile, and Argentina are some countries in which a process of class realignment is under way.

ATTITUDES AND MENTALITIES: CHANGE AND RESISTANCE TO CHANGE

Change was in the air of Latin America as it entered the last quarter of the twentieth century. Economic modernization demanded changes in family life, race relations, education, and the whole ideological superstructure of society, but the old attitudes and mentalities struggled hard to survive. As a result, Latin America presented dramatic contrasts between customs and mores that were as new as the Space Age and others that recalled the age of Cortés and Pizarro.

Woman's Place

The status of women was a case in point. In some ways, that status had improved; the struggle to obtain the vote for women, for example, began around World War I and ended successfully when Paraguay granted them the suffrage in 1961. More and more women held appointive and electoral offices, and in increasing numbers they entered factories, offices, and the professions. By 1970 in some countries, notably Brazil and Argentina, the number of working women classified as professionals was higher than the number of men, a significant fact because the proportion of economically active women was much lower than that of men. In Brazil, out of every 100 women working in nonagricultural sectors in 1970, 18 were engaged in professional and technical operations, whereas for men the figure was only 6 out of every 100. The ratios were reversed, however, for positions of higher responsibility; this reflected the persistence of discriminatory attitudes.

The small movement for women's rights could claim much less progress in such areas as family patterns, divorce laws, and sexual codes. The traditions of the patriarchal family, of closely supervised courtship and marriage, remained dominant, especially among the upper and middle classes. The ideology of machismo, the cult of male superiority, with its corollary of a double sex standard, continued to reign almost everywhere in the continent. "The Mexican family," wrote the sociologist Rogelio Díaz-Guerrero in 1967, "is founded upon two fundamental propositions: (a) the unquestioned and absolute supremacy of the father and (b) the necessary and absolute self-sacrifice of the mother." With small variations, the same statement could be made about the family structure in almost every other Latin American republic.

Socialist Cuba has made great advances in abolishing sexual discrimination in law and practice; in 1976 it introduced the Family Code, which gave the force of law to the division of household labor. Working men and women are required to share housework and child care equally, and a recalcitrant spouse can be taken by the other to court. But Vilma Espín, head of the Cuban women's movement, admits that the law is one thing and the way people live is another. "Tradition is very strong. But we have advanced. Before, the machismo was terrible. Before, the men on the streets would brag about how their wives took care of them and did all the work at home. They were very proud of that. At least now we have reached the point where they don't dare say that. That's an advance. And now with young people you can see the difference."

Nicaragua is another country where a liberating revolution has transformed the lives and roles of many women. Women, both rural and urban, took part in the struggle against the Somoza tyranny and made an immense contribution to its final triumph in July 1979. Their participation, writes Susan Ramirez-Horton,

"took many forms. Women in the countryside contributed food and served as cooks. Some made flags and bandanas for the rebels. They eventually served as spies and runners, transporting supplies across the country." Women, singly and in groups, prepared for the final offensive by stockpiling food, gathering medical supplies, and organizing communication networks to send messages to Sandinist fighters and their families. By the time of the final victory, from one-quarter to one-third of the Sandinist People's Army were female—some as young as 13. Three women were guerrilla commanders; two served on the general staff of the People's Army. Following the triumph of the revolution, women assumed responsible positions at all levels of the Sandinist government; innumerable women are active in the literacy program and other tasks of economic and social reconstruction. A similar process of women's liberation is taking place as part of the revolutionary struggle in neighboring El Salvador. As the Cuban experience shows, old ideologies die hard; neither in Cuba nor in Nicaragua have women achieved full consciousness of themselves as equals or full recognition of their equality by males, but significant progress has been made in that direction.

Race Prejudice

Notions of black and Indian inferiority are everywhere officially disapproved, but race prejudice remains strong, especially among upper- and middle-class whites. Even in Brazil, often touted as a model of racial democracy, the sociologist Florestan Fernandes found that the white man clung to "the *prejudice of having no prejudice,* limiting himself to treating the Negro with tolerance, maintaining the old ceremonial politeness in inter-racial relationships, and excluding from this tolerance any true egalitarian feeling or content." Socialist Cuba has made the largest progress in integrating its black minority into the national life and in combating the vestiges of racism.

The Indian remains the principal victim of racist exploitation and violence. In Brazil, according to one recent estimate, the number of Indians has dropped from 1 million to 180,000 since the beginning of the century. In the late 1960s, the Brazilian government revealed that hundreds of officials of its own Service for the Protection of the Indians had been implicated in crimes against the Indians that included the liquidation of whole tribes. In one case, the Indians were machine-gunned and bombed from the air; in another, they were distributed presents of sugar mixed with arsenic. The process of destroying the Indians by relocation in the interests of economic development continues. Wanton killings of Indians have been reported from the jungle lowlands of Colombia, and murders of Indians by land-grabbing hacendados or their *pistoleros* (gunmen) have occurred in Mexico, Guatemala, and other countries with sizable Indian populations.

In some countries, the Indians are subjected to a many-sided economic, social, and cultural exploitation. "The Indian problem," writes the Mexican sociologist Pablo González Casanova, "is essentially one of internal colonialism. The Indian communities are Mexico's internal colonies. . . . Here we find prejudice, discrimination, colonial types of exploitation, dictatorial forms, and the separation of a dominant population, with a different race and culture."

The Catholic Church

The ideological crisis of Latin America is illustrated by the rifts that have emerged in two of the area's oldest and most conservative institutions, the Catholic church and the armed forces.

The new reformist and revolutionary currents that have emerged within the Catholic church since about 1960 have different sources: a more liberal climate of opinion within the church since the Second Vatican Council, convened in 1962 under Pope John XXIII; concern on the part of some elements of the hierarchy that the church's traditional collusion with the elites risked a loss of the masses to Marxism; and a crisis of conscience on the part of some clergy, especially working clergy whose experiences convinced them that the area's desperate dilemmas required drastic solutions.

The Jesuits, more attentive than other clergy to the signs of the times, seem to have been the first to endorse radical reforms. In 1962 the Jesuit organ *Mensaje,* published in Santiago, Chile, warned that the masses were tired of waiting for reforms and demanded swift, thorough changes—a revolution, in short. *Mensaje* even had good things to say about Marxism. Praising it for its efforts to create a society based on fraternal equality, *Mensaje* called Marxism a "Christian heresy."

The new ferment within the Latin American church found dramatic expression in the life and death of the famous Colombian priest and sociologist Camilo Torres. Born into an aristocratic Colombian family, a brilliant scholar and teacher, Torres, who became convinced of the futility of seeking to achieve reform by peaceful means, joined the Communist-led guerrilla National Liberation Army. Defining his position, Torres claimed that "the Revolution is not only permissible but obligatory for Christians who see in it the only efficacious way of realizing love toward all men." Being a Christian and a priest, said Torres in another statement, he could not be a Communist, but he was fighting at the side of the Communists because "the Communist proposals to combat poverty, hunger, illiteracy, and lack of housing and public services are effective and scientific." He was killed in a clash with counterinsurgency forces in February 1966. Like the more famous Che Guevara, Torres has become a source of inspiration for many idealistic Latin American youths; he is also a symbol of the unity of believers and nonbelievers in the struggle for socialism.

The proper stand for the church to take in the face of Latin America's structural crisis was hotly debated at the second conference of Latin American bishops, held at Medellín, Colombia, in 1968. The presence of Pope Paul VI at its opening session underlined the importance of the meeting. Reflecting the leftward shift of portions of the clergy, the bishops at Medellín affirmed the commitment of the church to the task of liberating the people of Latin America from neocolonialism and "institutionalized violence." This violence, declared the bishops, was inherent in the economic, social, and political structures of the continent, dependent on what Pope Paul called "the international imperialism of money."

Even before Medellín, a group of Latin American bishops had taken a position in favor of socialism. Their leader was Helder Câmara, archbishop of Recife (Brazil). He and seven other Brazilian bishops had signed a pastoral letter issued by seventeen bishops of the Third World that called on the church to avoid identification of religion "with the oppression of the poor and the workers, with feudalism, capitalism, imperialism." Rejecting violence as an instrument of revolutionary change, Helder Câmara expressed sympathy and understanding for those who felt that violence was the only effective tactic. Another convert to socialism was Bishop Sergio Méndez Arceo of Cuernavaca (Mexico), who declared in July 1970: "Only socialism can give Latin America a true development. . . . I believe that a socialist system best conforms to Christian principles of true brotherhood, justice, and peace." The revolutionary current within the church gained momentum as a result of the first convention of Christians for Socialism, held in Santiago, Chile, in April 1972. Although the Chilean hierarchy did not participate in it, it was attended by more than four hundred delegates, including two hundred priests.

These developments were accompanied by the emergence and growing acceptance by many clergy of the so-called "theology of liberation," the product of the study and reflection of leading church scholars in various Latin American countries. This doctrine taught that the church, returning to its roots, must again become a Church of the Poor. It must cease to be an ally of the rich and powerful and commit itself to the struggle for social justice, to raising the consciousness of the masses, to making them aware of the abuses from which they suffered and of the need to unite in order to change an oppressive economic and political system. "Liberation theology" rejected Marxism's atheist world view, but drew heavily on the Marxist analysis of the causes of the poverty and oppression in the Third World. On the subject of revolution, while deploring all violence, liberation theologians taught that revolution, or counterviolence, was justified as a last resort against the greater violence of tyrants—an orthodox Catholic teaching that goes back to St. Thomas Aquinas. It was in this spirit that Archbishop Oscar Arnulfo Romero of San Salvador, in one of the last sermons he gave before he was murdered by a right-wing assassin in March 1980, declared: "When all peaceful means have been exhausted, the Church considers insurrection moral and justified."

In order to implement the teachings of liberation theology, progressive clergy set about developing a new type of Christian organization, the comunidad de base, or Christian grass-roots organization. Composed of poor people in the countryside and the barrios of cities, assisted and advised by priests and students, these communities combined religious study and reflection with efforts to define and solve the practical social problems of their localities. The great landowners and the authorities frequently branded their activities as subversive, and both laity and priests were subjected to severe repression. This led to a growing politicization and radicalization of many communities and their involvement in revolutionary movements. In Nicaragua, the Christian communities were integrated into the revolutionary struggle led by the Sandinist Front for National Liberation (FSLN) to a degree not found elsewhere in Latin America. "The experience brought the Christian community together in a powerful way," write Michael Dodson and T. S. Montgomery. "The centrality of prayer in their daily life was dramatically heightened. In September 1978, when the general uprising began, Christians throughout Nicaragua had accepted the need for revolution. When the final insurrection began the following May, they were prepared to fight until victory."

This unity of rank-and-file Catholic clergy and laity with the revolution has continued since the Sandinist triumph in July 1979. Five priests hold high office in the revolutionary government and have defied a 1980 Vatican ruling barring direct priestly involvement in political life. Many priests and nuns enthusiastically support and participate in the literacy campaign and other reconstruction projects of the new regime. Typical of this activist clergy is a priest described in the *Christian Science Monitor* (March 3, 1983):

The Rev. Angel Arnaiz lives on an agricultural cooperative with 14 other Christians in Nicaragua's northern Chinandega Province.

Besides ministering to farmworkers, the energetic Dominican priest tends cotton fields and cattle, teaches in the government's literacy program, works in agrarian reform projects, and hunts down community development funds.

Fr. Arnaiz says his mission is to "lift people out of poverty so they can lead dignified lives." He preaches the goodness of God—as well as the perceived evils of capitalism.

The church hierarchy, headed by Archbishop Miguel Obando y Bravo, has grown increasingly critical of the new government, however. Before the revolution, the hierarchy, historically aligned with the wealthy class, gradually moved toward anti-Somoza positions, but never became pro-Sandinist. The bishops may fear the gradual growth of atheism among the people and the loss of their influence over the faithful. The Sandinist government claims that the hierarchy is again aligning itself with the rich and is playing the game of the Reagan administration by trying to destabilize the revolutionary regime. Whatever the motives of the hierarchy, its attitude threatens to create a large rift between itself and the Catholic rank and file, intensely loyal to the new order.

The conflict between traditionalists and progressives concerning the role of the church was high on the agenda of the third conference of Latin American bishops, convened at Puebla, Mexico, in March 1979. Unlike Medellín, where the progressives had the upper hand, a conservative faction controlled the preparations for the Puebla conference and clearly intended to put down the troublesome liberation theology and its supporters. "The responsibility of the Puebla [conference]," said Cardinal Agnelo Rossi of the Vatican Curia, "is to put the Church in Latin America back on the right track." The dominant conservative faction prepared a working paper that urged resignation on the poor in the hope of a better hereafter and placed its trust for the solution of Latin America's great social problems in the failed reformist models of the 1960s. This document raised a storm of criticism among progressive bishops and other clergy.

The unknown element in the equation at Puebla was the position of the new pope, John Paul II, who was to inaugurate the conference. Seeking a guide for their deliberations, the bishops anxiously awaited his arrival in January 1979. But the apparent contradictions in his message made his position uncertain: some of his speeches appeared to emphasize personal devotion and religious discipline, to condemn priestly involvement in politics and—by implication—the theology of liberation; others could be considered favorable to liberation theology and even inflammatory, as when he told a gathering of forty thousand Indians at Oaxaca that "you have a right to be respected and not deprived of the little you have, often by methods that amount to plunder," adding that "the goods of the world were destined by God for the good of all. And if the common good so demands, there is no doubt that expropriation is the best measure."

Despite their ambiguity, the pope's statements in general tended to reinforce the position of progressives and moderates at the Puebla conference. Its final document continued the line of Medellín, especially in its expression of overwhelming concern for the poor: "We identify as the most devastating and humiliating scourge, the situation of inhuman poverty in which millions of Latin Americans live, with starvation wages, unemployment and underemployment, malnutrition, infant mortality, lack of adequate housing, health problems, and labor unrest."

But this concern for the poor had to be translated into action. Recent history—Central America offers the most recent examples—suggests that the Catholic masses of Latin America are on the move and that for many the direction of their movement is toward a socialism whose form will be determined by the specific historical background and conditions of each country. Whether the institutional church accompanies the Latin American peoples "in the historical process of their own self-determination" may well determine whether it becomes a marginal or a potent force in the Latin American society of the future.

The Military

A similar differentiation is taking place within the Latin American armed forces. The phenomenon of the reformist or even social rev-olutionary military officer is older than is sometimes supposed. In Brazil, we recall, the tenente revolts of the 1920s paved the way for the triumph of Getúlio Vargas's reformist revolution of 1930. Juan Perón and other members of the Group of United Officers exemplified a similar tendency within the Argentine officer corps in the 1930s. In Guatemala in 1944, a group of progressive officers led by Colonel Jacobo Arbenz overthrew the Ubico dictatorship and installed a government that enacted a sweeping land reform and other democratic changes.

The massive influx of North American capital into Latin America after 1945, accompanied by the growing political influence of the United States in the area, altered the balance of forces between conservatives and progressives within the Latin American military. Many high-ranking officers became fervent converts to the North American system of free enterprise and accepted the inevitability of a mortal struggle between "atheistical communism" and the "free world." By the Treaty of Rio de Janeiro (1947), the Latin American republics committed themselves to join the United States in the defense of the Western hemisphere. In the context of the cold war, this commitment entailed collaboration with the United States in a global anticommunist strategy, to the extent of justifying military intervention in any country threatened or conquered by "communist penetration." Under the cover of this doctrine, Brazilian troops joined United States forces in intervening in the Dominican Republic to crush the progressive revolutionary government of Colonel Francisco Caamaño. The integration of Latin American armies into the strategic plans of the Pentagon converted many into appendages of the North American military machine.

This integration was accompanied by the establishment of the technical and ideological tutelage of the Pentagon over the Latin American military, aimed particularly at the destruction of Latin American revolutionary movements. After the victory of the Cuban Revolution in

1959, this program of training and indoctrination was greatly expanded. Thousands of Latin American officers were sent to take courses in counterinsurgency warfare at Fort Bragg, Fort Knox, Fort Monmouth, and other installations in the United States and in the Panama Canal Zone. An especially important role was played by the School of the Americas, founded in 1949 and run by the United States Army at Fort Gulick in the Panama Canal Zone for the training of Latin American officers. Since its founding, 33,534 Latin American military personnel, including many future generals and some presidents, have passed through its doors; one of its former students is General Augusto Pinochet, head of the Chilean military junta.

The formation of close ties between high-ranking officers and large foreign and domestic firms contributed to the making of a reactionary military mentality. In Argentina in the 1960s, 143 retired officers of the highest ranks held 177 of the leading posts in the country's largest industrial and financial enterprises, mostly foreign-controlled. In Brazil, according to Omar Díaz de Acre, "it is difficult to find a large North American consortium that does not count among its executives some prominent retired military figures." Latin America thus developed its own military-industrial complex.

Through all these means, the United States acquired an enormous influence over the Latin American military, an influence of which General Carlos Prats, former commander in chief of the Chilean army, who was assassinated by agents of the Chilean military regime in Buenos Aires in 1974, was well aware. In his journal of the Allende years, Prats wrote: "I believe that neither President Allende nor the government parties know how profound the North American influence is in our armed forces, and especially in the mentality of the Chilean military man." Prats described it as "an influence without counterweight that I wanted to limit or at least balance." He advised President Allende to send

officers to Europe, Africa, and Asia, "not to copy them, but to understand that the world does not begin and end with the schools of the Pentagon."

Pentagon influence over the Latin American military engendered not only an obsessive anticommunism but an implacable hostility to even moderate programs of social and economic reform. North American ideological influence undoubtedly played an important role in creating a favorable climate of military opinion for the wave of counterrevolutionary coups that has swept over Latin America in the last decade and a half.

Not all Latin American military, however, are reactionaries of the Pinochet type. Even in rightist-dominated countries like Chile, Brazil, and Uruguay, there continues a more or less subterranean struggle within the military between extreme rightists and moderates who favor the restoration of democracy. In other countries, the military has seized power not to preserve the status quo but to change it. Although the military regimes in Peru (1968), Panama (1968), and Ecuador (1972) differed considerably in the scope and depth of their reforms, they demonstrated the existence of a reformist or even revolutionary officer class. We have already surveyed the Peruvian and Ecuadorian revolutions in Chapter 16. In Panama, a group of officers of the Panamanian National Guard organized a revolt that overthrew President Arnulfo Arias, a representative of the traditional oligarchy, in 1968. The rebels formed a military junta, headed by General Omar Torrijos, which soon displayed an unexpected reformist and nationalist fervor: It demanded the liquidation of the American military presence in Panama and a revision of the ancient Treaty of 1902 that would restore Panamanian sovereignty over the Canal Zone. The junta proceeded to enact the expropriation and division of large estates, the formation of peasant cooperatives, and an educational reform.

THE FLOWERING OF LATIN AMERICAN CULTURE

By mid-century, Latin American culture had attained maturity in a number of fields. Art and scholarship drew closer to the people and its problems and at the same time displayed a growing mastery of the refinements of technique. The swelling output of Latin American art and scholarship has grown into a torrent; we can only note some major trends in each field, with special attention to literature, a faithful mirror of Latin American history and problems.

The Social Sciences

Latin American social scientists, continuing the tradition of such nineteenth-century enlighteners as Sarmiento, Alberdi, and Lastarria, for the most part reject an impossible neutrality and openly take sides in the political and social struggles of the area. In Latin America, even history, the most aristocratic of the social sciences, walks hand in hand with politics. "History," says the distinguished Brazilian historian José Honório Rodrigues, "can and should be an instrument for political change." The liberal current, which dominated nineteenth-century historiography, was represented in the twentieth century by such major figures as the Mexican Daniel Cosío Villegas, who directed and took part in the writing of a monumental *Modern History of Mexico* (1955–1972), and the Argentine Ricardo Levene, who founded a historical school stressing archival research, rigorous critical method, and economic factors.

But there also existed a conservative current whose hallmarks were nostalgia for the colonial period and enthusiasm for such right-wing nineteenth-century caudillos as Alamán and Rosas. In Mexico this tendency was typified by José Vasconcelos, who proclaimed that Cortés was the creator of Mexican nationality; in Argentina it was represented by a group of re-

visionist historians who sought to rehabilitate the federalist caudillo Juan Manuel Rosas and bitterly criticized such fathers of Argentine liberalism as Mitre and Sarmiento.

Less involved in such historical quarrels were younger scholars who applied the new methods of social and quantitative history to the study of history, especially the colonial period; in Mexico this new school was represented by Enrique Florescano, in Chile by Mario Góngora, Alvaro Jara, and Rolando Mellafe. The Marxist historical method also had its able practitioners, such as Germán Carrera Damas in Venezuela, Caio Prado Júnior in Brazil, and Enrique Semo in Mexico.

The rise of Latin American anthropology was linked to that of nationalist, reformist movements whose programs stressed the redemption of the Indians and their integration in the national society. The triumph of the Mexican Revolution of 1910 gave a large impetus to such indigenismo. With modest official support, and in an atmosphere of widespread and sometimes emotional interest in Mexico's Indian past, Mexican anthropology made large quantitative and qualitative advances after 1920. The long roster of its distinguished names includes Manuel Gamio, Alfonso Caso, Wigberto Jiménez Moreno, and Miguel Covarrubias. In Peru the pro-Indian propaganda of APRA and other reformist or revolutionary movements stimulated a revival of interest in the study of Indians, past and present; two pioneers of Peruvian anthropology were Julio Tello and Luis Valcarcel. In the same period, Gilberto Freyre and Arturo Ramos in Brazil and Fernando Ortiz in Cuba began to explore the cultural contributions of the Negro and to attack racial myths. In recent decades, the emphasis in Latin American archaeology has been on patient field work designed to establish sequences and relations in the culture histories of different groups.

The first task of modern Latin American sociology was to rid itself of its nineteenth-century

A lithograph by Mexican artist Rufino Tamayo
(1899–   ), *Aztec Landscape*, 1950. (© Sotheby
Parke-Bernet. Agent: Editorial Photocolor Archives)

Spencerian heritage, which accounted for the area's disorder and backwardness by the racial inferiority of its Indian and other nonwhite groups. Since about 1960 there has arisen a "new sociology" that rejects the "impartial," empirical sociology in vogue in the United States. The new school openly identifies itself with the struggle for radical social change. "We know," says Colombian sociologist Orlando Fals Borda, "that science cannot remain a virgin in her ivory tower, claiming a theoretical neutrality in the face of the problems that assail her." A Marxist perspective illuminates the writings of such scholars as Fals Borda, Rodolfo Stavenhagen, Pablo González Casanova (Mexico), Octávio

Ianni, and Florestan Fernandes (Brazil). The new school has made contributions to the understanding of such problems as the causes of rural violence, internal colonialism, the social basis of Latin American populism, and race relations in Brazil.

Economics is a relatively young science in Latin America. Its rise is largely connected with the great crisis of 1930 and its disastrous impact on the economy of the area. In the 1940s, the UN's Economic Commission for Latin America (ECLA), led by the Argentine economist Raúl Prebisch, advanced a series of propositions, collectively given the name of structuralism, which attempted to explain Latin America's economic stagnation. Prebisch argued that countries of the "periphery," like those of Latin America, were at a permanent disadvantage in their terms of trade with the "center," the industrialized lands of Europe and North America. Two other alleged obstacles to growth were the traditional structure of agriculture, which led to the stagnation of agricultural output, and the excessive concentration of wealth and power in a few hands, which hampered social mobility, capital formation, and industrial development. The theories of the ECLA and Prebisch gave an important rationale and stimulus to the movement for Latin American industrialization, economic integration, agrarian reform, and social reform in general. A Brazilian economist, Celso Furtado, applied the structuralist thesis to Brazil in his scholarly *Economic Formation of Brazil* (1963).

Prebisch and Furtado appear to believe that Latin America can achieve economic independence and balanced development within a capitalist framework. Disappointment with the ECLA reform program and the Latin American economic performance in the 1960s and 1970s, however, has produced a progressive radicalization of Latin American economists, whose writings increasingly stress Latin America's structural dependence on multinational corporations. Pointing to the deformed, dependent character of Latin American capitalist industrialization and the persistence of such problems as the latifundio, Marxist economists like Theotonio dos Santos argue that socialism alone can cure the area's economic ills.

The Arts

The arts, like the social sciences, combined mastery of modern technical resources with increased use of national subject matter and local folk traditions. National schools of music arose that achieved a synthesis of those traditions with advanced European techniques and styles; examples of such synthesis are the compositions of Heitor Villa-Lobos in Brazil and Carlos Chávez in Mexico, the first two Latin American composers to achieve world renown. In painting, the Mexican school, led by Diego Rivera, José Clemente Orozco, and David Alfaro Siqueiros, won world acclaim with its bold, socially conscious art. Almost equally famous are the monumental murals of the Brazilian Cándido Portinari, which portray with moving simplicity and sympathy the bleak lives of Brazilian workers and peasants.

In recent decades, however, there has been a movement in the plastic arts toward a more cosmopolitan aesthetic, illustrated by the magical paintings of the Mexican Rufino Tamayo, very different from the art of Rivera, Orozco, and Siqueiros in theme and technique, yet as intensely Mexican in their own way. Modern Brazilian architecture impresses foreign observers with its audacity and its skillful solutions of problems of light and air, as evidenced by the work of the architect Oscar Niemeyer, who planned and directed the building of the new city of Brasilia.

It was in the field of literature, however, that Latin American culture of the twentieth century burned with the most brilliant flame. It may appear surprising that poor, backward countries with masses of illiterates and very small literary markets should produce such a multitude of distinguished poets and novelists, including four Nobel Prize winners in literature,[1] but the phenomenon has its reasons. In the first place, by the first decades of the twentieth century, the advance of the export-import economy had created the necessary economic and social conditions for the rise of literary circles whose members closely followed European artistic developments, plus a small reading public. Second,

---

[1] They are the Chilean poet Gabriela Mistral (1945); the Guatemalan novelist Miguel Angel Asturias (1967); the Chilean poet Pablo Neruda (1971); and the Colombian novelist Gabriel García Márquez (1982).

since colonial times literary culture has enjoyed much greater prestige in Latin America than in the United States, illustrated by the fact that many of Latin America's greatest men of letters have been rewarded with diplomatic posts, which were often sinecures. Finally, the dramatic contrasts of Latin American life—the extremes of wealth and poverty, the barbarous dictator-ships, the rich variety of regional types, the still untamed nature—have stimulated the cre-ative imagination of Latin American writers to an extent that has not occurred in happier countries. To a very considerable degree, Latin American literature is a literature of protest and struggle. In this, it continues the tradition es-tablished by such great nineteenth-century ro-mantic writers as Sarmiento, Echeverría, Martí, and Montalvo.

Literature and Society, 1910–1930: The Search for Self-expression

After 1900 the art-for-art's-sake creed, of which Rubén Darío had given the supreme example, came under growing attack. Latin American in-tellectuals, increasingly concerned with back-wardness, weakness, and disunity of their con-tinent vis-à-vis its powerful neighbor, the United States, began to descend from Parnassus. In 1899, José Enrique Rodó had already argued that Darío, despite his great technical virtuosity, was not "the poet of America." In a famous poem, "Wring the Neck of the Swan" (1910), the Mexican poet Enrique González Martínez (1871–1952) attacked Darío's proud swan, symbol of beauty as an end in itself:

Wring the neck of the swan whose deceitful
   plumage
Gives a white note to the azure fountain;
It glides in grace, but never thinks upon
the soul of things, the voice from wood and
   mountain. . . .

Observe that sapient owl which spreads his wings
Departing from Olympus and the lap of Pallas.
To end on yonder tree his silent flight.
He has no swan's grace, but his sharp eye,
Cleaving the dark, interprets the mystery of
   night.[2]

This poem foreshadowed the rise of a new spirit of sincerity, realism, and social consciousness in Latin American literature. By this time, Darío himself had turned away from escapism and had begun to write such powerful public poetry as his "To Roosevelt" (1905).

The intellectuals' concern about the destiny of the continent, about the growing gap in economic and political power between Latin America and the Colossus of the North, inspired numerous essays that probed the causes of the area's problems and suggested solutions. Par-ticularly influential—no doubt because it ex-pressed views Latin Americans wanted to hear— was the essay *Ariel* (1900) by José Enrique Rodó. One of its key themes was the opposition be-tween Latin American spirituality and the ma-terialism of the United States. However, contrary to a common misreading of Rodó, he did not wholly condemn North American utilitarianism; instead, he urged a fruitful fusion of Latin American spirituality and the practical, energetic spirit of the United States. Another important work of stocktaking was *Les democraties latines de l'Amérique* (1912) by the Peruvian Francisco García Calderón, published in France to inform Europeans about Latin America. The book de-plores Latin American disunity and anticipates a modern complaint of Latin Americans by its statement that the "new continent, politically free, is economically a vassal." In the same period, there appeared a large number of books that analyzed the problems of individual coun-tries and often found the origins of their malaise

[2] From Benjamin Keen, ed., *Latin American Civilization: The National Era*, vol. 2 (Boston: Houghton Mifflin, 1974), p. 483. © 1974 Houghton Mifflin Company.

in the racial inferiority of Indians or mixed races; typical of such primitive sociological analysis was Alcides Arguedas's study of Bolivia, *A Sick People* (1909).

The essayists sometimes also stressed the need for artistic originality. García Calderón, for example, claimed that originality in art was as important as economic independence. In the 1920s, a time of preliminary skirmishes in some countries between traditional elites and emerging bourgeois groups, Latin American writers began to try to express the essence of their lands in an original and truly native way. Struggle against an untamed nature, the Indians, the various regional forms of Creole life, and the problems of the peon and the worker were among the varied subject matter of the new literature. Writers received guidance from one of Latin America's most eminent men of letters, Pedro Henríquez-Ureña, who pointed out in his *Seven Essays in Search of Our Expression* (1928) that every formula of literary Americanism could be useful but that there was only one secret of expression: "To work for it profoundly, to seek to purify it, going to the roots of the things we wish to say, to polish, to refine, with a desire for perfection."

Two postmodernist poets, the Peruvian José Santos Chocano (1875–1934) and the Mexican Ramón López Velarde (1888–1921), illustrate the turning away of the new generation of writers from swans, eighteenth-century palaces, and princesses reclining on velvet divans to the reality of their own lands. Santos Chocano used a wide range of subject matter. He had a certain taste for exotic pre-Columbian and colonial themes: One of his finest poems evokes the ancient city of Cartagena de las Indias, dreaming behind her great walls. Pirates disturb her sleep, but she awakes serene, then softly closes her eyes; fanned by her palm trees and rocked in the hammock of the waves, she falls asleep again. But Santos Chocano could also sound a note of social protest:

Indian who toils without rest
on lands that others own,
Do you not know that they are yours
by right of your blood and sweat?[3]

The intensely personal poems of Ramón López Velarde celebrated the provincial scenes of his youth in verse free from sentimentality. His most famous poem, however, is "Suave Patria" (1921), a poem in two tender, teasing "acts" in which the poet expresses his love for Mexico with complete freedom from rhetoric. In the "intermezzo" between the acts, the poet invokes the Indian hero Cuauhtemoc—an early illustration of the indigenismo that is a major aspect of twentieth-century Mexican culture. The intermezzo opens: "Young forebear: hear me praise you, the only hero of artistic stature." But there are no heroics: The mood is subdued, tragic, compassionate. Upon the poet's spirit weigh the terrible losses and sufferings of the Mexican Revolution. His Cuauhtemoc is a Man of Sorrows; he is also an instrument for the fusion of Spanish and Indian elements into a Mexican synthesis: "Anachronistically, absurdly/The rosebush leans toward your nopal cactus." But the note most intensely sounded is that of suffering, of grief for

All that you suffered, the captive canoe,
The terror of your children,
The sobbing of your mythologies, the Malinche,
*   the idols going down.*
And last of all, that you were torn from the curv-
*   ing breast of your empress*
As from a quail's breast.[4]

---

[3] "Quién sabe," quoted in Jean Franco, *The Modern Culture of Latin America* (New York: Praeger, 1967), p. 49.

[4] From *The Aztec Image in Western Thought* by Benjamin Keen. Copyright © 1971 by Rutgers University, the State University of New Jersey. Reprinted by permission of Rutgers University Press.

The Mexican Revolution, which subtly colors "Suave Patria," also pervades the somber novels of Mariano Azuela (1873–1952). Their main theme is the betrayal by middle-class leaders and cynical intellectuals of the peasants and workers whose ignorance and valor they exploit. Azuela's best novel, *The Underdogs* (1916), tells the story of a peasant, Demetrio Macías, who organizes a guerrilla band, rises to the rank of general, and is killed fighting for Villa. He is the victim of blind forces he does not understand, over which he has no control. His simplicity and naiveté contrast with the cunning of the demogogic medical student Luis Cervantes, who carefully keeps out of harm's way and uses looted diamonds to lay the foundation of his future professional career.

The new cultural nationalism also found expression in the novels of the Colombian José Eustasio Rivera (1888–1928) and the Venezuelan Rómulo Gallegos (1884–1969). In Rivera's best work, *The Vortex* (1924), a violent tale of rubber collectors in the Amazonian jungle, the implacable wilderness joins the "rubber lords" in debasing men, in shattering their hopes and bodies. A novel of protest against the barbarism of his country, it is also "an intensely national novel: the first Colombian novel to describe the reality of life among the cowherders of the plains and the rubber-workers of the jungle."

The novels of Rómulo Gallegos, an active opponent of long-time dictator Juan Vicente Gómez, depict the hitherto neglected life of Venezuela's *llanos* (plains and jungles) and suggest that the country's destructive regional conflicts can be solved by the fusion of the antagonistic elements: whites and blacks, indigenous and European cultures, barbarism and civilization. In *Doña Bárbara* (1929), the mulatta heroine whose name the novel bears embodies the barbaric vigor and lawless spirit of the people of the plains. Santos Luzardo, on whose land she has encroached, is a city-educated lawyer who finds that he himself must resort to violence to defeat her. Their duel is finally ended by Santos Luzardo's marriage to Doña Bárbara's daughter, a child of nature whom he carefully educates, with particular care that she drop the plebeian dialect of the llanos and learn to speak and act like the "exquisite young ladies of Caracas." The patent artificiality of the civilization-barbarism dichotomy, reflecting Gallegos's middle-class liberalism, weakens his works.

A different viewpoint on the quarrel between civilization and barbarism emerges in the gaucho novel *Don Segundo Sombra* (1926) by Ricardo Guiraldes (1886–1927). One of the most perfect of Latin American novels, it evokes with incomparable skill a regional type rapidly receding into the past, but the portrait is clearly touched with nostalgia. The gaucho hero emerges as a dignified and rounded individual, perfectly adapted to his milieu; he needs no transformation from without, for he is already a completely civilized human being.

Literature and Society, 1930–1983: A Social Consciousness

In the 1930s, a time of growing economic difficulties accompanied by the sharpening of class struggles in mines, factories, and plantations, the radicalization of Latin American writers gave rise to the novel of social protest, frequently influenced by Marxist ideology. Since the principal victims of capitalist exploitation in Latin America were Indians, the new novels of social protest were usually Indianist novels as well. Leading representatives of this genre were Jorge Icaza (b.1906) in Ecuador, Ciro Alegría (1909–1967) and José M. Arguedas (1901–1969) in Peru, and Miguel A. Asturias (1899–1974) in Guatemala.

The early Indianist novels, like *Birds Without a Nest* (1889) by Clorinda Matto de Turner or *Race of Bronze* (1919) by Alcides Arguedas, had found the roots of Indian misery and exploitation in the personal vices or weaknesses of the ruling classes or of the Indians themselves. In the new Indianist novel, the destruction of the Indians flows inexorably from the operation of blind economic forces, of which the grasping landlord or exploitive foreign company (the Indianist novel is often an anti-imperialist novel as well) are mere instruments. The new Indianist novelists also made a more serious effort to enter the Indian mind and sometimes prepared themselves for their task by living with the Indians to learn their speech and customs.

Jorge Icaza's *Huasipungo* (1934) reports with blazing anger the brutal exploitation of a group of Ecuadorian Indians, which culminates in an effort to expel them from their parcels of land (*huasipungos*) to make way for the exploitation of the area by foreign oil companies. But the Indians are shown as so degraded by their servitude, so brutish even in dealing with one another, that it is difficult to sympathize with them. More successful in this respect is Ciro Alegría's *Broad and Alien Is the World* (1941), which also relates the destruction of an Indian community by a landowner bent on acquiring its lands. Alegría's idealized portrayal of Indian life and virtues borders on the sentimental, yet he convincingly portrays a communal society whose driving force is mutual aid and, therefore, engages the reader's sympathy with the Indians.

Land and labor struggles also characterize the Indianist novels of José M. Arguedas, who knew Quechua before he knew Spanish and had a profound mastery of Indian culture and customs. His novels achieve an unusual penetration of the Indian mentality through his effort to reproduce the rhythm and syntax of Quechua and to evoke the religious world view of the Indians.

The Guatemalan writer Miguel A. Asturias is one of the founders of the school of magical realism, which attempts to depict Indian life as the Indians themselves would experience it, in terms of myth. In *Men of Maize* (1949), he records from this mythic perspective the losing struggle of the Indians to retain their land and way of life, using a style whose language and rhythms resemble those of the Maya language. The blend of fantasy and reality in Asturias's Indianist novels is far removed from the documentary tone of such regional novelists as Rivera, Gallegos, and Icaza.

In Brazil in the 1920s and 1930s, there arose a "northeastern school" that portrayed the varied social types and struggles of the drought-ridden *sertão* and the coastal sugar plantations. This group included Graciliano Ramos (1892–1953), José Lins do Rego (1901–1957), and Jorge Amado (b.1912). In *Barren Lives* (1938), Ramos deals with the struggle of a cowherder against drought and starvation and his eventual flight to the city. The "sugar cane cycle" of Lins do Rego (1932–1943) chronicles the decline and fall of the old sugar aristocracy—the rise of the great *usina* (sugar mill) and the impact of economic change on planters, slaves, and their descendants. Partly based on Lins do Rego's own childhood and adult experiences, these novels reconstruct the social history of Brazilian sugar. In his *Cocoa* (1933), Amado describes the life of the workers on the cocoa plantations south of Bahia; in *The Violent Land* (1943), he records the bloody struggles for economic and political power of the cocoa planters.

The Cuban novelist Alejo Carpentier applies the method of magical realism to West Indian blacks in *The Kingdom of This World* (1949); set in Haiti in the time of the French Revolution, it presents the rise and fall of the black dictator Henri Christophe and the emergence of a new mulatto ruling class as seen through the eyes of a house slave. Revolution and the corruption of revolutionaries are major themes of Carpentier's *The Age of Enlightenment* (1962), which is also set in the period of the French Revolution but deals with the Caribbean as a whole.

Poetry, like the prose, revealed a new social consciousness. At the same time, poets struggled to free their verse from rhetoric and the tyranny of old forms. The difficult poetry of Cesar Vallejo (1892–1938), though concerned from first to last with human anguish, with the inherently tragic human condition, reveals in its later phase a compassion for the victims of war and exploitation, a vision of a possible better life, that reflects his new socialist ideology. For the Chilean poet Pablo Neruda (1904–1973), as for Vallejo, the Spanish Civil War was a turning point; in a poem written at the beginning of the war he declares that henceforth he will unite his "lone wolf's walk" to the "walk of man." At the end of the war, he joined the Communist party and combined his poetic career with political activism until his death in 1973. His major work is *Canto general* (1950), an epic attempt to tell the history of the American continent from the point of view of figures neglected by the textbooks—workers, peasants, and fighters for freedom. Another major poet of left-wing tendencies, the Cuban Nicolás Guillen (b.1902), founded the Afro-Cuban poetry movement, based on the rhythms and images of Cuban black folk poetry. With the passage of time, his poety acquired strong social revolutionary and anti-imperialist tones.

The period since 1940 has seen a continuing revolution in the technique of the novel. This technical revolution is marked by intensive use of such devices as stream of consciousness, flashbacks, symbolism, and fantasy. Some writers, like Jorge Luis Borges in his *Ficciones* (1944), employ fantasy and other avant-garde techniques to demonstrate the absurdity and senselessness of life. Others, however, employ them to heighten our awareness of an abhorrent social and political order. To one degree or another, these writers continue the Latin American tradition of employing literature as an instrument of social protest and change. Typical of such novelists is Mario Vargas Llosa, author of *Conversations in the Cathedral* (1970), whose structural and verbal disorder appears to re-enact the disorder of Peruvian life and geography. Vargas Llosa writes:

Novelists who speak well of their country should be distrusted: patriotism, which is a fruitful virtue in soldiers and bureaucrats, is usually a poor one in literature. Literature in general and the novel in particular are expressions of discontent. Their social usefulness lies principally in the fact that they remind people that the world is always wrong, that life should always change.

We noted Miguel Asturias's use of magical realism in such Indianist novels as *Men of Maize*. His powerful *Mr. President* (1941), deals with a sinister dictator who rules with a vast apparatus of repression. In it dreams, memories, and imaginings replace the truth the characters cannot speak. Fantasy and reality blend in Asturias's anti-imperialist trilogy, *Strong Wind* (1950), *The Green Pope* (1954), and *The Eyes of the Buried* (1960), which deal with the formation of a monopolistic banana company and the struggles of small farmers and workers against it. In *Strong Wind*, when those struggles fail, a hurricane summoned by an Indian witch doctor destroys the company's plantations.

Fantasy is the means employed by Gabriel García Márquez to attack a monstrous social and political order in *One Hundred Years of Solitude* (1967), which records the history of an imaginary town set in the remote Colombian *ciénaga* (swampland) where García Márquez grew up. The book describes extraordinary people and events in deadpan fashion; in this magical world, miracles occur in the most natural way. But many of the fantastic situations "are absurd but logical exaggerations of real situations." The fantasies are a parody of Colombian history itself. Indeed, no event in the book is as fantastic as *la Violencia*, the civil war unleashed in the Colombian countryside by conservative repression in 1949, a war that took perhaps 300,000 lives in the course of a few years.

Accelerated urbanization and industrialization have placed their stamp on the new novel; frequently, it is set in the great city and deals with the psychological problems of the urban middle class. In the urban novels of the Mexican Carlos Fuentes (b.1929), a major theme is the betrayal of revolutionary ideals by the men who made the revolution. In *Where the Air Is Clearer* (1958), *The Clear Consciences* (1959), and *The Death of Artemio Cruz* (1962), Fuentes skillfully depicts the life of a cynical, cosmopolitan society. Alienation and the emptiness of middle- and upper-class life are also common themes in the Argentine urban novel; a good example is *A November Party* (1938) by Eduardo Mallea (b.1903).

Continuing a tradition established by the founders of Latin American culture, modern Latin American scholars, writers, and artists have often tended to view their work not only as a means of self-expression but as an act of social protest, an instrument of social and political change. To be sure, in Latin America as elsewhere, there are poets who write very private verse, novelists who deal with intensely personal themes, and painters whose abstract or surrealist art conveys no explicit social message. But to a greater extent than elsewhere, perhaps, the Latin American poet, novelist, and painter have also been the voice and the conscience of the people.

CHAPTER TWENTY

The Two Americas:
United States–Latin American
Relations

Two consistent themes appear when the relations of the United States with Latin America over the past one hundred and eighty years are examined. First and foremost, the United States has sought to protect and expand its economic interests in the region. Ever since the administration of James Monroe, American governments have attempted to establish and maintain Latin America as an economic appendage of the United States. American policy makers have displayed resourcefulness and flexibility in pursuit of this goal, adapting their methods to meet the varying domestic political pressures, the changing requirements of American economic enterprise, and the shifting conditions in Latin America. Second, the United States has generally subordinated Latin America to its other concerns abroad. Consequently, American policy makers have tended to deal with Latin America either by employing frameworks formed for other regions or by grouping the nations of the area under one heading and ignoring their individual problems and needs.

UNITED STATES POLICY

American policy toward Latin America has changed over time to accommodate burgeoning American economic activities in the region. During the early years of the nineteenth century, U.S. commerce with its southern neighbors demanded little more than policing the Caribbean from marauding pirates. As the United States grew into a commercial, industrial, and, eventually, financial power, its foreign policy broadened in scope. The hunt for new markets brought it into competition with European nations, especially Great Britain. As a result, it became one of the major aims of American policy to check the further penetration of European commerce and capital into Latin America.

By the turn of the century, Latin America had become not only a substantial market for American products but an important source of raw materials and a major area for capital investment as well. Having recently built a powerful navy, the United States assumed the responsibility of protecting American commerce and investment by forcibly maintaining order in the region. Uninvited, it assumed the role of policeman of the Western Hemisphere. In this capacity, the United States focused its attention on the weak and chaotic nations of the Caribbean and Central America, where American economic activity was concentrated.

At mid-century, South America replaced the Caribbean as the focus of American economic expansion. Geography, logistics, and the anti-imperialist temper of the times required the United States to abandon the old policies of military intervention in favor of more subtle and sophisticated ways of achieving its ends; these new methods included the lure of grants and loans, the threat of economic sanctions, and subversion. When these methods failed, however, as they did in Guatemala in 1954, in

Cuba in 1959, and in the Dominican Republic in 1965, the United States did not hesitate to resort to the open or covert use of force.

Ideology has always figured in United States policy toward Latin America. Thus, Theodore Roosevelt vowed to "civilize," Woodrow Wilson to "democratize," and John F. Kennedy to "reform" Latin America. But ideology has always been subordinated to the material needs of United States–Latin American policy, and the presidents who made these pious professions were ready to use the sword in defense of the American Empire in Latin America. They were also ready to support the most oppressive regimes in the area as long as they cooperated with the United States.

The two Americas, both born in wars of national liberation, have followed very different historical paths. In two centuries, the United States has risen to become the industrial and financial giant of the capitalist world; despite its many economic and social problems, it provides the majority of its people with a high material standard of living. Latin America has fallen far behind the other America and belongs to the underdeveloped part of the world; 50 percent of its population earned less than $200 a year in 1965, and the living standards of the lower income groups have actually declined since 1950. By no coincidence, perhaps, the decline has been especially evident in such countries as Brazil and Mexico, which have some of the highest concentrations of American capital.

Many Latin Americans are convinced that these divergent trends are not unrelated, that Latin American underdevelopment is the other side of American development, that Latin American poverty and misery have accumulated as the economic and political power of foreign (chiefly American) multinational corporations has grown. A growing number of Latin Americans also believe that they must recapture their national resources from foreign control if they wish to make the structural economic and social changes needed by the area. How the United

States adjusts it policies to this trend may well determine the substance of its Latin American relations in the future.

PRELUDE TO EMPIRE, 1810–1897

Manifest Destiny, 1810–1865

During the early decades of the nineteenth century, westward expansion and nascent commerce brought the United States into its first contact with its southern neighbors. However, American military weakness, lack of information, and British predominance in the area limited U.S. activities in Latin America. U.S. trade with Latin America began in earnest in 1797, when Spain opened the ports of its New World colonies to foreign trade. By 1811 the Spanish colonies accounted for 16 percent of all American trade. A dozen years later, despite the disruptions of the War of 1812, the figure had increased to 20 percent.

From 1815 to 1825, pirates endangered this growing American trade in the Caribbean. The small United States Navy fought repeated engagements against these pirates to secure the region; American forces staged several landings in Cuba, Puerto Rico, Santo Domingo, and Yucatán.

With only a small navy and few funds at its disposal, the American government could offer little aid or comfort to the Spanish-American nations during their wars of independence (1810–1826). During the first stage of these wars, the War of 1812 consumed America's attention and resources. From 1819 to 1821, the United States undertook delicate negotiations with Spain for the purchase of Florida and did not choose to jeopardize these dealings by helping the Spanish-American insurgents.

When it was clear that the Latin American independence movements had succeeded, the United States acted to prevent other European nations from acquiring colonies or undue influence in the region, developments that could shut off American access to potentially lucrative markets. In his message to Congress on December 2, 1823, President James Monroe declared that as a matter of principle, "the American continents, by the free and independent condition they have assumed and maintain, are henceforth not to be considered subjects for future colonization by any European powers. . . . We should consider any attempt on their [the European powers'] part to extend their system to any portion of this hemisphere as dangerous to our peace and safety." Monroe went on to say that the United States would not interfere with existing colonies, nor would it meddle in European affairs.

The Monroe Doctrine was ineffective for much of the nineteenth century because the United States had neither the resources nor the inclination to back it up. Fortunately, the British fleet stood squarely in the way of any attempt by Europe to reconquer Latin America. Great Britain, with a virtual monopoly of trade in the area, saw no need to establish a formal empire and would not permit others to intrude. The doctrine, furthermore, failed to prevent repeated European interventions in Latin America. Following the accepted practice of the time, French and British gunboats regularly bombarded or blockaded Latin American ports to force payment of debts or reparations. The United States, too, adopted this practice, landing troops in the Falkland Islands, Argentina, and Peru during the 1830s, in Argentina, Nicaragua, Uruguay, Panama, Paraguay, and Mexico during the 1850s, and in Panama, Uruguay, Mexico, and Colombia during the 1860s.

Westward territorial expansion involved the United States in two wars during the nineteenth century. After the purchase of Louisiana (1803) and Florida (1821), the country began to cast covetous looks toward the northern provinces of Mexico, where Americans had begun to con-.

duct flourishing commerce. In 1825, President John Quincy Adams authorized the United States minister to Mexico to negotiate the purchase of Texas. The Mexican government rejected the proposal. During the early 1830s, American settlers poured into Texas and quickly found themselves at odds with Mexican authorities over the issues of local autonomy and the illegal introduction of slavery into the area. In 1836 the settlers rebelled, defeated Mexico in a short war, and won their independence. Texas remained an independent nation for ten years, for the bitter debate over the extension of slavery prevented its annexation to the United States until 1845.

In 1845, President James Polk sent an emissary, James Slidell, to Mexico to arrange the acquisition of California. Outraged at the annexation of Texas, the Mexicans refused to cede any of their territory. Consequently, Polk trumped up a border incident along the Rio Grande, provoking a military clash that led to the Mexican-American War (1846–1848). The victorious United States took the territories of Arizona, New Mexico, and California. Barely a half-century old, the United States had successfully waged a war of territorial acquisition.

Commerce and the Canal

From 1815 to 1860, American foreign commerce increased dramatically; exports grew by nearly 400 percent and imports by 300 percent. The nature of American trade was transformed, for instead of re-exporting foreign-made goods, U.S. merchants exported agricultural commodities and manufactured goods produced in the United States. Because of the increased economic activity in the Caribbean, especially Cuba and Central America, the United States began to pay close attention to the region. Cuba became one of the most important U.S. overseas markets, ranking third behind Great Britain and France in total American trade. Throughout the 1850s,

there was a strong sentiment, particularly among southerners, to annex the island. President Polk tried unsuccessfully to purchase Cuba from Spain in 1852.

Central America became important because of the prospect of a canal through the region. Americans had talked of a canal through the Central American isthmus as early as 1825. In 1846 the United States signed an agreement with New Granada (Colombia) that guaranteed American access to any canal built in Panama, then a province of New Granada. This concern over a canal and its commercial interests in Central America brought the United States into direct confrontation with Great Britain, which had colonies in the region. Both nations sought to keep the other from dominating the area or controlling any canal that would be built. As a result, in 1850 they agreed to the Clayton-Bulwer Treaty, which provided that neither would try to dominate Central America or any part of it or would acquire exclusive rights to a canal. Thus, they eliminated a potential cause of hostilities.

The gold rush to California in 1849 increased the importance of transportation across the isthmus. American entrepreneurs invested heavily in steamships and railroad construction in the region to satisfy the demand for cheap and fast transport across the isthmus to California. Despite the treaty with Britain and these heavy investments in transportation, U.S. interest in a canal continued.

The Awakening Giant, 1865–1887

After a short pause during the Civil War (1861–1865), the United States resumed its active role in Latin America under the guidance of the expansionist Secretary of State William H. Seward. In February 1866, Seward demanded that France remove its troops from Mexico, where they were supporting the short-lived imperial regime of Maximilian. Napoleon III, already concerned by the prospect of war with Prussia in Europe, decided to liquidate his unprofitable Mexican venture and complied. Seward had engineered the first successful application of the Monroe Doctrine and won a significant victory for American foreign policy. In 1867, the secretary negotiated the purchase of the Virgin Islands from Denmark, but the Senate refused to ratify the agreement.

During his two terms (1869–1877), President Ulysses S. Grant aggressively sought to expand American hegemony southward. Only the efforts of his more cautious secretary of state, Hamilton Fish, kept him from intervening in Cuba's Ten Years' War (1868–1878). In 1870, Grant arranged the annexation of Santo Domingo, but the Senate rejected the transaction. Grant and Fish also attempted to weaken European interests in Latin America. At the beginning of his term, Grant proclaimed the nontransfer principle, which maintained that "hereafter no territory on this continent shall be regarded as subject to transfer to a European power," thereby continuing the vigorous application of the Monroe Doctrine initiated by Seward. Twice in the 1870s, the president cautioned European nations not to interfere when they threatened intervention in Venezuela.

American policy was beginning to acquire a definite shape and direction. The American people were distrustful of overseas territorial acquisition; many believed that the nation had more than enough land, that time and money would be better spent on industrialization at home, and that expansion in Latin America would sharpen race problems in the United States. American leaders, however, responding to changes in the American economy, gradually widened the scope of American policy and adopted more aggressive methods to implement it in response to the requirements of the economy.

Several important developments influenced American foreign policy makers during the last quarter of the nineteenth century. Despite the burgeoning commercial and industrial power of the United States, it periodically suffered from severe economic depressions; the first such depression lasted from 1873 to 1878. American business and government leaders became convinced that surplus production caused these crises. The only solution, they concluded, was to expand American markets abroad. In order to increase its exports to Latin America, the United States had, first, to reduce the influence of its European competitors and, second, to obtain more favorable trade terms with the nations of the region.

Grant's meddling in Venezuela represented one effort to limit European influence. President Rutherford B. Hayes continued Grant's policy when he tried unsuccessfully to thwart the French attempt in 1878 to build a canal through Panama. Hayes claimed that the treaty with New Granada in 1846 had given the United States exclusive rights to construct the canal. Colombia rejected this interpretation. The decisive showdown with the Europeans was not to take place until the 1890s.

Simultaneously, the United States attempted to achieve favorable conditions for trade with Latin America. As part of this effort, American statesmen proposed to form a Pan-American movement, which, it was hoped, would promote friendly trade relations and help to create a desirable climate of political stability in the hemisphere. They also sought to negotiate reciprocal trade treaties that would facilitate the access of American products to the Latin American market. In 1881, Secretary of State James G. Blaine tried to establish an Inter-American Conference, but his plans were canceled in the aftermath of President James Garfield's assassination. F. T. Frelinghuysen, secretary of state in the Arthur administration (1881–1885), managed to negotiate bilateral reciprocal trade treaties with six Latin American nations. The administration of Grover Cleveland (1885–1889) abandoned most of these efforts, but in 1888 the president called for a meeting of nations of the

Western Hemisphere. When Blaine returned as secretary of state in the Harrison administration (1889–1893), he took up this initiative, organizing the first Inter-American Conference, which met in Washington, D.C., in 1889. The conferees could agree on very little. Suspicious Latin American delegates, led by Argentina, rejected American proposals for a customs union and treaties of arbitration. They did, however, agree to set up the Commercial Bureau of the American Republics (later the Pan-American Union).

A major impediment to trade with Latin America was the high protective duties placed on imported products by the United States Congress. Reciprocal trade agreements were impossible as long as Congress refused to allow the president to lower duties on goods from nations that lowered their tariffs on American goods. Finally, with the McKinley Tariff Act of 1890, the Harrison administration won acceptance of a provision for reverse reciprocity; sugar-producing nations would lose their duty-free status unless they lowered tariffs on American products. Under the threat of exclusion from the U.S. market, most Latin American countries signed reciprocal trade pacts. With the exception of the major sugar-producing areas, such as Brazil and Cuba, whose output found a large market in the United States, these treaties were generally unsuccessful in expanding trade. After the enactment of the McKinley tariff, Cuba's exports to the United States increased by 50 percent in three years. When the 1894 tariff revoked reciprocity, however, the Cuban economy collapsed, leading to the rebellion that culminated in the Spanish-Cuban-American War in 1898.

Adventures in Latin America, 1888–1896

American adventurism in Latin America in the last years of the nineteenth century stemmed from severe domestic economic and social problems and from the country's growing stake in commerce and investment in the region. The United States experienced a deep depression from 1893 to 1898, the third such downturn in twenty-five years (the others occurred in 1873–1878 and 1882–1885). It became evident that the domestic market could not absorb the rapidly growing output of American agriculture and industry. American leaders unanimously agreed that the answer to the problem was to expand foreign markets. The depression of 1893 created deep-seated social unrest, as well, resulting in a series of bitter and bloody strikes. Businessmen and politicians alike feared that continued depression would lead to class warfare.

At the same time, American capitalists increased their investment in Latin America. Paradoxically, despite the depression, U.S. banks had surplus funds to invest. Because investments in the United States were unattractive, the bankers turned to potentially more lucrative foreign enterprises. American investors poured millions of dollars into Cuban sugar and Mexican mining and railroads. By 1900 the American stake in Mexico alone had reached $500 million.

American interest, however, was not limited to areas like Mexico and Cuba, where the United States already had large investments. The United States was willing to go to great lengths, even at the risk of war, both to protect potential markets and to reinforce its political dominance in the region. This was particularly true of the Caribbean, which American leaders tended to view as an "American lake." Thus, in 1888 the United States intervened in a civil war in Haiti to secure a favorable commercial agreement and a naval base at Môle St. Nicolas. The U.S. fleet actually broke a blockade to bring about the victory of the faction it favored. Once entrenched in power, however, this group reneged on its promises to the Harrison administration. Secretary Blaine also tried unsuccessfully to obtain Samaná Bay from Santo Domingo.

In 1892 the United States came within a hairsbreadth of war with Chile. Chilean-American relations had been strained since the War of the Pacific (1879–1883), when the United States had failed in attempts to soften the harsh peace terms victorious Chile imposed on defeated Peru and Bolivia. In the following decade, American policy had tried to counterbalance the growing European influence in Chile, especially in its valuable nitrate regions.

In 1891 the United States became involved in the civil war between the supporters of President José Balmaceda and the Chilean Congress. The congressional faction enjoyed the support of both the British and the Germans. German warships actually patrolled the northern coast of Chile to protect the nitrate trade. As his military position deteriorated, Balmaceda, in desperation, appealed to the United States for help. The United States Navy confiscated a supply ship bound for the congressional faction. The United States also offered to mediate the conflict; this proposal met an icy refusal from the Chilean Congress. In October 1892, a contingent of American sailors on shore leave in Valparaíso was attacked by a Chilean mob, and two sailors were murdered. The congressional faction, now in control of the Chilean government, dragged its feet in investigating the incident. President Harrison demanded "full and prompt reparation" for the murders. After receiving an insulting note from the Chilean foreign minister, Harrison ordered the navy to prepare for action. In a message to Congress, the president strongly intimated that war was imminent. In the face of this threat, the Chileans backed down, eventually paying an indemnity of $75,000.

As the depression of 1893 deepened, American leaders looked southward with growing anxiety. President Cleveland declared in his annual message to Congress in 1893 that unrest and European meddling had threatened American interests in Nicaragua, Guatemala, Costa Rica, Honduras, and Brazil in 1892; the United States fleet was finding it difficult to keep up with its "responsibilities." Markets desperately needed by the United States were threatened by disorders and competition from European nations, particularly Britain.

In 1894 the United States became involved in another revolution when it intervened in Brazil to protect a potentially important market and to check British influence there. The United States had signed a reciprocal trade agreement with the newly proclaimed republic of Brazil in 1891, but the rebels who rose up in 1893 opposed the pact. The main strategy of the rebel forces was to blockade the harbor of Rio de Janeiro, the nation's principal city; they hoped to strangle the government by denying it the all-important customs revenue. The United States helped to undermine this strategy by refusing to recognize the blockade. American vessels unloaded their cargoes without interference.

Late in 1894, however, with clandestine aid from the British, the rebellion regained its momentum. At this time, important mercantile and oil (Rockefeller) interests, fearing the loss of their Brazilian market, brought pressure on the State Department to intervene. The United States responded by sending most of the Atlantic fleet to the harbor of Rio de Janeiro. By maneuvering to prevent rebel bombardment of the capital, the American warships played a crucial part in the defeat of the revolt.

Shortly thereafter, the United States intervened in Nicaragua to protect American rights to an isthmian canal and the substantial holdings of American investors. In 1893 a nationalist government, headed by General José S. Zelaya, took power in Nicaragua; it threatened to cancel a concession granted by a previous administration to the Maritime Canal Company to build a canal through Nicaraguan territory. Later, Zelaya also threatened the prosperous American-run banana plantations in the Mosquito Indian reservation (an area claimed by Nicaragua but controlled by the British) by invading the reservation in 1894. In response, British troops landed and quickly subdued the Nicaraguan force. American interests, with a $2 million stake in the Mosquito region, were unwilling to accept either British or Nicaraguan rule. To protect American property, the United States stationed two warships off the coast and in July dispatched marines to restore order. United States troops landed three more times, in 1896, 1898, and 1899, to protect American lives and property. In 1897 Secretary of State Richard Olney threatened war to prevent cancellation of the canal treaty.

The Turning Point: Venezuela, 1895–1896

The Venezuelan crisis of 1895–1896 ended in full British recognition of American hegemony in the Western Hemisphere. The United States intervened in a boundary dispute between Venezuela and Great Britain that had festered for over half a century. The controversy concerned the region at the mouth of the Orinoco River, the major artery for northern South America, which was claimed by both Venezuela and the British colony of Guiana (present-day Guyana). In the 1880s, Britain extended its claims, causing Venezuela to break off diplomatic relations.

During 1893 and 1894, the Venezuelan government, confronted with mounting economic difficulties and political unrest, appealed to the United States to help settle the controversy. President Cleveland's entrance into the dispute reflected his deep concern about the apparent resurgence of European intervention in Latin America. Between 1891 and 1895, the British had actively intervened in Chile, Brazil, and Nicaragua. The French had become involved in a dispute with Brazil over the boundary of their colony of Guiana and had threatened intervention in Santo Domingo to obtain satisfaction for the killing of a French citizen. The simultaneous scramble for territories in Africa magnified the threat; what the European rivals did on one continent, they could do on another.

Specifically, President Cleveland feared that British control of the mouth of the Orinoco would exclude American commerce from northern South American markets.

In 1895, in an obvious effort to intensify American support, the Venezuelan government granted a lucrative concession to an American syndicate for the exploitation of rich mineral resources located in the disputed zone. In July 1895, Secretary of State Richard Olney spelled out the American attitude toward European meddling in Latin America. Citing the Monroe Doctrine, he declared that the United States would intervene whenever the actions of a European power in the Western Hemisphere posed a "serious and direct menace to its own integrity and welfare." In effect, Olney claimed hegemony for the United States in Latin America.

The British initially responded to Olney's claims with disdain; the English foreign secretary denied the validity of the Monroe Doctrine in international law and brushed aside the American assertion of supremacy in the Western Hemisphere. President Cleveland, however, firmly supported Olney's position and made it clear that the United States was willing to go to war to uphold it. Meanwhile, international developments worked to soften the British stand; the threat of a war with Germany and British problems in South Africa took precedence. Accordingly, in late 1896, the British agreed to submit the dispute to arbitration. The government of Venezuela neither participated in nor was informed of this agreement.

The Venezuelan affair marked the end of British military predominance in Latin America. Its attention now focused on the growing German power and the competition for territory in Africa, Britain could no longer commit substantial resources to the region. With the growing threat of a general war in Europe, British leaders could also not afford to alienate the United States, a powerful potential ally. Thus, the British formally recognized American hegemony in

Latin America with the signing of the Hay-Pauncefote Treaty of 1901, which allowed the United States unilaterally to build, control, and fortify an isthmian canal. In 1906, Britain withdrew its fleet from the Caribbean. Great Britain retained its predominant economic position in southern South America but was fated to lose that also to the United States after World War I.

AN IMPERIAL POWER, 1898–1933

By 1898 the United States had emerged as an industrial, financial, and naval power. It surpassed Great Britain as the world's leading manufacturing state. Its giant banks and corporations invested heavily overseas. Increasingly, the nation looked abroad for markets, raw materials, and profits. Recurring economic difficulties and mounting social unrest spurred American leaders to seek solutions in overseas economic expansion and foreign adventures.

The War with Spain

The war with Spain in 1898 established the United States as a full-fledged imperial power. The primary goal of American Cuban policy during the 1890s was to protect the very large (over $50 million) American investment in the island by stopping the chronic political disorder there. When Spain proved unable to end the turmoil, and it appeared that ungovernable native rebels might take over, the United States intervened. In declaring war against Spain, the United States Congress pledged to free Cuba from Spanish tyranny and in the Teller Resolution disavowed any intention to annex the island. However, the American government proceeded to conduct the war and negotiate the peace without consulting the Cubans.

The United States occupied and ruled the island from 1898 to 1902, departing only after the Cubans agreed to include in their constitution

the notorious Platt Amendment, which made the country a virtual American protectorate. American forces occupied the island three more times, 1906 to 1909, 1912, and 1917 to 1922. As we have seen in Chapter 17, instead of bringing the Cubans liberty and economic progress, the American intervention promoted and perpetuated corruption, violence, and economic stagnation.

An American Lake: The "Big Stick" and "Dollar Diplomacy" in the Caribbean

From 1898 to 1932, the United States intervened militarily in ten Caribbean nations[1] a total of thirty-four times. Its occupation forces ran the governments of the Dominican Republic, Cuba, Nicaragua, Haiti, and Panama for long periods; Honduras, Mexico, Guatemala, and Costa Rica experienced shorter invasions. In their efforts to protect expanding American commerce and investment in the area, every American president from Theodore Roosevelt to Calvin Coolidge dispatched the marines to some part of the Caribbean. Military intervention was not the only method employed by the United States to control the region; other effective means included threats, nonrecognition, and economic sanctions.

The American economic stake in the Caribbean was substantial. Moreover, the nature of this investment, which was concentrated primarily in agricultural commodities, mineral extraction, oil production, and government securities, made it particularly vulnerable to political disorders. From 1897 to 1914, American investment in Cuba and the West Indies rose by 685 percent—from $50 million to $336 million. Investment in Central America increased 442 percent—from $21 million to $93 million. By 1914, American investment in Mexico had risen to over $1 billion. In 1914, 43 percent of this investment was in mining,

[1] The Caribbean nations include the West Indies, Cuba, Central America, and Mexico.

18.7 percent in agriculture, and 10 percent in oil. An additional 13 percent was invested in railroads, which were built to transport the export products to market. The owners of these enterprises often had considerable influence on American policy.

The United States justified its actions in the Caribbean by the so-called Roosevelt Corollary (1904) to the Monroe Doctrine, so named because President Theodore Roosevelt maintained that the United States, as a "civilized" nation, had the right to end "chronic wrongdoing" and thus could intervene in the Caribbean to maintain order. The Roosevelt Corollary was a logical outgrowth of the increasingly aggressive policies successively advanced by Seward, Grant, Cleveland, and Olney. As American economic interests in the Caribbean expanded and the tendency of the nations of the region to fall into disorder and fail to meet their financial obligations became progressively more evident, the United States assumed the self-appointed role of a hemispheric policeman, charged with maintaining law and order in the area.

The Panama Canal

U.S. interest in a canal across Central America to join the Atlantic and Pacific oceans intensified as the nation filled out its continental boundaries and expanded its commercial activities throughout the Western hemisphere. A group of New York businessmen initiated a project to build a canal in 1825 but failed to obtain financial support. In 1846 the United States signed a treaty with New Granada to assure American access to any future canal constructed in the province of Panama. The California gold rush three years later created a large demand for transportation across the isthmus en route to the West Coast gold fields. In response, a group of New York capitalists constructed a railroad across the 48-mile width of Panama between 1851 and 1855. No sooner was the railway finished than U.S. troops landed to

protect American interests from Panamanian insurgents rebelling against Colombian rule. In 1865, U.S. troops again landed to protect American lives and property during another rebellion.

Americans were not the first to attempt to build a canal. Ferdinand de Lesseps, the Frenchman who had constructed the Suez Canal, began a project to dig a sea-level canal across Panama in 1878. After eleven years of effort, de Lesseps, thwarted by tropical disease and engineering problems, gave up the project. Throughout this period, the United States pressured France to abandon the undertaking; it asserted its "rightful and long-established claim to priority on the American continent." During the 1890s, American commerce and investment in Latin America continued to grow, and interest in the canal grew apace. The growth of a large United States Navy, which had two coasts to defend, added to the urgency of constructing an isthmian passageway.

In the 1880s and 1890s, support grew for building a canal through Nicaragua. In 1901 a presidential commission endorsed the Nicaraguan route, despite the more favorable engineering and logistical characteristics of the Panamanian alternative, because the French company that controlled the canal concession in Panama wanted the fantastic sum of $109 million for its rights. At this point, two extraordinary entrepreneurs, William N. Cromwell, an influential New York attorney, and Philippe Bunau-Varilla, chief engineer of the de Lesseps project and an organizer of the New Panama Canal Company (the French company that had rights to the canal) acted to change the course of U.S. policy. Cromwell, as lawyer for the canal company, bribed the Republican party to end its support of the Nicaraguan route. He and Bunau-Varilla then convinced the company to lower the price for its concession to a more reasonable $40 million.

The two men were faced with the problem of convincing the United States to purchase their company's concession before it expired in

The construction of the Panama Canal. (Courtesy
of the National Archives)

1904. In 1902, Bunau-Varilla and Cromwell
managed to push through Congress the Spooner
Amendment, which authorized President Roosevelt to buy the New Panama Canal Company's
rights for the asking price of $40 million if he
could negotiate a treaty with Colombia. In 1903,
Secretary of State John Hay pressured the Colombian ambassador to the United States to
sign a pact that gave the United States a 99-
year lease on a strip of land across the isthmus
in return for $10 million and an annual payment

of $250,000. The Colombian Senate, demanding
more money, rejected the proposal. Roosevelt
reacted stormily, calling the Colombians insulting names.

In the meantime, Bunau-Varilla undertook to
exploit the long tradition of Panamanian nationalism and rebelliousness for his own end.
From the time that Colombia won its independence from Spain in 1821, it had never been
able to establish its rule in Panama. During the
nineteenth century, the Panamanians revolted

fifty times against their Colombian masters. On two occasions, when the Panamanian rebels seemed near success (1855–1856 and 1885), the United States intervened militarily to protect American interests and end the revolts. After a terrible civil war (1899–1902) had severely weakened Colombia, Panamanian nationalists again prepared to rise in revolt. Working closely with the U.S. State Department and the Panamanians, Bunau-Varilla triggered a successful uprising in early November 1903. With the help of the United States Navy and liberal bribes paid to the Colombian officers who were supposed to crush the revolt, Panama won its independence.

The Panamanians, to their own undoing, entrusted to Bunau-Varilla the subsequent negotiations with the United States over the canal concession. Feverishly working to complete the arrangements before the New Panama Canal Company's rights expired, he produced a treaty that gave the United States control over a 10-mile-wide canal zone "as if it were sovereign of the territory." The United States was to have "in perpetuity the use, occupation, and control" of the zone. In return, the United States was to pay Panama $10 million and assume a virtual protectorate over the new nation. The Panamanian government indignantly protested the terms of the agreement but eventually accepted the pact, fearing that the United States might either seize the canal with no compensation or build one in Nicaragua instead.

United States Marines were stationed in Panama from late 1903 until 1914 to protect American interests while the canal was built. During this period, the United States disbanded the Panamanian army and assumed the responsibility of defending Panama against any external threat. The United States established its own postal system, custom houses, and commissaries in the Canal Zone, privileges that seriously undermined the Panamanian economy and badly injured Panamanian pride. The canal was completed in 1914.

The Dominican Republic, Haiti, and Nicaragua

The United States occupied and administered the governments of the Dominican Republic (1916–1924), Haiti (1915–1934), and Nicaragua (1912–1925 and 1926–1933) to the detriment of these nations' long-range political and economic development.

President Ulysses S. Grant had sought to annex the Dominican Republic (then known as Santo Domingo) in 1869; only rejection of the agreement by the United States Senate prevented him from acquiring the nation, which shares the island of Hispaniola with Haiti. In the decades that followed, a series of venal and brutal dictators, often supported by loans from American banks, produced a debilitating cycle of repression and rebellion. In 1893 the Santo Domingo Improvement Company, an American firm, purchased the country's heavy foreign debt in return for the right to collect its customs revenue. In both 1903 and 1904, the United States dispatched marines to protect the interests of the influential New York financiers who were principals in the company. In 1905, the United States government assumed the administration of Dominican customs.

Unrest, however, persisted. In 1916, President Woodrow Wilson sent in the marines after the Dominican government refused to accept broader American control over the nation's internal affairs, and the United States Navy maintained a military dictatorship until 1924. The marines brutally repressed guerrilla activities, which threatened American-owned sugar plantations, and several American officers were subsequently court-martialed for the commission of atrocities.

The U.S. occupation forces attempted administrative and fiscal reforms and built some roads, but these projects were abandoned when the soldiers departed. One institution that remained intact after the occupation ended was the *Guardia Nacional*, the national police force. Rafael Trujillo, with American support, rose through the ranks of the Guardia to become dictator of the Dominican Republic in 1928. His rapacious rule, extending over three decades (he was assassinated in 1961) was the bitter legacy of intervention by the United States.

Events in Haiti followed a similar course. For a century after winning independence from France in 1804, Haiti experienced ruinous political turmoil. Reacting to the brutal murder of the Haitian president in 1915, Woodrow Wilson sent in the marines, ostensibly to prevent Germany from taking advantage of the chaos to establish a base on the island, which would endanger U.S. commerce and the access routes to the Panama Canal. A treaty signed the next year placed the United States in full control of the country. Although Haitians held public office, they served only at the pleasure of the American authorities. Here, too, American troops committed atrocities while engaged in the suppression of rural guerrillas, and civil liberties were ignored. U.S. control lasted until 1934.

The United States also intervened in Nicaragua to protect the interests of American companies operating there. The American investment totaled only $2.5 million, but the largest American company, the United States–Nicaraguan Concession, had considerable influence in the Taft administration (1909–1913); Secretary of State Philander C. Knox had been the company's legal counsel. In 1909, General José Zelaya, an old nemesis of the United States, canceled a concession to one American company and threatened the Nicaraguan Concession. The same year, the United States backed a revolution that overthrew Zelaya. In 1912, at the request of the Nicaraguan government, Taft sent in the marines to crush a new rebellion; the marines remained for thirteen years. In 1916 the United States and Nicaragua agreed to the Bryan-Chamorro Treaty, which gave the United States sole rights to build a canal through Nicaragua in return for payment of $3 million.[2] President

Calvin Coolidge withdrew American troops for a short period in 1925, but dispatched them again to subdue yet another revolution the following year; the soldiers stayed until 1933.

The Mexican Revolution

We have already discussed some aspects of United States policy toward the Mexican Revolution (1910–1920) in Chapter 12. That policy was directed above all at safeguarding the vast American investment below the border and securing the favorable political and economic climate required by American interests in Mexico. The specific policies and tactics employed by the administrations of Presidents Taft and Wilson varied with the shifting conditions in Mexico, political pressures in the United States, and the changing international background. We recall that the United States twice resorted to military intervention in Mexico. In 1914, United States Marines occupied the gulf ports of Veracruz and Tampico in an effort to bring down General Victoriano Huerta by denying his government the use of customs revenues and arms imports from Europe. The second intervention, Pershing's incursion into northern Mexico in 1916 in pursuit of Pancho Villa, served only to unite the Mexican nation behind the regime of Venustiano Carranza.

The United States exerted more decisive influence on the military course of the revolution by regulating the flow of arms and munitions across the United States–Mexican border. Through selective application of its neutrality laws, the American government prevented "undesirable" factions from instigating disruptive activities on the American side of the border. Woodrow Wilson introduced a new tactic in United States relations with Mexico by announcing that he would withhold recognition of governments that did not measure up to his standard of "morality." Wilson used this ploy against Huerta, Carranza, and Obregón. Another tactic employed by the United States to influence the course of the revolution was the

---

[2] This treaty gave the United States control over the two best routes for a canal in Central America.

threat of invasion. President Taft's shift of American troops to the border area in Texas, a veiled threat of intervention, may have helped to convince Porfirio Díaz to abdicate in 1911.

American efforts to control the course of the revolution were diluted by stubborn resistance on the part of nationalist Mexican leaders like Carranza, divisions among American investors in Mexico—some favoring and others opposing military intervention—and, finally, America's growing involvement in World War I. America's entry into the war in 1917 sharply limited policy alternatives, since the country lacked the military resources to fight in both Mexico and Europe. The threat of a Mexican alliance with Germany—a threat strongly posed by the famous Zimmerman telegram[3]—forced the United States to adopt a more moderate policy toward its neighbor.

Wilson and Latin America

In the presidential election campaign of 1912, Woodrow Wilson disavowed the Republican policies of "gunboat" and "dollar" diplomacy. Yet he surpassed his predecessors in the use of military force to impose American hegemony in Latin America. Under the banner of "morality" and "democracy," Wilson occupied most of the Caribbean even as the United States took part in a gigantic struggle whose aim, according to Wilson, was the defense of liberty and freedom in Europe. During the Versailles treaty talks, in which Wilson eloquently argued for national self-determination, he maintained a harsh American rule over five major Caribbean republics (Panama, Nicaragua, Haiti, Cuba, and the Dominican Republic). Wilson, to be sure, saw no inconsistency in his policies in Europe and Latin America. He believed his first priority in both areas was to establish order, without which, he claimed, there could be no democracy.

Wilson's secretary of state, William Jennings Bryan, also appeared to have a double standard in dealing with Latin America. The great populist, who had railed against "corporate interests," appointed as his main adviser on Latin America a former vice president of the New York City Bank, one of the biggest lenders to the governments of the Caribbean. Bryan, who later resigned in protest against Wilson's aggressive policy toward Germany, was the most ardent supporter of the American intervention in Haiti in 1915.

Quiet Imperialism:
The Post–World War I Years

American investment in Latin America grew rapidly in the period between 1914 and 1929. The world war enabled American entrepreneurs to buy up much of the large British and German investment in the region. Total American investment in Cuba and the West Indies, for example, rose from $336 million in 1914 to $1.2 billion in 1929, nearly a 400 percent increase. American capital in Central America more than tripled, from $93 million to $286 million. Investment in South America skyrocketed from $365 million to $3 billion, an increase of almost 1,000 percent; American investment in South America doubled every five years. In 1929 total American investment in Latin America had reached the staggering sum of $5.4 billion, or 35 percent of all U.S. investment in foreign lands.

Much of the new investment went into oil. U.S. companies channeled $235 million to Venezuela, $134 million to Colombia, $120 million to Mexico, and $50 million to Peru for oil exploration and production. Another $163 million went to manufacturing enterprises in South America. U.S. companies also invested heavily in Chilean copper and nitrate, in Argentine beef, and in Cuban sugar.

---

[3] In this dispatch the German government, not yet at war with the United States, offered to return to Mexico the southwestern part of the United States (lost during the Mexican War, 1846–1848), if Mexico would invade the United States. This telegram was a major factor in President Woodrow Wilson's decision to go to war in 1917.

This period marked the full-fledged involvement of giant U.S. corporations, later called multinationals, in Latin America. Such giants as Standard Oil of New Jersey, the American Smelting and Refining Company, International Telephone and Telegraph, American Foreign Power, and Armour established or added to their vast stake in the region.

The basic goal of United States policy in Latin America did not change during the postwar period; it remained the protection of American economic interests. However, public opinion and realism dictated modifications. The American people were badly disillusioned by the negotiations over the Versailles treaty and the subsequent rejection of the treaty and the League of Nations by the U.S. Senate. Americans were weary of overseas adventures and crusades. The United States remained dominant in the Caribbean, exerting decisive influence in the affairs of Mexico and Cuba and continuing to occupy the Dominican Republic, Haiti, and Nicaragua during the 1920s, but there was growing opposition, especially within the progressive wing of the Republican party and in academic and religious circles, to the old-style imperialism.

American foreign policy makers also realized that growing anti-American feeling in Latin America, primarily a response to U.S. actions in the Caribbean, posed a serious long-term danger to American economic interests. An early sign of a shift in United States policy came in 1921, when the Colombian government threatened to cancel the concessions of American companies to explore and drill for oil. The United States responded by paying Colombia $25 million to compensate for the loss of Panama. This act had a dual meaning: It served to protect American economic interests, and it symbolized a less aggressive policy toward Latin America. The shift in American tactics became even clearer when the United States removed its troops from Cuba in 1922, from the Dominican Republic in 1924, and from Nicaragua in 1925. Despite these actions, the United States encountered bitter

criticism of its role in the hemisphere at the Pan-American conferences held in Santiago in 1923 and Havana in 1928.

The most important indication that the United States had largely abandoned military intervention as a major tactic was its restraint in dealing with Mexico, the biggest trouble spot in the hemisphere during the 1920s. The Mexican constitution of 1917, as noted previously, was a most radical document by contemporary standards. The constitution's provisions on land ownership and ownership of subsoil rights seriously endangered American investments. American oil companies, in particular, objected to the new laws, which sought to reclaim Mexico's rich natural resources from foreign control.

Throughout the 1920s, the United States and Mexico haggled over application of the constitution. Several times, they reached temporary compromises, but the basic disagreement inflamed relations until World War II. The United States did not intervene militarily to protect the very large American investments in Mexico because three circumstances discouraged such action. First, public opinion opposed further foreign adventures. Second, a military invasion would have been prohibitively costly in terms of both manpower and finances. Finally, American entrepreneurs with interests in Mexico disagreed sharply over the proper course of action. The oil companies, who were most threatened by the constitution, favored intervention. The banks and the mining companies, whose interests would have been in greater danger in the event of war between the United States and Mexico, opposed intervention. The controversy abated during the late 1920s, when the Calles regime made significant concessions with regard to American oil interests in Mexico.

President Herbert Hoover and Secretary of State Henry L. Stimson continued to shift toward moderation and stepped up American efforts to win goodwill in Latin America. During the interim between his election and inauguration, Hoover toured Latin America. On taking office, he abandoned Wilson's policy of denying recognition to "unworthy" governments. The Clark memorandum, published in 1930, was a milestone in Hoover's efforts. It declared that the Roosevelt Corollary had no support in the Monroe Doctrine; consequently, the United States would no longer interfere in the internal affairs of Latin American nations under the provisions of the doctrine. However, the president carefully refrained from rejecting intervention outright. In 1933 he withdrew United States troops from Nicaragua and would have removed them from Haiti as well had the Haitians not objected to the terms of withdrawal.

A NEW ERA:
THE GOOD NEIGHBOR
IN DEPRESSION AND WAR,
1933–1945

Franklin D. Roosevelt assumed the presidency in 1933 amid a severe economic depression. Rejecting "interference in the internal affairs of other nations" and proclaiming the United States to be a "good neighbor" to the rest of the world, Roosevelt built his relations with Latin America on the foundations laid by his predecessor. First, expanding Hoover's initiative, Roosevelt renounced the right to intervene in Latin American affairs. Secretary of State Cordell Hull announced this position at the seventh Pan-American Conference in Montevideo in late 1933 and reiterated it at the Inter-American Conference in Buenos Aires in 1936. Hull toured several countries in Latin America in 1933, proclaiming American friendship and goodwill. The following year, the United States reached an agreement with Cuba to abrogate the Platt Amendment, thus abandoning its protectorate over the island; the same year, it withdrew its occupation troops from Haiti. In 1937 the United States gave up its right to intervene militarily to protect transit across the Isthmus of Tehuantepec in Mexico.

The nonintervention policy was soon put to the test in Cuba. In 1933 political unrest there threatened the substantial American investment on the island. Roosevelt dispatched Sumner

Welles to Havana to try to arrange an accommodation between dictator Gerardo Machado and his opponents. After several months of unsuccessful negotiations, Machado fled, and power fell into the hands of a disorganized and disunited junta. Eventually, Dr. Ramón Grau San Martín emerged as leader of the government. He quickly fell into disfavor with the United States when he suspended loan repayments to a large New York bank and seized two American-owned sugar mills. As a result, the United States refused to recognize the Grau government. With U.S. warships lingering in Havana harbor, Grau was forced to relinquish his leadership. Supported by the United States, Fulgencio Batista emerged as the strongman of Cuba. Despite the protestations of the United States to the contrary, it was evident that it had not entirely abandoned the "big stick."

Nonintervention was put to another severe test in Mexico in 1938. The long dispute between the Mexican government and the oil companies culminated in the expropriation of foreign oil holdings when the oil companies defied an order of the Mexican Supreme Court in a labor dispute. While the oil companies clamored for reprisal, Roosevelt tried to settle matters peacefully. In the face of isolationist sentiment in the United States, intervention was unthinkable. Moreover, with war in Europe on the horizon, the United States did not want to endanger an important source of oil. A settlement was eventually reached during the 1940s.

Another aspect of Roosevelt's "good neighbor" policy toward Latin America was the effort to achieve reciprocal trade agreements as a means of increasing American trade with the area. Secretary of State Cordell Hull ardently supported such agreements, believing they would help the United States emerge from the Great Depression. From 1934 to 1941, Hull succeeded in signing reciprocal trade treaties with fifteen Latin American nations. Had these treaties succeeded in significantly increasing American trade, which they did not, they would have adversely affected Latin America's nascent industrialization, which was critically dependent on protective tariffs for its survival. In this area, therefore, United States policy was in direct conflict with the goal of Latin American economic development.

In the 1930s, the United States grew increasingly concerned over the spread of German economic and political influence in Latin America. The large communities of German and Italian immigrants in Argentina, Chile, and southern Brazil were viewed as potential foci for the growth of German influence in the area. Both the Chilean and Argentine military establishments had long-standing ties with Germany. In the early 1930s, moreover, Germany began to compete for Latin American trade with the United States through barter agreements.

In response to this growing German economic and political activity, the United States pushed for closer cooperation among the nations of the Western Hemisphere by promoting a series of meetings to consider common problems. In December 1936, the participants in the Inter-American Conference for the Maintenance of Peace, held in Buenos Aires, agreed to consult in the event of war among themselves or outside the hemisphere. Two years later, the eighth Pan-American Conference met in Lima, Peru; the conferees decided that the mechanism for consultation would be foreign ministers' meetings. In September 1939, shortly after the German invasion of Poland, the First Meeting of Foreign Ministers of the American Republics approved a joint declaration of neutrality and established the Inter-American Financial and Advisory Committee to consider common problems brought on by the war. The foreign ministers proclaimed the existence of a safety zone around the hemisphere and warned belligerents not to wage war within it. In July 1940, after the fall of France, the Second Meeting of Foreign Ministers was held in Havana; the representatives agreed to administer French and Dutch colonies in the Western hemisphere in the event they were in danger of Nazi take-over. They also proclaimed that an attack on any of the conferring nations would be construed as an attack on all.

As war approached, Latin American nations were generally very cooperative with U.S. efforts to establish mutual defense. The Dominican Republic offered land for bases in 1939; Panama did the same in 1941. Several Latin American nations agreed to sell their raw material production to the United States.

The Third Meeting of Foreign Ministers was held shortly after the Japanese attack on Pearl Harbor in early 1942. The ministers agreed to cooperate against the Axis; most Latin American nations severed diplomatic relations with the Axis powers. During the war, Brazilians fought with distinction in Italy, and a Mexican air squadron served in the Philippines. With the exception of Argentina, every Latin American country contributed to the Allied war effort.

The war strengthened the economic links between the United States and Latin America. The United States served as the sole market for the region's exports and the only supplier of its requirements of arms, munitions, industrial equipment, and manufactured goods. American investment diversified geographically, going increasingly into South America whereas it had previously focused on the Caribbean. A growing proportion of U.S. capital went into manufacturing enterprises instead of raw material extraction. By the end of the war, Argentina accounted for 16 percent of American investment in Latin America, Chile 16 percent, Brazil 13 percent, and Peru 4 percent. For the first time, South America accounted for over half the total U.S. investment in Latin America.

DEFENDING THE EMPIRE AND CAPITALISM, 1945–1983

In the postwar era, three factors have determined United States–Latin American relations: the need for the United States to protect large investments

Bolivian women demonstrating in favor of the government's expropriation of U.S.-owned oil companies in 1969. (Wide World Photos)

in the region, the desire of Latin American nations to industrialize and otherwise diversify their economies, and the rivalry between the United States and the Soviet Union known as the cold war.

American Investment and Trade

After stagnating during the depression and much of World War II, American investment and trade in Latin America increased dramatically during the next two decades. It was an era of intensive investment in manufacturing enterprises and massive involvement of multinational corporations in the economies of the region. Direct American investment in Latin America totaled $3 billion in 1946. By 1961 this sum had grown to $8 billion, and by 1969 to $13 billion. By 1974, American investors had channeled $19 billion into the area. In those twenty-eight years, American investment in absolute figures increased by $16 billion, or 633 percent. (Nevertheless, Latin American investment made up a shrinking share of total U.S. investment in foreign countries. In 1950, Latin American investment accounted for 40 percent of all American investment abroad; by 1970 it accounted for only 16 percent.)

As American investment in Latin America grew, it became increasingly concentrated in a few large companies. In 1950 there were two thousand separate American-owned firms operating in Latin America; three hundred of them accounted for 90 percent of the capital invested. In 1957 forty-five firms with over $100 million invested abroad accounted for 57 percent of all American investment abroad; 80 percent of American investment in foreign countries was held by one hundred and sixty-three companies. In specific industries, the concentration was even more evident: Twenty firms held 95 percent of U.S. foreign investment in mining, twenty-four companies accounted for 93 percent of the oil investment, twelve held 89 percent of the public utilities, and six held 83 percent of the agricultural property. A similar tendency toward concentration of capital characterized American investment in Latin America. In the same period, big American banks greatly expanded their activity abroad, especially in Latin America. The Chase Manhattan Bank (Rockefeller), the First National City Bank of New York, and the Bank of America controlled 80 percent of the foreign branches of U.S. banks and 70 percent of the assets deposited in them. Fifty-one percent of American foreign branch banks were located in Latin America.

Since the 1950s, Latin American trade with the United States has declined in relative importance to both the United States and Latin American economies. In 1948, the region accounted for 29 percent of total United States trade. This figure dropped to 25 percent in 1958 and 12.6 percent in 1970, but rose to 15 percent in 1974. In 1960, 40 percent of Latin American exports went to the United States, and the region received 43 percent of its imports from the United States. In 1973, the totals had declined to 32 percent and 36 percent, respectively.

Despite the overall decline in the relative importance of Latin American–United States trade, the region remained a major supplier of critical minerals. In 1969, Latin America provided almost all the bauxite (from which aluminum is derived) imported into the United States, 36 percent of the manganese, 60 percent of the copper, 43 percent of the iron ore, 35 percent of the zinc, and 31 percent of the oil.

Although some analysts have interpreted the relative decline in the economic importance of Latin America to the United States in the postwar era to mean that American policy makers no longer base their decisions primarily on American economic interests in the region, this clearly is not the case. American trade and investment in Latin America continue to be huge in absolute terms. Moreover, every overt or covert American intervention in Latin America during this period—in Guatemala, Cuba, the Dominican Republic, Chile, for example—has taken place in countries where the security of large American investments appears to be endangered.

In the past three decades, anticommunism has become synonymous with efforts by the United States to defend its interests in Latin America. As a result of the triumph of the Cuban Revolution, successive American administrations have been determined to check the advance of communism in the hemisphere. The defense of U.S. economic interests and of capitalism has fused into a single goal, which the United States has consistently pursued, although its tactics have changed to meet the varying conditions of each successive stage of the postwar period.

Post–World War II Adjustments

Despite the high degree of wartime cooperation, sharp differences between the United States and Latin America surfaced in the immediate postwar years. These disagreements emerged initially at the Chapultepec Conference (Inter-American Conference on the Problems of War and Peace) in February 1945. Latin American leaders felt they should be rewarded for their contributions and sacrifices during the war. The United States, however, regarded European recovery as its first priority. There were also major disagreements over trade, industrialization, the overall direction of Latin American economic development, and the role of the United States in this development. The United States insisted on an open door to Latin American markets and investment opportunities but was unwilling to make any concessions that might injure its own producers. Latin Americans, however, feared that such free access to Latin American markets would destroy much of the industrial progress the region had made in the preceding two decades.

United States and Latin American interests were clearly opposed. The United States wanted to protect and maintain its markets and investment in Latin America, whereas Latin American nations sought to industrialize and diversify their economies. American leaders regarded private capital investment and free trade as the best routes to development. Latin American nations, on the other hand, favored a massive government role in industrialization and restrictions on foreign trade and investment as the only means of modernizing and regaining control over their economies.

After the war, Latin America vainly sought American help to finance industrialization and access to American manufactured goods, especially capital equipment in order to further industrialization. These efforts, however, were hindered further in the next few years as high prices for manufactured products dissipated the dollar reserves Latin American nations had accumulated during the war, while declining prices for raw materials eroded Latin America's terms of trade even further.

There was increasing evidence, moreover, that the United States had reverted to its traditional disregard for Latin American sensitivities and to intervention in the internal affairs of nations of the region. Latin America was pointedly snubbed in the meetings at Dumbarton Oaks (1944) that led to the formation of the United Nations. In addition, President Roosevelt would not permit Latin American participation in the San Francisco Conference, which organized the United Nations, until every nation of the region declared war against the Axis. This position deeply offended Latin Americans, who objected to being forced to dance to the tune of the United States. In 1946 the United States interfered in the internal political affairs of three South American nations. It meddled disastrously in the Argentine presidential campaign of that year, assuring the election of Juan Perón; it forced the González Videla government in Chile to oust the Communist members of its coalition cabinet; and it helped to undermine a revolutionary regime in Bolivia that had been wrongly accused of fascist tendencies.

The Cold War

American alarm over the vast expansion of Communist influence in Eastern and Central Europe as a result of World War II, the Communist victory in the Chinese civil war, and the gains of Communist parties in Western Europe as a result of their leading role in wartime resistance movements had the effect of pushing Latin America to the back burner. In this initial stage of the cold war, which lasted roughly until the 1950s, the United States focused its attention on checking the further spread of communism in Western Europe by aiding the revival of the shattered capitalist economy of that region through the Marshall Plan. From 1950 to 1954, the United States fought the Korean war, designed to stem the advance of Communist influence in Asia.

During this first stage of the cold war, American leaders tended to look on the world as being divided into two camps, one committed to the United States and its free enterprise system, the other loyal to communism. Since it regarded the world in such black and white terms, the United States viewed with implacable hostility governments and movements that disagreed with American policy or attempted to institute structural social and economic reforms.

On two occasions, in Guatemala and Iran, the United States helped to topple two such governments through the subversive activities of the CIA.

A second stage of the cold war began in the mid-1950s, when a "third world" emerged, made up of the many newly independent states of Africa and Asia, which proclaimed themselves unaligned in the struggle between the blocs led by the Soviet Union and the United States. The two superpowers, faced with the unacceptable consequences of nuclear war, fought out the cold war in the Third World. In this second stage, the United States became intensely concerned with Latin America only after the Cuban Revolution of 1959 led to the establishment of the first socialist state in the Americas. U.S. preoccupation with the threat of more Cubas in the hemisphere produced the Alliance for Progress as an alternative to the Cuban model.

The third and present stage of the cold war followed the disastrous American experience in Vietnam. The Vietnam war taught the American government and people, at very heavy cost, the limitations of American power and the difficulty or impossibility of preventing the success of indigenous social revolution. Nonetheless, the United States remained determined to maintain its empire in the Western Hemisphere, adapting its methods to suit new conditions. American policy makers substituted economic sanctions and diplomatic pressure for force in order to achieve their goals.

The Latin American Policies of Truman and Eisenhower

The Truman administration (1945–1953) focused its attention on fighting communism in Europe and the Far East. However, as we have seen, it meddled with mixed success in the political affairs of Chile, Bolivia, and Argentina in 1946. Under Truman, the movement for hemispheric cooperation continued, at least outwardly. The Rio Treaty of 1947 brought Central and South America into a military alliance with the United States. The ninth International Conference of American States, held in Bogotá the following year, resulted in the formation of the Organization of American States (OAS). The OAS was to provide collective security, with an attack against one member being viewed as an attack on all. The organization also was to be a mediator in disputes between members. Truman and his chief advisers (one of whom was Nelson Rockefeller) were primarily concerned with maintaining the status quo in the region.

The Eisenhower presidency (1953–1961) marked a revival of strong corporate influence in American foreign policy. Eisenhower took office in the middle of the Korean war and at the height of the McCarthy "Red Scare." His administration, particularly the fanatical anticommunist Secretary of State John Foster Dulles, divided the world into two categories: nations that supported the United States and those that did not. Any foreign government that restricted the activities of American corporations under its jurisdiction was adjudged to be communist and a threat to the security of the United States. During his two terms, Eisenhower faced four challenges of this kind in Latin America: Bolivia, British Guiana, Guatemala, and Cuba. In each case, his administration reacted according to the scale of the American economic interests involved and the prevailing domestic and international conditions.

In Bolivia in 1952, a successful revolution headed by Victor Paz Estenssoro and the National Revolutionary Movement (MNR) ushered in sweeping economic and political reforms; in its first year, the new government nationalized the nation's tin mines, wiped out the latifundio system, replaced the old army with workers' and peasants' militias, and greatly increased the number of eligible voters. The MNR, however, encountered serious economic difficulties that arose from the obsolescence of the tin industry, the disruption to agricultural production caused by the land reform, and massive inflation.

The outgoing Truman administration, anxious over the radicalism of the regime, withheld recognition and aid from Bolivia. The middle-class leadership of the MNR eventually managed to convince the Eisenhower administration that it was not communist; as a result, Bolivia received millions of dollars in grants and loans and substantial technical assistance over the next decade. American aid had a significant moderating influence on the MNR reform program. Indeed, U.S. assistance decisively altered the whole course of Bolivian development; the United States re-established, equipped, and trained the Bolivian army, which overthrew Paz Estenssoro in 1964, ushering in a period of conservative rule that continued almost uninterruptedly until 1981.

The United States employed different tactics to achieve the same general results under the differing conditions of another Latin American country. In 1953, Cheddi Jagan, an avowed Marxist, was elected on a program of structural reform to head the government of the British colony of Guiana. Guiana, however, was an important source of bauxite and other metals; several large American companies, including Reynolds Metals and Kennecott Copper, had substantial holdings in the colony. Alarmed at the prospect of nationalization of these holdings by a Marxist regime, the United States urged the British to nullify the election; the British government duly sent troops to Guiana and deposed the new government.

The Eisenhower administration employed yet other tactics in Guatemala in 1954; in this case, it conspired to overthrow a democratically elected government whose reforms threatened the interests of a large and influential American corporation. In 1944 a revolution toppled the oppressive regime of Jorge Ubico, who had ruled Guatemala since 1931. The victorious middle-class revolutionaries favored a capitalist course of development and were friendly to the United States. However, the reform programs of Presidents Juan José Arévalo (1945–1951) and Jacobo

Arbenz (1951–1954) provoked the hostility of the United Fruit Company (UFCO) and Secretary of State John F. Dulles. UFCO had operated in Guatemala since the 1890s, when it acquired a virtual monopoly on banana production and distribution. It was Guatemala's largest employer, with ten thousand workers, and its largest landowner. It owned several hundred thousand acres of land, much of it held in uncultivated reserve for the day when its producing land wore out or was ruined by disease. The company also controlled the nation's main transportation artery, the International Railways of Central America (IRCA), and major port facilities on the Gulf of Mexico.

The Guatemalan government clashed with UFCO over labor and land reform. Arévalo enacted a new labor code in 1947. The company, charging that it was being discriminated against, protested sharply. The ensuing labor agitation severely hampered banana production for several years. In 1952 the Guatemalan Congress enacted a land reform program, expropriating large tracts of uncultivated land for distribution among landless peasants. Again, UFCO charged the government with discrimination.

Unfortunately for the Guatemalan government, UFCO enjoyed great influence with the United States government. It was a client of Secretary Dulles's law firm. In addition, the company's headquarters were in Boston, which made it a constituent of three of the most powerful men in the United States Congress: Senator Henry Cabot Lodge, Speaker of the House Joseph Martin, and Democratic party leader John McCormack. What was more, the family of the assistant secretary of state in charge of Guatemalan relations, John Moors Lodge, was a major stockholder in United Fruit.

Guatemala's independent foreign policy sharpened its differences with the United States. The Guatemalan labor movement, closely linked to the Arévalo and Arbenz administrations, refused to cooperate with the American Federation of Labor's anticommunist international labor organization. Guatemala was critical of the United States at both the Rio (1947) and Bogotá (1948) conferences; the United States responded by cutting off arms supplies to Guatemala in 1948. In both the United Nations and the Organization of American States, Arbenz resisted American efforts to make it mandatory for members to send troops to Korea.

Seizing on allegations of communist participation in the Arbenz government to justify its actions, the United States trained and outfitted a rebel group under the command of Carlos Castillo Armas. Castillo Armas invaded Guatemala through UFCO property and overthrew Arbenz in June 1954. His repressive regime, which lasted until his assassination in 1957, erased all of the postwar reforms and restored UFCO's privileges.

The Cuban Revolution and United States– Latin American Relations

Eisenhower's successful interventions in Bolivia, British Guiana, and Guatemala produced bitter criticism of the United States in Latin America and contributed to the hostile and violent reception accorded Vice President Richard Nixon on his tour of the region in 1958. No major change in policy, however, occurred until the victory of Fidel Castro in Cuba in 1959.

After an initial period of confusion over the goals of the new revolutionary government, the United States embarked on a two-pronged program designed to destroy Castro and avert new Cubas. American policy makers simultaneously sought to undermine the rebel regime and to placate the rest of Latin America with various concessions. The United States imposed economic sanctions on Cuba and began clandestinely to train an invasion force of Cuban exiles. To insure Latin American backing, the United States committed limited funds to a new Social Trust Fund for the region and agreed to support plans for common markets in the area, such as the Latin American Free Trade Association

(LAFTA) and the Central American Common Market, proposals which it had long opposed.

Cuba was the first major crisis to confront the new administration of John F. Kennedy in 1961. Fearing a proliferation of Cuban-style revolutions throughout Latin America, the administration responded with a comprehensive plan for the region, the Alliance for Progress. The Alliance was a double-edged program, based on the theories of the economist Walt W. Rostow. In his theory of the stages of economic growth, derived from his study of British and American economic development, Rostow maintained that every nation on its path to modern development (or industrialization) passed through specific stages. The most important of these was the takeoff stage, from which nations jumped to industrialization. The object of American policy, therefore, must be to help underdeveloped nations, such as those in Latin America, reach the takeoff stage. Toward this end, the United States pledged to spend $10 billion in the region, over ten years, to build badly needed transportation facilities and to buy technology and industrial equipment. In return, Latin American governments were to institute programs of social and political reform. The United States proposed to foster democracy and economic justice in Latin America through a program of incentives. Rostow also argued that the stage prior to takeoff was peculiarly vulnerable to communist movements like the Castro-led guerrilla movement in Cuba. To guard against this type of insurgency, the American government undertook to strengthen the military forces of the region with arms and training.

The lessons of Cuba reinforced Rostow's theories. The United States had stood idly by while the regime of the dictator Batista created the preconditions for revolution on the island. A timely reform, the new policy makers believed, would have prevented Castro's take-over. These men also feared that the Caribbean was especially ripe for revolution; "Papa Doc" Duvalier terrorized Haiti; Rafael Trujillo ran the Dominican Republic like a fiefdom; the Somozas plundered Nicaragua. To desist from reform was to invite more Castros.

As it turned out, the Alliance for Progress failed to bring economic development and democracy to Latin America. In the first place, the program was not intended as philanthropy; it was designed to foster capitalist private-sector economic development and to expand American trade and investments. Much of the aid to the region was in the form of loans, which had to be repaid eventually. Moreover, U.S. aid had restrictions that actually hampered Latin American development. Most of the funds had to be spent on American-made goods transported in American vessels, provisions that added greatly to the cost of these purchases. Although the United States pumped $10 billion into Latin America between 1960 and 1968 and private sources added another $2.6 billion, there was a net outflow of capital from the area. Debt service payments ate up an increasing share of the budgets of Latin American nations, leaving little for social welfare expenditures and economic development. Often, these nations had to obtain new loans just to pay off their old debts. Unfortunately, too, a significant percentage of aid funds was dissipated through corruption and inefficiency.

American support for the Latin American military was the most effective program of the Alliance. From 1961 to 1964, the United States channeled $500 million, an average of $125 million a year, into this military. Officers from the region received the most modern training in counterinsurgency tactics against both rural and urban guerrillas and were indoctrinated to the American world view. Allegedly, sophisticated torture techniques formed part of the curriculum. One indication of the thoroughness of the training was the success of American-trained and American-equipped Bolivian rangers in hunting down Che Guevara and his comrades. The United States also urged Latin American military leaders to take a more active and positive role in their nations' development by participating in civic action programs in which military personnel built roads and other public facilities.

It was clear, however, that despite the Kennedy administration's avowed goal of helping Latin America "strike off the remaining bonds of poverty and ignorance," its major concern was to maintain friendly capitalist regimes in the region. Kennedy continued to interfere in the internal affairs of countries in the area, even after the debacle of the Bay of Pigs. In 1961 he attempted to destroy the regime of Cheddi Jagan in British Guiana for a second time by refusing to grant much-needed aid and pressing the British to overturn the democratically elected premier. The CIA also helped to subvert the Jagan government. Kennedy was involved in attempts to rid the Dominican Republic of Rafael Trujillo, and there are allegations that the CIA was responsible for the assassination of the unwanted dictator in 1961.

Like its predecessors, the Kennedy administration supported dictatorial regimes in Latin America when American policy makers considered them the only alternative to disorder and possible revolution. In March 1962, the United States made no protest when the Argentine military overthrew the democratically elected President Arturo Frondizi. Four months later, the American-trained and American-equipped Peruvian army seized power to prevent a democratically elected president from taking office. For a time, the United States withheld recognition and cut off aid, but it soon reached an understanding with the military regime. Like its predecessors, the Kennedy administration preferred order, even at the expense of democracy.

Lyndon Johnson carried on Kennedy's program in Latin America, although he increasingly shifted the emphasis of American policy from reform to the maintenance of order. Johnson was determined that he, unlike Kennedy, would not "lose" any nation in any part of the world to communism. In the Dominican Republic in

1965, Johnson faced a rebellion against a re-actionary military regime that less than two years before, had overthrown the nation's first democratically elected president. Johnson claimed that the United States had the right to intervene unilaterally in Latin America to prevent what he feared would be a Castro-like communist take-over. He dispatched the marines to suppress the rebellion. Johnson was undoubtedly worried about another Cuba in the Dominican Republic, but there is considerable evidence to indicate that his administration's main concern was to assure Dominican sugar production for several important American firms. Not coincidentally, several of Johnson's key foreign policy advisers, including Ellsworth Bunker and W. Averell Harriman, had close links to the sugar industry.

Under Johnson, the United States also played a major role in the military overthrow of the leftward-leaning regime of João Goulart in Brazil in 1964. Disapproving of Goulart's proposed "radical" reforms—which included a mild land reform and the grant of the vote to illiterates—the United States cut aid to Brazil to a minimum in 1963 and began to channel funds instead to pro-American state governors. In April 1964, the Brazilian military toppled Goulart and instituted fifteen years of brutal, repressive dictatorship. The Johnson administration immediately recognized the new government. In the next five years, the United States poured more than $1.5 billion in economic and military aid into Brazil, one-quarter of all U.S. aid to Latin America.

The lavish aid funneled to the Brazilian military helped to persuade the Argentine military that they should overthrow the faltering regime of President Arturo Illia in June 1966. The United States gave the military government $135 million in aid during the three years following the coup.

In political as well as socioeconomic terms, the results of the Alliance under Kennedy and Johnson were dismaying. When Kennedy took office, Alfredo Stroessner in Paraguay was the only dictator in power in South America. By

1968 military dictators ruled in Argentina, Brazil, and Peru, as well as in Paraguay. In Bolivia and Ecuador, civilian-elected governments served as figureheads for the military. In Central America, the record was worse. Rightist military overthrew democratically elected governments in Honduras, Guatemala, and El Salvador. The Somozas tightened their grip on Nicaragua. In 1968 a military coup ousted the elected president of Panama. More importantly, by every measure, the Alliance failed to stimulate economic development or rectify the immense economic and social inequalities of Latin America.

The Vietnam Era

Since the late 1960s, the repercussions of the disastrous American experience in Vietnam and related developments have produced some readjustments in U.S. foreign policy toward its southern neighbors. But the main goal of this policy—to protect and expand American economic interests and maintain capitalism as the dominant economic system in the region—has remained constant.

In the aftermath of Vietnam, American policy makers no longer regard overt military intervention as a realistic option. They now rely on such indirect methods as economic sanction and subversion. Chile in the period from 1970 to 1973 offers an excellent case study in the use of such methods to undermine and topple a democratically elected government working to achieve socialism by peaceful means.

The story goes back to 1958, when the Socialist Salvador Allende narrowly missed victory in the Chilean presidential election. For the next fifteen years, the American government poured millions of dollars into Chile, first to prevent Allende from winning subsequent elections, and then, after his election in 1970, to subvert his administration. The scare caused by Allende's near victory in 1958 led the United States to channel funds into the 1964 campaign of the Christian Democratic candidate, Eduardo Frei, a moderate reformer, helping him win the presidency. During Frei's term in office (1964–1969) the United States sent an average of $130 million a year in aid to Chile. Despite this enormous effort, the mild success of Frei's reform program, and the injection of more millions of dollars in the 1970 campaign, Allende was elected president in 1970.

The United States then imposed economic sanctions on the Allende government, cutting aid by 90 percent and denying credit. U.S. aid fell from $80 million in 1969 to $10 million during Allende's first year in office. The withdrawal of credit was especially damaging, because the Chilean economy operated on credit; government and industry needed credit to pay for spare parts and capital to increase productivity. Meanwhile, the CIA cooperated with opposition groups, such as striking truck owners, to destabilize the Chilean economy. Amid growing economic difficulties and political turmoil, the Chilean military overthrew Allende in a bloody coup in September 1973. The United States promptly recognized the military junta and resumed aid and credit.

The American economic stake in Chile, as we saw in Chapter 14, was large and concentrated primarily in copper mining. The first act of the Allende government, supported by the unanimous vote of the Chilean Congress, had been to expropriate the holdings of the American copper companies without compensation. Later, it expropriated the International Telephone and Telegraph Company, whose president enjoyed considerable influence in the Nixon administration. The United States intervened both to protect these investments and to teach a salutary lesson to other Latin American nations that might wish to construct a socialist society in the future.

Carter's Latin American Policy: Nationalism, the Canal, and Human Rights

Jimmy Carter took office in 1977 proclaiming a "new approach" for United States foreign policy based on "a high regard for the individuality

and sovereignty of each Latin American and Caribbean nation . . . our respect for human rights, . . . [and] our desire to press forward on the great issues which effect the relations between the developed and developing nations." He immediately put these principles into practice in two major initiatives; the reopening of negotiations with Panama over the canal and the beginning of talks with Cuba about normalization of relations.

Periodically since the signing of the original canal treaty, Panamanians violently protested the U.S. presence in the middle of their country; serious anti-American riots erupted in 1931, 1947, 1959, and 1964. These riots occurred in times of economic hardship in Panama and wrung minor concessions from the United States. One such concession came in 1936 in the form of the Hull-Alvaro Treaty, which ended the United States protectorate over Panama. (The Americans did not always react indulgently to Panamanian demands; during World War II, a Panamanian government that demanded concessions was overthrown with American connivance.)

In the 1950s, the Panamanians began a new effort to renegotiate the canal treaty, and talks toward that end opened in 1954. However, it took two major riots, the Castro revolution, and ten years to push the United States into serious negotiations; Lyndon Johnson renewed talks after the bloody riots of 1964. There was a plan afoot at the time to build a new canal through Nicaragua to replace the already obsolete Panama Canal. When this plan fell through, however, consideration of a new treaty was also abandoned. Ten years later, General Omar Torrijos, head of a revolutionary military junta in Panama, renewed the push for a new pact. After four years of sometimes bitter negotiations, the United States and Panama agreed to a new treaty that should gradually hand over control of the Canal Zone to Panama by the year 2000. The United States Senate ratified the treaty in April 1978. Although Panamanians were unhappy with a Senate reservation to the treaty that gave the United States the right to intervene to maintain the operation of the canal, it was received with general satisfaction in Panama and throughout Latin America.

Negotiations with Cuba led eventually to the opening of United States and Cuban Interest Sections in Havana and Washington in September 1977. These initiatives were short-lived, however, for the two nations came into conflict early in 1978 over Cuba's extensive military involvement in Africa, particularly in Angola and Ethiopia. The Carter administration strenuously objected to the presence of upwards of 35,000 Cuban troops and advisers in Africa and broke off further talks as a result. Relations worsened during 1980 as a consequence of the exodus of 125,000 Cuban refugees to the United States.

Relations with Mexico also proved thorny. Two difficult issues—the terms under which Mexico would supply gas and oil to the United States and the influx of undocumented workers from Mexico into the United States—troubled relations between the two nations. All of this was complicated by Carter's embarrassing lack of sensitivity to Mexican national pride and his inability to establish a working rapport with Mexican President José López Portillo. With the discovery of Mexico's vast petroleum reserves and its development into the United States' third largest trading partner (behind Canada and Japan), Mexico has taken on increased importance.

Carter's pursuit of human rights proved to be the most controversial aspect of his foreign policy. He centered his attention on Chile, Argentina, and Brazil, the harshest practitioners of repression in the region. The United States instituted sanctions against all of these nations, ending or reducing economic and military aid and impeding their ability to obtain credit from international lending agencies. In the last two years of his term, as a result of stepped-up pressure from American business and concern about growing communist influence in Central America, Carter backed off his human rights activism. His earlier efforts, however, had shown

some success. In 1978, nine Latin American nations held elections (though some, like Stroessner's re-election in Paraguay, were pro forma). Carter's criticism of Chile helped bring about some lessening of oppression there; the ruling junta released many political prisoners and disbanded the hated secret police, DINA. The intensity of repression eased in Brazil as the military dictatorship pursued its process of abertura (political opening), proclaiming an amnesty in 1979. Carter's greatest human rights triumph was in assuring the democratic transfer of power in the Dominican Republic in 1978. That year when it became clear that Antonio Guzman would defeat the conservative, long-time incumbent and U.S. ally Joaquín Balaguer (who had ruled since the U.S. intervention in 1965), the army stopped the balloting. The United States, however, quickly made it clear that it would not tolerate a coup. Guzman subsequently took office peacefully.

Nicaragua proved to be Carter's most difficult and pressing problem in Latin America. At the beginning of his term Carter's attention focused on South America, despite the abysmal human rights record of the Somoza dictatorship. After the assassination of Somoza critic Pedro Joaquín Chamorro in early 1978, the United States seemed to go out of its way to support the tyrant. The growing insurrection of the Sandinist Front for National Liberation, a broad coalition of religious, civic, and business opposition, led Somoza to conduct a desperate, criminal war against his own people. Carter cautiously stood by, clearly worried by the leftist overtones of the Sandinistas. As the Somoza regime crumbled in early 1979, the United States looked for a moderate alternative to the Sandinistas. Failing this, Carter tried to reach accommodation with the rebels after they ousted Somoza in July 1979. The United States offered economic aid to rebuild the nation ruined by civil war. The Carter administration, however, was further alarmed about events in Central America, when guerrilla insurgents, inspired by the *Sandinista* victory, took to arms in El Salvador to topple another repressive government.

Carter's term ended on an uncertain note for Latin America. On one hand, relations with the Sandinistas fluctuated; neither side was completely able to trust the other. Relations were complicated further by United States accusations that Nicaragua was sending arms to rebels in El Salvador (though the extent and importance of this aid was widley disputed).

A democratic wave rolled over Latin America in 1980. Peru elected its first democratic government since 1963. Bolivia struggled valiantly for several months to install an elected president before succumbing to a coup by right-wing military cocaine dealers. Ecuador had its first democratically elected president.

Ronald Reagan and the New Cold War

Ronald Reagan became president in 1981 determined to turn back communism in Latin America. In doing so, he openly courted repressive right-wing regimes in Argentina and Chile, heightened the rhetorical war against Cuba and Nicaragua, and committed substantial amounts of American money and military advisers to the antiguerrilla war in Central America. Especially during Alexander Haig's term as secretary of state, the anticommunist saber rattling was reminiscent of the early 1950s.

The new Republican administration almost immediately cut off new aid to Nicaragua, claiming that the Sandinistas were supplying Salvadoran rebels with arms from Cuba and the Soviet Union. Reagan proposed massive new military aid to the beleaguered government of El Salvador; the aid package included fifty American military advisers. The United States followed up these initial measures by financing anti-*Sandinista* rebels operating from Honduras, blocking Nicaraguan efforts to obtain foreign credit, and generally harassing the Nicaraguan government.

In the meantime, the United States moved to shore up Honduras and Guatemala by increasing economic and military aid. President Reagan also proposed his Caribbean Basin Initiative, which promised a modest U.S. investment in the region, much like the Marshall Plan in post–World War II Europe, to forestall the spread of communism.

The guerrilla wars in Central America continued in 1983. The Reagan administration stepped up aid to the Salvadoran government and openly backed the opposition to the *Sandinistas,* the so-called *contras,* who operated counterrevolutionary bands out of Honduras and Costa Rica. With extraordinary lack of historical judgment President Reagan called this conglomeration, which included many former followers of the Somozas, "freedom fighters." Reagan also defied congressional limitations on United States involvement by setting up training bases for Salvadoran government troops in Honduras. In one especially disconcerting period of a few weeks, he also expelled a large number of Nicaraguan diplomats from the United States and sacked most of the State Department's Central America team, replacing them with more ardent hard-liners. Reagan's tough stance against the Nicaraguan revolution and guerrilla insurgents in El Salvador and Guatemala polarized the region and worsened its political and economic chaos.

The Malvinas/Falklands War

One of the biggest disasters of the Reagan administration's Latin American policy has been the war between Argentina and Great Britain over the Malvinas Islands in the South Atlantic. Encouraged by Ambassador to the United Nations Jeane Kirkpatrick, an expert on Latin America, Reagan sought to repair relations with both military regimes in the southern cone, Argentina and Chile. Argentina became an important ally in Central America, providing military advisers to the government of El Salvador.

Misinterpreting the Reagan administration's

friendly overtures as a blank check, the shaky military junta in Argentina (see Chapter 13) sought to divert attention from its domestic woes by settling an old dispute with Britain over possession of the Malvinas. A last-minute telephone call from President Reagan to President Galtieri failed to deter the Argentines, who believed the United States would remain neutral in the conflict. On April 2, 1982, the Argentines invaded the islands. Secretary of State Haig vainly tried to mediate as the British fleet made its way 8,000 miles south to retake the islands. When he failed to bring an end to the war, the United States shifted to full support of the British. In a short, bloody war the British recaptured the Falklands. Casualties were in the thousands. The war badly damaged the inter-American security network and shook Latin American trust in the United States as a reliable ally. Most importantly, it was U.S. actions in the months before the invasion that had conveyed to the Argentines a false impression of support, which had helped convince them to go to war.

In Chile, United States overtures to the Pinochet regime have enabled it to step up repression, which had actually lessened during the late 1970s under pressure from Carter's campaign for human rights.

Another key problem that faced the Reagan administration was the enormous foreign debt accumulated by Latin American nations. Argentina, Brazil, and Mexico together owed private banks and international lending institutions more than $200 billion. Chile and the Central American nations were also heavy borrowers; and several nations technically defaulted. The United States was forced to take extraordinary steps—granting large bail-out loans and increasing its contributions to lending agencies like the International Monetary Fund—in order to prevent others from going into default. Because of the enormous involvement of the largest U.S. banks in these loans, the American government acted to forestall any damage to its banking system.

The outlook for Latin America has brightened since the late 1970s. The three Andean countries have elected governments. Two of the harshest military regimes, those of Argentina and Brazil, have promised new elections in the near future. Of course, the great problems of economic development and injustice will not soon go away. What remains to be seen is whether the repayment of the enormous foreign debts of Latin American nations will consume funds rightfully earmarked to alleviate poverty. Much depends on the role of the United States. Will it oppose moderate or leftist solutions to Latin America's problems? Will it continue to support brutal rightist governments, fearing communist takeovers and loss of America's enormous Latin American investments? While the United States alone cannot determine what is to happen in Latin America, its actions will have a great deal to do with whether the inevitable change is violent or peaceful.

Suggestions
for Further Reading

BIBLIOGRAPHICAL AIDS

The indispensable *Handbook of Latin American Studies,* published annually since 1936, attempts, with the aid of specialists in various disciplines, to digest published material on Latin America in the social sciences and humanities. C. C. Griffin, ed., *Latin America: A Guide to the Historical Literature* (University of Texas Press, Austin, 1971), provides "a selective scholarly bibliography, accompanied by critical annotations, covering the whole field of Latin American history." R. A. Humphreys, *Latin American History: A Guide to the Literature in English* (Oxford University Press, New York, 1958), is an exemplary reference work whose critical and occasionally pungent comments on entries enhance the book's value, but an updated edition is badly needed.

For assessments of trends in historical writing in the recent period, see Roberto Esquenazi-Mayo and M. C. Meyer, eds., *Latin American Scholarship Since World War II: Trends in History,*

Political Science, Literature, Geography, and Economics (University of Nebraska Press, Lincoln, 1971). For the literature on economic history, see Stanley Stein and Roberto Cortes Conde, eds., *Latin America: A Guide to Economic History, 1830–1930* (University of California Press, Berkeley, 1977).

Students can also keep abreast of the most recent writing in the field by consulting the review sections in *The American Historical Review* (1895–), the *Hispanic American Historical Review* (1918–1922, 1926–), *Revista de Historia de América* (1938–); *The Americas: A Quarterly Review of Inter-American Cultural History* (1944–), *The Review of Inter-American Bibliography* (1951–), *Latin American Research Review* (1965–), and the British *Journal of Latin American Studies* (1969–).

For well-informed coverage of current events in the area, see the *Latin America Weekly Report* and the *Latin America Regional Reports* (Andean Group, Brazil, Caribbean, Mexico and Central America, Southern Cone), published by Latin American Newsletters Ltd. (London, Eng.). For more extended coverage of particular topics and events, marked by a high level of scholarship and perceptive analysis, see the bi-monthly *NACLA Report on the Americas,* published by the North American Congress on Latin America (1967–) and focusing on the political economy of the area.

GENERAL WORKS

Charles Gibson, *Spain in America* (Harper & Row, New York, 1966), the best short survey of the colonial period, incorporates recent scholarship and has a valuable bibliographical essay; J. H. Parry covers the same ground somewhat more amply in his well-written *The Spanish Seaborne Empire* (Knopf, New York, 1966). Stanley J. and Barbara H. Stein, *The Colonial Heritage of Latin America: Essays on Economic Dependence in Perspective* (Oxford University Press, New York, 1970), which is brief but insightful, shows the continuity of Latin American economic patterns

from colonial times to the present. Among older works, C. H. Haring, *The Spanish Empire in America* (Oxford University Press, New York, 1947), remains indispensable for colonial institutions. B. W. Diffie, *Latin American Civilization: Colonial Period* (Stackpole, Harrisburg, Pa., 1945), is a work of formidable scholarship and sharply defined viewpoints on various controversial topics. For a comprehensive collection of source materials on the colonial period, see Benjamin Keen, ed., *Latin American Civilization*, Vol. 1, *The Colonial Origins* (Houghton Mifflin, Boston, 1974).

There are few satisfactory general accounts of the period since independence. Perhaps still the best in English is Harry Bernstein, *Modern and Contemporary Latin America* (Lippincott, Philadelphia, 1952), which is notable for its pioneering stress on the importance of regional conflicts in the development of various Latin American countries. Simon Collier, *From Cortés to Castro: An Introduction to the History of Latin America, 1492–1973* (Macmillan, New York, 1974), is excellent on economic and social developments, but sketchy in its survey of political history. For the student with some mastery of Spanish, we recommend the very useful work of Tulio Halperin-Donghi, *Historia contemporánea de América Latina* (Alianza Editorial, Madrid, 1969). For source materials on the modern period, see Benjamin Keen, ed., *Latin American Civilization*, Vol. 2, *The National Era* (Houghton Mifflin, Boston, 1974).

CHAPTER ONE:
ANCIENT AMERICA

J. H. Steward, ed., *The Handbook of South American Indians,* 7 vols. (Bureau of American Ethnology, Washington, D.C., 1946–1959), and Robert Wauchope, ed., *Handbook of Middle American Indians,* 15 vols. (University of Texas Press, Austin, 1964–1975), are two points of departure for the study of Indian America. The best recent synthesis is Friedrich Katz, *The Ancient American*

Civilizations (Praeger, New York, 1972), valuable both for its up-to-date factual content and its probing questions. J. H. Steward, *Theory of Culture Change* (University of Illinois Press, Urbana, Ill., 1955), is a major source of the evolutionist theory that dominates thinking about ancient America today. W. T. Sanders and B. J. Price, *Mesoamerica* (Random House, New York, 1968), apply evolutionist theory to the study of ancient Mexico; another example of such application is Robert McCormick Adams's stimulating *The Evolution of Urban Society: Early Mesopotamia and Prehistoric Mexico* (Aldine, Hawthorne, N.Y., 1966). For important new insights into the nature of the Aztec and Inca civilizations, see G. A. Collier, R. I. Rosaldo, and J. D. Wirth, eds., *The Inca and Aztec States, 1400–1800: Anthropology and History* (Academic Press, New York, 1982).

For a brilliant and sometimes poetic short account of the history and culture of Middle America, see E. J. Wolf, *Sons of the Shaking Earth* (University of Chicago Press, Chicago, 1959). The intriguing Olmec culture has attracted much attention recently; three outstanding works are M. D. Coe, *America's First Civilization: Discovering the Olmec* (American Heritage, New York, 1968), Ignacio Bernal, *The Olmec World* (University of California Press, Berkeley, 1969), and Charles Wicke, *Olmec* (University of Arizona Press, Tucson, 1971). For an excellent summary of knowledge about Teotihuacán, see René Millon's introduction to Part I, Vol. I, of his *Urbanization at Teotihuacán, Mexico* (University of Texas Press, Austin, 1973). Nigel Davies, *The Toltecs: Until the Fall of Tula* (University of Oklahoma Press, Norman, Okla., 1977), attempts to separate fact from legend in the shadowy Toltec history. Joseph Whitecotton, *The Zapotecs* (University of Oklahoma Press, Norman, 1977), forms a valuable companion study to John Paddock, ed., *Ancient Oaxaca* (Stanford University Press, Stanford, Calif., 1966).

Much of our knowledge of Aztec civilization is based on two ancient sources, Bernardino de Sahagún, *General History of the Things of New Spain, Florentine Codex*, tr. and ed. by A. O. J. Anderson and C. E. Dibble, 12 vols. (School of American Research, Santa Fe, N.M., 1950–1969), and Alonso de Zorita, *Life and Labor in Ancient Mexico*, tr. and with an introduction by Benjamin Keen (Rutgers University Press, New Brunswick, N.J., 1963). Although partly outdated, G. C. Vaillant, *Aztecs of Mexico*, rev. ed. (Penguin Books, New York, 1955), retains much value. Two important modern surveys are Jacques Soustelle, *The Daily Life of the Aztecs on the Eve of the Conquest*, tr. by Patrick O'Brian (Macmillan, New York, 1962), and Nigel Davies, *The Aztecs: A History* (Putnam, New York, 1974). Miguel León-Portilla, *Aztec Thought and Culture: A Study of the Ancient Nahuatl Mind* (University of Oklahoma Press, Norman, Okla., 1963), is richly informative, but perhaps exaggerates the Aztec intellectual achievement. For a survey of four centuries of interpretation of Aztec culture, see Benjamin Keen, *The Aztec Image in Western Thought* (Rutgers University Press, New Brunswick, N.J., 1971).

Diego de Landa, *The Maya: Account of the Affairs of Yucatan*, tr. and ed. by A. R. Pagden (O'Hara, Chicago, 1975), remains our most important source on Maya civilization. *Popol Vuh, The Sacred Book of the Ancient Quiche Maya*, tr. and ed. by Adrian Recinos (University of Oklahoma Press, Norman, 1952), is an interesting collection of Maya creation myths, legends, and beliefs. The literature on the Maya is immense; three older syntheses are Sylvanus Morley, *The Ancient Maya*, 3rd ed. (Stanford University Press, Stanford, 1956); J. Eric Thompson, *Maya History and Religion* (University of Oklahoma Press, Norman, 1970); and M. D. Coe, *The Maya* (Praeger, New York, 1966). For a well-written summary of current points of view and knowledge about the Maya, see Norman Hammond, *Ancient Maya Civilization* (Rutgers University Press, New Brunswick, N.J., 1982). T. P. Culbert, ed., *The Classic Maya Collapse* (University of New Mexico

Press, Albuquerque, 1973), inquires into one of the most difficult problems of Maya history.

E. P. Lanning, *Peru Before the Incas* (Prentice-Hall, Englewood Cliffs, N.J., 1967), is an excellent introduction to the subject. Paul Kosok, *Life, Land, and Water in Ancient Peru* (Long Island University Press, New York, 1965), studies the role of irrigation in pre-Inca Peru, with a focus on the Chimu Empire. Garcilaso de la Vega, *Royal Commentaries of the Incas and General History of Peru*, tr. by H. V. Livermore, 2 vols. (University of Texas Press, Austin, 1966), is an indispensable source, but its idyllic picture of the relations between the Inca rulers and their subjects must be viewed with caution. J. M. Rowe, "Inca Culture at the Time of the Spanish Conquest," in Vol. 2 (1946) of the *Handbook of South American Indians,* cited above, remains a useful summary. Alfred Métraux, *The History of the Incas* (Pantheon, New York, 1969), incorporates modern findings on Inca society. S. F. Moore, *Power and Property in Inca Peru* (Columbia University Press, New York, 1958), was among the first works to question the collectivist conception of the Inca Empire. J. V. Murra has shed much light on Inca economic and social organization in a series of searching essays; his important doctoral dissertation on the subject has finally seen the light in a Spanish edition, *La organización económica del estado inca* (Siglo Veintiuno, Mexico, 1978).

For new high estimates of pre-Conquest Indian populations, see Woodrow Borah and S. F. Cook, *The Aboriginal Population of Central Mexico on the Eve of the Spanish Conquest* (University of California Press, Berkeley, 1963), and S. F. Cook and Woodrow Borah, *Essays in Population History, Mexico and the Caribbean,* 3 vols. (University of California Press, Berkeley, 1971–1979). For a defense of traditional lower estimates, see Angel Rosenblat, *La población indígena de América, desde 1492 hasta la actualidad,* rev. ed. (Editorial Nova, Buenos Aires, 1954). W. M. Denevan, ed., *The Native Population of the Americas in 1492* (Uni-

versity of Wisconsin Press, Madison, 1976), brings together conflicting viewpoints and attempts to generalize from the evidence.

CHAPTER TWO:
THE HISPANIC BACKGROUND

For the general Hispanic background, see S. G. Payne, *A History of Spain and Portugal,* 2 vols. (University of Wisconsin Press, Madison, 1973). On the *Reconquista,* see Derek W. Lomax, *The Reconquest of Spain* (Longman, New York, 1978). Americo Castro, *The Structure of Spanish History,* tr. by E. L. King (Princeton University Press, Princeton, 1954), argues that certain fixed traits of the Spanish character reflect the enduring stamp of Moslem and Jewish cultural influence. The distinguished medievalist Claudio Sánchez Albornoz rejects Castro's determinism in a work that is more solidly rooted in economic and social realities, *Spain, a Historical Enigma,* tr. by C. J. Dees and D. S. Reher, 2 vols. (Fundación Universitaria Española, Madrid, 1975)—but the work deserves a better English translation. John Elliott, *Imperial Spain, 1469–1716* (New American Library, New York, 1964), and John Lynch, *Spain Under the Hapsburgs,* 2 vols. (Basil Blackwell and Oxford University Press, Oxford, Eng., 1964–1969), usefully complement each other.

J. H. Mariéjol, *The Spain of Ferdinand and Isabella,* tr. and ed. by Benjamin Keen (Rutgers University Press, New Brunswick, N.J., 1961), remains the best general account of the life, manners, and institutions of Spain under the Catholic Sovereigns. Henry Kamen, *The Spanish Inquisition* (New American Library, New York, 1965), is a reliable synthesis. Ruth Pike shows that nobility did not exclude the practice of commerce in *Aristocrats and Traders: Sevillian Society in the Sixteenth Century* (Cornell University Press, Ithaca, N.Y., 1972). Bartolomé Bennassar combines learning and literary grace in *The Spanish Character: Attitudes and Mentalities from the Sixteenth to the Nineteenth Century,* tr. and with a preface by Benjamin Keen (University of California Press, Berkeley, 1979). For economic trends, see Jaime Vicens Vives, *An Economic History of Spain*, tr. by F. M. López-Morillas (Princeton University Press, Princeton, 1969).

CHAPTER THREE:
THE CONQUEST OF AMERICA

C. E. Nowell, *The Great Discoveries and the First Colonial Empires* (Cornell University Press, Ithaca, N.Y., 1954), provides a good introduction to the subject. J. H. Parry, *The Age of Reconnaissance* (World, Cleveland, 1963), is especially informative on the techniques of navigation, ship construction, armaments, and the like. For the impact of the New World on the mind of the Old, see John Elliott, *The Old World and the New, 1492–1650* (Cambridge University Press, Cambridge, Eng., 1970); the subject is studied in much greater detail in Fredi Chiapelli, ed., *First Images of America*, 2 vols. (University of California Press, Berkeley, 1976).

On the background of the Portuguese outward thrust, see B. C. Diffie, *Prelude to Empire: Portugal Overseas before Henry the Navigator* (University of Nebraska Press, Lincoln, 1961). S. E. Morison, *Portuguese Voyages to America in the Fifteenth Century* (Harvard University Press, Cambridge, Mass., 1940), subjects those voyages to careful scrutiny. For a masterful survey of the Portuguese colonial experience, see C. R. Boxer, *The Portuguese Seaborne Empire, 1415–1825* (Knopf, New York, 1969).

S. E. Morison, *The European Discovery of America: The Southern Voyages, 1492–1619* (Oxford University Press, New York, 1974), is written with the author's customary verve and takes decided positions on such questions as the character and achievements of Vespucci; for a more favorable view of Vespucci, see German Arciniegas, *Amerigo and the New World: The Life and Times of Amerigo Vespucci*, tr. by Harriet de Onis (Octagon Books, New York, 1955). Mor-

ison's *Admiral of the Ocean Sea: A Life of the Admiral Christopher Columbus*, 2 vols. (Little, Brown, Boston, 1942), comes close to being the definitive biography of the discoverer. The most important primary source on Columbus is *The Life of the Admiral Christopher Columbus by His Son Ferdinand*, tr. and ed. by Benjamin Keen (Rutgers University Press, New Brunswick, N.J., 1959), the first modern version of this classic work. On the grim consequences of the discovery for the natives of the Antilles, see Carl Sauer, *The Early Spanish Main* (University of California Press, Berkeley, 1966). For the great voyage of Magellan, see C. E. Nowell, ed., *Magellan's Voyage Around the World: Three Contemporary Accounts* (Northwestern University Press, Evanston, Ill., 1962); and the fine biography by C. M. Parr, *So Noble a Captain: The Life and Times of Ferdinand Magellan* (Crowell, New York, 1953). Kathleen Romoli's carefully researched *Balboa of Darien: Discoverer of the Pacific* (Doubleday, New York, 1953), remains the standard biography.

Miguel León-Portilla, ed., *The Broken Spears: The Aztec Account of the Conquest of Mexico*, tr. by Lysander Kemp (Beacon Press, Boston, 1961), presents the neglected native vision of the Conquest. The major Spanish eyewitness accounts are by Cortés himself, *Letters from Mexico*, tr. and ed. by A. R. Pagden (Grossman, New York, 1971), and Bernal Díaz del Castillo, *A True History of the Conquest of New Spain* (many editions); Díaz del Castillo wrote his book in part to correct the hero-worshiping account of Francisco López de Gómara, *Cortés: The Life of the Conqueror by His Secretary*, tr. by L. B. Simpson (University of California, Berkeley, 1966). For the military side of the Conquest, see C. H. Gardiner, *Naval Power in the Conquest of Mexico* (University of Texas Press, Austin, 1956). A Cortés biography worthy of the man remains to be written; for the first part of his life, see the prosaic but reliable book of H. R. Wagner, *The Rise of Fernando Cortés* (The Cortés Society, Los Angeles,

Calif., 1944). R. C. Padden, *The Humming Bird and the Hawk: Conquest and Sovereignty in the Valley of Mexico, 1503–1541* (Ohio State University Press, Columbus, 1967), presents interesting new interpretations, but is marred by speculative and even fictional touches. W. H. Prescott, *History of the Conquest of Mexico*, 3 vols. (Phillips, Sampson, Boston, 1843, and many other editions), remains unsurpassed for breadth of conception and literary charm, but its romantic attitudes clearly reveal the book's age.

John Hemming, *The Conquest of the Incas* (Harcourt Brace Jovanovich, New York, 1970), supersedes all previous accounts, but Prescott's *History of the Conquest of Peru*, 2 vols. (Harper & Bros., New York, 1847), retains much informative value. James Lockhart, *The Men of Cajamarca: A Social and Biographical Study of the First Conquerors of Peru* (University of Texas Press, Austin, 1972), sheds light on the backgrounds of the conquistador group. For the sequel of civil wars in Peru, see the work of Garcilaso de la Vega, *Royal Commentaries of the Incas and General History of Peru*, tr. by H. V. Livermore, 2 vols. (University of Texas Press, Austin, 1966).

Morris Bishop, *The Odyssey of Cabeza de Vaca* (Century, New York, 1933), is a well-written account of his great trek over the plains of the Southwest. H. E. Bolton, *Coronado, Knight of Pueblos and Plains* (University of New Mexico Press, Albuquerque, 1949), remains a standard work. On Jiménez de Quesada's quest for El Dorado, see German Arciniegas, *The Knight of El Dorado: The Tale of Don Gonzalo Jiménez de Quesada and His Conquest of New Granada* (Viking, New York, 1942). On the origins of the El Dorado legend and its ramifications, see the well-written and beautifully illustrated book by John Hemming, *The Search for El Dorado* (E. P. Dutton, New York, 1978). On the origins, motives, and occupations of the conquistadors and other Spanish settlers, see Lockhart's *Men of Cajamarca*, cited above, and James Lockhart and Enrique Otte, eds., *Letters and People of the Spanish Indies:*

Sixteenth Century (Cambridge University Press, Cambridge, Eng., 1976).

CHAPTER FOUR:
THE ECONOMIC FOUNDATIONS
OF COLONIAL LIFE

For the juridical and moral aspects of the struggle over Spain's Indian policy, see Lewis Hanke, *The Spanish Struggle for Justice in the Conquest of America* (University of Pennsylvania Press, Philadelphia, 1949), and *Aristotle and the American Indians: A Study in Race Prejudice in the Modern World*, 2nd ed. (Indiana University Press, Bloomington, 1970). For messianic and utopian influences on the Conquest, see J. L. Phelan, *The Millennial Kingdom of the Franciscans in the New World* (University of California Press, Berkeley, 1956). On Las Casas, who played so large a part in the debate on Spain's Indian policy, see, amid a voluminous literature, Lewis Hanke, *Bartolomé de Las Casas: An Interpretation of His Life and Writings* (Nijhoff, The Hague, 1951), and Juan Friede and Benjamin Keen, eds., *Bartolomé de Las Casas in History* (Northern Illinois University Press, De Kalb, 1971), an anthology that presents varied points of view on the "Apostle of the Indians."

On the so-called black legend of Spanish cruelty, see the exchange between Benjamin Keen and Lewis Hanke: Benjamin Keen, "The Black Legend Revisited: Assumptions and Realities," *Hispanic American Historical Review*, 49 (1969), 703–721; Lewis Hanke, "A Modest Proposal for a Moratorium on Grand Generalizations: Some Thoughts on the Black Legend," *Hispanic American Historical Review*, 51 (1971), 112–127; Keen, "The White Legend Revisited: A Reply to Professor Hanke's Modest Proposal," *Hispanic American Historical Review*, 51 (1971), 336–351. For studies of Spanish-Indian relations that reveal the practice rather than the theory of Spain's Indian policy, see P. W. Powell, *Soldiers, Indians, and Silver: The Northwest Advance of New Spain,*

1550–1600 (University of California Press, Berkeley, 1952), and E. H. Korth, *Spanish Policy in Colonial Chile: The Struggle for Social Justice* (Standard University Press, Stanford, Calif., 1968). For an important case study of the impact of conquest on native peoples, see S. J. Stern, *Peru's Native Peoples and the Challenge of Conquest: Huamanga to 1640* (University of Wisconsin Press, Madison, 1982).

There is an abundant literature on the Spanish colonial labor and tribute systems. For an important source on conditions in sixteenth-century Mexico, again see Alonso de Zorita, *Life and Labor in Ancient Mexico*, tr. and with an introduction by Benjamin Keen (New Brunswick, N.J., 1963). L. B. Simpson's important pioneering study, *The Encomienda in New Spain*, rev. ed. (University of California Press, Berkeley, 1950), argues that the encomienda was eventually "tamed." For the devastating impact of the primitive encomienda on the Antilles, see again Carl Sauer, *The Early Spanish Main* (Berkeley, 1966). For a reassessment of the relation of encomienda to hacienda, see James Lockhart, "Encomienda and Hacienda: The Evolution of the Great Estate in the Spanish Indies," *Hispanic American Historical Review*, 49 (1969), 411–429.

Indian labor, tribute, and land are major themes in Charles Gibson's monumental *The Aztecs Under Spanish Rule: A History of the Indians of the Valley of Mexico* (Stanford University Press, Stanford, Calif., 1964). Gibson's book, like that of François Chevalier, *Land and Society in Colonial Mexico*, tr. by L. B. Simpson (University of California Press, Berkeley, 1963), documents the triumph of the hacienda over the Indian pueblo in central Mexico, but W. B. Taylor, *Landlord and Peasant in Colonial Oaxaca* (Stanford University Press, Stanford, Calif., 1972), shows that Indians retained much of the land in that province. For the development of the hacienda in Peru, see R. G. Keith, *Conquest and Agrarian Change: Emergence of the Hacienda System on the Peruvian Coast* (Harvard University Press, Cambridge,

Mass., 1976). For a concise survey of the status of the Indian in colonial Peru, see J. H. Rowe, "The Incas under Spanish Colonial Institutions," *Hispanic American Historical Review*, 37 (1957), 155–199. Juan A. and Judith E. Villamarín, *Indian Labor in Mainland Colonial Spanish America* (University of Delaware Press, Newark, 1975), shows how different patterns of Indian labor management were employed in different times and places.

For a good general survey of the subject of slavery, see L. B. Rout, Jr., *The African Experience in Spanish America: 1502 to the Present Day* (Cambridge University Press, Cambridge, Eng., 1971), and, for a concise history of black slavery in the area, Rolando Mellafe, *Negro Slavery in Latin America* (University of California Press, Berkeley, 1975). On black slavery in specific colonies, see, amid a growing literature, the fine monographs of F. P. Bowser, *The African Slave in Colonial Peru, 1524–1650* (Stanford University Press, Stanford, Calif., 1973); F. W. Knight, *Slave Society in Cuba during the Nineteenth Century* (University of Wisconsin Press, Madison, 1970); and G. M. Hall, *Social Control in Slave Plantation Societies: A Comparison of St. Domingue and Cuba* (Johns Hopkins University Press, Baltimore, 1971). For the dimensions of the slave traffic, see P. D. Curtin, *The American Slave Trade: A Census* (University of Wisconsin Press, Madison, 1969), and for various aspects of colonial slavery, Stanley Engerman and E. D. Genovese, *Race and Slavery in the Western Hemisphere: Quantitative Studies* (Princeton University Press, Princeton, 1975).

On the *encomendero* as entrepreneur, see José Miranda, *La función económica del encomendero en los orígenes del régimen colonial* (Universidad Nacional Autónoma de México, Mexico, 1965), and F. V. Scholes, "The Spanish Conquistador as Businessman: A Chapter in the History of Fernando Cortés," *New Mexico Quarterly*, 28 (1958), 1–29. G. M. Riley studies the Cortés economic interests in more detail in *Fernando Cortés and the Marquesado in Morelos, 1522–1547: A Case Study in the Socioeconomic Development of Sixteenth-*

Century Mexico (University of New Mexico Press, Albuquerque, 1973); see also W. J. Barrett, *The Sugar Hacienda of the Marqueses del Valle* (University of Minnesota Press, Minneapolis, 1970). On the short-lived Mexican silk industry, see Woodrow Borah, *Silk Raising in Colonial Mexico* (University of California Press, Berkeley, 1943). For the history of the stock raisers' guild in New Spain, see William Dusenberry, *The Mexican Mesta* (University of Illinois Press, Urbana, 1963). L. B. Simpson, *Exploitation of Land in Central Mexico in the Sixteenth Century* (University of California Press, Berkeley, 1956), chronicles, among other things, the replacement of men by sheep. M. J. MacLeod, *Spanish Central America: A Socioeconomic History, 1520–1720* (University of California Press, Berkeley, 1973) is the story of the economic rise and fall of a region. On the interplay of colonial politics and trade, see B. R. Hamnett, *Politics and Trade in Southern Mexico, 1750–1821* (Cambridge University Press, Cambridge, Eng., 1971).

There is a substantial literature on colonial mining. Studies of Mexican silver include R. G. West, *The Mining Community in Northern New Spain: The Parral District* (University of California Press, Berkeley, 1949); P. J. Bakewell, *Silver Mining and Society in Colonial Mexico: Zacatecas, 1546–1700* (Cambridge University Press, Cambridge, Eng., 1971), a work that calls into question older views on the availability of Indian labor and silver production trends; and David Brading, *Miners and Merchants in Bourbon Mexico, 1763–1810* (Cambridge University Press, Cambridge, Eng., 1971), a book that throws as much light on political and social themes as it does on mining. For Peruvian mining, see, in addition to the classic work of A. P. Whitaker, *The Huancavelica Mine* (Harvard University Press, Cambridge, Mass., 1941), J. R. Fisher, *Silver Mines and Silver Miners in Colonial Peru, 1776–1824* (University of Liverpool, Liverpool, 1977), a work that fills a serious gap in the literature.

Historians continue to dispute whether the seventeenth century was a century of colonial depression. Woodrow Borah's classic *New Spain's Century of Depression* (University of California Press, Berkeley, 1951) links a supposed drop in mining and food production to a drastic decline in Indian population; the depression thesis finds support in Murdo MacLeod's book on Central America, cited above, but is challenged with cogent arguments by John Lynch in the second volume of his *Spain Under the Hapsburgs*, 2 vols. (Basil Blackwell and Oxford University Press, Oxford, Eng., 1964–1969).

On the general character of the colonial economy, see, among other works, André Gunder Frank, *Capitalism and Underdevelopment in Latin America* (Monthly Review Press, New York, 1967), which claims that it was basically capitalist, and Enrique Semo, *Historia del capitalismo en México, los orígenes, 1521–1763* (Ediciones Era, Mexico, 1973), which offers a closely reasoned argument that the colonial economic system was composed of three modes of production: tributary despotism, feudalism, and embryonic capitalism.

On colonial commerce, see the classic study of C. H. Haring, *Trade and Navigation Between Spain and the Indies in the Time of the Hapsburgs* (Harvard University Press, Cambridge, Mass., 1918). For the Italian role in colonial trade, see Ruth Pike, *Enterprise and Adventure: The Genoese in Seville and the Opening of the New World* (Cornell University Press, Ithaca, N.Y., 1966). John Campbell, *The Spanish Empire in America* (M. Cooper, London, 1747), provides valuable information on legal and illegal trade. W. L. Schurz, *The Manila Galleon* (E. P. Dutton, New York, 1939), deals with the important silk trade between Manila and Acapulco. For piracy, see the still valuable work of C. H. Haring, *The Buccaneers in the West Indies in the Seventeenth Century* (Methuen, London, 1910), and the memoirs of a pirate, John Esquemeling, *The Buccaneers of America* (Swann Sonnenscheim, London, 1893).

CHAPTER FIVE:
STATE, CHURCH, AND SOCIETY

C. H. Haring, *The Spanish Empire in America* (Oxford University Press, New York, 1947), is particularly good on the political and administrative system. Mario Góngora, *Studies in the Colonial History of Spanish America* (Cambridge University Press, Cambridge, Eng., 1975), the work of a great Chilean scholar, sheds light on a variety of themes ranging from the organization of conquests to "the institutions and founding ideas of the Spanish state in the Indies." J. H. Parry, *The Spanish Theory of Empire in the Sixteenth Century* (Cambridge University Press, Cambridge, Eng., 1940), is a useful background study. Good studies of viceroys include A. S. Aiton, *Antonio de Mendoza, First Viceroy of New Spain* (Duke University Press, Durham, N.C., 1927), and B. E. Bobb, *The Viceregency of Antonio Maria Bucareli in New Spain, 1771–1779* (University of Texas Press, Austin, 1962). Peggy Liss, *Mexico under Spain, 1521–1556: Society and the Origins of Nationality* (University of Chicago Press, Chicago, 1975), fills a major gap in the literature on Spanish rule in Mexico. Karen Spalding, ed., *Essays in the Political, Economic and Social History of Colonial Latin America* (University of Delaware, Newark, 1982), focuses on the role of the state in the colonial economy.

Two excellent audiencia studies are J. H. Parry, *The Audiencia of Galicia in the Sixteenth Century* (Cambridge University Press, Cambridge, Eng., 1948), and J. L. Phelan, *The Kingdom of Quito in the Seventeenth Century: Bureaucratic Politics in the Spanish Empire* (University of Wisconsin Press, Madison, 1967). Phelan has also illuminated the conflict of goals and standards in the colonial political system, "Authority and Flexibility in the Spanish Imperial Bureaucracy," *Administrative Science Quarterly*, 5 (1960), 630–664. On the problem of venality, see J. H. Parry, *The Sale of Public Office in the Spanish Indies Under the Hapsburgs* (University of California Press, Berkeley, 1953). For the Bourbon effort at political reform, see John Lynch, *Spanish Colonial Administration, 1782–1819: The Intendant System in the Viceroyalty of the Rio de la Plata* (Athlone Press, London, 1958), and J. R. Fisher, *Government and Society in Colonial Peru: The Intendant System, 1784–1814* (Athlone Press, London, 1970). J. P. Moore has written two useful cabildo studies: *The Cabildo in Peru under the Hapsburgs* (Duke University Press, Durham, N.C., 1954) and *The Cabildo in Peru under the Bourbons* (Duke University Press, Durham, N.C., 1966). M. A. Burkholder and D. S. Chandler, *From Impotence to Authority: The Spanish Crown and the American Audiencias* (Columbia, Missouri, 1977), studies changes over time in the composition and functioning of the colonial audiencias.

R. E. Greenleaf, ed., *The Roman Catholic Church in Colonial Latin America* (Knopf, New York, 1971), is a collection of informative texts with a useful introduction. On the process of Indian conversion, see Robert Ricard, *The Spiritual Conquest of Mexico*, tr. by L. B. Simpson (University of California Press, Berkeley, 1966). On the colonial inquisition, see the old but still valuable work of H. C. Lea, *The Inquisition in the Spanish Dependencies* (Macmillan, New York, 1908), and two works by R. E. Greenleaf, *Zummáraga and the Mexican Inquisition, 1536–1543* (Academy of American Franciscan History, Washington, D.C., 1961) and *The Mexican Inquisition in the Seventeenth Century* (University of New Mexico Press, Albuquerque, 1969). H. E. Bolton, *Rim of Christendom: A Biography of Eusebio Francisco Kino, Pacific Coast Pioneer* (Macmillan, New York, 1936), is a model biography of the great missionary; for the career of another remarkable missionary, see F. B. Warren, *Vasco de Quiroga and His Pueblo-Hospitals of Santa Fe* (Academy of American Franciscan History, Washington, D.C., 1963).

On the Jesuits, see Magnus Mörner, *The Political and Economic Activities of the Jesuits in the La Plata Region: The Hapsburg Era* (Stockholm, 1953), and Mörner's anthology on *The Expulsion of the Jesuits from Latin America* (Knopf, New

York, 1965). For the fate of Jewish conversos at the Inquisition's hands, see S. B. Liebman, *The Jews in New Spain: Faith, Flame, and the Inquisition* (University of Miami Press, Coral Gables, Fla., 1970). On crown-church relations, see W. E. Shiels, *King and Church: The Rise and Fall of the Patronato* (Loyola University Press, Chicago, 1961), and, for those relations in the eighteenth century, see N. M. Farriss, *Crown and Clergy in Colonial Mexico, 1759–1821: The Crisis of Ecclesiastical Privilege* (Athlone Press, London, 1968).

On the structure of class and caste, see Magnus Mörner, *Race Mixture in the History of Latin America* (Little, Brown, Boston, 1967), and a collection of essays edited by Mörner, *Race and Class in Latin America* (Columbia University Press, New York, 1970). For new perspectives on colonial social history, see F. P. Bowser, "The African in Colonial Spanish America: Reflections on Research Achievements and Priorities," *Latin American Research Review*, 7 (1972), 77–94; James Lockhart, "The Social History of Colonial Spanish America: Evolution and Potential," *Latin American Research Review*, 7 (1972), 6–46; and Karen Spalding, "The Colonial Indian: Past and Present Research Perspectives," *Latin American Research Review*, 7 (1972), 47–75.

For the Indian adjustment to Spanish rule, see Charles Gibson's *The Aztecs Under Spanish Rule: A History of the Indians of the Valley of Mexico* (Stanford University Press, Stanford, Calif., 1964) and *Tlaxcala in the Sixteenth Century* (Yale University Press, New Haven, 1955); for Peru, see J. H. Rowe's article, "The Incas Under Spanish Colonial Institutions," *Hispanic American Historical Review*, 37 (1957), 155–199, and George Kubler, "The Quechua in the Colonial World," in Vol. 2 of the *Handbook of South American Indians*, J. H. Steward, ed. (Bureau of American Ethnology, Washington, D.C., 1946–1959). Pierre Duviols discusses Spanish efforts to extirpate Indian heresy in Peru, *La Lutte contre les religions autochtones dans le Perou colonial* (Editions Ophrys, Paris, 1971), and Nathan Wachtel describes the stubborn Indian resistance to acculturation in *The Vision of the Vanquished: The Spanish Conquest of Peru Through Indian Eyes, 1530–1570* (Barnes and Noble, New York, 1977).

Karen Spalding has carefully studied economic and social changes among the Peruvian colonial Indians; her scattered articles have been published in a Spanish edition, *De indio a campesino. Cambios en la estructura del Perú colonial* (Instituto de Estudios Peruanos, Lima, 1974). On the colonial blacks, in addition to the study of Bowser and other works cited in the bibliography to Chapter 4, see for conflicting views on the condition of slaves and black freedmen, Eugene Genovese and Laura Foner, eds., *Slavery in the New World* (Prentice-Hall, Englewood Cliffs, N.J., 1970); D. W. Cohen and J. P. Greene, eds., *Neither Slave nor Free: The Freedmen of African Descent in the Slave Societies of the New World* (Johns Hopkins University Press, Baltimore, 1972); and C. A. Palmer, *Slaves of the White God: Blacks in Mexico, 1570–1650* (Harvard University Press, Cambridge, Mass., 1976).

For Spanish immigration to the Indies, see Peter Boyd-Bowman, *Patterns of Spanish Immigration to the New World, 1492–1580* (State University of New York at Buffalo, Buffalo, 1973). James Lockhart, *Spanish Peru, 1532–1560: A Colonial Society* (University of Wisconsin Press, Madison, 1968), is a valuable study of the first generation of Spanish settlers, but the virtual absence of any discussion of Indian commoners inevitably distorts the colonial economic and social reality. For a good study of a colonial city, see Lewis Hanke, *The Imperial City of Potosí: An Unwritten Chapter in the History of Spanish America* (The Hague, 1955). C. R. Boxer, *Women in Iberian Expansion Overseas, 1415–1815* (Oxford University Press, New York, 1975), is a slight, often anecdotal study. Studies of colonial women are included in an important volume edited by Asunción Lavrin, *Latin American Women: Historical Perspectives* (Greenwood Press, Westport, Conn., 1978). D. M. Ladd, *The Mexican Nobility at Independence, 1780–1826* (University of Texas

Press, Austin, 1976), is a valuable study of a special social group.

CHAPTER SIX:
THE BOURBON REFORMS AND SPANISH AMERICA

Richard Herr, *The Eighteenth-Century Revolution in Spain* (Princeton University Press, Princeton, 1958), lucidly describes the Bourbons' effort to reconstruct Spain. R. J. Shafer, *The Economic Societies in the Spanish World, 1763–1821* (Syracuse University Press, Syracuse, N.Y., 1958), deals with an important agency of that effort. H. I. Priestley, *José de Galvez, Visitor-General of New Spain, 1765–1771* (University of California Press, Berkeley, 1916), studies the Mexican career of a leading Bourbon reforming official. For the intendant reform, see John Lynch, *Spanish Colonial Administration, 1782–1819: The Intendant System in the Viceroyalty of the Rio de la Plata* (Athlone Press, London, 1958), and J. R. Fisher, *Government and Society in Colonial Peru: The Intendant System, 1784–1814* (Athlone Press, London, 1970). For one aspect of the Bourbon trade reform, see R. D. Hussey, *The Caracas Company, 1728–1784* (Harvard University Press, Cambridge, Mass., 1934). S. M. Socolow, *The Merchants of Buenos Aires, 1778–1810* (Cambridge University Press, New York, 1978), is an important study of one merchant community. A major source of information on New Spain in the late Bourbon era is Alexander von Humboldt, *Political Essay on the Kingdom of New Spain* (Longman, London, 1811). For the impact of the Enlightenment on the colonies, see A. P. Whitaker, ed., *Latin America and the Enlightenment* (Cornell University Press, Ithaca, N.Y., 1961), and the works of A. J. Lanning, notably *The Eighteenth-Century Enlightenment in the University of San Carlos de Guatemala* (Cornell University Press, Ithaca, N.Y., 1956). For the rise of a colonial military elite, see the pioneering monograph of L. N. McAlister, *The "Fuero Militar" in New Spain, 1765–1800* (University of Florida Press, Gainesville, 1957). For economic trends in the colonies in the Bourbon era, see David Brading, *Miners and Merchants in Bourbon Mexico, 1763–1810* (Cambridge University Press, Cambridge, Eng., 1971); B. R. Hamnett, *Politics and Trade in Southern Mexico, 1750–1821* (Cambridge University Press, Cambridge, Eng., 1971); and J. R. Fisher, *Silver Mines and Silver Miners in Colonial Peru, 1776–1824* (University of Liverpool, Liverpool, 1977). Eric Van Young's important *Hacienda and Market in Eighteenth-Century Mexico: The Rural Economy of the Guadalajara Region, 1675–1820* (University of California Press, Berkeley, 1981) documents, among other findings, the growing domination of the great estate.

On colonial culture, see the basic study by J. T. Lanning, *Academic Culture in the Spanish Colonies* (Oxford University Press, London, 1940). Mariano Picón-Salas, *A Cultural History of Spanish America, from Conquest to Independence*, tr. by Irving Leonard (University of California Press, Berkeley, 1962), is a sprightly as well as informative survey. Irving Leonard combines literary and social history in his well-written *Books of the Brave* (Harvard University Press, Cambridge, Mass., 1949) and *Baroque Times in Old Mexico* (University of Michigan Press, Ann Arbor, 1959). George Kubler studies the relations among economics, society, and art in *Mexican Architecture in the Sixteenth Century*, 2 vols. (Yale University Press, New Haven, 1948). For the dawning of Creole national consciousness and its religious expression, see Jacques Lafaye, *Quetzalcoatl and Guadalupe: The Formation of Mexican National Consciousness*, tr. by Benjamin Keen (University of Chicago Press, Chicago, 1976); on Creole efforts to refute European charges of the New World's inferiority, see Antonello Gerbi, *The Dispute of the New World: The History of a Polemic, 1750–1900*, tr. by Jeremy Moyle (University of Pittsburgh Press, Pittsburgh, 1973), a learned and sometimes witty book.

L. E. Fisher surveys the revolt of Tupac Amaru in *The Last Inca Revolt, 1780–1783* (University of Oklahoma Press, Norman, 1966); for the revolt of the Comuneros, see the posthumous work of J. L. Phelan, *The People and the King: The*

Comunero Revolution in Columbia (University of Wisconsin Press, Madison, 1977), which argues that the Comunero movement was neither a frustrated social revolution nor an early effort to achieve political independence.

CHAPTER SEVEN:
COLONIAL BRAZIL

Despite its age, Robert Southey's *History of Brazil,* 3 vols. (Longman, London, 1810–1811), possesses much factual value and remains unsurpassed in style and the breadth of its vision. Caio Prado Júnior, *The Colonial Background of Modern Brazil,* tr. by Suzette Macedo (University of California Press, Berkeley, 1967), the best general survey, stresses economic and social aspects. A series of authoritative studies by the British Brazilianist Charles Boxer spans almost the whole course of Brazil's colonial history; see especially *The Dutch in Brazil, 1625–1654* (Clarendon Press, Oxford, Eng., 1957), *The Golden Age of Brazil, 1695–1750* (University of California Press, Berkeley, 1962), and *Salvador de Sá and the Struggle for Brazil and Angola, 1602–1686* (University of London Press, London, 1952). Dauril Alden, ed., *The Colonial Roots of Modern Brazil* (University of California Press, Berkeley, 1972), is a valuable collection of studies on socioeconomic topics, introduced by a historiographic essay by Boxer. James Lang, *Portuguese Brazil: The King's Plantation* (Academic Press, New York, 1979), is a useful synthesis, with a stress on the distinctive features of Brazil's colonial history.

For the early economic history of Portuguese Brazil, see Alexander Marchant, *From Barter to Slavery* (Johns Hopkins University Press, Baltimore, 1942). Dauril Alden, *Royal Government in Colonial Brazil* (University of California Press, Berkeley, 1968), focuses on the problems faced by an able viceroy of Brazil in the eighteenth century. For the backgrounds of colonial officials and their relations with other social groups, see S. B. Schwartz, *Sovereignty and Society in Colonial Brazil: The High Court of Bahia and Its Judges,*

1609–1745 (University of California Press, Berkeley, 1973). K. R. Maxwell, *Conflicts and Conspiracies: Brazil and Portugal, 1750–1808* (Cambridge University Press, New York, 1973), is a competent study of the emerging conflict between mother country and colony. On Portugal's Indian policies, see R. M. Morse, ed., *The Bandeirantes: The Historical Role of the Brazilian Pathfinders* (Knopf, New York, 1965); Clodomiro Vianna Moog, *Bandeirantes and Pioneers,* tr. by L. L. Barrett (G. Braziller, New York, 1964); and M. C. Kiemen, *The Indian Policy of Portugal in the Amazon Region, 1614–1693* (Catholic University of America Press, Washington, D.C., 1954); and John Hemming, *Red Gold: The Conquest of the Brazilian Indians* (Macmillan, London, 1978), which records "an appalling demographic tragedy of great magnitude." A. J. R. Russell-Wood, *Fidalgos and Philanthropists: The Santa Casa da Misericordia of Bahia, 1550–1575* (University of California Press, Berkeley, 1968), studies the social function of charitable activity in colonial Bahia. For the Jewish role in Brazil, see Arnold Wiznitzer, *Jews in Colonial Brazil* (Columbia University Press, New York, 1960).

Gilberto Freyre, *The Masters and the Slaves,* tr. by Samuel Putnam (Knopf, New York, 1946), is a literary and historical masterpiece, but its nostalgic portrayal of black-white relations must be viewed with caution. For a corrective, see Charles Boxer, *Race Relations in the Portuguese Colonial Empire, 1415–1825* (Clarendon Press, Oxford, Eng., 1963). For a valuable account of life and manners in Brazil at the end of the colonial period, see Henry Koster, *Travels in Brazil,* 2 vols. (Longman, London, 1816).

CHAPTER EIGHT:
THE INDEPENDENCE OF
LATIN AMERICA

John Lynch, *The Spanish-American Revolutions, 1808–1826* (Norton, New York, 1973), is an admirable synthesis, based on thorough research and supplied with a comprehensive annotated bibliography. R. A. Humphreys and John Lynch, eds., *The Origins of the Latin American Revolutions, 1808–1826* (Knopf, New York, 1965), brings together conflicting interpretations of the causes of the great upheaval. For the revolution in Haiti, see T. O. Ott, *The Haitian Revolution, 1789–1804* (University of Tennessee Press, Knoxville, 1973), and two biographies: Ralph Korngold, *Citizen Toussaint* (Little, Brown, Boston, 1944), and Hubert Cole, *Christophe, King of Haiti* (Viking, New York, 1967).

No completely satisfactory life of Bolívar exists; the best is Gerhard Masur, *Simon Bolívar*, 2nd ed. (University of New Mexico Press, Albuquerque, 1969). J. J. Johnson and D. M. Ladd, *Simon Bolívar and Spanish American Independence, 1783–1830* (D. Van Nostrand, New York, 1968), introduce well-chosen selections from Bolívar's writings with an informative brief biography; for a larger collection of selected writings, see Vicente Lecuna and H. H. Bierce, eds., *Selected Writings of Bolívar*, 2 vols. (Colonial Press, New York, 1951). On Miranda, see the standard work of W. S. Robertson, *The Life of Miranda*, 2 vols. (University of North Carolina Press, Chapel Hill, 1929). San Martín, like Bolívar, still awaits a biography in English worthy of the man, but there is an adequate short life by J. C. J. Metford, *San Martín the Liberator* (Longmans, Green, London, 1950). Bartolomé Mitre's massive nineteenth-century work, *Historia de San Martín y de la emancipación sudamericana* (many editions), remains the best biography in Spanish. John Street, *Artigas and the Emancipation of Uruguay* (Cambridge University Press, London, 1959), is an excellent study of the Uruguayan hero and the process of Uruguayan independence. For that process in Chile, see Simon Collier's thorough study, *Ideas and Politics of Chilean Independence, 1808–1833* (Cambridge University Press, New York, 1969), and Jay Kinsbruner, *Bernardo O'Higgins* (Twayne, Boston, 1968).

On the background of the movement for Brazilian independence, see the work of K. R. Maxwell, *Conflicts and Conspiracies: Brazil and Portugal, 1750–1808* (Cambridge University Press, New York, 1973); see also A. J. R. Russell-Wood, ed., *From Colony to Nation: Essays on the Independence of Brazil* (Johns Hopkins University Press, Baltimore, 1975).

An older work by L. E. Fisher, *The Background of the Revolution for Mexican Independence* (Christopher, Boston, 1934), retains much of its value; N. L. Benson, *Mexico and the Spanish Cortes, 1810–1822* (University of Texas Press, Austin, 1966), sheds light on the troubled relations between Mexico and Spain during the revolutionary period. The best full-scale life of Hidalgo is Luis Castillo Ledón, *Hidalgo, La vida del héroe*, 2 vols. (Mexico, 1948–1949), but H. M. Hamill, Jr., *The Hidalgo Revolt: Prelude to Mexican Independence* (University of Florida Press, Gainesville, 1966), is basic for an understanding of the causes and character of the revolt. W. H. Timmons, *Morelos of Mexico, Priest, Soldier, Statesman* (Texas Western Press, University of Texas at El Paso, El Paso, 1963), is competently done; W. S. Robertson, *Iturbide of Mexico* (Duke University Press, Durham, N.C., 1952), is a good biography of the traditional political type.

On the attitude of foreign powers toward Latin American independence, see W. W. Kaufmann, *British Policy and the Independence of Latin America, 1802–1828* (Yale University Press, New Haven, 1951); A. P. Whitaker, *The United States and the Independence of Latin America, 1800–1830* (Johns Hopkins University Press, Baltimore, 1941); and C. C. Griffin, *The United States and the Disruption of the Spanish Empire, 1800–1822* (Octagon Books, New York, 1941). For a case study in early inter-American relations, see Benjamin Keen, *David Curtis DeForest and the Revolution of Buenos Aires* (Yale University Press, New Haven, 1947).

The social and economic results of the revolutions still await intensive study. Tulio Halperin-Donghi ably discusses some of these results in *The Aftermath of Revolution in Latin America* (Harper & Row, New York, 1973). For an important pioneering essay, see C. C. Griffin, "Economic and Social Aspects of the

Era of Spanish-American Independence,"
Hispanic American Historical Review, 29 (1949),
170–187.

CHAPTER NINE:
DICTATORS AND REVOLUTIONS

For some new perspectives on Latin American
politics in the nineteenth century, see Richard
Graham and P. H. Smith, eds., *New Approaches
to Latin American History* (University of Texas
Press, Austin, 1974), and Tulio Halperin-Donghi,
The Aftermath of Revolution in Latin America
(Harper & Row, New York, 1973). See also Harry
Bernstein, *Modern and Contemporary Latin America*
(Lippincott, Philadelphia, 1952), which carefully
studies the impact of regional rivalries on the
political development of selected countries.

M. C. Meyer and W. L. Sherman, *The Course
of Mexican History* (Oxford University Press, New
York, 1979), supersedes all previous general
histories of Mexico, but Jan Bazant, *A Concise
History of Mexico from Hidalgo to Cárdenas, 1805–
1940* (Cambridge University Press, New York,
1978), contains a valuable brief account of the
first half-century after independence by a spe-
cialist in the period. Useful older works include
H. B. Parkes, *A History of Mexico*, rev. ed.
(Houghton Mifflin, Boston, 1969), and L. B.
Simpson, *Many Mexicos*, 4th ed. (University of
California Press, Berkeley, 1966). C. A. Hale,
Mexican Liberalism in the Age of Mora, 1821–1853
(Yale University Press, New Haven, 1968), is
a thoughtful analysis of the Mexican liberal
creed. Ralph Roeder's full-scale biography, *Juárez
and His Mexico*, 2 vols. (Viking, New York, 1947),
remains the best available work in English on
the subject. The important conservative Lucas
Alamán still awaits a biography in English, but
the flamboyant Santa Anna is the subject of
two biographies: W. H. Calcott, *Santa Anna:
The Story of an Enigma Who Once Was Mexico*
(University of Oklahoma Press, Norman, 1936),
and O. L. Jones, Jr., *Santa Anna* (Twayne, Boston, 1968).

On the key church issue, see W. H. Calcott,
Church and State in Mexico, 1822–1857 (Duke
University Press, Durham, N.C., 1926); M. P.
Costeloe, *Church Wealth in Mexico: A Study of
the Juzgado de Capellanías in the Archbishopric of
Mexico, 1800–1856* (Cambridge University Press,
Cambridge, Eng., 1967); and Jan Bazant, *Alien-
ation of Church Wealth: Social and Economic Aspects
of the Liberal Revolution, 1856–1875* (Cambridge
University Press, Cambridge, Eng., 1971). On
the Mexican War, see R. S. Henry, *The Story
of the Mexican War* (Bobbs-Merrill, Indianapolis,
1950); on the Maya revolt, see Nelson Reed,
The Caste War of Yucatan (Stanford University
Press, Stanford, Calif., 1964). For a panorama
of Mexican life in the age of Santa Anna, see
Fanny Calderon de la Barca, *Letters from Mexico*,
ed. by H. T. and M. H. Fisher (Doubleday,
Garden City, N.Y., 1966).

For the first half-century of Argentina's independent existence, see the reliable survey by
H. S. Ferns, *Argentina* (Praeger, New York, 1969),
and the older but excellent work of Y. F. Rennie,
The Argentine Republic (Macmillan, New York,
1945). Miron Burgin, *The Economic Aspects of
Argentine Federalism, 1820–1852* (Harvard University Press, Cambridge, Mass., 1946), is a
work of fundamental importance. On Rosas,
see the fine biography by John Lynch, *Argentine
Dictator: Juan Manuel Rosas, 1829–1852* (Oxford
University Press, New York, 1981). J. C. Brown,
A Socioeconomic History of Argentina, 1776–1860
(Cambridge University Press, New York, 1979),
is an excellent history of trade and agriculture
but seriously underestimates the emerging pat-
tern of a new dependency. For the lives of
Sarmiento and Mitre, see A. W. Bunkley, *The
Life of Sarmiento* (Princeton University Press,
Princeton, 1952) and W. H. Jeffrey, *Mitre and
Argentina* (Library Publishers, New York, 1952).
Studies of caudillos include the classic work of
Sarmiento on Facundo, *Life of the Argentine Re-
public in the Days of the Tyrants: Or, Civilization
and Barbarism*, tr. by Mrs. Horace Mann (Gordon
Press, New York, 1968), and Roger Haigh, *Martin*

Guemes: Tyrant or Tool? A Study of the Sources of Power of an Argentine Caudillo (Texas Christian University Press, Fort Worth, 1968). R. A. White, *Paraguay's Autonomous Revolution, 1810–1840* (University of New Mexico Press, Albuquerque, 1978), is an important revisionist study of the Francia era.

For the first decades of independent Chile, see the relevant sections of Brian Loveman, *Chile: The Legacy of Hispanic Capitalism* (Oxford University Press, New York, 1979) and Jay Kinsbruner's study of the conservative titan, *Diego Portales* (Nijhoff, The Hague, 1967), and consult again Simon Collier, *Ideas and Politics of Chilean Independence, 1808–1833* (Cambridge University Press, New York, 1969). On the Chilean great estate and its social consequences, see A. J. Bauer, *Chilean Rural Society from the Spanish Conquest to 1930* (Cambridge University Press, New York, 1975).

For independent Brazil's early history, see E. B. Burns's excellent *A History of Brazil* (Columbia University Press, New York, 1970) and his *Documentary History of Brazil* (Knopf, New York, 1966). Leslie Bethell deals with the crucial issue of abolition in *The Abolition of the Brazilian Slave Trade: Britain, Brazil, and the Slave Trade Question, 1807–1869* (Cambridge University Press, Cambridge, Eng., 1970). A key work on the British influence is A. K. Manchester, *British Preeminence in Brazil* (University of North Carolina Press, Chapel Hill, 1933). Gilberto Freyre, *The Mansions and the Shanties: The Making of Modern Brazil*, tr. by Harriet de Onis (Knopf, New York, 1963), carries his study of Brazilian society and race relations into the period of the empire. On the crisis of slavery in this period, see two important revisionist studies: Robert Conrad, *The Destruction of Brazilian Slavery, 1850–1888* (University of California Press, Berkeley, 1973), and R. B. Toplin, *The Abolition of Slavery in Brazil,* (Atheneum, New York, 1972). Stanley Stein has written two model socioeconomic studies: *The Brazilian Cotton Manufacture: Textile Enterprise*

in an Underdeveloped Area, 1850–1900 (Harvard University Press, Cambridge, Mass., 1947) and *Vassouras: A Brazilian Coffee County* (Harvard University Press, Cambridge, Mass., 1957). On Dom Pedro II, see M. W. Williams, *Dom Pedro the Magnanimous, Second Emperor of Brazil* (University of North Carolina Press, Chapel Hill, 1937), and Harry Bernstein, *Dom Pedro II* (Twayne, Boston, 1973). For the Paraguayan War, which contributed to the crisis of the empire, see H. G. Warren, *Paraguay: An Informal History* (University of Oklahoma Press, Norman, 1949); a good account of its military aspects is C. J. Kolinski, *Independence or Death! The Story of the Paraguayan War* (University of Florida Press, Gainesville, 1965).

CHAPTER TEN: THE TRIUMPH OF NEOCOLONIALISM

On the emergence and flowering of the neocolonial economy, see Celso Furtado, *The Economic Development of Latin America,* tr. by Suzette Macedo (Cambridge University Press, New York, 1970); Roberto Cortes Conde, *The First Stages of Modernization in Spanish America* (Harper & Row, New York, 1974); and A. G. Frank, *Capitalism and Underdevelopment in Latin America* (Monthly Review Press, New York, 1967). For an interpretation of modern Latin American history from the perspective of dependency theory, see Tulio Halperin-Donghi, *Historia contemporánea de América Latina* (Alianza Editorial, Madrid, 1969).

The following works contain good brief discussions of the Díaz era: M. C. Meyer and W. L. Sherman, *The Course of Mexican History* (Oxford University Press, New York, 1979); Jan Bazant, *A Concise History of Mexico from Hidalgo to Cárdenas, 1805–1940* (Cambridge University Press, New York, 1978); and C. C. Cumberland, *Mexico: The Struggle for Modernity* (Oxford University Press, New York, 1968). J. K. Turner,

Barbarous Mexico (C. H. Kerr, Chicago, 1910), is a blistering contemporary assessment of the results of Díaz's rule. No completely satisfactory life of Porfirio Díaz exists in English; still the best is Carleton Beals, *Porfirio Díaz: Dictator of Mexico* (Greenwood Press, Westport, Conn., 1971; 1st ed., 1932). The Northern Illinois University Press is publishing a series of monographs on the Porfiriato; studies already published are R. J. Knowlton, *Church Property and the Mexican Reform, 1856–1910* (Northern Illinois University Press, De Kalb, 1976), R. D. Anderson, *Outcasts in Their Own Land: Mexican Industrial Workers, 1906–1911* (Northern Illinois University Press, De Kalb, 1976), L. B. Perry, *Juárez and Díaz: Machine Politics in Mexico* (Northern Illinois University Press, De Kalb, Ill., 1979), and J. H. Coatsworth, *Growth Against Development: The Economic Impact of Railroads in Porfirian Mexico* (Northern Illinois University Press, De Kalb, 1981). For an excellent survey of intellectual dissent in the late Porfiriato, see J. D. Cockcroft, *Intellectual Precursors of the Mexican Revolution, 1900–1913* (University of Texas Press, Austin, 1968).

On Argentina in the same period, see H. S. Ferns, *Argentina* (Praeger, New York, 1969), and Y. F. Rennie, *The Argentine Republic* (Macmillan, New York, 1945), and especially Thomas McGann, *Argentina, the United States, and the Inter-American System, 1880–1914* (Harvard University Press, Cambridge, Mass., 1957), for an excellent account of oligarchical politics in the period from 1880 to 1914. For the British connection, see H. S. Ferns, *Britain and Argentina in the Nineteenth Century* (Clarendon Press, Oxford, Eng., 1960). James Scobie, *Argentina: A City and a Nation* (Oxford University Press, New York, 1964), is especially good for economic and social developments; see also his *Revolution on the Pampas: A Social History of Argentine Wheat* (University of Texas Press, Austin, 1964). On the rise of radicalism, see David Rock, *Politics in Argentina, 1890–1930* (Cambridge University

Press, New York, 1975), which is carefully researched and original in its conclusions.

On the political and economic evolution of Chile in the same period, see again Brian Loveman, *The Legacy of Hispanic Capitalism* (Oxford University Press, New York, 1979). On the agrarian structure, consult A. J. Bauer's excellent book, *Chilean Rural Society from the Spanish Conquest to 1930* (Cambridge University Press, New York, 1975), and an older but still useful work, G. M. McBride, *Chile: Land and Society* (American Geographical Society, New York, 1936). For opposing interpretations of the revolt of 1891, see Hernán Ramírez Necochea, *Balmaceda y la contrarevolución de 1891* (Editorial Universitaria, Santiago, 1969), and Harold Blakemore, *British Nitrates and Chilean Politics, 1886–1896: Balmaceda and North* (Athlone Press, London, 1974).

For Brazil in the period under review, see especially E. B. Burns's *A History of Brazil* (Columbia University Press, New York, 1970), and José Maria Bello, *A History of Modern Brazil, 1889–1954* (Stanford University Press, Stanford, Calif., 1966). On the decisive slavery issue, see Robert Conrad, *The Destruction of Brazilian Slavery, 1850–1888* (University of California Press, Berkeley, 1973), and R. B. Toplin, *The Abolition of Slavery in Brazil* (Atheneum, New York, 1972). Euclides da Cunha, *Rebellion in the Backlands*, tr. by Samuel Putnam (University of Chicago Press, Chicago, 1957), is a magnificent portrayal of a religious protest movement and its defeat. P. L. Eisenberg, *The Sugar Industry in Pernambuco, 1840–1910* (University of California Press, Berkeley, 1974), studies the transformation of a major industry. Richard Graham ably discusses British economic and cultural influence in *Britain and the Onset of Modernization in Brazil, 1850–1914* (Cambridge University Press, New York, 1968). On the political role of the military, see S. W. Simmons, *Marshal Deodoro and the Fall of Dom Pedro II* (Duke University Press, Durham, N.C., 1966). An important work on early Brazilian industrialization and its social aspects is Warren

Dean, *The Industrialization of São Paulo, 1880–1945* (University of Texas Press, Austin, 1969).

CHAPTER ELEVEN:
SOCIETY AND CULTURE
IN THE NINETEENTH
CENTURY

Tulio Halperin-Donghi's book, *The Aftermath of Revolution in Latin America* (Harper & Row, New York, 1973), is excellent on social and cultural change in the postindependence period. Travel accounts are valuable sources on life and manners in the nineteenth century; some good examples are Fanny Calderon de la Barca's *Letters from Mexico*, ed. by H. T. and M. H. Fisher (Doubleday, Garden City, N.Y., 1966); J. L. Stephens, *Incidents of Travel in Central America, Chiapas, and Yucatan*, 2 vols. (Dover, New York, 1969; 1st ed., 1841); James Orton, *The Andes and the Amazon* (Harper & Bros., New York, 1870); and D. P. Kidder, *Brazil and the Brazilians* (Sampson, London, 1866). For the process of social and cultural Europeanization, see Richard Graham's book on British influence in Brazil, *Britain and the Onset of Modernization in Brazil, 1850–1914* (Cambridge University Press, New York, 1968), and Frank Safford's excellent study, *The Ideal of the Practical: Colombia's Struggle to Form a Technical Elite* (University of Texas Press, Austin, 1976). Novels and poems are other important sources of information on Latin American society in the nineteenth century; some good examples are cited in the text. The literature on women in the nineteenth century is very meager, but there is some background material in Ann Pescatello, ed., *Female and Male in Latin America* (University of Pittsburgh Press, Pittsburgh, 1972); see also the relevant essays in Asunción Lavrin, ed., *Latin American Women: Historical Perspectives* (Greenwood Press, Westport, Conn., 1978).

J. L. Mecham, *Church and State in Latin America: A History of Politico-Ecclesiastical Relations*, rev. ed. (University of North Carolina Press, Chapel Hill, 1966), is the standard work on the subject; see also Frederick Pike, ed., *The Conflict Between Church and State in Latin America*, a useful anthology. The distinguished Mexican philosopher Leopoldo Zea ably discusses Latin American nineteenth-century thought in *The Latin American Mind* (University of Oklahoma Press, Norman, 1963) and *Positivism in Mexico* (University of Texas Press, Austin, 1974). See also the lively and informative book of W. R. Crawford, *A Century of Latin Thought*, rev. ed. (Harvard University Press, Cambridge, Mass., 1961), and R. L. Woodward, Jr., *Positivism in Latin America, 1850–1900* (D. C. Heath, Lexington, Mass., 1971), a well-chosen collection of texts.

The older works of Pedro Henríquez-Ureña, *Literary Currents in Hispanic America* (Harvard University Press, Cambridge, Mass., 1945) and Arturo Torres-Rioseco, *The Epic of Latin American Literature*, rev. ed. (Oxford University Press, New York, 1946), provide excellent guides to the subject. But Jean Franco, *An Introduction to Spanish-American Literature* (Cambridge University Press, London, 1969), and *The Modern Culture of Latin America: Society and the Artist* (Pall Mall Press, London, 1967), are especially recommended for their perceptive treatment of the relations between literature and society. Two very readable accounts of Brazilian literature are Samuel Putnam, *Marvelous Journey: Four Centuries of Brazilian Literature* (Knopf, New York, 1948), and Erico Verissimo, *Brazilian Literature* (Macmillan, New York, 1945). There are few studies in English on the social and political roles of the nineteenth-century Latin American historians; see, however, the stimulating essay of E. B. Burns, "Ideology in Nineteenth-Century Latin American Historiography," *Hispanic American Historical Review*, 58 (1978), 409–431, and Allen Woll, *A Functional Past: The Uses of History in Nineteenth-Century Chile* (Louisiana State University Press, Baton Rouge, 1982).

CHAPTER TWELVE:
THE MEXICAN
REVOLUTION—AND AFTER

Stanley Ross, ed., *Is the Mexican Revolution Dead?* (Knopf, New York, 1966), brings together conflicting views and offers his own assessment in the introduction. Frank Brandenburg, *The Making of Modern Mexico* (Prentice-Hall, Englewood Cliffs, N.J., 1964), is valuable for its discussion of the relation between politics and economic development and the workings of Mexican political machinery. Roger Hansen, *Politics of Mexican Development* (Johns Hopkins University Press, Baltimore, 1971), shows that since 1940 the revolution has benefited Mexican entrepreneurs at the expense of the masses. Raymond Vernon, *The Dilemma of Mexico's Development* (Harvard University Press, Cambridge, Mass., 1963), argues that Mexican revolutionary governments, whatever their rhetoric, have been committed to economic development based on private property and profit. R. E. Ruiz, *The Great Rebellion: Mexico, 1905–1924* (W. W. Norton, New York, 1980), provides much useful new information, particularly on economic development, but is marred by its unconvincing and not particularly novel thesis that the Mexican Revolution was no such thing, but a mere "rebellion." Friedrich Katz, *The Secret War in Mexico: Europe, the United States and the Mexican Revolution* (University of Chicago Press, Chicago, 1981), based on massive archival research, illuminates all major aspects of the Mexican Revolution, both foreign and domestic.

For the prerevolutionary background of intellectual dissent, see James Cockroft's *Intellectual Precursors of the Mexican Revolution, 1900–1913* (University of Texas Press, Austin, 1968). On Madero, see C. C. Cumberland, *Mexican Revolution: Genesis under Madero* (University of Texas Press, Austin, 1952), and Stanley Ross, *Francisco I. Madero, Apostle of Mexican Democracy* (Columbia University Press, New York, 1955); on Carranza,

see Cumberland's *The Mexican Revolution: The Constitutionalist Years* (University of Texas Press, Austin, 1972). John Womack, *Zapata and the Mexican Revolution* (Knopf, New York, 1968), is the standard life, but R. P. Millon, *Zapata: The Ideology of a Peasant Revolutionary* (International Publishers, New York, 1969), is an interesting Marxist effort to show that his movement transcended the limits of a peasant struggle for land. M. C. Meyer attempts the difficult task of partially rehabilitating Huerta in *Huerta, a Political Portrait* (University of Nebraska Press, Lincoln, 1972).

Special topics are covered by R. E. Ruiz, *Labor and the Ambivalent Revolutionaries: Mexico, 1911–1923* (Johns Hopkins University Press, Baltimore, 1976); R. E. Quirk, *The Mexican Revolution and the Catholic Church, 1910–1929* (Indiana University Press, Bloomington, 1973); and Edwin Lieuwen, *Mexican Militarism: The Political Rise and Fall of the Revolutionary Army, 1910–1940* (University of New Mexico Press, Albuquerque, 1973). For a classic study of the Mexican "culture of poverty," see Oscar Lewis, *Five Families: Mexican Case Studies in the Culture of Poverty* (Basic Books, New York, 1959). J. W. Wilkie, *The Mexican Revolution: Federal Expenditures and Social Change since 1910*, 2nd ed. (University of California Press, Berkeley, 1970), attempts to gauge the extent to which the revolution has benefited the masses. For a disillusioned portrayal of contemporary Mexico, see Pablo González Casanova, *Democracy in Mexico*, tr. by D. Salti (Oxford University Press, New York, 1970).

CHAPTER THIRTEEN:
ARGENTINA: THE
FAILURE OF DEMOCRACY

J. R. Scobie, *Argentina: A City and a Nation*, 2nd ed. (Oxford University Press, New York, 1971), is the best overview of Argentine history and society but is relatively weak for the post-1940 period. H. S. Ferns, *The Argentine Republic, 1516–1971* (Barnes and Noble, New York, 1971), is a comprehensive economic history. Three other standard economic studies are: Carlos F. Díaz Alejandro, *Essays on the Economic History of the Argentine Republic* (Yale University Press, New Haven, 1970), Aldo Ferrer, *The Argentine Economy* (University of California Press, Berkeley, 1967), and Laura Randall, *An Economic History of Argentina in the Twentieth Century* (Columbia University Press, New York, 1978).

Notable studies of the Argentine military are: Robert A. Potash, *The Army and Politics in Argentina, 1928–1945* (Stanford University Press, Stanford, Calif., 1969), and *The Army and Politics in Argentina, 1945–1962: Perón to Frondizi* (Stanford University Press, Stanford, Calif., 1982), and Marvin Goldwert, *Democracy, Militarism, and Nationalism in Argentina, 1930–1966* (University of Texas Press, Austin, 1972). The twentieth-century agricultural sector has received less scholarly attention than it deserves, but Peter H. Smith, *Politics and Beef in Argentina* (Columbia University Press, New York, 1969), is a well-done study of the landowning elite. Samuel L. Baily, *Labor, Nationalism, and Politics in Argentina* (Rutgers University Press, New Brunswick, N.J., 1967), attempts to separate myth from reality in Argentine labor history.

Several authors have tried to make sense out of the complexity of Argentine politics. P. H. Smith, *Argentina and the Failure of Democracy* (University of Wisconsin Press, Madison, 1974), employs sophisticated quantitative methods to produce some provocative hypotheses. Guillermo A. O'Donnell, *Modernization and Bureaucratic Authoritarianism: Studies in South American Politics* (University of California, Institute of International Studies, Berkeley, 1973), offers useful insights into Latin American politics in general.

The best study of the radical era (1912–1930) is David Rock, *Politics in Argentina, 1890–1930: The Rise and Fall of Radicalism* (Cambridge University Press, London, 1975), a superb analysis of political parties and their social bases. Mark Falcoff and R. H. Dolkart, eds., *Prologue to Perón: Argentina in Depression and War, 1930–1943* (University of California Press, Berkeley, 1976), is a valuable work; the studies of economic development (Javier Villanueva) and foreign policy (Joseph Tulchin) are especially useful.

The Perón era has attracted much scholarly interest: G. I. Blanksten, *Perón's Argentina* (University of Chicago Press, Chicago, 1974), is a classic work that has withstood the test of time. Other notable studies are: Jeane Kirkpatrick, *Leader and Vanguard in Mass Society: A Study of Peronist Argentina* (M.I.T. Press, Cambridge, Mass., 1971); R. J. Alexander, *The Perón Era* (Russell, New York, 1965); and A. P. Whitaker, *Argentine Upheaval: Perón's Fall and the New Regime* (Praeger, New York, 1956). J. R. Barager, ed., *Why Perón Came to Power* (Knopf, New York, 1968), is a useful reader. Two studies deal with Eva Perón: M. Navarro and N. Fraser, *Eva Perón* (Norton, New York, 1980) and J. M. Taylor, *Eva Perón: The Myths of a Woman* (University of Chicago Press, Chicago, 1979). Gary Wynia, *Argentina in the Post War Era* (University of New Mexico Press, Albuquerque, 1978), deals with both the Perón and post-Perón years.

David Rock, ed., *Argentina in the Twentieth Century* (University of Pittsburgh Press, Pittsburgh, 1975), contains some outstanding essays, including one by Rock on the Perón restoration. Jorge Fodor's piece on Perón's economics is also excellent, as is Walter Little's essay on the origins of *Peronismo*. D. C. Hodges, *Argentina, 1943–1976: The National Revolution and Resistance* (University of New Mexico Press, Albuquerque, 1976), studies Argentine guerrilla movements with the aid of some rare sources.

Finally, H. F. Peterson, *Argentina and the United States, 1810–1960* (S.U.N.Y. Press, Albany, N.Y., 1964), and A. P. Whitaker, *The United States and Argentina* (Harvard University Press, Cambridge, Mass., 1954), are useful surveys.

CHAPTER FOURTEEN:
THE CHILEAN WAY

The best and most up-to-date survey of Chilean history is Brian Loveman, *Chile: The Legacy of Hispanic Capitalism* (Oxford University Press, New York, 1979). F. G. Gil, *The Political System of Chile* (Houghton Mifflin, Boston, 1966), is a concise political history. Jay Kinsbruner, *Chile: A Historical Interpretation* (Harper & Row, New York, 1973), and F. B. Pike, *Chile and the United States, 1880–1962* (University of Notre Dame Press, Notre Dame, Ind., 1963), are useful overviews.

For an excellent overall economic history, see M. J. Mamalakis, *The Growth and Structure of the Chilean Economy from Independence to Allende* (Yale University Press, New Haven, 1976). Mamalakis and C. W. Reynolds, *Essays on the Chilean Economy* (R. D. Irwin, Homewood, Ill., 1965), provides a comprehensive study of the copper industry. Andre Gunder Frank, *Capitalism and Underdevelopment in Latin America: Historical Studies of Chile and Brazil* (Monthly Review Press, New York, rev. ed. 1969), helped to set off the debate on dependency theory.

James Petras, *Political and Social Forces in Chilean Development* (University of California Press, Berkeley, 1969), is an excellent examination of the development of the left-wing parties in Chile. Alan Angell, *Politics and the Labor Movement in Chile* (Oxford University Press, London, 1972), is the best study of Chilean labor. F. M. Nunn, *Chilean Politics, 1920–1931: The Honorable Role of the Armed Forces* (University of New Mexico Press, Albuquerque, 1970), and *The Military in Chilean History* (University of New Mexico Press, Albuquerque, 1976), are objective and well researched.

Sound studies of the Chilean agricultural sector are: R. F. Kaufman, *The Politics of Land Reform in Chile, 1950–1970* (Harvard University Press, Cambridge, Mass., 1972); Brian Loveman, *Struggle in the Countryside: Politics and Rural Labor in Chile, 1919–1973* (Indiana University Press, Bloomington, 1976); and A. J. Bauer, *Chilean Rural Society from the Spanish Conquest to 1930* (Cambridge University Press, New York, 1975).

The Allende regime and its violent overthrow have attracted much scholarly and journalistic interest. Perhaps the best study of the Allende period is Stefan de Vylder, *Allende's Chile* (Cambridge University Press, London, 1976). P. E. Sigmund, *The Overthrow of Allende and the Politics of Chile, 1964–1976* (University of Pittsburgh Press, Pittsburgh, 1977), A. Valenzuela, *The Breakdown of Democratic Regimes: Chile* (Johns Hopkins University Press, Baltimore, 1978), and B. Stallings, *Class Conflict and Economic Development in Chile 1958–1973* (Stanford University Press, Stanford, Calif., 1978) are other useful works. There are two impassioned but well-documented accounts of the military revolt and the complicity of the United States: James Petras and Morris Morely, *The United States and Chile* (Monthly Review Press, New York, 1976), and P. M. Sweezy and Harry Magdoff, eds., *Revolution and Counterrevolution in Chile* (Monthly Review Press, New York, 1974). Ian Roxborough, Jackie Riddick, and Philip O'Brien, in *Chile: The State and Revolution* (Holmes and Meier, New York, 1977), have written from a sympathetic view of the Allende program for social and economic reconstruction, but they question the likelihood of a peaceful transition to socialism. Edward Boorstein, *Allende's Chile* (International Publishers, New York, 1977), is a first-hand account of an American economist employed by the Allende government. See also Regis Debray, *The Chilean Revolution* (Random House, New York, 1971). Dale Johnson, ed., *The Chilean Road to Socialism* (Peter Smith, New York, 1973), is a useful collection of essays on the background and early stages of the Allende reform program.

CHAPTER FIFTEEN:
REPUBLICAN BRAZIL

E. B. Burns's *A History of Brazil* (Columbia University Press, New York, 1970) and Rollie Poppino, *Brazil: The Land and the People* (Oxford University Press, New York, 1968), offer good brief accounts of developments since 1914, but the most thorough recent study of modern Brazil is Peter Flynn, *Brazil: A Political Analysis* (Ernest Benn, London, 1978). J. M. Young, *The Brazilian Revolution of 1930 and the Aftermath* (Rutgers University Press, New Brunswick, N.J., 1967), R. M. Levine, *The Vargas Regime: The Critical Years, 1934–1938* (Columbia University Press, New York, 1970), and J. D. Wirth, *The Politics of Brazilian Development, 1930–1954* (Stanford University Press, Stanford, Calif., 1970), study various aspects of the Vargas era. See also Richard Bourne's fine biography, *Getúlio Vargas of Brazil, 1883–1954* (C. Knight, London, 1974). T. L. Skidmore, *Politics in Brazil, 1930–1964: An Experiment in Democracy* (Oxford University Press, New York, 1967), is especially good on the events leading to the coup of 1964. On the role of the military, see Alfred Stepan, *The Military in Politics: Changing Patterns in Brazil* (Princeton University Press, Princeton, 1971). For a critical analysis of the coup of 1964 by one of its victims, see Octávio Ianni, *Crisis in Brazil* (Columbia University Press, New York, 1970).

The apparent economic success of the Brazilian military regime has focused much scholarly interest on it; studies that view it as an example of the "bureaucratic-authoritarian model" or from the perspective of corporatist theory include Alfred Stepan, ed., *Authoritarian Brazil: Origins, Politics, and Future* (Yale University Press, New Haven, 1973); Philippe Schmitter, *Interest Conflict and Political Change in Brazil* (Stanford University Press, Stanford, Calif., 1971); R. M. Schneider, *The Political System of Brazil: Emergence of a Modernizing Authoritarian Regime, 1864–1970* (Columbia University Press, New York, 1971); and G. A. Fiechter, *Brazil Since 1964—Modernization Under a Military Regime* (Macmillan, London, 1975). See also Riordan Roett, *Brazil: Politics in a Patrimonial Society*, rev. ed. (Praeger, New York, 1978), which concludes that in the last analysis the military regime has always acted to preserve the existing economic and social structures. The reader's attention is again called to Peter Flynn's recent book, cited above; it offers an incisive analysis of the military regime that correctly stresses the elements of class interest in Brazilian corporatism.

Outstanding works on special topics in this period include Ralph della Cava, *Miracle at Joaseiro* (Columbia University Press, New York, 1970), a study of a religious protest movement and its leader, Padre Cícero; J. L. Love, *Rio Grande do Sul and Brazilian Regionalism, 1882–1930* (Stanford University Press, Stanford, Calif., 1971), on the politics of a key Brazilian state; Neil Macaulay, *The Prestes Column: Revolution in Brazil* (Franklin Watts, New York, 1974), the most complete study of the movement; and Warren Dean, *The Industrialization of São Paulo, 1880–1945* (University of Texas Press, Austin, 1969).

CHAPTER SIXTEEN:
STORM OVER THE ANDES:
PERU'S AMBIGUOUS
REVOLUTION

H. S. Klein, *Bolivia: The Evolution of A Multi-Ethnic Society* (Oxford University Press, New York, 1982), provides an excellent introduction to its subject. The best account of the events leading to the revolution of 1952 is H. S. Klein, *Parties and Political Change in Bolivia, 1880–1952* (Cambridge University Press, New York, 1969). For assessments of the revolution and its aftermath, see James Malloy, *Bolivia, the Uncompleted Revolution* (University of Pittsburgh Press, Pittsburgh, 1970), and James Malloy and R. S. Thorn, eds., *Beyond the Revolution: Bolivia Since 1952* (University of Pittsburgh Press, Pittsburgh, 1971). D. B. Heath, ed., *Land Reform and Social Revolution in Bolivia* (Praeger, New York, 1969), and W. E. Carter, *Aymara Communities and the Bolivian Agrarian Reform* (University of Florida

Press, Gainesville, 1964), survey the achievements and limitations of the Bolivian land reform.

The literature on Ecuador is very meager. G. I. Blanksten, *Ecuador, Constitutions and Caudillos* (University of California Press, Berkeley, 1951), is a competent study of the country's modern political history. A. B. Franklin's *Ecuador: Portrait of a People* (Doubleday, New York, 1943) and Lilo Linke's *Ecuador: Country of Contrasts*, 3rd ed. (Oxford University Press, New York, 1960), are designed for the general reader.

F. B. Pike, *The Modern History of Peru* (Praeger, New York, 1967), is the best general account. François Bourricaud, *Power and Society in Contemporary Peru*, tr. by Paul Stevenson (Praeger, New York, 1970), carefully studies class and political alignments. J. C. Mariátegui, *Seven Interpretive Essays on Peruvian Reality* (University of Texas Press, Austin, 1971), is a brilliant and highly influential Marxist analysis. For particular episodes of Peruvian nineteenth-century history, see Watt Stewart, *Chinese Bondage in Peru: A History of the Chinese Coolie in Peru, 1849–1874* (Duke University Press, Durham, N.C., 1951), and his biography of a colorful North American impresario in Peru, *Henry Meiggs, Yankee Pizarro* (Duke University Press, Durham, N.C., 1946). On the economic and social origins of the still influential Aprista movement, see P. F. Klaren, *Modernization, Dislocation, and Aprismo: Origins of the Peruvian Aprista Party* (University of Texas Press, Austin, 1973). On the Indian and land question, see, amid a substantial literature, T. M. Davies, Jr., *Indian Integration in Peru: A Half-Century of Experience, 1900–1948* (University of Nebraska Press, Lincoln, 1974); Howard Handelman, *Struggle in the Andes: Peasant Political Participation in Peru* (University of Texas Press, Austin, 1974); and F. L. Tullis, *Lord and Peasant in Peru: A Paradigm of Political and Social Change* (Harvard University Press, Cambridge, Mass., 1970).

The Peruvian Revolution of 1968 has produced conflicting assessments. For some generally favorable views, see A. F. Lowenthal, ed., *The Peruvian Experiment: Continuity and Change under Military Rule* (Princeton University Press, Princeton, 1975), and E. V. K. Fitzgerald, *The State and Economic Development: Peru Since 1968* (Cambridge University Press, Cambridge, Eng., 1976). For sharply critical views from the left, see "Peru: Bourgeois Revolution and Class Struggle," *Latin American Perspectives*, 4, No. 3 (1977). See also an excellent economic history by Rosemary Thorp and Geoffrey Bertram, *Peru 1890–1977: Growth and Policy in an Open Economy* (Macmillan, London, 1978), which concludes that "despite the Military's repeated claims that Peru has definitively broken with its past, the issue remains in doubt." S. M. Gorman, ed., *Post-Revolutionary Peru: The Politics of Transformation* (Westview Press, Boulder, Co., 1982), is an excellent survey of developments since 1975.

CHAPTER SEVENTEEN:
THE CUBAN REVOLUTION

Hugh Thomas's monumental *Cuba: The Pursuit of Freedom* (Harper & Row, New York, 1971), is a superb overview of Cuban history. R. F. Smith, ed., *Background to Revolution: The Development of Modern Cuba* (Knopf, New York, 1966), is a useful collection of selections from important sources. Ramón Ruiz, *Cuba: The Making of a Revolution* (Norton, New York, 1970), provides an excellent introduction to the subject.

There are several fine studies of Cuban society and political economy during the nineteenth century: Ramiro Guerra y Sánchez, *Sugar and Society in the Caribbean* (Yale University Press, New Haven, 1964); Fernando Ortiz, *Cuban Counterpoint: Tobacco and Sugar* (Knopf, New York, 1947); F. W. Knight, *Slave Society in Cuba During the Nineteenth Century* and V. Martínez Alier, *Marriage, Class, and Colour in Nineteenth Century Cuba* (Cambridge University Press, London, 1974).

Dudley Seers et al., *Cuba: The Economic and Social Revolution* (University of North Carolina Press, Chapel Hill, 1964), is a comprehensive economic history, focusing on the early years of the revolution. L. A. Pérez, Jr., *Army Politics in Cuba, 1898–1958* (University of Pittsburgh Press, Pittsburgh, 1976), is the best work on the Cuban military.

F. S. Foner, *The Spanish-Cuban-American War, 1895–1906* (Monthly Review Press, New York, 1972), drastically revises the traditional historiography of the Spanish-American War. L. E. Aguilar, *Cuba 1933: Prologue to Revolution* (Norton, New York, 1974), is a fine monograph on the unsuccessful moderate revolution of 1933.

The Cuban Revolution and Fidel Castro have attracted numerous studies by historians, sociologists, anthropologists, and journalists. R. E. Bonachea and N. P. Valdez, eds., *Cuba in Revolution* (Anchor Books, New York, 1972), brings together essays that assess the progress achieved in the first decade of the Cuban Revolution. Herbert Matthews, *Revolution in Cuba* (Scribners, New York, 1965), is based in part on Matthews's firsthand contact with Castro as a *New York Times* reporter who interviewed Castro in his mountain hide-out and helped to publicize his cause in the United States. J. N. Goodsell, ed., *Fidel Castro's Personal Revolution* (Knopf, New York, 1975), brings together different viewpoints on Castro and his regime. J. R. O'Connor, *The Origins of Socialism in Cuba* (Cornell University Press, Ithaca, N.Y., 1970), is a masterful study of the background of the Cuban Revolution and its economic program. K. S. Karol, *Guerrillas in Power* (Hill and Wang, New York, 1970), is a highly critical assessment by a disillusioned European leftist. Edward González, *Cuba Under Castro: The Limits of Charisma* (Houghton Mifflin, Boston, 1974), is equally disapproving. By contrast, Lee Lockwood, *Castro's Cuba, Cuba's Fidel* (Random House, New York, 1969), is highly favorable to the Cuban Revolution.

Carmelo Mesa-Lago has attempted to evaluate the revolutionary regime in three books: *Revolutionary Change in Cuba* (University of Pittsburgh Press, Pittsburgh, 1971); *Cuba in the 1970s*, rev. ed. (University of New Mexico Press, Albuquerque, 1978), and *The Economy of Socialist Cuba: A Two Decade Appraisal* (University of New Mexico Press, Albuquerque, 1981), which are notable for their objectivity. The second book is a particularly useful effort to define and analyze the various stages through which the Castro regime has passed. Jorge Domínguez, *Cuba: Order and Revolution* (Harvard University Press, Cambridge, 1978), is an encyclopedic, critical effort to measure the achievements of the revolution. The anthropologist Oscar Lewis, in *Living the Revolution: An Oral History of Contemporary Cuba*, Vol. 1, *Four Men* (University of Illinois Press, Champaign, 1975), and Vol. 2, *Four Women* (University of Illinois Press, Champaign, 1977), attempts to reveal the lives and thoughts of ordinary Cubans. C. Mesa-Lago and C. Blasier, *Cuba in the Third World* (University of Pittsburgh, Pittsburgh, 1979), studies Cuba's foreign relations, especially its involvement in Africa.

CHAPTER EIGHTEEN: REVOLUTION IN CENTRAL AMERICA: TWILIGHT OF THE TYRANTS?

R. L. Woodward, Jr., *Central America: A Nation Divided* (Oxford University Press, New York, 1976), provides a sound, clear overview of the history and problems of the area. T. L. Karnes, *The Failure of Union: Central America 1824–1975* (Arizona State University Press, Tempe, 1976), surveys the many failed efforts to unite the region. M. L. Wortman, *Government and Society in Central America, 1680–1840* (Columbia University Press, New York, 1982), is a carefully researched socioeconomic study. For the Walker episode in Central America, see W. O. Scroggs, *Filibusters and Financiers: The Story of William Walker and His Associates* (Macmillan, New York,

1916). T. P. Anderson, *Politics in Central America: Guatemala, El Salvador, Honduras, and Nicaragua* (Praeger, New York, 1982), is a useful guide to the complex politics of the area. *Revolution in Central America*, ed. by the Stanford Central America Action Network (Westview Press, Boulder, Co., 1983), brings together a wide variety of sources on the Central American crisis.

Susanne Jonas and David Tobis, eds., *Guatemala* (NACLA, New York, 1974), is an excellent introduction to its subject. For some new light on the U.S. role in the 1954 coup in Guatemala, see R. H. Immerman, *The CIA in Guatemala: The Foreign Policy of Intervention* (University of Texas Press, Austin, 1982), and Stephen Schlesinger and Stephen Kinzer, *Bitter Fruit: The Untold Story of the American Coup in Guatemala* (Doubleday, Garden City, New York, 1982). On the consequences of the counterrevolution, particularly the terror against the Indian peasantry, see R. N. Adams, *Crucifixion by Power* (University of Texas Press, Austin, 1970), and Thomas Melville and Marjorie Melville, *Guatemala—Another Vietnam?* (Penguin, London, 1971).

T. W. Walker, *Nicaragua: The Land of Sandino* (Westview Press, Boulder, Co., 1981), is a well-informed, well-written introduction to its subject. On the Somoza era, see Richard Millett, *Guardians of the Dynasty: A History of the U.S.-Created Guardia Nacional de Nicaragua and the Somoza Family* (Orbis Books, Maryknoll, New York, 1977). On Sandino, see Gregorio Selser's fine biography, *Sandino*, tr. by Cedric Belfrage (Monthly Review Press, New York, 1981), and Neil Macaulay, *The Sandino Affair* (Quadrangle Books, Chicago, 1967), which focuses on his military activity. George Black, *Triumph of the People: The Sandinista Revolution in Nicaragua* (Zed Press, London, 1981), is a carefully researched study of the origins and development of the Sandinista revolution. The contributors to T. W. Walker, ed., *Nicaragua in Revolution* (Praeger, New York, 1982), offer a comprehensive, sympathetic assessment of the revolution's first few years in power.

Alastair White, *El Salvador* (Praeger, New York, 1973), provides much useful background information. T. S. Montgomery's spirited *Revolution in El Salvador: Origins and Evolution* (Westview Press, Boulder, Co., 1982), studies the development of the revolutionary movement in engrossing detail. T. P. Anderson has written model monographs on two milestones on El Salvador's road to revolution, *Matanza: El Salvador's Communist Revolt of 1932* (University of Nebraska Press, Lincoln, 1971), and *The War of the Dispossessed: Honduras and El Salvador* (University of Nebraska Press, Lincoln, 1981). Robert Armstrong and Janet Shenk, *El Salvador: The Face of Revolution* (South End Press, Boston, 1982), is a vivid, moving portrayal of the continuing struggle in El Salvador.

CHAPTER NINETEEN: LATIN AMERICAN SOCIETY IN TRANSITION

The *Economic Survey of Latin America*, published annually since 1948 by the Economic Commission for Latin America of the United Nations Economic and Social Council, is a valuable source of data on economic and social trends. Frank Tannenbaum, *Ten Keys to Latin America* (Random House, New York, 1962), remains a masterful account of some key facets of Latin American society and culture, but its liberal faith in a reformist solution to the area's problems seems pathetically dated. Typifying the grim or angry tone of much current writing on the Latin American scene are such books as John Gerassi, *The Great Fear in Latin America* (Macmillan, New York, 1965); E. R. Wolf and E. C. Hansen, eds., *The Human Condition in Latin America* (Oxford University Press, New York, 1972); and Sven Lindquist, *The Shadow: Latin America Faces the Seventies*, tr. by Keith Brandfield (Penguin Books, Harmondsworth, Eng., 1972). On urban problems, see G. H. Beyer, ed., *The Urban Explosion in Latin America* (Cornell University Press, Ithaca, N.Y., 1967); W. D. Harris, Jr., *The Growth of*

Latin American Cities (Ohio University Press, Athens, 1971); and Jorge Hardoy, ed., *Urbanization in Latin America: Approaches and Issues* (Doubleday, Garden City, N.Y., 1975). Nicolás Sánchez-Albornoz, *The Population of Latin America*, tr. by W. A. R. Richardson (University of California Press, Berkeley, 1974), is an excellent demographic history.

Two important collections of essays dealing with class structure and alignments are S. M. Lipset and Aldo Solari, eds., *Elites in Latin America* (Oxford University Press, New York, 1967), and I. L. Horowitz, ed., *Masses in Latin America* (Oxford University Press, New York, 1970). J. J. Johnson's classic *Political Change in Latin America: The Emergence of the Middle Sectors* (Stanford University Press, Stanford, Calif., 1958), assumes that industrialization and the rise of the middle sectors will lead to a growth of democracy and social change. For disillusioned views of the results of industrialization, see two symposia edited by Claudio Veliz: *The Politics of Conformity in Latin America* (Oxford University Press, New York, 1967) and *Obstacles to Change in Latin America* (Oxford University Press, New York, 1969).

On the problems of the peasantry, see Rodolfo Stavenhagen, ed., *Agrarian Problems and Peasant Movements in Latin America* (Doubleday, Garden City, N.Y., 1970); Ernest Feder, *The Rape of the Peasantry* (Doubleday, Garden City, N.Y., 1971); Gerrit Huizer, *Peasant Rebellion in Latin America* (Penguin Books, Harmondsworth, Eng., 1973); and Andrew Pearse, *The Latin American Peasant* (Frank Cass, London, 1975). Older, mainly descriptive surveys of the history of Latin American labor include R. J. Alexander, *Organized Labor in Latin America* (Free Press, New York, 1965), and Victor Alba, *Politics and the Labor Movement in Latin America* (Stanford University Press, Stanford, Calif., 1969). A superior work is the scholarly, analytical study by H. A. Spalding, *Organized Labor in Latin America: Historical Case Studies of Workers in Dependent Societies* (New York University Press, New York, 1977). A val-uable companion volume is a collection of essays edited by June Nash, Juan Corradi, and H. A. Spalding, *Ideology and Social Change in Latin America* (Gordon & Breach, New York, 1977), which deals with problems of worker and peasant class consciousness.

On the status of women in contemporary Latin America, see Ann Pescatello, ed., *Female and Male in Latin America* (University of Pittsburgh Press, Pittsburgh, 1972), and the November 1975 issue of the *Journal of Inter-American Studies and World Affairs*, which is devoted to the changing role of women in Latin America. A notable work on race relations is Florestan Fernandes, *The Negro in Brazilian Society* (Columbia University Press, New York, 1969), which demonstrates a continuing pattern of race prejudice in a country often cited as a model of racial democracy. Richard Arens, ed., *Genocide in Paraguay* (Temple University Press, Philadelphia, 1976), documents the destruction of Paraguayan Indians, a story with parallels in other Latin American countries.

There is a large and growing literature on the new reformist and radical tendencies within the Catholic church. See, among other studies, François Houtart and Emile Pin, *The Church and the Latin American Revolution* (Sheed & Ward, New York, 1965); H. E. Landsberger, ed., *The Church and Social Change in Latin America* (University of Notre Dame Press, Notre Dame, Ind., 1970); and, on the especially militant Brazilian clergy, Emanuel de Kadt, *Catholic Radicals in Brazil* (Oxford University Press, London, 1970), and T. C. Bruneau, *The Political Transformation of the Brazilian Church* (Cambridge University Press, London, 1974). For recent developments in the struggle of the church for human rights in Latin America, see the impassioned but carefully documented book by Penny Lernoux, *Cry of the People* (Penguin Books, New York, 1982).

For a comprehensive and very readable survey of modern and contemporary Latin American culture, see German Arciniegas, *Latin America: A Cultural History*, tr. by J. MacLean (Knopf,

New York, 1966). For the views of three leading Latin American social scientists, see J. A. Kahl, *Modernization, Exploitation, and Dependency in Latin America: Germani, González Casanova, and Cardoso* (Transaction Books, New Brunswick, N.J., 1976). The best brief explanation of the dependency theory that currently dominates Latin American economic thought is by Theotonio dos Santos, "The Structure of Dependence," *American Economic Review*, May 1970, pp. 231–236. For statements and applications of dependency theory by other Latin American and North American scholars, see R. H. Chilcote and J. C. Edelstein, eds., *Latin America: The Struggle with Dependency and Beyond* (Halstead Press, New York, 1974).

On twentieth-century literary trends see, in addition to the surveys of Henríquez-Ureña, Torres-Rioseco, Franco, Putnam, and Verissimo cited in the bibliography for Chapter 11, D. F. Gallagher, *Modern Latin American Literature* (Oxford University Press, New York, 1973), and F. P. Ellison, *Brazil's New Novel; Four Northeastern Novelists: José Lins do Rego, Jorge Amado, Graciliano Ramos, and Rachel de Queiroz* (University of California Press, Berkeley, 1954).

CHAPTER TWENTY:
THE TWO AMERICAS:
UNITED STATES-LATIN
AMERICAN RELATIONS

An excellent text based on a revisionist interpretation of American foreign relations and which assigns considerable space to Latin America is L. C. Gardner, Walter LaFeber, and T. J. McCormick, *The Creation of the American Empire* (Rand McNally, Chicago, 1976). J. L. Mecham, *A Survey of United States-Latin American Relations* (Houghton Mifflin, Boston, 1965), offers a more conventional view of inter-American relations. Several books of readings contain intelligent, critical essays on U.S. policy toward Latin America: Julio Cotner and R. R. Fagen,

eds., *Latin America and the United States: The Changing Realities* (Stanford University Press, Stanford, Calif., 1974); I. L. Horowitz, ed., *Latin American Radicalism* (Random House, New York, 1969); James Petras and Maurice Zeitlin, eds., *Latin America: Reform or Revolution?* (Fawcett, New York, 1968), and K. T. Fann and Donald Hodges, eds., *Readings in United States Imperialism* (Porter Sargent, Boston, 1971).

A. P. Whitaker, *The United States and the Independence of Latin America, 1800–1830* (Johns Hopkins University Press, Baltimore, 1941), is the standard study of United States-Latin American relations during the wars of independence. Dexter Perkins, *A History of the Monroe Doctrine*, rev. ed. (Little, Brown, Boston, 1963), is the standard work on this thoroughly exploited topic. D. M. Pletcher, *The Diplomacy of Annexation: Texas, Oregon, and the Mexican War* (University of Missouri Press, Columbia, 1963), is an excellent overview of the era of manifest destiny and the road to war with Mexico. R. E. May, *The Southern Dream of a Caribbean Empire* (Louisiana State University Press, Baton Rouge, 1973), and L. D. Langley, *Struggle for the American Mediterranean* (University of Georgia Press, Atlas, 1976), studies United States involvement in the Caribbean during the nineteenth century. The best treatment of the Mexican War from the United States perspective is Otis Singletary, *The Mexican War* (University of Chicago Press, Chicago, 1960). Walter LaFeber's brilliant *The New Empire* (Cornell University Press, Ithaca, N.Y., 1963), stresses economic factors in U.S. relations with Latin America from 1865 to 1898. D. F. Trask, *The War with Spain in 1898* (Macmillan, New York, 1981), is the most useful single volume on the Spanish-American-Cuban War.

Dana G. Munro's volumes on U.S. activities in the Caribbean, *Intervention and Dollar Diplomacy in the Caribbean, 1900–1921* (Princeton University Press, Princeton, 1964), and *The United States and the Caribbean Republics, 1921–1923* (Princeton University Press, Princeton, 1975), are scholarly, but apologetic in tone. C. N. Ronning, ed.,

Intervention in Latin America (Knopf, New York, 1970), is a useful anthology. J. R. Benjamin, *The United States and Cuba: Hegemony and Dependent Development 1880–1934* (University of Pittsburgh Press, Pittsburgh, 1974), is an excellent, critical study of the U.S. role in Cuba. R. H. Immerman, *The CIA in Guatemala* (University of Texas Press, Austin, 1982), details the overthrow of Arbenz in 1954. Peter Wyden, *The Bay of Pigs: The Untold Story* (Simon and Schuster, New York, 1979), uncovers the extraordinary blunders of the CIA and its betrayal of the Cuban exiles.

Two excellent monographs that furnish opposing interpretations of New Deal policy toward Latin America are Bryce Wood, *The Making of the Good Neighbor Policy* (Columbia University Press, New York, 1961), which offers a traditional view, and L. Gardner, *The Economic Aspects of New Deal Diplomacy* (University of Wisconsin Press, Madison, 1964), which is a more critical study emphasizing the less altruistic goals of American policy.

For the post-World War II period, there are several excellent, generally critical studies of United States policy toward Latin America. S. L. Baily, *The United States and the Development of South America, 1945–1975* (New Viewpoints, New York, 1976), is a dispassionate plea for a change in American policy. Harry Magdoff, *The Age of Imperialism* (Monthly Review Press, 1969), levels a harsh attack on American political and economic influence in Latin America.

The North American Congress on Latin America (NACLA), *Yankee Dollar* (NACLA, New York, 1971), is an exposé of the harmful effects of American economic influence. David Green, *Containment in Latin America* (New York Times Book Co., Scranton, Pa., 1971), sets United States-Latin American relations within the context of worldwide policy. Jerome Levinson and Juan de Onis, *The Alliance that Lost Its Way* (New York Times Book Co., Scranton, Pa., 1970), is a critical evaluation of the Alliance for Progress. Alonso Aguilar, *Pan Americanism from Monroe to the Present* (Monthly Review Press, New York, 1969), is a bitter indictment of United States policy by a Latin American.

Cole Blasier, *The Hovering Giant* (University of Pittsburgh Press, Pittsburgh, 1976), and Richard J. Barnet, *Intervention and Revolution* (New American Library, New York, 1972), attempt to assess American responses to revolution in Latin America.

Two recent works try to evaluate United States policy toward specific regions of Latin America: F. B. Pike, *The United States and the Andean Republics* (Harvard University Press, Cambridge, Mass., 1977), and A. P. Whitaker, *The United States and the Southern Cone* (Harvard University Press, Cambridge, Mass., 1976).

Finally, Walter LaFeber has written a superb volume, *The Panama Canal* (Oxford University Press, New York, 1978), which skillfully explains the issues involved in the recent negotiations between Panama and the United States.

Index

Student Evaluation of
A SHORT HISTORY OF LATIN AMERICA, Second Edition

While a textbook is being written, the publisher works closely with the author(s) and with course instructors to be sure that the book is useful and interesting. Since the main reader of this textbook is you, the student, we at Houghton Mifflin Company would also like to know what you think about the quality of this text.

Please answer the questions below, and mail this response sheet to

College Marketing Services
Houghton Mifflin Company, One Beacon Street
Boston, MA 02108

We will appreciate reading your comments on the textbook.

1. Does the textbook cover the information necessary to master your course? Circle the appropriate number.

1	2	3	4
No, none of the information is there	Yes, some of the information is there	Yes, most of the information is there	Yes, almost all of the information is there

2. Was the textbook excessively difficult to read?

1	2	3	4
Yes, I often had to consult a dictionary	No, although there were some unfamiliar words	No, the book was not too difficult to read and understand	No, the textbook was almost too easy to read

3. Did the textbook hold your interest?

1	2	3	4
No, I often had trouble concentrating	Yes, but a few parts are dull	Yes, the text held my attention	Yes, I enjoyed many parts of the book

4. Which three chapters are the best?　　　　　Why?

5. Which three chapters are least effective?　　　　Why?

6. Do any parts of the book stand out in your mind? Please identify them by page number or topic, and please explain why you remember these sections.

7. Do you have any general suggestions for improving the text?

Thank you for giving your reactions to this textbook.

(Optional)

Course Title _____

Name _____

College _____

City _____*State* _____